MW01630304

TECHNIQUES OF THE ARTISTS OF THE AMERICAN WEST

TECHNIQUES OF THE ARTISTS OF THE AMERICAN WEST

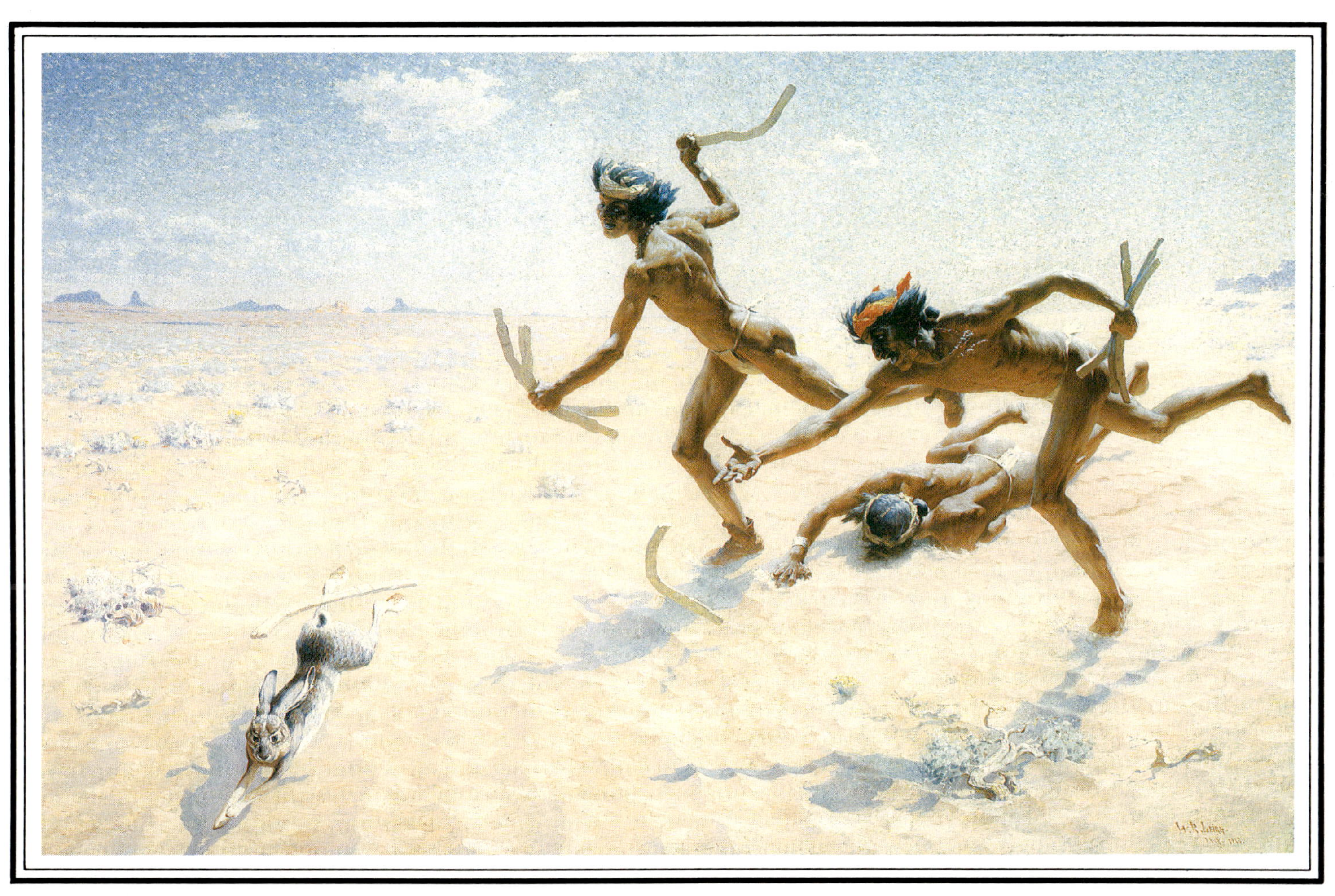

Peggy and Harold Samuels
Joan Samuels
Daniel Fabian

THE WELLFLEET PRESS

Publishing Director: Frank Oppel
Editorial Director: Tony Meisel
Design Director: Carmela Pereira
Editor: Theresa Stiles
Composition: Meadowcomp Ltd.
Origination: Regent Publishing Services Ltd.
Printing: Leefung-Asco Printers Ltd.

Manufactured in Hong Kong
ISBN: 1-55521-662-5

TABLE OF CONTENTS

PREFACE

When I started collecting Western art in the 1970s, I appeased my appetite for knowledge of my new avocation by digesting texts such as Janson's *History of Art,* and by constantly snacking on reference books, such as Samuels' *The Illustrated Biographical Encyclopedia of Artists of the American West*, for example. Were *Techniques of the Artists of the American West* available then, I would have found it "a must." However, I had to settle for bits and pieces. R.H. Rush warned me in his *Art as an Investment* that the value of a damaged painting may be but a small fraction of one in prime condition. Input from conservators and a layman's proficiency with a black light served me fairly well in my search for Western art tops in quality and fettle. Recently I have become somewhat more proficient with the help of Samuels' *Everyone's Guide to Buying Art.*

Besides sating the curiosity of artists, restorers, museum-goers and collectors about the construction processes employed in the works studied here, this book will enable each of us to be better at what we do. Many a decades-old painting or sculpture is in poor condition today for one of two reasons: either the artist was a poor technician or the painting was not well cared for by the owner, dealer, or restorer.

I bought a Grant Wood painting without hesitation after discovering that it was accurately dated the year after he stopped using composition board, which absorbs the paint over the years. A conservator who worked on George Caleb Binghams for years in St. Louis told me that the crackle in mine was due to the artist's use of a type of paint for an *imprimatura* that was improper. I have passed on fine Remington bronze casts with poor patinas as well as one of the artist's major oils whose once beautiful impasto had been squashed by a famous, incompetent reliner. The dealer was competent; he got his rich Texan.

Typed above the artist's signature on a label tacked to the back of its frame are instructions on what to do and not do when cleaning my Thomas Hart Benton. Finally, after reading that Jackson Pollock often flicked house paint and at least once a cigarette butt on his canvases, I thought it prudent to put mine in a translucent plexiglass asylum.

If you are an incurable admirer of good Western art, as I am, you have a desire to know the artist, his environment and his work. Unlike laws and sausage, I think art can be enjoyed even more if we see it made. The authors have given us this opportunity.

W.C. Foxley
Chairman of the Board
The Museum of Western Art
Denver, Colorado

INTRODUCTION

Twenty-one classic paintings of the American West are illustrated, separated into their details, and analyzed in this book. The pictures are by 21 different master painters. As background for investigating how these painters worked, there is also a brief exploration of their lives in relation to their careers.

The approach is to scrutinize these distinguished artists and pictures of the Old West to provide the basis for a sound appreciation of the art in its context. The analysis is in depth but this is not a textbook. Rather, the historians and conservators contributing to the study have adopted a conversational and pictorial approach designed to make the biographical and technical information easily accessible.

Painterly technique has been a neglected way of looking at all American artists, particularly at the master painters of the American West. By correcting this omission, investigating the artists' techniques gives a new dimension to the meaning of their work.

The book asks basic questions: How was the painting conceived? What was the procedure the artist followed in applying paint? What pigments were used? Were traditional methods employed or did the artist experiment? Did the artist adhere to the composition originally planned or were changes made? In the course of answering these questions, each of the artists is discovered to have been more of a distinct individual than first appearances indicated, with sometimes surprising strengths and weaknesses.

There is after all a reason why certain paintings evoke a positive reaction in viewers. Subject matter is the first and obvious clue, but the real reason lies deeper. Probing below the surface provides insight into the artist's particular genius and discloses the singularity of "the hand behind the brush."

The purpose of this book, then, is to inform and entertain while examining mostly traditional Western art to see what is significant about each picture and each painter. The primary intent is broad, to present a new way of looking at any painting, regardless of subject. More specific goals are to enhance the appreciation of Western art, to substantiate the current appraisal of these Western master painters as equal to American painters of other subjects, and to offer guidance to today's artists who desire to learn how the masters worked. The approach lends itself to the production of a book that is beautiful as well as informative.

The method used here examines thoroughly the one characteristic painting chosen for each artist, not the artist's entire *oeuvre*. The focus is on the painter and the method, not on mechanical improvements in art supplies. The period of the book is roughly the hundred years from ethnologist George Catlin's arrival in St. Louis in 1830 to the mature Georgia O'Keeffe's summer in New Mexico in 1929. The artists were the most influential of the Americans who worked in the West. They employed substantially all of the various painting techniques that were popular in their day.

Each analysis starts with the whole painting. The painting is then broken down into a series of photographs of details to show which effects were special to each artist and how the artist achieved these effects. The photographs were taken individually for every illustration, either the actual size of the segment of the painting or through an enlarging lens on the camera. Some were taken through a microscope.

The relationship of the detail to the whole picture is also indicated on a location sheet. Finally, there is a step by step summary of the particular artist's working process.

The book was written by two teams. One was concerned with art history in terms of who the artists were, what their training was, what brought them West, and what their experiences were beyond the Mississippi. The other team was the painting conservators who did the connoisseurship and the technical analyses.

Until recently, a study of the painting methods employed by the principal American artists of the Old West might not have been received well. With the exception of O'Keeffe and Fechin, Western artists were usually the butt of cruel Eastern jokes about training, competence, and hackneyed subject matter. Museum curators and art critics debunked Western painting exhibitions. Current studies, however, are forcing them to upgrade their opinions and to discuss Western paintings in terms of realism, romanticism, impressionism, aestheticism, symbolism, and abstraction.

The most recent of these Western landscape or genre master painters to be resurrected on a grand scale was Frederic Remington, the paramount cowboy, Cavalry, and Indian artist of the Old West. A 1982 biography of Remington demonstrated that he was not just the cowboy dauber he himself had pretended to be. Rather, he had matured into an American Impressionist of the first rank. Since then, scholarly investigations and retrospectives touring nationally have confirmed the revised evaluation of "he who knew the horse." His paintings grace the covers of important current catalogs.

Other master painters of the Old West are earning the same improved ratings. Under similar scrutiny, these men and women were far from potboilers. Most of them were in fact the products of years of overseas training in the prestigious art schools of Germany, France, Holland, Italy, and Russia, as well as in the United States. They popularized the Western scenes that have become familiar. Like Remington, they painted at least as well as their contemporaries who devoted themselves to more conventional subjects.

This book provides enough biographical background to document who these newly appreciated painters were and how they lived. They are listed alphabetically for easy usage. That puts Oscar Berninghaus ahead of Albert Bierstadt and so on.

It also helps to look at the American master painters of the West chronologically, by birth dates and when they first entered the West. George Catlin was the only 18th century man among them. Born on the frontier, he was an amateur explorer-ethnologist who abandoned a profitable practice as a Pennsylvania lawyer to record Plains Indians and their artifacts on canvas for more than 40 years. His jumping off point was Missouri when he was 34.

The group of artists who penetrated the West next were the landscapists of the Rockies and the Plains. Each had his own style and specialty. Realist and panoramist Albert Bierstadt reached the Rockies in 1859 by accompanying a government wagon train. Two years later Thomas Hill, "the fastest brush in the West," rode a prairie schooner to San Francisco. He concentrated on Yosemite. In 1865 Worthington Whittredge went to the Rockies with another government wagon train, disliked the heights, and looked back eastward to paint the more intimate Plains. A third government party escorted the romanticist Thomas Moran to the Yellowstone in 1871.

Then came a disparate pair of Indian genre painters who went beyond Catlin's turf. Both were born in 1847. The mystic Ralph Albert Blakelock preceded Thomas Moran across the frontier in 1869 when he was 22. After he returned to New York City, ghostly images of amorphous Indians in primeval forests dominated his vision for the rest of his creative life. Henry Farny did not reach the Plains until 1881. He painted aspects of Indian culture from the white man's viewpoint.

The fourth group to arrive were the story tellers chronicling the Indian fighting army, the Indians, the frontiersmen, and the cowboys. Frederic Remington, "the greatest of us all," was in Wyoming in 1881 when he was 20, drawing his first rough sketch of cowboys for *Harper's Weekly*. Charley Russell was in Montana the following year when he was 18. Joseph Sharp, the founder of the Taos art colony, visited New Mexico in 1882 when he was 23. Charles Schreyvogel, who was Remington's age and his unwilling antagonist, did not go West until 1893. He concentrated on the Indian-fighting Cavalry.

The fifth group were more derivative genre painters and landscapists. Although born in 1865, Sidney Laurence appears to belong with the early panoramists. His style was much like theirs, if not his technique, but he did not depict Alaska until 1913 when the West was already settled.

The others in the fifth group were genre painters. Grace Hudson was born in the West in 1865. She started portraying Pomo Indian children in 1890. William R. Leigh was born in 1866. He did not visit the West until he was 40.

Ernest Blumenschein and Frank Tenney Johnson were born in 1874. Blumenschein arrived in Taos by accident in 1898 and became the most celebrated member of the Taos Society of Artists. Johnson was born near a prairie schooner trail in Iowa but did not begin illustrating the West until he was 30.

Maynard Dixon and Oscar Berninghaus were born the following year. Berninghaus visited Taos immediately after Blumenschein. He was the only self-taught master who became a teacher. Dixon was a native Westerner who was illustrating professionally when he was 20.

The last three of the master painters were modernists. Nicolai Fechin emigrated from Russia. He was born in 1881 when Remington and Farny were already on the Plains and he did not arrive in Taos until 1926. The illustrator N.C. Wyeth was born in 1882. His exposure to the West was brief, starting in 1904, so his Western paintings were few but they were memorable. Georgia O'Keeffe was born in 1887, making her the youngest of the master painters. When she travelled to New Mexico in 1929, she was the last of the group to reach the West. Her abstracted vision of the landscape was quite different from the others.

The biographies of these master painters provide both similarities and differences. For example, most of them lived the artists' long span. At a time when American life expectancy was less than 50 years, they averaged more than 74 years. This was 50 percent greater than could have been statistically expected, even though four of the 21–Remington, Schreyvogel, Wyeth, and Johnson–had their careers shortened by casualties. Remington's appendix burst. Schreyvogel gummed a chicken bone. Johnson received the kiss of death from a woman friend. Wyeth was hit by a train.

Remington's wife Eva liked "to talk horoscopathy and astrologitio." Remington was sympathetic to fortunetelling. He was a Libra with his scale balanced between painting and sculpture. Six others were Libras, Berninghaus, Blakelock, Laurence, Leigh, Sharp, and Wyeth. Perhaps coincidentally, all of the seven were native born. Six of them were genre painters. Only Laurence was different and he did not fit well any place. None of the master painters was passionate Aries or violent Taurus.

The Western artists had surprisingly little encouragement from their parents. Johnson's mother and Sharp's father had studied painting but they died too early to teach their offspring. Laurence's mother was an amateur artist but she did not support his Alaskan venture. Berninghaus' father sold prints. The rest of the fathers were soldiers, doctors, musicians, lawyers, politicians, tailors, weavers, farmers, and bakers. Many actively disapproved of art as a way for their children to make a living.

Nevertheless, the master painters knew when they were very young that they would be artists. Dixon and Leigh were drawing at seven. Berninghaus sold sketches at 10, Fechin at 13. O'Keeffe was sure at 10 that she would become a painter. Hudson was in art school at 13, Sharp at 14, Wyeth at 17. Blakelock and Blumenschein coupled music and art as youths.

More than half of the painters were exceptionally well taught: Whittredge, Bierstadt, and Farny were in Düsseldorf, Germany. Leigh and Schreyvogel were in Munich. Hill, Sharp, Laurence, and Blumenschein were in Paris. Fechin was at the Imperial Academy in Russia.

Moran copied Turner paintings in London. Johnson and O'Keeffe were taught in New York City, Dixon and Hudson in San Francisco. Remington and Wyeth attended schools as illustrators. Russell in mid-life learned from other painters. Only Catlin, Blakelock, and Berninghaus could honestly claim to be completely self-taught, and two of them worked where they could see other trained artists painting nearby.

There is, though, no "school" of Western artists as there is, for example, for the Hudson River School painters. Even the Taos artists were bound primarily by shared isolation and the need to combine in exhibitions for financial reasons rather than by style. The backgrounds, training, techniques, and goals of the artists of the American West are almost as varied as any group of artists would be if chosen at random. Consequently, Western artists are usually grouped by subject matter and chronology, not by technique or philosophy.

The first of these artists, Catlin, already realized that much of the West he saw and painted in 1830 would disappear in his lifetime. His work and the work of the master painters who followed him record this vital period in American history. They also document a romantic sentiment that is an intrinsic part of American culture.

Western expansion was the lifeblood of America. Only Western art preserves the nation's heritage that would otherwise have been lost.

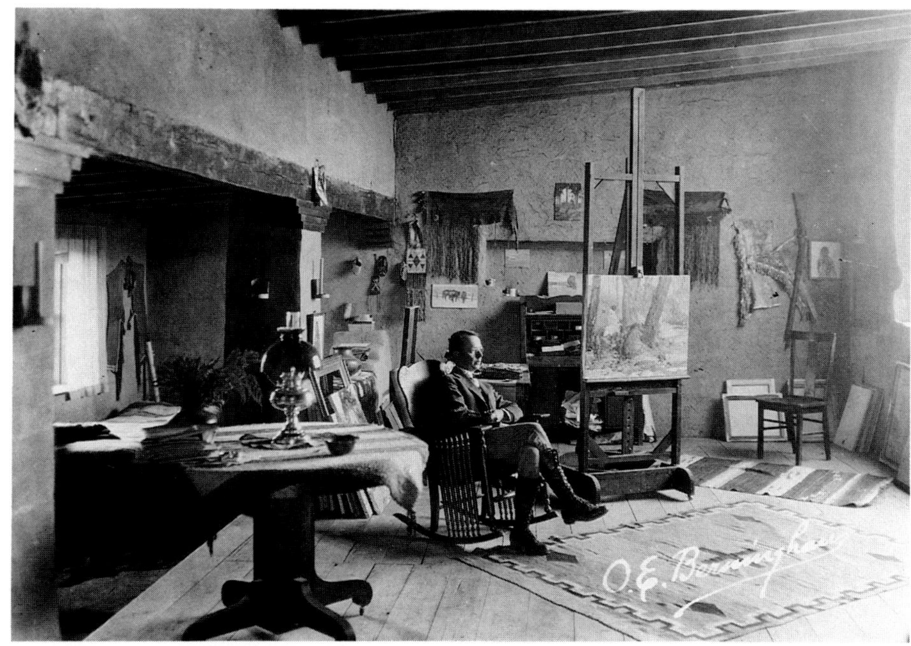

OSCAR EDMUND BERNINGHAUS

Oscar Berninghaus was the odd man among the six painters who migrated one after the other to northern New Mexico at the turn of the last century and initiated a singular flowering of Western American art. Five of the six were highly trained in prestigious art schools. They had attended sophisticated salons in Antwerp, Paris, or Munich.

The sixth man was the quiet one, Oscar Berninghaus. He was a St. Louis illustrator. His whole art education was three terms of night classes in the Washington University School of Fine Arts.

Berninghaus was born October 2, 1874 in St. Louis to immigrant German parents. His father was a salesman of lithographic prints, so Berninghaus was exposed to professional art as a child. At 10 he was a prodigy of self-taught drawing. In days when cameras were rare and photographs were less suited to reproduction than line drawings, he hurried to newsworthy events such as fires and accidents. He sketched what he saw and sold the drawings to the local newspapers. At 19 he was apprenticed to a large printing company. His first drawings were signed with his nickname, Bern.

One of his employer's clients was the Denver & Rio Grande Railroad. In 1899 the Railroad hired Berninghaus to travel its lines in Colorado and New Mexico to sketch the landscape for use in advertisements. The train crews cooperated by strapping him to the top of a car to give him unobstructed views. Berninghaus recalled that "the brakeman pointed out Taos Mountain and I started on a 25 mile wagon trek. I found it all as the brakeman had described, a barren plaza, few Anglos. I stayed but a week and became infected with the Taos germ." By "Taos germ" he meant the special quality that attracted artists to the remote village. Bert Phillips who had studied art in Paris was already in residence. Including Phillips, only 26 Anglos lived in Taos. Some of them were hiding from the law.

Taos was a painter's dream. The attraction was the paired but unmixed cultures, Spanish and Pueblo Indian, in an uncontaminated landscape under a clear sky and a brilliant sun in front of the sacred mountain. Friendly but primitive and unspoiled natives were prominent against an ideal background of light and land.

When Berninghaus returned to St. Louis, thoughts of Taos stayed with him. He decided that he would try to become a painter of the West, another Remington, so he could live in New Mexico permanently. The following year, 1900, he spent the summer in Taos as the second resident painter. In the winter he went back to St. Louis where he was a successful commercial artist earning the funds for successive summers dedicated to fine art in Taos.

His conservative German appearance gave comfort to his staid commercial customers in St. Louis by demonstrating that he was not given to Bohemian whims like the unreliable artists who had studied in Paris. In Taos, however, he was a strange looking duck. When he rose each morning in the village, which was without electricity, indoor plumbing, or telephone, he put on a clean white shirt and a tie before starting work in the studio. For excursions outdoors to paint landscapes he donned the jacket to his gray business suit and topped his apparel with a soft gray felt hat. He was never seen in a cowboy outfit or in an artist's smock.

His hair was cut short and he wore gold-rimmed spectacles that gave his gray-brown eyes an owlish look. "In fact," he admitted with characteristic good humor, "people could mistake me for an undertaker." He was less than medium height and slightly built, weighing 150 pounds. He smoked a pipe. His friends thought of him as a gentle man, calm and unaggressive, except those times when he relaxed by playing combative games of poker or bridge.

His studio was neat, with everything in place. He kept books of account covering all his business transactions. He never bought anything on the installment plan. Although he tried to disguise his emotions, he was a bit of a sentimentalist. He wrote his friend Bert Phillips, "Sometimes when you get a little sketch that don't amount to much and you want to sell cheap, I should like it for my home" in St. Louis. "I have quite a few of various artists" from Taos and Santa Fe.

His paintings were as tidy and consistent as his person and his habits. Foreground, middle distance, and background spaces were generally defined. He liked working out of doors. The Indians and the horses he depicted were placed in their natural setting, but not usually in a position to dominate the painting. *Ceremony of the Rabbit Hunt* is an exception.

In the studio he used the Indians as models to portray their domestic lives in a straightforward, illustrative, objective manner. One criticism was that he settled for the merely picturesque rather than striving for insightful treatments of his Indian subjects. That objectivity was, however, a common practice among the Taos artists. They were there simply because of the availability of the distinctive pictorial features, not as crusaders for racial justice.

He prepared most of his own canvases. The landscapes were usually painted directly from nature, without preliminary sketches on paper to define the composition. Instead, outlines were drawn on the canvas with charcoal. Then the shapes were blocked in, generally with a very thin blue oil underlayer for the shadows. Refinements were added while he was sitting at the easel in the studio where he used a maulstick to rest his painting hand.

Like Remington, Berninghaus prided himself on his ability to depict the horse, particularly the Indian ponies. He said "the Indian models know the pose. The horses are kept in place and brought back to almost the same position after each rest" from posing.

New Mexico became a state in 1912. Berninghaus was still wintering in St. Louis to secure plum commercial assignments such as an historical booklet of illustrations commissioned by the Anheuser-Busch brewing company. In the summers he joined the thriving Taos art colony. The number of painters had grown to the six who were the founders of the colony.

Marketing arrangements for the art emanating from this remote village had been difficult to establish. Phillips for example had no sooner found a gallery in Chicago to handle his output than he felt he was being cheated in the division of the selling prices. In 1915 the artists formed a sales cooperative they named the Taos Society of Artists. The Society was immediately successful in organizing group shows that toured the national museum and dealer circuit to exhibit and sell paintings. The Society became one of the best known painters' groups in the United States.

Berninghaus and the other Taos artists were similar in choice of subject and concept. They were no longer young and experimenting. They painted what they chose to see, with romantic overtones. The Indian was their principal subject but he was not the maltreated fighting Indian, the unfortunate victim of the winning of the West. The local models were dignified white-robed red men from the peaceful pueblo. Nevertheless, the artists' seemingly straightforward depiction of the Taos Indian was not his reality. The Indian's true lot was poverty and isolation.

The Taos painters were satisfied to continue to emphasize the Pueblo Indians' surface picturesqueness, a retrograde look that was repeated until the image became a stereotype. As a result, the Eastern art historians of the period ignored the Taos painters as an insignificant group traveling on a backward warp in American art. They were said to be recluses, working apart from the modernist movement that was winning the great critical plaudits.

In 1918 Berninghaus was still spending only six months of the year in Taos. In the winters he taught illustration at his old school, Washington University. He counseled his students to "draw–draw–draw. The painter must first see his picture as paint–as color–as form–and not as a landscape or a figure. Paint with feeling, not with seeing."

The next year he finally bought a residence in Taos but he did not move there permanently until 1925. That was the year after he exhibited a painting at the National Academy of Design in New York City. The Academy purchased the painting for its collection, a great honor, and elected him an associate member in 1926. He never became an Academician, however, because of a blackball from his feuding neighbor Blumenschein who was already an Academician.

In his later years Berninghaus abandoned the use of models in the studio and the plein air landscapes in order to paint from memory. His focus was wider and the figures smaller as they receded into the middle distance. He concentrated on composition, rhythm, and color with softened lighting in pastel tones. His brushstrokes were shortened and loaded with pigment. There was a controlled texture, compared to the freer application in earlier pictures.

He maintained his belief in the validity of what he was doing. "We have had French, Dutch, Italian and German art," he remarked. "Now we have American art. I feel that from Taos will come that art." When he was 76 he wrote, "I belong to the vintage of yesterday and I still paint that way. At the same time I respect the present-day movement. I have tried to do the best I could."

No one doubted his perseverance. He died April 27, 1952 in Taos.

1. THE PAINTING

Berninghaus was an intense observer of the Indian scene around him. He remarked that the Indians preserved their ancient hunting skills in the ritual pursuit of the rabbit: "From my studio window I have a view of 30 miles. Every now and then I see whirlwinds. Looking out now, I see one but as it approaches it is a band of Indians out on the ceremonial rabbit hunt. These rabbits are hunted with bows and arrows, clubs and dogs– but no firearms, such is the reverence for the old days. The band comes on–all mounted on their ponies, helping make the sight picturesque."

The dynamic spiral composition and prismatic palette of *Ceremony of the Rabbit*

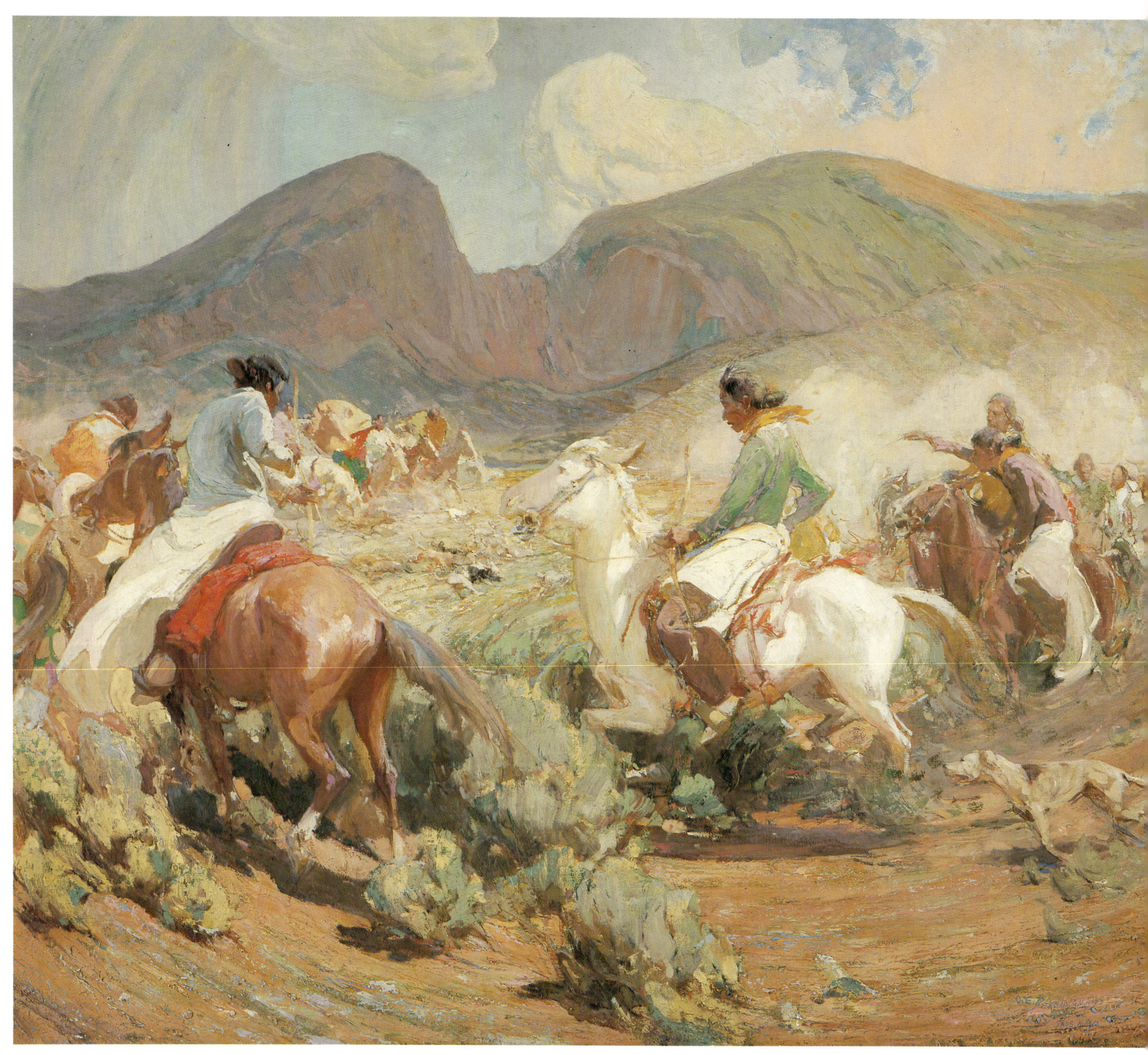

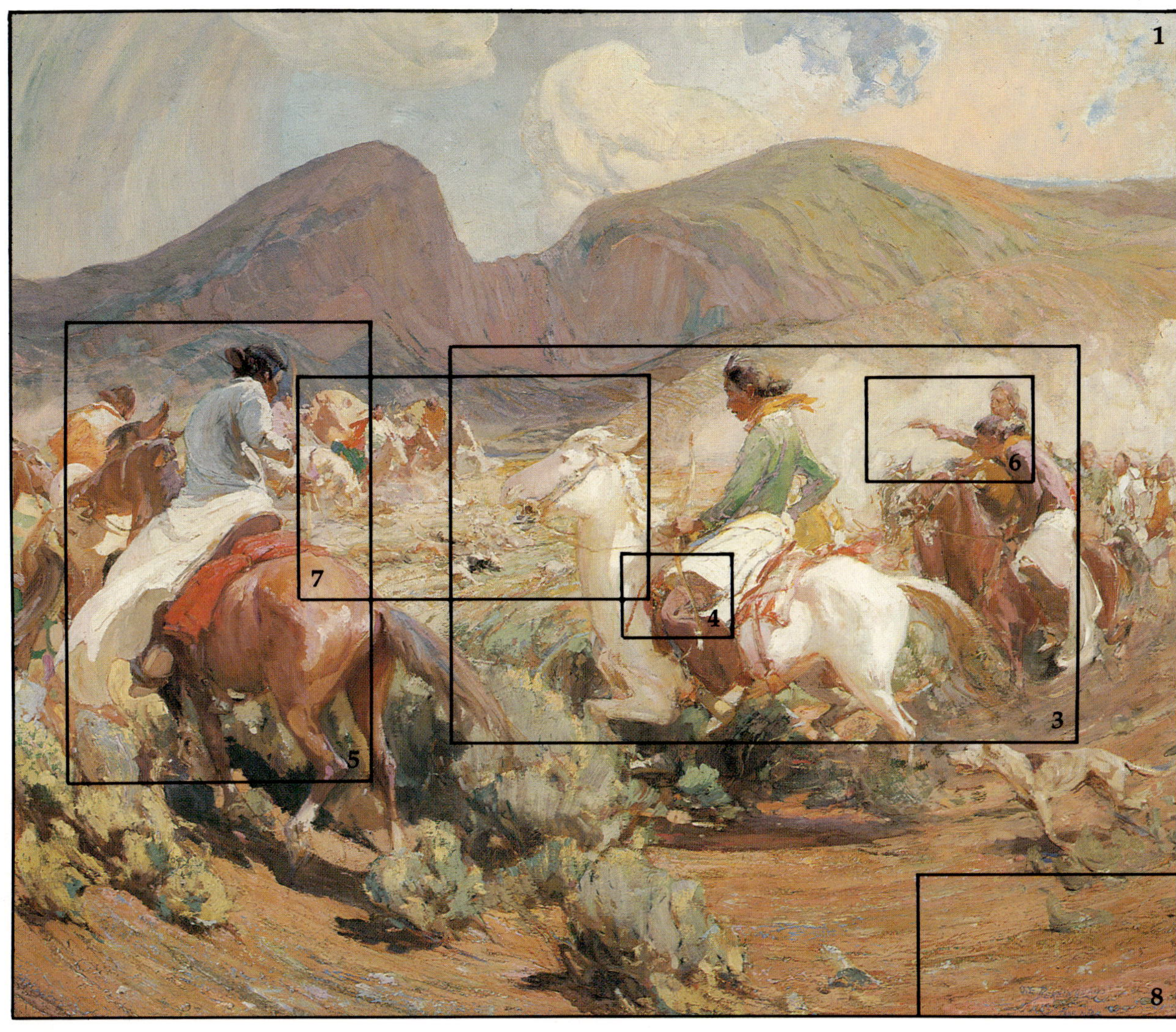

O.E. Berninghaus. Ceremony of the Rabbit Hunt *is in the collection of the Museum of Western Art, Denver, Colorado. Oil on canvas, lined. 35 1/8 inches (89 cm) height x 40 1/4 inches (102.2 cm) width. Signed lower right. Not dated.*

Hunt re-creates this kaleidoscope of color and action. Both composition and palette were exaggerated and manipulated by Berninghaus to duplicate the effect of this vivid scene.

Focus was achieved by the spiral composition leading the eye to the center of the painting where the rabbit must be. As in stop action photography, the two foremost riders and their horses are captured sharply. The surrounding blur of the landscape and even bushes in the foreground are swept into this vortex of motion. This circular composition is framed by clouds that curve over the top to complete the circle.

To attract the viewer's eye, Berninghaus utilized daring color combinations based on the principle of complementary colors. A color gives a greater degree of contrast to its complement than to any other color. A strong red, for example, is balanced and emphasized by its complement green. Light yellow-green is complemented by lilac, and yellow appears with violet. The excitement of the composition is thus enhanced. The contrast achieved through use of complementary colors, however, remains harmonious to the eye because these colors strengthen and purify each other. The association between complementary colors is so strong that it holds true even when the colors are dulled with gray, as is the case with some of the shadows.

Berninghaus' colors are fantastic and unnaturalistic. Shadows and highlights reflect the colors of the Indian garb, trappings, and surrounding foliage and landscape in complementary combinations of yellows and violets or greens and reds. Use of these colors is conceptual and heightens the effect of the whirling action.

Berninghaus also used contrasts in his brushwork to set off shapes against each other, and to emphasize their spatial positions. A solidly painted figure, for example, is set against a sketchy background. The figure appears bolder and more distinct than his surroundings and as a result is more prominent.

For *Ceremony of the Rabbit Hunt*, a plain weave, medium coarse canvas was used. A thin gray ground was applied, probably by the artist. The extensive underdrawing for the horses and other figures appears to have been done with charcoal. The shadows, modeled in the underdrawing, were often left exposed in the final work. The underdrawing is less apparent in the background.

The main composition was applied directly onto the underdrawing with paint that ranges from thin with ground and underdrawing left exposed to quite thick with moderate impasto. In the next stage of the painting process, thick brushstrokes indicating the spiraling motion of the composition were applied to the perimeter of the composition. When this paint was dry, thin lines of light blue, mauve, lilac, green, and yellow paint were dragged across the surface in a fast and circular movement, catching only on the tops of the impasto of the previous layer, and further enhancing the circular direction of the paint beneath. The result of these many layers is a lively, highly textured surface of crusty impasted peaks with different colors from underlayers showing through the gaps.

The movement of the ceremony was what caught Berninghaus' interest. The combinations of complementary colors, from pure hues such as red with green, to less saturated mixtures such as shades of purple-reds with yellow-greens, give the effect of colors whirling by in bright sunlight. Like a fast ride on a carousel, the colors mingle and reflect one another.

The viewer's attention is caught by the prominent figures. From there, the circular composition leads in a spiral motion to the center of the painting where only a few blurs and indistinct dabs of color indicate the target of the hunt: the rabbit is dissolved in the whirlpool of action. The swell of the mountains and clouds in the background rise like great waves, threatening to pull the scene into itself in a great undertow.

2. COLOR CIRCLE

The color circle is an artist's aid in which the colors of the spectrum are depicted in their intrinsic order, that is, as they would be in a rainbow. In this circular arrangement, the complementary colors naturally fall opposite each other. The complements of primary colors are formed by the combination of the other two primaries. These combined colors are called secondary colors. By following this system, an infinite range of complements can be formed.

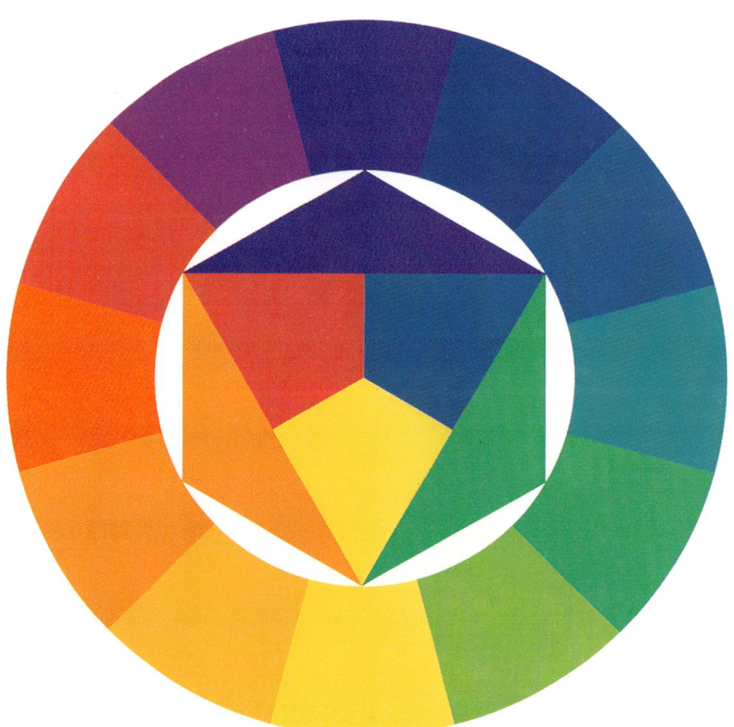

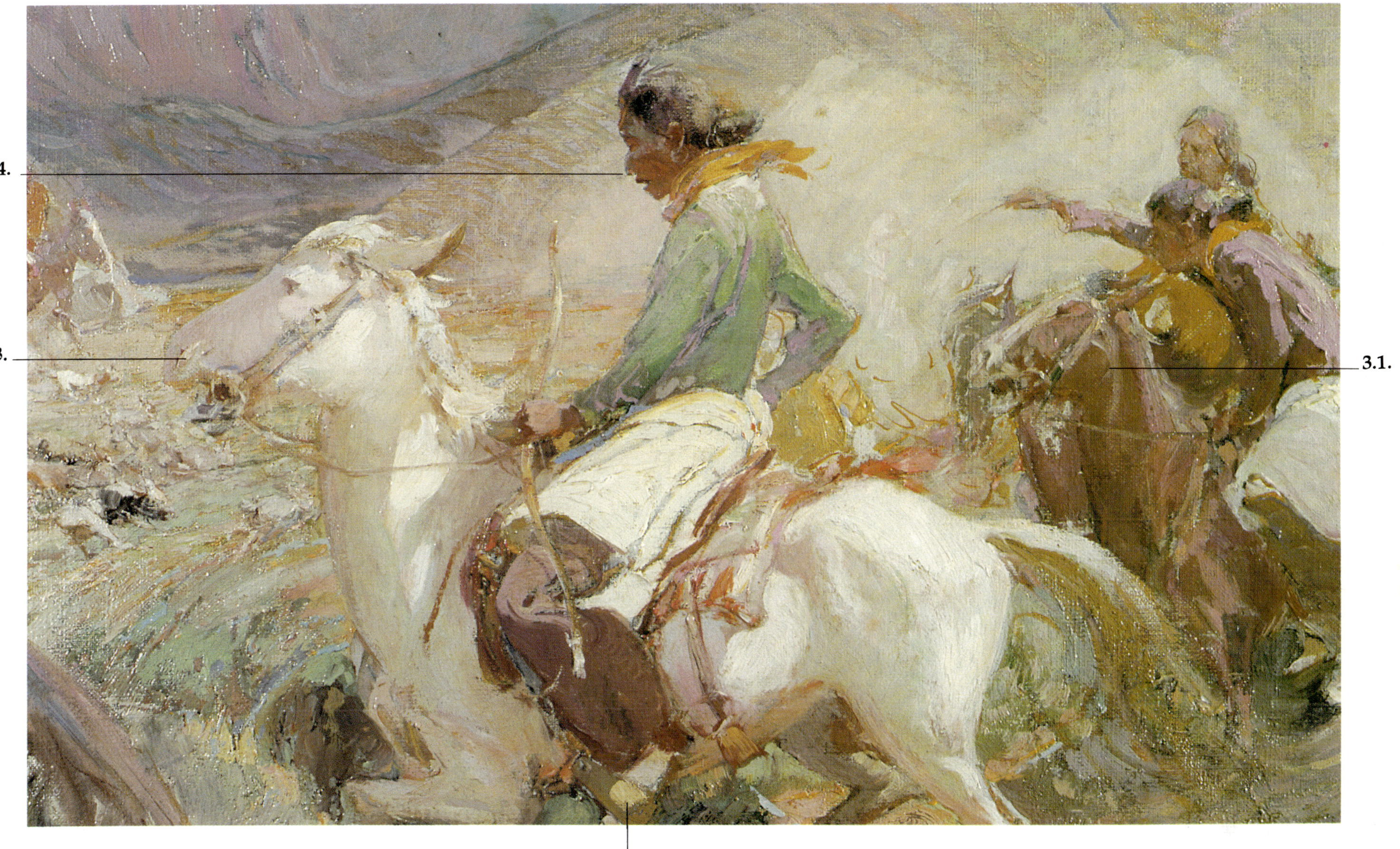

3. DETAIL OF CENTRAL FIGURE ON WHITE HORSE

The modeling of this vivid white horse has been done in complementary combinations of pale yellow-green and lilac, with less saturated hues of the same colors used for the rider's blouse.

3.1. The heads of these two horses in the distance are sketchily painted. The more distant horse is made up of sparse details painted directly onto the gray ground. The contrast between the less detailed, grayer horses and the vividly painted white horse in the foreground creates a sense of depth.

3.2. The colors for the stirrup were partially mixed on the canvas in a wet-into-wet technique.

3.3. The light pink and white paint for the horse's head was applied directly onto the gray ground, leaving the gray partially exposed as a middle tone. The ground was left completely uncovered for the gray color of the nostril and reins.

3.4. The head of the figure follows a dark blue-black painted line. This line probably served as an outline or a sketch to guide the artist in applying the colors.

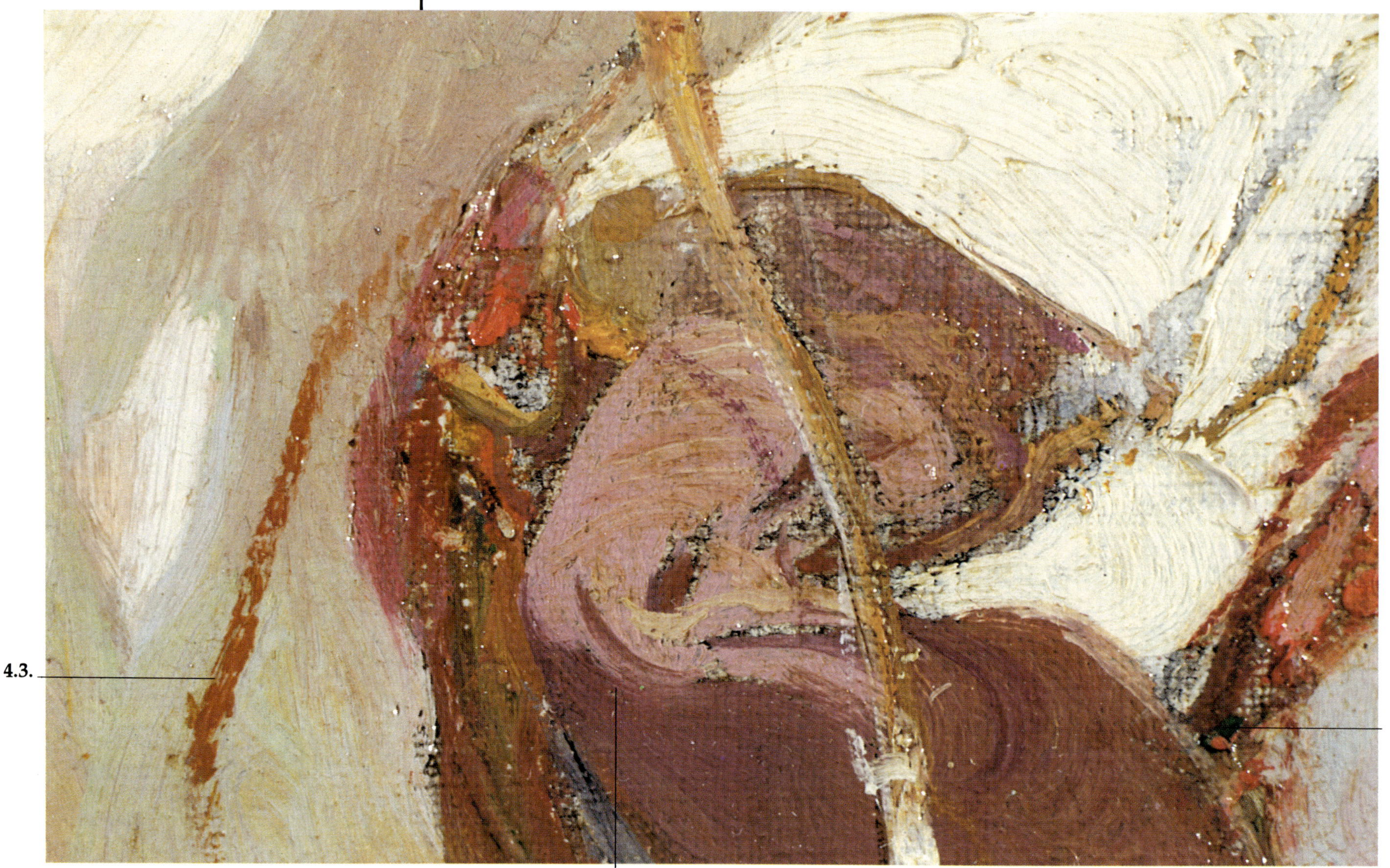

4.1. A tiny pure red dot sitting in a bed of its complement green enlivens this area.

4.2. The knee was painted in a wet-into-wet technique. The colors were not mixed on the palette but directly on the surface of the painting.

4.3. Dragged lines were added as refinements when the paint beneath was dry.

4. DETAIL OF CENTRAL FIGURE'S KNEE

The extensive charcoal underdrawing can be seen between the color areas as broken black lines. Outlines, shadings, and contours were drawn completely. The paint was confined to these outlines, often without covering them. The gray ground was often unobscured by paint, remaining visible as gray lines between the color areas. Like the visible underdrawing, the gray ground was used as a pictorial device, adding to the definition of the forms.

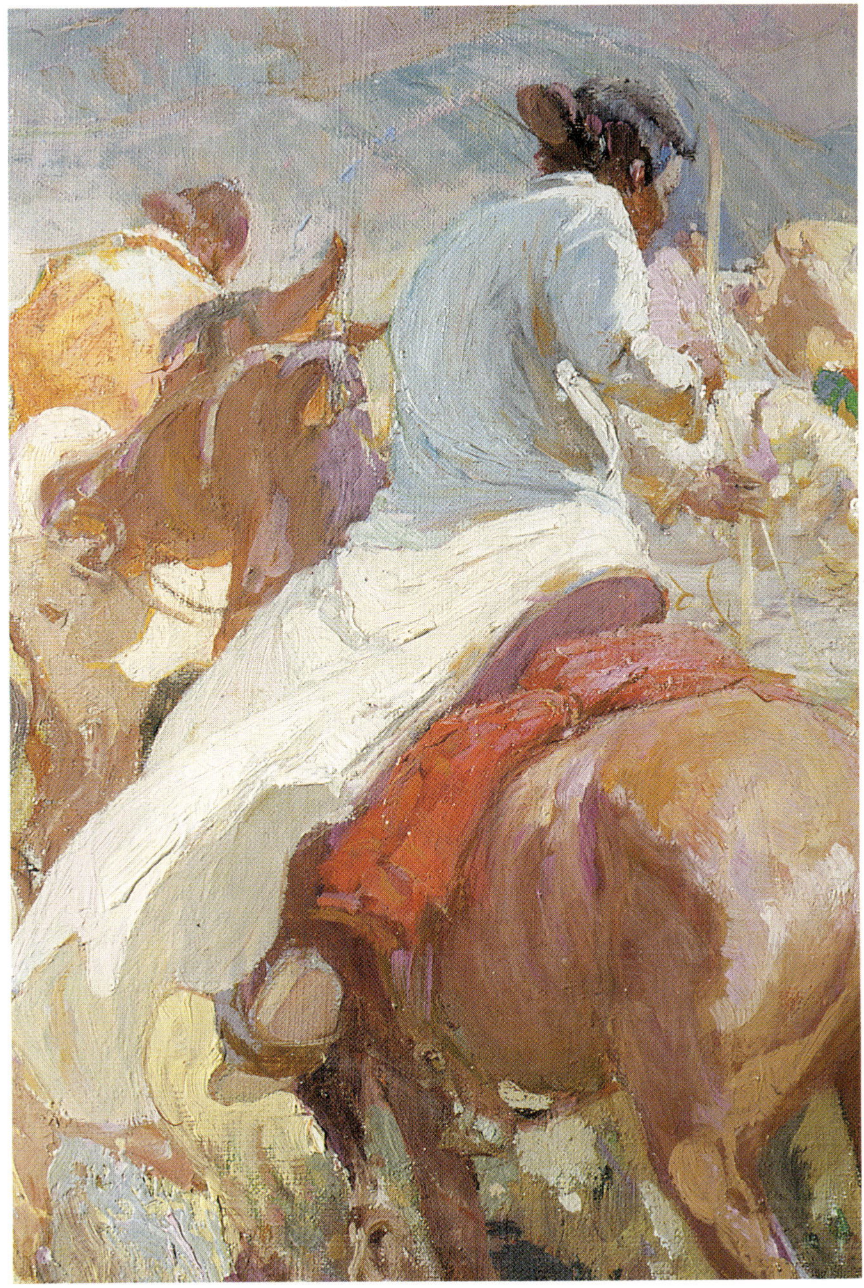

5. DETAIL OF RIDER ON BROWN HORSE TO LEFT

The rich paint application sculpts the rider's clothing. Thick highlights were added to his shoulder and arm. The rich paint and intense colors of the horse and rider stand out against the sketchily applied, less saturated colors of the background, creating a sense of depth. This receding space was amplified by the curved motion of the brushwork for the light blue shirt which follows the circular direction of the composition.

Enlargements of details are an array of colorful shapes that make little sense when taken out of the context of the entire composition, and resemble fitted colored patches of a puzzle assemblage. The rider's shoe is set off against a frame of pale yellow that fits snugly between the boot and the light gray shadow of the man's outfit. The same importance given to this yellow frame was given to the object within the frame. The detail does not read as three dimensional objects located in the picture plane but as abstract puzzle pieces. It is only by viewing the entire painting that the shapes form images, and only by following the spiral composition that spatial relationships are established.

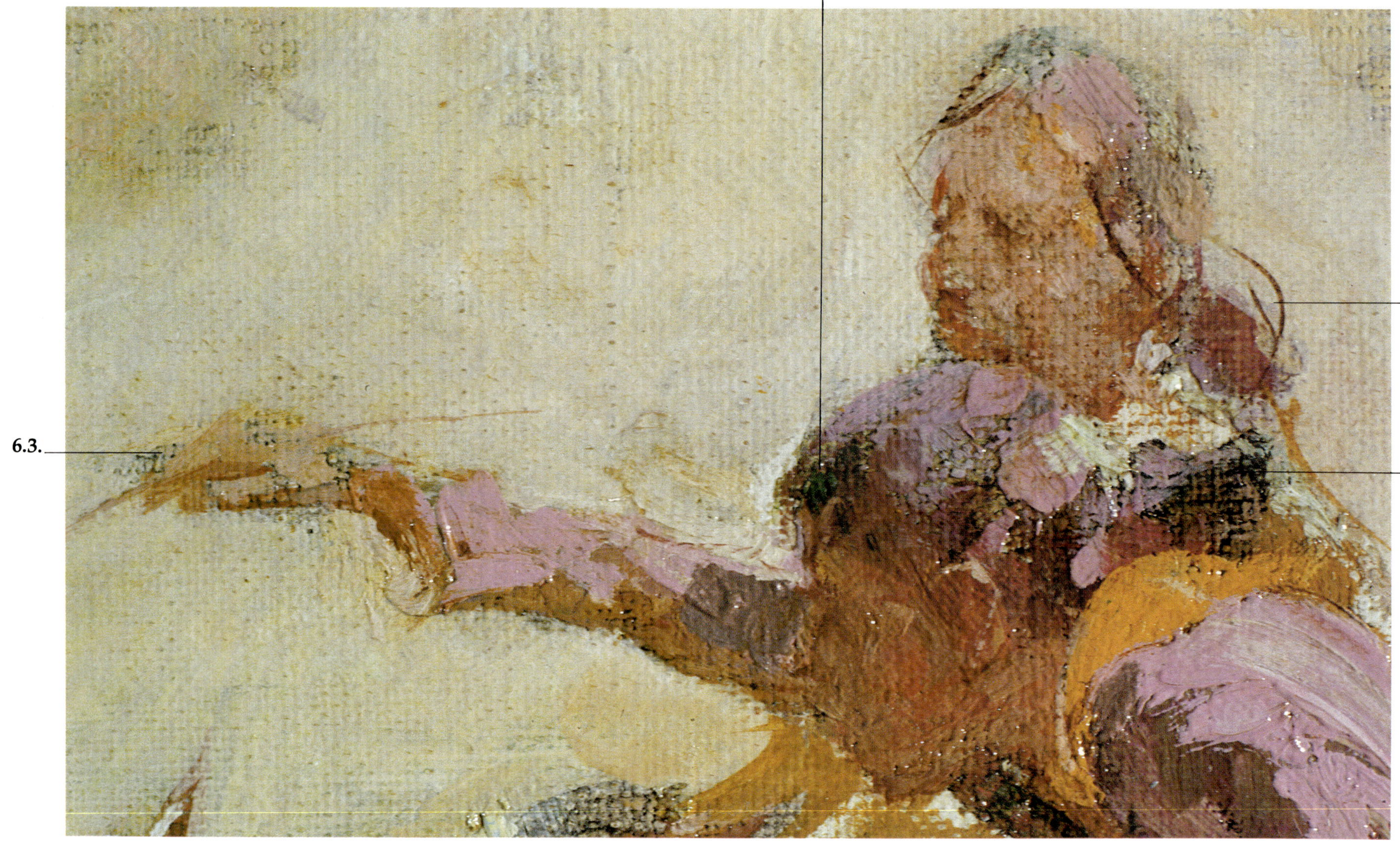

6.1. Thin calligraphic lines for the hair were added last.

6.2. The underdrawing was left exposed here as a dark shadow.

6.3. The terse brushwork of the hand leaves the gray ground and underdrawing exposed.

6.4. On top of the thin paint a few dabs of strong color were added to define the features. The seemingly random dot of green serves to make a contrast with its complement red.

6. DETAIL OF TWO HEADS ON RIGHT

These faces in the middle distance are minimally indicated, yet the strong modeling is achieved by applying impasted dabs of rich color on the bare ground or on a thinly applied paint layer. The features are rendered without detail, only with this sharp contrast between light and shadow. The sketchiness of the figures is balanced by impasted dabs of strong colors. Complementary colors are juxtaposed: yellow is alongside lilac, red alongside green.

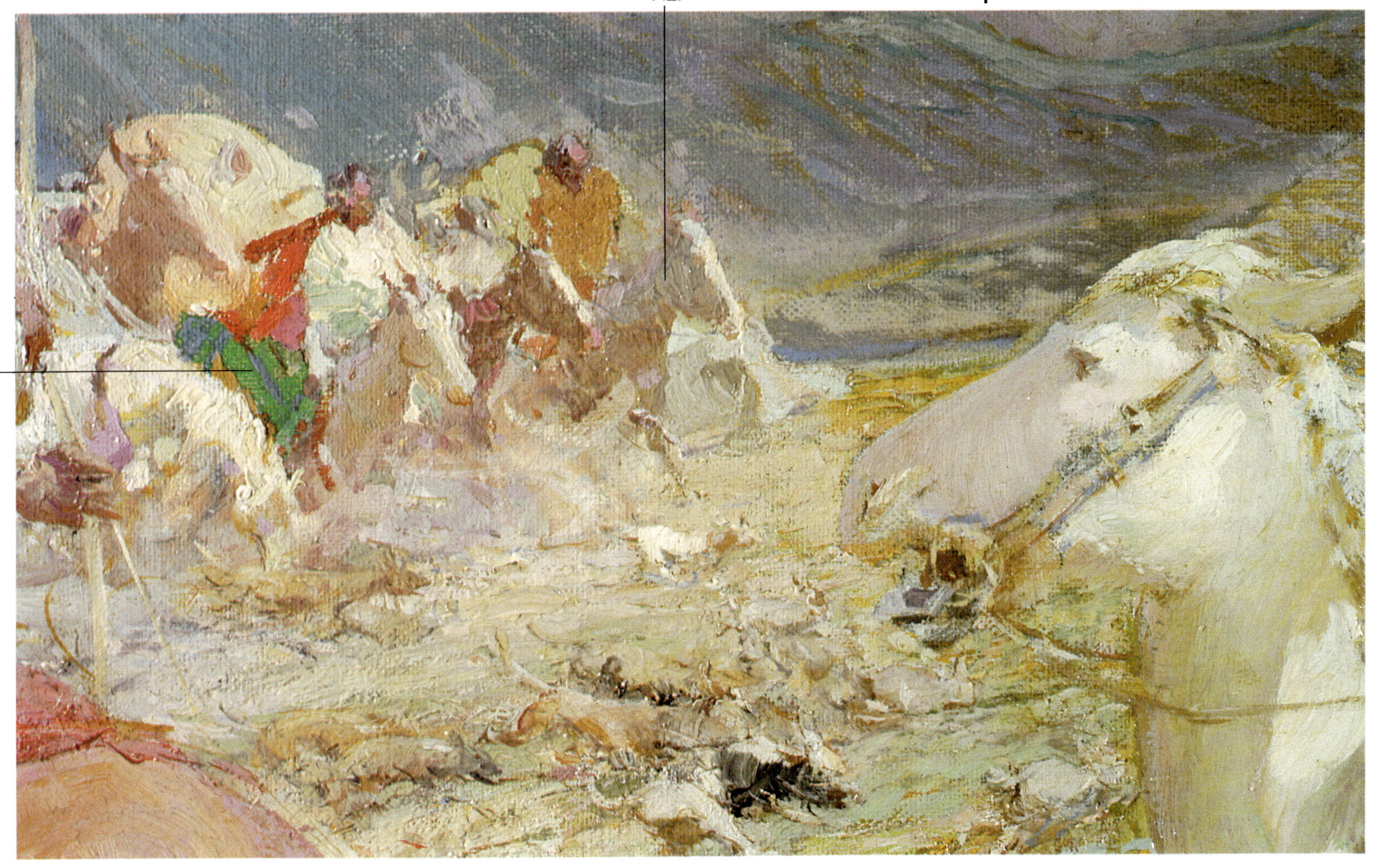

7. DETAIL OF DOGS AND RABBIT IN CENTER OF PAINTING

An enlarged view of the center of the action reveals only a few dabs of color and some fine lines to indicate the focal point where the rabbit is about to disappear behind the white horse's neck. The dogs following the prey are merely suggested by dabs of highlights against shadow. The viewer can only anticipate that the dogs will catch their quarry. The figures and inevitable outcome of the chase are of secondary importance to the whirlwind of the chase.

7.1. A saturated red is juxtaposed with its complement green to draw the eye into the center of the composition.

7.2. Completing the spiral of the painting's composition, the parallel white faces of the three horses in the background all point toward the rabbit.

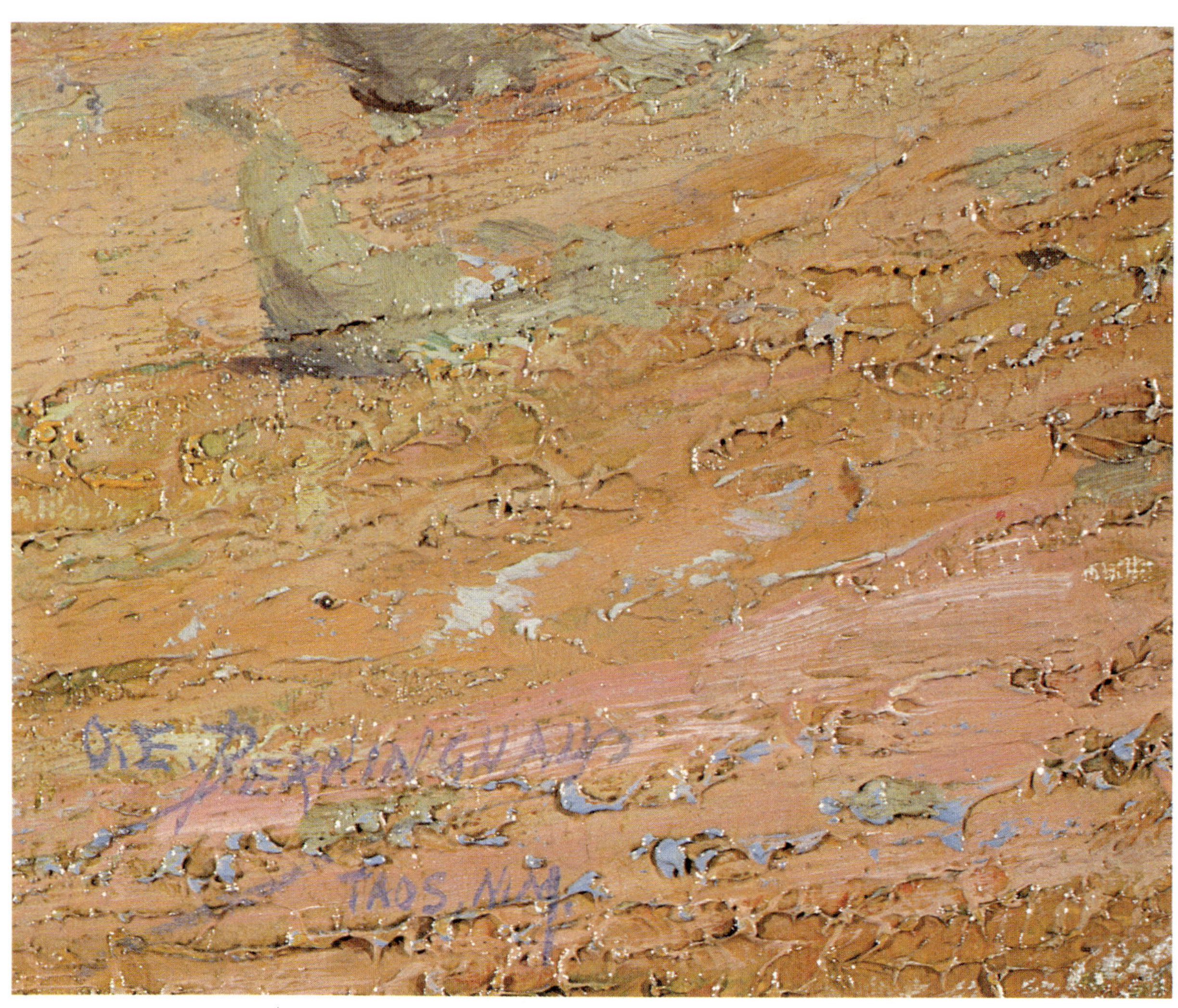

8. DETAIL OF SIGNATURE

O.E. Berninghaus

SUMMARY OF PAINTING TECHNIQUE

a. The canvas was mounted on the stretcher.
b. The fabric was sized and a thin gray ground was applied, probably by the artist.
c. An extensive underdrawing was carried out for the horses and figures, with what appears to be charcoal.
d. The main composition was painted, often leaving the ground and underdrawing exposed.
e. The thick brushstrokes indicating the spiraling motion of the composition were then applied to the perimeter.
f. Final thin lines of pastel colors were dragged in a swift and curved motion across the surface, catching only on the tops of the impasto of the previous paint layers, to further enhance the circular composition.

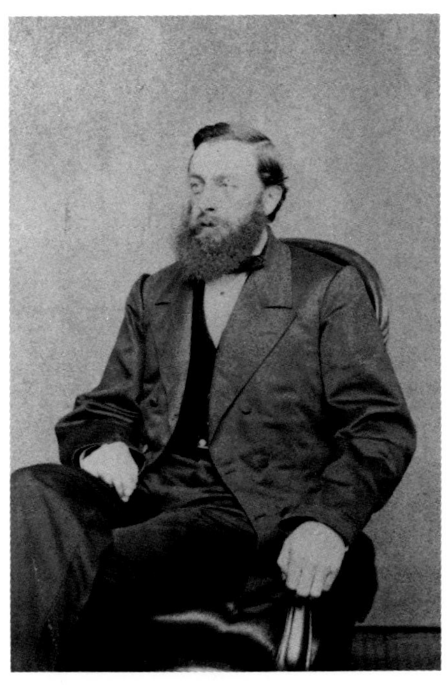

ALBERT BIERSTADT

Appreciation of Albert Bierstadt's art has been on a rollercoaster ride for more than a century. Even during his lifetime, the ups and downs of critical acceptance of his work were extreme compared to other master painters of the Western landscape.

At the crest of his popularity in the winter of 1865, New York City hung a banner across Broadway to announce the exhibition of the new Bierstadt panoramic painting *Storm in the Rocky Mountains*. After reading his obituary in 1902, however, a surprised art critic confessed, "I did not know he was alive until I saw he had died." In the trough in 1940, 100 of his paintings sold at auction for $2 each. Today his major works bring millions of dollars.

Bierstadt was born in Solingen, Germany on January 7, 1830. His father, who had been conscripted as a German soldier, emigrated to New Bedford, Massachusetts with the family "to escape the hostile atmosphere" in Europe. The senior Bierstadt labored as a cooper in the peaceful whaling port, making casks for water storage on board ship.

Bierstadt wanted to become an artist. There were fine marine painters like William Bradford, Benjamin Russell, and Charles Raleigh in New Bedford, but proximity to the sea had no appeal for Bierstadt. His bent was to depict people.

In the beginning of his career, Bierstadt kept no diary. The details of how he came to be an artist are sketchy. He did not study with the famous New Bedford painters. Instead, he began as a cake decorator and later was employed by a manufacturer of picture frames. At the age of 20 in June 1850, however, he emerged as a fine artist and a teacher of "mono-chromatic painting," that is, in black and white. The following year he was exhibiting paintings in New Bedford and the year after that his work was competent enough to be reviewed by Boston critics.

Soon Bierstadt had established a circle of customers. He recognized, though, that he needed more training. As a proud German-American he was attracted to the Düsseldorf Academy near where he was born. The Academy and the masters with studios in the town comprised the Düsseldorf School of 300 artists from all over the world. The most celebrated genre painter in Düsseldorf was a distant cousin, Johann Peter Hasenclever, who agreed to serve as Bierstadt's master.

With money advanced by his patrons, Bierstadt went to Düsseldorf in 1854. On his arrival, he found that his cousin had died. Painting the landscape was a new subject with growing popularity in the Academy. Bierstadt discovered that he had more talent for scenery than for people, so he concentrated on the landscape as taught by Karl Friedrich Lessing and Andreas Achenbach.

The leading young painter in Düsseldorf was another German-American, Emanuel Leutze who specialized in historical subjects. At first Leutze disparaged Bierstadt as a man of little ability. He considered Bierstadt to be just "another waif to be taken care of," but he arranged for the newcomer to share a studio with the more established American painter Worthington Whittredge.

To Whittredge, Bierstadt was a revelation: "After working in my studio for a few months, he fitted up a paint box and started off to try his luck" at drawing the peasants and the countryside. After five months had gone by without a word, Bierstadt came back "loaded down with innumerable studies. For one who had little instruction, it was marvelous." The drawings and oil studies were fresh and direct from nature.

Bierstadt used these field sketches to produce larger paintings in Whittredge's studio. In each picture he combined elements of several studies to create a composite view that no longer represented any single location. Then he sent the completed paintings to New Bedford for sale to his old clients.

The poetic Düsseldorf styling of his work was new to America. The high finish and sentimental treatment took the public by surprise. The critics could not believe that young "mono-chromatic" Bierstadt had achieved such virtuosity so quickly. They remembered him as having been merely competent. Before the Düsseldorf paintings could be sold, Bierstadt's mother had to obtain certificates of authenticity from the great Leutze. Only then did New Bedford accept Bierstadt's romantic mannerisms as having actually been painted by him.

Bierstadt's "pockets soon had money in them." Even in Düsseldorf he was accepted as the peer of the older American artists. He went on long sketching tours with Leutze, Whittredge, and Sanford Gifford. By 1857 he was finally satisfied with his polished technique. He sailed back to New Bedford where he continued to paint European themes in the Düsseldorf style.

There was a financial panic in the United States in 1857, along with worldwide unrest. Nevertheless, Bierstadt was promptly accepted as a successful New England painter of European scenes. He exhibited at the National Academy of Design in 1858 and 1859 and organized a New Bedford show of works of major living American painters. He included his friends from Düsseldorf and himself.

The American West had been in the back of Bierstadt's mind since adolescence. At the age of 12 he had written an account of an imaginary trip to the Rocky Mountains. His interest coincided with the start of the national movement toward Western expansion and the strong public involvement with the unknown territory. After the mature Bierstadt heard a lecture on the experiences that the American explorer Bayard Taylor had beyond the Mississippi, he determined to find out for himself what the West had to offer as a subject for his landscapes.

At the time, the best way West for any artist was with Colonel F.W. Lander. The Colonel was not only the government's most famous surveyor of the Overland Trail but he was also a published poet and an art critic. He solicited painters and photographers to accompany and record his surveys, as long as the artists paid their own expenses.

Bierstadt learned that Lander was preparing for an 1859 venture to find a trail to California safer than the existing one endangered by hostile Indians in Mormon territory. The painter secured an introduction from Lander's boss, the Secretary of War, and started for St. Joseph, Missouri to join Lander's wagon train.

For a young man of 29 who had walked across Germany, Switzerland, and Italy, the trek that started in a Lander's wagon in May was not arduous. Bierstadt was following the earlier painters Alfred Miller and George Catlin past the frontier into the wilderness. Unlike his predecessors, his primary interest was the landscape, not the Indian.

Lander's route was to the Platte River, then through Nebraska Territory to South Pass in what has become Wyoming. In the beginning, Bierstadt was not taken by the scenery. While describing the Wind River chain on July 10, he played down the uniqueness of what he saw: "The mountains are very fine; they resemble very much the Bernese Alps. Many spots remind us of our New Hampshire and Catskill hills."

Soon after voicing these chauvinistic geologic comparisons, Bierstadt left Lander and started home while the weather was favorable. With only a couple of civilian companions he wandered casually across Indian territory, sketching and living off the land. He grew increasingly enamored of the rugged mountains and finally decided to spend the rest of his life painting the West. The polished Düsseldorf technique would be employed to convey to Eastern viewers the majestic terrain he had come to revere.

He arrived in New Bedford in November. The following year he found quarters in New York City near friends in the Tenth Street Studio Building. He was elected to the National Academy in recognition of his proficiency in European subjects while he was beginning the long series of pictures of the West. To avoid disrupting his career, he bought an exemption from military service in the Civil War.

In 1863 he went West again. This time he was with Fitz Hugh Ludlow, a writer whose fame resulted from his confessional published as "The Hasheesh Eater." When they returned to New York, Ludlow's wife divorced him and married Bierstadt. Ludlow never again referred to Bierstadt by name.

The year 1863 also saw the issuance of Bierstadt's professional challenge to America's greatest landscape painter to that time, Frederick Church, who was the panoramist of remote parts of the hemisphere other than the West. Both painters were familiar with the philosophic discussion about beauty versus the sublime, where beauty was small and serene while the sublime was huge and powerful. When Church painted a colossal canvas of turbulent Niagara Falls, Bierstadt also went for the sublime. He countered Church with a 6x10 foot *The Rocky Mountains*.

Because his two exposures to the grandeur of the Western mountains had eventually overwhelmed Bierstadt, he painted the landscape on the monumental scale needed to convey the magnitude of what he had seen. To show the splendor, he added theatricality equivalent to the lushness of a German opera. That way he stunned his Eastern viewers with his paintings, precisely as the real mountains had awed him.

Bierstadt's panorama was an immediate, tremendous success just when the leadership of the Düsseldorf school was being eroded in Europe by French and German realists. There were also some American critics who called his Düsseldorf style skillful rather than imaginative. These critics described his self-promoting salesmanship as mere "puffery."

As part of Bierstadt's marketing plan, *The Rocky Mountains* was first shown to a few influential guests who informally spread the word about the painting's magnificence. Next the picture was taken to Boston for a preview that aroused a furor. Then it was unveiled and engraved in New York. Finally, the painting was exhibited at the New York Metropolitan Fair. By that time the picture was as well-known as the face of George Washington. The promotion enabled Bierstadt to sell the painting for $25,000, a huge amount for the day.

The next year Bierstadt started exhibiting the *Storm in the Rocky Mountains* that raised the Broadway banner. The size had increased to 84 square feet and the price to $35,000. The height of his success was the 9 1/2x15 foot *Domes of the Yosemite* in 1867.

With the proceeds of these paintings, Bierstadt built a $100,000 villa overlooking the Hudson River. The studio alone was 75x50 feet. He returned to Europe in 1867 for a two-year grand tour. The urbane and good-natured artist was honored everywhere. Nobility were his hosts.

By 1876, though, the roller coaster was commencing a long downward slide. Critics were complaining that "Mr. Bierstadt seems to be under the delusion that the bigger a picture is, the finer it is." The book of the Philadelphia Centennial decried his "lapse into sensational and meretricious effects."

There was a changing taste in American landscape painting. The trend was toward the Munich school and the romantic Barbizons. To compensate, Bierstadt's sales methods verged on high pressure to produce the funds he needed for his gracious living and his extensive travels.

Inevitably, he reached the point where he could not pay his creditors. His villa burned. His paintings were rejected for exhibitions in London and Washington. After his wife died he married a rich widow but he was declared bankrupt in 1895. The sheriff seized his effects including the pictures in his studio. His painting, *The Last of the Buffalo*, was refused by the American selection committee for the Paris Exposition of 1899. His death on February 18, 1902 at 71 did not cause "a ripple in the art pond."

In two decades Bierstadt had won and lost a reputation as America's greatest landscape painter. His fall as an artist was blamed on his lifelong adherence to the precepts of the Düsseldorf school, but the other panoramic painters were also forgotten and they had favored different schools. All of them simply went out of style. As the perceptive artist Frederic Remington noted in 1908, Bierstadt's "big canvases won't do as we understand painting [today]. The old men saw things darkly. Small canvases are best." In 1988, however, the medium sized 26x36 inch *The Last of the Buffalo* returned to the market to sell for $1,870,000 at public auction in New York City.

1. THE PAINTING

In *Cho-looke, The Yosemite Fall* Bierstadt portrays the newly discovered Fall in all its grandiosity. Few had seen this wild, untouched, and romantic place by 1864. The campers at the bottom of the Valley in the painting probably included artists Enoch Wood Perry, Virgil Williams, and Bierstadt, as well as Dr. John Hewston, a scientist, and Fitz Hugh Ludlow, the writer. The small figures are not only true to life, but in this context they effectively demonstrate the gigantic scale of the cataract.

The men had their first glimpse of the Yosemite from Inspiration Point on August 1, 1863. Ludlow wrote in his book, *The Heart of the Continent*, "That name [of the Point] had appeared pedantic, but we found it only the spontaneous expression of our own feelings on the spot. We did not so much seem to be seeing from that crag of vision a new scene on the old familiar globe, as a new heaven and a new earth into which the creative spirit had just been breathed. I hesitate now, as I did then, at the attempt to give my vision utterance. Never were words so beggared for an abridged translation of any Scripture of Nature."

Ludlow also wrote that during the artists' stay in the Yosemite, most of them got up at dawn and took a bath in the ice-cold Merced. They breakfasted on flapjacks and coffee—sometimes game. "Then the artists with their camp-stools and color boxes, the sages with their goggles, nets, botany-boxes, and bug-holders, the gentlemen of elegant leisure with their naked eyes and a fish-rod or a gun, all rode away, firing back Parthian shots of injunction about the dumpling in the grouse-fricassee.

"Sitting up in their divine workshop, by a little after sunrise our artists began labor in that only method which can ever make a true painter or a living landscape, –*color*-studies on the spot; and though I am not here to speak of their results, I will assert that during their seven weeks' camp in the Valley they learned more and gained greater material

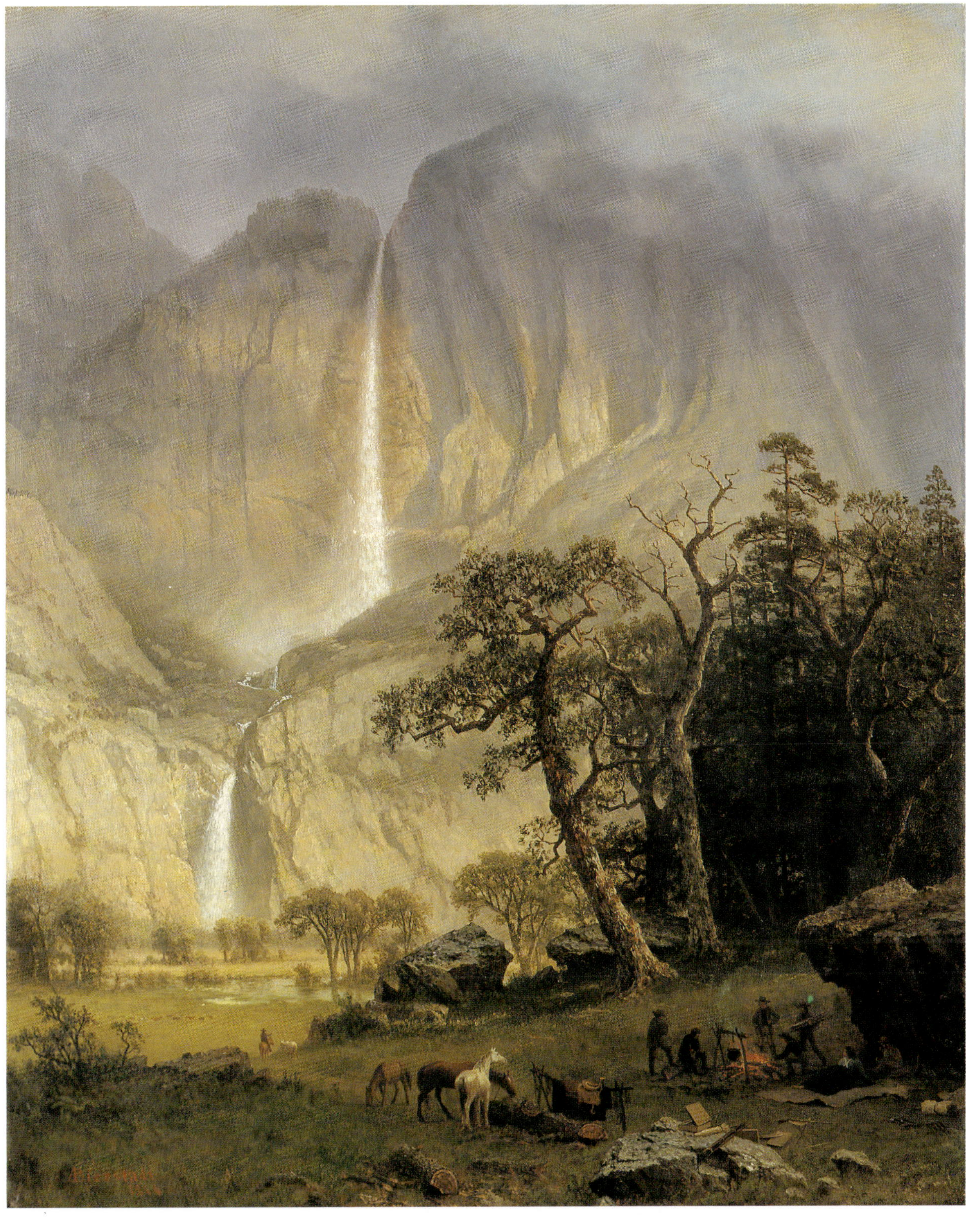

A. Bierstadt. Cho-looke, The Yosemite Fall, *also known as* Camping in the Yosemite, *is in the collection of The Timken Art Gallery, The Putnam Foundation, San Diego, California. Oil on canvas, wax lined. 34 1/8 inches (86.7 cm) height x 27 inches (68.7 cm) width. Signed lower left and dated 1864.*

for future triumphs than they had gotten in all their lives before at the feet of the greatest masters.... At evening, when the artists returned, half an hour was passed in a 'private view' of their day's studies; then came another dinner, called a supper; then the tea-kettle was emptied into a pan, and brush-washing with talk and pipes led the rest of the genial way to bed-time."

Bierstadt used these oil sketches when he painted *Cho-looke, The Yosemite Fall* back in his New York studio. The picture was immediately acclaimed as one of his finest paintings. The New York *Evening Post* wrote that "Bierstadt, who is one of the most indefatigable workers among the artists–for even in mid-June the days are not sufficiently long for his purpose, and he is obliged to work by gaslight–is engaged, in the moments he spares from his large picture, in painting an upright of a view of the Yo-Semite valley, including the Great Fall, which leaping from the brow of a precipice about whose crest the clouds rest in thick, dark folds, drops in the descents into the sunshiny valley two thousand eight hundred feet below. In the foreground of the picture, sheltered from the setting sun by massive rocks, a party of travellers, which we may presume was the artist and his friends, is encamped, engaged in preparing the evening meal. Three or four horses are tethered near by, and a solitary horseman is driving as many more down to the water. The picture promises to be one of the artist's best works."

Cho-looke, The Yosemite Fall has a cream colored ground. There is no evidence of underdrawing. This does not rule out a separate preliminary sketch on paper as a guide for the composition. The work sequence seems to be back to front, that is, starting with the sky and working toward the foreground of the picture. The paint application is fairly even and smooth with some low impasto in the waterfall and in the foliage of the trees.

The mountains were painted dark to light. The dark gray color of the mountains was applied directly in one thin paint layer without completely concealing the ground. Where the light color of the ground shows through between thicker paint strokes, highlights are created. Overall, the ground produces a warm, yet bright tonality, closely imitating sunlight reflecting off the rock faces.

A cool gray scumble was added for the water spray and the clouds. This lighter gray creates an atmospheric effect as though the viewer was looking at the mountains through a light haze. The clouds were painted with scumbles containing a blue pigment. Pentimenti of the trees are visible near the left edge of the painting. They were scumbled over with the beige color of the rocks, leaving the green layer of the foliage partially exposed.

The beige colored rocks and the meadow have a distinct texture which resembles the effect of stippling with a brush. For the river in the middle distance, light blue was applied in a horizontal direction using dry paint. A beige color was dragged across the water to depict the reflection.

The trunks of the large trees to the right were painted fairly thickly in a wet-into-wet technique. The foliage of the trees was done with short brushstrokes while the layer beneath was still wet. For the distant trees a darker olive green was applied in horizontal strokes, with dabs of lighter green paint added.

The paint of the foliage appears to have an admixture such as resin in the binding medium of the paint. Adding resin would make the paint more fluid while retaining its viscous properties, allowing Bierstadt to apply precise dabs of rich paint. The paint would flow enough to feather at the edges, yet would maintain a distinct shape. The effect is of sharp focus in strong light.

The rocks were then painted using a dark brown underlayer for the shadows. The figures, horses, flowers, and grass were added to the foreground. The sharp highlights on the branches, grass, and rocks give this picture a photographic quality. These highlights were created by leaving the cream colored ground exposed in areas, and by adding touches of lighter paint. Both techniques were employed throughout.

Bierstadt's style was greatly influenced by his student years in Düsseldorf. From a technical point of view, he was not an innovative painter. Instead, he continued to perfect his academic training during his entire career. His technique was surprisingly simple, yet effective.

The surface appearance of his paintings is generally smooth, in keeping with the academic tradition. The colors were brushed onto the canvas neatly. The mountains and the clouds were painted quite freely without neglecting the warm sun rays hitting the cool granite surface of the rocks. Scumbles were applied in a skillful and precise manner, creating the thundering waterfall and enhancing the mystical atmosphere. Small objects on the other hand were recorded with almost photographic accuracy. The particulars were

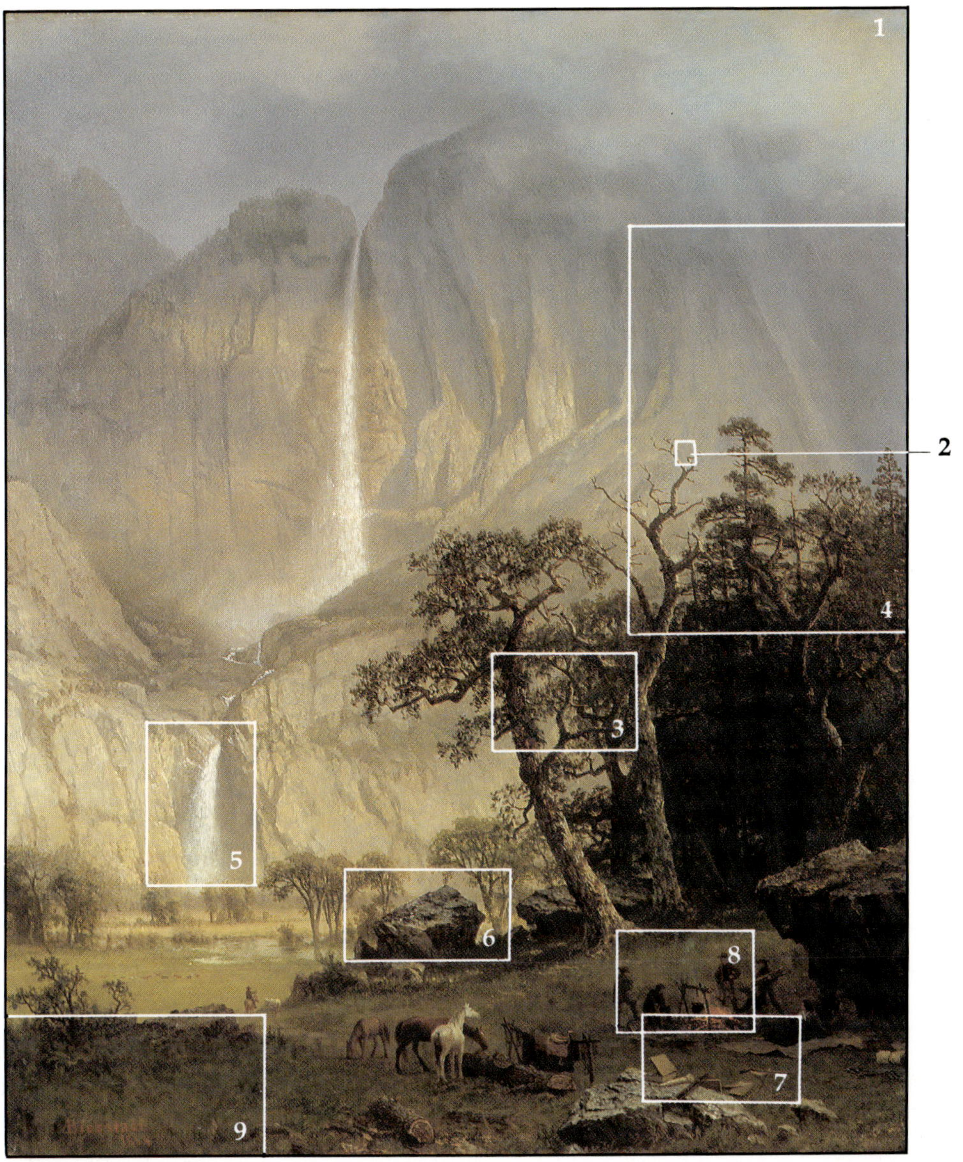

added with a fine brush.

Bierstadt was concerned with the true depiction of light. Every highlight has been placed with great care. The amount and quality of light reflected by an object determine its form. Value, or where a color falls on a scale from light to dark, rather than color or line, was used to achieve photographic precision.

Moran and Bierstadt are commonly paired because both artists depicted grandiose scenes of the American West. A comparison of the two from a technical point of view, however, shows very few similarities.

Moran was interested in the effects of combining texture, color, and glazing. He employed a complicated and sophisticated painting technique using underlayers and glazes to create an optical richness. His subjects are often idealized. His concern was not so much with accurately depicting nature, but with creating a romantic interpretation. He tended to prefer fantastic locations and dramatic luminous effects.

Bierstadt's technique, on the other hand, employed straightforward paint layers, and his imagery was more realistic. The viewer can almost touch the cold granite stone, feel the wet meadowland, and get a chill from the rising mist and clouds. With an analytical, almost photographic eye, the scene and even the time of day, were recorded.

It is precision in handling the paint and applying the highlights that makes his technique very distinct. Bierstadt should properly be recognized as a leading realist painter of the landscape of the American West. After all, color photography did not exist in his day to duplicate and deprecate his achievements.

2.1. The blue-gray paint of the rocks in the background was fluidly applied. The brush texture is retained in the paint which does not completely cover the cream colored ground. Under this magnification particles of the pigment can be seen in the background.

2.2. On top of the already dry blue-gray paint, the dark brown of the branch was applied fluidly with a quick movement and calligraphic precision. The rapid stroke left little gaps and skips in the paint. The paint is rich in medium, possibly containing a resin along with the oil, allowing the paint to be fluid yet cohesive. The paint maintains its shape and a sharp focus is depicted.

2.3. The highlights of a brown such as raw sienna mixed with white were laid in with a few distinct brushstrokes. The color was not completely mixed on the palette before it was applied, resulting in a marbled effect.

2.4. A very fluid green was dabbed on for the foliage where it flowed into puddles in the pockets of the paint. A diluent such as turpentine was probably added to the paint, making it more liquid. The effect is of a leaner, less viscous paint than if oil or resin had been added, as for the branch.

3.1. The foliage was applied first with a darker green in broad brushstrokes in various directions. The branches were then laid on top, followed by the highlights. Finally, light green dabs were added to achieve highlighted leaves.

3.2. Bierstadt achieved a very realistic rendering of nature without losing the painterly quality. Great care was taken to place the fluid highlights in exactly the right places. The photographic quality was obtained by the sharp focus and careful attention to the depiction of light, the essence of this painting. The depiction is so accurate that the viewer can feel the time of day.

3.3. The light blue-gray for the mountain was painted thinly, not altogether hiding the cream colored ground.

3.4. The trunks and branches were painted with great elaboration and precision by mixing the various colors wet-into-wet. Here again, highlights were created by the light ground showing through as well as by adding lighter paint on top.

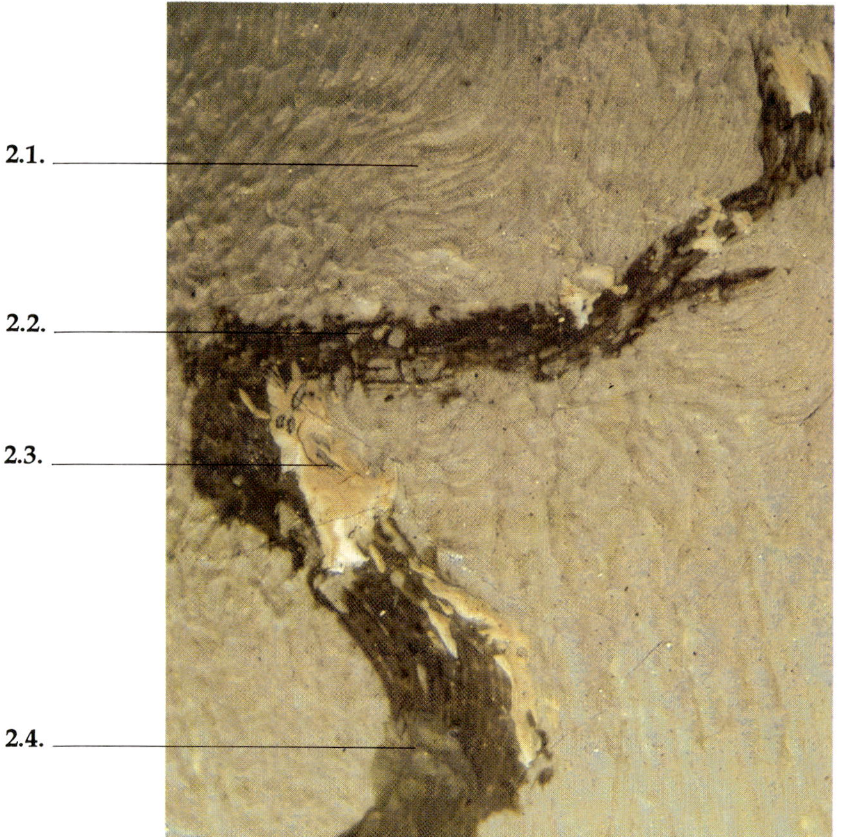

2. ENLARGED DETAIL OF SINGLE BRANCH

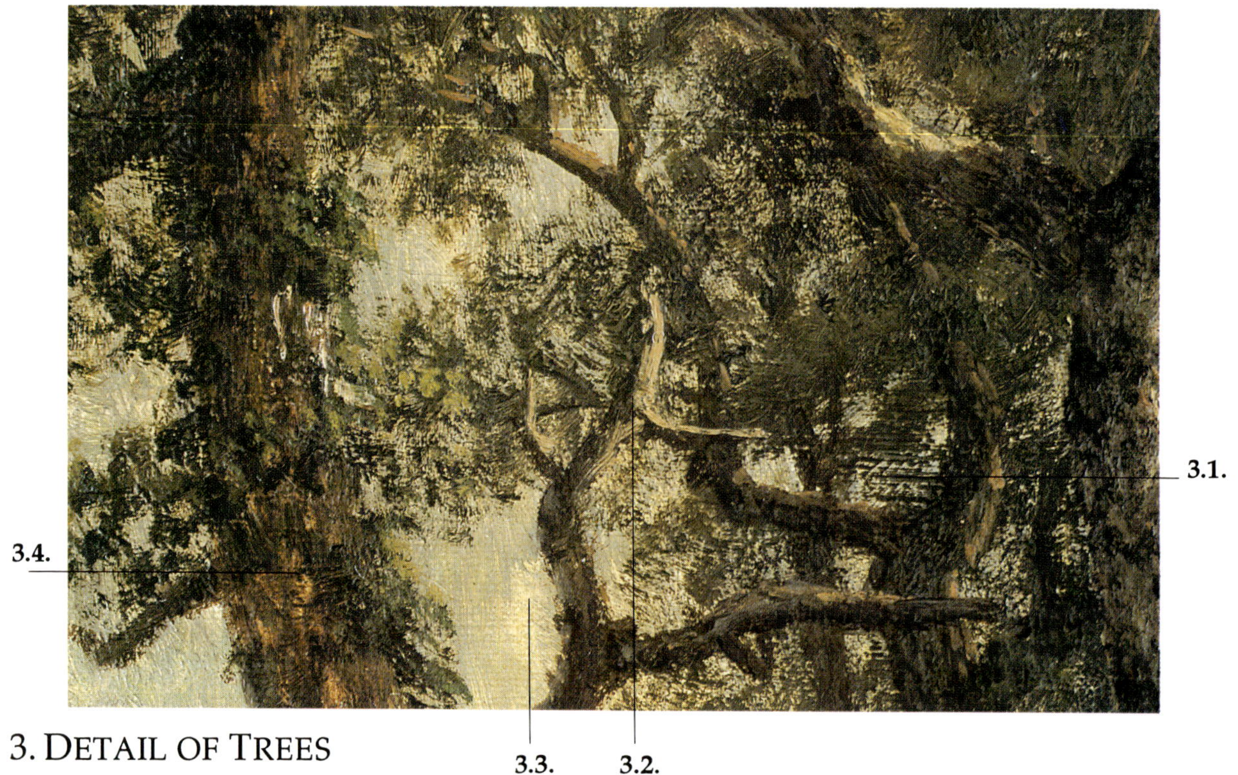

3. DETAIL OF TREES

Bierstadt used a wide variety of techniques to depict the different elements in this picture. Despite the small scale of this detail, different solutions were found to depict highlights, mass foliage, single leaves, branches, and tree trunks for the background.

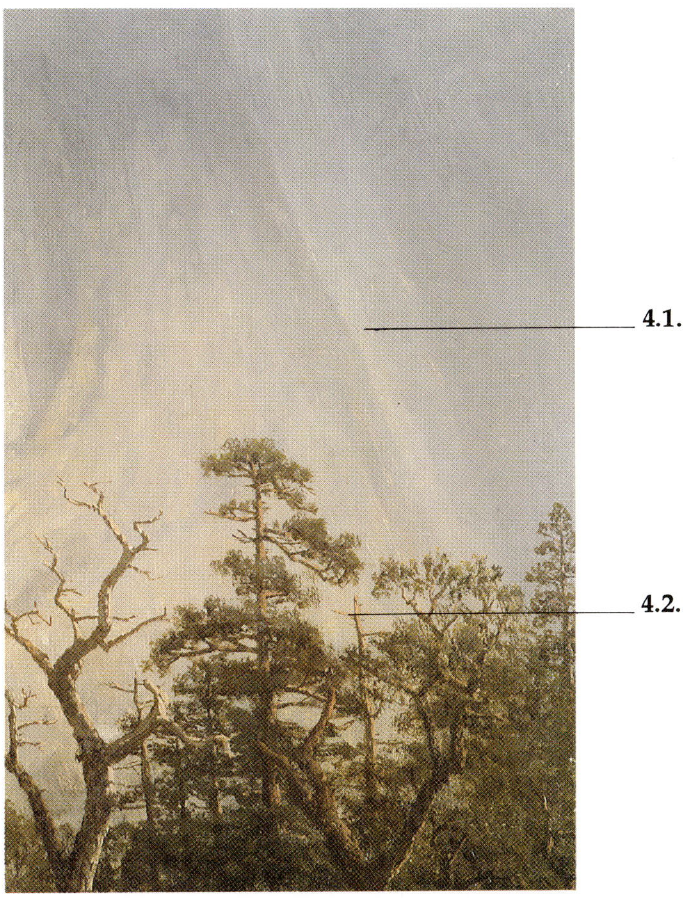

4. DETAIL OF TREES AND MOUNTAINS

4.1. The mountains were painted quickly. This illustration again demonstrates that the gray paint of the granite does not completely conceal the cream colored ground. The effect enhances the luminosity of the sun's rays hitting the rocky wall.

4.2. The light is strong on the tree trunks to which the viewer's attention is first drawn. It was painted with sharp observance of the interaction of highlights and shadows that is photographic in its accuracy. In addition to sketches, Bierstadt may have used photographs as aids. His brother Charles, a photographer, had taken a series of pictures of Yosemite.

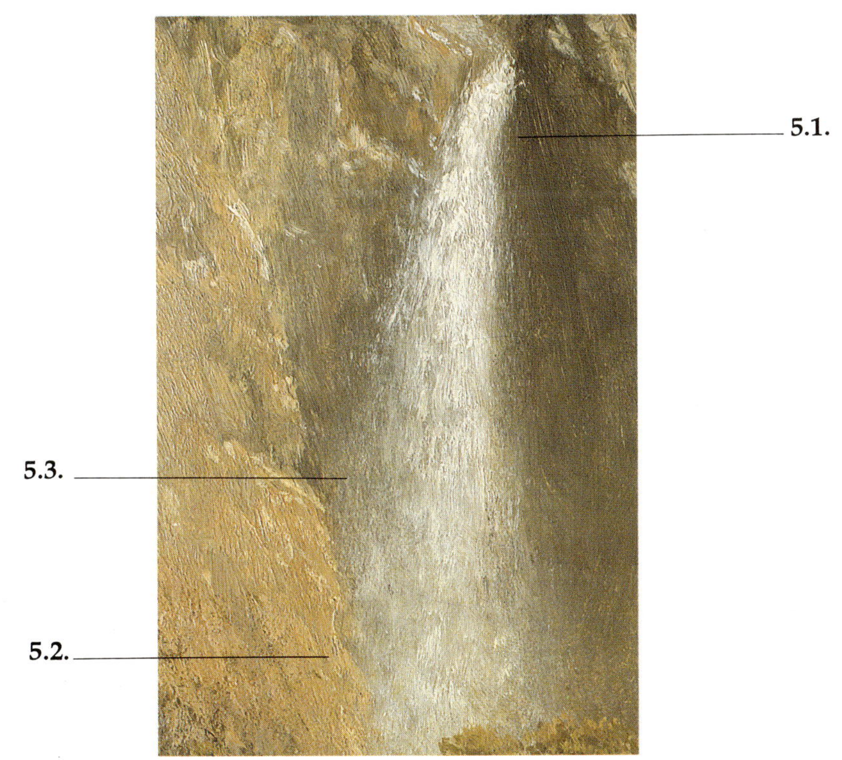

5. DETAIL OF WATERFALL

5.1. The cream colored ground was left partially exposed in the shadowy patch of the dark brown to the right of the water.

5.2. The beige colored mountain wall was painted after the waterfall. Lighter colored highlights were added.

5.3. The waterfall was painted with pure white color and slightly impasted paint. The spray of the wild water was achieved by a thin scumble of white paint.

Artist's license created this thundering cataract. The volume of water is surprising because the painting was done from sketches made in August, a dry time of year.

6.1. Slightly impasted gray, dark green, white, and ochre paint were added in a wet-into-wet technique on top of the dark brown shadows. Great care was taken for the correct placement of the highlights on the cold granite.

6.2. A dark brown paint was used for the shadows of the rock that were applied mainly with horizontal brushstrokes. Some of the cream colored ground is visible.

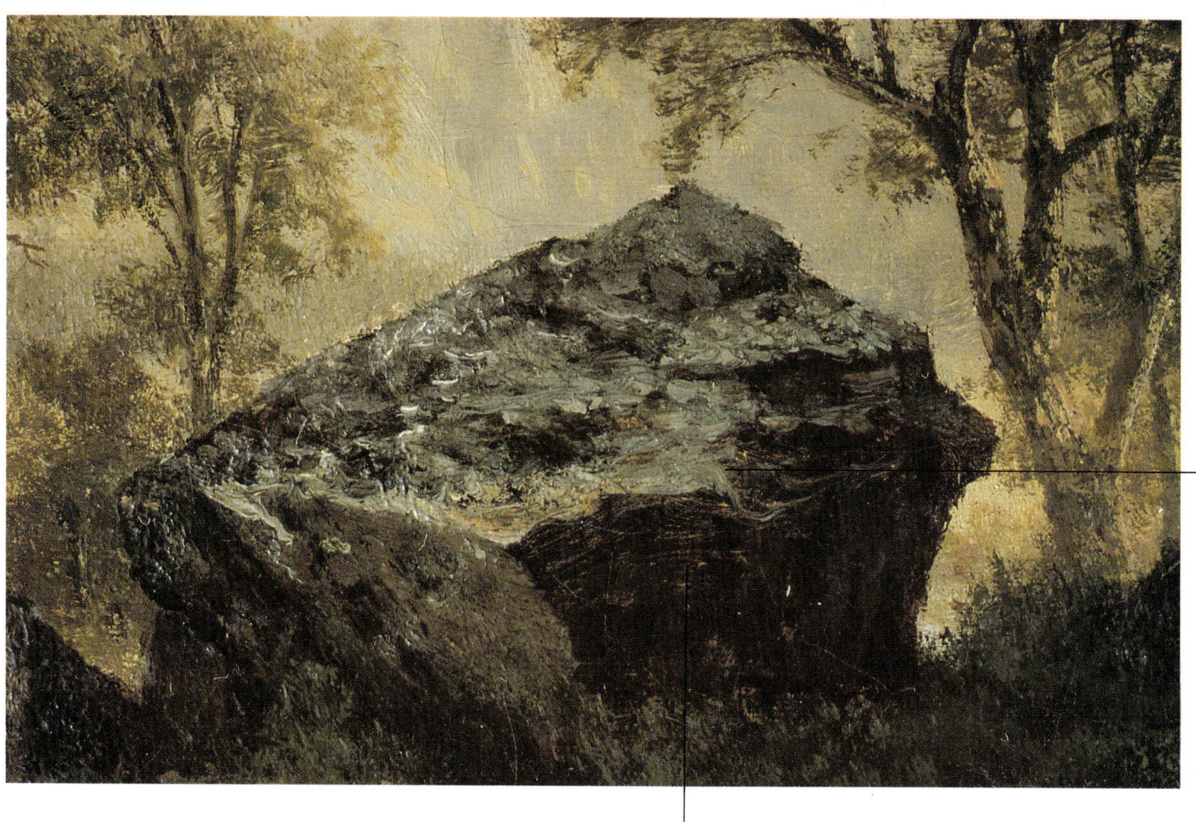

6. DETAIL OF ROCK

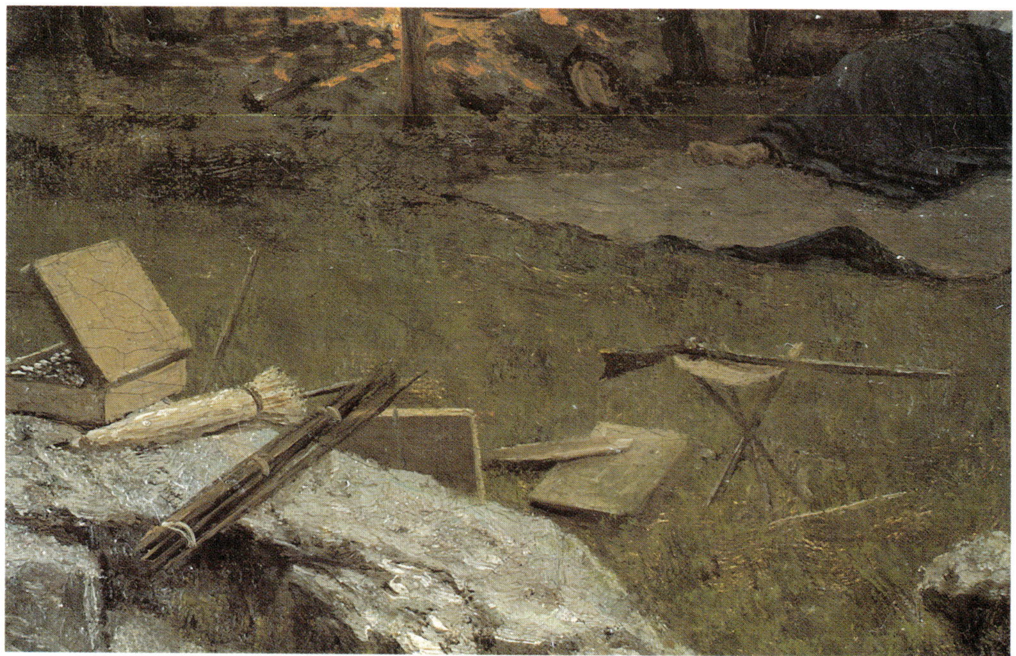

7. DETAIL OF ARTIST'S EQUIPMENT

An open paint box lies on a rock, along with an umbrella and a folding easel. Leaning against the stone is an artist's canvas and on the ground perhaps a panel or a sketchbook. A rifle rests upon a stool.

Bierstadt did not paint this picture on the spot but later, back in the studio, from the oil sketches that Ludlow called color studies. Pains were taken to depict the minutest object in the correct light.

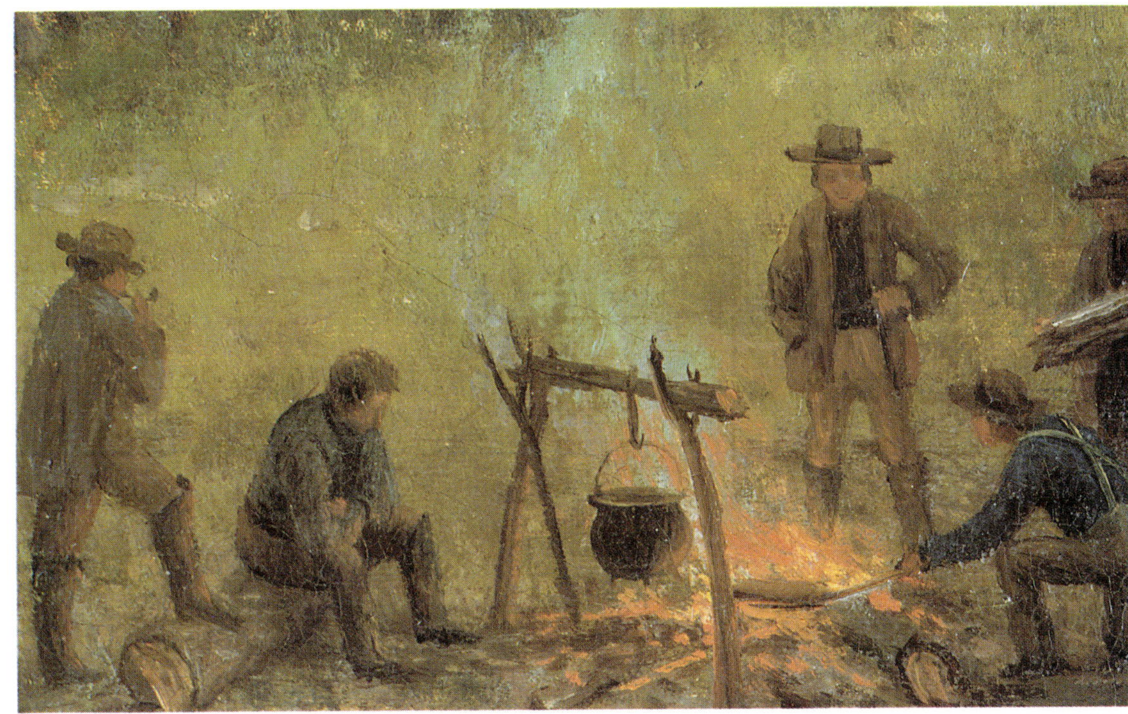

8. DETAIL OF CAMPERS

There is no evidence of underdrawing for the figures. They are, however, painted with care as they prepare the meal and heat the large kettle. The warm orange light from the fire is reflected on the garments, hands, and faces, highlighting them. The smoke rising from the fire was depicted by a bluish scumble painted on top of the grass.

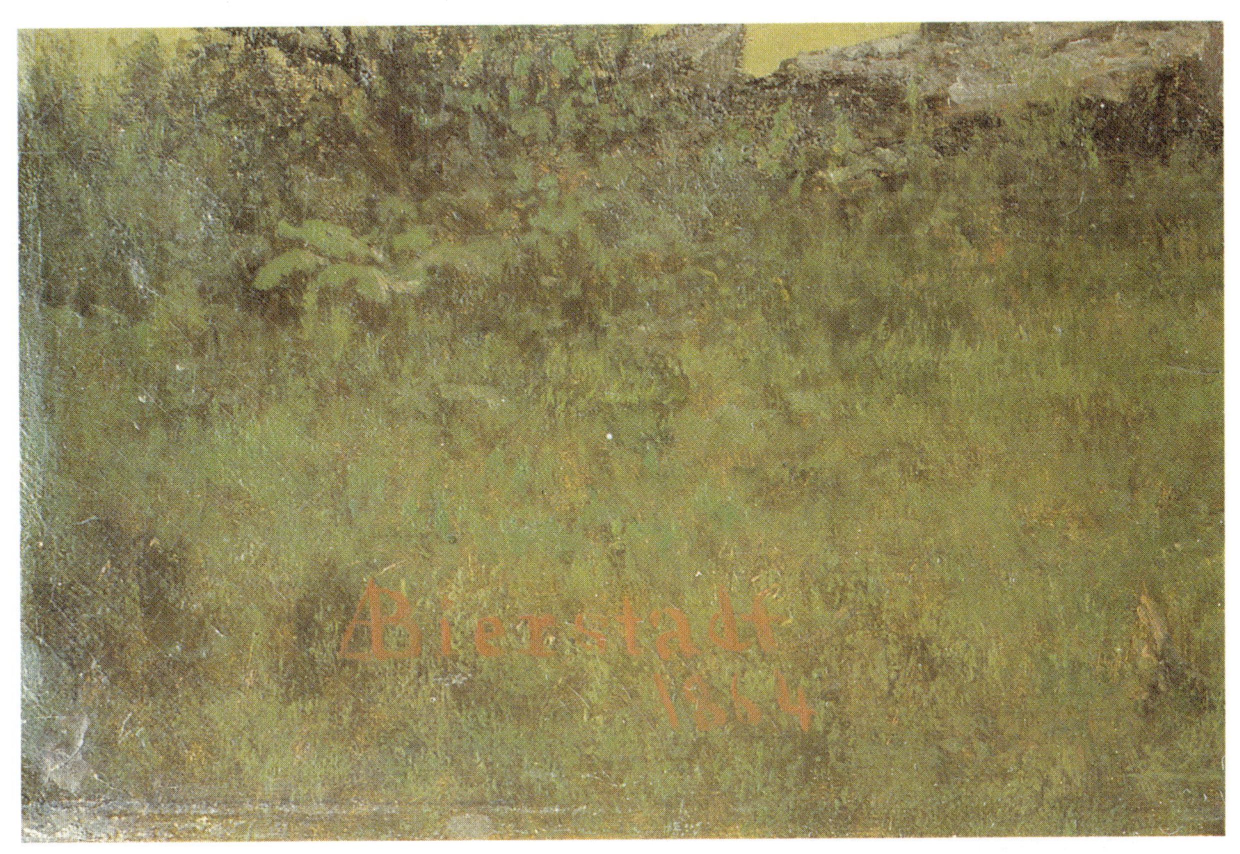

9. DETAIL OF SIGNATURE

A. Bierstadt

SUMMARY OF PAINTING TECHNIQUE

a. Bierstadt used a cream colored ground. There is no evidence of an underdrawing.

b. The work sequence begins with the sky and progresses to the foreground.

c. The ground gives the thinly applied underlayers a warm luminosity. Dark underlayers create shadows in the final image. Forms were built up with slightly thicker paint, though the overall surface remains relatively smooth. Highlights, consisting of bare ground or of bright touches of paint, define the sharp focus.

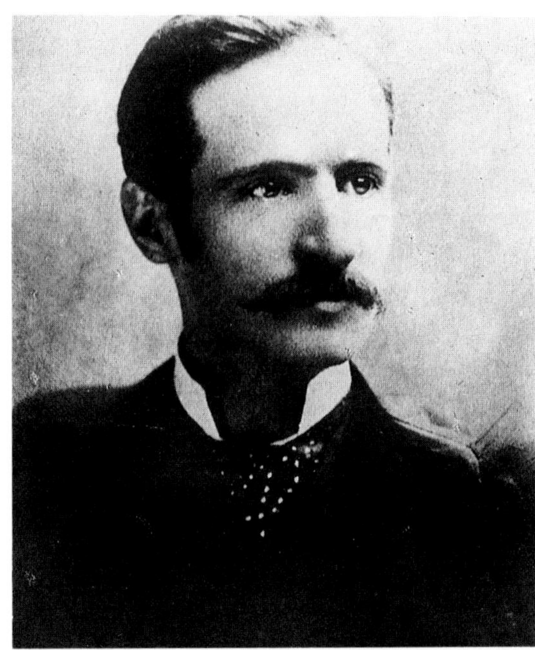

RALPH ALBERT BLAKELOCK

Even when compared to other American painters who were self-taught, Ralph Blakelock was special. Thomas Moran had his Turner and Maynard Dixon had his Remington, but Blakelock never sought any model to emulate. In technique and in treatment of subject matter, he was entirely his own man.

When recognition came to him, the accolades were overwhelming. In 1900 when he was 53, a collector submitted one of Blakelock's paintings to the Paris Universal Exposition. The picture won an honorable mention. By 1904 his works were shown in museums and galleries across the country.

In 1912, his painting *Moonlight* brought $13,900 at public auction, the highest auction price recorded for a living American artist to that time. He was elected an Associate member of the National Academy of Design.

Three years later, his *Brook by Moonlight* was sold for $20,000, again the highest auction price for a living American painter. He was elected an Academician. This was the greatest honor his peers in the National Academy could bestow on him. By 1916 he was receiving more publicity in the press than any other American artist.

There was, however, a monumental irony in this belated recognition. Blakelock had not painted at his best for almost 20 years. He was schizophrenic, an American Van Gogh. He had been confined to insane asylums since 1899. He was not aware of the honors he was receiving in absentia. Not one dollar from the public sales of his pictures came to him. Instead, the auctions were of his paintings from before 1899 that collectors were selling to each other at rapidly rising prices.

Meanwhile, Blakelock was a charity patient in a state hospital for the deranged poor. His wife and large family were even worse off. They were destitute, living in a one-room farmhouse in the remote Catskill mountains.

Blakelock was born October 15, 1847 on Greenwich Street in New York City. He was the 12th in the line of Ralph Blakelocks. His father was a well-to-do but eccentric homeopathic physician who had emigrated from England. Blakelock attended city schools. He was a shy, nervous, and imaginative child, short and slender with a high forehead. His father wanted him to be a doctor but his twin interests were painting and the piano. He was adept at watercolors and pastels while he was still in school.

After doing well on the college entrance examination he matriculated in the city's Free Academy. His interest in a formal education soon flagged, however. The first term he ranked 58th of the 297 students. The second term he was 72nd of 223. The third term he had dropped to 82nd of 116. The fourth term he left. That was February 1866. Soon afterward he met 9-year-old Cora Bailey while on vacation in Vermont and told her he was depressed. His sister, who was Cora's age, had died the previous summer.

He had no training in art other than trial and error, but the next year his first oil painting, *View of Mount Washington,* was accepted for the annual National Academy exhibition. His technique was similar to the traditional style of the Hudson River School artists, without the grandiosity. The realistic rendering of the picture with dilute paint and fully drawn details was in the popular mode. He was encouraged to continue to paint and he offered similar landscapes in the Academy's 1868 and 1869 exhibitions.

Most young artists with his family connections, aspirations, and achievements went to art schools in Europe. Rather than going abroad, however, Blakelock obtained his father's financial encouragement to head West when he was 22.

He left by railroad in 1869. He kept no diary but the notations of dates and places on hundreds of his surviving pen and ink drawings indicate that he continued by stagecoach and then strayed off the traveled roads, on horseback and alone. He crossed Kansas and Colorado, went north to Wyoming Territory, and then west again to Utah, Nevada, and California. Later he proceeded south to Baja California, Mexico, and Panama, north across the isthmus, and by ship to Jamaica.

He sent a few paintings back to family and friends. His father entered *View Near Acapulco, Mexico* in the 1872 Academy exhibition. That was the year Blakelock returned to New York City. He offered *The Hunting Grounds of Nebraska* for sale at the Academy in 1873.

In the course of his solitary travels, however, he had become obsessed with the primeval woodlands of the American West, the diffused lighting in the forests at night, and the mysterious Indians celebrating unfathomable rituals in their ephemeral camps.

His painting underwent a complete change. From then on, his pictures tended toward romantic abstractions of what he had observed in the West. The subject remained the landscape, but it was no longer a specific place. The treatment was in terms of light and shade, color, tone, and texture. Figures were subordinated to the overall design. *Moonlight* and *Indian Encampment* were frequent titles.

His new style was ahead of its time, though. He had lost touch with the art public. Romantic Western visions that were neither realistic nor panoramas were not readily salable in the 1870s. The Academy denied him a place in the 1874 exhibition. He had no dealer to represent him and his income from painting suffered drastically.

Despite the economic hardship, he grew more introverted in his art. He drew an arrowhead around his signature to indicate his ties to the symbolic Indian, but he was reduced to holding exhibitions in his own studio over the Vienna Bakery at Broadway and Tenth Street in New York City. Few customers came.

He married Cora Bailey 10 years after he had been attracted to her when she was a youngster in Vermont. Since he had no money to pay the minister, he traded a painting for the marriage service. He worked briefly at crafting imitation Cordovan leather, coloring and coating the leather repeatedly as he did his paintings. After he lost this job there was little money to pay the rent and the growing family was forced to move often.

Blakelock did not write about himself or his technique but a fellow painter, Elliott Daingerfield, watched him at work. He said Blakelock got his effects by starting with a rough silvery surface on an impasted ground. The ground was spread haphazardly.

Some areas were thick and even. Others were thin, but the pattern of the knife or brush that had applied the ground remained.

Sometimes the disposition of the ground corresponded to the final image. Other times there was no relationship. The image was generally conceived as spontaneously as the ground had been. There was a lack of method in favor of seizing and developing an accidental arrangement that caught his eye.

Because he had no schooling in art, he experimented. A number of paintings were in process all the time, so there was always one with a ground hard enough to satisfy him. On a typical canvas with underlayers in place, he started with bituminous washes for the dark areas. Then he created the shapes by floating on rich colors thinned with his own "Blakelock varnish" consisting of copal resin with a few drops of cold-pressed linseed oil. While the top layer of paint was still partially wet, he flattened the surface with his palette knife. He used costly Winsor & Newton colors rather than scrimping on pigments and materials.

If the surface remained gummy or he considered the picture overglazed, he wiped the surface selectively with a rag or he abraded it with a pumice stone to bring up sections of the silver tones of the textured ground. With the silver as his color key he again developed his theme, drawing the details with darker lines and relieving any overglazing with the rag or stone. Alternately, he scraped with the wooden handle of his brush or even with a metal meat skewer. This layering of the colors was repeated many times until he was satisfied.

Viewers asked, "Did Blakelock paint those silvery tones deliberately?" The answer was no. He removed the overlayers to expose the silver that had been hidden there all along. Today the silver tonality may appear golden.

Because of his lack of training Blakelock built two physical problems into his paintings, copal and bitumen. The copal turned dark and cracked. In the 1880s, experts recommended sunlight to freshen the copal. A generation later, his colors were even duskier than he had intended. In addition, the bitumen never dried completely. Heat from the sun caused the bitumen to run and the surface to crack in an alligator pattern.

Exaggerating a bit, Daingerfield reported that a collector who owned nine Blakelocks told him, "You remember my Blakelocks. Well, I found two of them on the floor this morning." Daingerfield remonstrated with him: "You should have used stronger wire." The collector was angry. "Wire, nothing! The frames are hanging on the wall all right, but the pictures just slipped off the canvas and were lying on the floor in a mass of brown gum!"

Daingerfield observed Blakelock at the National Academy: "He was slight of figure, stooped, thin and very sad of face. Hair brushed back from a high white forehead was long and curly at the ends, falling to the shoulders." Blakelock's usual mood was melancholy. His gentle sadness was reflected in his work.

His release and inspiration were at the piano he kept in his studio. When his painting included an Indian ritual, he repeated a primitive rhythmic phrase on the keyboard until ideas for the painting came to him. Once he asked his friend, the painter Harry Watrous, about the figures in a picture, "Do they dance? Do they dance? I've been trying to make them dance all day and now I think I've got them going!"

Next to his art, his strongest love was for his family. Watrous had the adjoining space in the old Sherwood Building. One day, Watrous recalled, "Blakelock came into my studio and asked for a loan. He said 'A new baby came to us yesterday and money goes fast.' 'Yes,' I said, 'but you already had a big family. How many have you now?' 'Eight, Watrous, eight! I just had to have an octave.' "

His curse was his continuing inability to support his family. When the need arose, he sold his paintings any way he could, for any price he could get. A famous collector purchased two masterpieces for $35 for the pair. A Third Avenue junk dealer bought 33 pictures for $100. There was never enough money.

His wife disclosed that "it was in 1891 that we first suspected that Mr. Blakelock was acting in a strange manner. I thought he was merely worrying but at last we were obliged to have him taken away. He was gone but a week when he was pronounced cured. He did seem to be in his right mind." After two years "I found that his mind was again unbalanced," she added. "We would live but a short time in a place before it would be known that there was something wrong and we would be requested to move. Still he was harmless and retained his love for me and the children.

"At this time he had a beard and wore his hair even longer. He made himself all sorts of sashes of old embroidery, and to these attached long strings of trinkets. He also carried an old dagger he made no effort to conceal. People were afraid but he wore it only because he thought it artistic. I was never afraid of him but at last the doctors said it was necessary to have him taken away. On that day September 12, 1899 my youngest child was born." That was the ninth child.

Blakelock's climactic disappointment had been in 1891. It involved the famous painting *Brook by Moonlight*. Needy as ever, he removed the large painting from its stretcher and rolled it for easier handling. With his son Carl for company, he went cheerfully to the wealthy collector Catholina Lambert's New Jersey castle to collect the $1,000 that he said had been agreed upon as the price for the painting. Lambert denied the arrangement and offered to pay only half. Blakelock was forced by circumstance to accept, but outside the castle he burned the banknotes in a violent rage. This was the same painting that later brought $20,000 at Lambert's estate sale.

A similar episode completed his mental breakdown in 1899. Another collector offered $400 for a painting priced at $1,000. Blakelock refused. When Blakelock returned because he could find no other customer, the collector reduced the offer to $300. Blakelock refused again. He went home but there was no food in the house and no rent money. On the third visit, the collector decreased the offer to $200. Blakelock was compelled to accept the $200 but he was found outside, tearing the bills. He was then confined to the asylum.

He died in 1919, ending one of the most tragic stories in art. He had lived the American dream, in reverse.

1. THE PAINTING

Blakelock's paintings are as complex as was his mind. The usual terminology for describing elements of paintings such as "ground" and "underlayer" cannot consistently be used for any individual layer throughout a single painting because his technique led him to work back and forth within the space, literally up and down through the paint layers. The result makes logical progression meaningless. What one looks for instead is texture, design, patterns–the factors that led Blakelock himself through the painting process.

Indian Encampment, North Dakota is built up of multiple layers and seems to have been worked over and over until the composition reached the state of perfection the artist had in mind. His work procedure was generally very complicated and continued for an extended period of time.

According to Lloyd Goodrich, Blakelock "had a strongly sensuous feeling for texture and surface, for the purely physical properties of the pigments and materials. Often he seems to be emulating luxurious materials like jewels, enamel, velvet, or leather. In his early years when he earned part of his living by making imitation old Cordova leather for an art firm in New York, the process was one of painting and varnishing over and over until richness and depth of tone had been achieved–a process similar to his own painting. His technical methods were his own, and by no means simple."

Examination of the surface reveals the structure to be of many superimposed layers of paint. Some of the layers appear to have been varnished selectively, in between the various steps. The allover golden tonality was achieved by using glazes and possibly a pig-

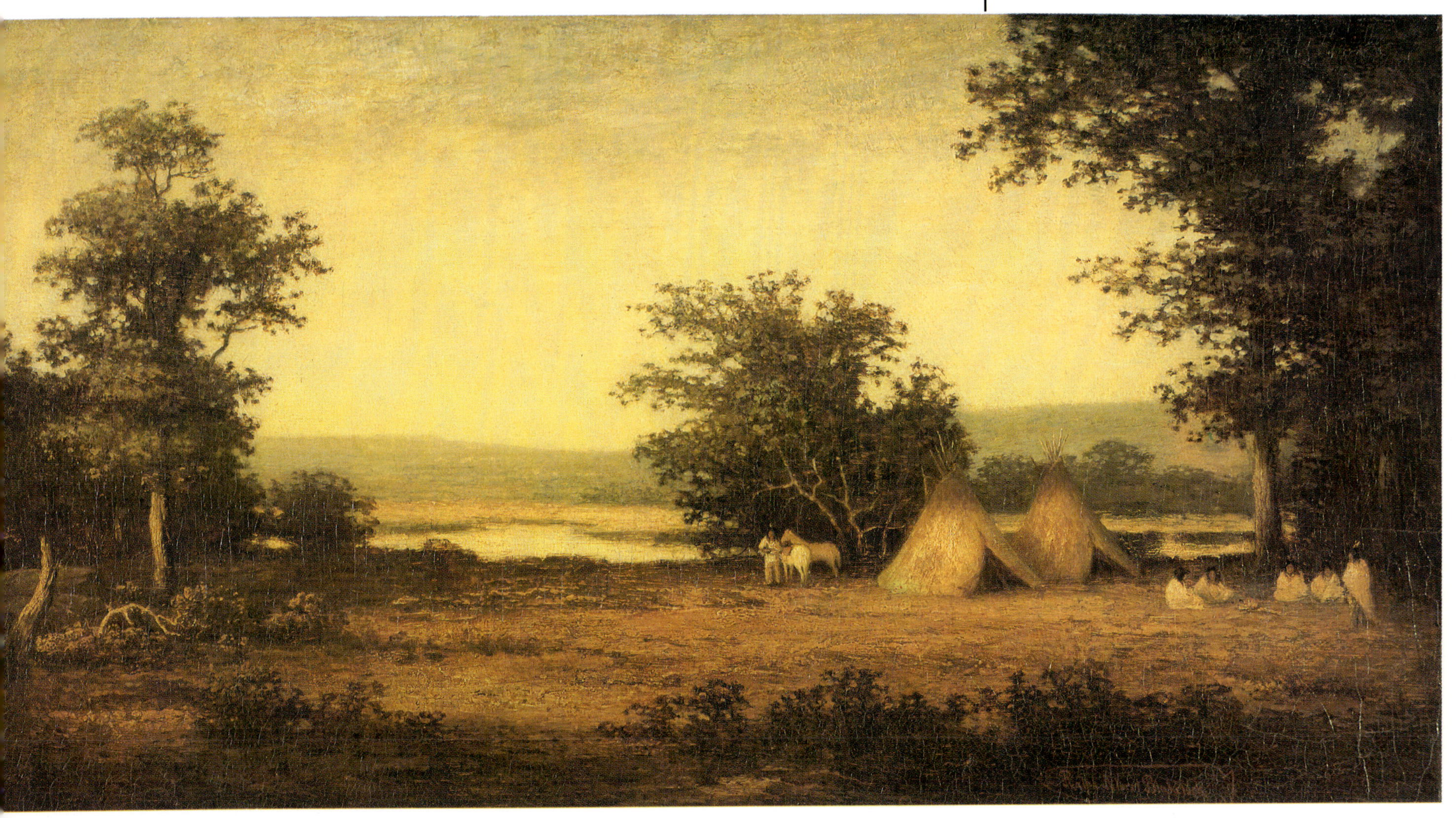

mented varnish. The aged appearance of the painting seems to have been the intention from the outset.

Goodrich also observed that "many canvases were painted first in light color and the surface roughened and made uneven with a meat skewer, which he often used. These pictures, meaningless to anyone else, would be set aside for months or years until they had thoroughly hardened. Such heavily loaded, uneven surfaces were evidently much more attractive for him to work on than blank canvas or panel.

"Often he would rub down the surface with a pumice stone until the high points were worn through, allowing the light underpaint to gleam out. Planing down the several surfaces of color would allow the different colors to come through with an opalescent effect—a method that can be recognized in many of his skies."

It would be difficult to reconstruct the work sequence of a typical Blakelock painting. The artist routinely went back to improve and add more texture, perhaps overpainting areas, only to start again. When making these changes, it appears that Blakelock generally painted over existing layers rather than rubbing the paint down.

Frederick Morton pointed out that "his process was slow and laborious; sometimes years would elapse from the beginning to the end of his pictures, and many years at that. He piled on pigment and he scraped, he varnished and he repainted, and he was likely at the last to completely change his theme once he had the proper foundation of paint on the canvas or panel.... It was something he could never by any means repeat once the

Ralph Albert Blakelock. Indian Encampment, North Dakota *is in the collection of the Fine Art Museums of San Francisco, a gift of Mr. and Mrs. Robert Gill through the Patrons of Art and Music. Oil and resin on hardwood panel. 15 3/4 inches (40 cm) height x 28 5/8 inches (72.5 cm) width x 1/2 inch (1.25 cm) thickness. Signed lower right. Not dated.*

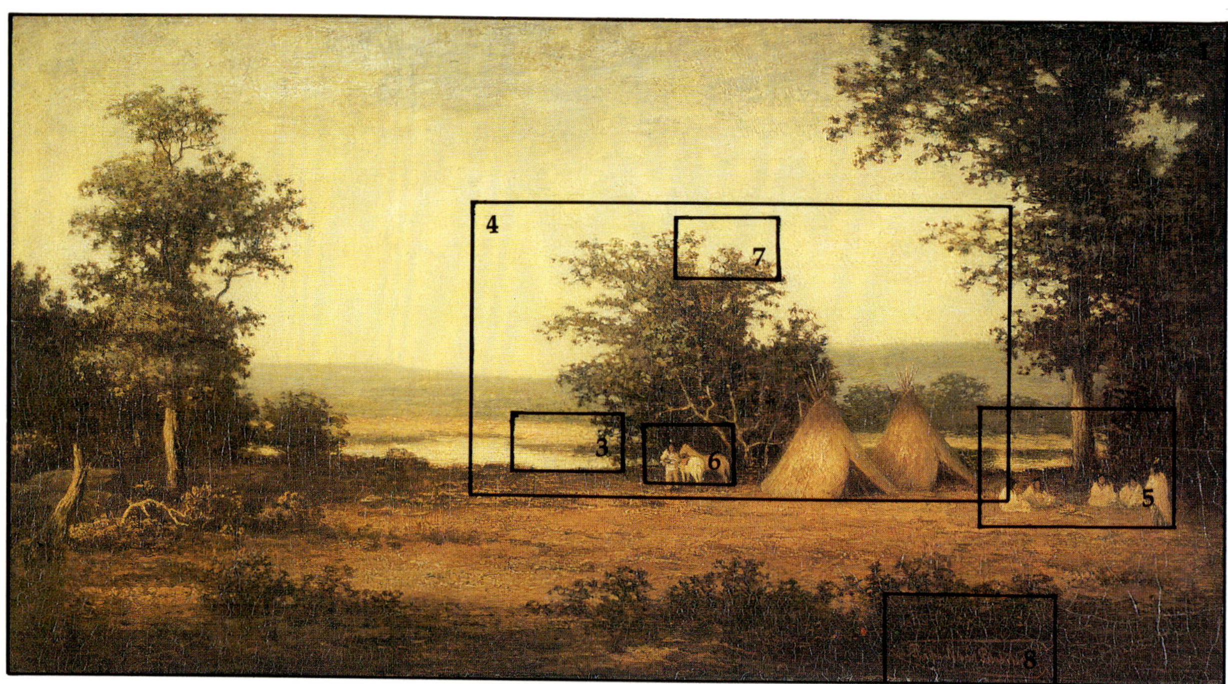

work was finished, for he least of all knew how the effect was secured. It was feeling, pure and simple, like the improvisations of some gifted musician."

Indian Encampment, North Dakota was done on a wood panel that was covered by a white ground. It is not possible to determine whether the panel was primed commercially or by the artist because the ground has been obscured by the subsequent accumulation of the multiple paint layers which lie under the final image. Some parts of these lower layers can be seen in the finished picture as underlying brushwork and texture that do not correspond to the image.

In constructing a base by applying paint and glazes and then scraping down through the layers, Blakelock was looking for inspiration in the textures and patterns of any step. His working technique resulted in a complicated build up of layers that became his underlayers as he proceeded. Serendipity played a large role.

On top of the base he eventually selected, he laid in dark brown underlayers or underpaint for areas he intended as shadows, much as if he was working directly on top of the ground in a normal painting procedure. The use of these planned underlayers can be seen in the trees and the landscape in the middle distance of *Indian Encampment, North Dakota*. The subsequent paint layer does not completely conceal these dark underlayers. As the following paint layers were built up, varnish and glazes were also applied.

He was a painstaking artist, sometimes requiring years to complete a painting. "He could paint a really good picture in less time than anyone else I ever saw, but more often he would lay in a picture and not touch it again, perhaps for months. But he never forgot it. It had to be in just the right condition to rub down before beginning work on it again. He was always busy as there was always some picture in the right condition."

While Blakelock was painstaking he was also spontaneous. Much depended on intuition and accidental inspiration by images he saw in his own unfinished paintings. It is thus virtually impossible to reconstruct his work sequence. He sculpted three-dimensional space in a two-dimensional representation. He interpreted space in a tactile way. The act of composing and the actual paint application were inextricably combined. He allowed himself to be inspired by his own work process. The final image was not necessarily a foreseen goal but rather an evolution ended by the attainment of his own satisfaction or by financial pressures to sell.

Blakelock was more sensuous than other painters of his day. He created beauty by means of color "until it seems to flow upon the senses, as some melody."

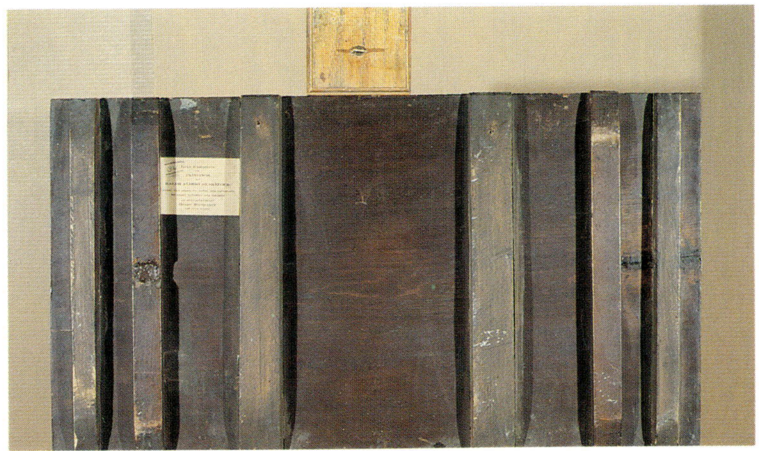

2. Reverse of the Panel

The original construction of the panel included the reinforcing bars or battens visible on the reverse. The location of the tops of the pegs that hold the battens in place can be seen on the front of the panel although they are covered by many layers of ground and paint.

The purpose of the battens was to prevent the panel from warping in response to climatic changes. In this instance the panel has remained stable, but more often than not battens can be the cause of damage. A restricted panel still responds to changes in the environment. With no allowance for expansion and contraction of the wood, the panel may split to release tension. An insignificant split can be seen on the right side of the reverse of this panel.

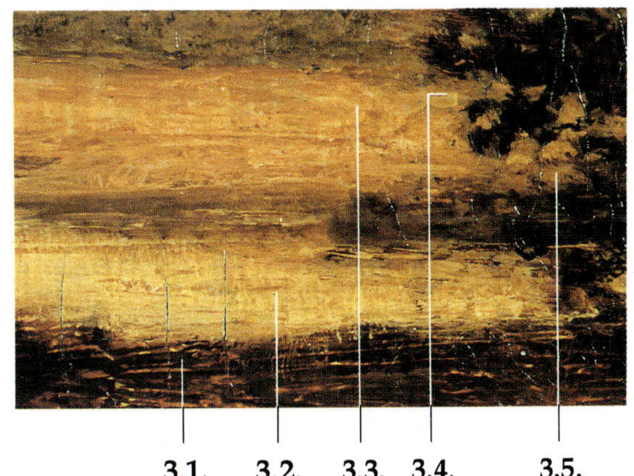

3. Detail of Middle Distance

3.1.   3.2.   3.3. 3.4.   3.5.

At the bottom of this detail, traces of a lighter layer of paint can be seen through the brown paint layer. This underlayer is not necessarily the ground or even a bottom layer of paint. Its thickness and complicated brushwork indicate that there are paint layers beneath it.

Further evidence of multiple layers are the crack patterns in this area. The cracks seen throughout the picture are of various origins, but the ones that supply the most technical information are the early drying cracks caused by the use of excess medium or of a non-drying medium like bitumen. When the top paint layers dry before the underlayer, stresses are formed. The top layer is pulled apart by the movement of the non-drying layer beneath.

There are some age cracks present here as well. Age cracks are caused by movement of the panel as a result of climatic changes. These cracks occur in the direction of the grain of the wood, that is, horizontally.

3.1. Blakelock used an opaque paint for the brown. Its transparency comes from the thin application that does not completely conceal the brighter paint beneath. This earlier layer reflects the light and thus adds to the luminosity of the brown. The result is a rich and deep color.

3.2. A white layer has been applied over the brown, and appears golden in tone due to the use of the glazes and thick varnish. The brushstrokes of the various layers beneath can be seen where they cross under the horizontally applied white paint layer.

3.3. The green paint in the upper half of the detail was applied over thick whitish paint. A scumble on top of the green created atmospheric distance.

3.4. The foliage of the tree consists of a brown underlayer left exposed. Darker brown and green dabs were added to indicate the individual leaves.

3.5. Here and elsewhere in the painting, lighter dabs of paint were applied around the foliage to allow the sky to silhouette the trees.

4.1. Here again, a warm brown underlayer was used for the tepees and trees. The foliage and branches of the trees were then applied, using the underlayer as a shadowy base. These color patches in the foliage break up the form of the trees and the leaves seem to quiver in the wind.

4.2. There is a noticeable difference in height between the darker brown of the receding river bank and the thicker light brown paint applied over it to form the foreground. This paint build-up pushes the foreground even farther forward, enhancing the sense of dimension.

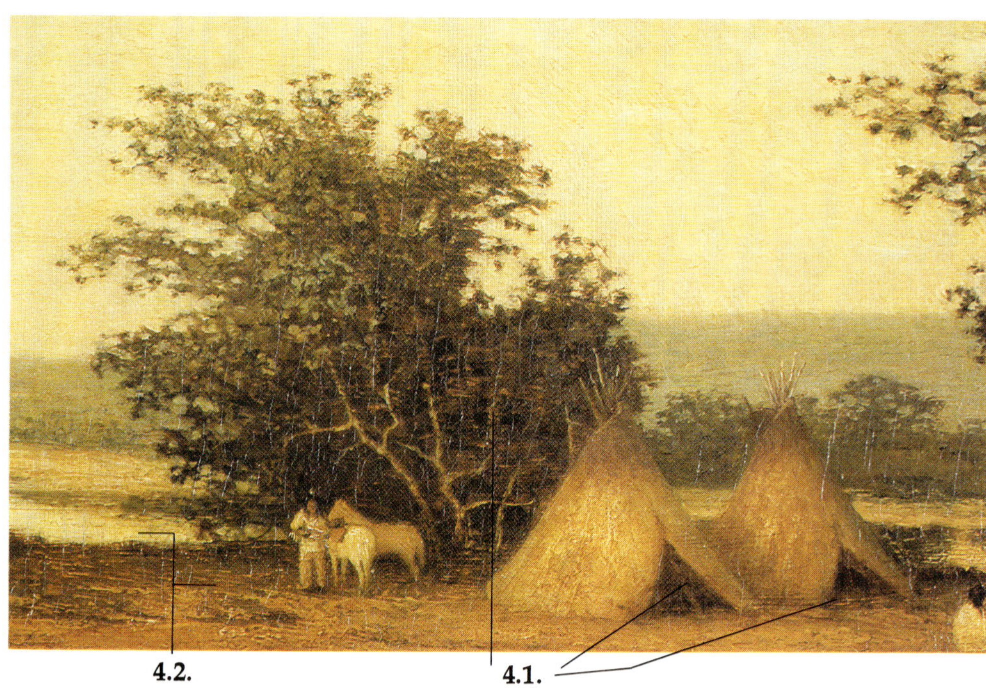

4. DETAIL OF TREES, TEPEES, AND FIGURES

A warm golden glow was achieved by layering glazes and varnishes over the opaque, light colored, and reflective underlayer. Though the painting has certainly darkened with time, the composition still reads well.

Blakelock imitated the patina and textured surface of old age. This intentionally antiquated look has combined with the natural aging of the paint to create a tonal unity.

5.1. The energetic pattern of Blakelock's criss-crossing brushwork can be seen in the brown underlayer above the two Indians seated to the left.

5.2. The foreground was created not so much with various shades of color but with the physical texture of the paint. Added glazes and varnish form the structure of the earth. Where the glazes and varnish were captured in the interstices of the paint layer beneath, the resulting thicker layer caused rich and deep shadows.

5.3. The smoke of the fire was achieved by adding a subtle scumble over the darker brown.

5.4. Rough tree bark was achieved by thick vertical strokes of paint. The contrast between the impasted highlights and the thinner brown underlayer enhances the textural qualities. Here, too, Blakelock "saw" the coarse texture with his brush.

5.5. The same technique was used to define the forms of the Indians. The figures were created from the structure of the paint. The final form emerged when the glazes were applied. For example, a highlight on the standing Indian was created by a hill of paint showing through glaze that has settled around it.

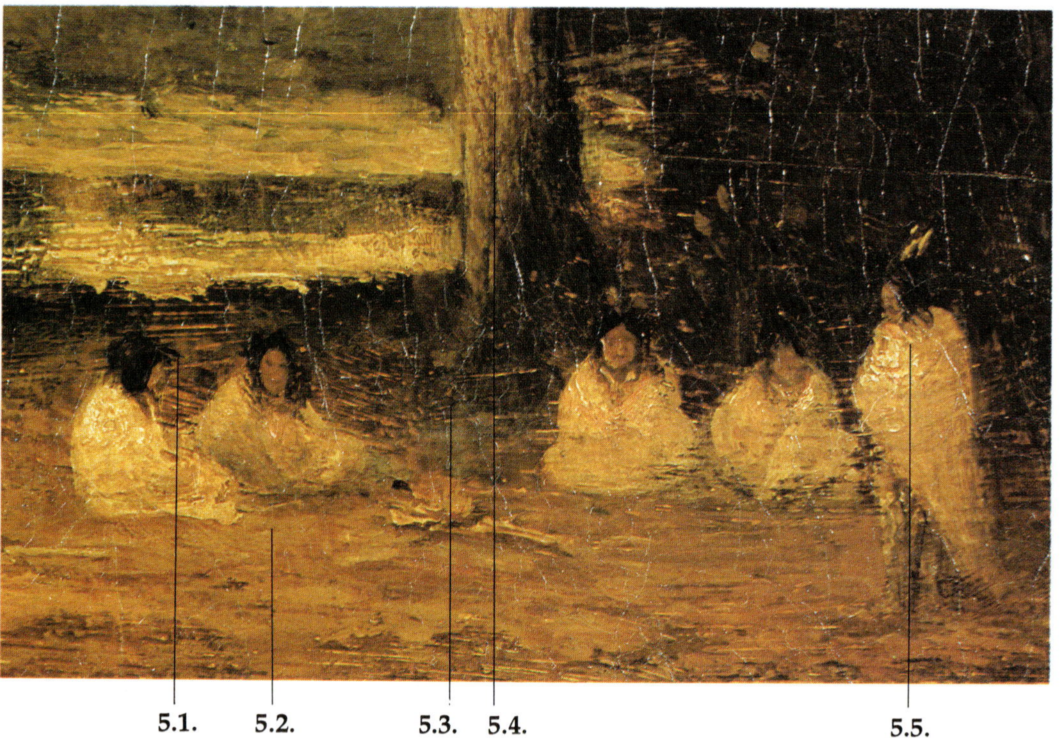

5. DETAIL OF INDIANS SEATED AROUND A FIRE

Close inspection reveals that some of the figures are garbed in delicate pink, a color that is now obscured by the brown tonality of the varnish and glazes.

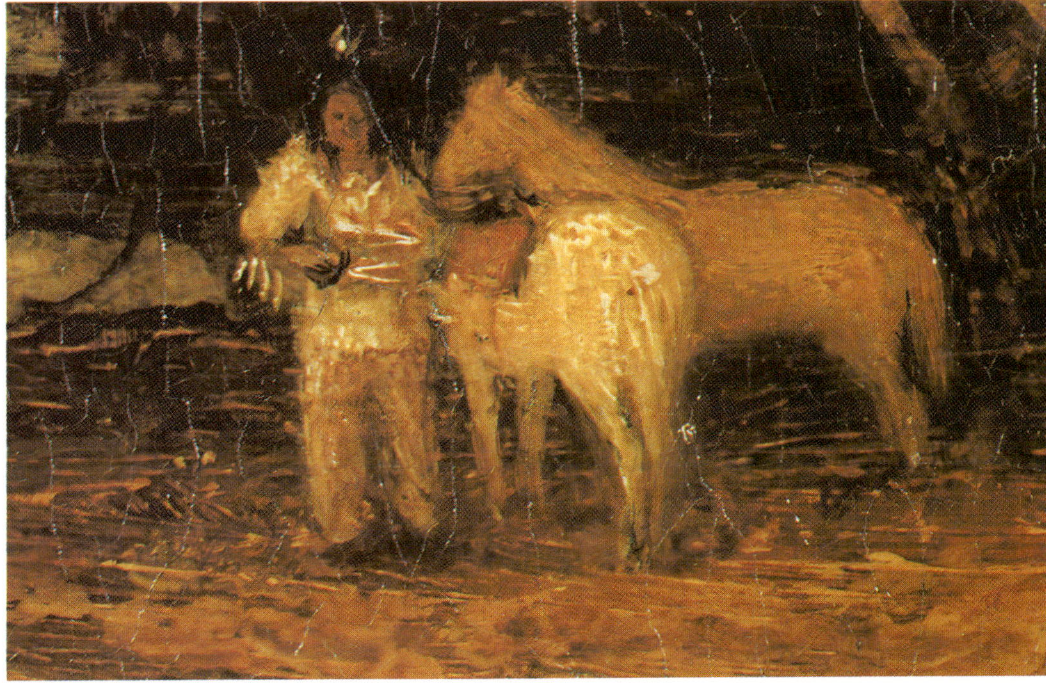

6. DETAIL OF INDIAN AND HORSES

Here, too, Blakelock sculpted the paint into impasted forms that took shape when he applied glazes over them. These glazes settled into the impasto, resulting in darker areas where the interstices were deep. Shadow and highlight are created, thus distinguishing contours by tonal differences, instead of with conventional means such as line, color, or painted detail.

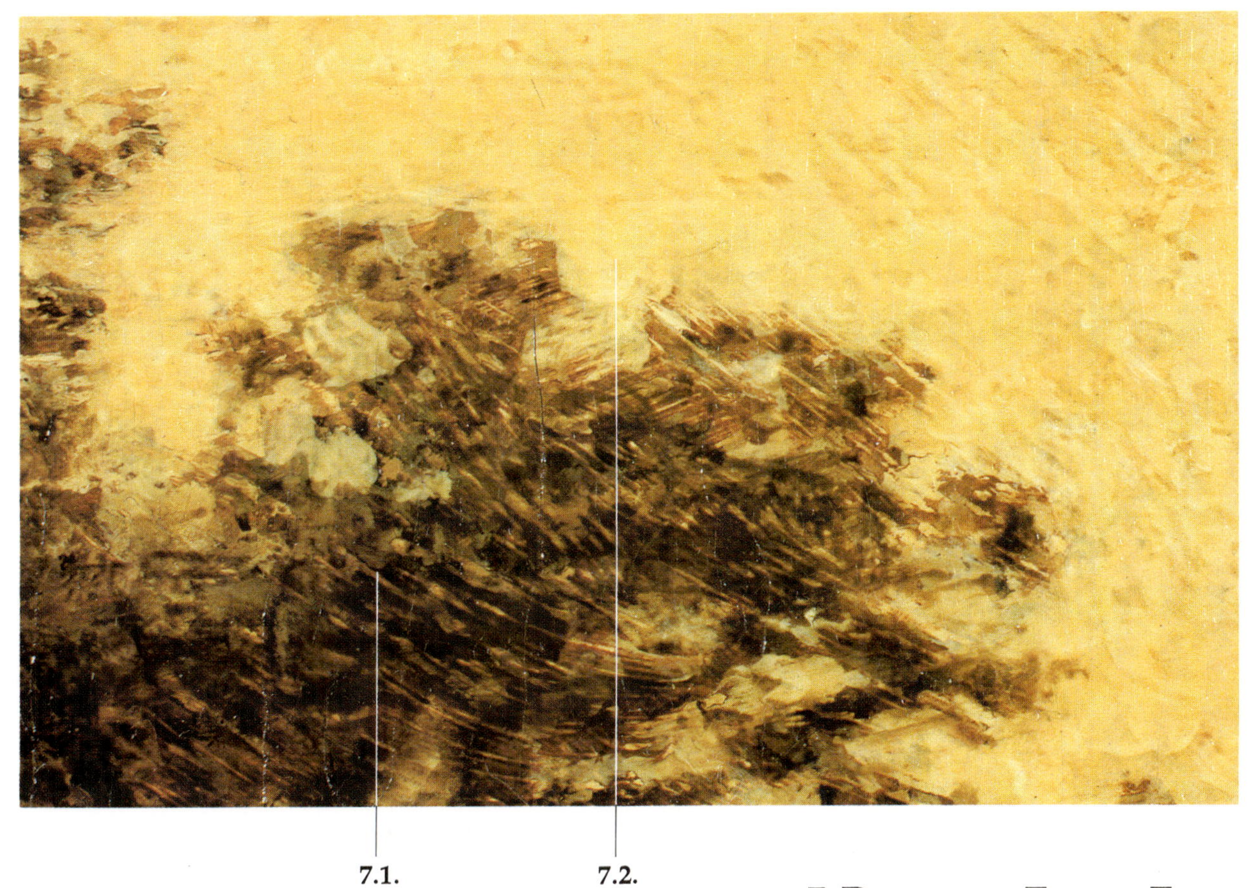

7.1. *Here again, the crosshatched pattern originates from the white underlayer. The thin dark brown paint was brushed over this, catching only in the interstices of the brushwork of the underlayer, creating a pattern of sunlit foliage.*

7.2. *The thick white paint of the sky was brushed in to shape the tree. Additional small dabs of white were applied to the tree to depict breaks in the foliage where the sky shows through.*

7.1.   7.2.

7. DETAIL OF TOP OF TREE

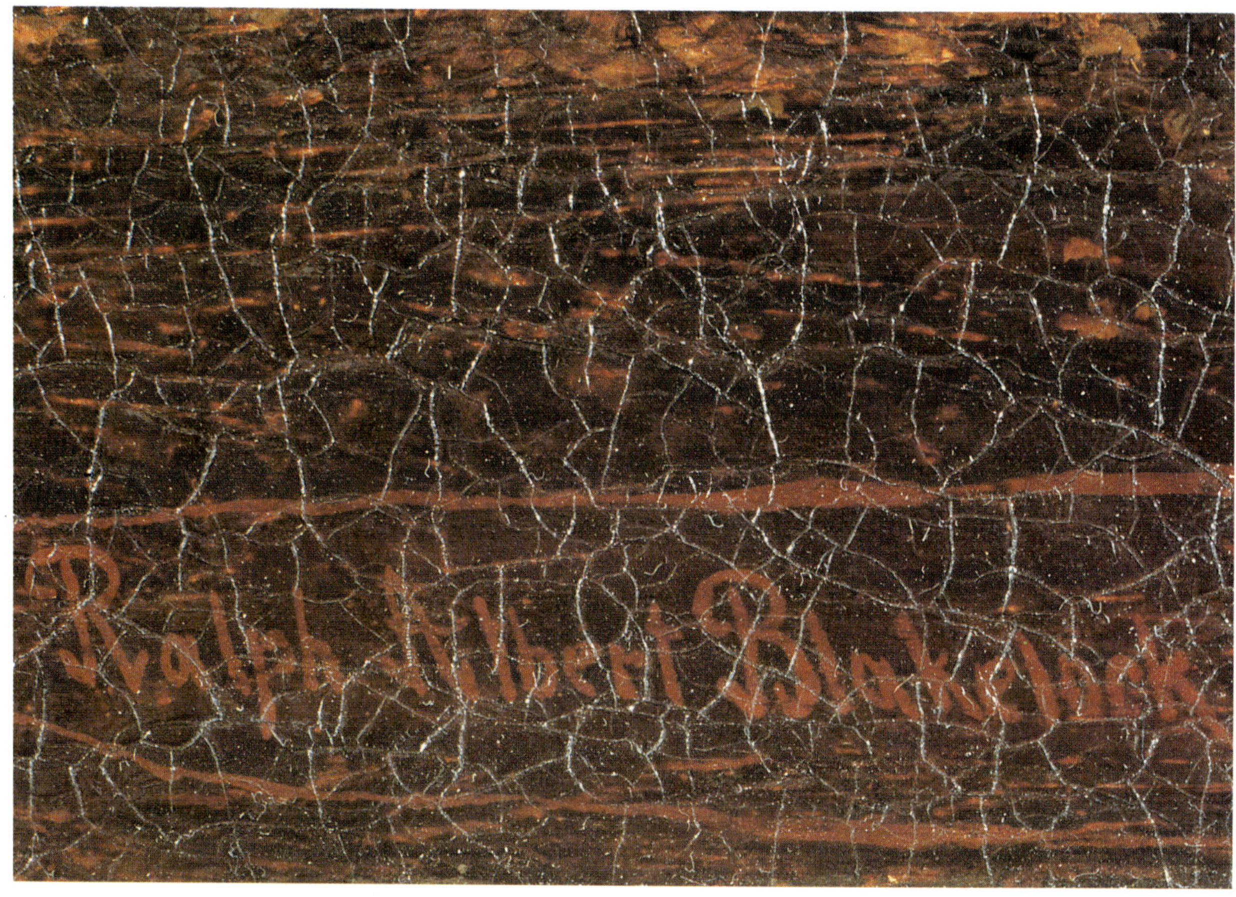

8. DETAIL OF SIGNATURE

Ralph Albert Blakelock (enclosed in the outline of an arrowhead)

The signature to *Indian Encampment, North Dakota* shows Blakelock's full name within a crude arrowhead. This form of identification was so widely accepted that forgeries of Blakelock's work feature the same enclosing arrowhead. Yet, Daingerfield pointed out that many of Blakelock's paintings were unsigned.

The question of forgeries is complex. In 1902 while Blakelock was institutionalized, Morton was already warning that "Blakelock was a very uneven painter. In his duller moods he plagiarized his own pictures and it would not be strange if his inferior work should come to be condemned as forgeries."

After Blakelock died, a dealer put on a big exhibition of "Blakelocks." Many fake Blakelocks were said to have come from that exhibition. In addition, a flood of near-Blakelocks painted by other artists entered the market signed Blakelock.

Blakelock's daughter, Marian, became a painter to support the indigent family. Her style was like her father's. It was tragic that a dealer took advantage of the similarity and secretly substituted her father's signature for her own. When she learned of the forgeries, she too had a nervous breakdown and was institutionalized.

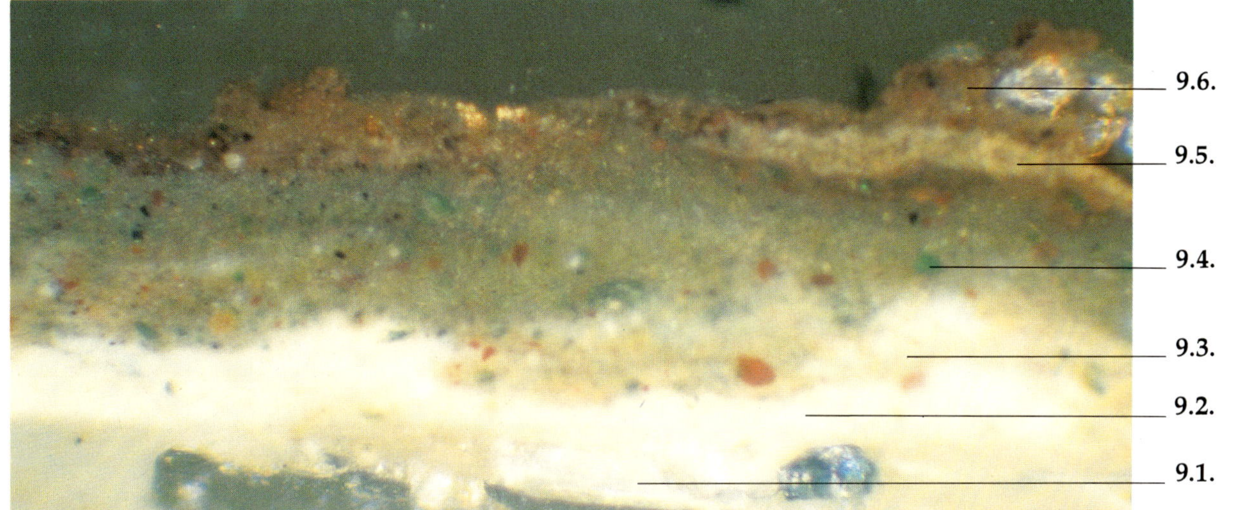

9.1. *A wood fiber from the panel.*

9.2. *The white, gesso-type ground.*

9.3. *A light green layer containing zinc white, lead white, viridian, burnt sienna, and possibly yellow ochre.*

9.4. *A darker green, medium rich layer containing viridian, sienna, a yellow such as ochre, black, and white.*

9.5. *A light brown layer containing white and earth pigments.*

9.6. *The dark brown layer on top appears to be a pigmented resin.*

9. Cross-Section from Trees at Left Edge

This cross-section (see glossary) has been taken from the trees at the left edge. Complex layers of different colors have been worked in together. The colors themselves are complex combinations of many pigments.

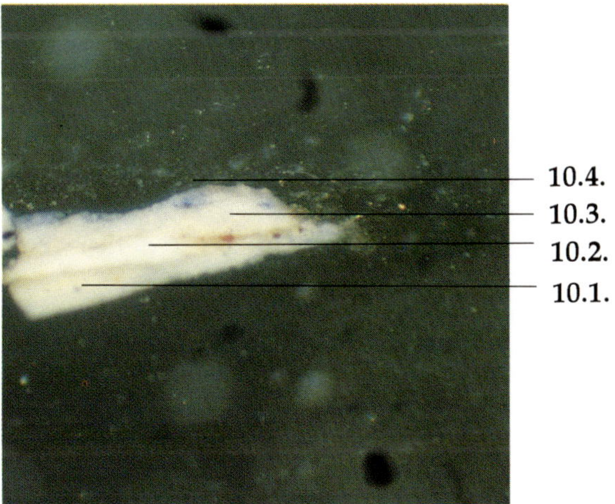

10.1. *A zinc white layer containing traces of black and ochre.*

10.2. *A white layer.*

10.3. *A white layer containing lead white.*

10.4. *A layer containing blue and white.*

10. Cross-Section from Sky

This cross-section was taken from the sky. It shows the true nature of the vivid blue of the sky, now obscured by the discolored varnish.

SUMMARY OF PAINTING TECHNIQUE

The complex nature of the working procedure of Blakelock makes it difficult to give an exact step-by-step description. The following is therefore an indication of a possible work sequence.

a. A white ground was applied onto the panel.
b. It could not be determined whether there is an initial sketch present.
c. A multitude of layers were superimposed, resulting in a complex build-up. Dark underlayers were applied for areas intended to be shadows. More paint was applied without completely concealing the underlayers. Blakelock worked up and down through the layers, sometimes scraping down to lower layers, but more often adding paint. He made constant changes.
d. Glazes and layers of pigmented varnish were applied. In places, the glazes were used to add shadows where they settled thickly into recesses in the impasto.

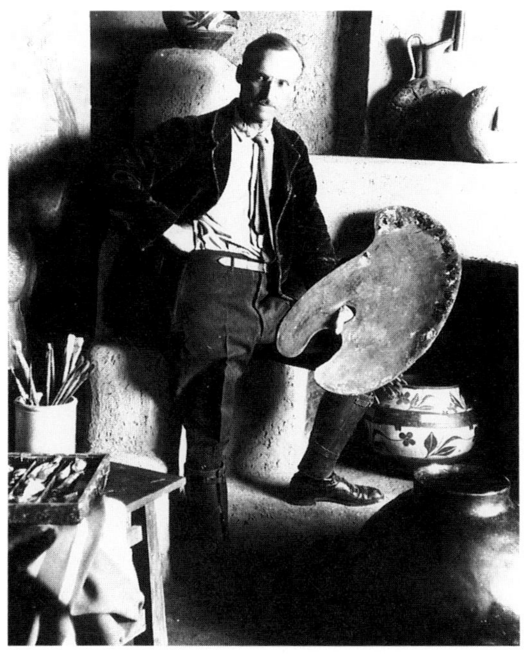

ERNEST BLUMENSCHEIN

The articulate Ernest Blumenschein was the most celebrated member of the Taos art colony in northern New Mexico. He was the group's creative and intellectual leader. "I was born lucky and happy," Blumenschein boasted. The date was May 26, 1874, the place Pittsburgh, Pennsylvania. As a youth he was an outdoorsman and an athlete, the captain of his high school football team. Friends called him Blumey.

His father was a professional musician of German descent who insisted on a high standard of education for his son. Blumenschein was trained as a violinist and was talented enough to win a scholarship to the Cincinnati College of Music. He preferred drawing, however, to music. To prove his ability he sent sketches to the magazine *Harper's Young People* for an evaluation. The reply was, "You show talent" but a warning was added that "the ranks of the illustrators are very full."

Blumenschein accepted this practical advice. He continued his musical studies in Cincinnati. At the same time he took one art course with the transplanted California painter Fernand Lungren who encouraged Blumenschein to become an artist. With his father's reluctant permission Blumenschein went to New York City to enroll in the Art Students League. He supplemented his allowance from home by playing first violin in a symphony orchestra.

From 1894 to 1896 Blumenschein was in Paris studying at the *Academie Julien*. He and another student, Bert Phillips, met the older painter Henry Sharp there. Blumenschein recalled that "from Sharp I heard for the first time of the Indian village of Taos. Returning soon to America, *McClure's* [magazine] assigned me to visit Arizona and New Mexico" as an illustrator. "When I got back I induced Phillips to accompany me the following summer.

"At Denver we purchased a light wagon and away we drove, headed for Mexico. June, July, part of August we spent sketching in Colorado. The second of September we crossed into New Mexico. On a miserable road the wagon suddenly sat down, collapsed. The nearest blacksmith was at Taos, 20 miles away. We flipped a $3 gold-piece to see which of us stayed. It was my fortune to carry the wheel on horseback.

"Sharp had not painted for me the mountains and plains and clouds. No artist had ever recorded the New Mexico I was now seeing. When I came to the valley I saw paintings perfectly organized, ready to paint, everywhere I looked. I was receiving the first great unforgettable inspiration of my life. Dark skinned [Hispanic] people greeted me pleasantly. Then I saw my first Taos Indians. New Mexico had gripped me. Mexico could wait." The first of the pictures of Taos to be published was said to be by Blumenschein.

Phillips remained in Taos while Blumenschein returned to New York City after three months. He was only 24 and his ambitions soared beyond portraying New Mexico. He went back to the *Academie Julien* in September 1899. His letters often referred nostalgically to Taos, but apart from a visit in 1901, he remained in Paris for a decade. He was such a fine illustrator that the New York magazines were willing to send commissions to him in Europe.

Blumenschein did not return to Taos until 1910 when he began a regular summer residency there. Talking about his fellow Taosenos he observed that "we all drifted in like skilled hands looking for a good steady job. We found it. We lived only to paint." In the winters he taught at the Art Students League in New York City.

The critics praised his work for "the systematic and balanced order of his composition." He was fascinated by the Indians. His early Taos paintings featured them, with diagrammable abstract patterns and shapes, built-in tensions, a play on tonality, and reliance on the effects of opposing and compensating colors. In short, he displayed the benefits of his Parisian education.

In 1913 the resident and summer painters in the village formed the Taos Society of Artists. They were six: Blumenschein, Phillips, Sharp, Irving Couse, Buck Dunton, and Oscar Berninghaus. The reason was the need for better sales opportunities. In northern New Mexico they were isolated from customers. There was no way for all of them to market their paintings individually. Through the Society, however, they organized group exhibitions that traveled the national circuit. The paintings were for sale as well as for show so the members prospered in both reputation and reward.

In addition to his share of the proceeds from these group shows, Blumenschein earned large monetary prizes at competitions. The magic of Taos was liberating him from the 19th century style he had learned abroad. A more modern touch was replacing the academic. Compositions were simpler. Figures were flatter, silhouetted, and placed on a plane of limited depth. They told stories. Colors were muted.

"I do not take out my easel and set it up before a scene to copy," he explained. "My usual procedure is to make a drawing from memory of the scene that moved me. This is not a line drawing but hulks of abstract charcoal masses.

"When I believe I have reproduced the effect I saw, a dramatic movement of masses and lines with certain qualities of light and color, and above all a mood with character, strength, and the virility of my first impression, then I must stop. There may be errors of proportion, of values, but whatever is in my composition is right if it gives me the jolt I received [originally]. This is the most important detail of all, as the composition must not only give my emotional reaction but also be well built structurally. All I have to do now is transfer this black and white drawing to a large canvas and paint." He also "painted a thumb note of the color effect."

An inheritance his wife received enabled the Blumenschein family to move to Taos permanently in 1919. He bought four rooms of an 11 room adobe structure that had been built in 1797. Although there was no electricity, telephone, or indoor plumbing in the village, he claimed that "music is all I miss, but we have that in the storms and in the quiet nights." He was 45 years old. From then on he refused all commercial work. He did not realize that the bloom of the Taos founders was already fading for the moment due to the repetitiousness of the themes.

Over the years he purchased the remaining seven rooms in the adobe. The Blumenschein living room was a gathering place for the villagers. His wife, Mary, brought her Continental manners and elegant taste along with her artistic skills. She had been elected an associate member of the National Academy in 1913, three years after her husband.

Blumenschein was wiry and witty. Jauntily he walked their groomed cocker spaniel on a leash through the dirt streets. His sympathy for the Indians he painted contrasted with the antagonism he directed at his peers. He wrote to Oscar Berninghaus, who was Secretary of the Taos Society of Artists in 1922, complaining that Irving Couse had told Buck Dunton that Berninghaus had referred to him as that "bald-headed S.B." He meant S.O.B.

The following year Blumenschein resigned from the Society. He had asked to be excused from serving as Secretary in his turn because of his obligations to another society of painters. He was refused after a stormy session.

Blumenschein did not suffer from his professional disassociation from the other Taos painters. He was elected a National Academician in 1927. His paintings progressed to a more humanistic awareness of the emotions of his subjects, in addition to displaying the decorative qualities. His palette became brighter.

He painted his masterpiece in 1936. This was his best known work, *Jury for the Trial of a Sheepherder for Murder*. He considered the painting to be his finest. At a time when other Taosenos were losing their power, critics called *Jury for Trial* as important to American art as any other American work.

The painting started with one of Blumenschein's memory sketches. The composition is from his recollection of an episode he had observed a year earlier. The setting for the painting was not the real courtroom but was constructed in the artist's studio. The figures were not the actual jury but types Blumenschein saw in the street and drew from memory.

The artist's choice of subject reflected the social realism of the day. As depicted, the attitude of the Hispanic jurors was resentful but resigned. A crazed Hispanic sheepherder who was one of their own had killed an "Anglo." They were unwillingly deciding his fate under Anglo law, not by the ancient Hispanic way of life in the village.

Starting in the 1940s, Blumenschein began to experience difficulty in finishing a painting. As he grew older he was dissatisfied with the quality of his work. Many of the paintings were labored over repeatedly for 10 years or more. The paint grew thicker. Brushstrokes made a dense pattern. Surface effects seemed to have been sought for their own sake.

In the 1950s Blumenschein became artistically conservative. He had been a defender of modern art. Now he changed his mind, saying, "I will never again compare these [newer] works that build no form, with the grandeur expressed in our [older] masterpieces."

He was subject to depression and destroyed 150 paintings that had been stored in his studio. He often painted at night and then repainted the same canvas the next day when the colors were seen to be off in sunlight. He had been an expert tennis player and a champion at bridge, but had to give up both of them because his eyesight was failing and he suffered from arteriosclerosis. Then his wife died.

After a prolonged illness, Blumenschein died in Albuquerque, New Mexico on June 6, 1960 at the age of 86. His ashes were buried near the Indian pueblo in Taos.

1. THE PAINTING

What interested Blumenschein was not so much the tragic incident of the sheepherder who had unwittingly killed a man, but the larger story of the change forced on the long existing Hispanic laws and culture. The weightiness of the drama is emphasized by the stage-like setting.

Ernest Blumenschein. Jury for the Trial of a Sheepherder for Murder *is in the collection of the Museum of Western Art, Denver, Colorado. Oil on canvas. 46 inches (116.8 cm) height x 30 1/8 inches (76.5 cm) width. Signed bottom right. Not dated.*

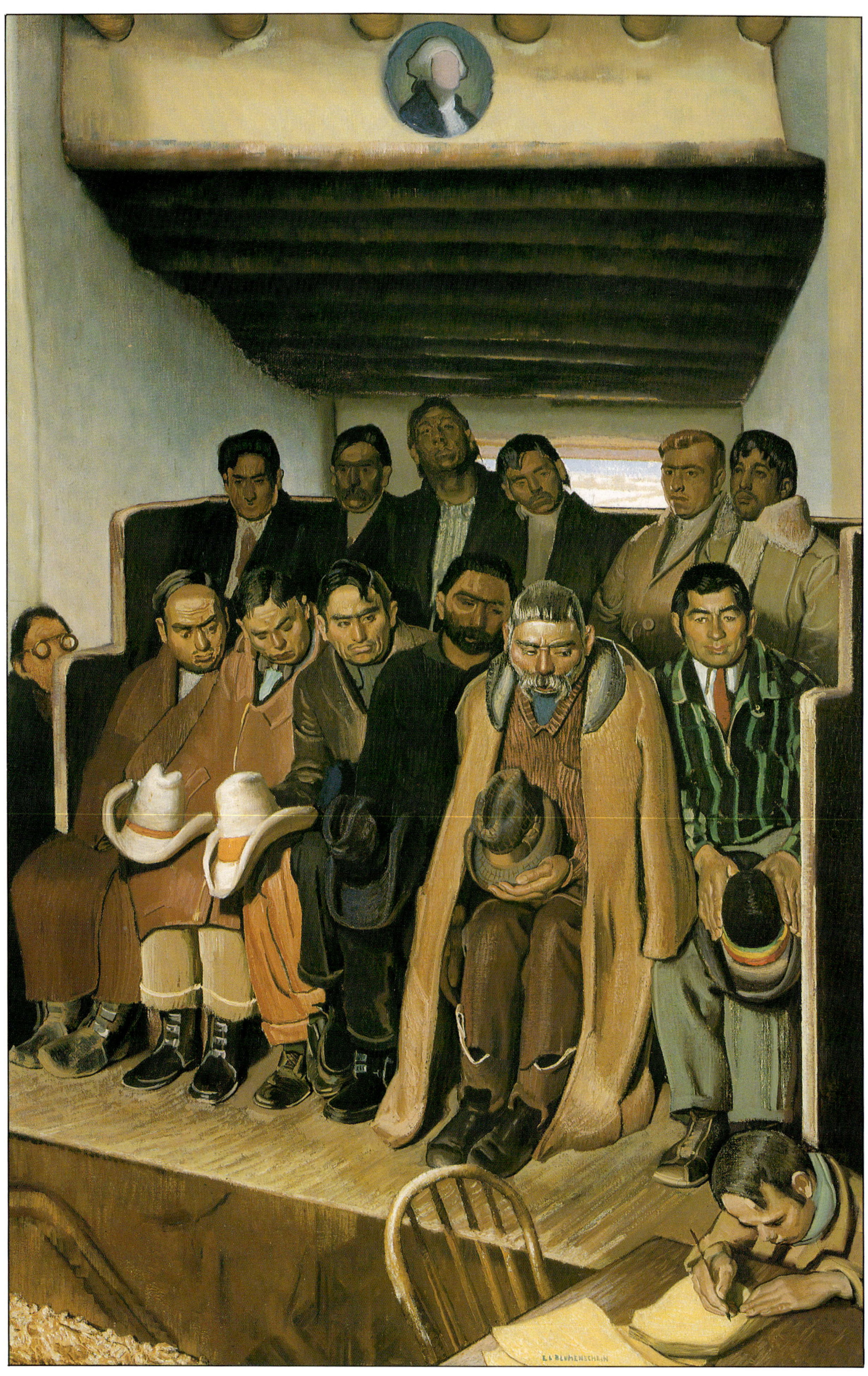

Blumenschein captured the sober attitude of the jurors during the trial in the remote village. With a restrained hand, he depicted the restrained emotions on the grave faces. The portraits were not all finished to the same extent. Some are sketchier than others.

The viewer's attention is first drawn to the more detailed heads, especially the foremost older man whose somber demeanor and slumped pose represent the traditional way of life that is grudgingly being subordinated to the newly imposed Anglo laws. The well-dressed man to his left smiles very slightly while looking directly at the viewer.

The others in the front row look with great interest at the court recorder, as though he is performing a special and unusual task. It appears as if the recorder's simple art of writing may be as new to him as the Anglo legal system is to them all. Another figure is partially hidden behind the platform. He is said to be the artist himself observing the court proceedings.

The men in the back row are painted with much less detail, forming a contrast with the more solidly painted figures in the front row. The faces in the back are simplified into revealing character studies carried out with only highlight and shadow. This emphasizes the greatly foreshortened space of the room in which the ceiling and back wall meet in an impossibly small space. The desk of the recorder is sharply cut off at the front edge of the picture plane, engaging the viewer and drawing him into the proceedings.

A plain weave, medium weight canvas of what appears to be mixed cotton/linen fibers was used. The canvas is coarse, textured with slubs and irregularities in the threads. The ground was commercially applied, though the fabric appears to have been attached to the stretcher by the artist.

A sketch not visible to the naked eye but revealed by infrared photography was drawn on the ground. The sketch was followed by dilute colored underlayers that blocked in the main elements of the painting. These underlayers were applied thinly, leaving the coarse texture of the canvas apparent and, in places, leaving the ground exposed.

The underlayers often represent the darkest color of an area, thus serving as a shadow in the final work. They are often not the same color as subsequent paint layers, serving instead as optical devices to increase depth and luminosity. For example, a dark brown such as burnt sienna underlies the faces. Violet was employed for the setting, the outlines of the bench, and one of the hats. Green-gray is the underlayer for the walls.

The underlayers were generally followed by a single, thicker paint layer to build up the main elements of the composition. In the final stage, details and highlights were added, with additional shadows where necessary.

Despite the simple build-up of paint layers indicating that Blumenschein had a clear concept of where to lay in his colors, artist's changes are evident. Visible to the naked eye is the original location of a set of stairs leading down from the front of the platform, now partially covered by the chair back. An infrared photograph also reveals that the resulting composition does not exactly follow the underdrawing.

The surface of the painting is textural. Where the paint was thinly applied, the coarse-grain canvas was exploited, to emphasize in particular the rough setting and the weathered faces and hands of these provincial people that marked their way of life. Where there is a thicker build-up of paint, for example to indicate the heavy clothes of the men, the paint has often been manipulated by dragging one layer of paint over another to create a broken surface. This effect was achieved by pulling the tip of the brush handle through the still wet paint to produce furrows, or by pulling a loaded brush slowly so that the paint builds up in low ridges along the edges of the strokes.

The gravity of the drama is emphasized as much by the composition as by the painting technique. The low focal point pulls the composition down toward the court recorder in whose unpracticed hands justice seems to rest. A faceless portrait of George Washington, floating in relatively empty space at the top of the setting, is the symbol of the sovereignty of the federal government. The fanciful perspective and childlike rendering

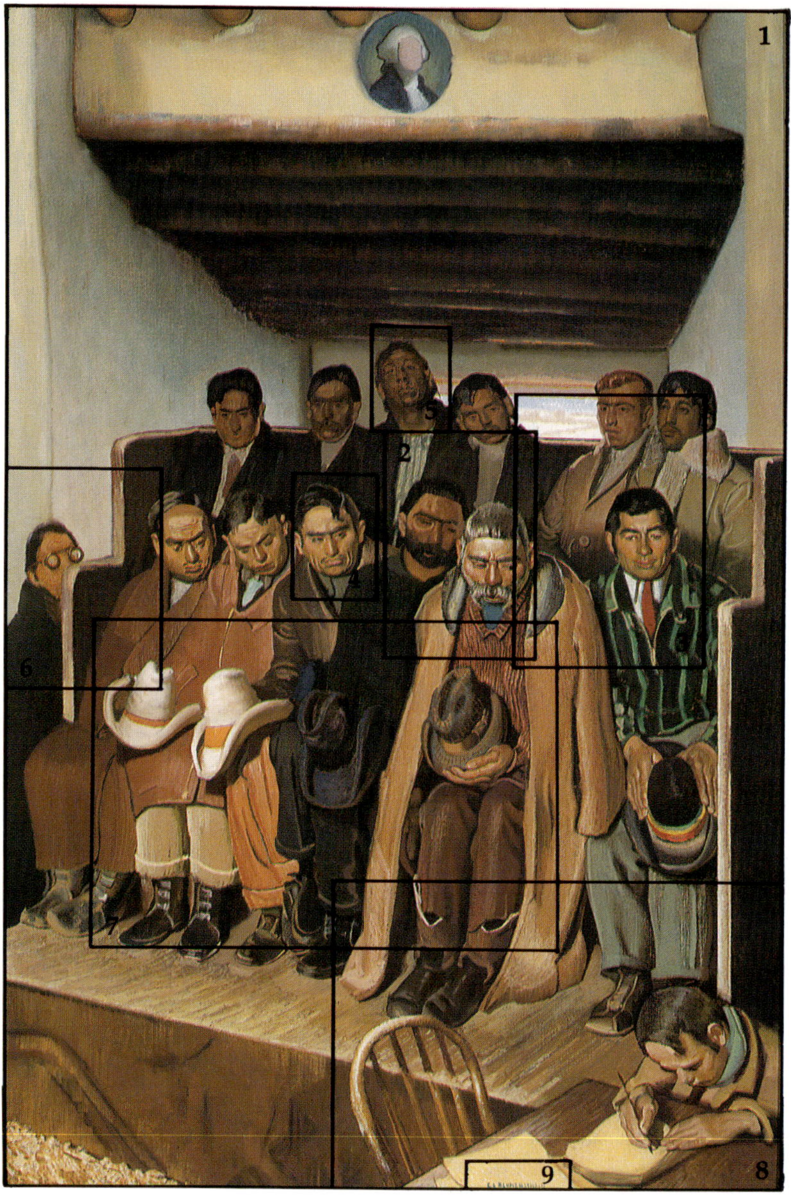

of the figures resemble naive painting, perhaps consciously to indicate an innate innocence. The hand behind the brush seems heavy, as though influenced by the ponderous proceedings.

The six rules given by Blumenschein to his students describe the brilliant technique of *Jury of the Trial of a Sheepherder for Murder*. Do not approach painting with preconceived formulas. Trust your subconscious taste. Establish planes with color as well as perspective. Search for distinguished tonalities. Make memory sketches. And finally, ask yourself: Are the masses big enough? Is the design vigorous? Are the proportions beautiful? Is the work decorative as well as realistic?

The dramatically foreshortened space engages the viewer. The energetic diagonal compositional lines lead the eye from the lower right corner, along the edge of the front of the platform, and then back into the rapidly receding space. The figures, though sketchily carried out with cartoon-like features, convey mass and character. The palette, comprised largely of opaque earth colors, is given depth and luminosity by the transparent colored underlayers.

Equally important to technique is the social realism. At a time when the Taos painters were being criticized for painting romanticized views of the Indian in an obsolete milieu, Blumenschein painted an actual event which represented the changes forced on the lives of these Hispanic people.

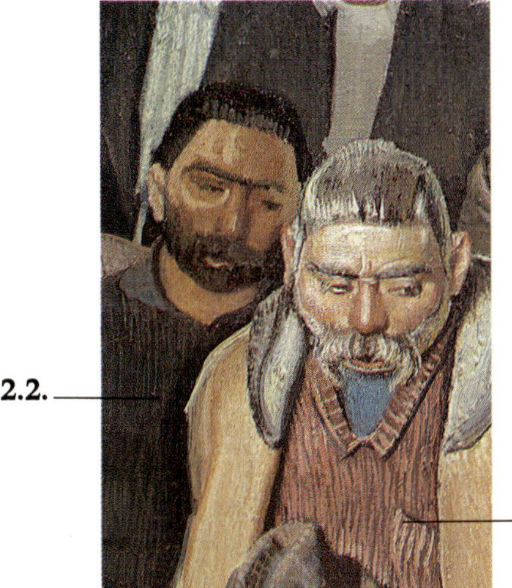

2. DETAIL OF OLD MAN

The physiognomy of the senior juror is the most completely executed, emphasizing his importance. The colored underlayer was thinly applied, not concealing the texture of the canvas. This is especially noticeable in the old man's face where the irregular texture is used to emphasize his roughhewn nature. The texture breaks up the paint application, increasing its sketchiness. For the shirt and coat, however, thicker and richer paint covers the texture of the canvas completely, yet connotes the heavy coarse clothes of the outdoor man. Black outlines for the face and the collar were left partially exposed for sharpness and contrast.

The man immediately to his right was painted in an abbreviated manner with exaggerated modeling. The cartoon-like highlight around his right eye makes his face almost unreadable at close inspection. In the context of the composition, the contrast between the two heads serves to make the senior juror's face even more prominent.

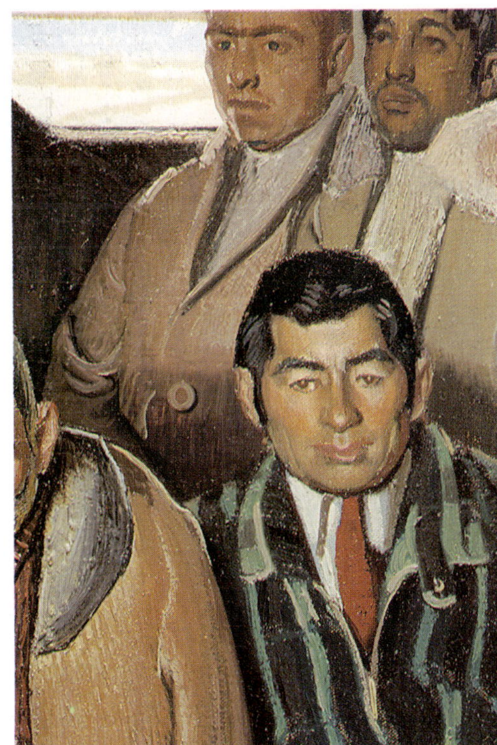

3. DETAIL OF WELL-DRESSED MAN IN FRONT ROW

Unlike the others dressed in earth-toned work clothes, this man sports a striped green jacket with a red tie. These complementary colors, as well as his direct look, attract the viewer's eye.

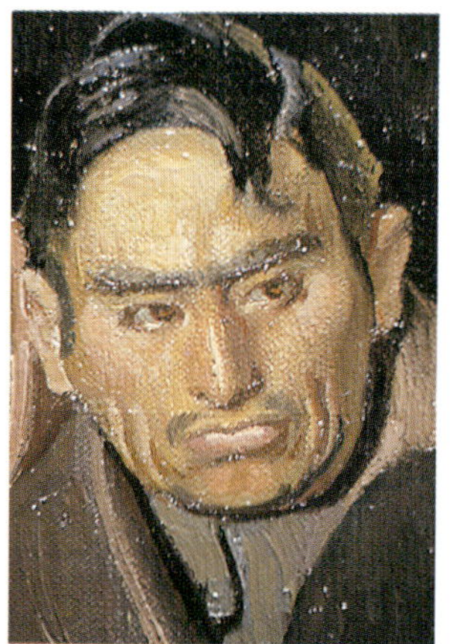

4. DETAIL OF SECOND FACE (4TH FIGURE FROM RIGHT, FRONT ROW)

This face appears to have been sculpted out of the paint. The canvas texture gives the rough, weathered skin a tactile quality. For example, a slub in the canvas passes horizontally through the man's face, between his nose and lips, and deep gaps occur in his flesh where the paint has caught only on the prominent tops of the canvas weave. The thick paint used for hair, eyebrows, nose, lips, and chin accentuates these heavy features.

In contrast, the pupils of the eyes are painted with thinner, more saturated paint, giving them a deep, clear look. Despite the unpolished appearance, this is a revealing portrait of a sensitive, intelligent man.

The first layer of paint is quite thin. Highlights with thicker, richer paint stand out against the texture. Black outlines emphasize form and add shadow to the face and clothing. The shirt consists of a few multicolored brushstrokes. Highlights on the coat were indicated by scumbling lighter paint around the collar.

5.1. A thin dark brown underlayer was used for the head. The modeling of the features has been sketchily carried out with thicker opaque paint broadly applied for highlights and shadows.

5.2. A gap was left between the hair and the light gray rear wall, leaving the brown underlayer exposed.

5.3. The violet underlayer used for the ceiling is visible above the man's head.

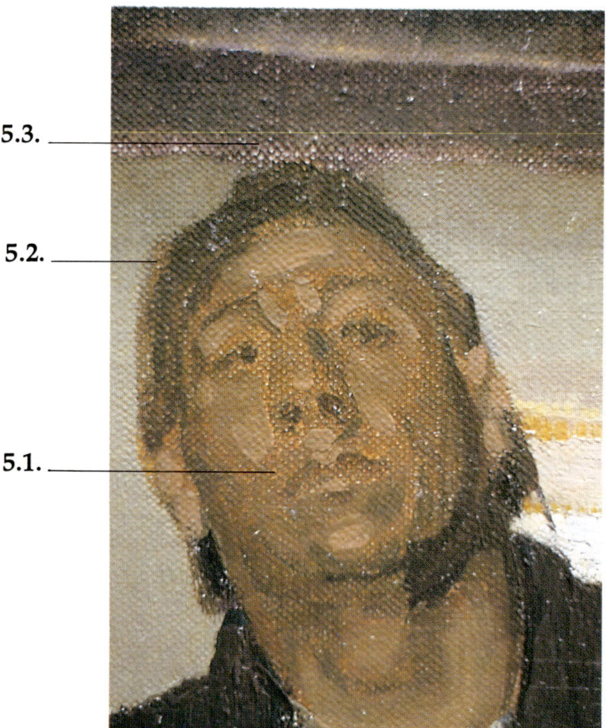

5. DETAIL OF FACE (4TH FIGURE FROM RIGHT, BACK ROW)

The underdrawing for this figure, visible by means of infrared photography, indicates that the eyes did not originally look toward the spectator but rather up to the ceiling of the courtroom.

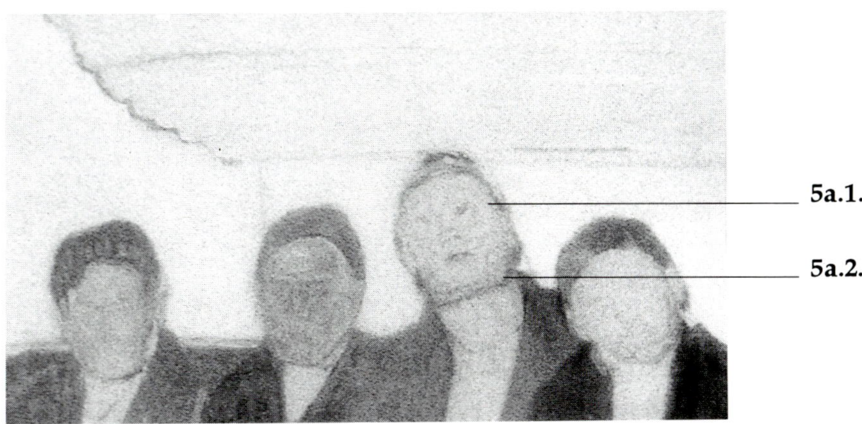

5A.   INFRARED PHOTOGRAPH

This infrared photograph reveals the artist's underdrawing.

5a.1. In the underdrawing, the eyes look upward; not at the viewer.

5a.2. The geometric style of Blumenschein's sketch is visible in the square lines of the jaw.

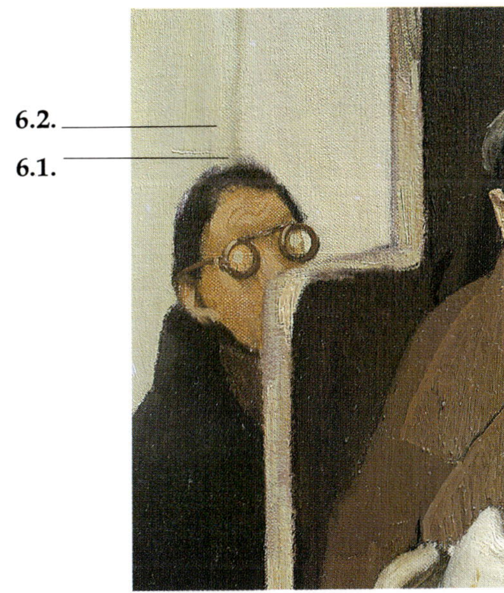

6. DETAIL OF FIGURE ON FAR LEFT

The figure observing the scene from behind the bench is said to be a self-portrait of Blumenschein. The inclusion of an artist in his work is not uncommon and dates back to the beginning of painting. Probably the most famous example is Van Eyck's *Arnolfini Wedding Portrait* of 1434 in which the artist portrayed himself in the reflection of a mirror. Among the master painters of the West, Remington frequently included himself in his pictures.

In this detail a thin, warm, dark-brown underlayer was used for the face, leaving the ground partially exposed on the tops of the canvas weave. A few lighter opaque brushstrokes indicate the facial features.

6.1. The violet underlayer can be seen between the black hair and the light gray wall. The same violet color can be seen in the opening of the figure's coat and along the edges of the bench which was then further built up with greenish paint and thicker yellowish highlights.

6.2. The gray-green underlayer was left exposed here to create the shadow along the corner of the room.

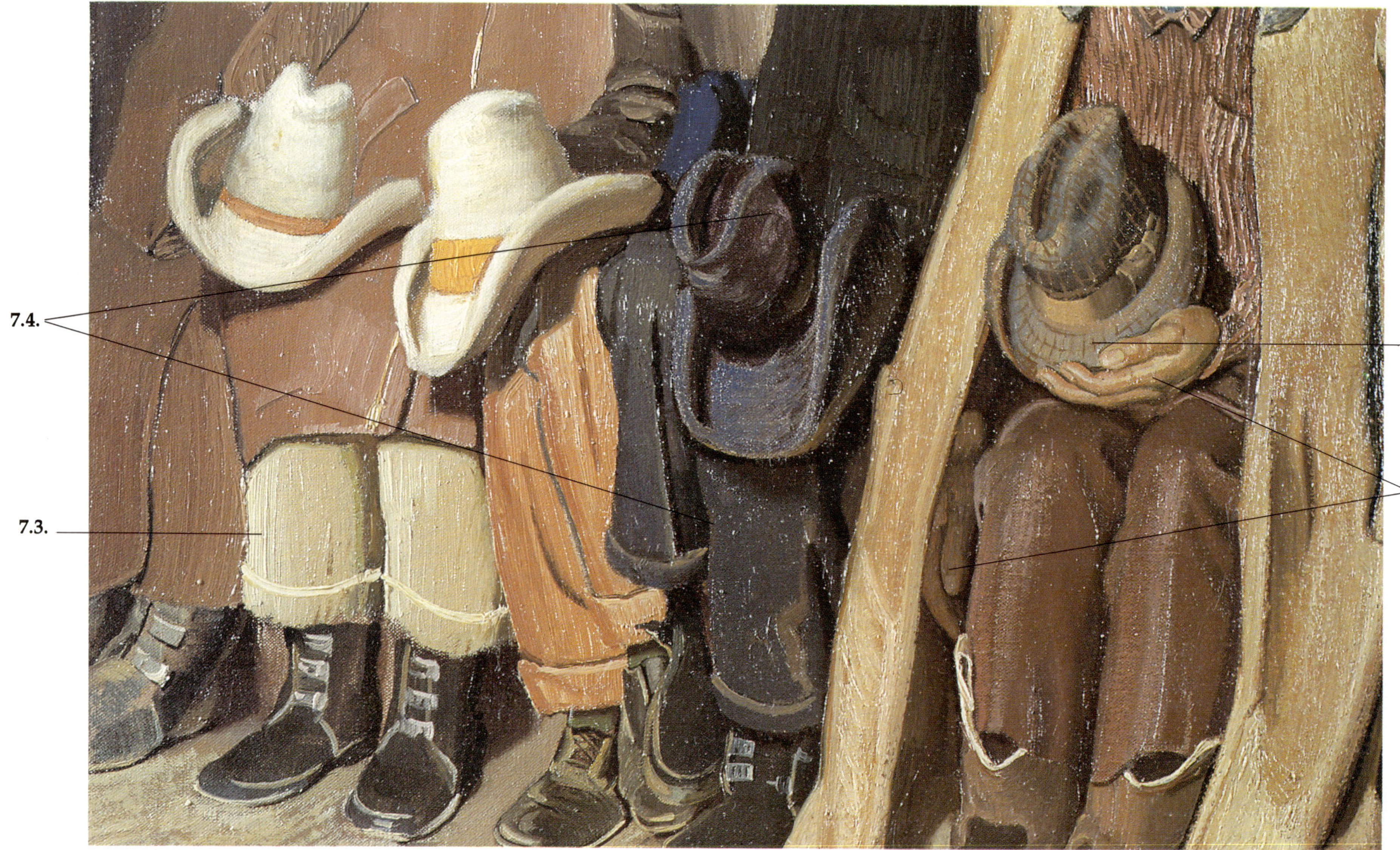

7.4.

7.3.

7.1. *Details such as the pattern on this hat were added when the paint beneath was dry.*

7.2. *The older man's hands were painted with great detail and expressive gesture. The hat is held as though precious within the big hand. The other hand which is located farther back in space was minimally indicated, yet the gesture conveys the man's serious attitude.*

7.3. *A 3/8 inch brush loaded with buttery paint was pulled in long vertical strokes which left ridges in the sides of the brush-strokes to create the effect of a ribbed fabric such as corduroy.*

7.4. *Even though the hat and trousers appear to be a similar color, a violet underlayer was employed for the hat and brown for the trousers.*

7. DETAIL OF HATS

The hats are treated as significant objects. They are held gingerly in the hands of out-doorsmen who would be more comfortable in the open with the hats on their heads.

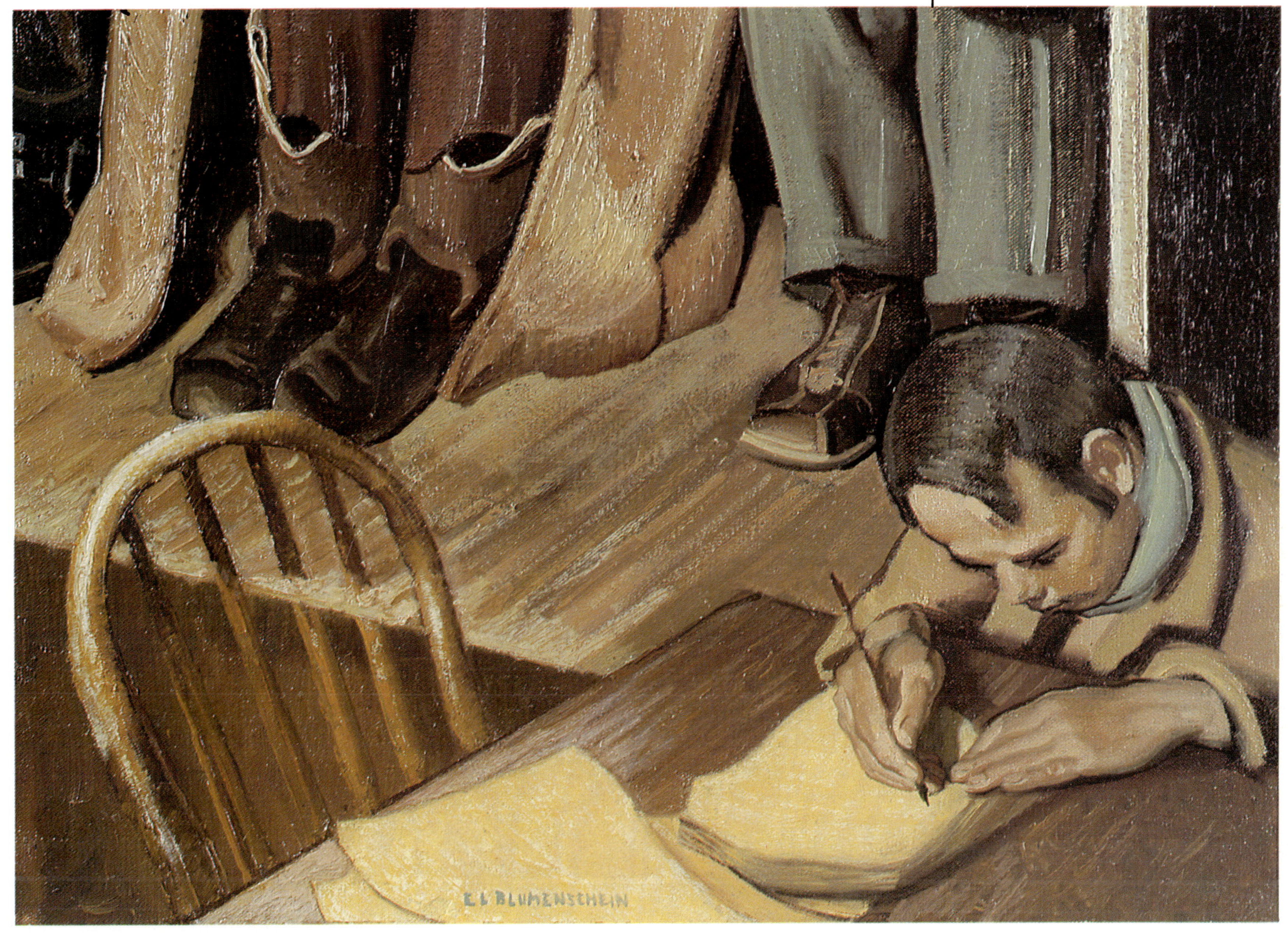

8. DETAIL OF COURT RECORDER

The young scribe records the proceedings, absorbed in his own world. The meticulous writing is an effort which requires great concentration. Nothing could disrupt his work. The foreshortened face and hands of the figure are painted with great accuracy and detail.

The pen, however, appears to be incomplete. Lost in his big hand, it consists of only the brown underlayer with the flesh of the hand painted around and over it. Final details and modeling were never added.

The disrupted spokes of the chairback present another anomaly. When Blumenschein added the highlights to the floor of the platform, two of the spokes of the chair were partially covered. As with the unfinished pen, the final paint layer was never added to these spokes, leaving them to disappear mysteriously into the platform.

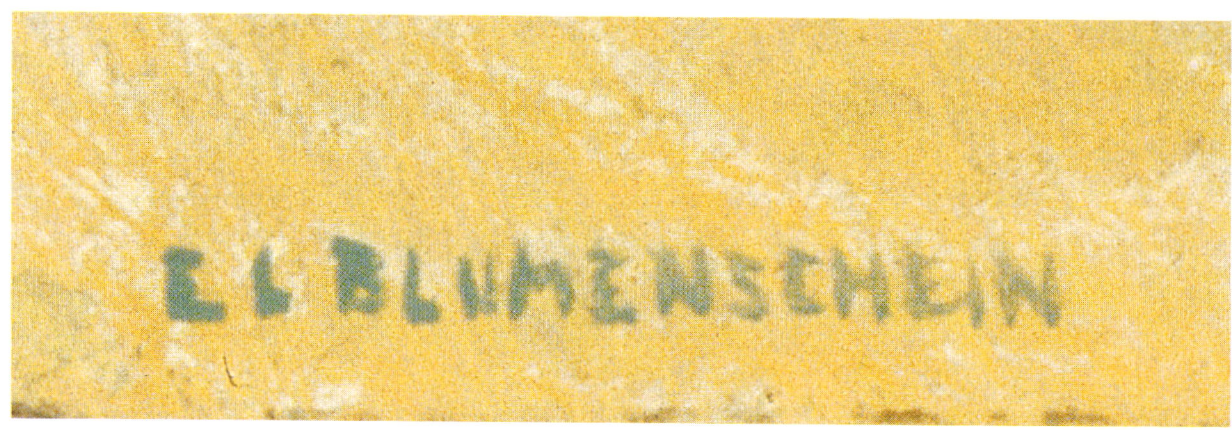

9. DETAIL OF SIGNATURE

E.L. Blumenschein

SUMMARY OF PAINTING TECHNIQUE

a. A mixed fiber canvas with a commercially prepared ground was attached to the stretcher, probably by the artist.
b. An underdrawing was laid in either with a fine brush or a pencil.
c. The main elements of the composition were blocked in with dilute colored underlayers that do not conceal the texture of the canvas. They often represent the darkest color of that area, serving as a shadow though not always the same color as the subsequent paint layers. Thus they influence the final visual appearance of the painting.
d. The main paint layer was added, generally consisting of a single layer. The optical effect of depth was achieved by leaving the preparatory local underlayers partially exposed.
e. Details and refinements to the figures were added, as well as highlights and some shadows.

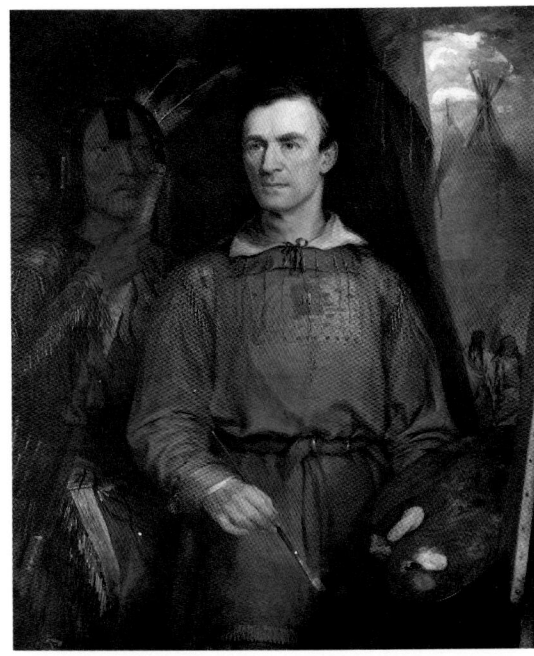

GEORGE CATLIN

George Catlin was the first American artist to dedicate his life to painting portraits of Western Indians. His emotional involvement with the red men was learned at his mother's knee. She had been captured by the Iroquois during an Indian attack when she was eight years old. She had fantastic tales to tell her children about experiences she recalled as frightening but not otherwise unpleasant.

In 1830 Catlin went beyond the frontier where some of the Indians who were his hosts had never before seen a white man. The pictures he made of them were of real people, recognizable as individuals.

By painting more than 1,200 Indian portraits and genre scenes during the next 41 years, he set a pattern for other artists who followed him into the American West. Most of the later Indian painters became rich through their development of a subject that initially was his. Catlin died poor.

He was born July 26, 1796, the only 18th century child among the master painters of the frontier. The place was Wilkes-Barre, Pennsylvania which was then the gateway West, the farthest advance of white civilization. Explorers, Indian fighters, and trappers were frequent guests at the Catlin residence. They had exciting stories to relate that concerned the original Americans.

The fifth of 14 children, Catlin was educated at home by his mother. Despite the attraction of her old relationship with the mysterious Indians who had caught her and freed her, he was influenced by his more prosaic father to study law. At 21 he traveled to Connecticut to read statutes and cases in America's first law school. Then he returned to Pennsylvania to practice.

Although he had no training, he undertook the painting of portraits as an absorbing hobby. By the time he was 27, his growing aptitude for art gained precedence over jurisprudence. He moved first to Philadelphia and then to Washington, D.C. where he became established as a miniaturist and painter of political and society portraits.

Catlin was still dissatisfied, however. Although he was elected a National Academician in 1826, his second career was proving to be almost as pedestrian as the law had been. For relief he began painting portraits of peaceful Eastern Iroquois on their reservations in New York State. Then a chance meeting in Philadelphia with a delegation of dignified looking Indians from the Western plains re-oriented his goals. He made a bold statement of a new personal purpose. He was determined, he said, "to use my art and so much of the labors of my future life as might be required in rescuing from oblivion the looks and customs of the vanishing races of native man in America." He vowed that "nothing short of the loss of my life shall prevent me from visiting their country and of becoming their historian."

That was a great resolve and he fulfilled it beyond question. True, some of the later Indian painters made equivalent declarations. Their task, however, was infinitely easier than Catlin's. He traveled without benefit of railroad or stagecoach. There was not even a government survey expedition he could join that would have suited his purpose. After the first year he was usually alone.

Yet Catlin was an enthusiast. At the end of six years as a lawyer and another seven as a society artist, he went to St. Louis on his own initiative and without outside financial support. The costs he incurred in studying the Indians had to be paid for with money he earned. His custom over the years was to spend winters in a city where he could solicit society portrait commissions, while in the summers he used the proceeds to travel among the Indians.

St. Louis was the jumping off point for the West in 1830. The headquarters of General William Clark who had led the 1804 expedition with Lewis was there. Catlin began his mission the easy way by painting the portraits of the Plains Indians who came to see Clark. When he was sure of his technique, he accompanied Clark to Prairie du Chien on the Mississippi, to Fort Leavenworth, and to Kansa Indian villages on the Kansas River.

Other artists generally make sketches in the field, preparatory to doing finished portraits back in their studios. Catlin was so facile with his quick brushstrokes, he was able to paint plein air portraits. He produced as many as six finished portraits and roughs on the spot in a single day, despite the reluctance of some Indians to pose and the jostling by a rapt primitive audience.

In the field he cut canvases to the size he wanted and rolled them in large tubes for transporting. His palette contained colors that were quite different from the colors he had used as a society painter in Washington. The exotic hues of the red men and their decorative costumes controlled his choices.

He spent no time sketching on the canvas in charcoal or pencil. Instead, the figure was outlined in sepia with broad, thin strokes so the paint would dry quickly and not crack when rolled back up to go into the tube. Next, the bust of the figure was painted in warm earth tones.

He was always working under pressure. If he was about to be interrupted because he had to change sitters or move on, he would sketch in the particulars of face and costume with unmixed touches of color. Enough detail had to be brushed on so the more important paintings could be completed accurately after he returned from the field.

The following year, Catlin started in the spring to paint the Pawnees and the Omahas along the Platte River. He was 35 years old, with blue eyes and black hair. Lean and agile at 5 feet 8 inches, he walked with the measured stride of the Indians he pursued.

In 1832 he boarded the American Fur Company's new steamboat, *Yellow Stone,* on the maiden trip to Fort Union at the mouth of the Yellowstone River. During the three months it took to voyage 2,000 miles up the Missouri, Catlin continued to paint Indian portraits at the many stops. His unbounded admiration for the Indian as a person survived all of the scrapes and privations he endured. He also took elaborate notes on what he saw. For a man without formal schooling, he expressed himself clearly and vividly. His findings were taken seriously in scientific circles.

Catlin's biographers differ as to where he was in a given year, but by the end of the summer of 1836 Catlin was satisfied that he had completed the record of the Indians of the Western plains. The usual lack of money prevented him from going on to the Indians of the Rockies and the West Coast, so the 40-year-old frontiersman turned lawyer turned society painter turned Indian anthropologist became a showman as a new career.

To that point in his years in the West, Catlin had painted hundreds of Indian portraits and genre scenes. He had also accumulated scores of artifacts. He had brought back Indian clothing and objects ranging in size from beads to a huge Crow tepee, but he had not permitted himself to sell one painting or artifact. He regarded his collection as a treasure to be held together for the nation and not to be offered for sale piecemeal.

He began by exhibiting the Indian portraits in Buffalo, New York in 1836 and in Albany in 1837. By the fall of 1837 he had perfected "Catlin's Indian Gallery" to bring to the public all that he had painted and collected. He had two goals, to promote his humane view of the Indian and to make his fortune.

He opened his exhibition in New York City on the evening of September 25, 1837. "There will be several hundred Portraits exhibited," he promised in the broadsides, "as well as Splendid Costumes–Paintings of their villages–Dances–Buffalo Hunts–Religious Ceremonies, etc. Collected by himself, among the wildest tribes of America, during an absence from this city of seven years. Mr. Catlin will be present at all his exhibitions, giving illustrations and explanations in the form of a Lecture. Each admission 50 cents."

In the beginning the Indian Gallery was so successful that Catlin needed a larger hall. He was called a genius, but as the novelty wore off he had to move to Washington, Philadelphia, and then Boston to attract enough spectators. To keep the collection together, he offered it to the United States government but Congress would not authorize funds for the purchase.

Disappointed by the legislative rebuff and by slackening public interest, he took his collection to England in 1840. He was immediately a celebrity again. He met European royalty, added live Indians to the Gallery to do demonstrations of ritual dances, and continued to paint from his sketches and notes. Many of the paintings were commissioned by private customers.

In London Catlin was able to use the money he earned to finance the publication of a book on the North American Indian. He also published a portfolio of 25 lithographs of his Indian paintings. In 1845 he exhibited the Gallery in Paris at the invitation of King Louis Philippe.

By 1852, however, European interest in the collection had subsided. Catlin's wife and only son had died in Europe and his three daughters were being raised by his wife's family in the United States. He was 56, deaf, and impoverished. Soon he was incarcerated in debtor's prison. The Indian collection was about to be seized by creditors when Joseph Harrison, a Philadelphia manufacturer of locomotives, paid Catlin's debts and took the collection as security. Catlin never recovered possession of his Indian Gallery.

Instead, "with no other means on earth than my hands and my brush, and less than half a life, at best, before me," the indomitable Catlin started over. He recreated the paintings that were in the Indian Gallery as well as he could from his notes, and traveled to South America and the American West Coast to paint additional Indian portraits. That became the basis of "Catlin's Cartoon Collection."

By 1870, the collection included hundreds of new paintings, most of them done on white cardboard rather than canvas. The Congress did not buy the Cartoon Collection either, but this time the executive branch showed its appreciation by having the paintings hung in the Smithsonian Building in Washington. Catlin was provided with an apartment in the tower. After he died in 1872 the Cartoon Collection was sold to the American Museum of Natural History in New York City.

Joseph Harrison's heirs gave Catlin's original Indian Gallery to the Smithsonian Institution. In the 1940s the American public became curious about what the Indians of the 1830s had been like. Catlin's paintings were restored and exhibited.

It was fashionable in the 1940s to debunk Catlin's ability as an artist. He was self-taught. He was also said to have painted standing figures poorly, to have lacked an understanding of perspective, and to have taken liberties with the landscape. From the beginning, however, Catlin himself had declared that the plein air paintings were intended only "as true and fac-simile traces of individual life and historical facts." To him, they were ethnographic records rather than works of art. Even the title "Cartoon Collection" meant that the pictures were large sketches, not finished paintings.

In retrospect, if there were failures among the paintings, the defect was neither artistic nor ethnographic. When Catlin wanted to paint a portrait as fine art instead of as a field sketch, he knew how to take the time required in a studio. The result then was at least as competent as the work of his urban contemporaries. Moreover, his standing figures suit the modern eye. He was an excellent advocate for the Plains Indian, if not a practical businessman for himself.

In sidelines not related to art, though, Catlin was the proponent of a few choice bits of nonsense. For one, he was certain that the Indians were the lost tribe of Israel. He professed to have found numerous similarities between the two peoples in the recognition of one God, use of sacred houses, employment of high priests and prophets, separation of women, bathing rituals, and feasts and fasts. Neither the Indians nor the Israelites acknowledged these connections.

A second humbug was *The Breath of Life*. This was a book Catlin wrote and illustrated in London in 1860 to document the harm he said civilized people do to themselves when they fail to keep their mouths closed while asleep. When a person "opens his mouth to its widest" in sleep, Catlin maintained seriously, "he lets the enemy in that chills his lungs–that racks his brain–that paralyses his stomach–that gives him the nightmare–brings him Imps and Fairies that dance before him during the night."

More than 40,000 copies of *The Breath of Life* were sold after the title was amended to *Shut Your Mouth and Save Your Life*. Catlin was offering good advice for any time.

1. The Painting

Catlin wrote in his *Letters and Notes on the Manners, Customs, and Conditions of the North American Indians*, "The prairies burning form some of the most beautiful scenes that are to be witnessed in this country, and also some of the most sublime. Every acre of these vast prairies (being covered for hundreds and hundreds of miles, with a crop of grass, which dies and dries in the fall) burns over during the fall or early in the spring, leaving the ground of a black and doleful colour....

"Over the elevated lands and prairie bluffs, where the grass is thin and short, the fire slowly creeps with a feeble flame, which one can easily step over; where the wild animals often rest in their lairs until the flames almost burn their noses, when they will reluctantly rise, and leap over it, and trot off amongst the cinders, where the fire past and left the ground as black as jet....

"There is yet another character of burning prairies ...the war, or hell of fires! where the grass is seven or eight feet high ...and the flames are driven forward by the hurricanes, which often sweep over the vast prairies of this denuded country. There are many of these meadows on the Missouri, the Platte, and the Arkansas, of many miles in breadth, which are perfectly level, with a waving grass, so high, that we are obliged to stand erect in our stirrups, in order to look over its waving tops, as we ride through it. The fire in these, before such a wind, travels at an immense and frightful rate, and often destroys, on their fleetest horses, parties of Indians, who are so unlucky as to be overtaken by it."

In *The Natural Man Observed: A Study of Catlin's Indian Gallery*, W.H. Truettner noted that Catlin traveled with only half a dozen pigments, and the unused canvas

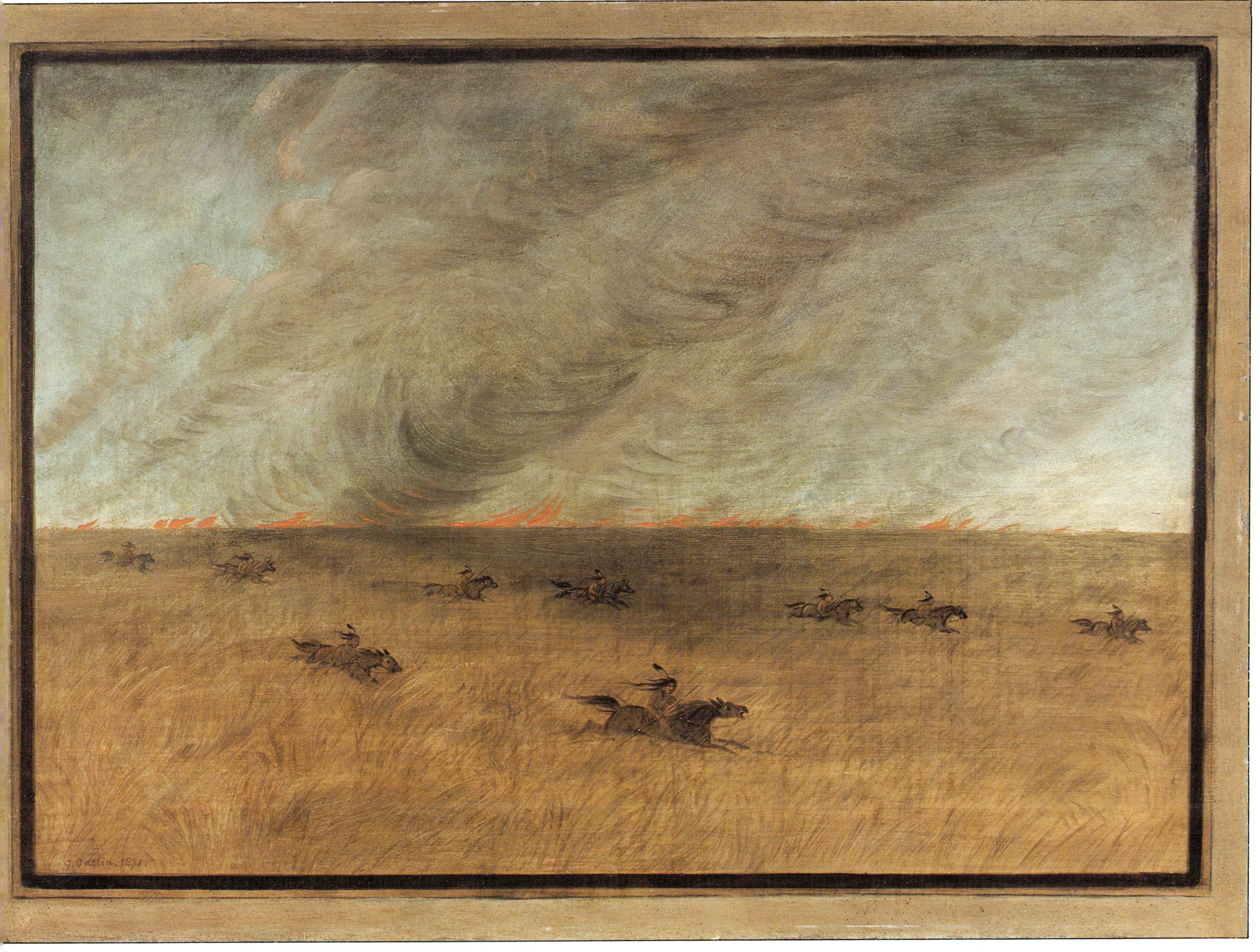

rolled up and kept in large cylinders. He wasted no time in doing his sketches, using broad sepia brushstrokes. He would then paint in the figures and clothing with pure vermilion, ultramarine, Prussian blue, and earth colors. The paint was applied thinly to speed the drying so the canvas could be rolled again for storage without cracking the paint. Final touches were added in the studio. In his landscapes Catlin followed the same painting method he used in the portraits. Small canvases were painted directly.

Fire in a Missouri Meadow fits into the "Cartoon Collection" painted late in the artist's life to replace his earlier works which he had lost to bankruptcy. This painting was done in 1871 from the artist's earlier notes, based on his trip up the Missouri in 1832. Paintings of the same subject survive from that earlier period. The colors were more vivid and the compositions more dramatic than the later painting discussed here. This is no surprise as there lay some 40 years in between. *Fire in a Missouri Meadow* was painted a year before Catlin died.

George Catlin. Fire in a Missouri Meadow, and a Party of Sioux Indians Escaping From It: Upper Missouri 1871 is in the Fine Arts Museums of San Francisco. Gift of Mr. & Mrs. John D. Rockefeller 3rd. Oil on thick paper glued overall to cardboard. 18 inches (45.7 cm) height x 24 3/8 inches (61.9 cm) width. Signed lower left and dated 1871.

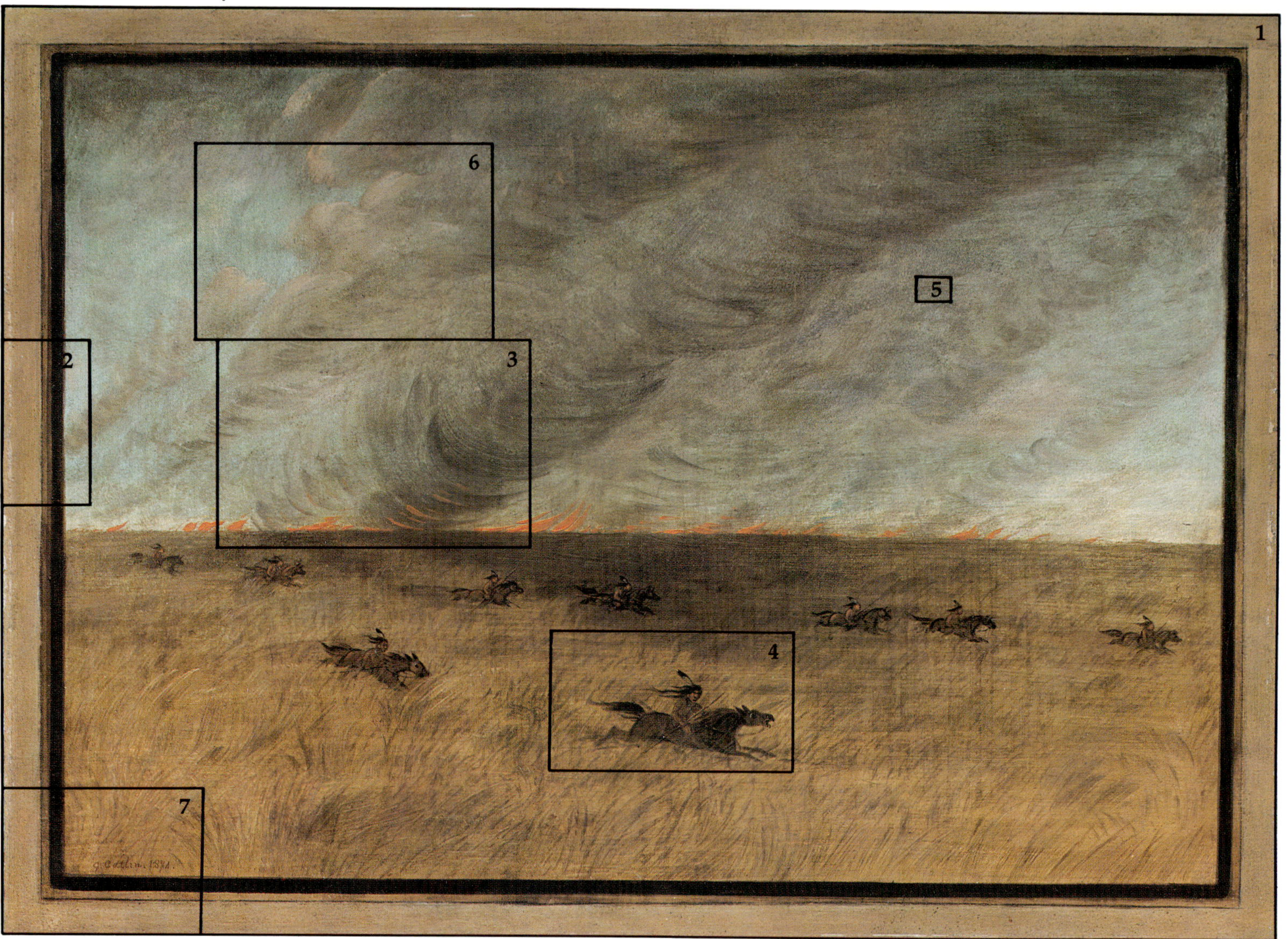

A comparison of Catlin's paintings shows striking stylistic and qualitative differences, regardless of when they were done. A primitive quality is easily detected in some of his pictures, whereas the technique of others is more sophisticated and an understanding of perspective and anatomy can be observed. Furthermore, inconsistencies may occur within a single painting.

It is easy to understand these intermittent ups and downs. One theory is that Catlin worked quickly on his bread and butter commissions. Another is that some paintings were done from life, in the field under difficult conditions, whereas others were completed in the studio. Or, as here, the paintings were done from memory very late in his life, when he thought the earlier collection had been lost forever. These variances also seem consistent with the artist's lack of formal training. In any event, the paintings will always be appreciated for their historic value.

Fire in a Missouri Meadow is very simple in composition and form. The picture is divided in two by the flat prairie skyline. The smoke clouds rise diagonally toward the upper right corner. Following the same wind pattern, the diagonal licks of flame and the blades of grass parallel the plumes of smoke. The Indians on horseback flee in the opposite diagonal direction, toward the lower right corner. The composition is enclosed in a *trompe l'oeil* frame.

This picture displays some unorthodox techniques. Catlin's untutored background, as well as the difficult conditions under which he often worked, freed him to experiment with a non-academic approach to painting materials. His oil paints were handled as dilute washes, similar to watercolor technique. Furthermore, it appears that paint of an aqueous nature, such as watercolor, was used in addition to the oil paint. Analysis of the paint media could not be carried out because the excellent condition of this painting did not permit samples to be taken for further study, yet observation of the intact paint surface through great magnification strongly suggests the final touches to be of an aqueous nature.

Fire in a Missouri Meadow was painted on a heavy paper support that has been attached overall to a cardboard mount. A white ground was brushed on in a horizontal direction, retaining some texture of the brushstrokes. This textured ground is evident throughout the painting because of the thin nature of the subsequent paint layers. It is not clear if the simple composition was sketched in. It is possible that the painting was carried out directly, especially as the theme is one from the artist's memory.

The blue sky was painted first. The brushwork in the sky follows many directions, but is mainly vertical. Skips and gaps in the blue expose the white ground beneath. The blue is composed of white, blue, and traces of green as well as a small amount of an earth color such as raw sienna. Some of the distinct pigment particles can be seen to be exceptionally large when viewed under a microscope and the larger blue particles can even be discerned with the naked eye. These may be very coarsely ground pigment particles or conglomerates of pigments. The proportion of white pigment to blue increases toward the horizon.

The dark smoke clouds were painted on top of the blue in a circular motion of the brush with opaque, but dilutely and thinly applied paint. They were painted generally from dark to light with light pinkish gray highlights added. Final scumbles were added to the clouds and to the sky to increase the smoky haze.

The foreground was begun with an underlayer of a light yellowish brown color for the prairie. This was applied thinly and uniformly over the ground. The grass was added with darker brown paint in individual diagonal brushstrokes. The Indians and horses were then laid in. More blades of grass were added around and partially over the horses. This grass is more yellow and lighter in color and the paint is more opaque. The flames were the last part of the composition to be painted. Red, orange, and yellow were applied together wet-into-wet over paint which had already dried, thus preventing contamination of the bright colored flames by the duller paint beneath.

In a final step, dark and light colored flecks of paint were added. Microscopic examination suggests that a different sort of paint was used, perhaps one with an aqueous medium as a binder. These flecks were applied to the surface in an irregular pattern. In the main composition they make up the clouds of soot sent up by the flames. The usual method of achieving this look is to flick dilute paint from a stiff brush by drawing a finger across the surface, or by hitting the brush shaft against the other hand, thus casting tiny drops onto the surface. The paint could also have been dispersed with an atomizer or mouth blower. Paint spatters are commonly used to achieve an antique appearance, such as with frame antiquing, and it may be that Catlin did intend an older appearance as this was a re-creation of a picture done many years before. By accident or not, the spatters do extend over the painted border.

To the viewer's sophisticated eye, *Fire in a Missouri Meadow* has a naive, almost childlike quality. In the first place, Catlin was untaught as a painter. He considered himself to be a recorder of the Indians, not a fine art painter. He worked, for the most part, under difficult, primitive conditions that did not allow leisure to refine and reflect. He was concerned with truth, not effects. Finally, this painting is part of a series intended to record his vast and unique knowledge of a rapidly disappearing West. Except for brief flashes of fame Catlin's works were unappreciated, and as he believed at the end of his life, lost altogether. This cartoon series was a valiant effort of an old man to preserve what he knew of the Indian, whether the public was interested or not.

2.1. These horizontal brushstrokes of the white ground show through the thin paint of the sky.

2.2. The spatters appear throughout the painting, and are clearly visible on the black strip of the painted frame. In the main composition they represent the debris thrown into the air by the fire. The same specks on the painted frame give it an antique appearance that would be appropriate for a subject Catlin had not seen for 40 years. Whether this "antiquing" was intentional cannot be determined, but its effectiveness is clearly seen.

2.3. The diagonal brushstrokes here are from the vertical application of the blue paint of the sky.

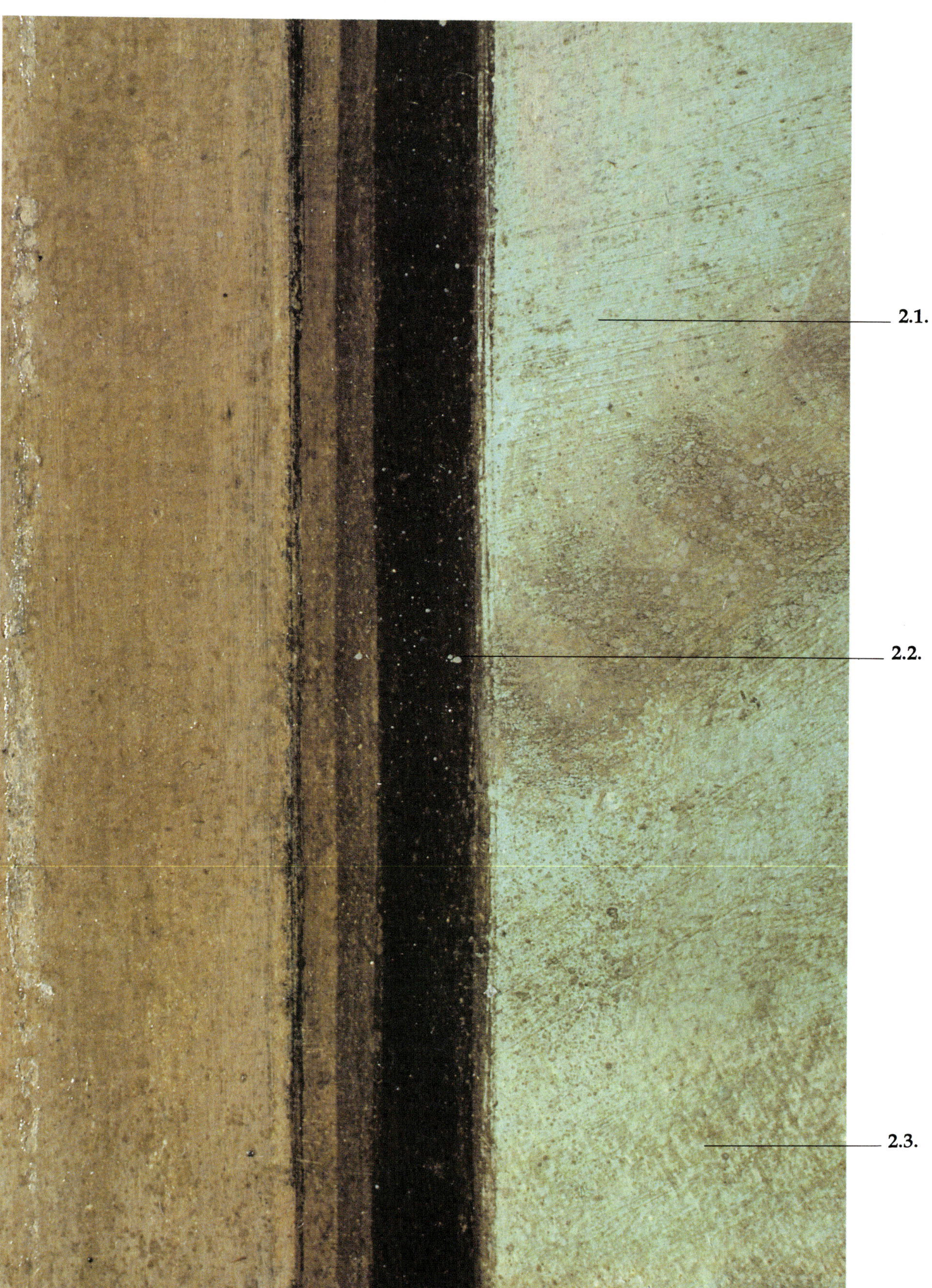

2. DETAIL OF LEFT EDGE

Catlin painted an imitation shadow box frame around this picture. Guidelines were drawn first and then the paint was neatly applied within the drawn boundaries.

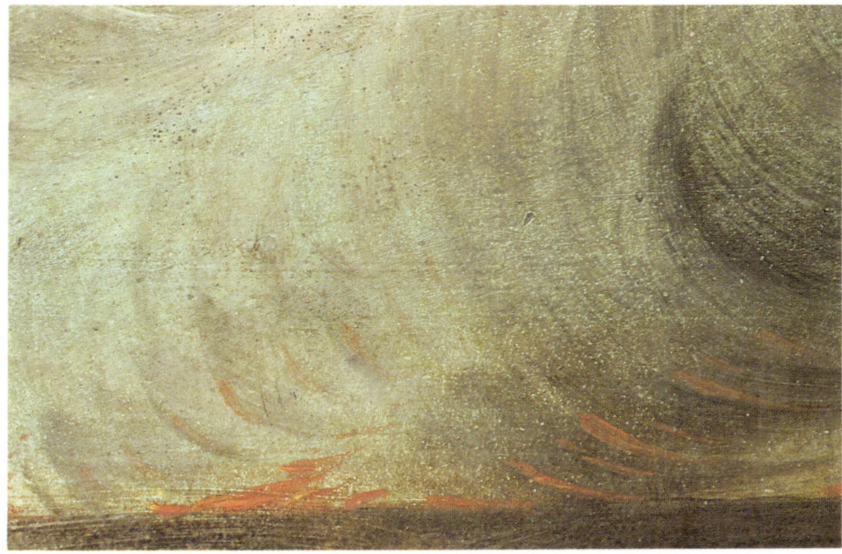

3. Detail of Flames

The horizontal brush texture seen across the middle of this detail is from the application of the white ground. The vertical brushwork that angles slightly diagonally to the left is from the application of the blue paint of the sky and can be clearly seen on this detail. This was followed by the darker paint for the smoke which was applied in broad and curved strokes. The smoke clouds were then scumbled over with a slightly warmer and lighter color seen in the top center of the illustration. The red flames were added next. Red, orange, and yellow paint was applied wet-into-wet over the dry paint beneath. Finally, the spatters were applied over the painting.

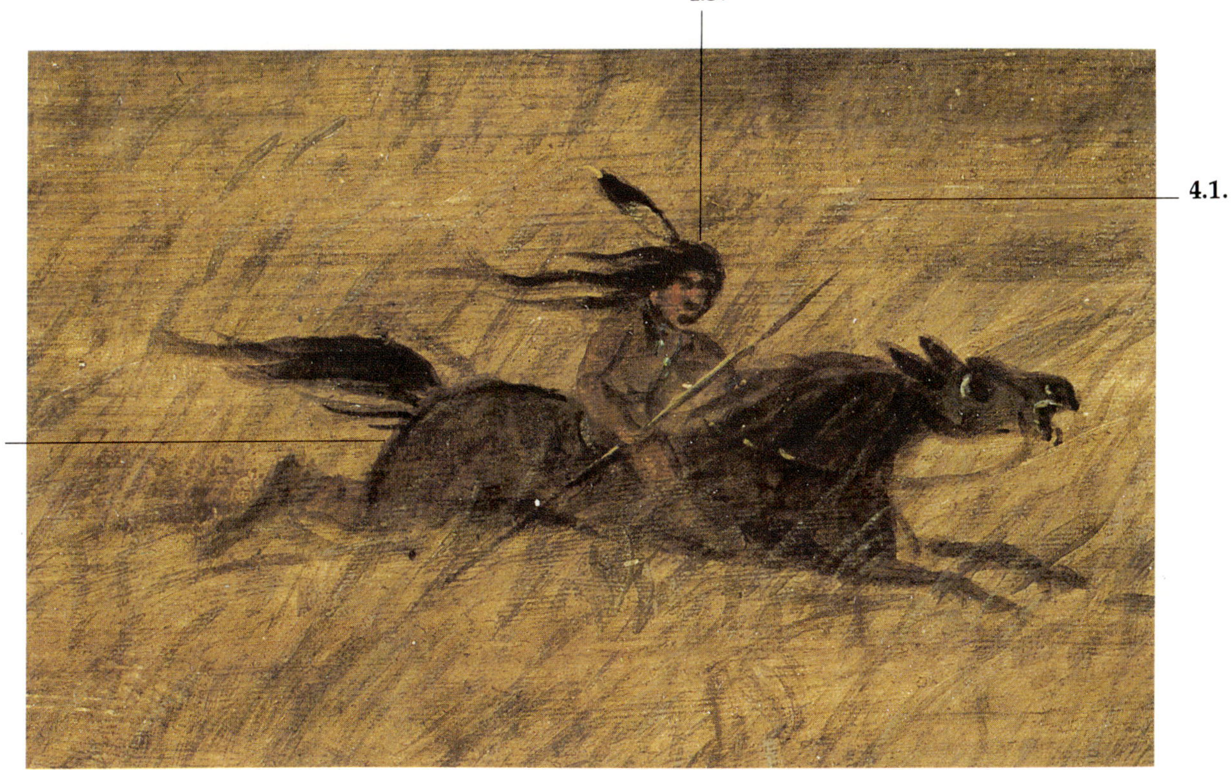

4. Detail of Indian on Horseback

4.1. The reflective white ground shows through at the tops of the strokes where the earth-colored paint is thinnest, producing a luminous base for the foreground.

4.2. The general shape of the horse and rider was laid in with opaque paint over the earth-colored underlayer. Darker outlines and details were added next.

4.3. The color of the grass was used as the main color for the Indian's face. Red dots complete the features. The hair was done with dark outlines added last.

5. DETAIL OF SKY

The image of this soot filled maelstrom was painted in the following order: first the blue sky was brushed in thinly over the white ground; darker paint for the smoke clouds was added in a circular manner; warm hued scumbles were added; these were followed by dark specks followed by lighter specks. The medium of the spatters appears to be aqueous, perhaps gum arabic, the medium used for watercolor, indicating that Catlin used a mixed media technique. In the composition the spatters represent soot, though where they extend over the painted frame their role becomes more obscure. In any case, it is an individual and effective touch.

6.4.

6.3.

6.2.

6.1.

6. DETAIL OF SKY AND CLOUDS

6.1. The impression of the artist's accidentally-affixed thumbprint can be seen in the blue.

6.2. The sky was applied thinly over the white ground allowing the white to show through in places. A darker paint for the smoke clouds was laid over the blue, followed by the more opaque, pinkish paint for the highlights.

6.3. A scumble was added to increase the smoky haze.

6.4. In a last step, flecks of paint were added.

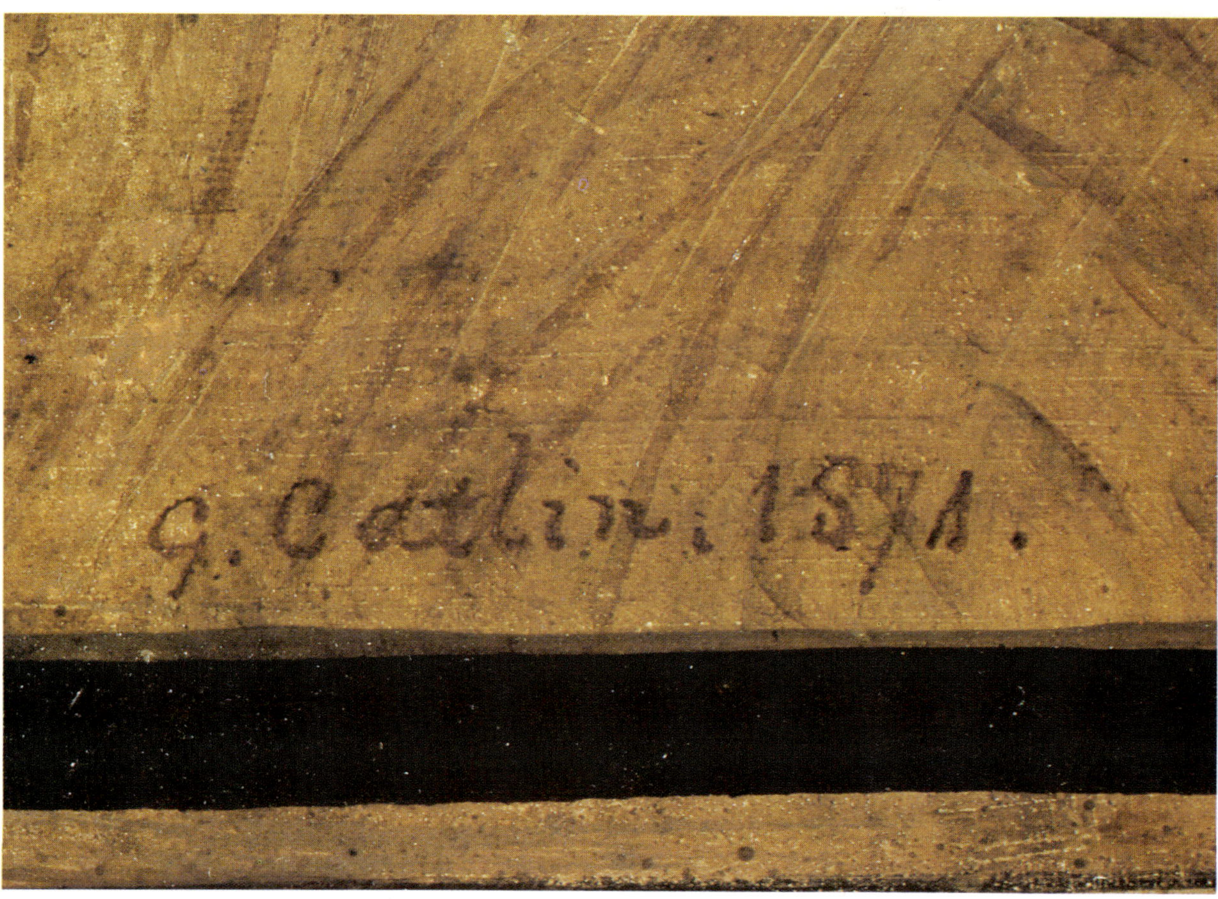

7. DETAIL OF SIGNATURE

G. Catlin, 1871

SUMMARY OF PAINTING TECHNIQUE

a. A white ground was brushed in a horizontal direction onto a heavy paper support that has been attached to a cardboard mount.
b. A *trompe l'oeil* frame was painted around the border. Guidelines for this frame can be seen where the paint is thin, though no underdrawing for the composition was detected.
c. The sky was painted first, beginning with the blue, and continuing with the smoke clouds painted from dark to light.
d. The bottom half of the composition was carried out next, beginning with an earth-colored base, followed by the grass, then the horses and riders, and finally more grass around the figures.
e. The flames were added last when the paint beneath was dry to prevent contamination of these bright colors.
f. In a final step, the spatters were added, first dark flecks, then lighter ones.

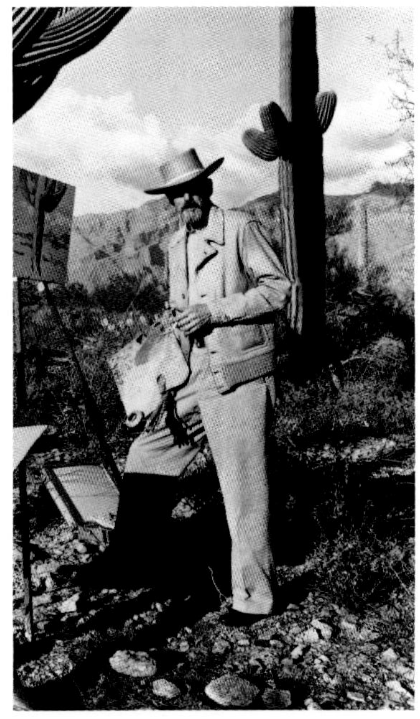

MAYNARD DIXON

As a painter and as a person, Maynard Dixon was independent to an extreme. He quit school to study art. He left art school to draw from nature. He refused to paint violent Western illustrations for Eastern editors who demanded conformity with violent Western texts.

He was divorced from two wives because of what he called "the absolute necessity of freedom, cost what it may." He declined to teach art because his students were not as self-reliant as he thought he had been. He stopped exhibiting with his fellow California artists when they criticized his murals. He experimented with bizarre religions and the occult to try to attain simplification of his life and work. He was radicalized politically by the suffering caused by the Great Depression of the early 1930s.

And that was only a part of the independence he made into a permanent personal rebellion. Yet, his own torment never showed in his paintings of the West. He was able to convey both the tranquility of ordinary people and what he described as the simple poetry of barren landscapes.

Lafayette Maynard Dixon was born on January 24, 1875 in the pioneer city of Fresno, California. His grandfather owned a nearby ranch. His father was county clerk and head of the local vigilantes. An asthmatic, Dixon was taken on camping trips into the Sierras and Yosemite to help his breathing.

He had been drawing since he was seven. At 16, he began to sketch full-time. His silent teachers were engravings of illustrations by Howard Pyle and Frederic Remington in the popular magazines. When he filled two sketch books, he had the courage to mail them cross-country to his idol Remington for criticism. The surprised but affable superstar told the young aspirant, "You draw better at your age than I did at the same age. Above all, draw–draw–draw–and always from nature." Dixon held on to the note and followed the advice.

In 1893, Dixon enrolled in the San Francisco School of Design. He studied under Arthur Mathews who had been a pupil of traditional Academicians in Paris. Dixon incurred Mathews' vicious sarcasm by his Remington-induced unwillingness to draw from plaster casts of antiques. He felt compelled to leave the school and return to unguided outdoor sketching for his art education.

Despite Mathews' faultfinding, Dixon was selling magazine illustrations by the end of 1893. In response to another Dixon inquiry, Remington suggested that the minimum price for a drawing be the same $10 that had been the older man's starting compensation a decade earlier. By 1895 the *Overland Monthly* was enthusiastically calling Dixon "perhaps the coming rival of Frederic Remington. He has made a national reputation." The same year, Dixon had his first exhibition of drawings. He produced his initial illustrations for books two years later. Dixon admitted that "all these drawings were terrible. I did not begin to hit the ball until 1898."

In 1899 he was hired by the *San Francisco Examiner* as staff artist but "the tension of the Hearst office finally got on my nerves," he complained. Moreover, the daily regimen interfered with his sketching trips. He quit and went off on another swing through the Southwestern deserts. He also travelled with the painter Xavier Martinez who had just come back from studies with the French Academicians. Next he left for a trip through the Northwest with Edward Borein whose untutored background in painting was similar to Dixon's.

As Dixon said, his status as an illustrator was assured when he was 23. His drawings appeared in national magazines. In addition, his easel paintings were exhibited in San Francisco. He maintained a studio there until the earthquake and fire of 1906 destroyed both his studio and his stock of paintings. The next year he went to New York City where he lost his savings in the bank panic.

In the East he obtained assignments for illustrations in competition with some of the great artists he had revered. His independence, however, alienated editors who wanted him to depict sensational frontier subjects. Dixon explained that "illustration is OK but too confining. I am being paid to lie about the West. The melodramatic Wild West idea is not for me. I'm going back home where I can do honest work."

Dixon wanted to concentrate on fine art. Although he exhibited easel paintings at the National Academy of Design in 1910 and again in 1911, he believed that "as a painter I date from 1912. My return from New York to the old studio on Montgomery Street marked the beginning of my real development. I was getting a new direction and beginning to find myself."

The influential magazine *International Studio* said about him that "the poetical feeling of the artist is the dominating quality. [He is] a signal success in interpretation of the mystery and silence of the Great Plains." At the Panama-Pacific Exposition in 1915 he was exposed to the Impressionists he credited with revising his ideas about color. That was when *Apache Land* was painted. He was 40 and just hitting his stride as an artist.

In a five-year period he produced 130 canvases and sold 80. Nevertheless, a nervous breakdown blamed on discord with his first wife and an inexplicable shortage of ready money caused him to go back to more restrictive employment as a commercial artist.

During World War I he was shaken by the hate propaganda in vogue and by the later Red-baiting. He was discouraged, too, by the increasing commercialization of his Old West "with dude ranches and show-off cowboys." He tried the esoteric religions and the occult after he was divorced in 1917.

Dixon married photographer Dorothea Lange in 1920 and finally discontinued commercial art. On camping trips Lange photographed while he sketched. He painted 140 oils in the next four years, selling half for an income adequate to support his two families. His brushwork was getting looser.

Lange's photography contributed to his staging of subjects with more depth. In addition, the California critics insisted that "he has absorbed and digested the newer movements of modern art, with vivid color, simplified form, and a larger decorative impulse," but he denied any artistic connection with the modernists. He repeated only that "my object has always been to get as close to the real thing as possible. I aim to interpret the poetry and pathos and the life of Western people seen amid grandeur, sternness, and loneliness."

During a 1923 visit to New York City to open an exhibition, he was emphatic about rejecting any association with the American abstract painters. He also ranted about "the hot-house atmosphere and false modernisms" of the avant garde movement led by the voluble Alfred Stieglitz in his 291 gallery that represented the rising Georgia O'Keeffe. "After listening to exploiter Stieglitz expatiate and observing so much cleverness and futility," Dixon exclaimed, "I was glad to quit that stale-air existence and come West."

For his purification, Dixon lived with the Hopis for four months, painting and writing poetry about his experiences: "Ascendant over the world grows the saffron dawn: Still and dim in the prairie–dark is the sod,/and dewy the cool curling blades of the buffalo grass...."

In the 1920s Dixon was the busiest mural painter in the West. He started even the largest walls with thumbnail sketches 1 1/2x1 inch. The drawings were enlarged to full size in stages and the final outlines were traced onto heavy linen. According to his biographer Wesley Burnside, Dixon's mural technique was his own. He diluted the paints to let him spray an undercoating onto the linen. Then he filled in details with his brushwork. The result was said to resemble hand-woven American Indian fabrics.

When his fellow artists criticized the murals Dixon responded that "the painter must go to the public with his work," not to other artists. He quickly disassociated himself from his California peers.

After the Depression commenced in late 1929, art sales were few. Dixon was saddened by the national malaise. He said he had "a feeling of something unavoidable impending, of complete helplessness in the grip of fate. To get it out of my system grew the idea of painting *Shapes of Fear*." This was a major symbolic work later bought by the National Academy of Design.

In 1934 Dixon drove "around the water front surveying the turbulence" during the maritime labor troubles in San Francisco. His *Strike* series of paintings was in dull colors to indicate his sympathy with the underdogs. He also painted *The Forgotten Man* series about the homeless.

Acknowledging that he was reaching beyond cowboys and Indians for subject matter, he remarked that "painting must be human. It is my testimony in regard to life." When he saw the sorrowful conditions faced by migrant farm laborers in 1935, he queried, "Is this my country?"

With the arrival of better economic times, he returned to using the West as his theme. His outburst of radicalism disappeared as his health declined. His style, however, was still emerging. Edges were sharper and colors fresher. The backgrounds were of shadows in geometric patterns. He called the technique "cubist realism," as much a self-contradiction as a "studied impressionism" would be. Dixon died in Tucson at 71. His ashes were buried at Zion Canyon in Utah.

Instead of the atmospheric vistas of Hudson River painters in the West, his landscapes were of dramatic desert mountains under a designed sky. He thought his paintings were closest to the Taos School depicting dignified pastoral Indians, but his simplified realism was really a station on the way to the abstracted shapes of the modernists he once abhorred.

1. THE PAINTING

In *Apache Land*, Dixon captured a tranquil desertscape in which the passing clouds provide the only motion. The horizon is far away and the sky fills the greater portion of the composition. The color range is fresh and bright, and could be a reflection of the artist's

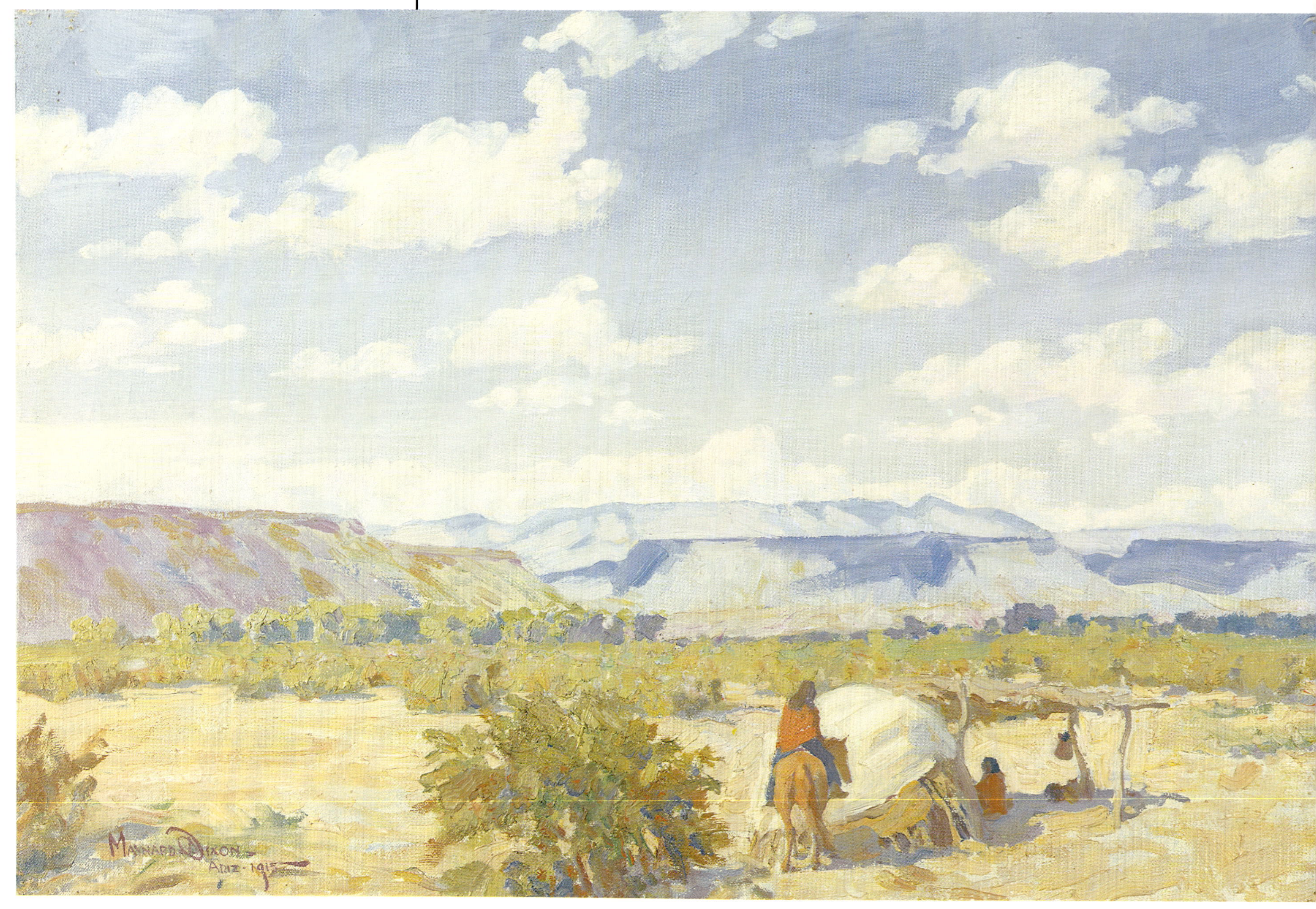

Maynard Dixon. Apache Land is in the collection of the San Diego Museum of Art, California. Oil on canvas. 20 1/16 inches (50.9 cm) height x 30 1/8 inches (76.5 cm) width. Signed lower left and dated 1915.

exposure to the French Impressionists at the Panama-Pacific Exposition the same year.

Similar to the works of the Taos painters, the Indians are depicted as an integral part of the landscape. The Indians blend in with the desert floor, and only the bright red of the blankets sets the figures apart from their surroundings.

It was Remington who advised the then novice Dixon some 25 years earlier to "see much and observe the things in nature which captivate your fancy and above all draw–draw–draw and always from nature. Do not try to make pictures. When you are studying–do the thing simply and just as you see it–use india ink–crayon or some broad medium at first–then color, either water or oil–solid simple subjects and work–work–work."

One phenomenon of nature that continued to "captivate" Dixon's fancy was the sky and the formation of clouds, vital components of a desert scene. When he visited Taos in the 1930s, he was particularly taken with the desert sky and noted that the bold cloud formations were in striking contrast to the haze and fog of his own San Francisco.

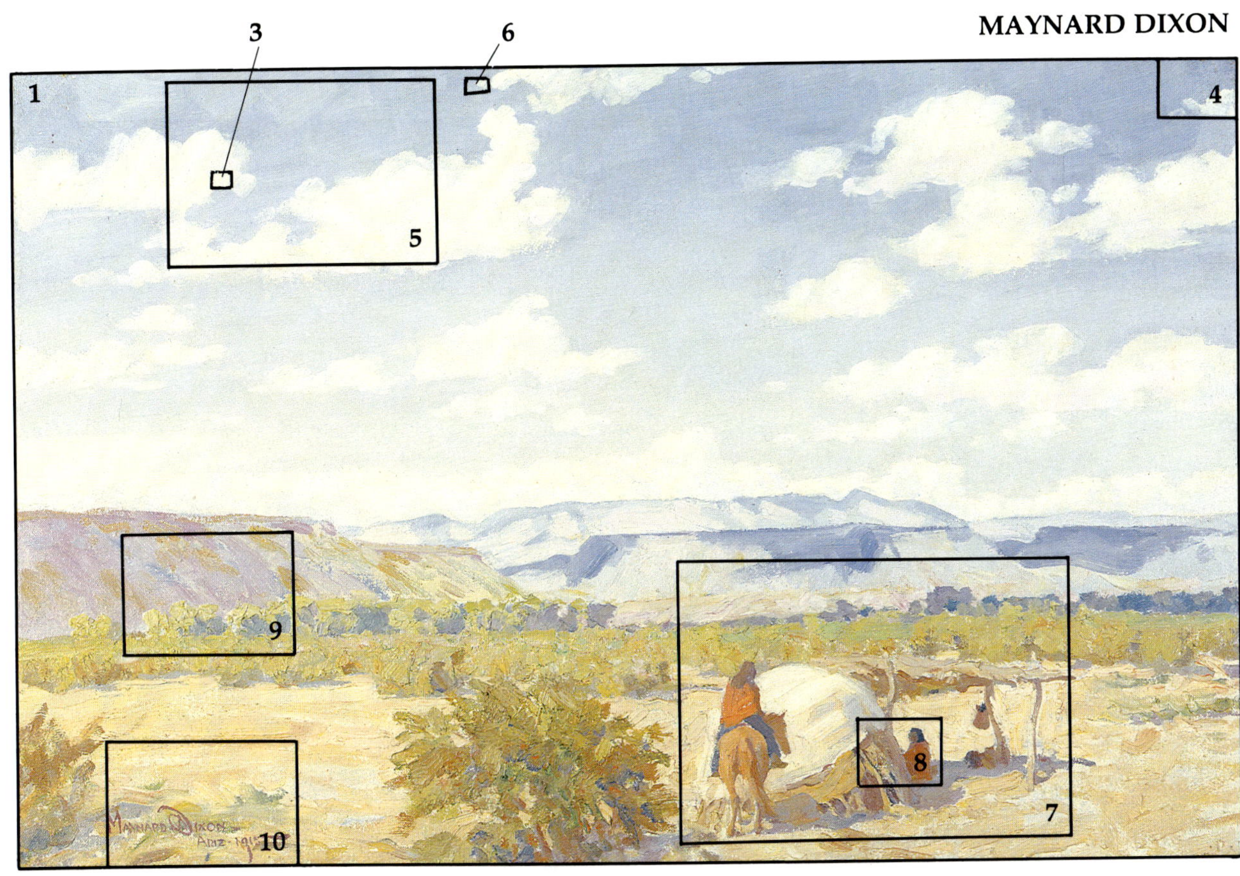

Apache Land may well have been painted from nature in the plein air tradition. Plein air, a French term meaning open air, refers to the Impressionist painters who in the 1880s-1890s strove to capture momentary effects of nature. In contrast to the Academic painters who preferred to work in the studio, the plein airists worked directly in the ambiance of natural light. Concerned with the observation of light and atmosphere out-of-doors, they challenged the existing doctrine, considering it to be a romantic and belabored view of the world.

Like the French Impressionists, Dixon felt compelled to leave the studio and paint in a fresher, more inspiring climate. Through the use of this technique, to which America had only recently been exposed, he captured a fleeting moment in the desert.

Apache Land was most likely done in one sitting. The structure of the paint layers indicates a rapid working process. For the most part, the paint has been applied in a wet-into-wet technique. Furthermore, the desert air would have sped the drying of the paint, allowing Dixon to work wet-over-dry within an hour or so.

Dixon primed the canvas himself with a very absorbent ground made up of chalk and lead white. This ground may have been deliberately chosen to facilitate the drying of the paint. The oil of the colors would have been soaked up by the ground, making the paint layers less vulnerable to damage and the picture transportable from the site sooner. The matte appearance of the surface is another consequence of the absorbent ground taking up the excess paint medium.

The painting has never been varnished. Plein air paintings were often left unvarnished by the artist. Varnish would uniformly saturate the paint, compromising the subtle variations in the surface which give these paintings their naturalistic, out-of-doors, atmospheric quality.

No underdrawing is apparent, adding to the evidence that the painting was done directly in an *alla prima* manner. The composition was laid in with a sure hand. The brushwork was rapid and direct and forms were created by single defined brushstrokes. The texture of the impasto and the calligraphic swirls of colors, partially mixed wet-into-wet on the painting surface, bear evidence of the artist's lively hand. The shape of the impasto forming some of the bushes in the middle distance indicates that they were done rapidly by squeezing paint directly from the tube onto the canvas, without the intervention of a brush.

The Impressionistic palette is influenced by the white ground which Dixon often left bare. The contrast of the white ground with the richer paint enhances the hazy, atmospheric depth typical of plein air paintings. As mentioned, the application of a varnish would have reduced this effect. Dixon relied on a simple palette consisting mainly of earth colors, blue and white, and strong purples and green.

Dixon made at least one compositional change as he worked, albeit a minor one. Large-size brushstrokes in the top left corner of the sky appear to have covered some clouds. These large strokes are paler than the surrounding blue, perhaps as a result of picking up the white pigment of the clouds beneath.

Plein air paintings reflect an unselfconscious aspect of an artist's *oeuvre*. Done on the spot, and in the case of *Apache Land* probably on a camping trip, Dixon was likely to have been inspired by the location and so stopped to paint it. The facile brushwork is free and spontaneous and a direct impression of the artist's sensitivity to this scene. *Apache Land* is a gentle and objective depiction of the Indians in their milieu, probably done just as Dixon saw it. The only artist's change was the position of the one fugitive cloud.

2.1. The cusping of the fabric corresponds to the location of the existing tacks, indicating that the canvas is mounted on its original stretcher.

2.2. The plain weave canvas, double threaded in one direction, appears to be cotton.

2.3. The white ground does not extend to the tacking edge of the canvas and is therefore likely to have been applied by the artist himself. A commercially applied ground would have covered the tacking edge. As mentioned, the ground is composed of a highly absorbent mixture of chalk and lead white. The sky is composed of cobalt blue and lead white applied in one paint layer on the ground.

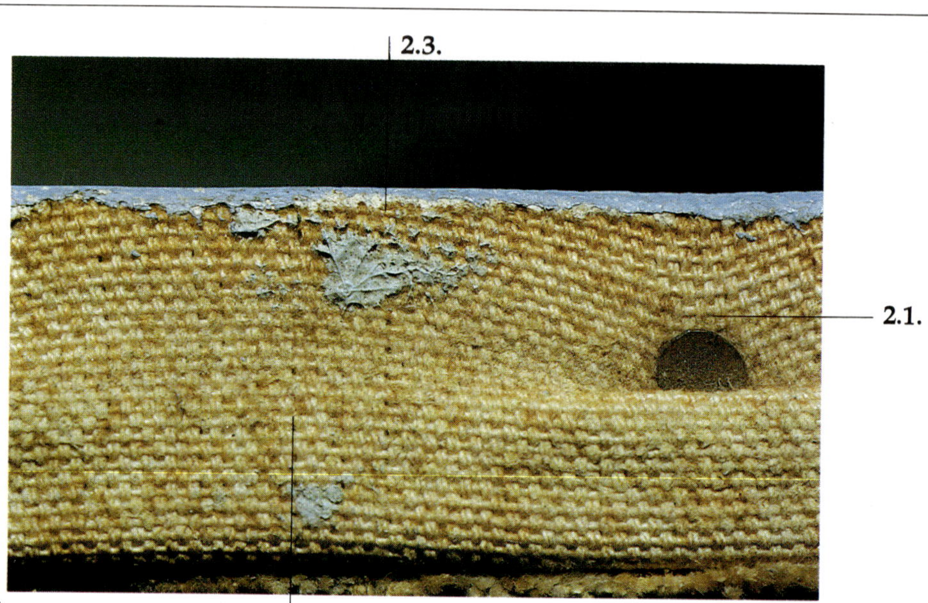

2. TACKING EDGE

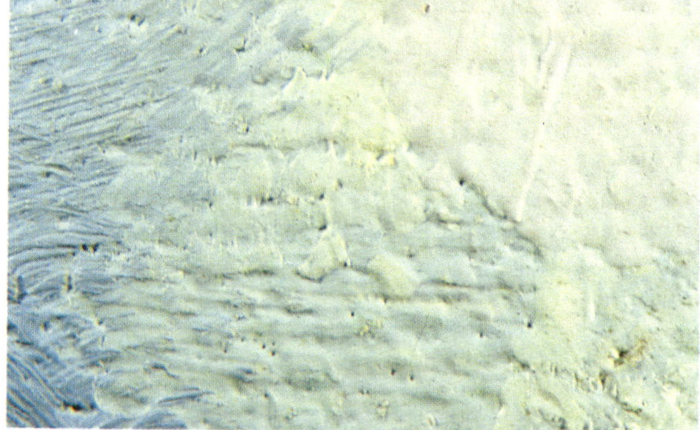

3. PHOTOMICROGRAPH OF PARTIALLY EXPOSED GROUND IN SKY

This photomicrograph shows the bubbly structure of the absorbent white ground which Dixon left partially exposed. These bubbles could be the result of the ground having been applied rapidly. The subsequent paint of the sky and clouds was also applied so quickly that it skipped over the bubbles, leaving them showing.

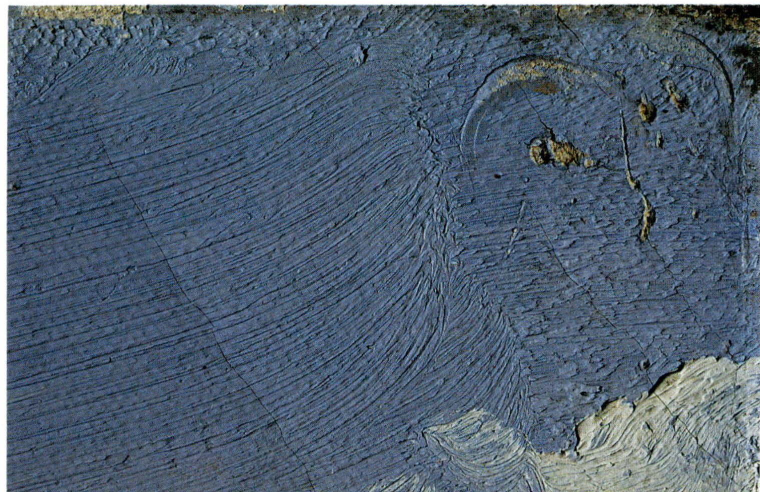

4. Tack Hole in Upper Right Corner

All four corners of the painting retain impressions from tacks that were pressed in while the paint was still wet. The reason for these impressions on the surface is unclear. One suggestion is that spacers were attached to the corners so that wet paintings could be stacked together while Dixon was travelling.

The possibility of the tack holes originating from a temporary mount during execution can be excluded. It is clear from the tacking edges that the fabric was attached to its permanent stretcher before paint was applied.

The impressions of the tacks are part of the painting's original structure. They should be left visible as evidence of the artist's working process.

5. Detail of Sky and Clouds in Upper Left Corner

5.1. The paint of the clouds has mixed with the still wet sky, creating the swirled effect typical of wet-into-wet painting.

5.2. These large-sized brushstrokes show what appears to be the artist's change referred to above, where possibly a cloud was painted out. The change would have been executed without delay, when the whiter paint of the cloud beneath was still wet, thus mixing the two slightly. This is the reason that the blue here appears paler than in the rest of the sky.

The sky was painted first and then the clouds were added in a partial wet-into-wet technique. The color of the clouds ranges from white to pale yellow, pink, and bluish. The paint has been applied with a few distinct brushstrokes.

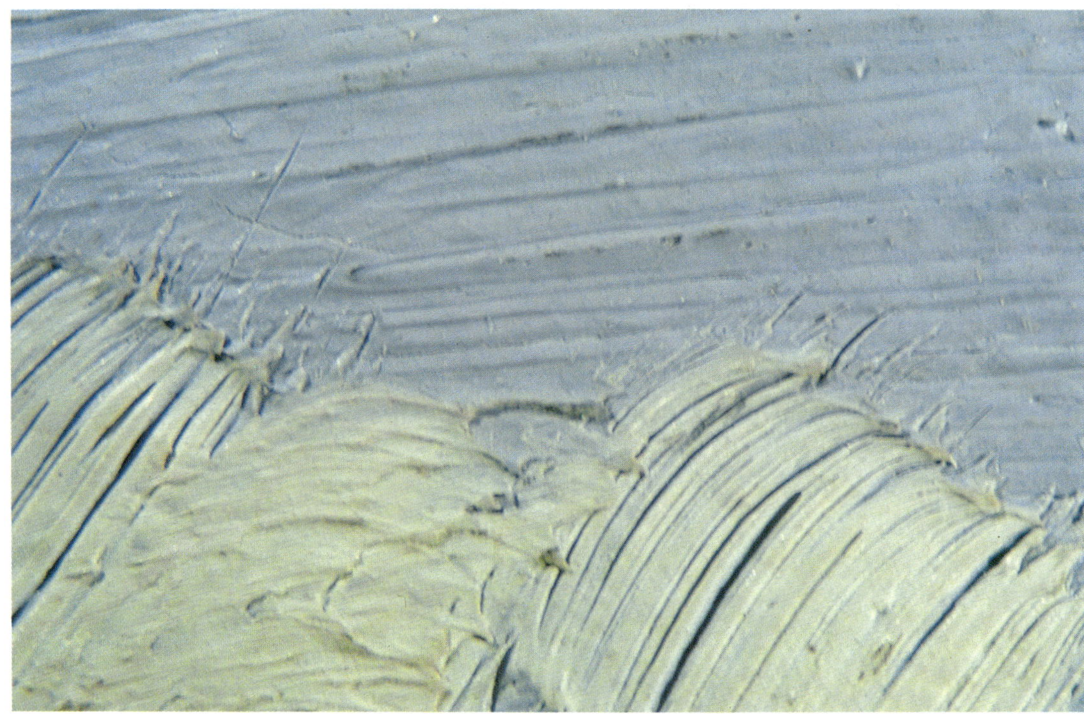

6. PHOTOMICROGRAPH OF SKY AND CLOUDS

The sky is made of mostly cobalt blue and lead white with a trace of red ochre. It was applied with horizontal brushstrokes. The white paint of the clouds was applied with a very stiff bristle brush while the blue paint layer was still wet, leaving sharp cutting marks.

7.1. For the most part, the foreground was built up simply of individual brushstrokes of lean ochre paint dragged across the white ground which was left partially exposed as areas of brightly reflective sand.

7.2. The gray shadows at the base of the horse were blended wet-into-wet with the ochre.

7.3. The horse was painted beginning with the head, moving on to the rider, and finishing with the tail.

7.4. Dabs of color mixed into still wet brushstrokes, to form the multi-textured foliage in the middle distance.

7.5. The darker beige roof was added while the middle distance paint was still wet, allowing the colors to mix and the boundaries to become indistinct.

7.6. The pronounced brushstrokes of the beige soil frame the seated figure with a sharp outline.

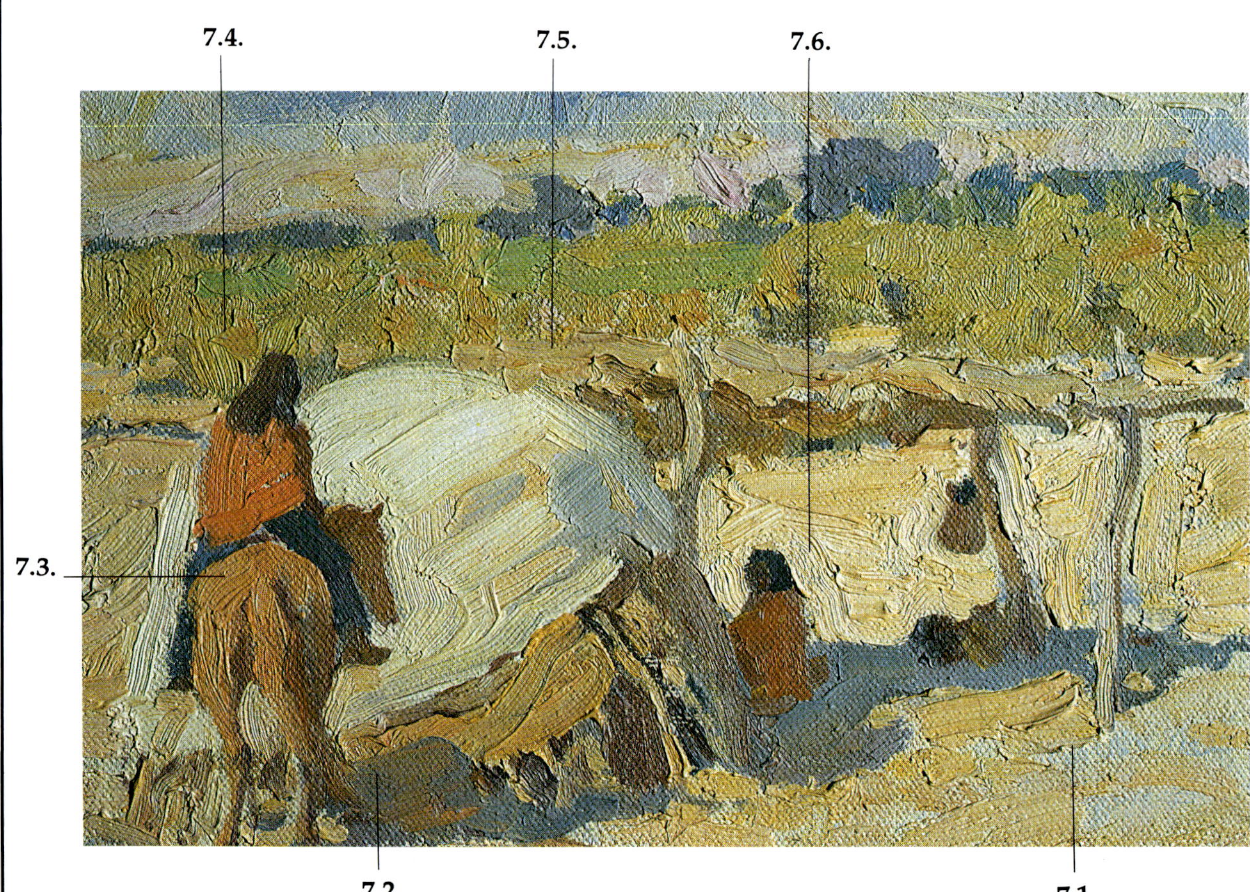

7. DETAIL OF INDIANS AND HORSE TAKEN WITH RAKING LIGHT

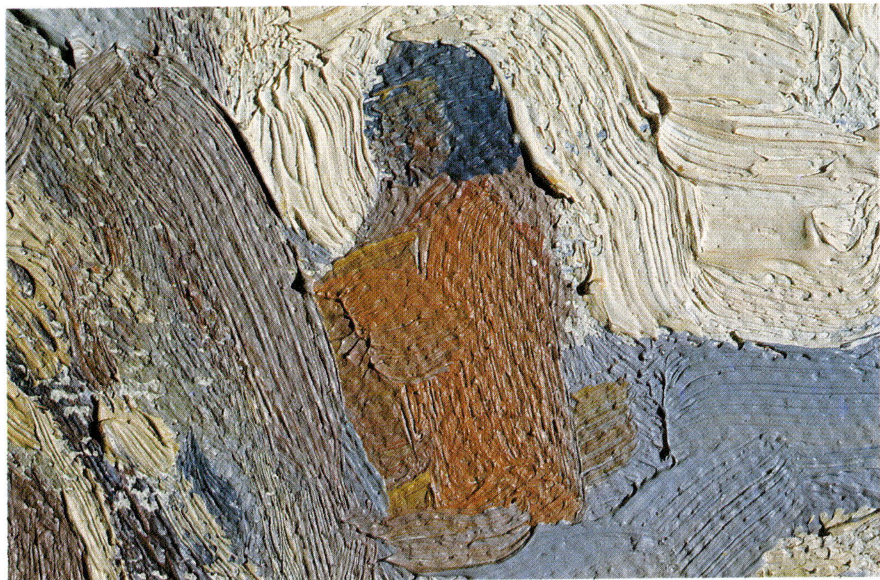

8. DETAIL OF SEATED FIGURE

The torso of the figure was created by a single short vertical brushstroke interrupted by a diagonal, slightly shorter stroke of the same color to indicate the arm. The figure was painted on top of the blue shadow cast by the roof and the colors mixed wet-into-wet at the base of the figure. The shadow was composed of cobalt blue, lead white, red ochre, and possibly zinc or chrome yellow. The face and hair consist of dabs of dark blue mixed into reddish brown. The cream colored paint of the sand was then applied around the figure, leaving distinct brush marks.

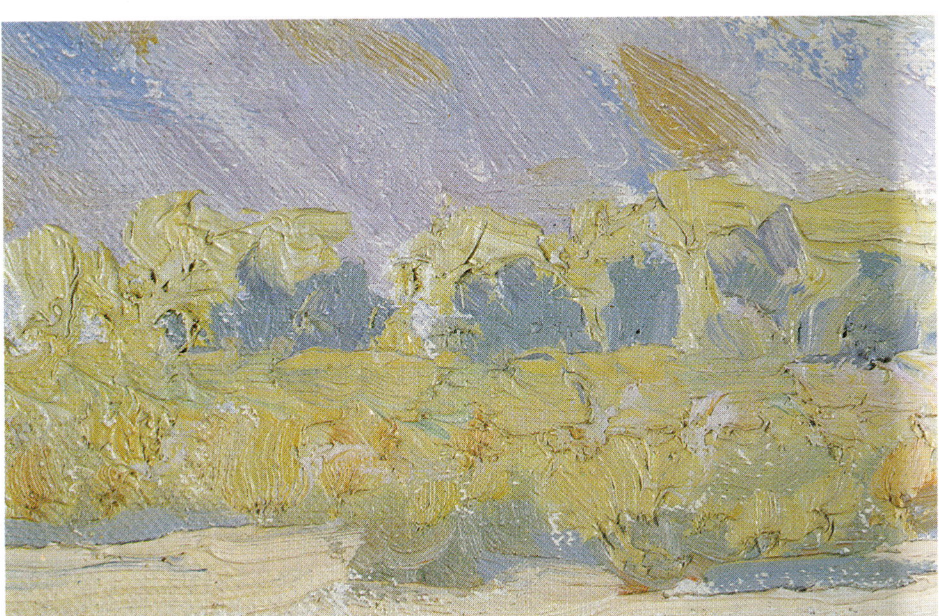

9. DETAIL OF IMPASTED TREES IN THE MIDDLE DISTANCE

The olive green impasto along the bottom of this illustration was painted with a small stiff brush. Blue was added, followed by more green which was applied with a horizontally scalloped brushstroke in a wet-into-wet technique. The squiggled green paint above appears to have been laid on straight from the tube.

The colors in this detail are quite startling but read well in the context of the whole picture. These strong colors of the middle distance and background create a balance with the large expanse of sky.

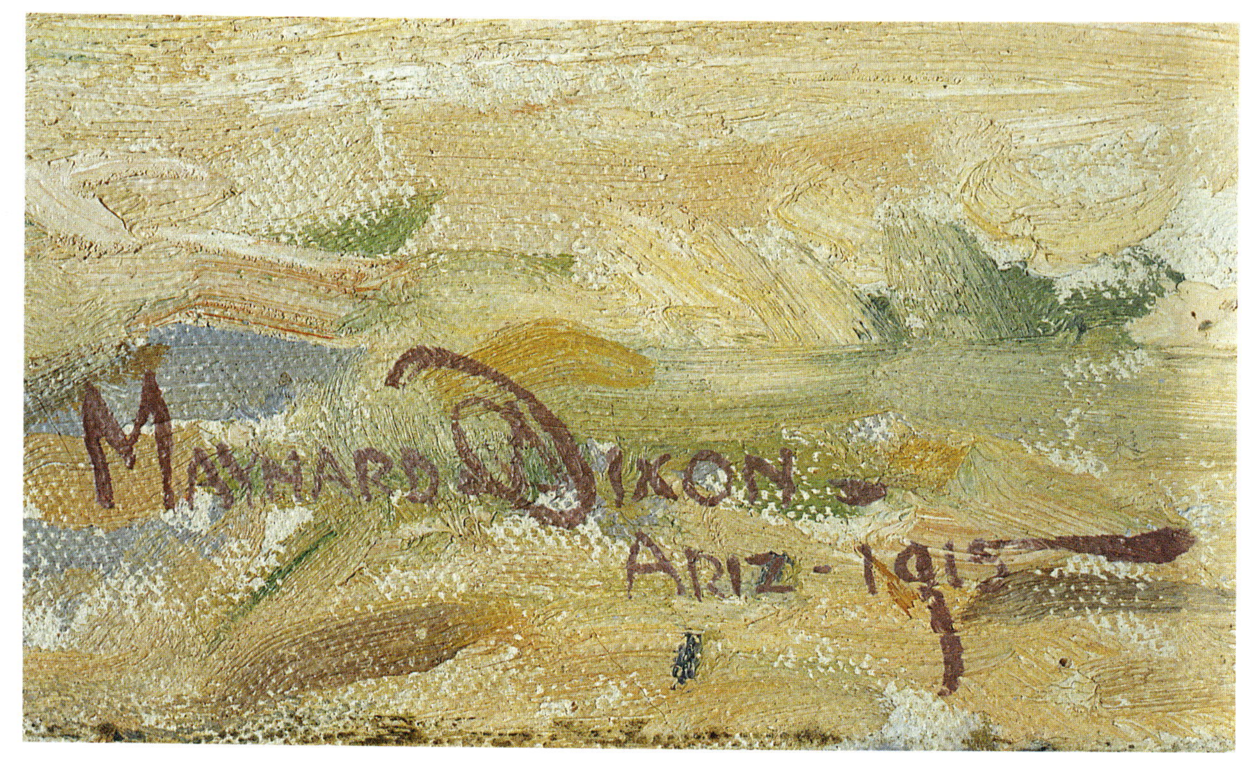

10. Detail of Signature

Maynard Dixon. Ariz - 1915.

SUMMARY OF PAINTING TECHNIQUE

a. The canvas was mounted on the stretcher and primed by the artist.
b. No underdrawing is apparent.
c. The picture was painted using a very simple build-up, consisting mainly of one layer on top of the ground. The lack of an underdrawing and the consistency of paint, for the most part applied wet-into-wet or in one simple layer, suggest that the painting was done out-of-doors in a rapid manner.
d. The painting has never been varnished.

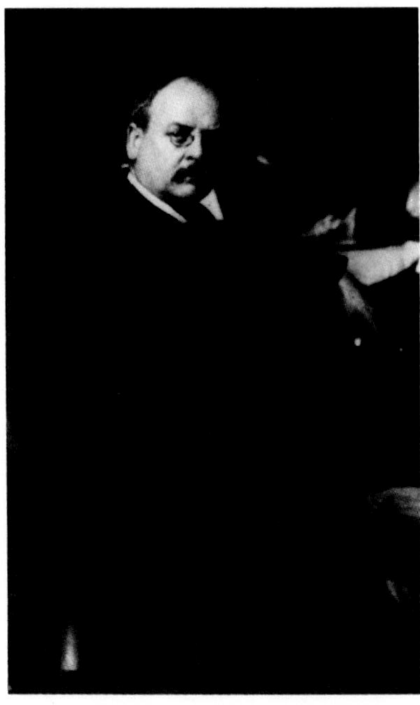

HENRY F. FARNY

Henry Farny was an Alsatian who had been christened Francois Henri Farny. The given names were French and seemingly inappropriate in a transitional French province on the German border that was more German than French.

His birthplace was Ribeauville near the Rhine River. The date was July 15, 1847, a generation earlier than Remington and Russell who became leading Western genre painters. His father was a well-to-do builder who had picked the wrong French side politically. He was a Protestant Republican opposing the Napoleonic monarchy. When Napoleon III came to power in 1852, the Farnys had to flee Alsace. They emigrated to the United States although they did not speak English. As an adjustment to the new country, Francois Henri was Americanized to Frank Henry.

The family settled in northwestern Pennsylvania near Warren. They bought 165 acres of isolated pine forest, built a log cabin, and set up a sawmill. The children were educated by an itinerant teacher who lived with the family for three months each year.

In addition, there was a Seneca tribe confined to a nearby reservation. These Iroquoian Indians were past their warring days in the area south of Lake Erie. When necessary they were doctored by the good samaritan Mrs. Farny. Frank Farny visited the encampment often enough to learn about the woodland Indians' way of life.

After six years in the forest, the Farnys opted for civilization. With their own timbers they built a 28 foot raft on the banks of the Allegheny River. Then they loaded their possessions including horses and chickens and a crew of 12 and embarked March 16, 1859. They floated past the junction with the Ohio River at Pittsburgh and in six weeks landed in the business, publishing, and art center of Cincinnati.

At 12, Farny's homemade education was sound enough to qualify him for Woodward High School. When his father died in 1863, however, Farny had to leave school to work as a bookkeeper and as a craftsman painting ornamental watercolors.

In 1865 he sent an unsolicited group of crude Cincinnati views to *Harper's Weekly* for publication. The sketches were redrawn by a staff artist as a two-page spread. When this first illustration was printed, the credit line was erroneously listed as Henry F. Farny. He chose to remain Henry Frank the rest of his life.

His success with *Harper's Weekly* impelled Farny toward art. The same year, he was apprenticed to a Cincinnati firm as a lithographer preparing Civil War scenes for printing. The next year he went to New York City to become a staff engraver for Harper & Brothers, starting a 30 year relationship as artisan and illustrator.

Farny's career in art was moving fast. The following year, 1867, he sailed for Rome. His job was to serve as secretary to fellow Cincinnatian and portrait artist Thomas Buchanan Read. Soon he became Read's studio assistant. He drew the preparatory outlines on canvases before Read started to paint. During the night he studied art in a Roman academy.

Like Read, however, Farny was interested only in painting the figures in the compositions. He did not want to handle the landscape backgrounds where Read needed the most help. His air of independence irked Read who sent Farny to study with the competent landscapist Hermann Herzog. Farny complained that "it is as if one put a young man who wished to become a priest in with a lawyer." At 21 he was on his own in the European continent.

By July 1868 Farny had found his way to the Düsseldorf art colony where he painted with the important Hungarian artist Michael Munkacsy who had arrived the same year. There Albert Bierstadt critiqued Farny's work favorably. Bierstadt recommended another year of study abroad and then a trip to the Rocky Mountains for subject matter.

In September Farny was touring Germany and Alsace when he received an unexpected inheritance that paid for two more years of European training. His surviving paintings of the period show broad brushstrokes in the background which may have been an influence of the Barbizon School. In the foreground are tightly drawn figures, typical of the Düsseldorf manner.

In 1870 Farny returned to Cincinnati after three years abroad. He was well trained in the Continental styles, as were many of the Cincinnati artists, but he found little acceptance for his easel paintings. His European subjects did not sell and he was forced into commercial work, painting circus posters and illustrating books. As he later observed, "When I first came here, for a year or two I almost despaired of being able to succeed. Unless an artist takes to designing tobacco labels, he will generally find it hard to make a living. Many of us take refuge in portrait painting, which is the best paying."

Farny did receive portrait commissions, but he handled them cavalierly. He took payment in advance and then sometimes failed to deliver. One of his frustrated patrons wrote to another, "His keeping away from us shows a consciousness that he has not acted well. I can't help thinking that Farny feels doubtful of his ability to make a picture to satisfy himself or us."

When a New Yorker paid in advance for a portrait to be finished by Christmas and became insistent the following June, Farny sent the money back. "I am not a house painter," he protested. "I can only paint when the spirit moves me."

He was equally high-handed concerning the portraits he did paint. A Chicagoan was dissatisfied because Farny's portrait of him had included a mole on the cheek. He asked that the mole be painted out. Farny refused: "God put that mole there, and I can't improve on his work."

When doing illustrative assignments for major publishers, however, Farny softened his arrogance with an awareness that time really was of the essence for periodicals. *Harper's Weekly* sent a telegram demanding the prompt shipment of an illustration on order and requesting an immediate reply. The messenger tracked Farny to a saloon where the artist was acting the part of Samson in a tableau. Farny's curt reply was that he would be in the bar "enjoying friends and beer till 3 a.m." After 3, though, he went back to his studio and labored the rest of the night to finish the picture by 10 a.m.

In 1873 he produced a 90 foot long painting for the Cincinnati Chamber of Commerce. When the Chamber was through with the painting, Farny rolled it and took it to the prestigious exposition in Vienna, Austria. He won a medal. He remained in Europe to study in Munich that year and again in 1875.

His most famous illustrations were done in 1879. The assignment was for a new edition of children's school books, the *McGuffey Readers*. The pictures he drew were said to be revolutionary because they were realistic. Even after a decade, 1,700,000 copies were sold in one year. A critic wrote, "These drawings reflect the contemporary American scene and its spirit as no other body of illustrative art has ever done." Farny became a star. Children recognized him and saluted him on the street.

As a local celebrity, he had many visitors to his studio which was described as "a perfect little museum of curiosities" he had obtained abroad. There were Egyptian and Oriental objects along with a book of Japanese designs and a screen he had decorated in the Japanese manner. Among his own works that were displayed were copies of Old Masters and character studies done in Germany.

Habitually, Farny entered his studio at 8 a.m. and worked until 11. He took 45 minutes for lunch and painted until 4 p.m. Frequently, though, he just sat motionless in an armchair with his eyes closed. Visitors assumed he was asleep but after he got up he insisted he had merely been planning the details of the next picture. As soon as he had the composition in his mind, he maintained, he would go to the easel, sit down, and paint steadily until the picture was done.

By 1880 he could look back at 16 years as a professional artist. He had studied abroad in Rome, Düsseldorf, Strasbourg, Munich, and Paris. Experts praised his figures painted in the confident calligraphic strokes of Düsseldorf and the broad handling of the background in the somber tonalities of Munich. Yet he was not able to support himself with his easel painting and had to depend on illustrative assignments to eke out a living.

Then Farny's fortunes improved abruptly. The change began in the early autumn of 1881 when he hastened to Fort Yates on the bank of the Missouri River. He was not on an illustrative assignment but rather was acting on his own initiative. The notorious Sioux chief, Sitting Bull, who had precipitated the massacre of General Custer only five years earlier, had been captured and taken to the Fort. Farny's goal was to become the first journalist to reach the war chief. His interviews and sketches would be the basis for feature material he could sell to a large number of Eastern publications.

The Sioux lived in tepees at the Standing Rock Agency near the Fort. Fearing an uprising, the army officers had moved Sitting Bull to more secure confinement. By the time Farny arrived the chief was gone, but the officers insisted on keeping the disappointed Farny as their guest.

The officers did not interest him as subjects. For two months, though, Farny sketched and photographed the Sioux. When he returned to Cincinnati November 5, he had scores of portrait sketches and 124 photographs, all of them of Indians. He had also collected hundreds of Sioux artifacts to use as props in studio paintings.

Most of the photographs had been taken by Farny. Others he bought and a few he clipped from magazines. Photography had become a new source of reference material for studio painters.

From 1881 on, Farny regarded himself as the paramount Indian artist. He resented competition from others and even warned away his pupil Henry Sharp. For the next 12 years he decreased the number of illustrations he drew in favor of the Indian oils and gouaches that found a ready market.

He had always favored romantic subjects to set off his dry narrative style. He claimed that "the plains, the buttes, the whole country, and its people are fuller of material for the artists than any country in Europe." A journalist added that Farny "gazes on his photographs of Indians, he draws Indians, he paints Indians, he sleeps with an Indian tomahawk near him, he lays great store by his Indian necklaces and Indian pipes, he talks Indian and he dreams of Indian warfare."

Although Farny thought he owned the Indian as a subject, Remington and Russell were already on the scene. Most of the Indians were on reservations. The buffalo had been slaughtered. The railroad had gone transcontinental. Sociologists were about to declare that the frontier had vanished. By then the Old West was really only nostalgia.

After Farny was a success, his big broad-shouldered frame went to fat around the waist. He appreciated his own gourmet cooking and the elaborate dinners where he was in demand as a speaker to relate Indian stories. His lifestyle was seen as Bohemian. Picturesque expletives punctuated any difficulty. Now that he had money, he was generous with it. Derelicts sat on a special bench outside his studio, waiting to run errands for him. At the end of the day Farny would give each of them 50 cents.

He had many famous friends. President Theodore Roosevelt told him in 1902, "The Nation owes you a great debt. It does not realize now, but it will some day. You are preserving phases of American history that rapidly are passing away." Roosevelt said similar things to many of the artists and authors of the West.

Farny did not marry until 1906 when he was 59. The bride was his 18-year-old ward. Illness halted his painting in 1914. He died in 1916 and was cremated in Cincinnati. When his wife died 25 years later, his ashes were dug up, mingled with hers, and reburied.

In 1981 the painting *Nomads* brought $460,000 at public auction in New York City.

1. THE PAINTING

Farny travelled to Europe many times and was exposed to the great currents of art during the second half of the 19th century. He was in Rome under the tutelage of Thomas Buchanan Read. Then he moved on to study with the landscapist Hermann Herzog in Düsseldorf where he met and was encouraged by Albert Bierstadt. In 1873 he participated in the technique class of Wilhelm Diez in Munich, considered to be the most innovative painting class of the time. There he most likely made the aquaintance of Frank Duveneck with whom Farny returned to Europe in 1875 in the company also of John Henry Twachtman.

Nomads demonstrates the sure hand and technical ability that resulted from his years of study. The fluid yet precise lines of the figural group and the somber palette are a result of his time in Düsseldorf. The social realism typical of late 19th century German painting was certainly an influence on Farny's choice of subject matter. *Nomads* emanates a power which goes beyond technical ability. The exaggeratedly simple, yet rhythmic composition draws the viewer into the painting and into the Sioux family's life.

The subject of the Indians' daily life in camp, or on the move as depicted here in *Nomads*, was a favorite of Farny's. This theme was painted as early as 1891, in the gouache *Breaking Camp*. The particular family group and landscape can be traced to a photograph which Farny had in his possession. The photograph has a dynamic composition, showing the family group moving toward the viewer along a diagonal line. The gouache remains true to the photograph, retaining the same composition and format.

In *Nomads*, Farny has rearranged the figures and landscape into static horizontal lines that are broken only by the parallel diagonals of the travois poles and trailing lead line. The resulting composition, with its heightened symmetry and frieze arrangement of the figural group, has an exaggerated sense of equilibrium that is very nearly unnerving.

Whereas the composition of *Nomads* may seem less painterly than the diagonal of the photograph, a psychological tension is created which stresses the Indians' trek through a bleak land. The forward lean and the raised hooves of the pulling horse are the only indications of motion; yet, the progress is so slow the dogs have time to stop.

The somber palette further emphasizes the stillness of this picture. The heavy gray sky

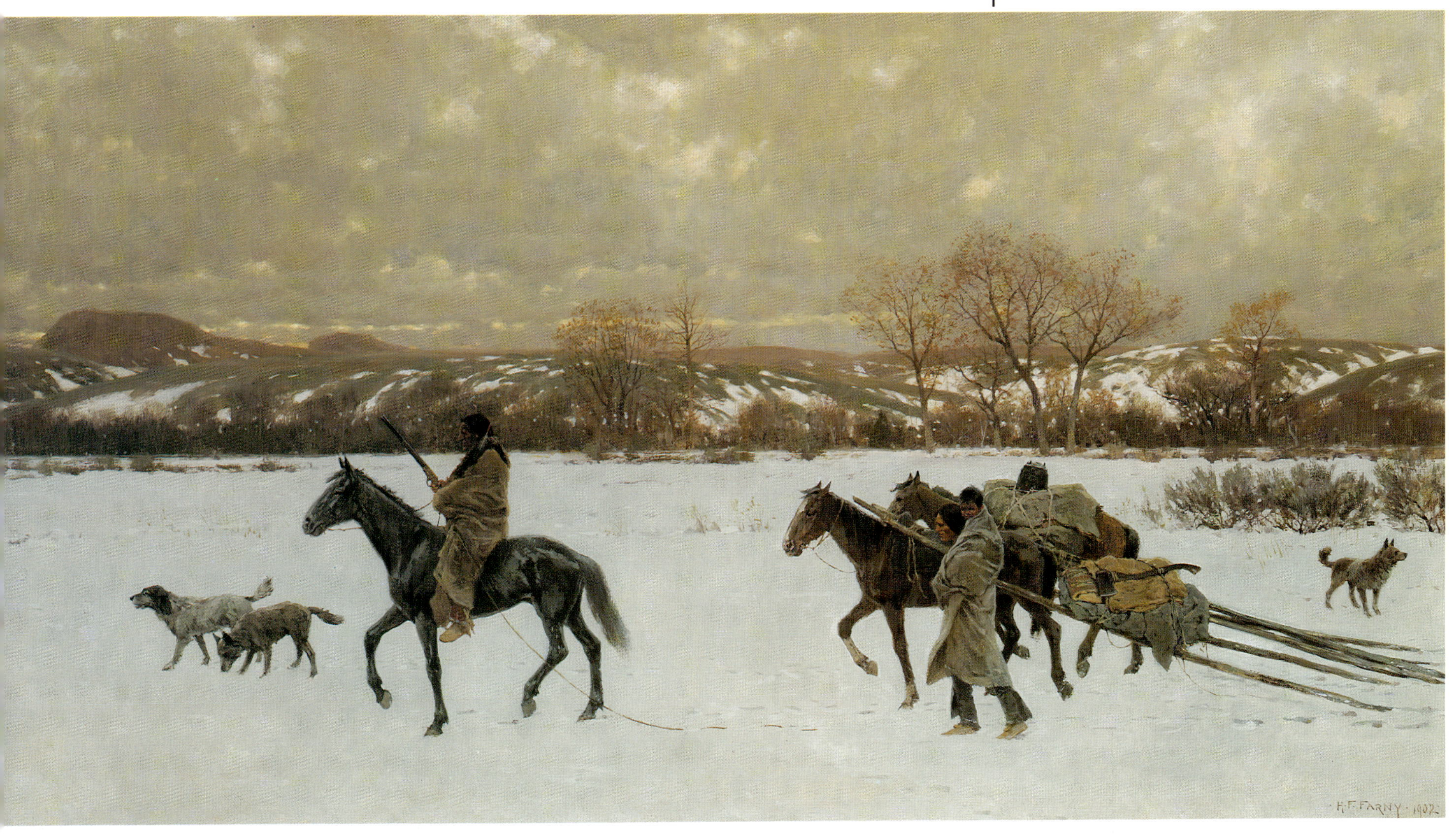

presses on the land, weighing down the meager belongings of the Indians, and seems to squeeze the composition into its exaggeratedly wide dimensions. In order to justify this unusually wide format Farny has adapted linear perspective to lead the viewer back into the receding expanse of snow. From a central viewpoint, the diagonal lines of the sledge poles to the right of the composition are enough to guide the spectator to the vanishing point in the distant hills.

Nomads was painted on a plain weave canvas. The ground is a warm gray color and extends evenly over the tacking edges indicating that it was commercially applied to the fabric. The technique appears to be fairly direct; if an underdrawing does exist, it has been obscured by the subsequent paint layers. One could assume that because Farny had made at least the one earlier version of this subject and was probably working from a photograph, an underdrawing was not necessary.

The order in which the various elements of the composition were applied can be determined with some accuracy by noting edges of overlapping paint. The snow was blocked out with an underlayer of bright white which has some local color variations such as a yellowish tone in the foreground. The figures and horses were then put in. A grayer layer was applied over the snow, around the figures and in places over the edges to correct the contours. The resulting snow looks darker and lighter in different places due to color variations in the underlayer. Farny covered the entire top half of the composition with sky, then when this paint was dry, he applied the rolling hills with fluid

Henry Farny. Nomads is in the collection of the Museum of Western Art, Denver, Colorado. Oil on canvas, wax lined. 22 inches (56 cm) height x 40 inches (102 cm) width. Signed H.F. Farny lower right and dated 1902.

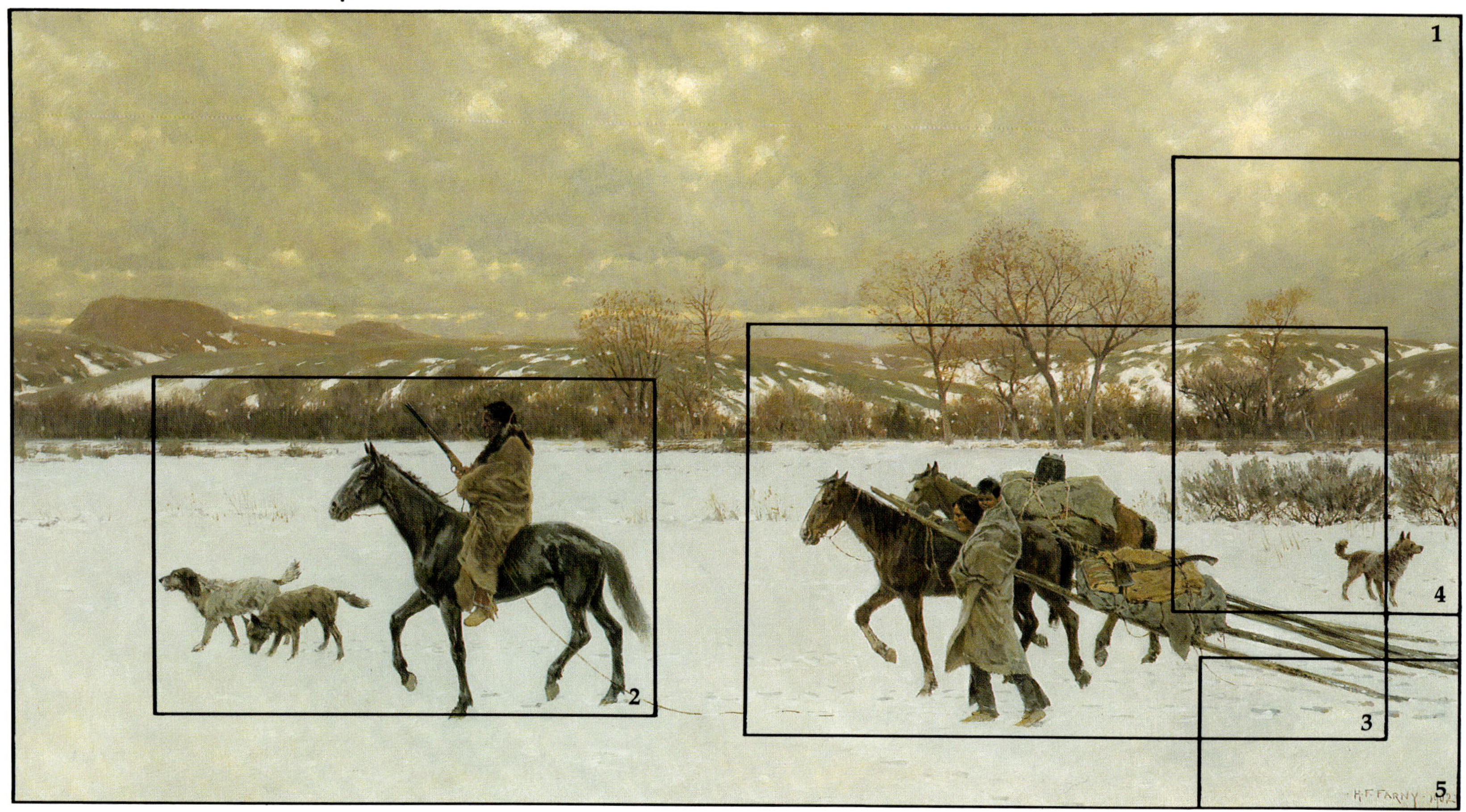

paint in a wet-into-wet technique.

Farny did make several changes as he worked. A pentimento of a higher hill can be seen through the clouds at the right side of the picture and in the position of the raised leg of the horse pulling the travois, as well as adjustments in the contours of the back of the man.

Nomads was painted at the height of Farny's career. On a visit to Cincinnati in 1902, President Roosevelt praised Farny paintings he had seen at an exhibition. In 1904, German Prince Hohenlohe paid a visit to Farny's studio. The Prince had been an admirer of the artist ever since he had seen a painting by Farny that had been presented to Emperor Wilhelm II years earlier.

To a prospective buyer Farny wrote: "Personally [*Nomads*] pleases me—as one of the most sincere things I have perpetuated in this vale of tears. But pictures are essentially 'affaires de gout'—one man likes a color scheme, another wants a crass recitative of facts. I had Loring Andrews and one or two other people of good taste see it—and their comments were of a most agreeable nature to the self esteem of [a] painter.... Should you decide not to take the picture please advise me at once—should it on the other hand please you—the price is $1500." In those days $1500 was a good price for any artist to ask.

Nomads is a sympathetic and romanticized view of the Indians' life as it once was. One dog looks forward, one stops to sniff the ground and another looks back, framing the Sioux family in a symbolic flow of time. By 1902, the Indians had long since been confined to reservations where their natural way of life, simple yet in balance with nature, no longer existed.

Farny no longer traveled to the West, preferring to work in his Cincinnati studio from photographs, sketches, souvenirs, and memories collected on his previous trips. He remarked in 1910, when asked if he planned to return to the West: "It breaks my heart to see the prairies cut up with barbed wire, and to see the once noble Red Man debauching himself with fire water on the reservations. The Golden West isn't what it used to be."

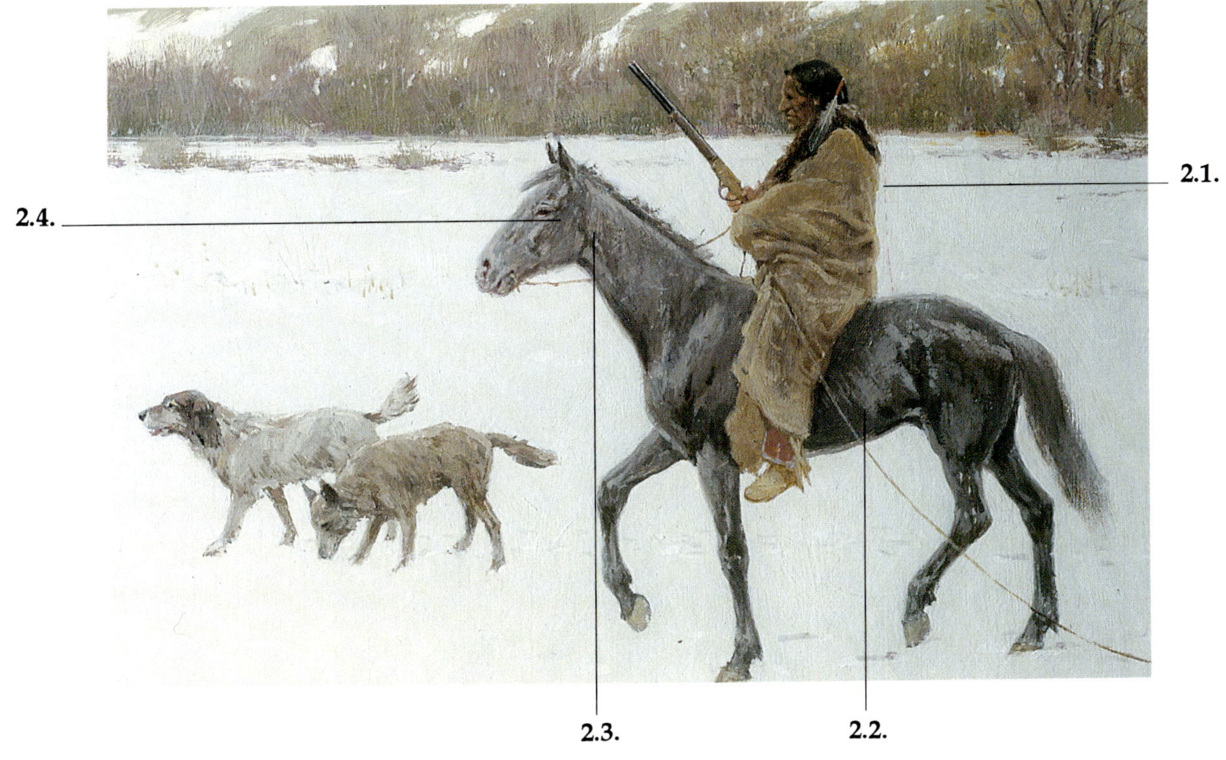

2.1. Farny has adjusted the contours of the man by adding additional snow around his back.

2.2. The lean dry oil paint of the horse has been handled in a manner similar to gouache, a medium familiar to Farny and one which he used for the earlier version of this subject, Breaking Camp.

2.3. The gray ground has been used as the middle tone for the horse.

2.4. A brilliant red touch of paint sets off the eye of the horse.

2. DETAIL OF HORSE AND RIDER

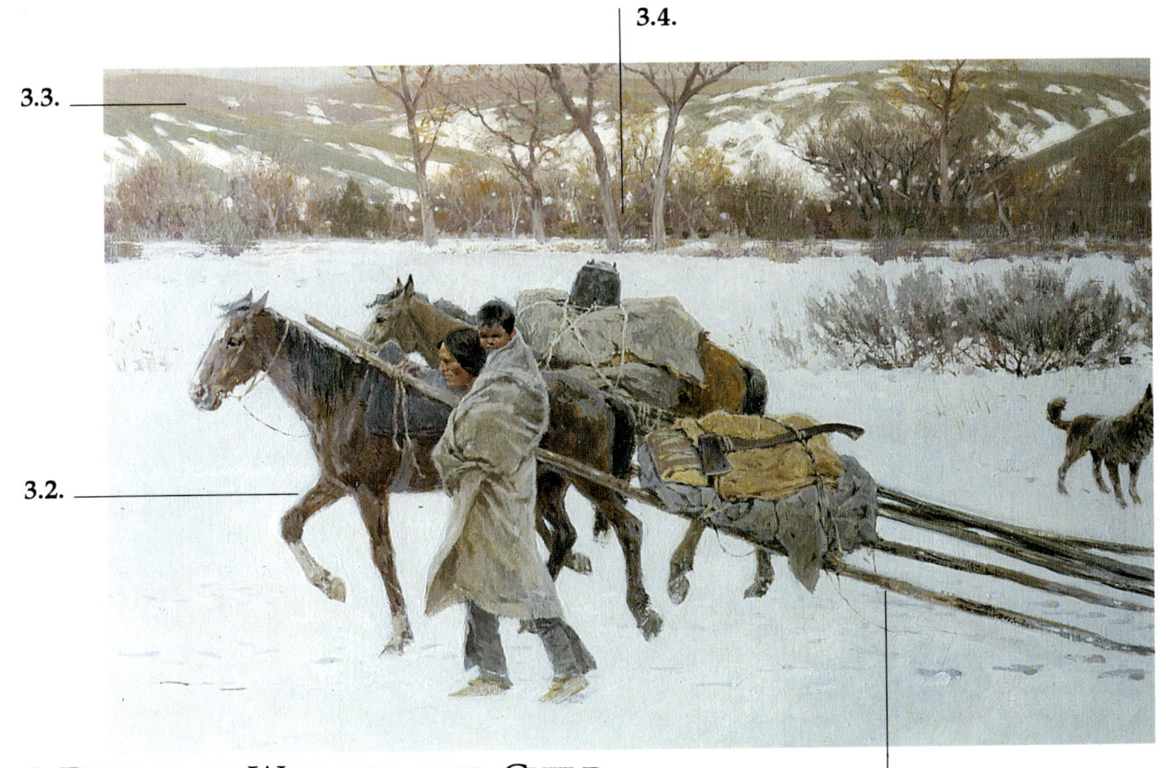

3.1. The diagonal sweep of the travois poles provides some contrast to the broad horizontal composition and is used as a device to create linear perspective, leading the eye back into space.

3.2. The position of the raised leg was lowered slightly by Farny.

3.3. The hills in the middle distance were applied wet-into-wet over the dry paint of the sky.

3.4. In a final step a fine brush and dry paint were used to add the trees and bushes.

3. DETAIL OF WOMAN AND CHILD

Nomads quietly dramatizes the hardships of the Indians' daily life. The gaunt weathered face of the woman, although she is probably young, contrasts sharply with the round faced baby who looks straight out at the viewer.

4.1. This darker triangular shaped area is probably a pentimento and could represent higher hills which have been overpainted by the artist. The change was probably made to strengthen the strong horizontal lines of the composition.

4.2. A bright white underlayer provides a reflective base for the snow. A darker grayish-white layer was applied next, wet-over-dry.

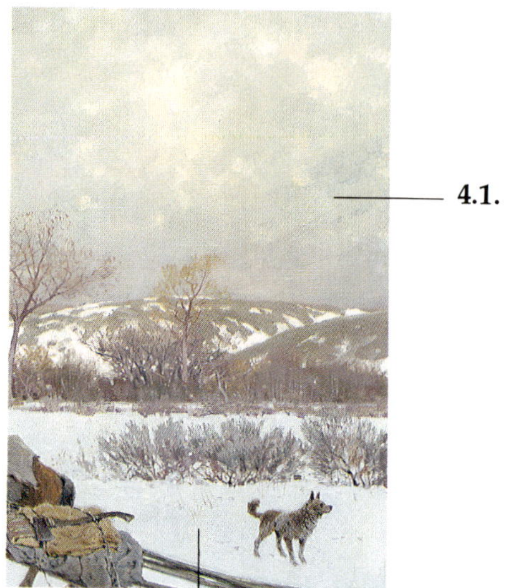

4. DETAIL OF SKY AND LANDSCAPE

The sky was painted from dark to light with the warm gray ground left uncovered in places to serve as a middle tone. The clouds were blocked out first with a dark gray underlayer. They were then worked up with rapid strokes of gray-green fluid paint. The richer paint of the pink, yellow, and white highlights is slightly impasted.

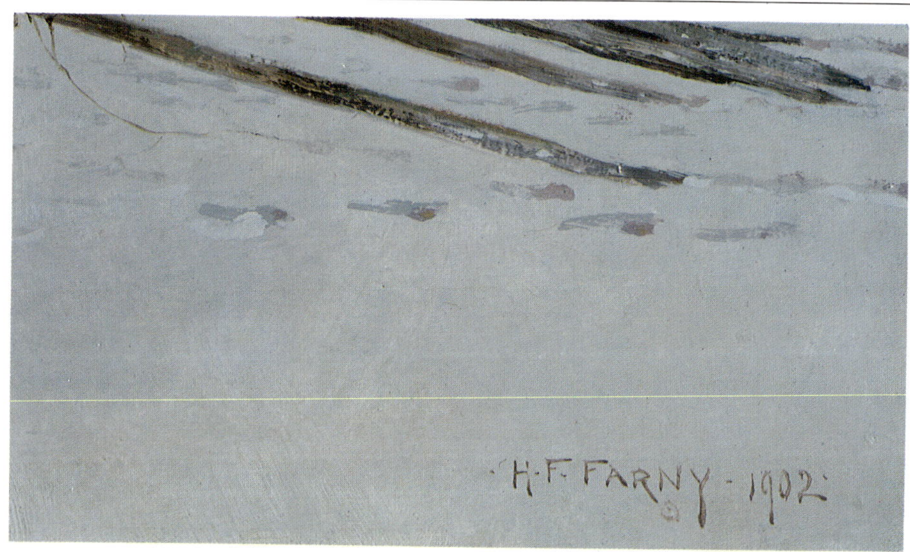

5. DETAIL OF SIGNATURE

H.F. Farny-1902.

SUMMARY OF PAINTING TECHNIQUE

a. Farny used a plain weave canvas preprimed with a warm gray ground.
b. The snow was blocked in with an underlayer of generally bright white that has some local color variations. The figures and horses were then painted, followed by a subsequent layer of grayer white which was applied over the underlayer and around the figures, adjusting outlines where necessary.
c. The sky was also built up in distinct layers beginning with a gray underlayer for the shadows of the clouds, then rapidly worked up with fluid gray-green paint.
d. The middleground was painted over the sky with fluid paint applied wet-into-wet.
e. Final details such as the trees and brush at the horizon were added last with a fine brush and dry paint.

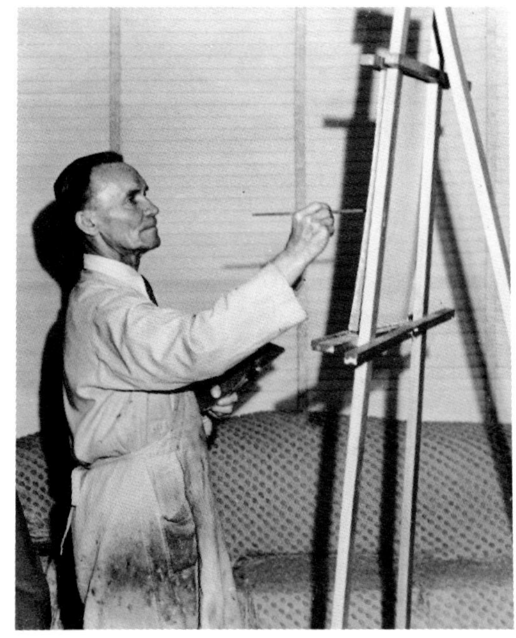

NICOLAI FECHIN

The least likely choice to be included as a master painter of the American West has to be Nicolai Fechin. Although he became a naturalized American citizen, he had emigrated from Russia when he was a mature 41 years old. His technique as a painter was already formed in the modern Russian tradition. Personally, he was the classic stereotype of a heavily-accented, irascible, stubborn, and temperamental Russian artist. He located in the West solely because of the climate.

Moreover, he was the only true portrait painter among the master artists. He painted likenesses of Western subjects in the bravura Russian style because he was living in the West as a displaced person, not because his primitive sitters were the category he might have preferred.

He ignored the dramatic Western landscape, for the most part, and he abhorred cowboys. He would have denied being a Western painter. He was an emigre Russian all the way. As a final rejection of commitment to America, East and West, his ashes were brought back to motherland Russia for final interment.

Nevertheless, Fechin lived and painted in the West for 29 years. He reached his peak as an artist in Taos. His singular portraits of the idealized but impassive Taos Indians and docile Spanish-American types were realized through his own special qualities as man and painter.

Fechin's ancestors had settled on a military outpost on the desolate Tartar border. He was born in central Russia November 26, 1881. He wrote that "my father moved to Kazan on the Volga River where he opened a crafts shop. For two weeks at the age of four I hardly showed any signs of life. It was meningitis. An ikon was brought to our house and I recovered.

"My father dreamed I would be his assistant [but] his business grew steadily worse. I liked best to draw. I executed a draft [drawing] for the building of a shrine. I was then 13. At this time the art school in Kazan opened. My father enrolled me. He was unable to help me [with money] and left. My mother went back to her parents. I was alone as I began studies. I lived with two comrades in one room.

"The school was a branch of the Imperial Academy of Art and offered a six-year course including regular high school. Those who could afford it paid tuition. Others were on scholarship. My aunt helped me.

"In due time I finished the Kazan Art School and went to the Imperial Academy in Petrograd [now Leningrad]. I was then 19. No payment was expected for tuition. Meals were free. It was the hope of all the students to be accepted into Professor I.E. Repin's studio. To my joy he granted me permission.

"In 1905 the Academy was temporarily closed during the first revolution [after the Russo-Japanese War]. The next year Repin left the Academy. There was no one to supervise [me] so my technique changed radically. The following summer I began painting my first large composition and received first prize.

"1909 was my final, competitive year. The Kazan School chose me to assist as a teacher, good for my work for the competition. I graduated with a scholarship enabling me to travel abroad. The next spring I left for Europe, wandering through Austria, Germany, Italy and France. I didn't paint and thus was not granted a second year scholarship.

"I settled down in Kazan in 1910. I began receiving invitations to international exhibitions and had a firm connection with America where a collector and his friends acquired 20 paintings." This was before World War I. American critics called Fechin "the most original" and "a striking emotional force."

In 1913 he married the daughter of the director of the School where he taught. "During the first year of the revolution the School lost central heating. Finally, a fire started," he continued. "My family were spared cruel results. My pupils saw to it that I would not be molested. In 1921 there arrived in Kazan the American Relief Administration." Fechin talked to the officials about life in America.

"There was no certainty of what tomorrow would bring. I was losing my creative energy as all art was used for propaganda. Having decided to leave our homeland, I received immigration papers to move to America signed by several Senators. It took a whole year to get permission from our own government. It was done with the help of my students in key positions.

"All the way to London, countless times we were washed, disinfected, vaccinated. The belief grew within us that we were bound for a land of paradisiacal cleanliness. On August 1, 1923 we first saw through a thick fog the skyline of New York."

American painter A.H. Gorson of Pittsburgh, where Fechin's clients lived, met the Fechin family at the dock and found them an apartment in the city. Illustrator Dean Cornwell rented a studio for Fechin and recruited students. Soon, however, the emotional Fechin was deprecating the quality of his American pupils who "are satisfied with the most superficial effects. They demand that I take the brush and correct their work, then they take the study and do not touch it again, signing to it their own name."

The first year in the United States, Fechin lived up to his artistic reputation by winning the prize for the best portrait in the annual exhibition of the National Academy of Design. He was quickly represented by New York City and Boston galleries and turned out a large amount of work. His paintings sold easily but he was depressed by the strange urban life. In 1926 he developed tuberculosis. His doctor recommended a dry and clean Western climate.

On the advice of the English painter John Young-Hunter, Fechin picked Taos, a still remote village in northern New Mexico. The inhabitants were the Indians and Spanish-Americans whose dignified primitive images had been depicted by the members of the Taos Society of Artists for the preceding quarter of a century.

Fechin was happier in Taos. The mountain reminded him of the Caucasus and he saw the Indians as related to the wild Tartar tribe in Russia. After a few months Mrs. Fechin agreed to settle permanently in Taos. Fechin began the legal proceedings to become a naturalized American citizen.

As a student in 1905, his compositions had been very bright in tone but complex. After his Paris trip in 1909 his paintings had assumed the appearance of spontaneity. His palette was generally lightened with zinc white which "at night he squeezed onto blotting paper and [the next day] painted with a thickened paint." When he was in New York City his brushstrokes became bolder. His technique was at its height, however, in his paintings of the Taos Indians.

In New Mexico his subjects were permitted only "a narrow range of emotions." There was no agony and no ecstasy. Yet, his brushwork became so fierce that his sitters were intimidated when he rushed at them to peer into their faces. The painter Leon Gaspard observed that "his canvas is rough as a heavy sea. He works with the savage violent temperament of his Tartar ancestry."

His procedure in painting usually started with a brilliant white ground made porous with highly individual additives. The underpainting was casein, followed by drained oil paints. The colors were placed both side by side and layered. They were applied with stiff bristle brushes, palette knife, and thumb. He wet his knife on his tongue until he suffered lead poisoning.

In 1933 his Taos idyll ended. His wife asked for a divorce he did not want. He acknowledged that his marriage had been impaired because his childhood illness had left him "high-strung. It was hard to reconcile art and family. I often ran away from home and went to my studio." Without the help of his wife he did not know how to write a check or make a travel reservation.

He became embittered and was seen as destructive and gaunt. He gradually withdrew from his neighbors, complaining about lack of communication with fellow artists. They described him as the uncommunicative one, aloof and stubborn. He wrote personal letters in Russian. He acknowledged that he "conversed entirely in Russian" with his little dog Pepper. The patron and writer Mabel Luhan told him "you are essentially and entirely a Russian soul. Go back."

Fechin remained in the United States but felt he had to leave Taos. He found New York City depressing once more so his art dealer persuaded him to try California. There he was an immediate success again. He soon had 80 students. His paintings sold well enough to make him independent.

In California his work was no longer the interpretive depiction of primitive people. He painted pictures on commission from the wealthy and the famous, employing a slick realistic style. When a client requested a picture of his daughter as a bride in her wedding gown, however, he declined. He announced that he did not paint portraits of dresses.

He moved to an isolated studio in a wooded canyon near Los Angeles. A burglar broke into his new residence and knocked him unconscious. He complained that "I went through Russian revolutions and here I get hit on the head in my own home." There was no more talk of returning to Russia, though. The silent, suspicious emigre had become gregarious. He gave informal dinner parties. As a host he was warm and friendly. He visited Mexico, Bali, and Japan.

His daily regimen was inflexible. He rose at 6 a.m. and did stretching exercises. Then he took a cold shower and appeared on his porch to hang his towel on the railing to dry. He made his own breakfast and ate while listening to the news on the radio. After taking Pepper for a brisk walk, he painted until the sun went down.

When his neighbors did not see him go through his fixed routine on October 5, 1955, they investigated. He had died quietly, painting until the end. He had been a troubled little man without much joy in his life, but collections of his paintings are still on display in the Kazan Art Museum in Russia and in the National Cowboy Hall of Fame in Oklahoma City.

He left behind not only this body of work in museums but also his sometimes-conflicting considered opinions about art. He wrote in his Notes that the most important part of painting is expertise in technique and that the value of the subject of the painting is transitory. Yet, Fechin's technical expertise did not work for the longevity of his own paintings and he survives as an American artist primarily because of his Indian subjects.

His conclusion was, "I can only say that when you find yourself in the presence of creativeness, take off your hat!"

Take off your hat.

1. THE PAINTING

Fechin was a technician and an intellectual. He was always concerned about the theoretical as well as the practical parts of the painting process. In his "Notes on Art," he provided a rare opportunity for access to the thoughts of both a master painter and a veteran teacher. He declared that "a high degree of expertise in technique has always had, and always will have, a predominant place in art. The subject, in itself, has value only according to the mode of the day. Tomorrow it will be superseded by a new fashion or fad. With the passing of time, the subject loses much of its meaning. But the fine execution of that subject retains its value....

"The more consummate his technique, the easier an artist will find it to free himself from all dependence upon a subject. What he uses to fill his canvas with is not so vital. What is vital is how he does it. It is sad if an artist becomes a slave to the object he seeks to portray. The portrayed object must serve as nothing more than an excuse to fill a canvas. Only when the subject passes through the filter of his creative faculty does his work acquire value for an artist...."

Fechin went on to observe that "actually the work of the artist begins the moment he takes the prepared canvas into his hand. A canvas has dimensions and a definite geometrical form. This already set form of the canvas is the very point of departure from which the construction of his future painting commences....

"The artist must never forget that he is dealing with the entire canvas, and not with any one section of it. Regardless of what he sets out to paint, the problem remains one and the same. With his own creative originality, he must fill in his canvas and make of it an organic whole. There must not be any particularly favored spot in the painting....

"My way of drawing and painting can be taught only through direct visual perception and it is almost impossible to describe it. An *attitude* toward painting and a few technical fundamentals can be discussed, however–but always with a warning not to take my observations in an overly literal or rigidly set manner....

"To me, technique should be unlimited and constant growth in ability and understanding. It must never be mere virtuosity but an endless accumulation of qualities and wisdom.... First comes the initial idea for a work–what the artist desires to portray, to bring into concrete manifestation. In order to fulfill this task, he must begin to build, to organize."

As a basis for his intellectualizing about art, Fechin studied treatises on the technique of painting. He read the 14th century manual of Cennino Cennini and the writings of Dmitri Kiplik. His investigations led him to experiment for a while with tempera painting on wood. He also started to manipulate paint more freely. By using spatulas and his fingers, his drawing with the paint became broader. The technique of using spatulas dated back to the Imperial Academy of Arts in Petrograd where he was influenced by his teacher Ilya Repin.

Despite the apparent spontaneity, a painting such as *Indian Maid Seated* took Fechin two weeks to a month to complete. He used a plain weave, double threaded, Belgian linen canvas reported to have been the best quality obtainable. He reputedly made some of his own stretchers. For this picture, however, he used a commercial stretcher.

Fechin gave a great deal of consideration to the appearance and function of his

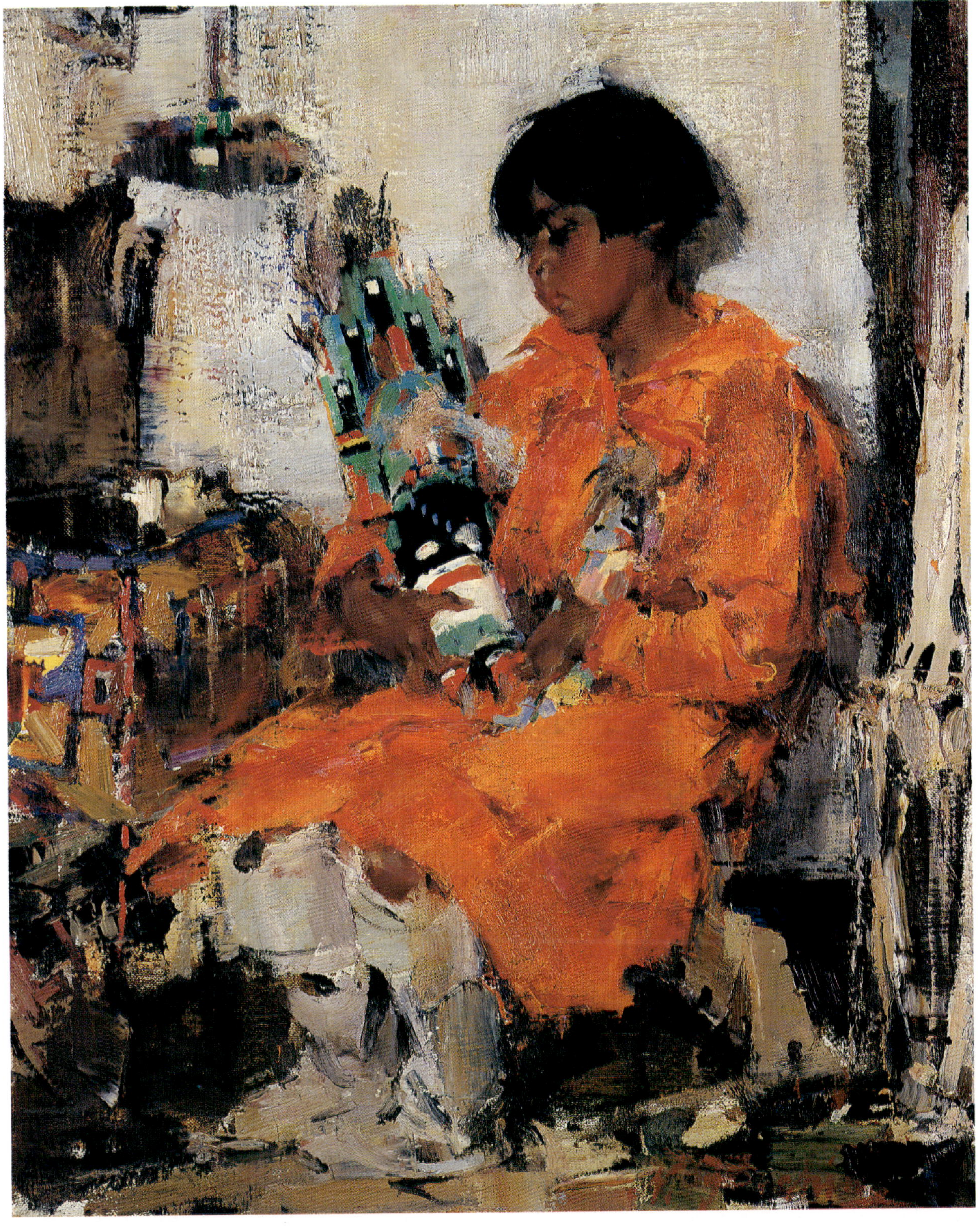

N. Fechin. Indian Maid Seated *is in the collection of the San Diego Museum of Art, California. Oil on canvas. 20 1/8 inches (51.5 cm) height x 16 1/8 inches (41 cm) width. Signed lower right. Not dated.*

grounds. It is thought that he prepared some of his canvases by sealing them in selective areas with cottage cheese, rabbit skin glue, and perhaps other ingredients before applying a casein ground. The porosity and the brilliant white of the gesso-type ground appealed to him. He remarked that it was a shame to spoil such a beautifully varied surface with paint. This selectively porous ground was designed to soak up excess medium from portions of the subsequent paint layers. As a result, the paint appears matte in some places and glossy in others, an effect Fechin intended. For this reason, he did not varnish his paintings. The application of varnish would have made the surface sheen uniform.

For *Indian Maid*, the white ground was applied in two layers. Analysis of the binding media indicates that the lower ground layer has a high protein content, probably casein.

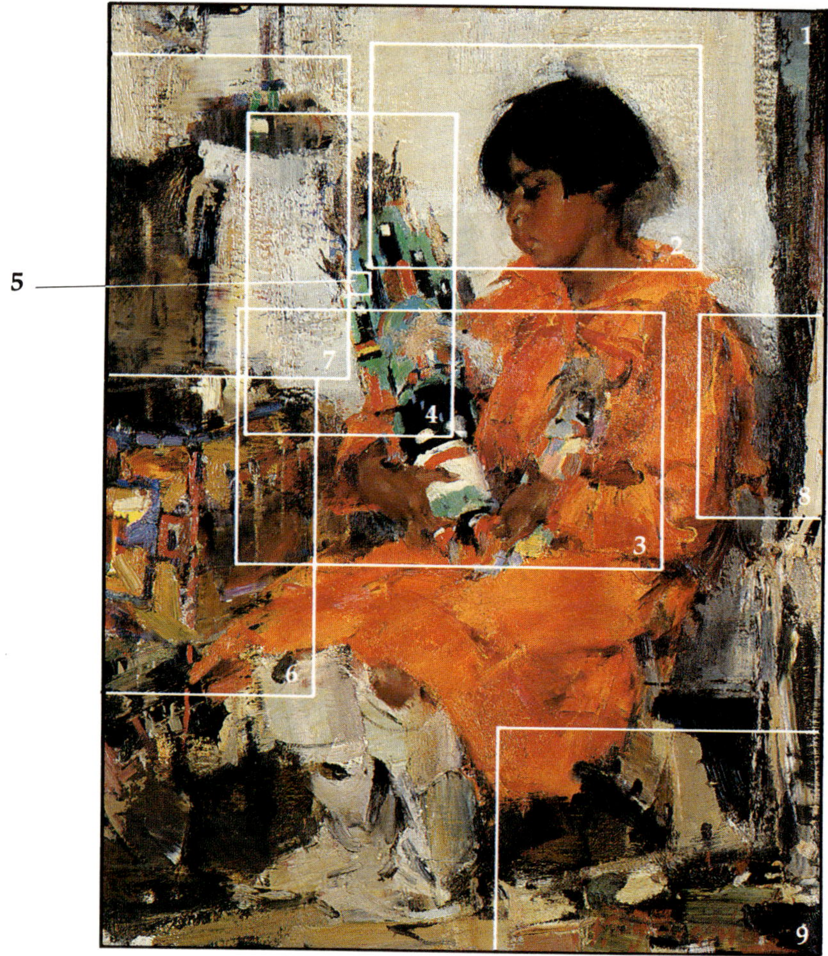

The upper layer has an oil medium. Cross-sections of the ground and paint layers show cracking in the ground into which the paint has flowed. This indicates the cracking occurred before the paint was applied.

These cracks occur because of the incompatibility of the physical properties of the different layers. The cracking, cupping, and interlayer cleavage are common Fechin ailments. They pose ongoing problems for the conservation of the paintings.

The initial sketch on the ground was probably done in casein tempera over which the oil colors were added. The complexity of this painting makes it impossible to distinguish the sketch from the subsequent paint layers. Only after Fechin worked out a perfectly correct sketch was it possible for him to abstract form, shape, and color.

The build-up of the paint layers in *Indian Maiden Seated* is very complex. There is, however, a sense of organization behind the colors. The paint was generally applied from dark to light and from thin to thick. Multiple layers of colors were superimposed over each other, without completely obscuring the one beneath.

Fechin used brushes, a spatula or palette knife, and his fingers to apply the paint. Often the paint layers were brushed in one direction and then smoothed in a perpendicular direction with a spatula, thus blending the colors wet-into-wet in those areas. A student observed that Fechin often drained his oil paint before using it. The thickened paint could then be spread onto the canvas with his fingers. Fechin handled the paint as though he was a sculptor modeling clay.

At first glance the paint application seems chaotic, but after studying Fechin's own "Notes" it is evident that the choice and the placement of every color served a specific purpose. Fechin was in his own way quite controlled while working. It would have been easy for him to be carried away and add too much paint. Mixing colors was minimized so that they would remain pure and strong. Instead, the layering and juxtaposition of the colors form vibrant combinations as they interact. His primary interest was in physically constructing and building up his pictures. As he wrote, the subject was not of the greatest importance to him.

Fechin's palette usually included zinc white, cadmium yellow, yellow ochre, burnt sienna, Vandyke brown, rose madder, emerald green, mineral (manganese) violet, Mussini Sunproof rose, cerulean blue, ultramarine blue, and ivory black. He noted that he did not like to use a "medium" because it thins the paint too much: "The pigments mix together and cannot retain their individual distinctness and thus again lose much of their fresh intensity. Likewise, it is bad to use too much zinc white. This makes colors chalky, anemic; color transparency is lost and it becomes difficult to produce nuances of tone."

2.3. 2.4.

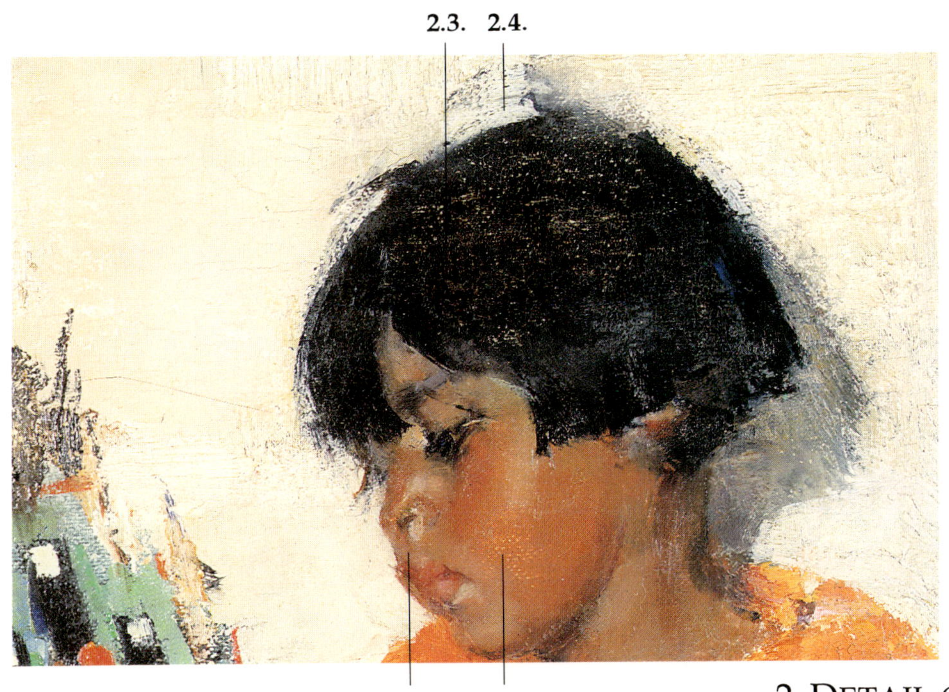

2.2.   2.1.

2. DETAIL OF HEAD

2.1. The flesh color was applied smoothly with a spatula, directly onto the white ground without entirely covering it. The work sequence was dark to light. Highlights were added in the form of thin scumbles over the neck, chin, cheek, nose, and forehead. Thicker impasted light paint was added in the eye socket and below the nose.

2.2. The red lips retain the imprint of the finger which pressed them into shape.

2.3. The black hair was painted on top of a brown underlayer. The ground shows through at the tops of the fabric weave. Light scumbles were added to the thick hair to indicate form and luster.

2.4. The heavily impasted white paint for the background was added around the head and extends over the edges of the girl's hair.

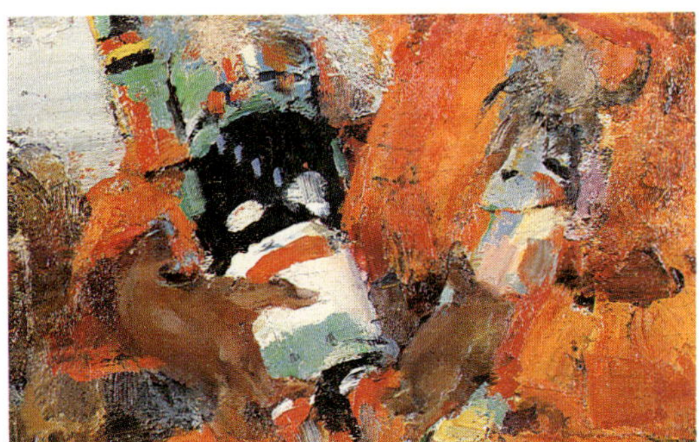

3. DETAIL OF GIRL'S HAND AND HER KACHINA DOLL

Kachina means supernatural in the Hopi Indian language. A kachina is an impersonated ancestral spirit deified by the Hopis. Doll-sized reproductions of kachinas like this one were carved from cottonwood roots and given to children as presents.

The orange of the dress is made up of a combination of red lake and an orange such as cadmium. The shadows were modeled with red lake glazes. The colors were treated with equal importance. Fechin took care not to spoil their pure vibration.

Analysis of the paint media shows that Fechin used a mixed media technique (an oil and a protein such as casein), as he did for the ground layers. Fechin either had something very complicated and specific in mind or he dipped his brush into the wrong pot.

4.1. A thin green wash lies directly on the ground as an underlayer for parts of the kachina doll. This green underlayer was left exposed in areas to form part of the body of the doll.

4.2. The texture and application of the paint for the kachina doll ranges from simple red, black, and green brushstrokes to a very impulsive stroke of multi-colored paint for the feathers.

4.3. The background was built up of multiple layers of differently colored paint. The final layer was light gray which was applied with the previous layers left visible in places. Superimposing colors appealed to Fechin: "If one wishes to produce this living vibration [of color] one must resort to the use of the pure basic colors and 'build' with them in such a manner as to give this living effect and vibrancy. To avoid murky results, it is necessary to learn how to use the three basic colors and to apply them, layer upon layer, in such a way that the underlying color shows through the next application...."

4.4. The light gray and black were first applied with a fast motion in a vertical direction. The paint was then smoothed horizontally across the lower part with a spatula.

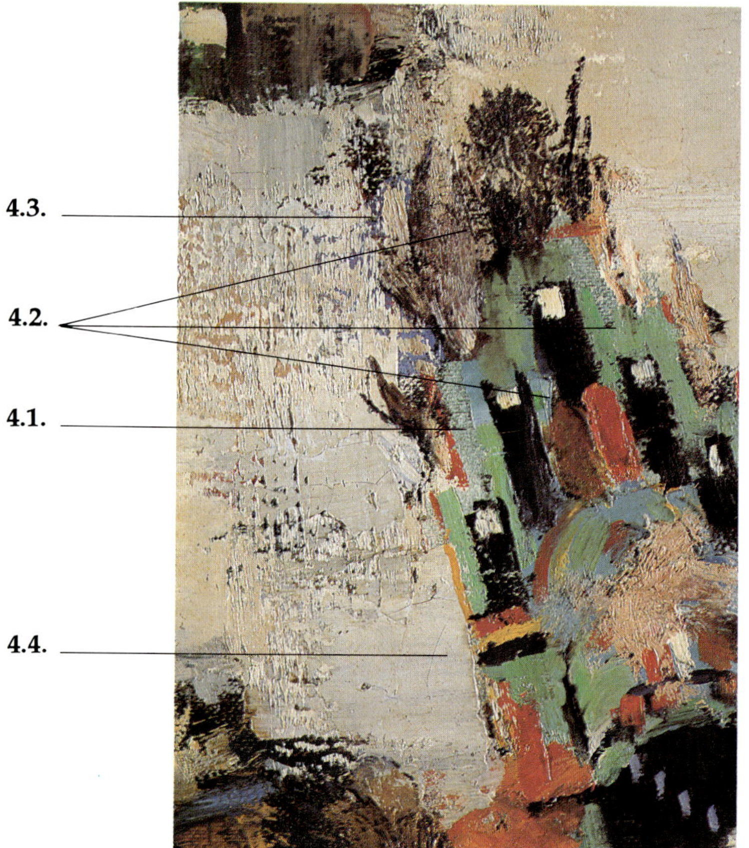

4. DETAIL OF KACHINA DOLL

5.1. The ground has been applied in two distinct layers. The top layer seems to have been applied with a brush in a horizontal direction. The incompatibility of these layers has resulted in the fine pattern of cracks seen here. This is common to Fechin's paintings as a result of his manipulation of the ground to suit his needs. He did not, of course, intend these cracks. Rather, they occurred accidentally because of the incompatibility of the materials he used.

5.2. A thin transparent layer of green was laid in over the white ground.

5.3. Bright red paint such as cadmium red was applied with a single brushstroke. The cracks correspond to the cracks in the ground.

5.4. Green was also applied in a single brushstroke. The green is made of a mixture of distinct blue and yellow pigment particles, despite the artist's advice not to mix colors. Cracks can reveal clues to the physical properties of the paint. The crack pattern of the ground does not affect the green paint, indicating that the green is less brittle than the red paint, perhaps because it is richer in medium. The green's mechanical crack is more recent, showing that the incompatibility of the different paint layers is ongoing.

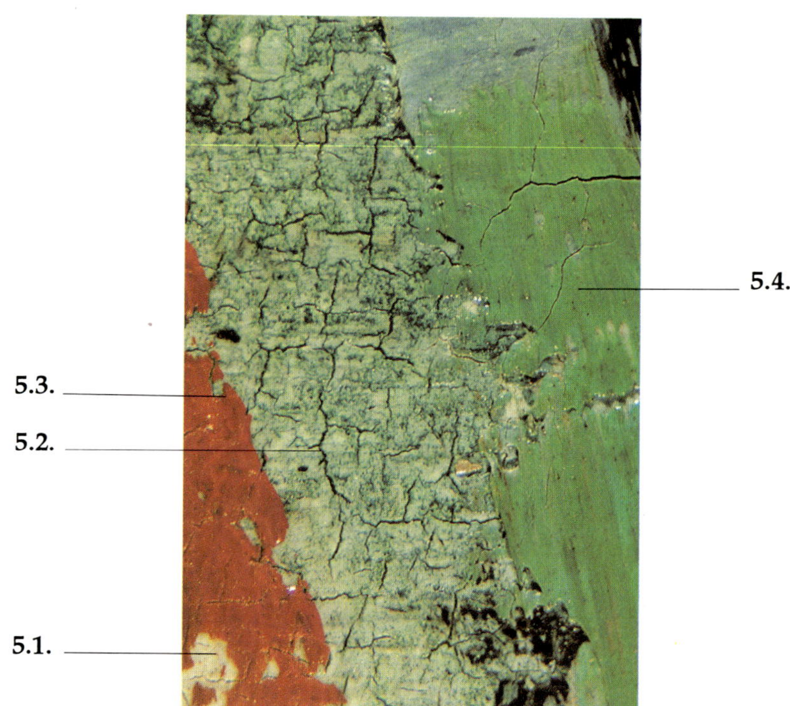

5. MICROGRAPH OF KACHINA DOLL

Cracking and cleavage in the ground and paint layers are ongoing problems with Fechin's paintings. It is odd that a mature painter with Fechin's intellect, studiousness, and experience would have selected a combination of painting materials that undermined the stability of his work.

5A./B. CROSS-SECTIONS OF SAMPLES STAINED FOR MEDIA IDENTIFICATION

5a.1.

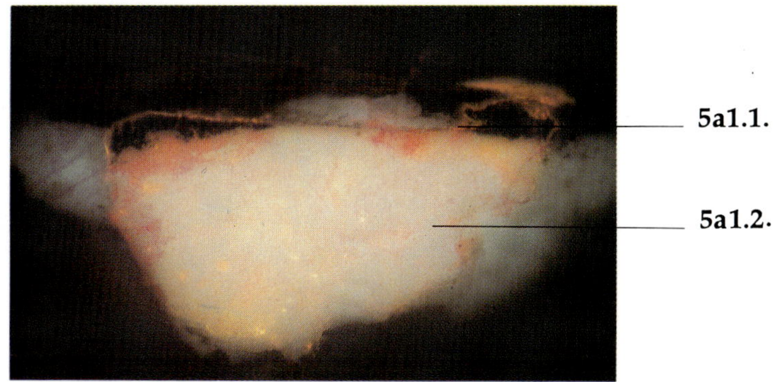

5a1.1.

5a1.2.

5a.1. This cross-section is from an area of matte and glossy black paint over the white ground. This sample has been stained with Rhodamine B, a dye which fluoresces red in the presence of oil when viewed under ultraviolet light.

5a1.1. This is the black paint layer. The bright red halo around the black suggests an oil medium that, in the normal drying process of oil paint, has separated to the top.

5a1.2. This is the ground layer. The upper portion seems to be richer in oil.

5a.2.

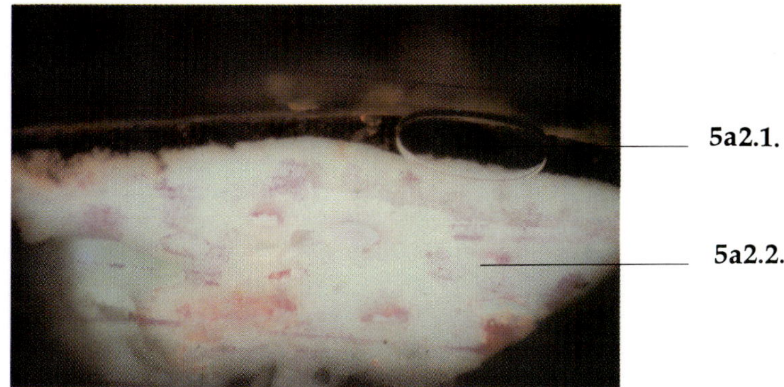

5a2.1.

5a2.2.

5a.2. This is the same sample stained with Lissamine, a dye which fluoresces in the presence of protein when viewed under ultraviolet light.

5a2.1. The black paint layer.

5a2.2. The ground layers. The speckling indicates that the ground is a "failed" emulsion. That is, that the components, perhaps an oil and a protein, have separated. This can be seen in other Fechin grounds as well.

5b.1.

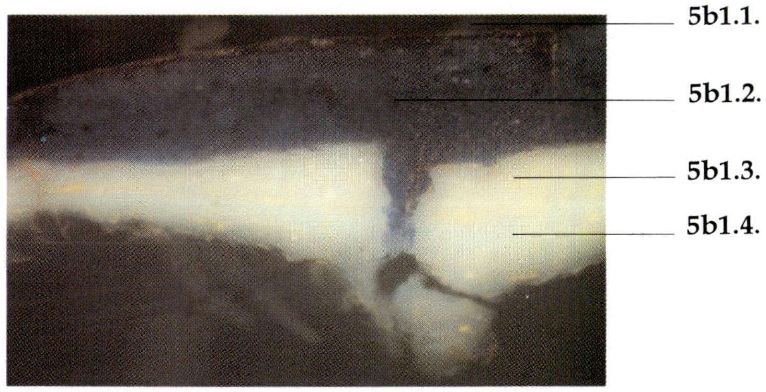

5b1.1.

5b1.2.

5b1.3.

5b1.4.

5b.1. This cross-section is of a thin black paint layer over blue on the white ground. It shows the cracking typical of Fechin's troubled grounds. The paint has flowed into the crack, indicating that the ground cracked before the paint was applied. This sample has been stained with Rhodamine to indicate the presence of oil when viewed in ultraviolet light.

5b1.1. Thin black paint layer.

5b1.2. The blue paint layer.

5b1.3. Upper ground layer. The yellowish fluorescence indicates a high oil content.

5b1.4. Lower ground layer.

5b.2.

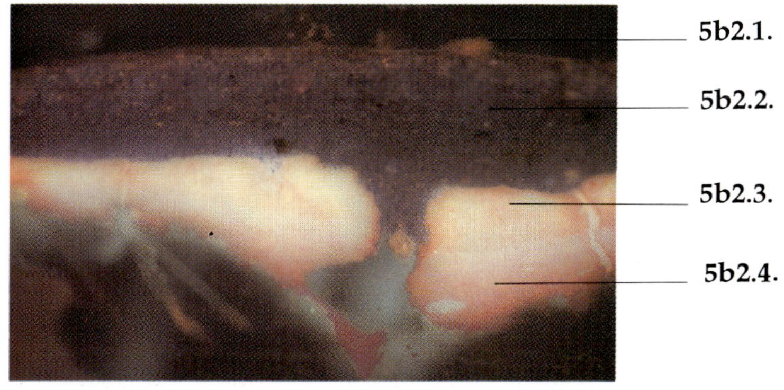

5b2.1.

5b2.2.

5b2.3.

5b2.4.

5b.2. This is the same sample stained with Lissamine which indicates the presence of protein when viewed in ultraviolet light.

5b2.1. The reddish tinge to the thin black layer indicates the presence of protein, perhaps a casein medium.

5b2.2. The blue also fluoresces red indicating a medium which contains protein.

5b2.3. The upper ground layer.

5b2.4. The lower ground layer fluoresces red indicating a high protein content.

6.1. A transparent red lake was applied along the left and right edges.

6.2. A spatula was drawn over the wet paint to blur the colors and to blend them.

6.3. The first layers tend to be thin washes of paint with the ground left partially exposed. The successive layers become more heavily impasted.

6.4. Refinements were added by dragging drier red paint such as cadmium across in a vertical direction.

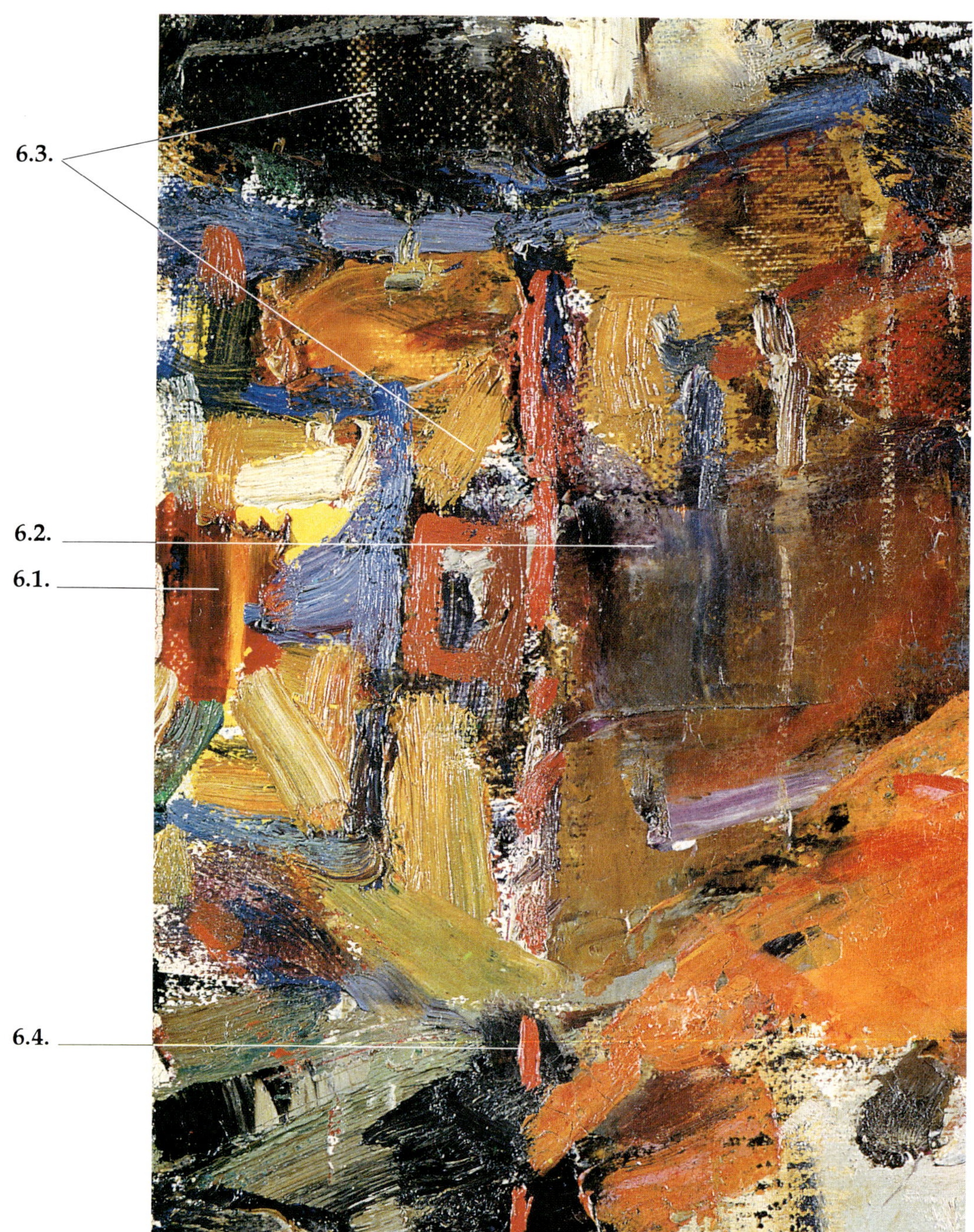

6. DETAIL OF LEFT EDGE

"As a matter of fact," Fechin wrote, "an artist actually has to deal with only three basic colors: red, blue, yellow (all the rest are combinations of these fundamental colors). Everyone knows this, but few pay any attention. Thus, the first step is for the artist to learn to see these primary colors and to distinguish them. It must not be forgotten that unadulterated paints fresh from the tube are beautiful, intense and clear, and only when one begins to mix them do they lose these vibrant qualities. The artist's problem of retaining the true pure strength of color depends on keeping the pigments separate and individually distinct. Mixing paints has definite limitations and only certain combinations of the three basic ones continue to provide clear and vital colors."

The palette here includes more than just the three basic colors, although they remain dominant. The procedure ranges from paint applied thinly with a spatula and then scraped, to paint put onto the canvas with a heavily loaded brush. The paint generally seems quite rich in medium though there are also areas of lean paint.

7. DETAIL OF BACKGROUND

7.1. *A dark brown-black was applied thinly, not covering the white ground completely. This paint was then scraped down, possibly with the handle of the paint brush.*

7.2. *Colored layers were built up, leaving gaps to reveal the underlying colors. By this additive process the varied hues combine visually to produce vibrating colors while retaining their individual qualities.*

7.3. *A thick, fairly dry white paint was applied, leaving gaps. The direction of the brushstroke is vertical. The wet paint was then shaped and partially mixed vertically with a spatula.*

7.4. *Finally, nuances of green and blue were added.*

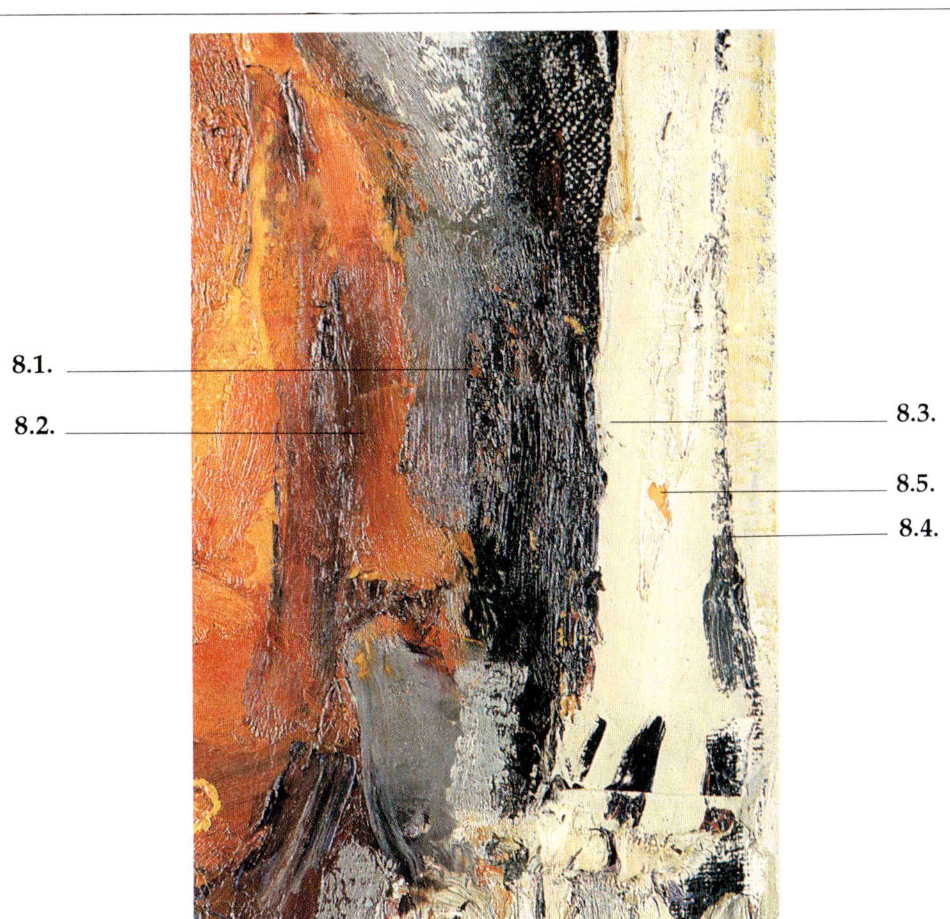

8. DETAIL OF DRESS AND BACKGROUND

8.1. *Black and white were applied around and partially over the orange dress to further define the shape and add shadows.*

8.2. *A red glaze was added over the orange to deepen the color in brilliant modeling.*

8.3. *Thick white paint was then applied and smoothed with a spatula.*

8.4. *Black and gray paint were partially dragged in a vertical direction.*

8.5. *The orange can be seen under the white paint. As usual, Fechin works here from rich to lean paint and from thin to thick and impasted paint.*

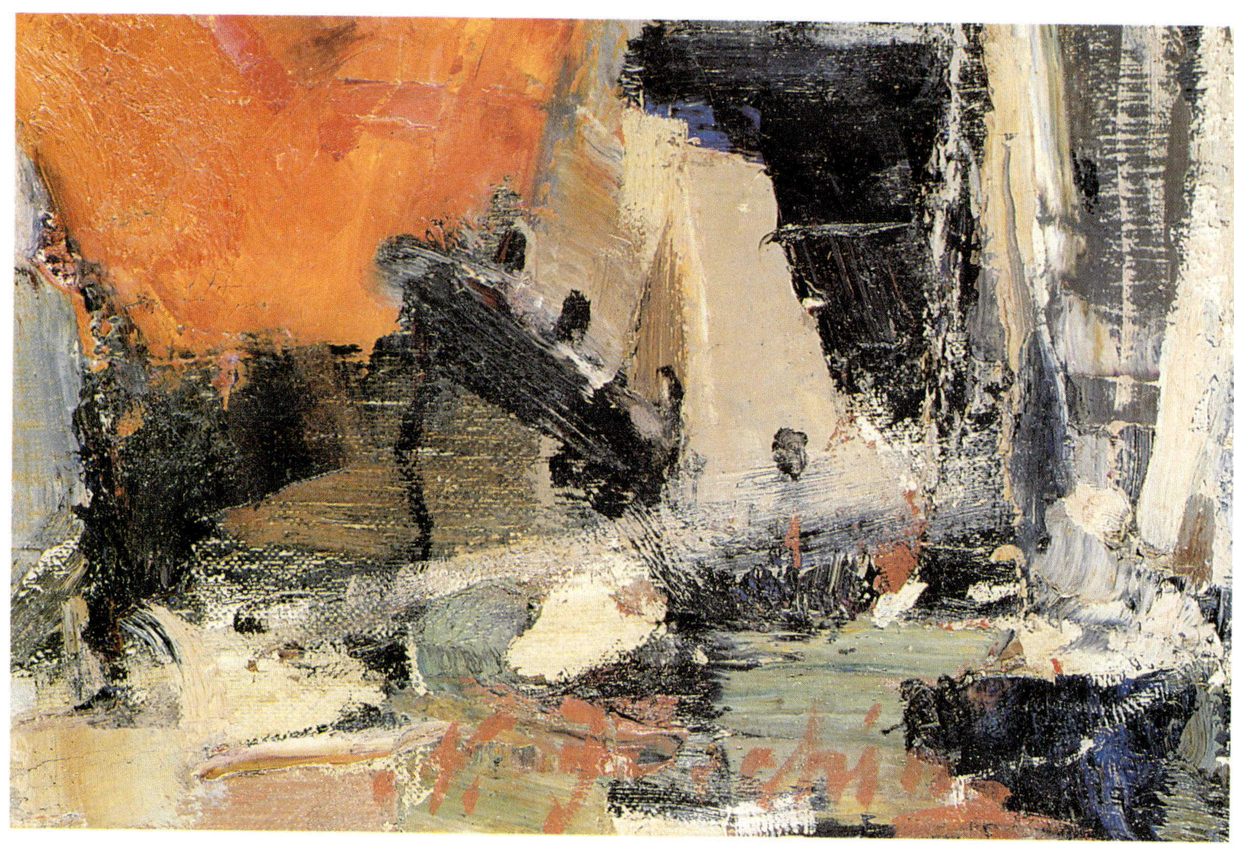

9. DETAIL OF SIGNATURE

N. Fechin

SUMMARY OF PAINTING TECHNIQUE

a. A plain weave, double threaded canvas was attached to a commercial stretcher.
b. A "failed" emulsion-type ground (a mixture of an oil and a protein such as casein or glue) was applied in two layers, the upper richer in oil. Shortly after application, the incompatibility of the components of the ground layers resulted in cracking.
c. The complex build-up of the paint layers was applied over this cracked ground. Fechin used various types of paint including oil and one with a protein medium such as casein. These were applied with a brush, palette knife, and fingers. Areas were scraped down and left raw or covered with more paint. The artist used varnish or resin locally to achieve gloss and saturation. The colors were applied from dark to light.

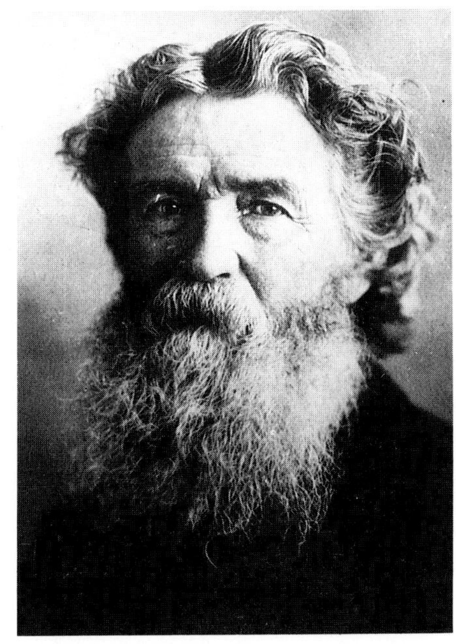

THOMAS HILL

Thomas Hill was the most maligned of the master painters of the American West. Detractors described him as an evil-tempered old man sitting like a 19th century spider in the studio his son-in-law built for him alongside the Wawona Hotel, at the approach to Yosemite Valley in California.

His critics' indictment was partly correct. The market for landscapes of the usual California scenery was eroded by the economic depression of the 1880s and by the switch to more eclectic tastes in art. Consequently, Hill's regular patrons for easel paintings were buying nothing from him. In their place, tourists with money to spend wanted Hill's paintings as souvenirs of the distinctive geological features of Yosemite. That was substantially all he was able to sell. His fame rested on these panoramas of the Valley he began painting as early as the 1860s.

Hill's principal subject was Yosemite because he believed he knew the terrain better than any other artist. He did not produce the large volume of work that came from his easel as intentional potboilers, but simply because he had the fastest brush in the West. He painted very rapidly whether the composition was for exhibition or for direct sale in his studio.

During the summer season, he turned out a huge supply of these variously sized paintings of the Falls and the Dome, finishing one picture every three hours or so. The total was barely enough to satisfy the seemingly endless demand for mementos more colorful than the ubiquitous black and white photographic postcards.

Hill was born in Birmingham, England on September 11, 1829. Much later he went through genealogical rigmaroles to document descent from a noble family, but his father was a tailor. The family was too impoverished to afford art materials. Hill made a brush out of horsehair and started painting when he was seven.

In 1843, Hill's father left England to seek a better job in the United States. While he was away, Hill's mother gave birth to another son in the Wolverhampton poorhouse. The next year the family was re-united in Taunton, Massachusetts. The father evaded the laws of the Commonwealth by putting 15-year-old Hill to work in a cotton mill instead of sending him to school.

In 1845 Hill secured employment more to his taste with a local carriage painter but he soon ran away from home to work for a firm of interior decorators in Boston. Because he was still a minor, he had to return to Taunton to buy his freedom from his father. The bargain was $20 down and "two dollars a week till he is of age and he is to bear all expenses."

When he was 24, Hill moved to Philadelphia to study painting at the Pennsylvania Academy of Fine Art. He supported himself by continuing to embellish carriages in his spare time. The following year he held himself out as a full-fledged fine artist. He painted landscapes in the White Mountains of New Hampshire, trading art for room and board as the Hudson River School painters Frederick Church, John Casilear, and John Kensett had before him. Albert Bierstadt was a sketching companion. One of his peers, Benjamin Champney, was already observing that Hill "can make more pictures in a given time than any man I have ever met." He painted with the broadest brush.

This first try at fine art was a failure. In 1859 he was forced to return to employment as a decorator, painting landscapes on furniture. The next year he was diagnosed as tubercular. After traveling overland in a wagon, he arrived in San Francisco in 1861 "because his health is not very good and he thinks he can do better there."

He was right about professional prospects in the Far West. San Francisco was an isolated community before the railroad became transcontinental in 1869, but there was pride in the local landscape and there were patrons for northern California pictures. Hill became the leader of the San Francisco artists. He painted portraits as well as mountain landscapes he explored with prospectors. These trips were into uncharted wilderness, dangerous enough so that on one occasion the members of the party were forced to eat their horses to survive.

With his health improved in 1862, Hill made his initial trip into Yo-Semite, the Indian name for Grizzly Bear. Hill estimated the Valley at 6 miles long and 1 mile wide. The Merced River was in the gorge, 150 miles east of San Francisco in the Sierra Nevadas, where he painted rapid sketches used as notes for panoramas to come.

After five years in the West, Hill was financially independent. He left his wife and children in San Francisco so he could travel to New York City where he exhibited a painting of Yosemite at the National Academy of Design. Then he went on to Paris where he studied not with a French master but in the atelier of the much younger German, Paul Meyerheim, a portrait and genre painter who had been at the Berlin Academy of Art.

When Meyerheim saw Hill's sketches of the Fontainebleau woods, he recommended that his senior pupil specialize in landscapes. Hill visited Barbizon to sketch with French painters there, but he retained his personal style of romantic realism. Brushstrokes, color selection, and tonalities were his own.

Hill exhibited his work at the Paris Universal Exposition in 1867. The pictures were favorably received. In the spring he returned to the United States, settling in Boston with his family. The newspapers reported that up one flight in the Studio Building, critics saw "several large pictures of wild scenery, and are told by the artist they are views of California."

His thoughts were of Yosemite even when he was in New England. Working from the old sketches, he started on a 6x10 foot masterpiece, *The Yo-Semite Valley*. When it was finished in 1868, the painting was priced at $10,000 and shown in Boston's Childs Gallery. A smaller version was done for reproduction as a Prang chromolithograph.

Hill's health failed again in February 1871. He sailed back to San Francisco via the Isthmus of Panama, shunning the railroad that reached across the United States by then. Buyers for his paintings were plentiful in the California city made prosperous by silver.

In addition, newly rich railroad tycoons were looking for art to decorate the mansions they were building. In 1872 the Crocker brothers bought two Hill paintings for $15,000.

Hill was soon wealthy. He exhibited in Boston and New York City as well as San Francisco. At the Philadelphia Centennial in 1876 he was awarded the medal for "best in landscape." Although he was spending more days in Yosemite and concentrating on the Valley as his favorite subject, he also found time to operate his own art gallery.

His pace was increasing. "Probably there is no painter in the country who paints more rapidly. On one occasion he painted six 18x24 pictures in nine hours." He still worked from his own sketches, not photographs, while "his strokes moved with the facility of a dancer."

His friends said that on casual observation he "would never be suspected of being an artist. His dress resembles a well-to-do rural resident, not at all aesthetic." He was of medium height and light complected with gray eyes and brown hair. He was a quiet, generous man, at ease with his intimates but never a bohemian. A late riser, he worked hard, wearing an old jacket instead of a smock. When he painted in the studio he liked to have friends around, laughing and telling stories while he applied broad strokes with his brush in one hand and a cigar in the other.

Hill's most frustrating encounter was with Leland Stanford, governor of California and president of the Central Pacific Railroad. In 1875 Stanford had called Hill into his office. He wanted paintings of the laying of rails across the Sierra Nevadas. Hill fulfilled the commission and Stanford paid him.

Next Stanford ordered a colossal rendering of the May 10, 1869 ceremony at Promontory Point, Utah where the Central Pacific tracks had joined the Union Pacific to complete the first transcontinental railroad. Stanford furnished Hill with a railway pass to Utah and introductions to scores of people Stanford wanted in the picture.

Hill began sketching the landscape and likenesses in 1877. As he proceeded with the massive painting, Stanford came to his studio frequently to supervise the composition. The railroad magnate demanded numerous alterations in the placement of the 400 figures to match his changing feelings about the individuals.

Hill was half finished with Stanford's commission in 1879 when the economic boom ended in California. Suddenly, all of Hill's patrons ceased buying his paintings. He had spent lavishly, had no capital other than his unsalable art, and could not meet the mortgage payments on his estate. His art gallery was sold to pay his debts. In 1880, the word in San Francisco was that "Thomas Hill has not sold a picture for eight months."

In desperation, Hill concentrated on completing Stanford's picture. After three years the painting was nearly finished in late 1880 when Charles Crocker, who had been in charge of building the railroad, visited Hill's studio. He looked at the arrangement of the various figures and exploded, "What damn nonsense is that?" Crocker was enraged because Stanford had improperly placed himself in the center of the composition where Crocker had actually stood. When the picture was completed in January 1881, Stanford was no longer interested in acquiring the painting. He refused to see Hill again.

The painting was *The Driving of the Last Spike*, framed in redwood the artist had shaped himself. Hill was never able to sell the painting or even to give it to an institution though the work is recognized today as one of the great American railroad pictures.

Because sales remained slow and Hill painted fast, he held an auction of the paintings accumulated in his studio in 1882. To drum up trade, the auctioneer claimed that "the pictures would be worth a fortune if the artist should die, and Tom may die, yes, he may die." Hill's health was in another decline but the prices were still low.

A decade later in 1893, Hill was too sick to paint, probably due to overexertion while preparing entries for the Columbian Exposition that year. Nevertheless, he attended the Exposition and was disappointed by the work of the Impressionists. He complained that "the French merely give you an impression which the observer must complete. This they call Poetic Art. I call it *Rott!*" The extra T was for emphasis.

Yet, Hill's own landscapes were still freely painted with sweeping brushstrokes. He said, "I depend entirely on accident. Accidental effects can only be gotten with a big brush." Many critics saw Hill as a transitional painter, a bridge between his teacher Meyerheim's Germans and the Barbizon School.

The complaint generally voiced was that Hill's mannerisms had not changed over the years. He had become old-fashioned. His former customers were now devoted to new European styles and they did not come back to him. His paintings sold only at Wawona where his daughter steered tourists into his studio.

In 1896 he had the first of a series of strokes. His disposition suffered and he never recovered his energy. The few paintings he managed to complete were exhibited but he was not able to maintain his former standards. The painter Will Sparks noted that "there seems to be something added and something lost." Regardless, "It all seems to please him."

A final high point came in May 1903 when President Theodore Roosevelt visited Hill's studio: "He admired a large painting of Bridalveil Fall, which the artist immediately gave him." Hill did not know that Roosevelt acquired all of his substantial art collection through similar gifts.

Hill died on June 30, 1908 at Raymond near Yosemite. He was almost 80 and unable to paint. The suspicion was that he took his own life.

1. THE PAINTING

The landscape is viewed from the lower elevations of the Sierra Nevadas looking east into the sunrise over the Great Basin. The scene is of distant buttes and brackish water making up one small depression of the large number that comprise the huge 200,000 square mile geologic formation. None of the many separate basins has an outlet for the small amount of water that enters from mountain streams and sparse rainfall. John C. Fremont in 1852 was the first to comprehend the uniqueness of the region.

Completed less than 20 years after Fremont's discovery, *Hunter and Setters* is a painting of contrasts. Low-keyed mauve hues are juxtaposed with vivid dabs, transparent paint with opaque, and purposeful touches with broad sweeping brushstrokes. When examined intimately, the colors can have a slightly jarring appearance and at times the brushwork seems to have no apparent reason.

Hill worked quickly and liked big brushes. He used "accidental effects" to his advantage. His paintings look as though his brush was slightly ahead of his thoughts, as if he thrived on a certain intensity he himself created during the application of the paint. The finished work conveys this energy. In 1879 a young student at the School of Design in San Francisco was chided by his teacher, Virgil Williams: Your sketch "is awfully careless. Do not try after Hill. Try ... any great French master. Tom Hill has a great deal of knowledge and can afford to neglect details, and there is always so much evidence of knowledge in his work that the most careless sketch of his passes for good. You have his carelessness without his knowledge."

Hunter and Setters was done on a plain weave canvas with a white ground. It cannot be determined whether the canvas was primed by the artist because the tacking edges were removed when the painting was lined.

There is no evidence of an underdrawing. Hill usually painted in the studio from sketches. This painting was probably done from more than one sketch, given the large area and variety of landscape encompassed. A small painting with what appears to be the same hunter and dog is in the collection of the Fine Arts Museums of San Francisco.

Hill began by brushing in broad areas of dilute color. Blue was applied for the sky and brown for the middle distance and foreground. The composition was developed with paint that becomes increasingly more opaque as the space recedes. Shadows and high-

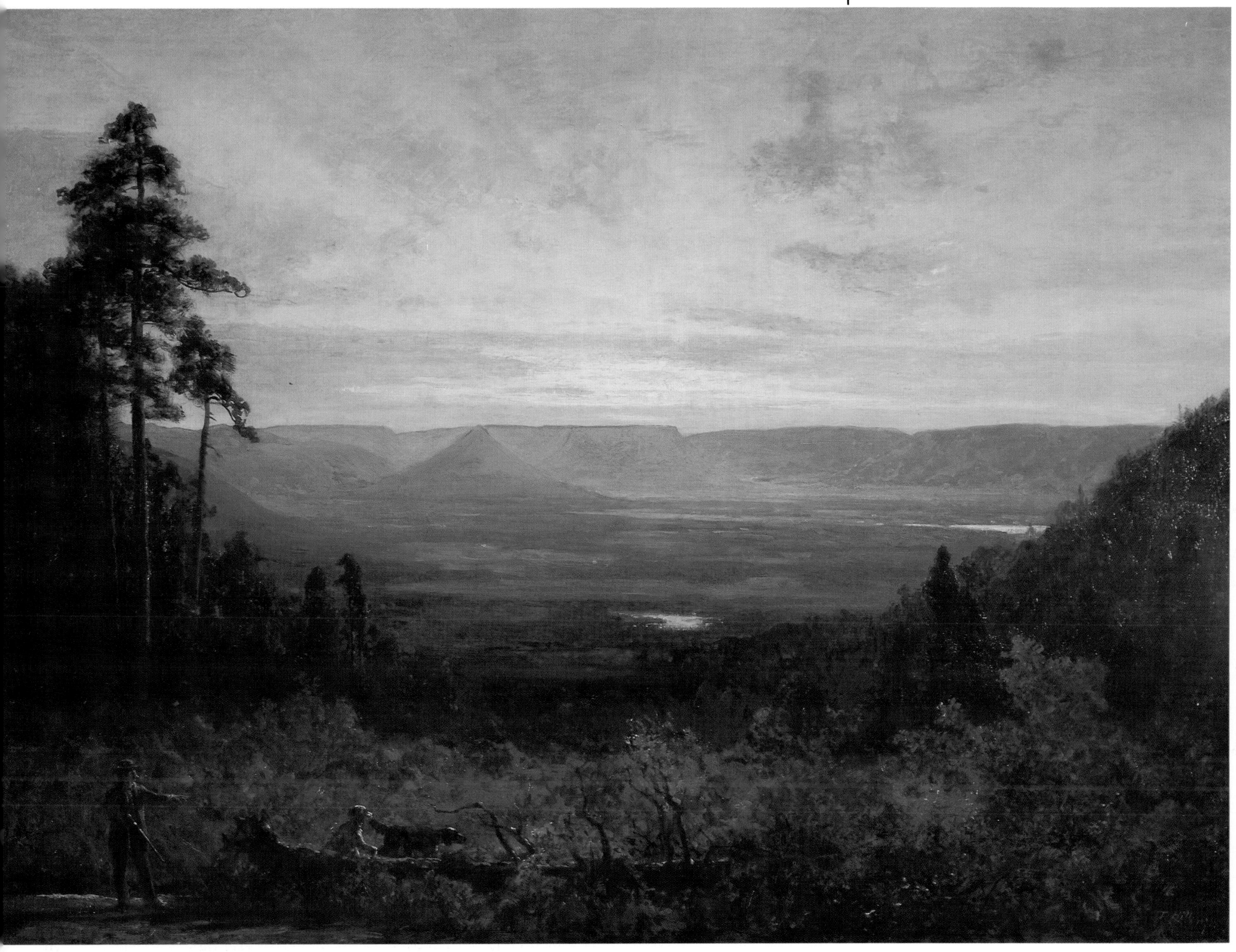

lights were applied together, often wet-into-wet. Scumbles were used in the distant landscape and sky to produce a hazy atmosphere. Hill's vigorous technique includes the use of large brushes, palette knife, the tip of the brush handle, and fingers.

The subject of *Hunter and Setters* embodies changes of mood as well as terrain. The lush foreground is redolent of a Hudson River scene while the more untamed, forested middle distance gives way to a vast, fantastic landscape. The separate peaks and mesas of the distant panorama form a single line along their tops, making a vibrating wall. The warning to the viewer is that beyond the safe and familiar forest lies an unsympathetic land where one does not wander when armed with only a shotgun and accompanied by two tame dogs.

Thomas Hill. Hunter and Setters in the Foothills with the Great Basin Beyond *is in the collection of the Palm Springs Desert Museum, Palm Springs, California. Museum purchase from the William Holden Acquisition Fund. Oil on canvas, wax lined. 27 inches (66.6 cm) height x 36 inches (91.5 cm) width. Signed lower right and dated 1871.*

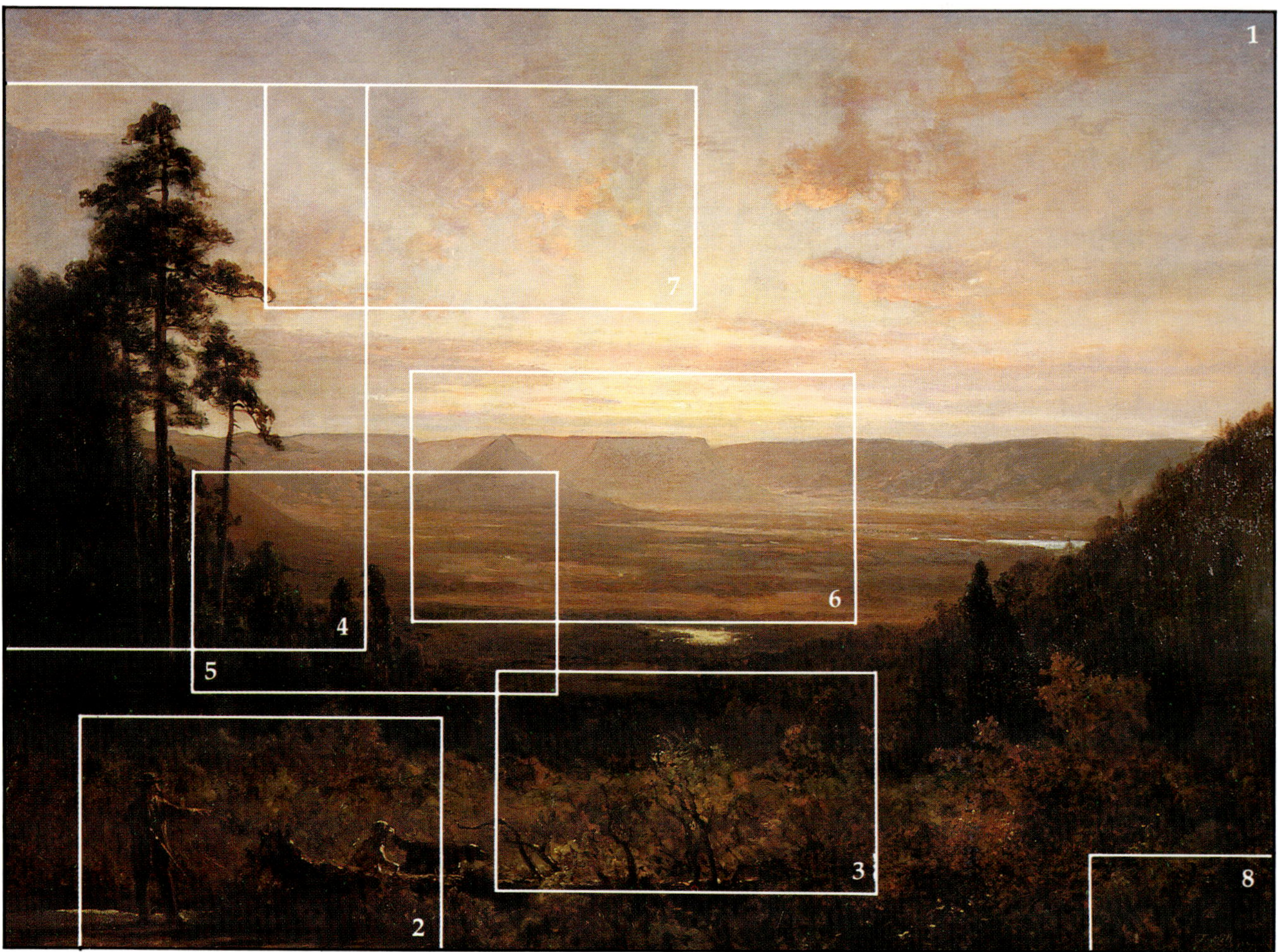

The luminous sky fills nearly half of the composition, giving the painting a bright and open feeling despite the dark forest foreground. Yet, the composition is contained by the bowl shape of the middle ground.

The foreground is dark, and the colors are rich and saturated. As the space recedes, the colors were diluted with more and more white, reducing the tonal contrasts and color intensities. For example, the hand of the figure and the upright dog have been brightly highlighted, creating a strong contrast between light and shadow. As the landscape extends into the distance, light and dark become less distinct and closer in tone. Hill's use of atmospheric perspective is well suited to this vast landscape because it imitates natural loss of visual clarity over a considerable distance due to the atmospheric effects.

Hill was a close contemporary of Bierstadt, Thomas Moran, and Whittredge in terms of years, and like them, his first experiences in art were influenced by the Hudson River painters. Hill's European exposure was brief and came after he had already established himself in the West as a painter. Europe did not tame him. His ways may have already been set, influenced by the wild American country that he had seen. His technique retained its verve.

Hill admitted that precise refinements, like those in the works of Bierstadt, did not interest him. In addition, he preferred broad brushwork to the delicate touches of Whittredge. His colors lacked the lucidity of Moran. Instead, Hill often muddied his colors by overmixing. Yet, in this one painting, Hill combined the terrains of all three: the intimate forest of Whittredge, the broad panorama of Bierstadt, and the fantastic land formations of Moran.

Hill's technique was very much his own. His work shows little direct influence of other painters or of European styles. He had a good eye, a direct approach, and a natural ability to convey the energy and wildness of this new land. He differed from Bierstadt, Moran, and Whittredge in that he chose to live in the West that he painted.

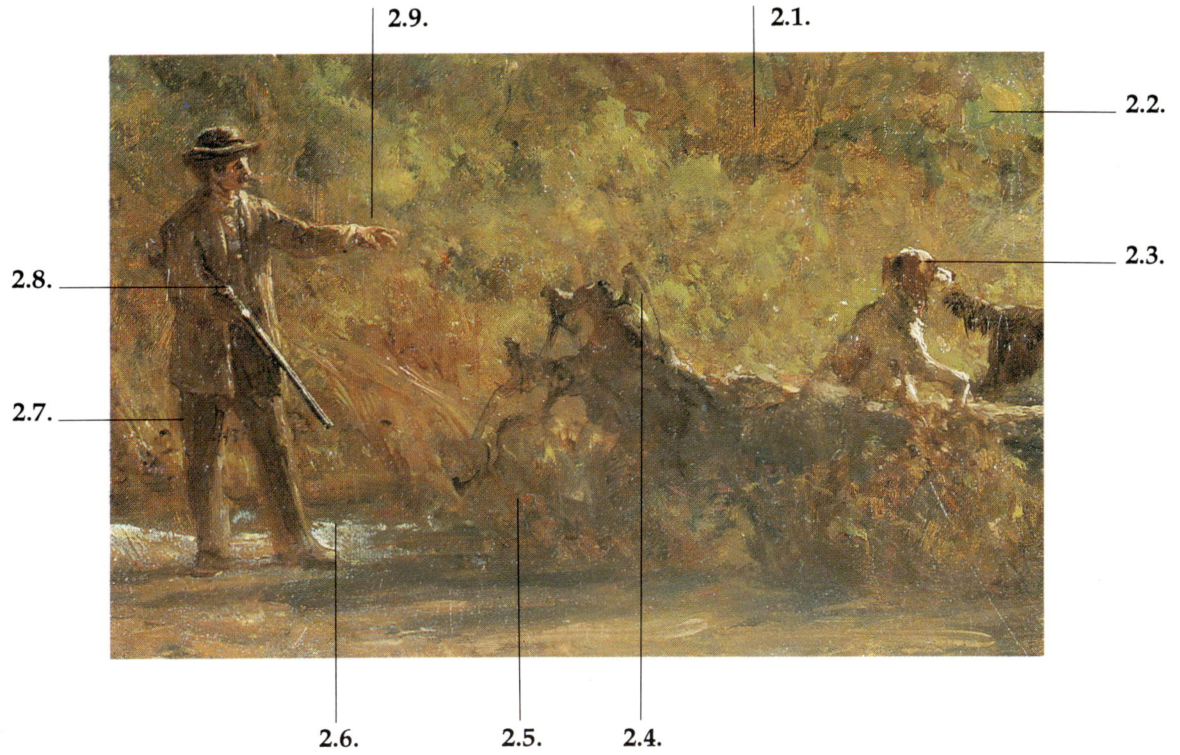

2. DETAIL OF FOREGROUND WITH HUNTER AND DOG

Hill advised his son who was also a painter, "Don't paint paws on your figures, a dab of color is enough…. Accidental effects can only be gotten with a big brush, I depend entirely on accident–you have no idea how much is produced that way."

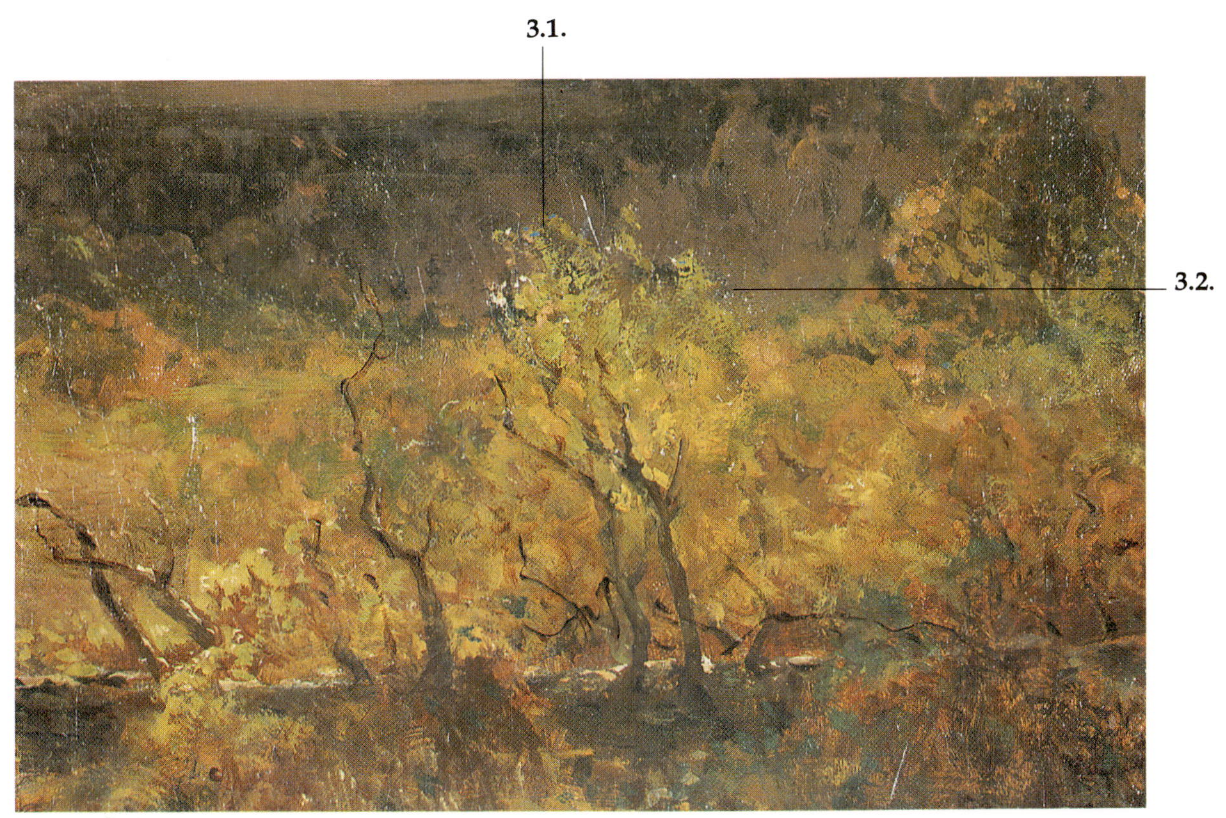

3. DETAIL OF FALLEN TREE LIMB IN FOREGROUND

2.1. A brown underlayer was broadly scrubbed in first for the foliage, using a large brush. This warm-hued underlayer was thinly applied, allowing the ground to show through in places and produce luminous middle tones.

2.2. Dark and light opaque greens were applied together over the brown underlayer in a wet-into-wet technique.

2.3. Vivid touches of orange paint highlight the tops of the dog's ears.

2.4. Rapidly applied saturated brown calligraphic lines delineate the roots of the tree.

2.5. A brilliant but seemingly random dot of contrasting red paint enlivens the surrounding duller green hues.

2.6. Drier white paint dragged across the surface of the forest floor sets off the hunter.

2.7. Bold directional brushstrokes form the hunter's legs.

2.8. The hand that holds the gun is suggested with minimal detail.

2.9. The pointing hand, formed simply of shadow and highlight, was painted wet-into-wet.

3.1. The bright foliage was animated by tiny but intense blue flecks that seem to have been haphazardly placed.

3.2. Warm mauve hues form a contrasting backdrop for the brilliant green and orange foliage. The colors play off each other: the duller mauve recedes and the bright colors jump forward. Not only is a deep space created, but the opposing intensities of hue set up a vibration, encouraging the eye to move on rather than to linger at particular details.

4.1. This foliage was painted on top of the sky. The light color of the sky serves as a bright underlayer, giving the trees a more luminous appearance than the foliage to the far left which was painted over a brown underlayer.

4.2. Dry dragged paint gives the rough effect of the fringed pine needles.

4.3. The tree trunks were painted with opaque dark brown paint and opaque highlights, placing them farther back in space than the saturated foreground.

4.4. In the foliage to the extreme left, the paint ranges from transparent to opaque. First a brown underlayer was thinly scrubbed in. More opaque dark green and then lighter green were added, forming shadow and highlights. In some places, the colors were mixed on the painting surface, causing them to lose their individual qualities and become somewhat muddied. Whether or not this was intentional, the effect successfully evokes dense foliage.

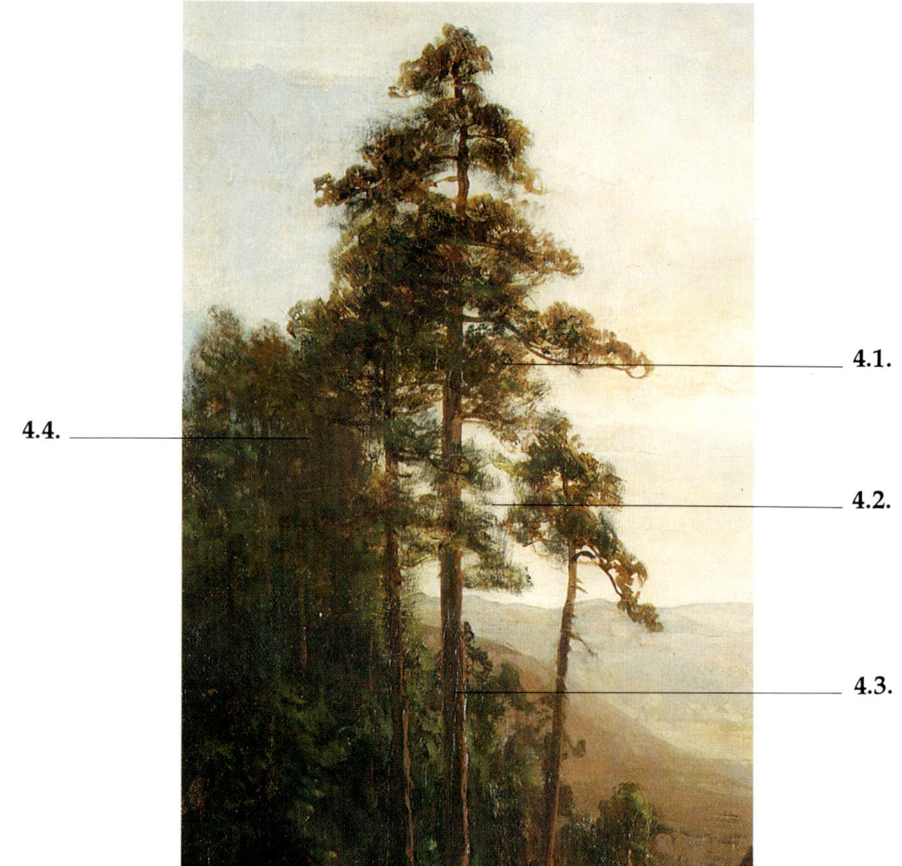

4. DETAIL OF TREES ALONG LEFT EDGE

5.1. Varying shades of browns and pinks were rapidly built up from dark to light for the basin. The colors slur and produce opaque, sometimes muddy combinations. Final white highlights dragged across the surface stand out against the duller paint, brightening the overall effect.

5.2. The brown underlayer for the basin floor was laid on broadly with a large brush.

5.3. Final dabs of mauve paint break up the foliage.

5.4. Vivid lighter green swirls of drier paint dragged across the surface make broken highlights which accentuate the ragged outlines of the trees.

5.5. Partially blended paint produces the frayed edges of the bristly foliage.

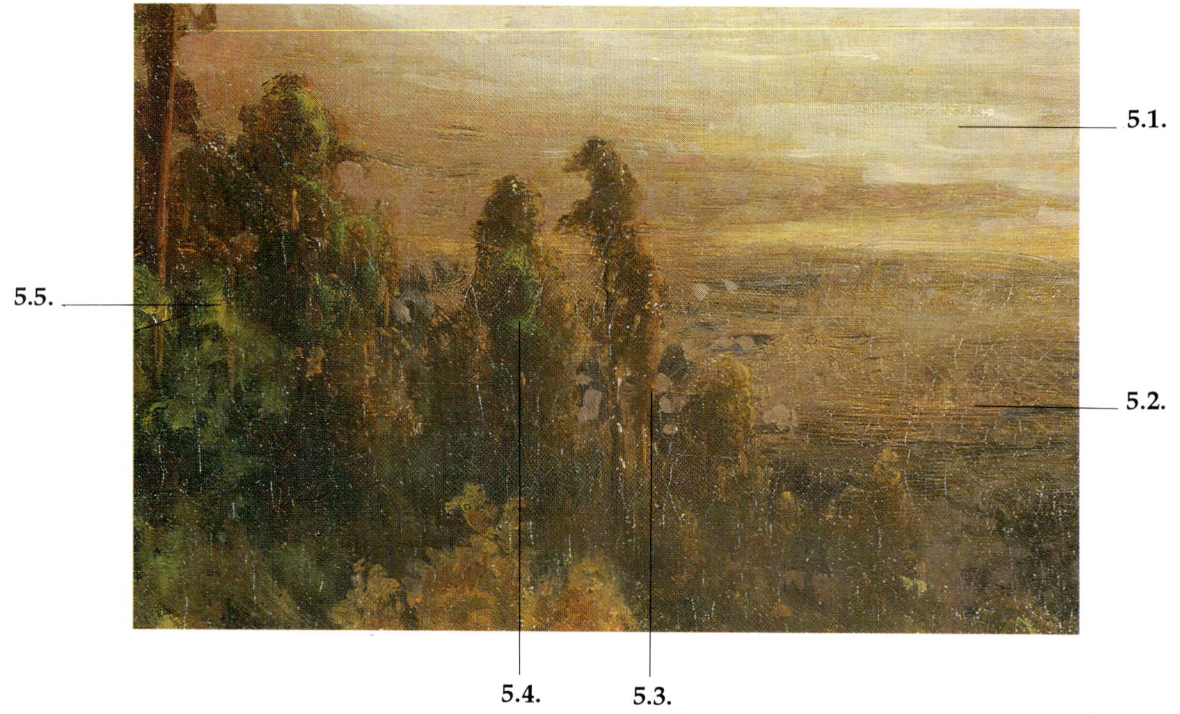

5. DETAIL OF MIDDLE DISTANCE

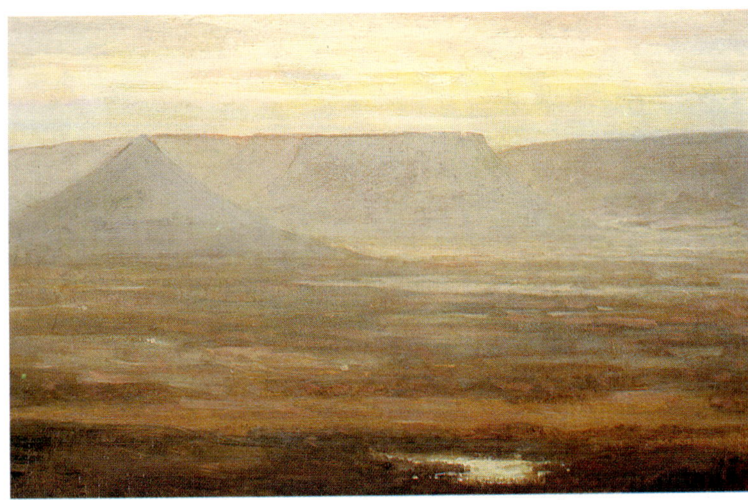

6. DETAIL OF DISTANT LANDSCAPE

The mesas and pointed hill meet along their crests to form a level line. No individual peak stands out from the rest to catch one's eye. They blend together into a single wall wavering in the distance. The bright yellow band across the sky backlights the mountains, making them appear flat against the intense light.

This atmospheric effect is strengthened by the use of scumbles for the mesas and hill. A dark opaque gray made of many colors mixed together was brushed on first. A lighter pinkish color was scumbled over this, allowing the underlayer to show through, defining the rock formation. The resulting color of these combined layers has a hazy, bluish hue. This cool tonality is caused by an optical phenomenon known as the turbid media effect, not necessarily by blue pigments being present.

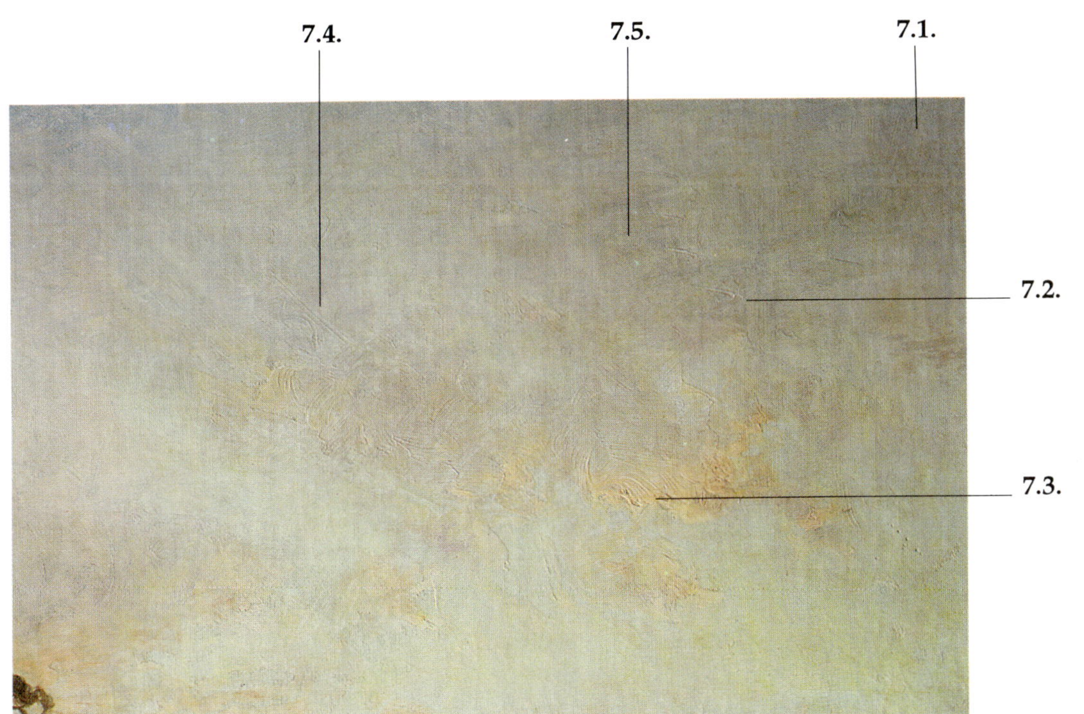

7. DETAIL OF SUN RAYS IN SKY

7.1. A thin application of blue paint was broadly brushed in first. The white ground was left exposed in places, especially at the tops of the fabric weave, creating a luminous effect.

7.2. The tip of the brush handle was used to draw a squiggled line in the wet paint.

7.3. A thin, dark-gray underlayer was applied for the clouds, then the somewhat impasted pinkish-orange paint was built up. The thicker paint retains the imprint of the brush, a palette knife, and fingers.

7.4. The rays of the sun were not done with added color but with long diagonal brushstrokes in the blue paint layer. These strokes left their tracks in the still wet paint, pushing the paint aside to form low ridges along their edges.

7.5. A milky scumble was applied over the blue sky and clouds. Here the curved strokes form a large arch over the sun's rays. Because of the turbid media effect, the strokes appear as cool shadows where they were applied over darker paint.

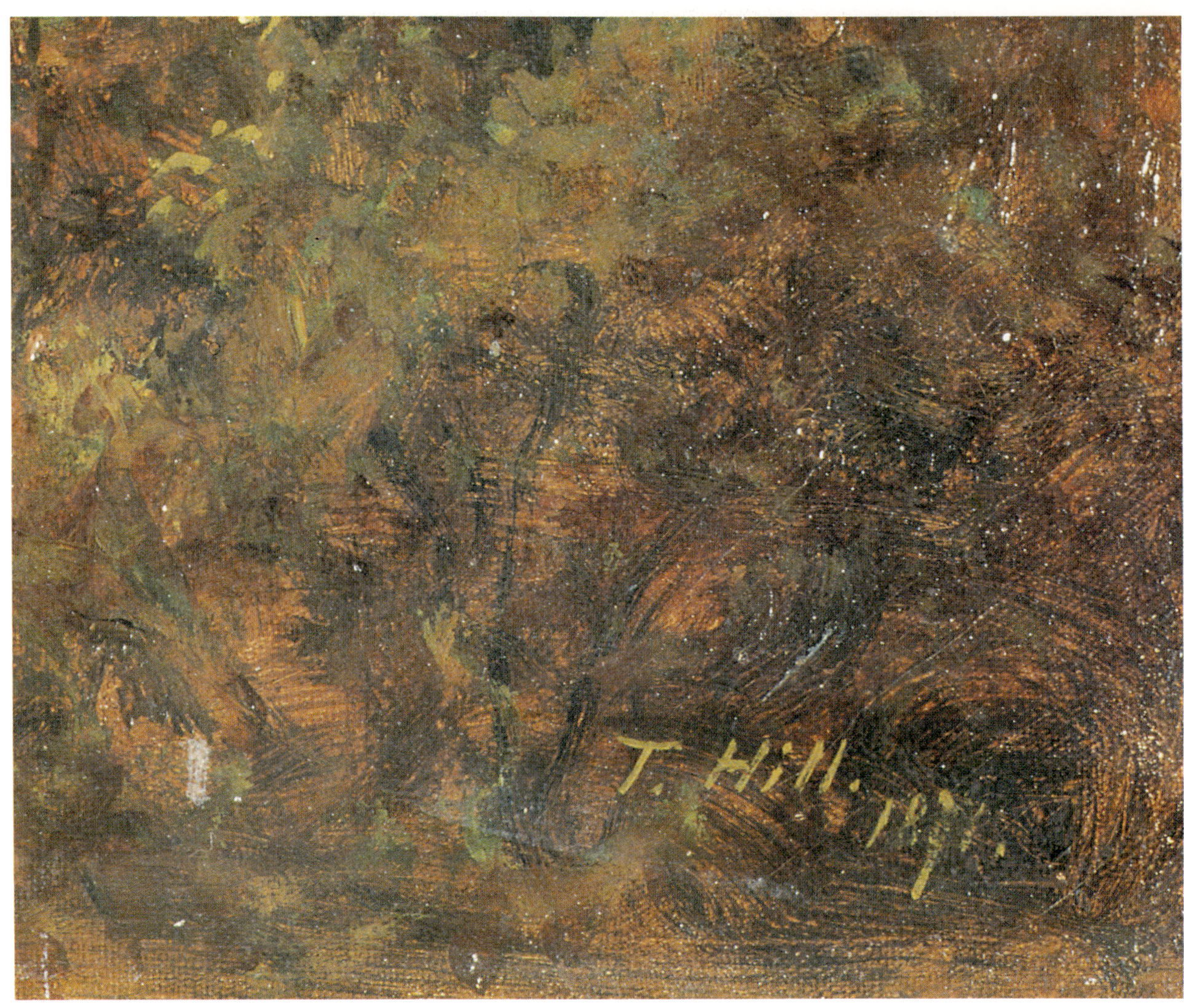

8. DETAIL OF SIGNATURE

T. Hill. 1871.

SUMMARY OF PAINTING TECHNIQUE

a. A white ground was applied to a plain weave canvas support.
b. First, broad areas of dilute color were rapidly brushed in: blue in the sky and brown in the foreground and middle distance.
c. More opaque paint was applied, both shadow and highlight together, often wet-into-wet. In the sky and distant landscape, scumbles were used to create a hazy, atmospheric effect.

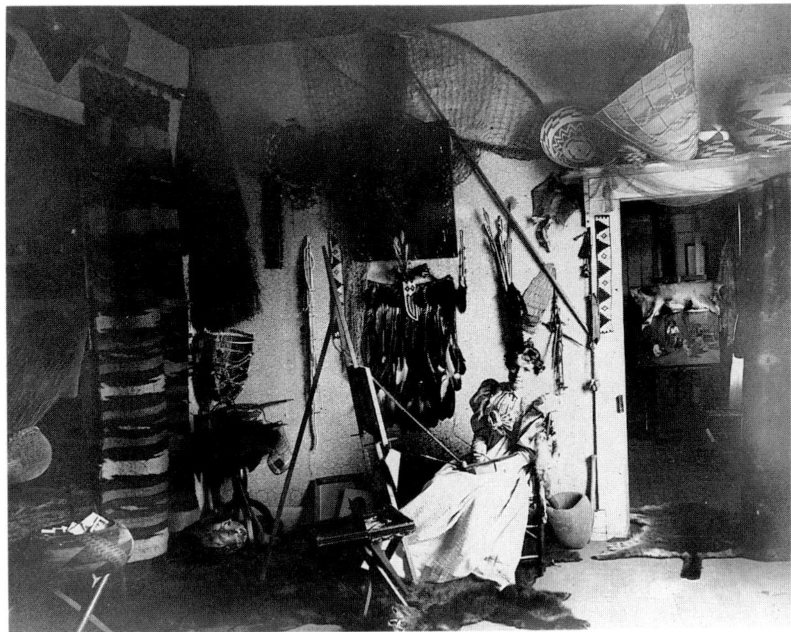

GRACE HUDSON

Paintings of the American West are sometimes disparaged on the basis that the subject had more to do with the success of a particular picture than the artist. Grace Carpenter Hudson and her depictions of appealing papooses are vulnerable to such an attack. She began painting Victorian portrayals of Pomo Indian babies propped against artifact-filled backgrounds in 1890. One year later she exploded onto the California art scene.

She had married for the second time in April 1890. Her husband was a medical doctor more interested in Indian ethnology than in medicine and they happened to live near a Pomo village that attracted his attention. She started painting realistic portraits of the Pomo infants not as works of art but as a detailed record to supplement her husband's cultural studies.

The same year, the Minneapolis Art Association purchased from her the first of the 684 numbered works she completed over the next four and a half decades. The title of the painting, *National Thorn*, was the improbable name of a Pomo infant. He was bound into a native baby basket with the family dog at the side. When the painting was exhibited at the Art Association, the gushing art critic of the Minneapolis *Journal* asked emotionally, "Did you ever see anything cuter?" The artistic style and subject were set and Hudson's reputation was made.

Her parents Aurelius and Helen Carpenter had been newly wedded pioneers when they rode an ox-drawn wagon across the wilderness from Kansas to California in 1857. They were both educated. He was a typesetter and she was a schoolteacher. They settled in Potter Valley, 16 miles northeast of the town of Ukiah, in the midst of the Pomos' little grazing farms between the Russian River and Clear Lake. The Pomos were world-famous for their basketry, among the finest on the continent, and for children's dolls carved to represent native gods.

On February 21, 1865 the Ukiah *Herald* reported the birth of the twins Grant and Grace Carpenter. They were a curiosity to the Pomos who ritually put their own twins to death because of the superstition that they would otherwise kill each other. In 1869 the Carpenters moved to Ukiah where Aurelius, who was known as Reel, opened a photography shop. Grace attended public school until 1878 when she left for Normal School in San Francisco. She was slated to become a teacher like her mother but her proficiency was in drawing, not in educating children.

In 1880 she was admitted to the California School of Design in San Francisco. After only one term her instructor told her parents that she was "one of my best pupils." Her father was aware of her skill. He was mailing her photographic portraits to be hand-colored for his customers. In her second year at the California School she won the prize for life drawing, but her art education ended in 1884 after four years. She never studied in the East or in Europe.

She had been without parental supervision in San Francisco where she was seeing William Davis, an older man. Her parents described him as coarse and disapproved of him as her suitor. In a burst of rebellion she eloped with Davis September 17, 1884, then contritely divorced him the next year. She returned to Ukiah to face down the shame small towns attached to the legal dissolution of a marriage. A few of her earliest paintings were signed Grace Carpenter Davis.

In the spring of 1889, John Hudson arrived in Ukiah from the South to practice medicine. Grace Davis was teaching art. In 1890 they married and moved into an addition to her studio. She had been surprised to learn the depth of his involvement with the culture of the Pomos who were as familiar to her as the river and the townspeople. She began painting pictures of the children to help him record data on the Pomos. Unlike other artists who went West to paint Indians, she had been brought up among the Indians she depicted.

The next year, the field collector for the Minneapolis Art Association was in Ukiah to buy some of the famous Pomo baskets. One of his vendors was Whisky Jennie. She told him that a local white lady was painting a portrait of her infant posed in one of the baby baskets he had purchased. He went to Hudson's studio, saw the painting in progress, recognized the quality, and bought it on the spot for the Association. That was the beginning of her career.

Hudson realized immediately that she was destined to become more than the local painter lady. To protect her artistic integrity she numbered each painting on the back, entered the description in a special notebook, and had her father photograph the canvas before it left her studio. With very few exceptions, she painted no duplicate of her work although other painters soon offered facsimiles for sale. There were even pirated postcard reproductions.

By 1892 her portraits of the Pomo children were in national exhibitions. Her fifth painting was exhibited at the Columbian Exposition in Chicago in 1893. She also drew pen and ink illustrations for *Overland Monthly*.

She was represented by major dealers across the country. Some came to her studio on behalf of private collectors and other museums. Meanwhile her husband was recording the Pomo language, learning tribal traditions, and collecting artifacts. He gradually gave up the practice of medicine, depending on her income from the sale of paintings. Her price was $500 for large pieces, $150 and up for the smaller ones. A century later in 1987, her *Mendocino Products* brought $56,100 at public auction.

From 1895 to 1900 she painted 125 pictures. Some were life-size at 30x30 inches. More than half were 8x10 inches or less. Except for three of these canvases, the Pomo children were her only subjects. It amused her to hear a visitor remark, "I suppose these paintings are bought by the children's parents."

There were feature articles about her in newspapers and magazines from coast to coast. She was described as dark blonde and slender, graceful and charming, bright and attractive, with a good sense of humor. She was also a crack shot at doves with a 12-gauge gun. She weighed 103 pounds.

By 1895 she was able to quit illustrating. She was an established professional fine artist even though she had made her first sale only five years earlier. Interviewers wanted to know how she captured the emotions the children evidenced. "I have much to contend against," she exaggerated. "When I see a baby I want to paint, I have to kidnap it. There is a superstition among the Indians that to be sketched is to bring some terrible calamity on the subject. If [some of] these Indians knew I painted their babies, I would be regarded as a murderess.

"If a child's face suits me, I enter into negotiations with the mother to work for me, usually scrubbing floors. She leaves the baby strapped in his basket, braced against the side of the house where it will be under her eye. The next maneuver is to get possession of that baby. That is where our St. Bernard 'takes his turn.' That will usually make an Indian baby cry. The mother is glad to let me take the papoose inside where it will be safe. In a jiffy, I have that baby propped against the front door of my studio.

"Then comes the task of getting a sketch of one fleeting expression on the face of the baby. They are little stoics. I worried, tormented, bullied and frightened one poor little fellow for two days, trying to make him cry. I grew ashamed of myself and gave it up.

"I am having a time with my last baby. The mother has been ill, so I have to paint from two other babies. I am seldom able to get the same child all through the painting of a picture, for an Indian can seldom be relied upon for anything and rarely comes when he agrees to, unless he is hungry."

One of the babies she painted died. "If its mother ever knew that I had painted him," she confessed, "she would have held me responsible." Neither Hudson nor the Pomos realized then that the Pomos were a disappearing race. Their numbers decreased from 8,000 to 800 during her lifetime. If the Pomos had been aware they were physically fading away, they might have blamed her for their misfortunes. Actually, the trouble was said to result mainly from the change in the Pomos' natural diet after white settlers civilized the valley and the food.

Hudson never had children of her own but she was recognized as the principal painter of Indian children. There were two main complaints about her work. The first was that she was a potboiler. From the first painting to the last, her primary subjects were the Indian children. When she branched out to Hawaiian and Asian children on her travels, they looked like Indians. The second criticism concerned "the painful faithfulness of her rendering. She justifies this by aiming at ethnological value, forgetting that the camera can do even more accurate work. We have the right to something more serious."

Compounding the charge, her twin brother quoted her as saying, "The only aid I get in my work is a tiny snapshot photograph. One day I will get a photograph of a baby's face and the next day a hand or a foot. Sometimes I get a little [white] boy to pose for me and then I put the little Indian face on him. My pictures are composites."

"I employed a squaw with a baby to do some work," she herself once added. "While she was busy I sent my niece to entice the child away. Out of sight of the mother, my niece seized the child from behind and gave it a shake. As it commenced to wiggle and cry, I photographed it, and just had time to hide before the anxious mother came running. My labor would be easier if I could paint from living models."

Mrs. Hudson vehemently denied her brother's quotation. She replied in the third person, "Grace Hudson does not depend on a Kodak for her studies. She is a thorough artist and not a copier of photographs."

Aficionados say that she did some of her best work between 1913 and 1925, despite influenza, surgery, and the death of her parents. Her subjects were still the Indian children she referred to as little "its."

In 1920 doctors had told her she would never be able to paint again because of a thyroid condition. Instead, radium tubes were implanted in her neck to control her goiter and she was soon working once more. She spent one year in Hawaii and made two trips to Europe.

Her last work was a sketch drawn December 14, 1935 and numbered 684. Her husband died January 20, 1936. She did not produce another painting, and died March 23, 1937.

1. THE PAINTING

"This is Alice. The basket she is weaving is a plaque basket and the design appears to be of multiple quail top-knots. She is amusing her child in the *seka* [the holding basket] and has her materials close at hand to finish the basket. In the background is a 'sweathouse' with its entrance door and airvent." So wrote Grace Hudson about this painting in her notebook, as was her custom.

During the five years before 1900 when Grace Hudson completed 125 paintings, portraits of Indian children were her primary subject. *Love's Labors* on the other hand is a genre painting of the mother weaving a basket.

The works tended to be small, many even smaller than *Love's Labors*. Despite Hudson's training as an artist, her main vision was to record the lives and culture of the Pomo Indians. Artistic concerns were secondary. Her technique was rapid and direct with cursory attention given to the background. She concentrated on accurate depiction of Indian artifacts and creation of portraits that captured the nature of the sitter both as to personality and as anthropological study. One would recognize Alice if one met her.

There is still some dispute about the extent to which Hudson worked from photographs. Her brother's suggestion that she relied on photos rather than live models was "not to her liking." Nevertheless, the use of snapshots as "sketches" was a common practice of artists at the time and Hudson was an accomplished photographer.

For *Love's Labors* Hudson used a plain weave linen canvas with a white commercially-prepared ground. There is no underdrawing apparent and no artist's changes seem to have been made. The paint has been handled precisely and without hesitation. It has been applied directly onto the ground in an *alla prima* manner.

Similar to watercolor technique, the background has been painted with washes of lean paint with the ground used throughout to supply white. The colors, though muted in tonality, appear brighter against the white ground. The effect is light and airy and brings to mind the Impressionist painters, Renoir in particular. This likeness is not surprising since the quality of light in California closely resembles the strong Provence sunshine that the Impressionist painters found so appealing. Hudson's artistic eye must have appreciated this climatic characteristic inherent to California.

Within the setting of soft pastel sunshine sits Alice with her baby. Unlike the Impressionists who tended to keep the entire composition in one tonal range, the figural group here has been done with thicker, richer paint than the background. The stronger and more saturated colors stand out against the surrounding atmospheric landscape, enhancing the sense of space.

The composition is made up entirely of interrelated triangles. Alice, the baby, and the sweathouse entrance and vent form a strong inner triangle that includes all the human elements. This is softly framed by the grassy hillside which is balanced by the triangle of the distant landscape and sky. It is an earth-oriented composition with little sky showing. The forms are gentle, rounded, and organic. The hillside of the sweat-house has an unmistakably pregnant look. The baby is but suggested by the shock of black hair, the plump shape of the *seka,* and the mother's intent gaze toward her child.

In the more socially conscious atmosphere of the late 20th century, it is easier to appreciate Grace Hudson's paintings of Pomo Indian children than it was when the work was done. It seems natural now that a white woman would make a career of depicting these indigenous people with warmth and tenderness. Compare, however, what well-known contemporary biographer Clara Erskine Clements wrote about Hudson in her

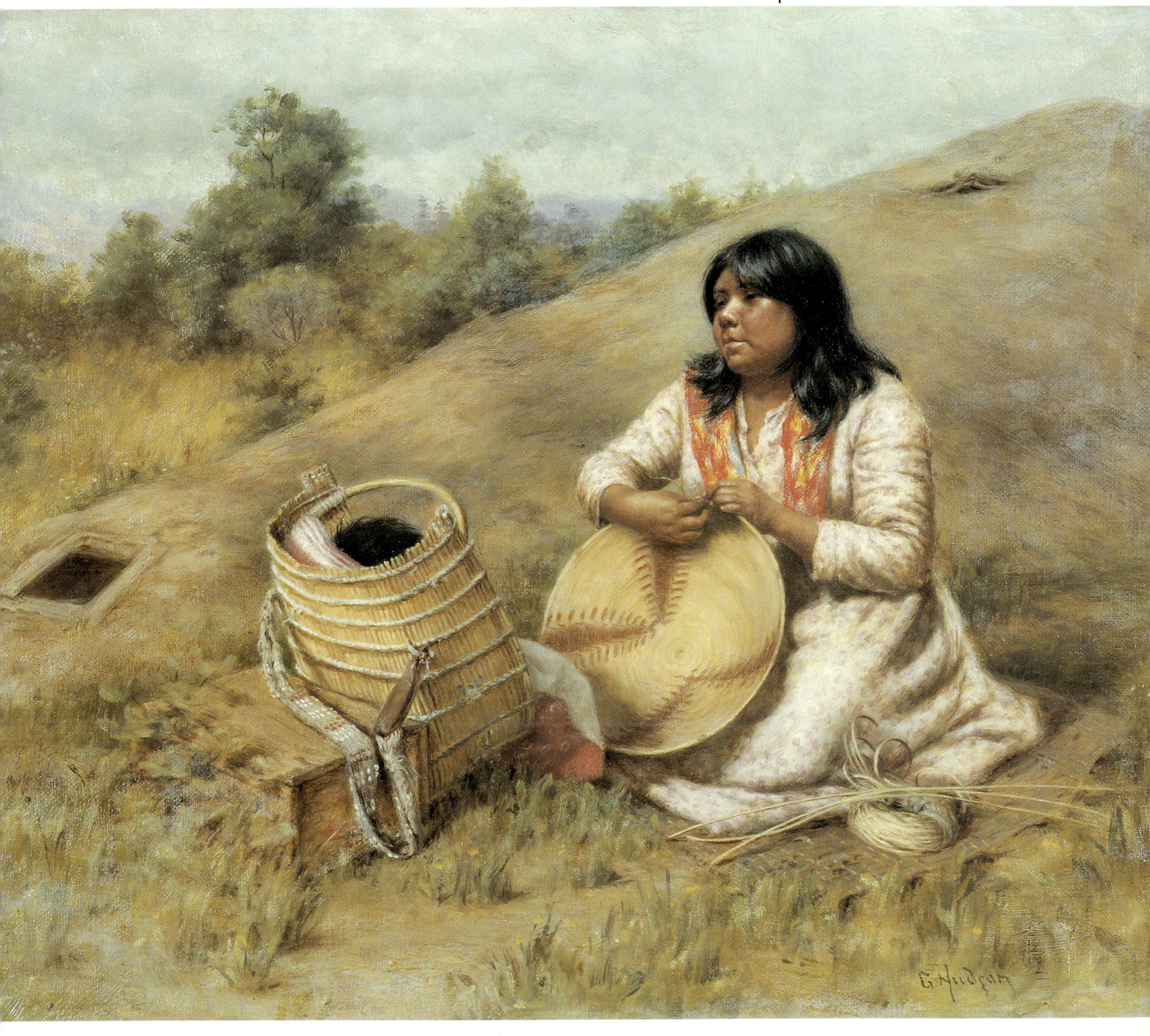

tribute to women artists, *Women in the Fine Arts*:

    Mrs. Hudson's pictures of Indians, the Pomos especially, are very interesting, although when one sees the living article one wonders how a picture of him, conscientiously painted and truthful in detail, can be so little repulsive–or, in fact, not repulsive at all.... If we do not sympathize with her choice of subjects, we are compelled to acknowledge that her pictures are full of interest and emphasize the power of this artist in

Grace Hudson. Love's Labors *is in the collection of the Palm Springs Desert Museum, Palm Springs, California. Museum purchase from the William Holden Acquisition Fund. Oil on canvas. 12 1/16 inches (30.5 cm) height x 15 inches (38.0 cm) width. Signed lower right and inscribed on the reverse, 1898.*

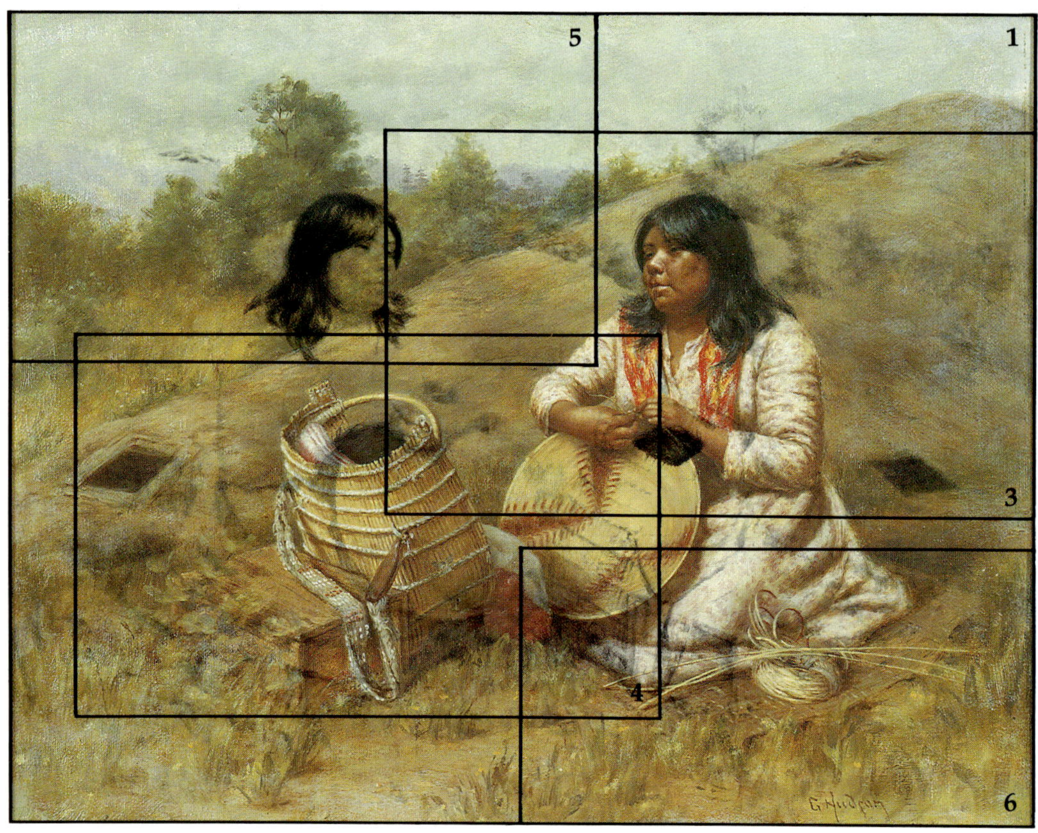

keeping them above a wearisome commonplace.... Her compositions are simple, and it can only be a rare skill in their treatment that gives them the value that is generally accorded them by critics, who, while approving them, are all the time conscious of surprise at themselves for doing so, and of an unanswered Why? which persists in presenting itself to their thought when seeing or thinking of these pictures.

Why Grace Hudson chose this subject as her life's career no longer troubles her advocates or critics. Her appreciators include a wider audience than simply lovers of art or children, for her realistic renderings provide the world with one of the few visual records of the vanished Pomos.

2. DETAIL OF REVERSE OF PAINTING

This is the inscription. The number 119 is the artist's record.

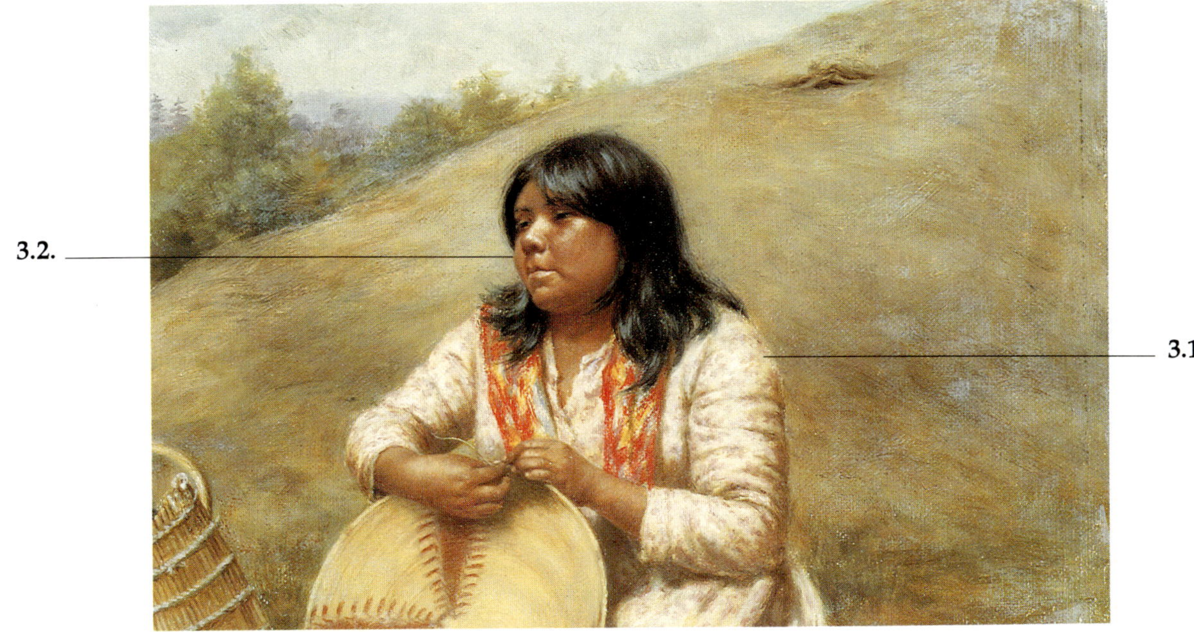

3. DETAIL OF ALICE

3.1. *The richer and denser paint of the figure stands out in sharp focus against the paler, more sketchily applied background, creating a sense of deep space.*

3.2. *The full modeling has been carefully done for the face with a warm underlayer set off by bright white highlights.*

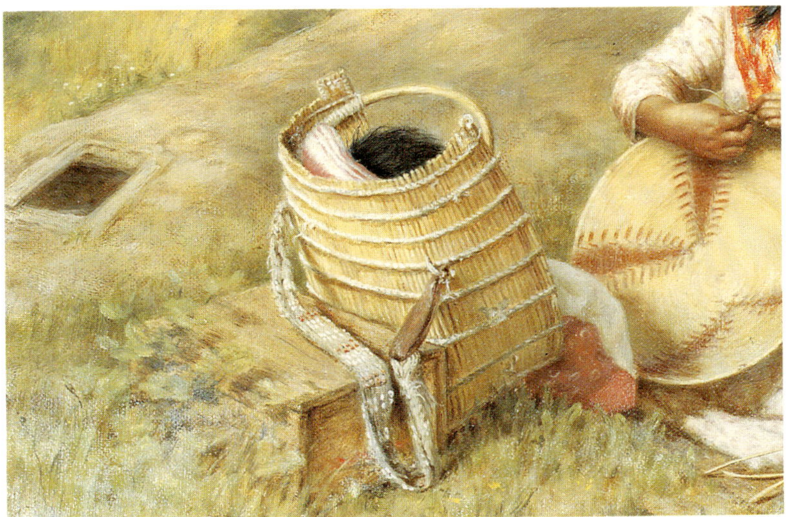

4. DETAIL OF *SEKA*

Hudson repeated simple geometric shapes in her composition, giving the painting a solid reassuring quality. The basket being woven by Alice reflects the round top of the *seka*. The rectangular opening of the sweathouse parallels the boxiness of the wooden crate.

Hudson painted what she saw. The Pomo culture was already in a dissipated condition. Alice's cast-off western-style dress and the wooden crate are evidence of the white man's intrusion into the Indian way of life. Hudson did not romanticize her subject beyond the natural inclination to depict mother and child tenderly.

5.1. The green foliage of the trees was applied wet-into-wet.

5.2. Details such as the tree trunk were added last, on top of the foliage.

5.3. The white was left exposed to create lighter areas.

5.4. The tip of the brush handle was used here to draw a line in the paint while it was still wet.

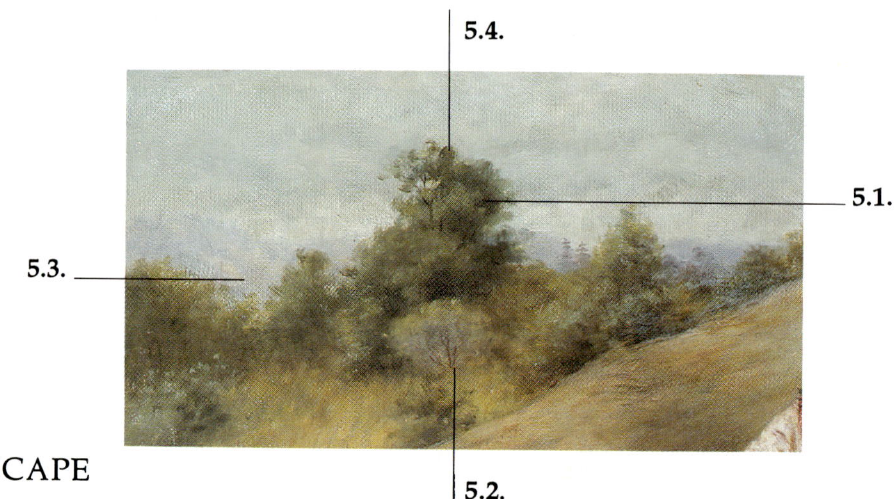

5. DETAIL OF LANDSCAPE

Loose brushwork and muted colors characterize the Impressionistic landscape in the background. The washes of paint are lean and the ground supplies the whites, especially in the sky.

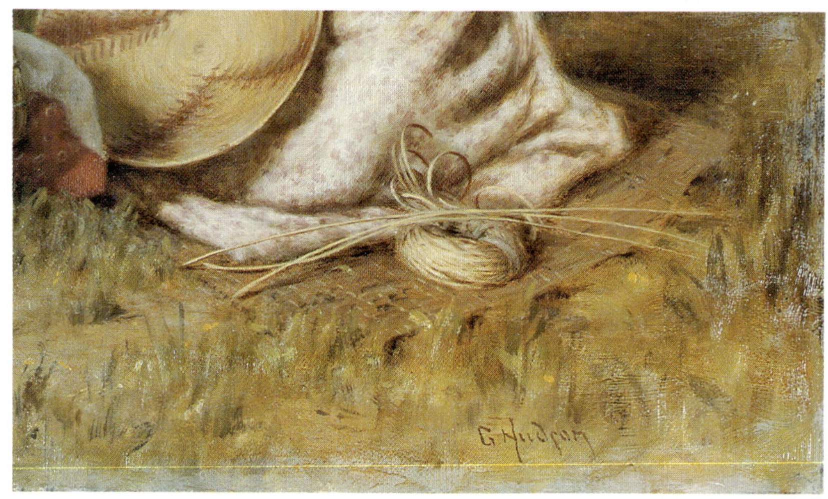

6. DETAIL OF SIGNATURE

G. Hudson

SUMMARY OF PAINTING TECHNIQUE

a. A commercially primed canvas was mounted onto a stretcher.
b. The figural group was painted with fairly rich, slightly impasted paint. The face and hands were carefully modeled with bright highlights added last with thick white paint. The paint appears to have been applied rapidly without hesitation or artist's changes.
c. The background was freely painted with dilute washes of lean paint, similar to watercolor technique. The white of the ground was used extensively for the light areas. Overall the white gives the background its light, airy, brightly sunlit quality.

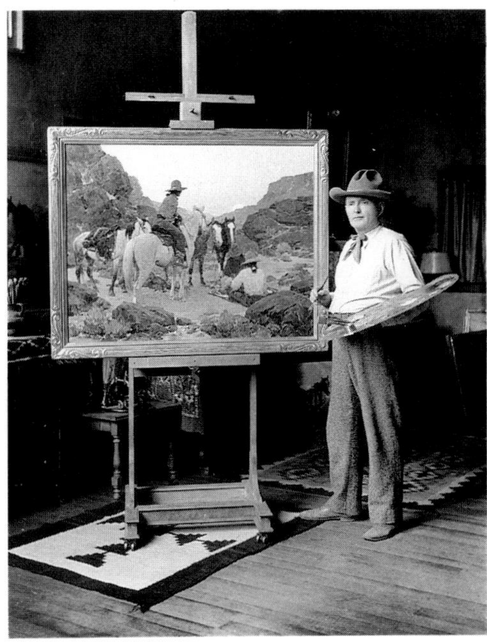

FRANK TENNEY JOHNSON

Frank Tenney Johnson attained prominence as a painter of the American West 20 years after the 20th century began. A full step behind the superstars, Frederic Remington and Charles Marion Russell, Johnson distinguished himself from the more versatile pair. He avoided scenes of violence as subjects and specialized in impressionistic night effects with subtle colors.

Johnson also received one honor that escaped the two giants of Western figurative art. He was elected an Academician of the National Academy of Design. In contrast, the abrasive Remington had been limited to a much lesser prize, an Associate membership. The elitist Academicians never even considered the self-taught Russell for election as one of them.

Johnson was born June 26, 1874 on a barren farm beset by grasshoppers, drought, and high winds near the eastern terminus of the Union Pacific Railroad at Council Bluffs, Iowa. Both of his parents were educated. His mother had studied painting at a private boarding school. A calf on the family farm was called Rosa Bonheur after the French female painter of domestic animals.

His unsuccessful father was proud of the family genealogy that was based on the rare claim of descent from a member of the Mayflower's crew rather than a passenger. Frank was named for a favorite Aunt Frankie, Mary Frances Louisa Tenney. This was a reversal of the more usual naming of female children for male relatives. Georgia O'Keeffe, for example, was identified with her grandfather George.

Johnson maintained that his "boyhood days were filled with the excitement of growing up alongside the Overland Trail that led directly past our pioneer farm. The occasional slow-moving prairie schooners and the weekly stagecoach traveling westward had a great deal to do with my painting the pictures I have." When his mother died in 1886, his father married maiden Aunt Frankie. They sold the unproductive Iowa farm and moved to supposedly greener pastures near Milwaukee, Wisconsin.

Johnson's ambitions as a painter were triggered by a visit to a public art gallery in

Milwaukee. When he was 15 he quit high school to apprentice himself to a sign painter. Fired after a year because he also sought his own commercial clients, Johnson took art lessons from Richard Lorenz, a German panoramist. Trained as an academic realist, Lorenz had exhibited paintings in Munich before emigrating to the United States. After Lorenz left to paint in the West, Johnson made a trip to South Dakota by himself to sketch Indians. Then he set up as an illustrator in Milwaukee.

Quickly recognizing his need for further schooling as a painter, Johnson spent a year at the Art Students League in New York City to learn commercial art. His teacher was John Henry Twachtman who had been an illustrator before becoming one of the impressionistic Ten American Painters. After returning to Milwaukee in 1896 Johnson married Vinnie Francis and devoted the next six years to commercial art.

His aspirations were still not fully realized, however, so the young couple moved back to New York City. His wife worked as a secretary to support him while he attended the New York School of Art. He studied under two more of the great artist-teachers of the day, Robert Henri and William Merritt Chase.

By 1904 Johnson was at last a successful New York illustrator. The magazine *Field & Stream* advanced him the railroad fare for a long Western tour. From Colorado he wrote, "I've been experimenting with colors, the way Maxfield Parrish gets his peculiar techniques." He tried to capture the clear starlit Western nights for the first time on a ranch near Steamboat Springs. Two years later, Johnson had all the assignments he could handle for illustrations of Western subjects. In 1910 he also began selling a few easel paintings of cowboys and Indians. He started exhibiting at the National Academy of Design in 1922.

Johnson and his wife found a new home in Alhambra, California near Los Angeles but they ignored the benefits of the seasons. They lived in New York during the busy and cold winters to obtain illustrative work and they lived in California during the hot summers to do easel painting. The first year, only one Johnson painting was sold in California and there was no commercial assignment in New York. Younger and cheaper illustrators were winning the commissions. Johnson's wife Vinnie took over the marketing end of the art, as Nancy Russell had done for her husband. The tide began to turn in 1923.

In 1926, Johnson's murals for the Carthay Circle Theatre in Los Angeles were seen by a million people. He earned almost $22,000 from his paintings. After Russell died that year, Johnson was generally acknowledged to be the foremost figurative painter of Western life. He was a founder of Painters of the West which marketed the members' work. Named an Associate of the National Academy in 1929, he was elected an Academician in 1937.

Johnson had more than 4,000 photographic negatives and scores of oil sketches from his numerous Western trips. Before he started an easel painting he generally selected the composition from the negatives and sketches for both figures and background. A favorite subject was the horse. He claimed that "horses have as much individuality as people when you get to know them."

His nocturnes were the most sought-after of his pictures as early as 1924. He called his technique the simulation of daytime colors under moonlight, but the method went beyond just the choice of colors. For these night scenes his usual practice was to tint the white ground on the canvas with a bright Spanish red. He believed the red provided luminosity for the finished painting. In other nocturnes the ground was tinted blue-green.

He used a palette knife for broad effects in the application of the paint. Brushwork filled in the details over the knife strokes. He frequently employed his left thumb to shape the wet paint. A photographic negative taken to the easel for guidance would show his fingerprint in paint whenever he had not cleaned his thumb.

When Johnson painted *In Old Isleta*, he was 60 and still in his prime. During these later years he became more finicky about his standards. When he was not pleased with what he had done he put aside the work in process rather than starting again by painting over unsatisfactory areas. His intent was to return to the unfinished pictures at a later date to correct and complete them. He seldom did.

Johnson was a gregarious man who liked plenty of people around him to participate in group singing and lively conversation. Many of the Southern California artists and the illustrators visiting from New York met at his studio.

He literally died for a kiss. On December 19, 1938 he and his wife went to a party at the home of friends, the Callahans. As Vinnie Johnson described the tragic episode, "Frank, always sociable with the ladies, kissed Mrs. Callahan–just a social greeting. But she was found to have spinal meningitis and died the following Tuesday–on which day Frank took to his bed with what we thought was just grippe.

"On Wednesday when his fever did not get better I called the doctor. He recognized the symptoms and got him to the hospital under quarantine. He lived only until the early morning hours of January 1. Being a contagious disease, we could not have a service in a chapel. We arranged with the Health Department to have a service at the graveside, keeping the people at a distance. Many told me everything was perfectly beautiful, and just like Frank."

Patrons wanted to buy Johnson's last painting. At his death, however, there were only unfinished and unsigned paintings in his studios. The multiplicity of choices made it difficult to pick the one painting that was the last.

Johnson's wife maintained that the final one was the one still on the easel. This was a nocturne of cattle bedded down for the night. Dim mountains were in the distance. In the foreground was a mounted cowboy with a spot of radiance from a struck match that illuminated his face as he lit a cigarette.

The painting was a characteristic Johnson subject. The work was unsigned but it was a heartwarming bread-and-butter composition the artist had done and re-done. Paintings like that had always been highly salable and this one was no exception.

In 1980 his 36x46 inch *Pack Horses from RimRock Ranch* sold for $120,000 at auction.

1. THE PAINTING

Johnson has created a bright moonlit nocturne that causes the viewer to strain his vision to make out the indistinct images of figures that blend into the background. In this way the viewer is soon drawn into the scene.

Johnson was known for his night pictures. To create this unusual halflight, he evolved a technique of employing a toned ground. This was achieved by applying a transparent veil of color over the ground, thus adding a color effect without sacrificing the bright reflective qualities of the white ground. To simply mix color directly into the ground would give a duller, less luminous effect.

To evoke the cool dark night atmosphere of *In Old Isleta*, a brilliant blue-green was washed over the white ground. This toned ground influences the value of the subsequent paint layers, making them darker and more saturated. By this fairly sophisticated technique, Johnson was able to paint a bright, coloristic scene and still achieve a night-time effect. The light is strong, but without warmth. The rich contrasting glow emitted by the window further heightens the cool evening hues.

A fine plain-weave lightweight canvas was used as the support. The canvas has been double primed, that is, the white ground appears to have been applied in two distinct layers. This is a standard priming technique used when a stiffer and smoother working surface is desired. It seems to be a commercially prepared ground, applied before the canvas was stretched. The canvas, however, was mounted onto the stretcher by the artist. The transparent blue-green tone was then washed over the ground to create the general tonality of the night scene.

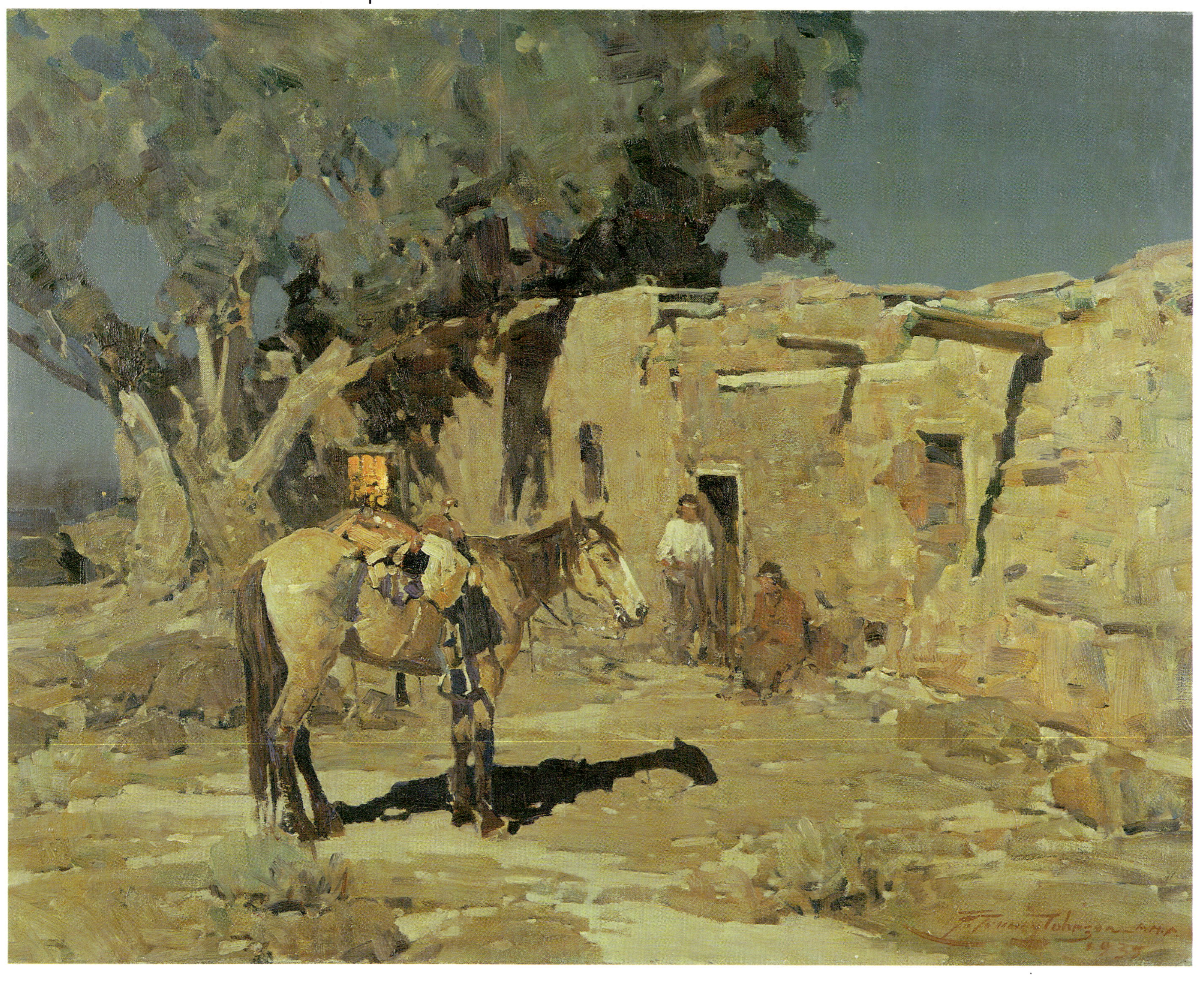

Frank Tenney Johnson. In Old Isleta *is in the collection of the San Diego Museum of Art, California. Oil on canvas. 24 1/8 inches (61.3 cm) height x 30 inches (76.2 cm) width. Signed lower right and dated 1935.*

The paint ranges from simple thin layers to a thick build-up made of many layers applied wet-into-wet. For example, the sky consists of a single blue paint layer that is rich in medium, glossy in appearance, and even in texture. The tree and building, on the other hand, were painted with multiple short brushstrokes applied wet-into-wet. Forceful marks can be seen in the detail enlargements where the paint was purposefully scraped away with a sharp tool.

The painting was not done in one session. The paint layers bear evidence that the

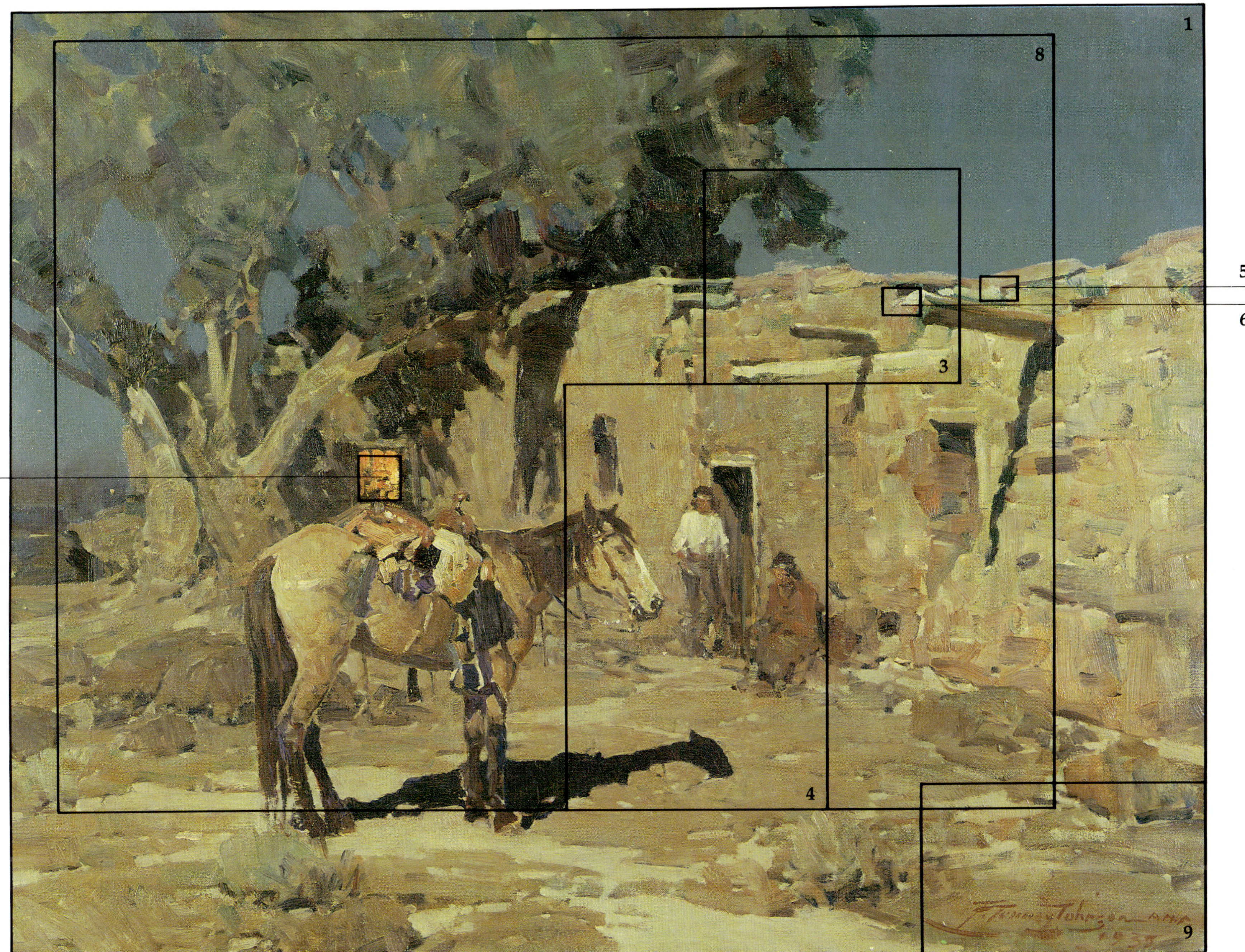

artist reworked some areas over and over again, resulting in a heavy accumulation of paint. It was not a spontaneous hand behind the brush, but one that had to correct often until the composition was satisfactory.

Johnson was primarily a colorist, forgoing line and detail in deference to the manipulation of hue and value to achieve his particular night effects. As he stated, Maxfield Parrish's gem-like colors were his great influence. The brilliant Western night sky was his inspiration.

Johnson's individual use of a tinted wash of vibrant color over the ground sets his technique apart from that of his contemporaries such as Remington and Russell, as illustrated in this book. The two examples of their typical work depict exciting moments. There is no apparent story to *In Old Isleta*, just the play of bright moonlight on a quiet evening scene.

One's first impression when viewing *In Old Isleta* is of a simple scene simply painted. Only on close scrutiny can one appreciate the subtle and well-conceived technique of interrelated layers of color. One understands why Johnson at the end of his life finally reached full Academician, a rank that eluded so many other painters.

2.1. The white ground covers the entire surface of the canvas including the tacking edge. From this one can deduce that the ground was commercially applied before the fabric was mounted onto the stretcher. A microscopic sample taken from the ground indicates the two distinct layers known as double priming. The unevenness of the placement of the tacks indicates that the fabric was not commercially mounted. It was probably purchased by the roll and stretched by the artist.

2.2. After the fabric was stretched, the greenish-blue tone was applied overall to the white ground. The cool tint influences the tonality and creates the night-time atmosphere. Analysis of this layer indicates that it consists mostly of viridian and prussian blue.

2.3. The deeply cut lines in the wood of the stretcher indicate that the edges of the canvas were trimmed after mounting onto the stretcher. The cuts caused the wood to "bleed" or exude a dark brown resin.

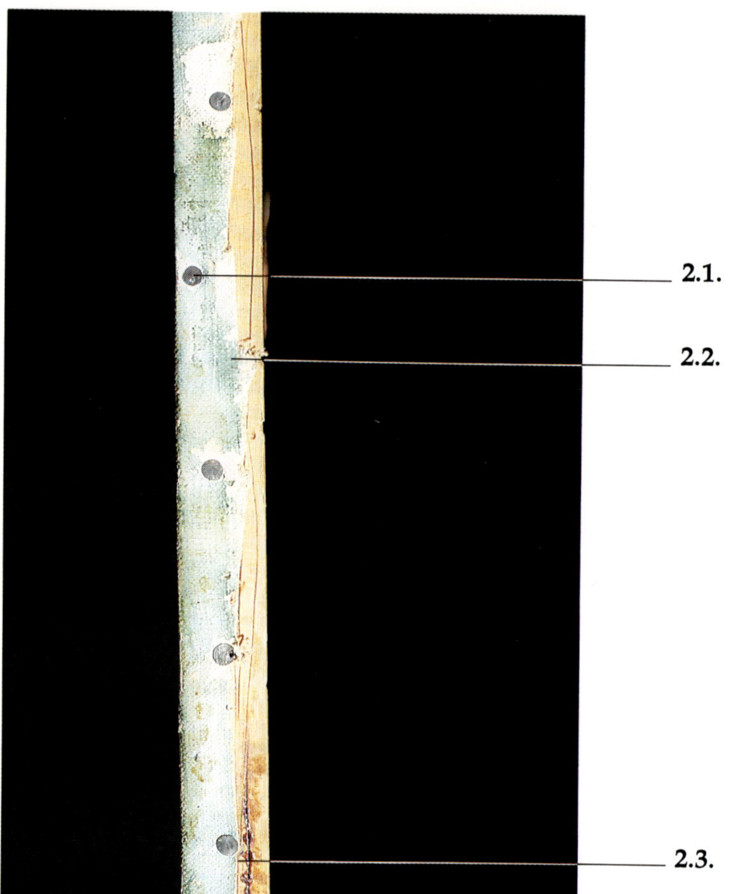

2. TACKING EDGE

3.1. For the tree, blurred edges were created with a wet-into-wet technique. Analysis shows these multicolored brushstrokes to contain a wide variety of pigments such as viridian, red lake, yellow lake, cobalt and prussian blue, and red iron oxide.

3.2. The paint in the sky is smooth and glossy. Little brush texture is evident, indicating that the paint was rich in medium and fluidly applied.

3.3. The thin and transparent blue-green tone that was applied directly onto the white ground can be seen here where the painting technique left it partially exposed in the foliage, the beams of the roof, and in the building.

3.4. Lean paint has been dragged across the surface, leaving little gaps that allow the underlayers to show.

3.5. Multiple color brushstrokes make up the adobe bricks. The colors were not mixed on the palette, but were picked up individually and applied in one stroke.

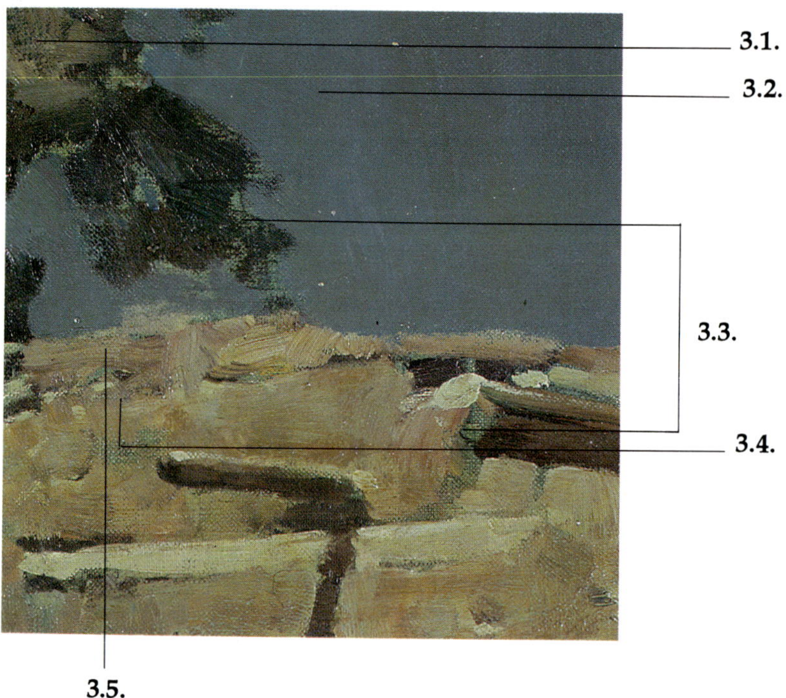

3. DETAIL OF SKY AND ROOF OF BUILDING

The tree was painted first, followed by the building. The sky was applied last and can be seen to overlap some of the foliage and the roof top.

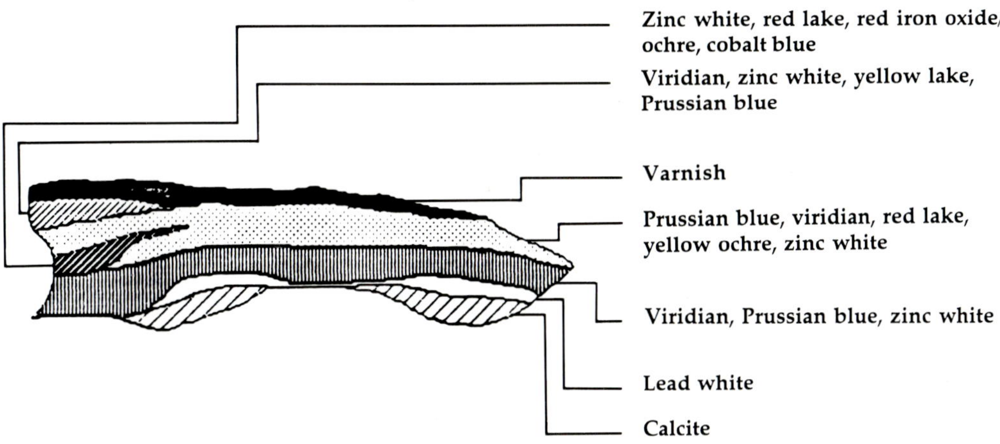

3A. Cross-Section from Sky and Roof of Building

This cross-section shows the complicated build-up of Johnson's paint layers. The bottom two layers are the double ground. The next layer, made up mostly of viridian and prussian blue, is the colored wash applied over the ground. The remaining pigmented layers indicate paint applied wet-into-wet. The top layer is varnish.

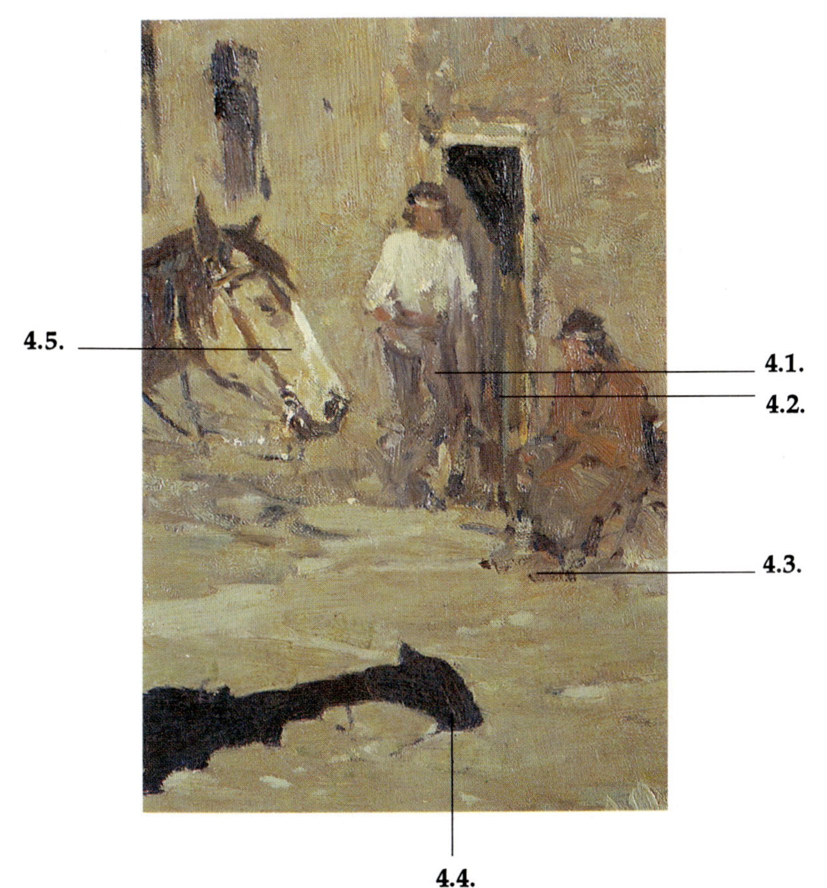

4. Detail of Figures and of Horse's Head

4.1. The paint has been worked and reworked wet-into-wet, creating a blurred image of the standing figure. The right side of the figure is indistinct and melts into the doorway.

4.2. The subsequent paint layers do not completely conceal the toned ground which is clearly visible in the doorway.

4.3. The seated Indian was painted with a few earth-colored brushstrokes in a very fast and sketchy manner. Some red lake brushstrokes were dragged rapidly to indicate the feet and the shadows.

4.4. The color of the shadow contains a wide range of pigments such as cobalt and prussian blue, viridian, red lake, and red ochre.

4.5. As a short cut, Johnson has painted the horse on top of the background, using the wall of the house as the body color for the head, thus limiting the color range. This would be in keeping with night vision which is partially monochromatic. Details of the head were added next. Spatially, the wall lies farther back in the picture plane so the use of the wall for the body color makes the horse's head seem slightly out of focus.

5.1. Johnson used a hard tool to scrape away paint and ground in a forceful, almost violent way. This exposed the bare fabric at the top of the weave, breaking up the surface to depict reflected moonshine.

5.2. The transparent blue-green wash has a yellowish tinge due to the varnish which covers the surface of the painting. The varnish has yellowed with age.

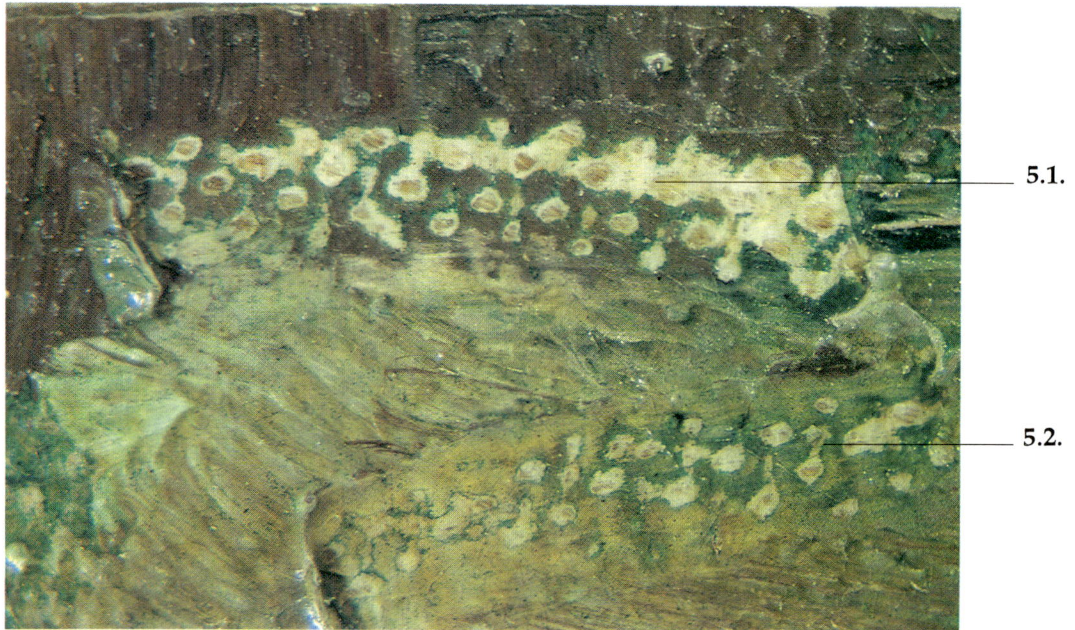

5. MICROGRAPH OF ROOF OF HOUSE

6.1. The brown paint of the viga has been dragged in a vertical direction.

6.2. The transparent blue-green tone has been rubbed to expose the white ground as well as the bare fabric on the top of the canvas weave.

6.3. The magnification of the micrograph shows an accumulation of surface dirt and discolored varnish in the impasted white dab of paint.

6.4. The light brown color contains some white and red lake, mixed in a wet-into-wet technique.

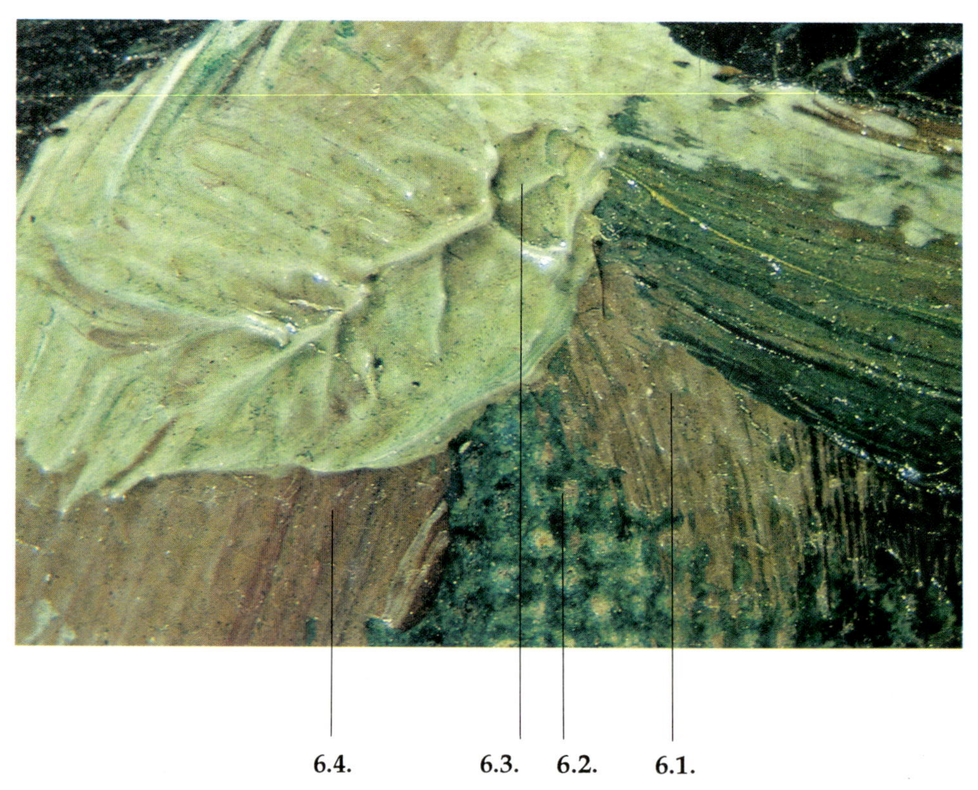

6. MICROGRAPH OF DAB OF COLOR ON TIP OF BEAM OR *VIGA*

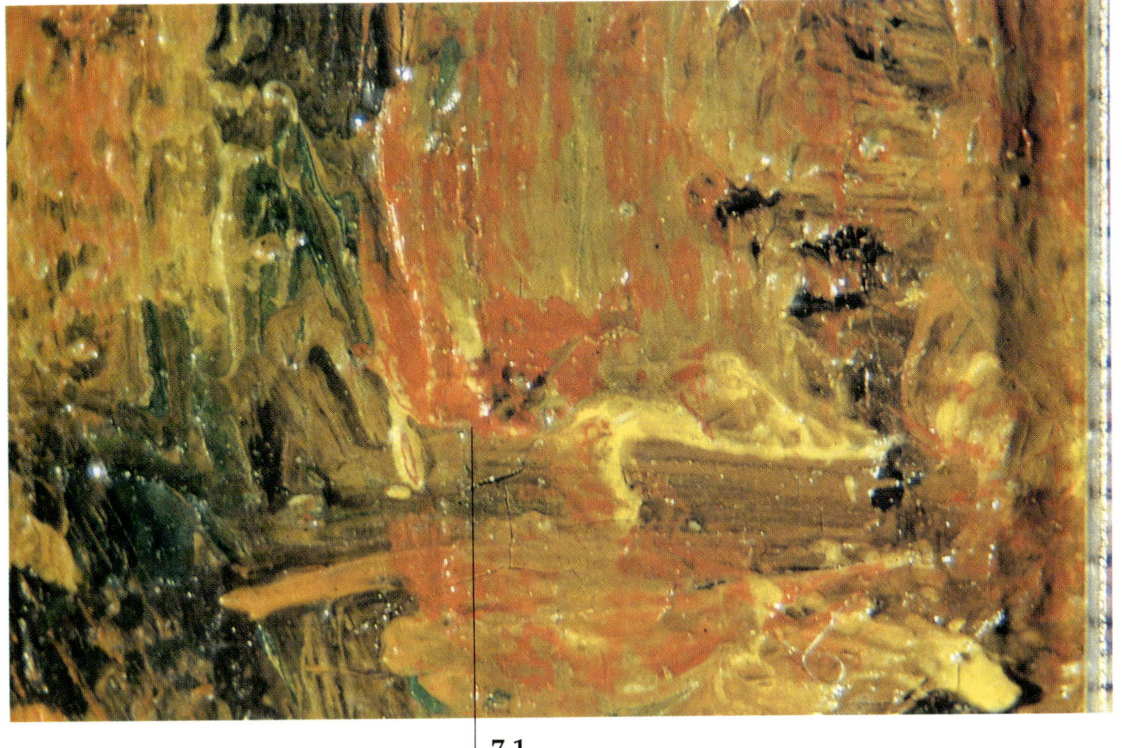

7.1.

7. MICROGRAPH OF RED-ORANGE LIGHT IN WINDOW

The scale on the right edge indicates millimeters. The great magnification of a micrograph dramatizes the mixing of colors resulting from a wet-into-wet technique.

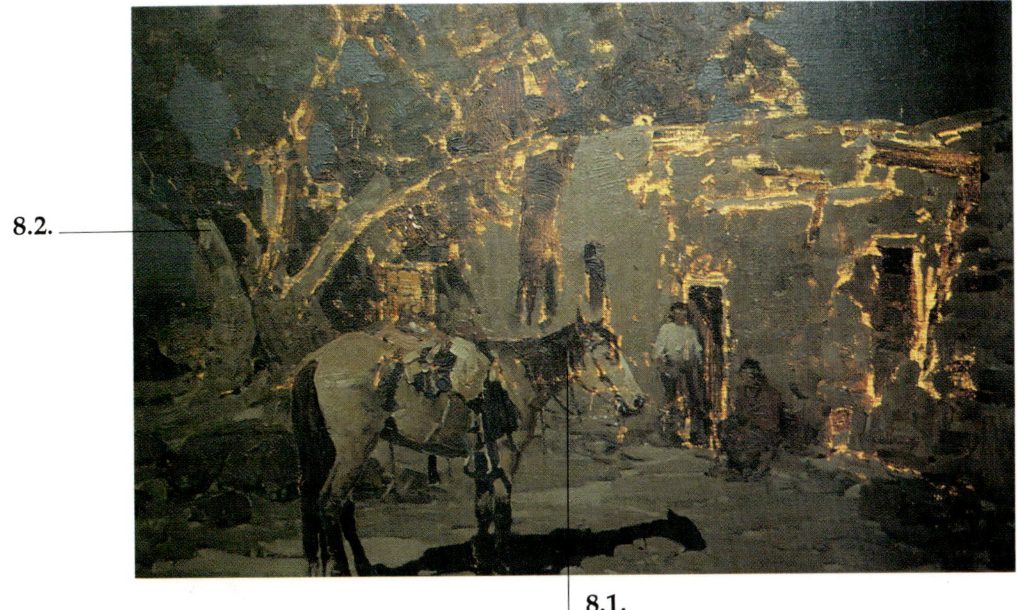

8.2.

8.1.

8.1. The bright line crossing the horse in a horizontal direction originates as part of the house. The absence of any bright line outlining the horse indicates that the animal was painted on top of all of the layers. Thus, the horse was painted last.

8.2. Some alterations are also evident in the tree. The center and right branches of the trunk are surrounded by bright lines indicating that in his original conception of the composition, Johnson knew where he wanted the sky to end and the tree to begin. The foliage and branches on the left side of the tree show no such bright lines or gap. A possible explanation would be that he added more foliage to the tree, overlapping into the sky, in order to build up the effect of depth by contrasting thicker paint on the left with the thinner paint on the right.

8. DETAIL OF PAINTING SEEN IN TRANSMITTED LIGHT

Here the source of illumination is placed behind the picture. Dark areas represent thicker paint where the light cannot penetrate. The areas of thinner paint let light through and appear a bright yellow-orange which is the color of light transmitted through canvas. This manner of viewing the painting gives some insight into the order in which various elements were painted as well as changes the artist made.

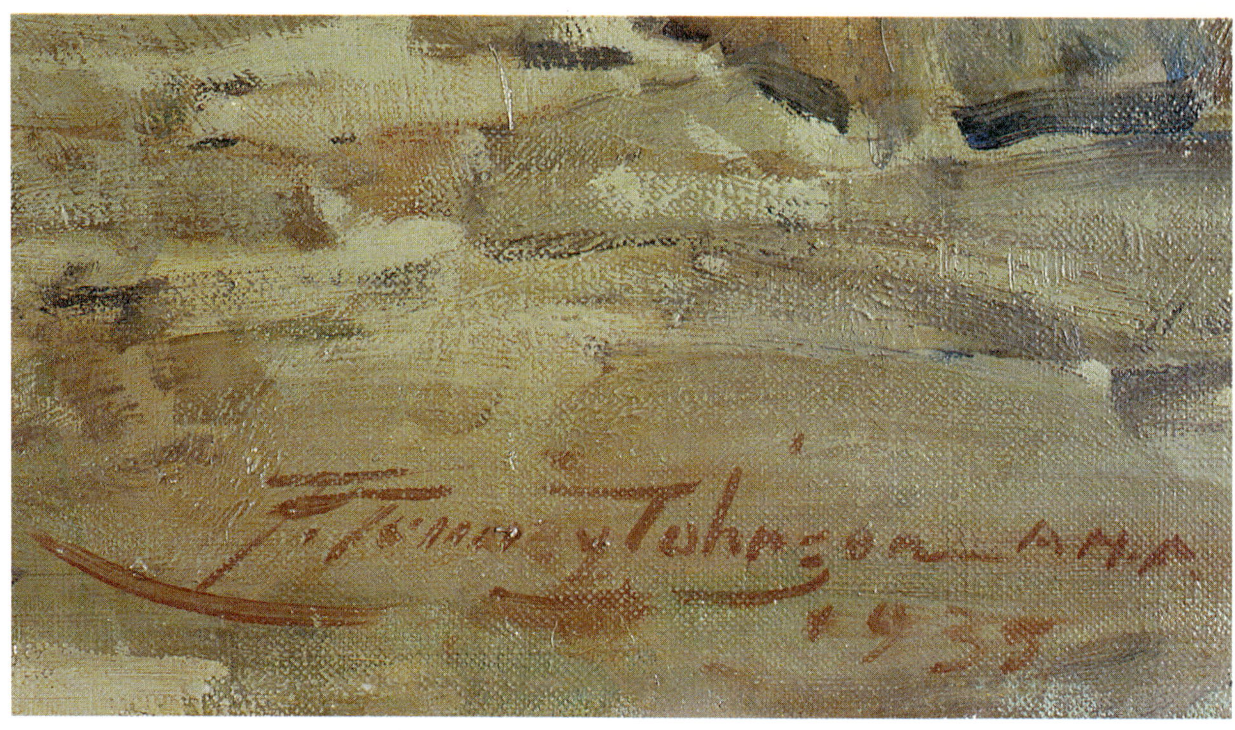

9. DETAIL OF SIGNATURE

F. Tenney Johnson A.N.A. 1935

Johnson's use of the designation A.N.A. indicates his pride in having been elected an Associate of the National Academy of Design in 1929. Some Western masters like Frederic Remington thought the honor too insignificant to acknowledge on paintings.

SUMMARY OF PAINTING TECHNIQUE

a. A canvas with a commercially prepared white ground was attached to the stretcher, probably by the artist.
b. A thin and transparent blue-green wash was applied over the white ground.
c. The main composition including the foreground, building, part of the tree, and the sky was done in this step.
d. Small sections of the paint and ground were scraped out with a sharp tool, leaving distinct marks on the canvas.
e. In a further step the horse and the figures as well as the rest of the tree were added.
f. Final touches were applied completing the painting and unifying the components.
g. The painting was varnished with a natural resin.

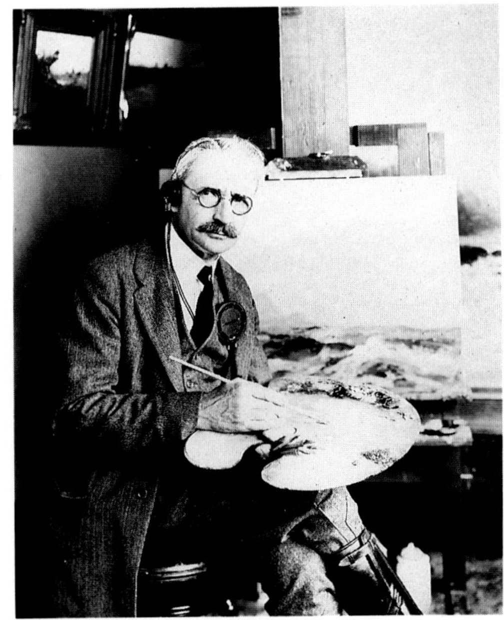

SYDNEY LAURENCE

The master painter of the American West who triumphed over the greatest physical hazards to reach his subject was without doubt Sydney Laurence. To become the first artist to paint Mount McKinley in the south-central Alaskan interior, he left the farthest outpost of civilization by himself in the late winter of 1913. He led five sled dogs over unmarked snow fields in sub-zero weather for almost three months, just to get to a suitable location for sketching this highest peak in North America. Even the native Indians would not go as far as he ventured.

In comparison, Albert Bierstadt was the first important landscape painter to penetrate the Western Rockies of the lower territories. His trip was in mid-summer 1859. Although that was more than 50 years before Laurence's solitary trek, Bierstadt rode in moderate comfort in a government wagon on an expedition guided by Colonel F.W. Lander, a professional surveyor familiar with the mountains.

By Laurence's time in 1913, Bierstadt's frontier beyond the Mississippi had officially been labeled "tamed" for almost a quarter of a century. The West was already said to be roads, mortgages, fences, and dude ranches rather than the United States Cavalry fighting rampaging Indians in the trackless wild. The wonder at transcontinental railroads had given way to automobiles on highways. In 1913 no relatively cossetted Westerner could conceive of the risks Laurence was taking and the privations he was enduring.

Unfortunately, the particulars of Laurence's adventures are among the least documented of the master painters. The details come from an unreliable source, the artist himself. Worse, what happened was filtered through his widow long after the events occurred. He had called her Kid. Her pet name for him was Sweetie. It would have been unusual for him not to exaggerate what he had achieved while recounting his experiences for an impressionable woman much younger than he was.

Sydney Mortimer Laurence was born in Brooklyn, New York on October 14, 1865, two years before Secretary Seward purchased Alaska from the Russians. According to the artist, his grandfather was an English admiral who had been the first governor of New

South Wales in Australia. Laurence claimed to have been named after the city of Sydney where his father Sir Lester Laurence II had supposedly been born. Laurence's story was that Sir Lester was the founder of the New York Life Insurance Company and the family was both noble and well-to-do.

His mother was an amateur artist. She taught him to paint. When he was nine his proud father took a few of his paintings to Edward Moran for an informal evaluation. Moran was a marine painter, the older brother of the Western panoramist Thomas Moran. Edward Moran's reaction was given by Laurence as, "Remarkable! I have never taught but bring the boy and I will take him under my wing. There is a great talent in that little fellow." Instead, Laurence's father sent him to Peekskill Military Academy in New York for disciplinary reasons.

After Laurence graduated from the Academy at 17, he asked his father for permission to join the crew of a sailing vessel. He wanted to become more familiar with the oceans he expected to paint a la Edward Moran. Sir Lester refused. Laurence demonstrated how ineffectual the restraints of the training at the Academy had been by stowing away on the *Edmond Yates*, a ship captained by a friend of his father. When Sir Lester was told of the act of defiance, his instructions to the Captain were, "Keep him on board for four years. Don't let him on shore. Make a seafaring man out of him."

Laurence said that by the fourth year, he was first mate. When a hurricane struck the ship, the crew took to the lifeboats and were drowned. Laurence remained on board with the injured Captain. They were rescued in five weeks.

After these unsubstantiated references to ancestor nobility and heroic sailing, the tales become a little more verifiable. In 1886 Laurence enrolled in the art school of the National Academy of Design in New York City to study at last with Edward Moran, who had presumably changed his mind about teaching. Laurence was 21. He left Moran in 1889 to enter the *Ecole des Beaux-Arts* in Paris.

At the end of five years in France, his schooling was over. He moved to a studio in the St. Ives art colony where he joined the ranks of English marine painters. Professional and social success came immediately. He was elected to the Royal Society of British Artists and claimed to be an intimate of the Prince of Wales.

His sketching trips were by bicycle rather than boat. As an artistic idiosyncracy, he built a covering for his cycles out of old canvases he had painted and discarded. When he was without a new painting to exhibit in the Paris Salon he took down, cleaned, re-stretched, and repainted the canvas that was the roof of his cycle shed. He titled the picture *Setting Sun, Coast of Cornwall* and won an award.

As a hobby he played the harp. An avocation was more serious. He loved the dangers involved in serving as a war correspondent. In 1894 he went to Zululand to cover an uprising. Although he took refuge in the center of a classic British defensive square, the Zulus overran the soldiers' lines. He was hit on the head with a knobkerrie that permanently impaired his hearing. Despite the handicap, he went to the Spanish-American War as a correspondent in 1898.

He relished shocking female audiences with earthy anecdotes. He told them he had returned to South Africa to cover the Boer War in 1899. While he was riding as an observer with the Rangers, his horse was shot and he was treated in the hospital for a wound in the buttocks. Two hours later, he said, another mount was shot from under him and he received a second wound in the buttocks. This time the doctor told the orderlies to "stick this man in the hospital before he comes back with his whole ass shot off." Laurence insisted he had the scars to prove the story. His audience took his word for the episode.

The following year he was in China for the Boxer Rebellion. He said he went to sleep in a freight car in the battlefield and woke up surrounded by hostile Chinese. According to Laurence, he proved he was a correspondent by drawing the faces of his captors and they let him go.

In 1904 Laurence was bitten by the Klondike gold bug. He ceased painting and sailed to New York where he visited his mother. She offered no financial support. He then took the train to Seattle and the boat to Juneau, wearing a stylish raccoon coat and hat he had bought in New York. After quickly making new friends, he decided to stay in Juneau where he found work as a photographer, a trade he had practiced in England. In the spring he sailed on to Valdez. Because of a shortage of laborers he was able to obtain a job as a skilled carpenter though he had no experience with woodworking.

For the next seven years he prospected during the summers. Each year he found enough gold dust to carry him into the winter when he took odd jobs. He was cook, lumberjack, and boat pilot. To explain his fascination with prospecting he quoted the plebeian poet Robert W. Service, "Once you've panned the speckled sand...."

Freakish outbursts of nature plagued him. He was caught on the fringes of a volcanic eruption. In 1912 a storm wrecked his dory and froze his limbs while he was sailing down Cook Inlet. He was cared for by Athapaskan Indians until he could be moved to the primitive hospital in Valdez.

The desire to paint again had surfaced two years earlier. He began carrying a sketch book wherever he went. During his recuperation in the hospital he was thinking, "I wonder why no artist has ever gone to Mount McKinley to paint?" On Christmas Eve he solicited fellow prospectors in the Seattle Saloon, promising that "when you boys are willing to grubstake me, I will paint you a $10,000 painting."

Five of the men raised $400 for a half interest in the possibility of a masterpiece. That was all the money they said they had. They also gave him a letter of credit of questionable value for the balance of what he might need. It could take 12 months for one man to get in to paint Mount McKinley and come out again.

Laurence boarded the boat for Seward the same night, without stopping to buy a ticket. He was afraid that his sponsors would change their minds and want their money back. From Seward he ordered painting materials to be shipped from Seattle. Then he bought five dogs, a sled, and provisions and started for Mount McKinley. His hands and feet were still sensitive. The time was March 1913 which remained a harsh part of the Alaskan winter.

The quantity of goods he needed for a project that might take a long time was too much for one sled load. He had to break the hauling down into a number of shorter trips. At the end of each, he would elevate the supplies into a cache and go back to Seward for another load. After 200 miles, the mapped trail came to an end at the Susitna River. From there on, he walked on snowshoes ahead of the dogs to break the surface of the snow that would otherwise have been too deep for them.

At last he gained sight of Mount McKinley. In May he pitched his tent to the south of the mountain, 45 miles from the top that had never been climbed. The camp was at the edge of the timber line.

The view from the camp was of the massive mountain overlooking the valley of the Tokositna River into which three glaciers descended. Measured from the base which was near sea level to the 20,320 foot crest, Mount McKinley was the highest in the world. Other great mountains rose from plateaus, so McKinley would be the most imposing of all to paint.

Laurence cut enough wood to last the summer and was ready to go to work. Before beginning, however, he had to backtrack to Seward to pick up the art supplies he had ordered months earlier. Downhill and with an empty sled, the trip took only a few lighthearted days.

Back in camp, he studied the mountain for hours. He was awed by the glorious sunrise, by the changing colors and atmospheres during the day, and by the sunset. For awhile he was afraid he might not have the talent to do justice to the scene but he made his sled into an easel and started painting. By fall he had done 45 oil sketches. Surprisingly, in view of his skill as a photographer, he had no camera with him.

It was necessary for him to leave before the first snow. He never said what happened to the sled dogs. He abandoned everything he could not carry on his back and was lucky to be able to join a few prospectors who were rafting down the river. A steamer took him from Seward to Valdez where he rented a small studio in December 1913. He had been away almost a year.

His sponsors were glad to see him. They had assumed he was dead. He soon set to work and painted a panoramic 6x8 foot view of Mount McKinley he called *Top of the Continent*. It was agreed to place the picture on loan at the National Collection of Fine Arts in Washington. Exhibiting the work would support a campaign to establish Mount McKinley as a National Park.

In November 1914 the massive painting was on its way to the capital. The 45 sketches were all sold and Laurence was prepared to start back to Mount McKinley in the spring of 1915 for more studies. He was well enough off financially to hire two Indians to carry his things as far as they would go toward the mountain.

He returned to Anchorage in the fall. To tide himself over the winter he again opened a photography shop where he also hung his watercolors. A tourist bought every picture he had. For the first time Laurence felt financially able to paint in Anchorage for the entire year. He sold the shop and rented a studio.

Summers he now prospected for gold only as a diversion from painting. Winters he spent in Anchorage, preparing his work for sale to tourists. His technique was a throwback to the early panoramists of the Rockies.

In 1926 he began wintering in Los Angeles and in 1928 he married there. In 1940 he started to complain about feeling tired. September 8 he asked to enter the hospital and the next morning he was in a coma. He died September 12.

Top of the Continent remained on loan to the Smithsonian Institution. The five grubstakers and their heirs tried to recover the painting to sell it but they could prove only a half interest. In 1967 the heirs to the other half showed up. While Laurence was in Seattle in December 1914 and the painting was on the way to Washington, he had secretly sold his share to W.A. Dickey for $1,000. More than a quarter century after Laurence's death, *Top of the Continent* was removed from the Smithsonian and sold for the benefit of the private owners.

1. THE PAINTING

Sydney Laurence was born only two years after the founding of the *Salon des Refusés* in Paris, which marked the break of the incipient Impressionists with the Academic establishment. The term Impressionism was coined by the time he began his studies and the modern art revolution was under way.

Working in Paris in the early 1890s, Laurence surely was aware of these dramatic changes in the art world, yet he chose to follow a more traditional artistic path. In the catalogue of the 1895 Paris Salon Laurence described himself as a "pupil of Edward Moran" even though he had been studying abroad for more than five years.

Thus, by Laurence's own admission and by the style of his works one can deduce that he was influenced by the mid-19th century Hudson River School of painting and more importantly by the seascapes of Edward Moran. Perhaps indirectly he was also influenced by Turner, with whom both Moran brothers were smitten. Turner was among the first to establish the colony at St. Ives, a center of marine painting where Laurence lived before going to Alaska.

In keeping with his training as a marine painter, the foreground of *Mt. McKinley* is dominated by the turbulent water of the Tokositna River, a view he painted many times. The space of the horizontal composition recedes in well organized planes, a formula

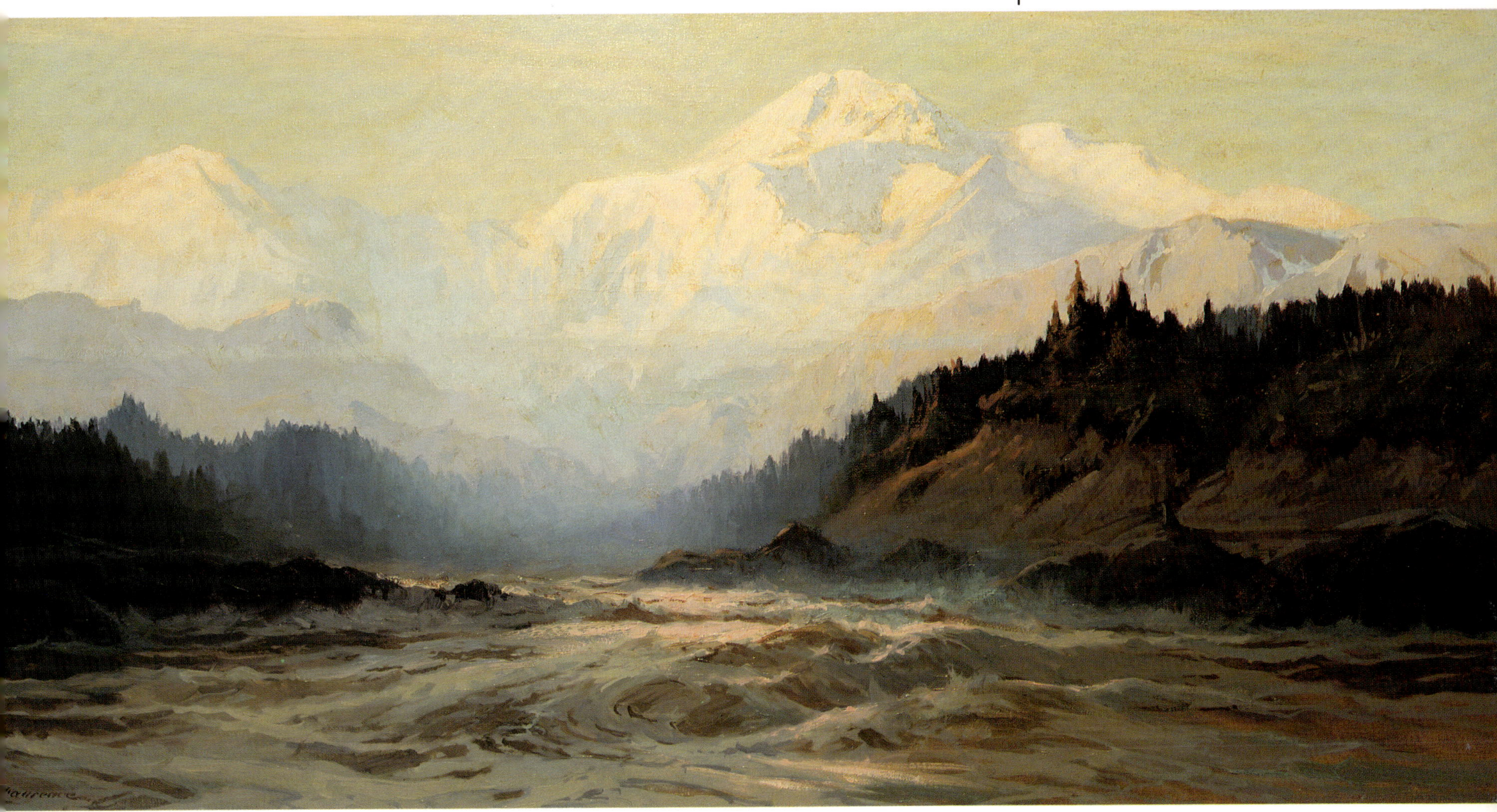

generally practiced by 19th century landscape painters.

Because of the use of this prescribed layout, the first impression is of an older painting. A closer look reveals bold brushwork which produces semi-abstract patterns, especially in the rushing water of the foreground. Furthermore, the incorporation of vivid colors such as purple and blue, particularly for the underlayers, shows a departure from the use of more conventional brown tones. Like the Impressionists, Laurence was a colorist, emphasizing hue rather than line as his mode of expression.

For *Mt. McKinley* Laurence used a cotton/linen mixed fiber canvas. This fabric might have been chosen because it was thought to be more stable when exposed to climatic changes than pure linen, or because it was a less expensive alternative to pure linen. The canvas was commercially prepared with a white ground. There is no evidence of an underdrawing. The artist's familiarity with the subject may have made this unnecessary.

The technique is quite simple. The uninhibited handling indicates a rapid working process. The application of paint is generally smooth and thin, not concealing the texture of the fabric. The mountains, however, were painted with thicker, slightly impasted paint. In the foreground and middle distance, tinted underlayers were used not only as shadows, but also as base colors onto which details and highlights were added. These underlayers add to the overall translucence, especially where thinly applied, allowing the reflective white ground to show at the tops of the canvas weave.

Linear perspective was used to create a sense of depth. The rocky shores of the river converge at a central vanishing point which leads the viewer's eye over the churning water. The viewpoint could only be from the middle of this unfriendly river, a location which engages one's attention and brings on an involuntary shiver.

Sydney Laurence. Mount McKinley is in a private collection on loan to the Museum of Western Art, Denver, Colorado. Oil on canvas. 24 1/8 inches (61.3 cm) height x 48 1/4 inches (122.5 cm) width. Signed lower left. Not dated.

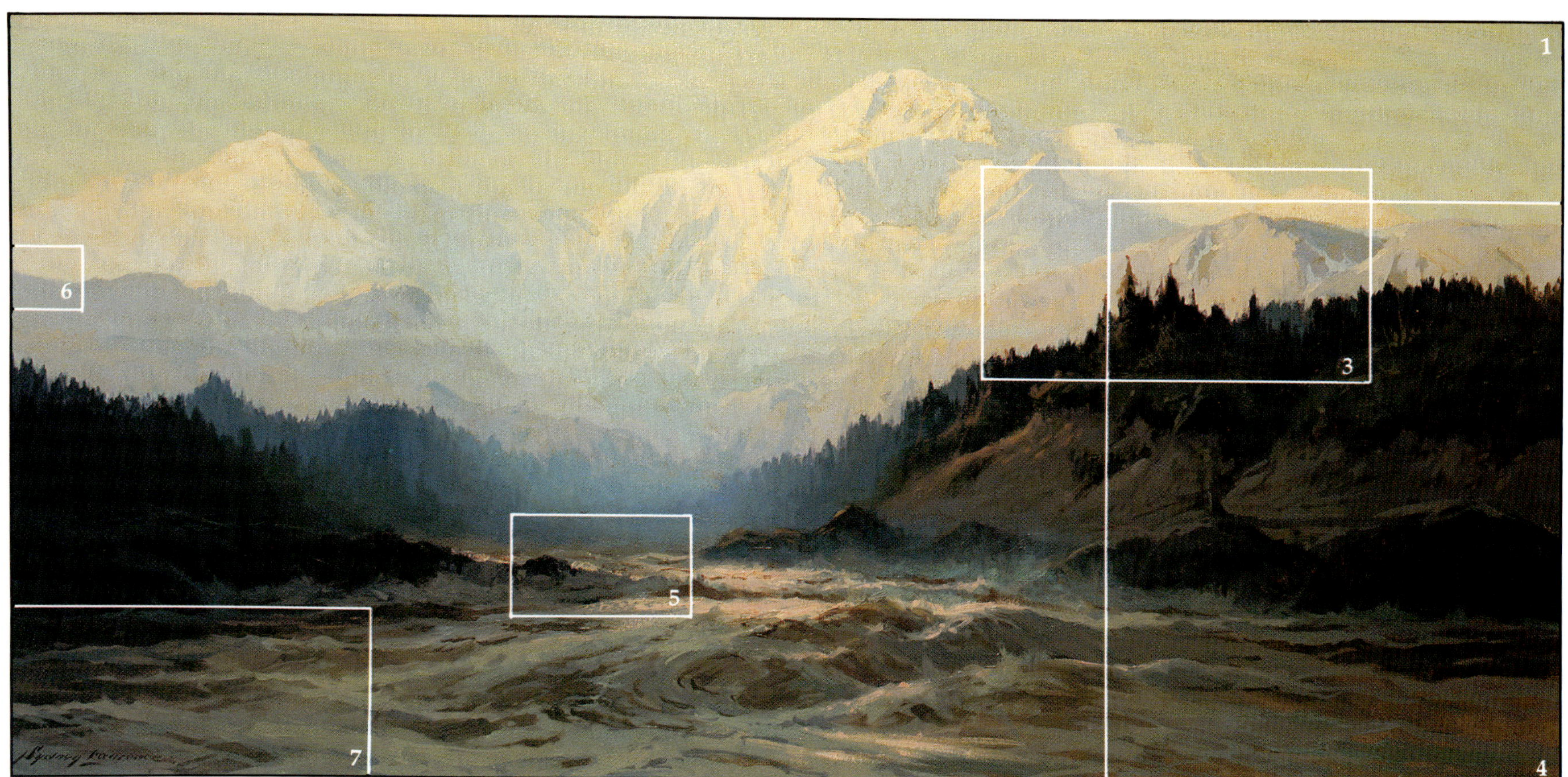

Depth is enhanced by the juxtaposition of freely applied dilute colors with opaque paint. For example, the brilliant, reflective snow of the sculpted mountain appears massive against the loose brushwork and varied palette of the foreground and middle distance. On a closer scale, the milky and opaque strokes applied across the transparent greenish river water stand out in high relief.

The slightly yellow, overall appearance originates from the varnish which has discolored with age. Other paintings by Laurence that remain in original condition have similar discolored and unevenly applied varnish, indicating that this is the original surface.

By the time Laurence was born, Whittredge, Hill, and Bierstadt had travelled to the West and Thomas Moran would soon be on his way. The West they captured in paint had already been explored, tamed, and trampled when Laurence was seeking adventure. The still remaining wilderness of the Alaskan frontier satisfied his need.

Laurence's desire to pioneer ended with his accomplishment of being first to depict Mount McKinley. His painting technique, however masterful, stayed within secure and accepted bounds.

His ability to abstract the forms by means of individual dexterous brushstrokes marks his break from the earlier, more representational painters. His mastery of color as a primary means of expression and his concern with the depiction of light shows his awareness of contemporary styles prevalent in France, particularly the Impressionists. Yet his paintings remain romantic renderings derived from a conventional mode that had been well established in the 19th century.

While the only new ground that he broke may have been the trail to Mount McKinley, he nevertheless forms an important bridge between the American School and the European avant-garde. Laurence denotes the end of the landscape tradition practiced by the Western artist-explorers.

2. Detail of Reverse

As noted, the canvas appears to be a mixed fiber fabric. The cotton threads are lighter in color than the linen.

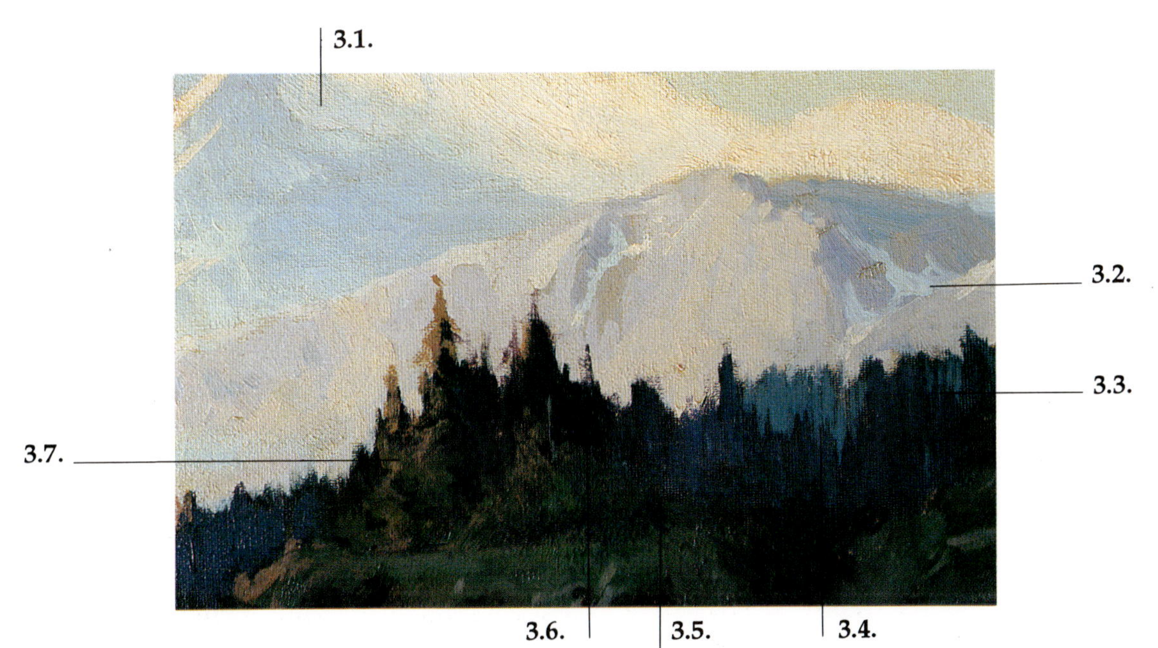

3. Detail of Trees and Mountains

By examining how the paint layers overlap, the work sequence can be determined. Laurence has used the logical working order of back to front, that is, starting with the sky, then the mountains, and finally the foreground. The brushwork is free, yet to the point. Each stroke is essential. The palette is varied with a range of vivid colors contrasted with mixed shades of gray and earth colors. Depth is enhanced by contrasting bright with dull hues, and contrasting thin with more densely applied paint.

3.1. The light blue was partially blended with the white of the mountains producing atmospheric cloud-shrouded peaks.

3.2. Liquid bluish-white paint creates a glacier-like effect of flowing ice.

3.3. Dark blue was applied beneath the blue trees, and blue-violet beneath the green trees. The bare white tops of the canvas weave add to the luminous properties of these thinly applied, pigmented underlayers.

3.4. Milky blue paint was sketched on with up-and-down passes of the brush. The darker blue underlayer shows at the edges of the strokes making shadowy fringes of the pine needles. Color rather than line was used to emphasize form.

3.5. To capture the cool northern light of Alaska, a transparent blue-violet underlayer was used for the green trees.

3.6. The paint caught on the weave texture of the canvas creates the bristly silhouette of a fir tree.

3.7. Warm highlights were applied wet-into-wet to the trees with long zigzagging strokes, creating a range of hues and values from the bright gold treetops and the blue-green dappled sun on the foliage to the dark blue shadows.

4.1. A violet underlayer was used for the shadow of the rocks. Murky shades of gray were dashed over the underlayer to indicate the stone. The same gray was slurred across the tops of the rocks for a fallen tree. The paint of the tree was partially blended with the rocks making the forms almost indistinguishable, yet precisely evoking decaying matter along a riverbank.

4.2. A transparent greenish-brown underlayer was used for the muddy river. The layer was left exposed in most areas as a body color for the water. Long and fluid strokes of light blue and pinkish white were added. These opaque highlights stand out against the translucent underlayer, giving the water icy depth. Blue was scumbled over the edge of the river for the breaking waves.

4.3. The river bank was painted with opaque patches of varying gray hues.

4.4. The dark underlayer was left bare for the shadowy forest floor.

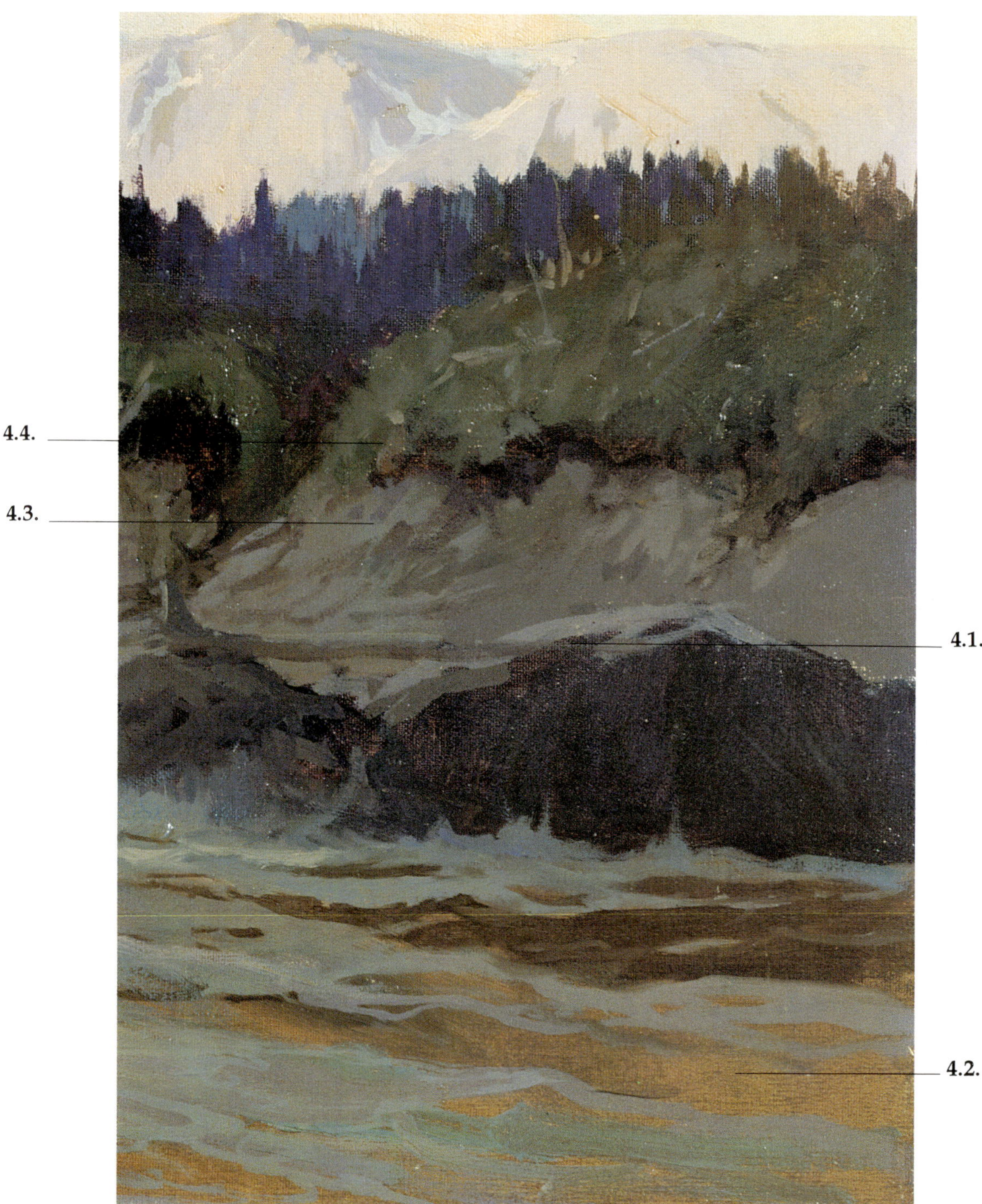

4. DETAIL OF RIVERBANK AND MIDDLE DISTANCE

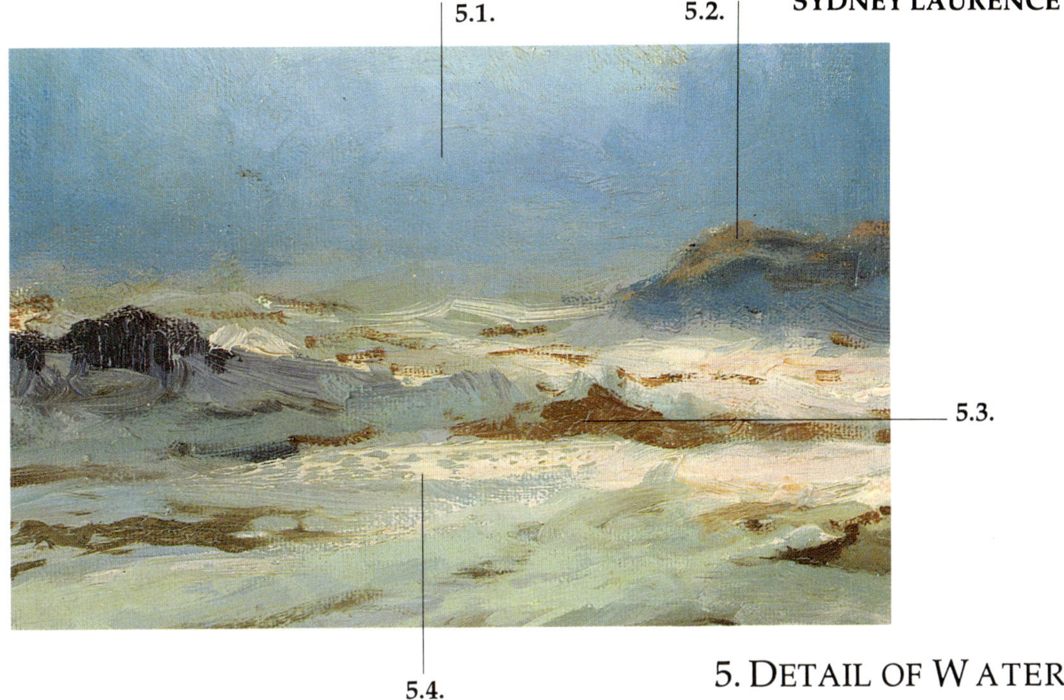

5. DETAIL OF WATER

5.1. Mixed blue scumbles create an atmospheric haze of sunlight filtering through mist.

5.2. Ochre was touched to a still wet, greenish-blue paint such as cerulean, and partially mixed in as a coppery highlight.

5.3 Early drying cracks occurred in the brown where it was applied diluted over richer, more slowly drying paint.

5.4 A deft stroke of pinkish-white was swiftly dragged across the surface, leaving small gaps in the paint that effect flickering light on frothing water.

This illustration demonstrates Laurence's painterly approach of juxtaposing individual brushstrokes to capture the image of energetic water. By its color, shape and consistency, each stroke has a precise meaning.

The facile brushwork is well suited to the depiction of freely flowing water. The paint ranges from thin and transparent to thick and opaque. The colors were mixed on the palette and applied, in places, wet-into-wet to be blended on the surface of the canvas. The paint varies from dry and dragged to rich and fluid.

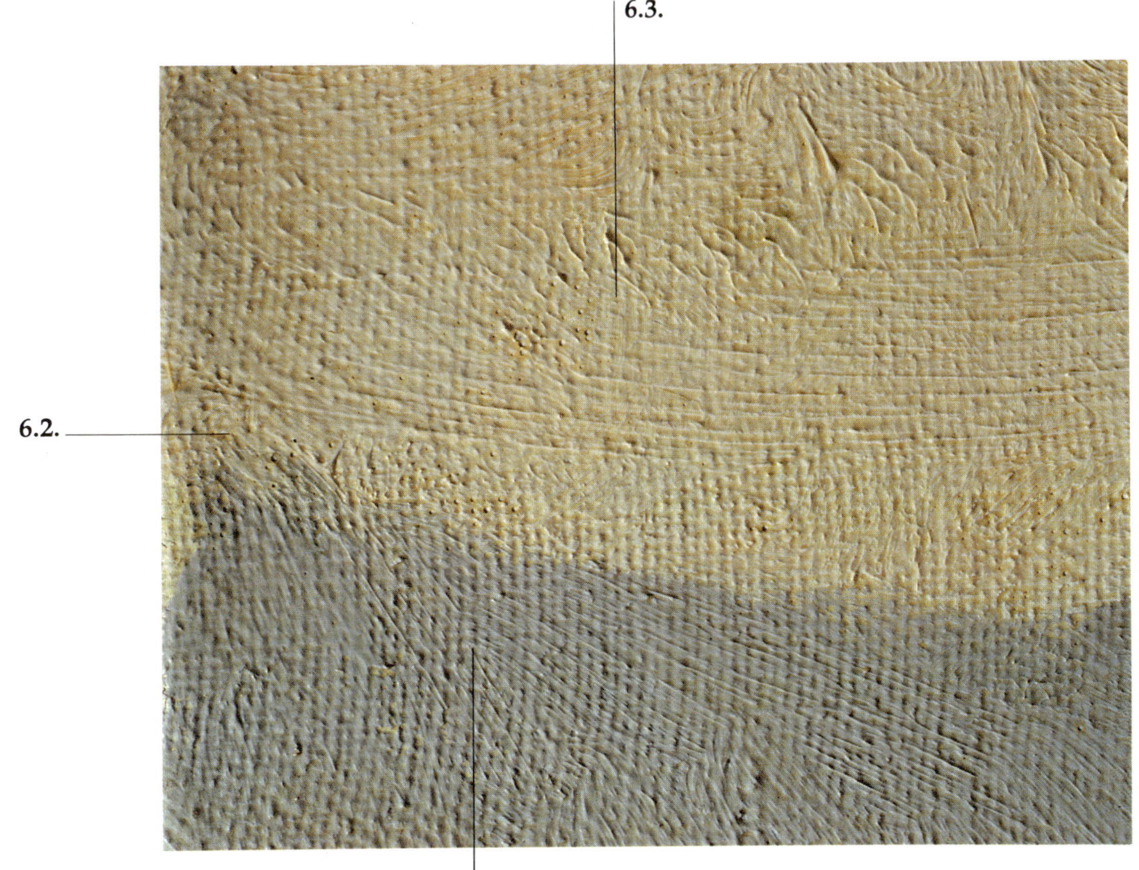

6. DETAIL OF HORIZON ON LEFT EDGE

6.1. Not all brushwork correlates to the top paint layer. The blue gets its diagonal pattern from brushstrokes of the paint layer beneath. This pattern of contrasting brushstrokes enlivens the sky.

6.2. The application of the paint is thin and does not conceal the texture of the fabric. Scallop shaped deformations along the edges of the fabric, referred to as cusping, are caused by the attachment of the canvas to the stretcher where the tacks have pulled the threads more tightly. By matching the points of the cusps with existing tacks, it can be determined whether or not the painting has been restretched. In this case, it has not.

6.3. Tiny air bubbles in the white paint may be caused by an absorbent ground and a rapid paint application.

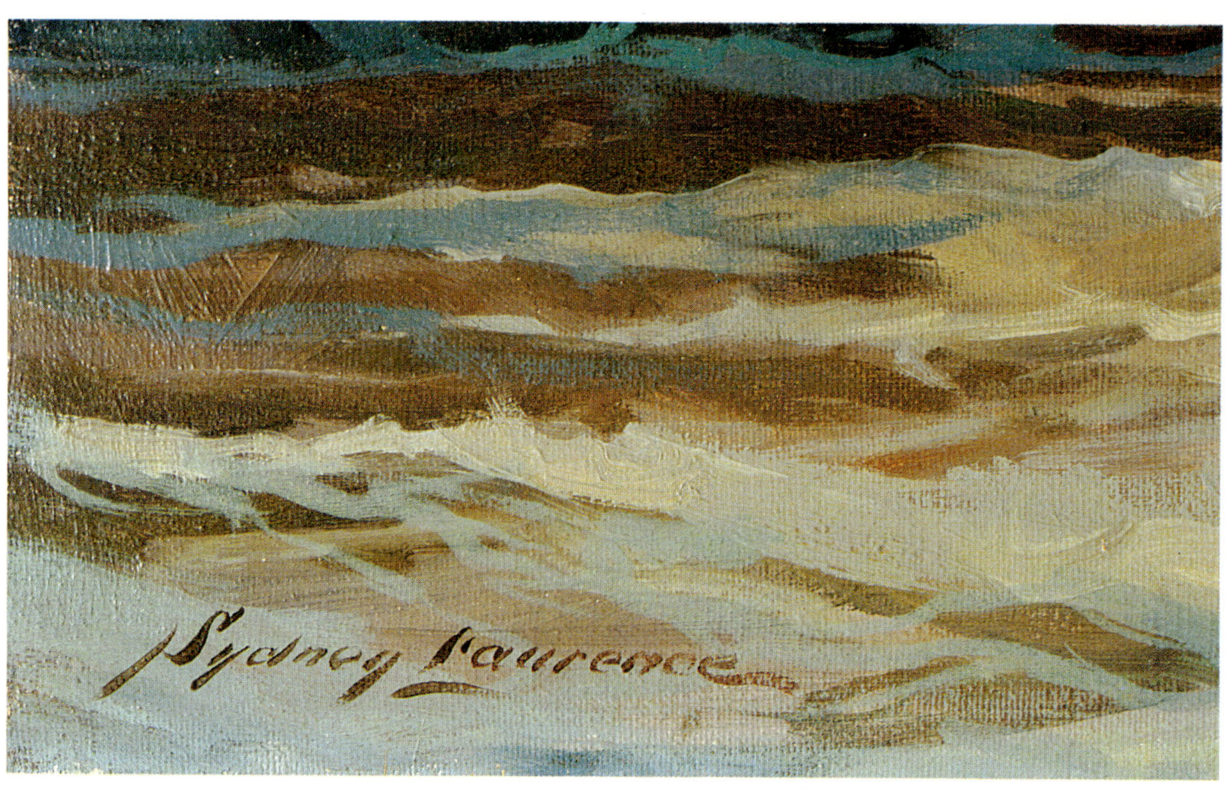

7. DETAIL OF SIGNATURE

Sydney Laurence

SUMMARY OF PAINTING TECHNIQUE

a. A white ground was commercially applied onto a plain weave, mixed cotton-linen fiber fabric.
b. Underlayers which serve as body colors and shadows were thinly applied. The white ground shows through at the tops of the canvas weave, increasing the overall luminosity.
c. Forms were built up with facile brushstrokes that are alternately impasted or fluid and dilute. This contrast enhances depth. Color rather than line was used to delineate shapes.
d. A natural resin varnish that has become yellowed with age was applied, probably by Laurence.

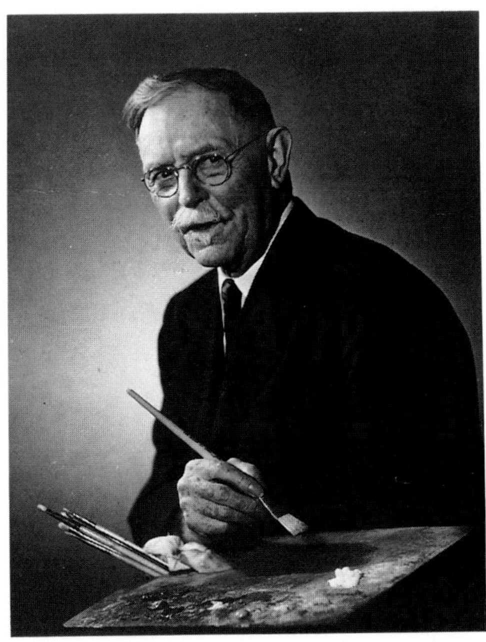

WILLIAM ROBINSON LEIGH

William Robinson Leigh was born September 23, 1866, within five years of his contemporaries Remington and Russell. He was frequently compared to them as an artist. He did not begin his career in the West, however, until 1906 when Remington was close to the end of his life and Russell was just gaining fame outside Montana.

Leigh's ultimate success as a Western painter did not come until he was past 70 and Remington and Russell were long dead. Then his honors and exhibitions lasted for another 20 years.

Part of the reason recognition eluded Leigh for so long was that fellow artists disliked him. He was constantly expressing delusions of persecution in his work. At other times he hallucinated about his own greatness as painter, author, actor, explorer, poet, and philosopher. He also showed himself to be a racist and a bigot. In spite of these serious emotional imbalances, however, he was professionally among the most highly trained artists and the best draftsmen of the master painters of the West.

Leigh's father had been a naval officer who married for money. Leigh's mother was delicate but testy and stubborn. By the time Leigh was born, his father's opulent West Virginia estate had been ruined in the Civil War. Yet, the artist was so proud of his ancestors in the Southern aristocracy, he even claimed false connections to Pocahontas and Sir Walter Raleigh.

Because the family was impoverished, Leigh had to be educated at home. The public school was not good enough to meet his mother's standards and private schools were prohibitively expensive. He never did learn how to spell. His father beat him because he was considered to be lazy and hostile but he actually felt inferior and defensive. He preferred the farm animals to his rich relatives.

The family thought of him as "a fool with a faculty for drawing." The greatest triumph of his childhood came when he was seven. He won a prize of $1 for figures he cut out of paper. When he was 14 an uncle took him to Baltimore and paid for his tuition at the Maryland School of Art. His teacher was Hugh Newell, a fine watercolorist who had studied extensively in Europe and had exhibited at the National Academy of Design.

Leigh was also financed by the collector W.W. Corcoran who later founded a Washington museum. Leigh said he soon "began to see the slow, sure, logical development of sincere painting." He became a teaching assistant to supplement the aid he was receiving and he broadened his social interests by attending plays including a performance of *Hamlet* by Edwin Booth.

After Leigh had been in Baltimore for three years, Newell recommended further study in Europe. Leigh wanted to go to Paris where Newell had been, but Paris cost $900 a year and Munich only $300. A second uncle agreed to pay the $300 but no more. France was out of the question.

Leigh was glad to leave home where he was still regarded as a freak. He sailed for Munich and the Royal Academy when he was 16. At the Academy he passed his competitive entrance examination along with two other youths from Baltimore. Typically, he thought they were mean and jealous of him.

While studying drawing for 13 hours a day six days a week he was a loner in a country where he did not yet speak the language. He saved his applause for Wagnerian operas. From the beginning of his training he would have preferred Paris where the art was graceful, as opposed to Munich where he thought the paintings were stiffly realistic, but the difference in cost remained insurmountable.

By the time he entered the fourth year at the Academy, there was no more money from home. Pressure was put on him to terminate his art education but he would not proceed faster than the pace that was comfortable for him and he would not be frugal.

"Willy" as his mother called him continually demanded more funds to support his trips, clothing, and entertainment as well as art, but the money well was dry. He had to come back to the United States in 1887 to earn enough by teaching to get back to Germany in 1888. That year at the Academy was "an indistinct blur of misery" because of poverty, until he found part-time work in Munich as a panoramist. His commitment in painting was to genre, so the employment suited him.

After 12 years at the Academy, he sold a prize-winning painting for $1,000 and returned to an 1896 America whose art appreciation was a cross between Currier & Ives and the mauve decade. Neither had any place for a 30-year-old thoroughly-Munich-trained painter who was long on drawing ability, draftsmanship, masterful manipulation of paint, and excessive detailing, but short on imagination and feeling.

When the profligate Leigh landed in New York, he had $40 in his pocket and no prospects. *Harper's Weekly* had sent scouts to Munich to search for younger and cheaper illustrators than those available in New York City, but Leigh had never attended one of their receptions. "At all costs," he explained, "I had hoped to avoid illustrating, yet it seemed as if I were doomed to do it." With no alternative he agreed to illustrate *Scribner's* magazine for $100 a page, a top rate. In 1897 Leigh was sent on his first Western trip to do pictures for a report on the wheat harvest.

In the small world of commercial art Leigh became known as fusty old "Buttons and Shoestrings" because of his meticulous depiction of minutiae. He was tired of the constraints of illustration, unable to obtain commissions for portraits, and divorced from his first wife. His break came in 1906 when a fellow Munich student, Albert Groll, invited him to visit the pueblo at Laguna, New Mexico in search of fresh subject matter. As usual, Leigh was penniless, but the Santa Fe Railroad gave him free transportation in exchange for a picture to be painted of the Grand Canyon.

At Laguna, Leigh exclaimed that "at last I was in the land where I was to prove whether I was fit or just a dunderhead." He "started in to paint, paint, paint!" When Leigh ran out of pocket money he made a quick trip to the Grand Canyon to satisfy the railroad and then went back to New York. "I knew now," he maintained, "that my field was in the frontier West." Though he was genre trained, half of his Western paintings in the next eight years were landscapes. His success was minimal.

He was still bound by the tightly realistic Munich mannerisms. He used engineering paper divided into squares for his preliminary drawings so there was no latitude for interpretation in producing the finished painting. In a 1913 depiction of a confrontation between man and grizzly, he photographed and sketched the man, the bear, and the actual background of the incident. Then he went back the next day to pace off the distances and count the exact number of trees to be in the composition.

He often complained about the vicissitudes of working in the open. Cloudy days defeated him because of the diffused lighting. He also had to protect his canvases against rain. Some of the Indians were unwilling models. Insects were a trial. He complained that "it took me an hour, with the point of a penknife blade, to pick the dead mosquitoes off my studies."

He did not find a New York dealer for his Western paintings until 1913. The critics were unfriendly. They reviled him as a photography-oriented illustrator with "a schoolboy's romantic vision of the West." He sought membership in the National Academy to help his sales but he was denied.

During World War I he was without painting commissions. He auditioned as an actor but was rejected there, too. Finally, he caught on as a painter of theatrical backdrops. Not until 1920 did his work begin to receive favorable reactions. He was 55 years old and his career as a painter was just starting.

He developed his personal Ten Commandments at this time. Featured were the agnostic "Thou shalt have no other God but Commonsense," the anti-black "Thou shalt not betray thy race," and the aesthetic "Thou shalt not cultivate the ugly."

He wrote unpublished essays opposing organized religion and favoring nature as exemplified by his Indian art with the idealized figures. Anglo-Saxons were praised at the expense of inferior blacks and exploiting Jews. Later in World War II he lauded Hitler. He excoriated jazz, cosmetics, and modern art. French painting was "Parisian sewer-psychology." Art critics were failed artists. The United States was an oligarchy of the 50 richest families.

His dignified appearance belied his peculiarities. He was tall, sturdy, and attentive, displaying the gracious manners of his Southern-planter forebears along with an appropriately massive mustache and goatee. His remarriage in 1921 was another demonstration of his eccentricity. The couple lived in separate apartments in different buildings. When he called on his wife, he had no key. He had to knock on her door.

In 1925 his career in art took its final detour. He was teaching a class in illustration when he heard that the American Museum of Natural History was planning an expedition to Africa and needed an artist. He secured the position, was gone for 14 months, and on his return was retained as supervisor of habitat painting in the Museum. He could portray native Africans scientifically, but American blacks he scorned.

His first published book was a never-performed drama claiming that Sir Francis Bacon wrote Shakespeare's plays. His second book, *The Western Pony*, was one of the 50 best books of 1933: "Since painting is an art, its mission is to produce impressions. It is photographically correct to paint the horse in action as the camera shows it, but it is artistically wrong because some of the phases of the stride do not convey the idea of rapid movement." Remington had practiced this 40 years earlier. Leigh's third book was on the African trip and it was a best seller.

He was financially able to return to painting full time in 1938. *Custer's Last Fight* was exhibited in 1939 and brought $10,000. His best years were the 1940s and his most widely publicized exhibition was in 1944. His trademark was the appearance of a burro in his pictures. He was 78 years old and his hand was still steady.

In the 1944 exhibition, Leigh was described as "the last great painter of the Old West" and "the only living member of the Remington-Russell-Leigh trio." His story was carried in 200 newspapers: "His principal admirers are not critics but western enthusiasts and anthropologists. They like his photographic realism and painstaking authenticity." Another reviewer wrote that in Leigh's work there was "no freakishness, no Freudian impulses wild-brushed for effete critics."

After World War II there was an increased demand for Western art. In 1948 Leigh painted 30 pictures. In 1949, he painted 17. He painted 32 in 1950 when he was 84. The National Academy elected him an Associate in 1953 and an Academician in 1955. There was a retrospective of his work the same year.

By 1955, however, his output had decreased to one painting every couple of months. March 11 he worked all day in his studio on 57th Street in New York City. His wife said that in the evening he told her he "was going to bed to read until sleep overtook him." Instead, it was death that caught up with him. Leigh's poetry remained unpublished but he correctly rhymed his own credo as, "My tameless soul/Has aye abhorred control."

In 1981 one of his earlier Indian paintings, the 25x30 inch *Zuni Pottery Painter* dated 1907, sold for $135,000 at public auction.

1. THE PAINTING

The vast Arizona desert is the stage for *Hopi Indian Runners*. The air is still and glimmers with heat. The desert floor resembles ocean waves as the calligraphic shapes of the blue shadows play across the rippled sand. The hunt stands out in vivid relief against the limitless land.

In sharp contrast to the pastel palette of the land and sky, the three men hunting their prey were painted in strong colors. The interplay of light on the bodies in motion was well planned and accurately depicted. Two different sources were used for the strong lighting. The warmer hued highlights reflect off the sand onto their bodies and the cool, silvery colored highlights come directly from the sun at its zenith. Leigh probably set up the scenario in his studio, using models with the light sources placed appropriately for this picture. Deep shadows contained within the modeling contrast with the exaggerated highlights to create a sculptural representation of the hunters.

The intensity of the hunt is dramatized by the headlong plunge of the runners. The composition is a simple and strong triangle. At the apex is the raised arm of the Indian still standing. The raised foot at the right edge of the composition locates another angle of the triangle and the fleeing rabbit the third corner. This triangular theme is used repeatedly in *Hopi Indian Runners*. The inverted V formed by the upper legs of the standing Indian is completed by the extended arm of the middle Indian. The forward arm and torso of the top Indian form another triangle, and so on throughout the pose.

Leigh appears to have been influenced by various styles that he combined freely in this painting. The terse, decisive brushstrokes of the Indians' gypsy-like heads resemble Frans Hals' bold directional brushwork. The anatomically correct running rabbit brings Dürer's very realistic studies of rabbits to mind. Both influences could be attributed to Leigh's traditional European training.

Leigh also used the pointillist technique of the Impressionist painters to create the glittering desert sky. The effect of heat waves rising from the hot sand was created by the optical phenomenon of the short dabs of colored paint that mix in the viewer's eye. The influence that the French Impressionists, Seurat especially, had on Leigh's work is undeniable, although his appreciation of French art seemed to stop with the technique. When Leigh visited the momentous 1913 Armory Show in New York, the same year that *Hopi Indian Runners* was painted, his remarks indicated that the modern art exhibited there was not to his liking: "When our country was first invaded by the excretions of French absinthe fiends & soul-debased moral prostitutes at the Armory exhibition in 1913, few including myself could have been brought to believe possible the aberrations of which our land is capable."

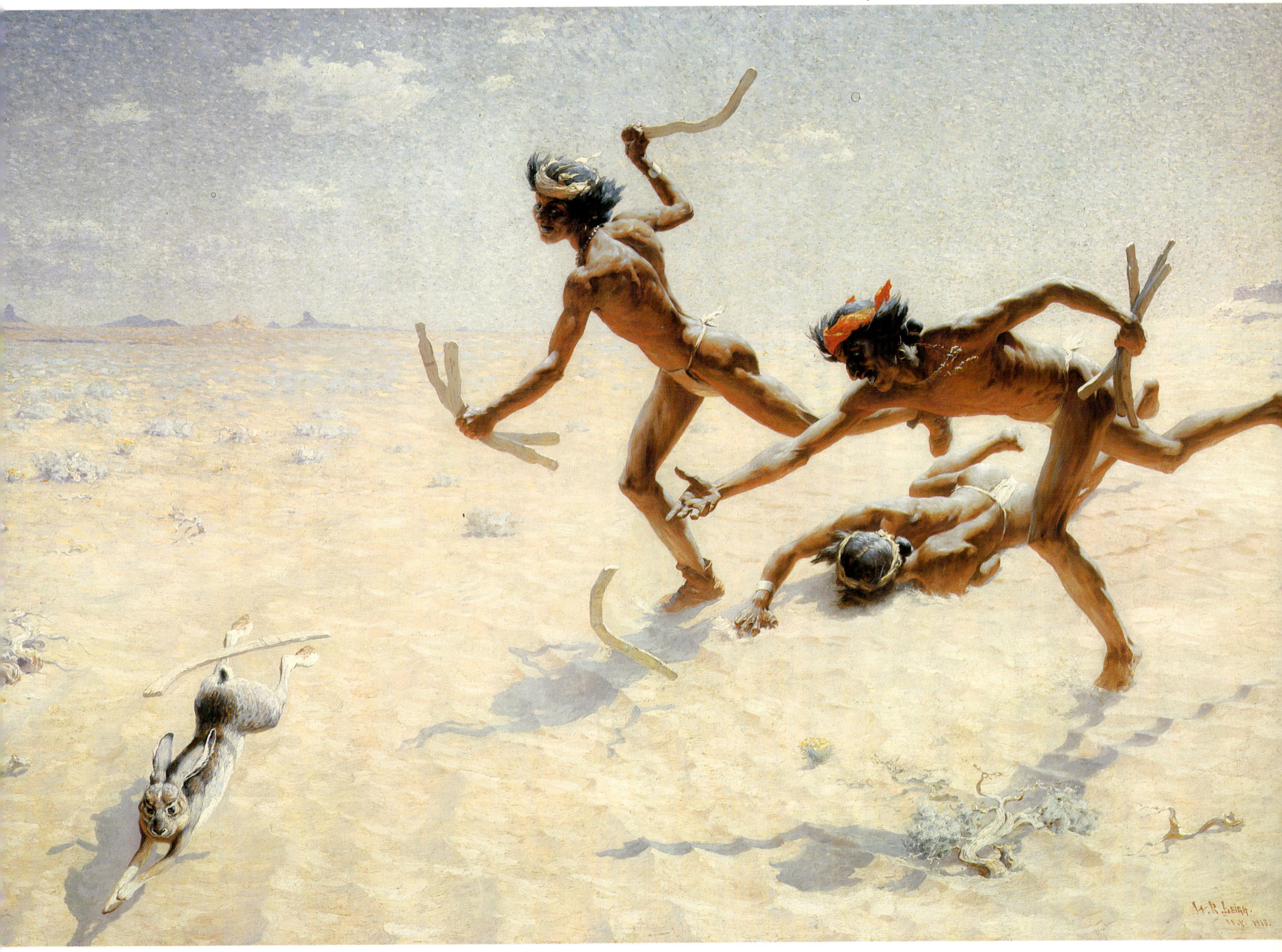

For *Hopi Indian Runners* Leigh used a very fine, lightweight canvas with a thin, light gray ground. A dark underdrawing can be seen along the edges of the figures where the paint is thin. The figures were methodically painted. First a thin underlayer of a warm brown middle tone was applied. This provided a ready base onto which the highlights and shadows were facilely added and in places blended slightly together to produce a smooth modeling. The thicker, more freely applied paint of the Impressionistic background was applied in an *alla prima* manner around the figures.

Like his contemporary Frederic Remington, Leigh was a masterful painter of dynamic motion. Both relied on deft hands to produce virtuoso brushwork. Both carefully choreographed their action to have the greatest impact. Both depicted romantic views of an exciting West that had already succumbed to the abuses of civilization. Where they differ is in the pervading spirit of the action.

Leigh's rigorous early training in Germany remained his greatest influence. His very

W.R. Leigh. Hopi Indian Runners *is in the collection of the Museum of Western Art, Denver, Colorado. Oil on canvas, lined. 40 inches (101.3 cm) height x 59 3/4 inches (151.7 cm) width. Signed lower right and dated 1913.*

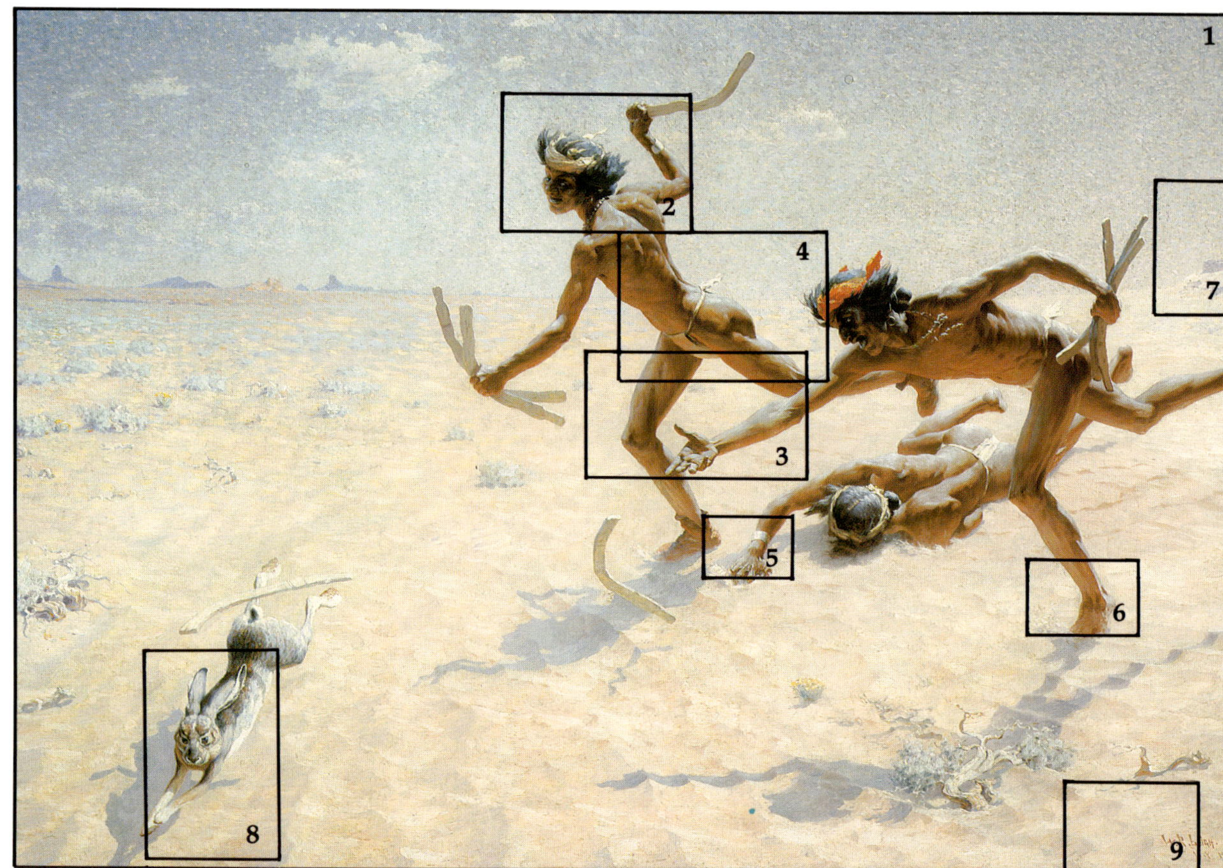

complete and almost exaggerated anatomy has been achieved with an economy of terse, directional brushstrokes. Every muscle and tendon stands out and has been accounted for. Despite the high drama depicted, all of this attention to anatomical detail serves only to give the picture a staged look. One has the feeling that the models had to hold their poses a little too long. Remington, on the other hand, was willing to forgo details in deference to capturing the action of the moment.

2.1. The dark brown shadows and cool bluish-white highlights were added over the dilute brown underlayer in the same step, and in places blended together to produce smooth modeling.

2.2. The paint for the face is drier than for the torso in order to maintain the sharp lines of the extreme features.

2.3. The Impressionistic sky and distant landscape were applied directly onto the gray ground after the figures were painted. The imprint of the brush remains in the malleable paint.

2.4. The white of the Indian's headdress was painted last, on top of the Impressionistic background.

2. DETAIL OF FACE

The facial features are extreme to the point of being almost bizarre. The modeling of the face was done in a terse manner with only a few firm brushstrokes. The cool bluish highlights stand out against the warm flesh tones. The anatomy of the shoulder and arm is correct and was painted with great sureness. Cool highlights contrast with glowing flesh tones, creating a roundness of form.

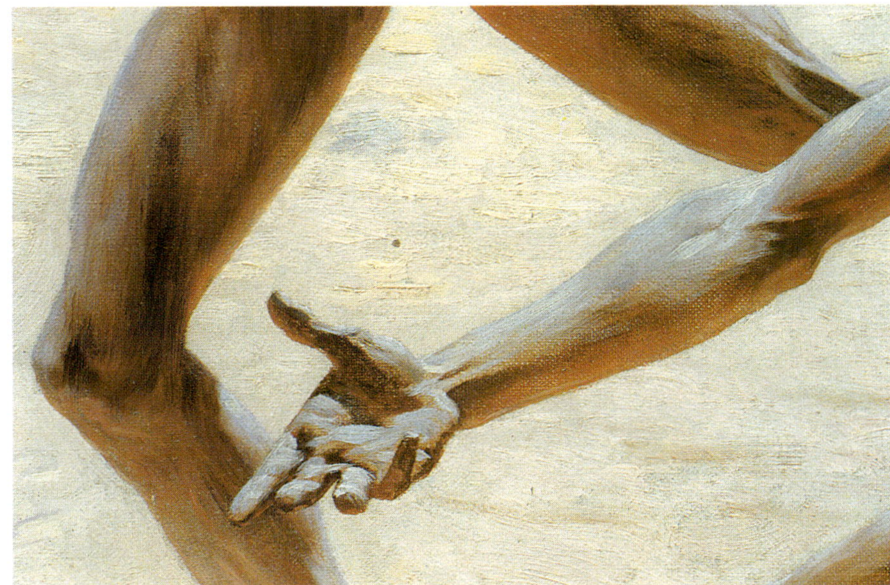

3. Detail of Arm

The triangular compositional theme is dominant throughout the picture. Here the triangle is composed of the two legs and the forearm. The studied gesture of the hand is reminiscent of Leigh's rigid German training.

   As noted, the fall of light and shadow on the bodies was accurately depicted, as if done from models arranged in the studio. The light from above has been focused intensely on the arm. The silvery, almost cold tonality contrasts with warm brown flesh tones to produce fullness of form.

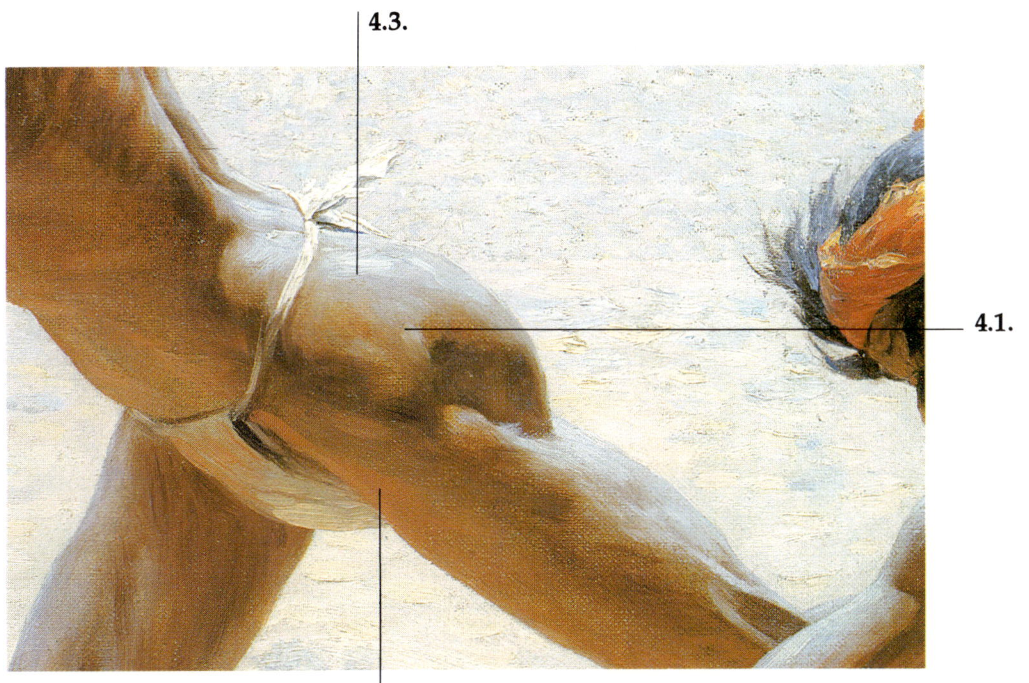

4. Detail of Buttocks and Thigh

4.1. A dilute brown layer was put in first, not completely obscuring the ground. This underlayer was used as a middle tone. Upon it, the lighter reddish-brown highlights reflecting from the sand, the cool white highlights from the strong sun, and the dark shadows contained within the modeling of the figures were applied in one step. In places they were blended together.

4.2. Fluid paint was used for these reddish highlights caused by the light reflecting up from the glowing sand.

4.3. The bluish highlights have small white touches added, the same paint that was used for the loin-cloth.

This section shows Leigh's mastery of the correct depiction of bodies in dynamic motion, as though he was illustrating an anatomical atlas. Leigh allowed himself more freedom while creating the desert background which contrasts with the smoothly applied and carefully modeled paint of the figures.

5.1. Consistent with the way Leigh painted the body, a thin warm brown layer was applied over the light gray ground, without concealing the tops of the canvas weave. Shadows were added, followed by a more opaque brown and highlights partially blended together.

5.2. The silver armband consists of blue paint with white highlights set off by a black shadow.

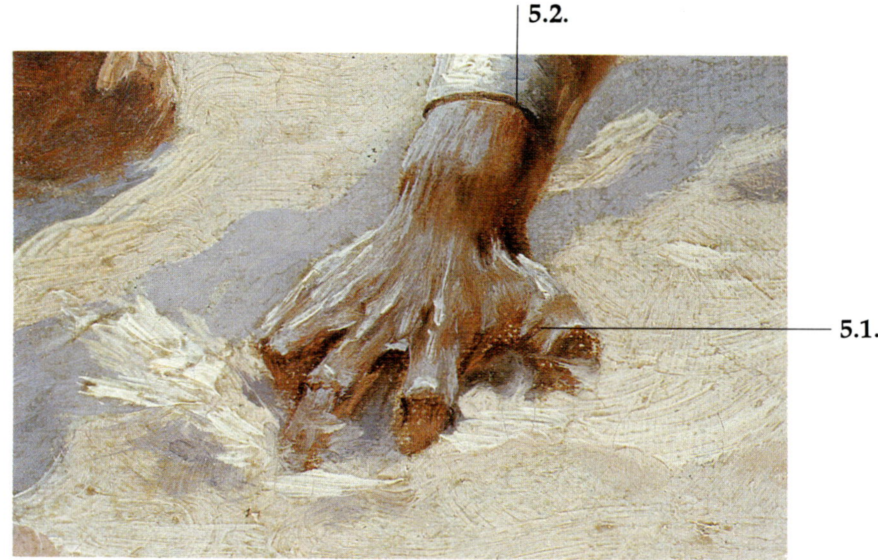

5. DETAIL OF HAND

The viewer anticipates the dramatic fall of the two Indians. The claw-like hand is grasping for a hold in the glowing sand. The ribbons of impasted white paint stand out as the straining tendons.

Unlike the realistic and mannered hand shown above in the detail of the arm, here Leigh has abbreviated unnecessary refinements to concentrate on conveying energy. The splash of sand depicted with highly impasted paint further emphasizes the impact of the hand on the ground. The wind-sculpted sand is depicted very fluidly, closely resembling the sea.

6.1. The black underdrawing for the figure can be seen along the bottom of the heel where it was not entirely covered by the paint.

6.2. The same technique can be seen here as for the rest of the figure. Beginning with a luminous middle tone, the modeling was done with opaque paint. The contrast between the transparent light-reflecting underlayer and the opaque shadows and highlights creates the three-dimensionality of the foot.

6.3. The blue shadows in the sand were applied over the toes.

6.4. The impasted paint, depicting the thrown up sand, stands out in sculptural relief.

6.5. The contours of the foot were adjusted slightly when the paint of the background was added.

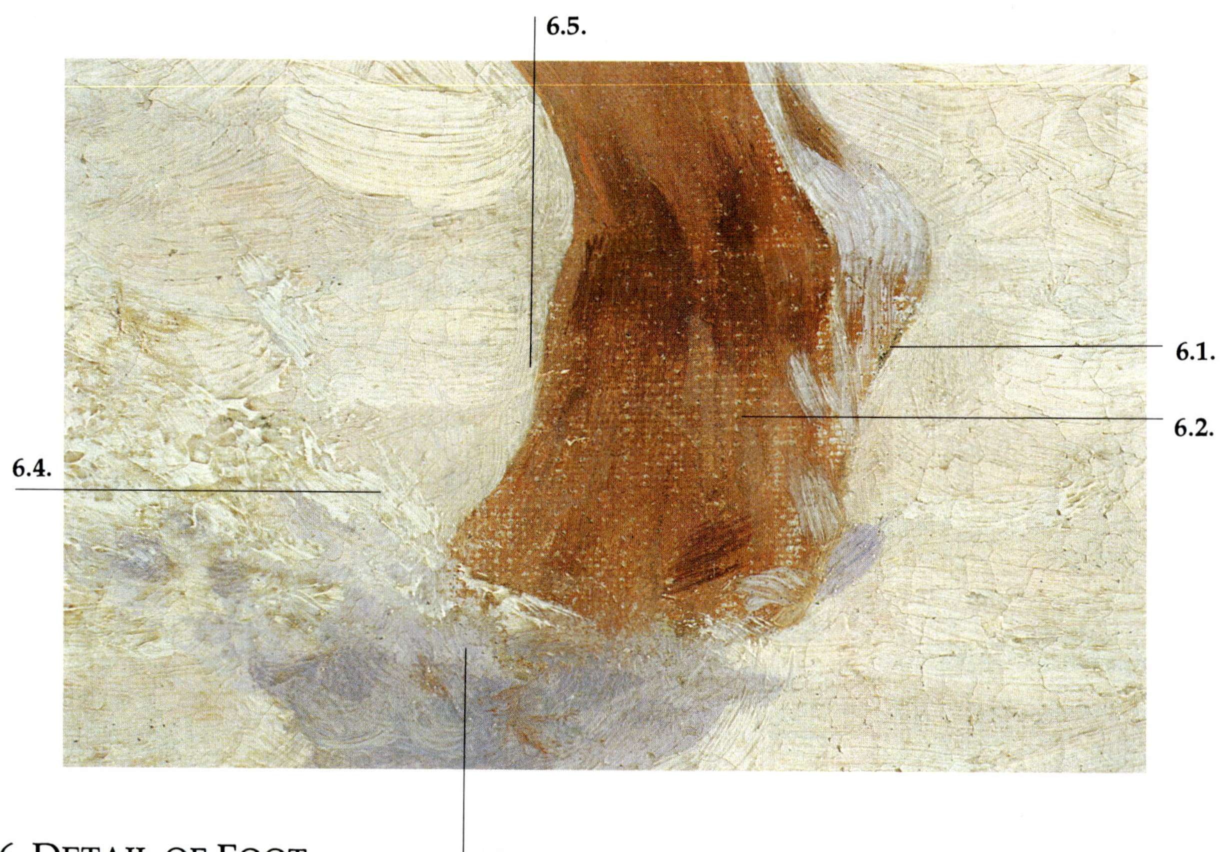

6. DETAIL OF FOOT

7. DETAIL OF LANDSCAPE

The background was done in a pointillistic style. Dabs of pastel shades were applied over the gray ground. Leigh employed the texture of the paint and the brushwork to create an image of shimmering heat waves in the desert air, though the colors used are cool and depict a harsh, uncompromising light. The rocks form a mirage-like image, indistinct and seeming to waver in the distance.

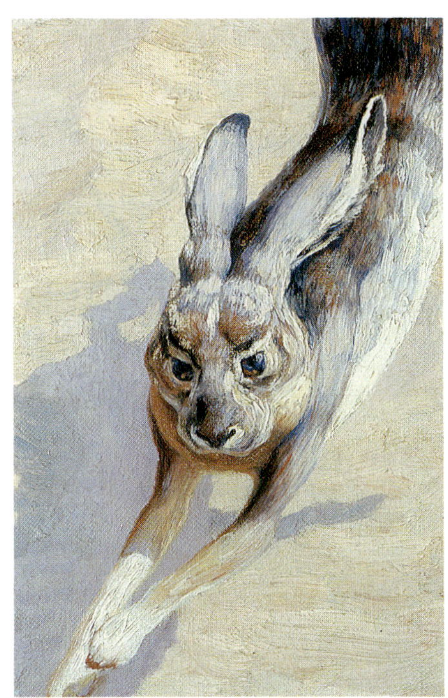

8. DETAIL OF RABBIT

The direction of the chase is indicated by the rabbit fleeing out of the picture plane, rushing past the viewer. The impasted paint of the opaque cool highlights was applied onto a thinner, warmer brown paint. This contrast of the cool-hued, impasted highlights with the thinner warmer underlayer again creates a three-dimensional form. The rabbit's shadow was painted last, on top of the landscape.

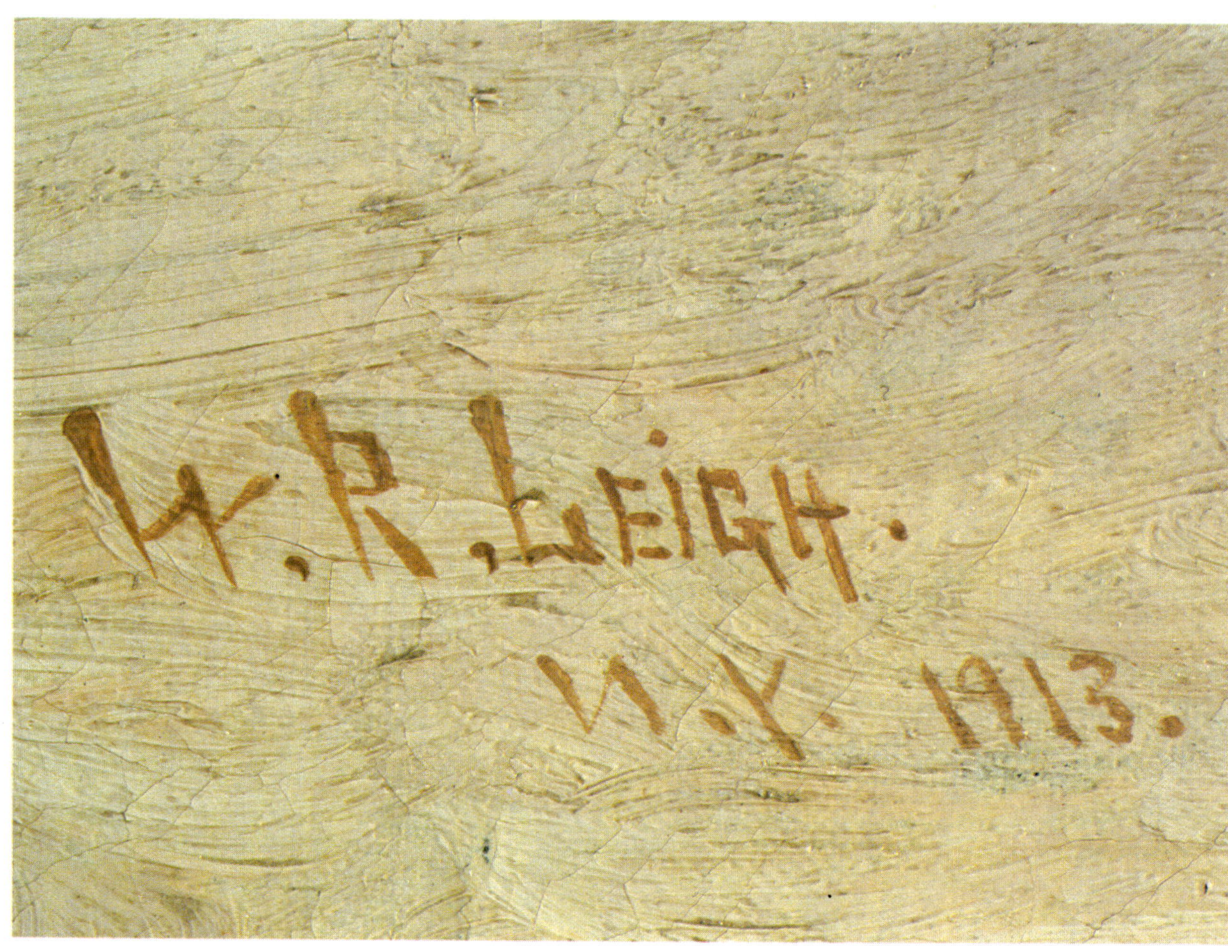

9. DETAIL OF SIGNATURE

W.R. Leigh. N.Y. 1913.

SUMMARY OF PAINTING TECHNIQUE

a. A thin, light gray ground was applied to a fine, lightweight canvas.

b. A dark underdrawing was made for the figures.

c. The figures were painted before the landscape. First, a thin warm-hued middle tone was applied. Then the shadows and highlights were worked in together and in places partially blended to produce a smooth modeling. The paint application varies from thin with ground exposed at the tops of the fabric weave to thicker where there are lighter highlights.

d. The background was put in around the figures. The soft paste-like paint is thicker and retains the imprint of the brush. The handling is freer and derived from the pointillist technique of the Impressionist painters.

e. The blue shadows were put in over the foreground.

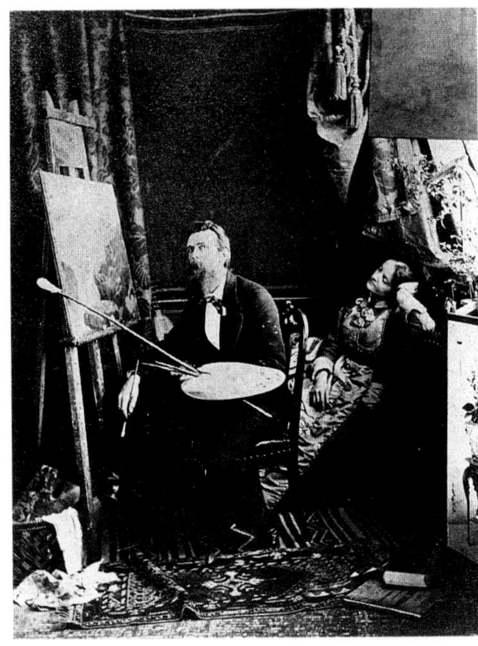

THOMAS MORAN

Thomas Moran was a dapper man. His eyes were clear and shining like a child's eyes. His mouth was delicate but hidden by a fair mustache and a full beard. He was only 5 feet 6 inches tall. Thin and wiry, he weighed 105 pounds. Except for his head which was small, he was perfectly formed for his size. He was quick on his feet, with the balance of a gentleman boxer.

Despite his diminutive stature, however, he was a giant as a painter of panoramic Western landscapes in the academic manner. To attain his realistic results, his concentration at the easel was complete. He even forgot his children while he worked. His younger daughter said she had no recollection of ever asking him for anything or of depending on him at any time. In later life, though, he was dependent on her.

Moran was born January 12, 1837 in Bolton, an industrial city in northwestern England. The family were cottage weavers and knew both poverty and harsh working conditions before emigrating to the United States. They settled in Philadelphia in 1845.

Moran was named Thomas Junior, the fifth of nine children. As an adolescent, he was determined "to be a painter and make pictures like those on the banknotes" he seldom saw. He left school at 16 for an apprenticeship to a wood engraver who made printing plates. In his spare time he painted watercolors. Soon his watercolors were selling to a modest extent.

Freed from his apprenticeship by temporary ill health, he found space in the art studio of his older brother Edward. He absorbed the traditional oil painting technique by observing his brother and James Hamilton, a luminist artist who was a disciple of the English painter of atmospheric effects J.M.W. Turner.

Despite his method of learning by seeing and then doing in the studio, Moran considered himself to be self-taught and so "never under any master." He believed formal art instruction would have been unproductive for him. As proof of his self-confident approach, one of his first oil paintings was accepted by the Pennsylvania Academy of Fine Arts for an 1856 exhibition. He was only 19.

Moran did not fight in the Civil War. Instead, he went to England in 1861 to learn more about Turner who had died a decade earlier. For months he sat in the National Gallery in London and copied Turner's paintings, striving for the same technique and palette. Stunned by the radiance of the paintings, he attempted by trial and error to identify the pigments the Englishman had employed and found Turner had used earth colors along with a wide range of yellows, vermilion and red lakes, cobalt and Prussian blues, (copper) blue verditer, and blacks.

He frequently thereafter expressed his enduring admiration for Turner. He explained that "Turner is a great artist, but he is not understood, because both painters and the public look upon his pictures as transcriptions of Nature. He certainly did not so regard them. All he asked of a scene was simply how good a medium it was for making a picture; he cared nothing for the scene itself.

"Literally speaking, his landscapes are false; but they contain his impressions of Nature and so many natural characteristics as were necessary adequately to convey that impression to others. The public does not estimate the quality of his works by his best paintings, but by his latest and crazier ones, in which realism is entirely thrown overboard."

In 1862 Moran returned to Philadelphia with enhanced technical concepts based on his study of Turner. He worked successfully as both a painter of fine art and a commercial illustrator.

One of his 1871 assignments for *Scribner's* magazine was to redraw an amateur's crude sketches of the previously unknown Yellowstone region in Wyoming. Thoughts of what the terrain might really be like intrigued Moran. He learned that a government survey party led by Dr. Ferdinand Hayden would be returning to the Yellowstone later in the year. This was his opportunity to see an untouched part of the West that might be a unique subject for his art. He induced the Northern Pacific Railroad to intercede with Hayden to permit him to join the group. To pay his way he borrowed money by pledging a favorite painting and he rushed off to meet Hayden.

The survey party also included the photographer William Henry Jackson. Moran and Jackson acted together in choosing the spots where the photographs would be taken and the sketches made. Because of Moran's enthusiasm for the grandeur of the terrain, his companions jokingly dubbed him T. Yellowstone Moran.

In the field, one traveling bag was enough to contain his personal belongings. The bag was outweighed, however, by his art supplies including sketch books, papers, pencils, watercolors, ink, and brushes. He used his portfolio as his lapboard. When Moran returned to the East, he employed the Jackson photographs and his own sketches to supplement his retentive memory of the scenes he had selected.

Launched by the *Scribner's* commercial assignment to redraw illustrations of the Yellowstone in 1871, Moran had now discovered his life's work in the portrayal of the Western vistas. He was not the first landscape painter to find his best subject matter in the West, but through Hayden he visited regions such as the Yellowstone that had not been seen by other artists.

His initial private reaction was that "the beautiful tints were beyond the reach of human art." He told Hayden, however, that "the business of the great painter should be the representation of great scenes in nature." To achieve this standard he painted *The Grand Canyon of the Yellowstone*, a 7x12 foot panorama. Congress purchased the picture for the nation in June 1872.

Moran's early forays into the West were numerous. He traveled regularly to Colorado, Arizona, New Mexico, Utah, Wyoming, and Idaho, as well as to Florida, Europe, and Mexico. His reputation and his fortune were soon made. Mount Moran in the Tetons was named for him.

His pattern in landscape painting was set. He preferred the horizontal view as more in keeping with the wide-angled scenery. Although his fame was for huge panoramas, his usual canvas was a more manageable size.

He generally portrayed far-off mountain peaks in light and delicate tones to contrast with the progressively darkening values of the middle distance and the foreground. When he visited Yosemite in California in 1872, he was disappointed because of the absence of a distant focus. He could not apply "the witchery of atmospheric gradation."

In later years he traveled less frequently. Although he still looked at his photographs and sketches while painting, he intentionally departed from their reality to idealize nature. In that way he became even closer to Turner, his most important model. He was even called "the American Turner."

He was also considered to be an expert on the authenticity of paintings supposed to have been done by the Englishman. Once he was asked to validate a small unsigned landscape painting thought to be by the master. Immediately, however, he felt a "tantalizing sense of familiarity." When he examined the painting more carefully, he recognized marks on the back and identified the picture as one of his own.

In 1877 some of the younger European-trained American painters rebelled against the tradition-bound National Academy of Design. They formed the Society of American Artists just as the French Impressionists had deserted the French Academy. Although Moran had vowed to "paint as an American on an American basis," he joined the Society to please friends who were members.

Two years later, Moran resigned because the Society's hanging committee headed by the Impressionist painter William Merritt Chase refused to exhibit his work. At the height of Moran's career he was being described by more modern artists as old-fashioned and therefore passe. The public sided with Moran. So did the established American artists. He was elected a member of the National Academy in 1884.

In 1900 Moran's paintings were again under attack. This time he was more vulnerable because he had retained his old mannerisms rather than becoming innovative or at least modernizing his style. His 19th century technique was being carried unchanged into the more turbulent 20th century. Some critics ridiculed him as "the postcard painter, slick, grandiose, and pretentious." They maintained that his style had deteriorated from a meticulous description of a real place into a generalized depiction of an idealized subject with soft atmospheric edges concocted in the studio.

Moran paid scant attention. He went on the attack himself. He reviled the Barbizon School as merely "one dish" and the Impressionist School as a fad. After visiting Corot in Paris he claimed the Frenchman's color effects were as poor as if he had used only black and white. In contrast, he pointed to an imaginative indigenous element in his own work that for him transcended the Impressionists and the Post-Impressionists.

The public continued to agree with Moran rather than with his critics. They looked to him as the premier landscape painter of the American West. He painted competently until he was 85 and died at 90 in 1926.

Approval of his work has grown in recent years. His paintings of the Western landscape are in great demand. The criticism has muted as he holds on to a distinguished niche in the history of American art. *The New York Times* has asserted that "more than any other artist he has made us acquainted with the [mountains of the] great West."

His 62x52 inch *Children of the Mountain* dated 1866 sold for $650,000 at public auction in 1980.

1. THE PAINTING

Indian Village is representative of Thomas Moran's mature, more romantic style. He explained, "I place no value upon literal transcriptions from Nature. All my tendencies are toward idealization. A place as a place has no value in itself for the artist. When I desire to tell truly of Nature, I do not wish to realize the scene literally but to convey its true impression."

T. Moran. Indian Village *is in the collection of the San Diego Museum of Art, California. Oil and resin on canvas. 20 inches (50.8 cm) height x 16 1/16 inches (41 cm) width. Signed lower right and dated 1915.*

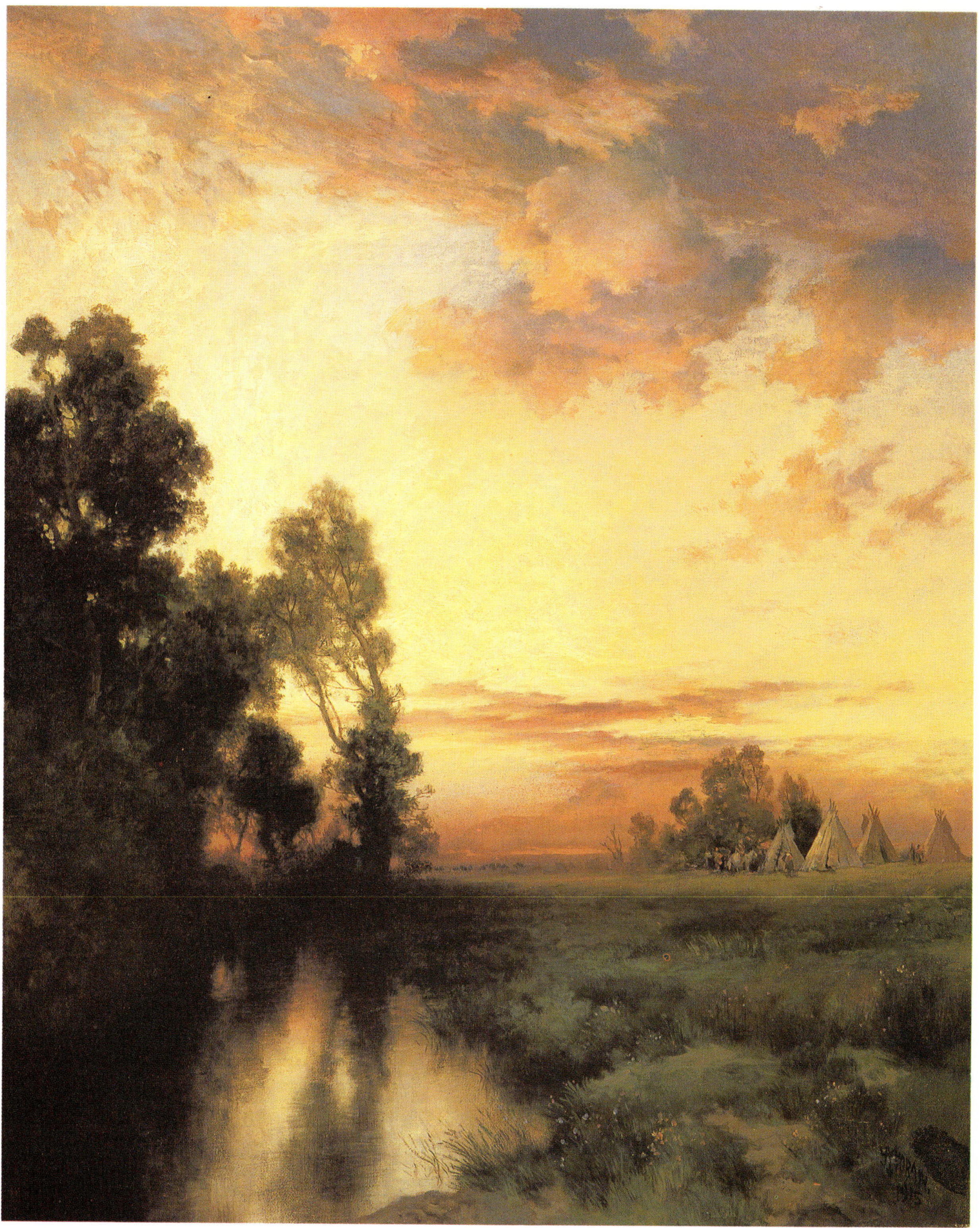

This painting is a masterful performance by a precise, well organized, creative, and confident artist. He started the work with a clear conception of his final composition, although he did ultimately change part of the background to create a more mystical atmosphere. He knew how to achieve the optimum optical advantage and he proceeded with an economical handling of the paint.

The painting is traditional in its execution. Broadly speaking, Moran's technique is academic. He followed the characteristic techniques of European and American luminist painters of the mid-19th century. Moran adopted this style as early as the 1860s, as a result of his training in his brother's studio and his European travels in that decade. This style was retained until the end of his career.

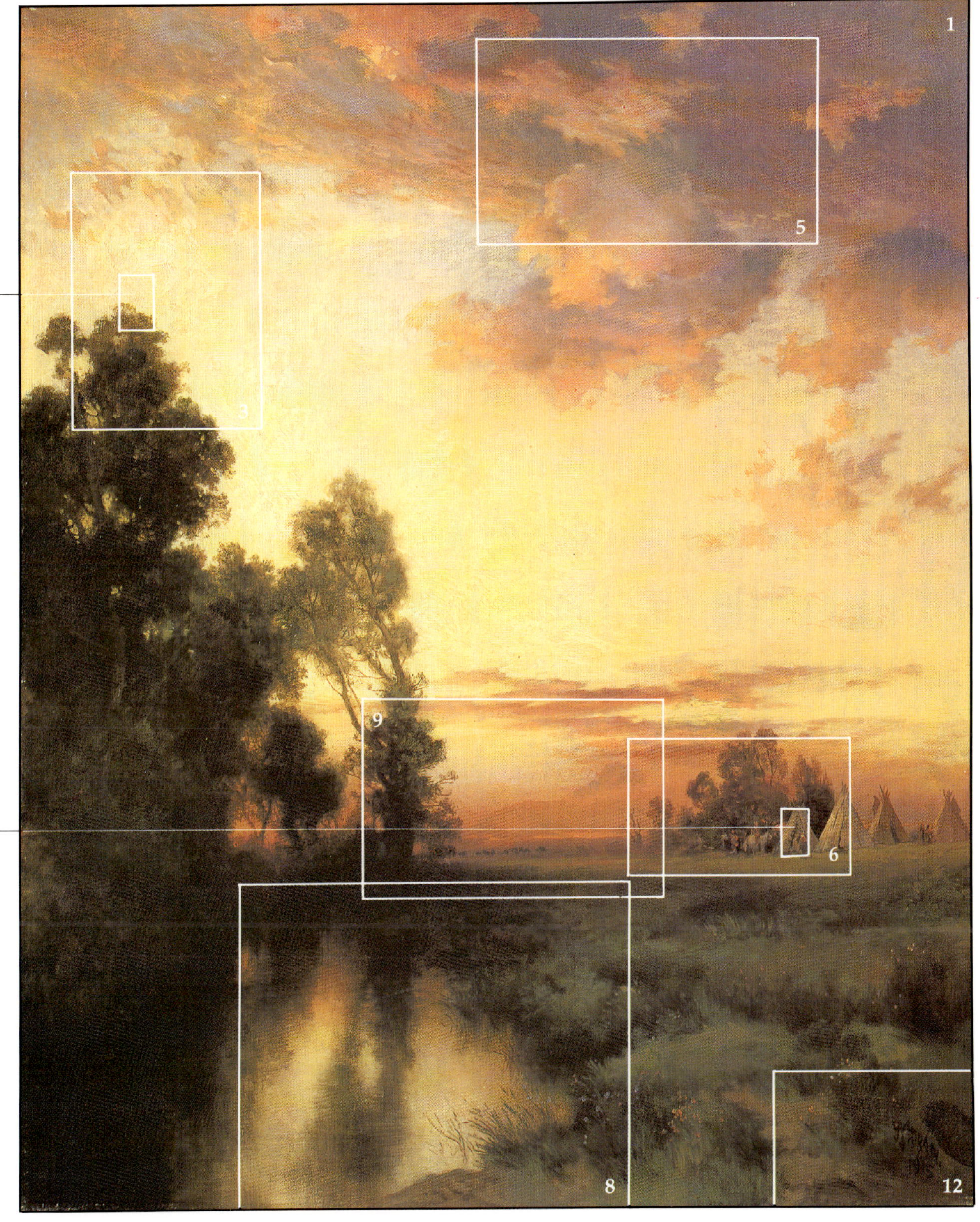

As a luminist painter, the rendering of space through the expression of light effects was the dominant concern of Moran. The full-bodied clouds were modeled in fiery highlights and leaden shadows. The reflection of the incandescent sky in the pond emphasizes the foreground. These luminous effects are heightened by the dark silhouettes of the trees. Soft greenish-yellow highlights of sunlight touching down on islands of foliage develop the middle distance where the tepees are gathered.

For *Indian Village* Moran used a fine, plain weave linen canvas with pronounced and regularly occurring slubs. He mounted the canvas to a typical tongue-and-groove stretcher of the period. The priming appears to have been carried out by the artist as well.

The white ground contains small coarse particles that give it tooth, as well as break up the surface, providing a reflective base for the paint. This had been the practice of luminist painters of the Hudson River School.

The composition was sketched in next. The sketch can be clearly seen with the unaided eye where the paint is thin, particularly along the edges of some clouds.

Moran built up his forms from dark to light. Thin, dark underlayers were applied that influence the tonality of the subsequent paint layers. For example, the recessive trees and their reflection on the water were applied over a dilute brown underlayer, and the clouds were painted over dark gray. Where left exposed, the underlayers create luminous shadows. Thicker paint for halftones and highlights was added to these shadowy bases to develop the modeling. The alternating layers of thin and thick paint create the illusion of deep space.

Glazes were applied to the sky to produce the radiant color range. Glazing was a popular method to produce radiant colors that are in fact an optical union of differently colored layers. Light rays penetrate the glaze layer to the opaque paint beneath, from which some light is reflected back through the glaze and some light is scattered. This phenomenon enhances luminosity of colors in a way that cannot be achieved by mixing colors within a single layer. Moran also used scumbles for some of the darkest clouds. These opaque touches contrast with the glazes to further enhance the sense of depth. Finally, deft strokes of color were used to adjust proportions, and the delicate details were added.

Despite this well conceived working process, Moran made a change in the composition. Upon close inspection, the faint shape of mountains can be detected in the background. These have been painted over with the orange clouds at the horizon. This artist's change can be seen more clearly with infrared photography.

An oddity in the technique is that some of the impasted paint was deliberately flattened with a tool such as a palette knife. The reason for this is not clear, though it is seen in other paintings by Moran. He may have copied the effect from paintings of Turner that demonstrate his flamboyant use of the palette knife to apply paint.

According to his daughter, Moran used the following pigments: chromes, raw sienna, burnt sienna, yellow ochre, bright red, cobalt blue, rose madder, asphaltum, and zinc green. Analysis of *Indian Village* identified the following pigments: lead white, ochre, iron oxide, cobalt blue, chrome yellow, red lake, and for the glazes red lake and probably sienna. A student of Moran noted the use of asphaltum throughout his career, particularly in glazes, though none was found in this painting.

The daughter's recollection of Moran's working procedure was that after he completed a painting, he would study the work for minutes at a time, backing steadily away until he was across the studio. Then he would hurry to the easel to make one or two additional strokes before retreating again, to one side or the other. If an effect still bothered him, he would paint it out with white lead and start that part over. This finalizing of the work would continue until he was satisfied, regardless of the time consumed.

Within the confines of his unchanging style, Moran was a confident and masterful painter. From his day to the present, Moran's paintings have inspired awe and wonder in viewers. They provide a world of supernatural beauty that is the essence of the romantic West: the sublime Western scenery that is now as precariously preserved in nature as in the delicate layers of Moran's paintings.

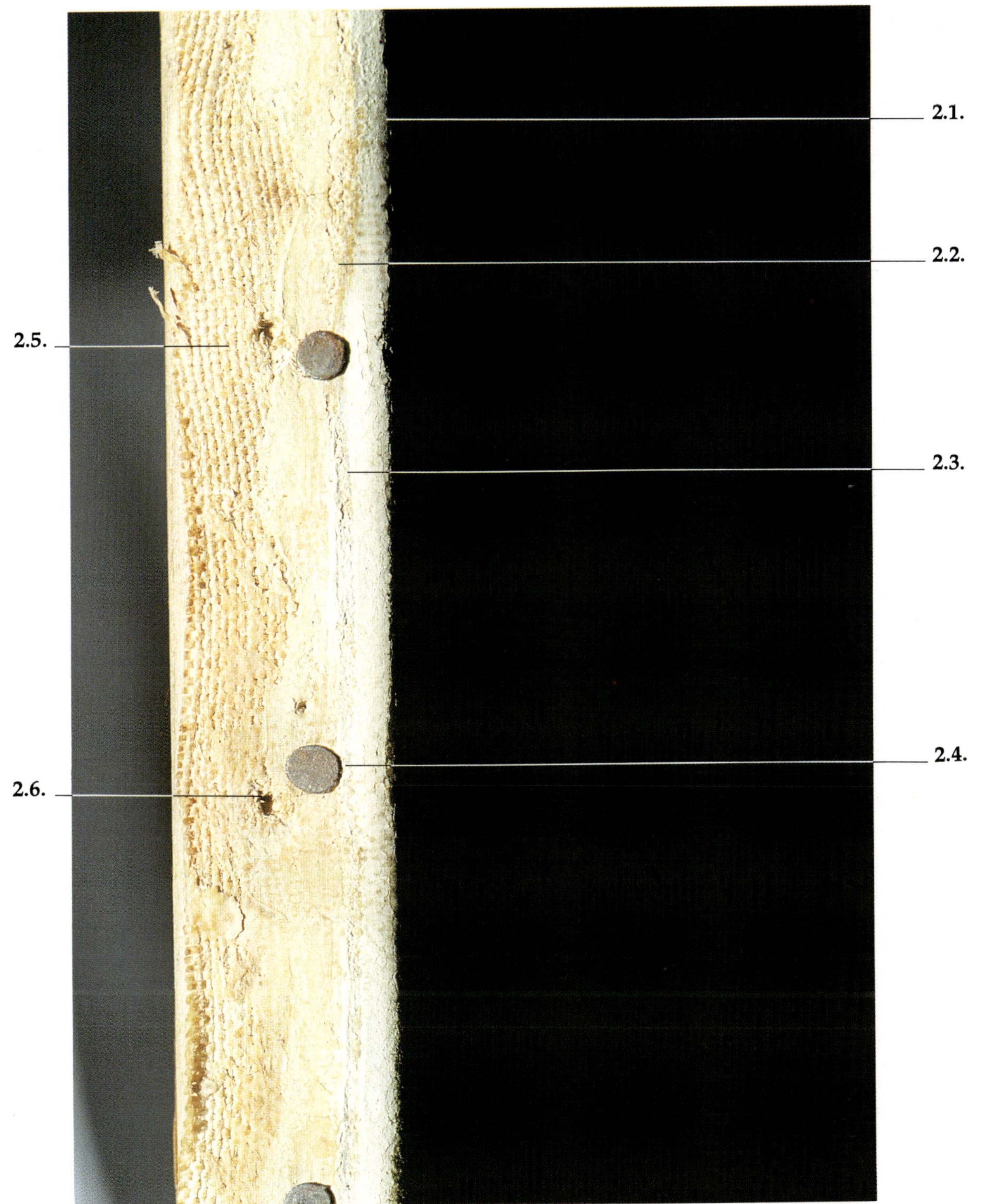

2.1. The picture plane.

2.2. The thick paste-like size has a smooth surface and appears to have been applied with a spatula.

2.3. The ridge at the edge of the white ground was caused by the application stopping at the tacking edge of the temporary mount. The current location of the ridge indicates that the dimensions of the temporary mount were slightly larger than the actual picture size.

2.4. The existing tack heads are bare, indicating that the fabric was primed before it was attached to its present stretcher.

2.5. The imprint of tack heads in the size layer shows that the size was applied after the fabric was stretched the first time.

2.6. The cusping of the fabric corresponds to tack holes originating from the previous mount.

2. TACKING EDGE

The tacking edge of a painting can reveal a great deal of information about the artist's technique and especially the process of canvas preparation. In the case of *Indian Village* it is particularly informative because the original state of the painting has not been altered by restoration.

Close inspection reveals a complicated canvas preparation. The ground material does not completely cover the tacking edges indicating that the ground was applied by the artist. A closer look reveals that the canvas was stretched twice. The cusping and corresponding tack holes indicate that the unprimed canvas was first stretched onto a temporary support, at which time it was sized and the ground was applied. The primed canvas was then remounted onto the slightly smaller, permanent stretcher to which it is still attached.

3.1. The sky is composed of a purplish gray underlayer with a lighter gray scumble over it. The resulting cool gray was achieved not by adding blue pigment, as might be assumed, but by the combined paint layers that produce a bluish optical phenomenon known as the turbid media effect.

3.2. The brighter clouds were then built up with thicker, slightly impasted light yellow paint. The impasto has been leveled with a tool such as a palette knife. This peculiar touch gives the impasto a unique flattened appearance. Finally, an orange glaze was applied that settled thickly in the interstices of the impasto.

3.3. The richly shaded trees were begun with an underlayer of dark brown paint brushed thinly over the ground. The green of the foliage was painted on top of the brown wash. The underlayer was left exposed in places, providing the shadows.

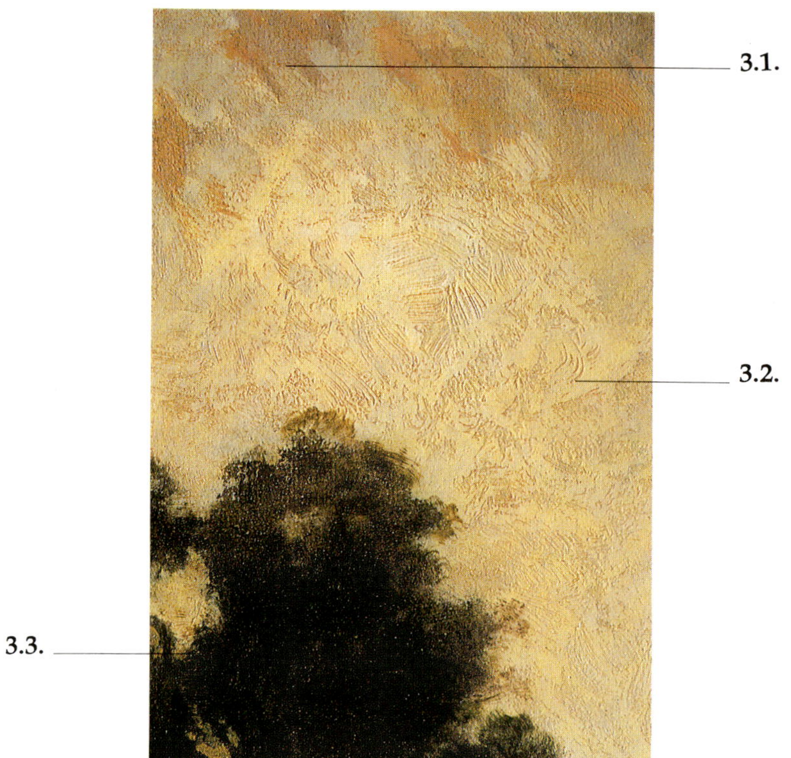

3. DETAIL OF TREE AND SKY

Moran created form, shadow, and depth by the layering of colors, proceeding from dark to light.

4.1. First a dark brown underlayer was applied.

4.2. Coarse particles in the ground appear as pinpricks of reflected light increasing the luminosity of the dark shadowy underlayer.

4.3. To refine the shape of the treetop, a final touch of yellowish-green was applied over the bordering sky.

4.4. The slightly impasted paint of the sky has been leveled by Moran with a tool such as a palette knife. The orange glaze has collected most thickly in the resulting interstices.

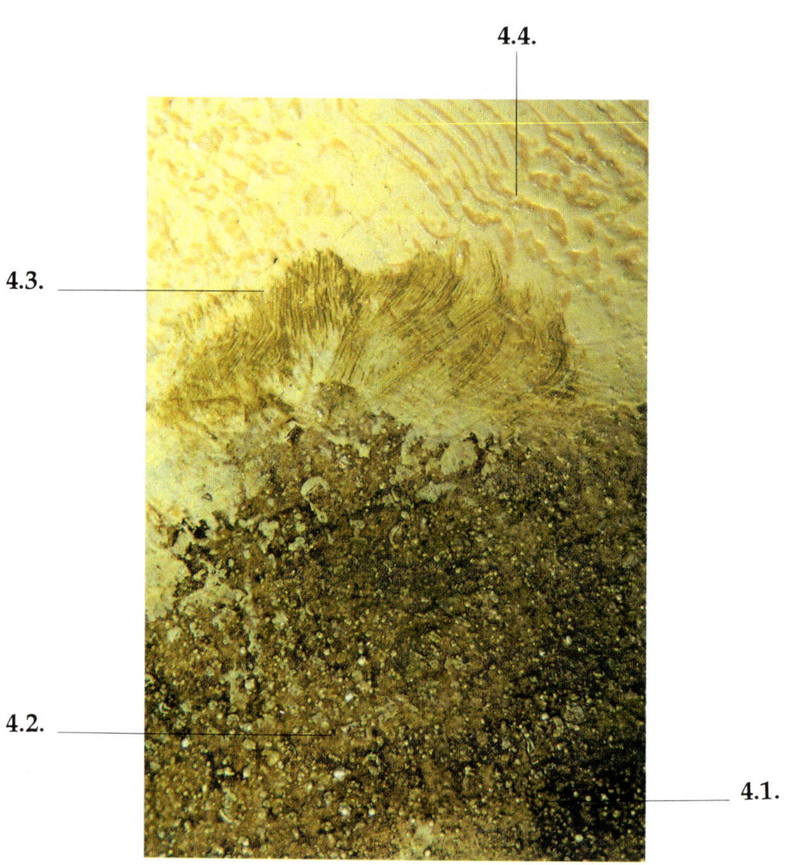

4. DETAIL OF TREETOP

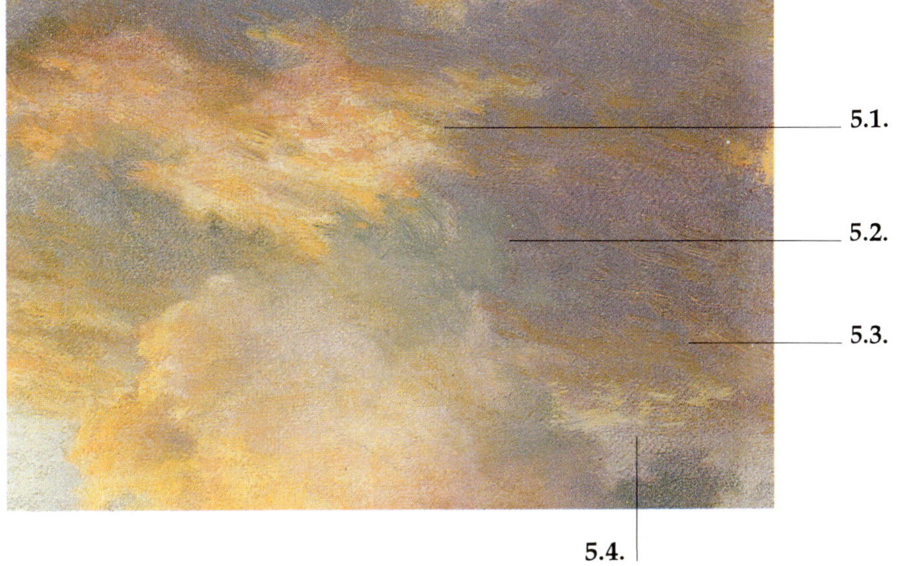

5.1. The underdrawing can be seen through a thin paint layer.

5.2. In a last step, purplish gray opaque shadows were added to heighten the effect of the layered clouds.

5.3. Calligraphic orange ribbons of paint form intense reflections of light from scattered clouds.

5.4. The paint of this bright cloud has been dragged over the surface leaving small gaps that reveal the darker layers beneath.

5. DETAIL OF CLOUDS

The mass and depth of this luminous sky have been created by the multiple layers of transparent and opaque paint. Beginning with the thin, dark gray underlayer, Moran proceeded to build up the modeling of the clouds with subsequent layers of cool gray and impasted light yellow with final additions of delicate pink and orange glazes. Last touches of opaque dark gray and orange were added to create the dark shadows and final intense highlights of the sunset. The luminous transparent layers contrast with the denser opaque layers to produce the radiant sky of coruscant colors and deep, contained shadows.

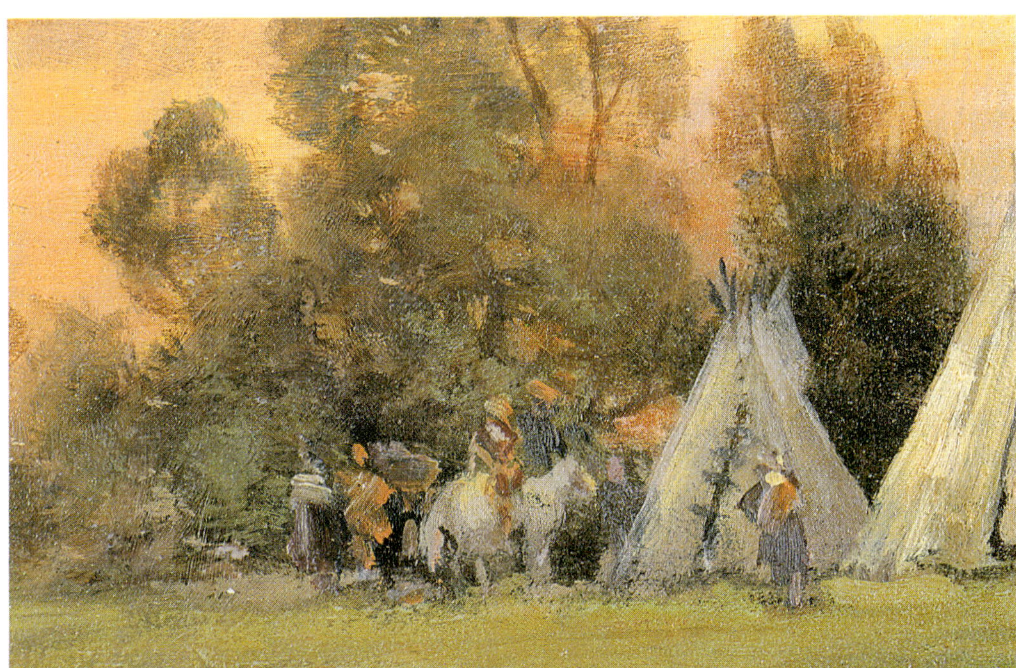

6. DETAIL OF FIGURES AND TEPEES

The figures were painted sketchily with just a few decisive strokes and dabs of almost pure yellow, orange, red, and black. In contrast, the tepees were formed by colors that were picked up individually from the palette, then applied together in long, multicolored brushstrokes.

7.1. The figure was painted with concise strokes and dabs of color. The brush, loaded with orange paint, touched down at the shoulder and was swiftly drawn down until empty.

7.2. The thin, dark brown underlayer was left exposed to create the shadow. Coarse particles in the ground break up the surface and reflect light.

7.3. The highlighted green foreground was added around the figure.

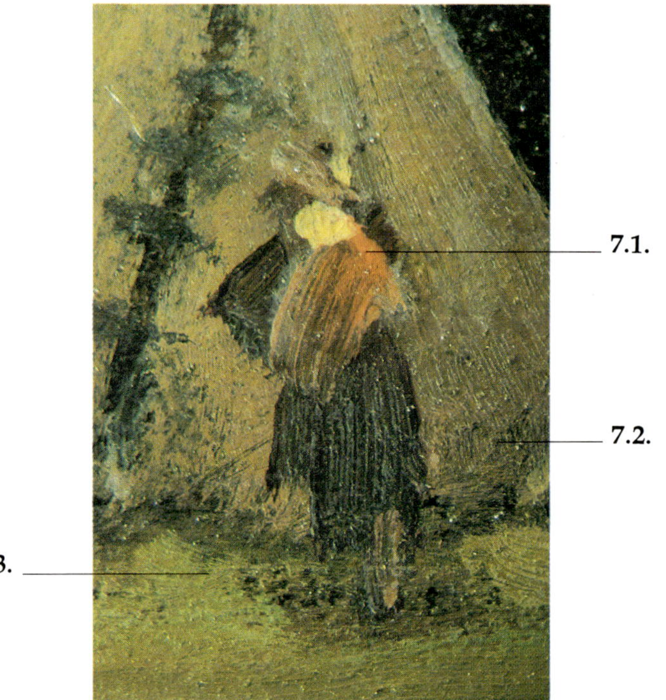

7. DETAIL OF FEMALE FIGURE

The actual size of the female figure is one centimeter. This enlargement reveals the fast and abbreviated manner of the paint application. Refinements were omitted, yet one still gets a sense of the figure's completeness.

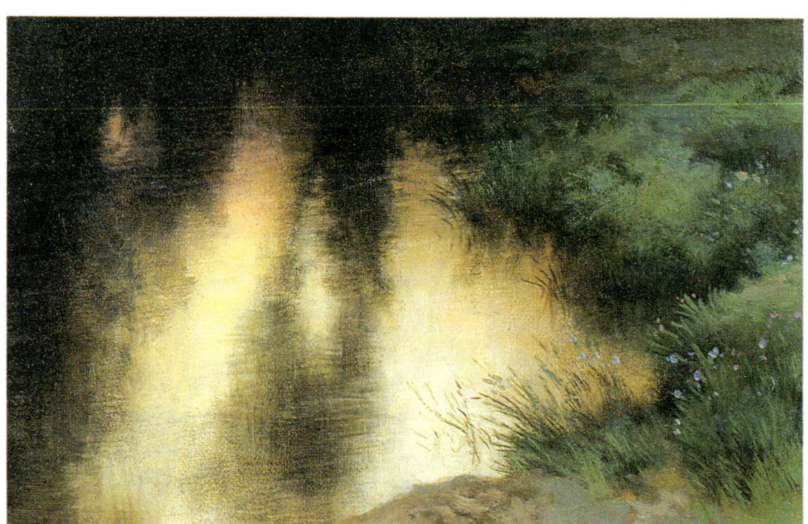

8. DETAIL OF REFLECTION OF TREES IN WATER

The viewer is enticed into the moist stillness of this crepuscular scene. The dark brown underlayer has been left exposed to create the shadows and reflection of the trees on the water. In places, the paint has been partially wiped away, leaving a thin layer that is influenced by the canvas texture. This broken surface further enhances the effect of shimmering light. Pale yellow and orange strokes have been lightly dragged across the reflections to simulate ripples in the water. Thin washes of green form the rich foliage at the edge of the water and in the last step, the individual blades of grass and dots of flowers were put in with the tip of a fine brush.

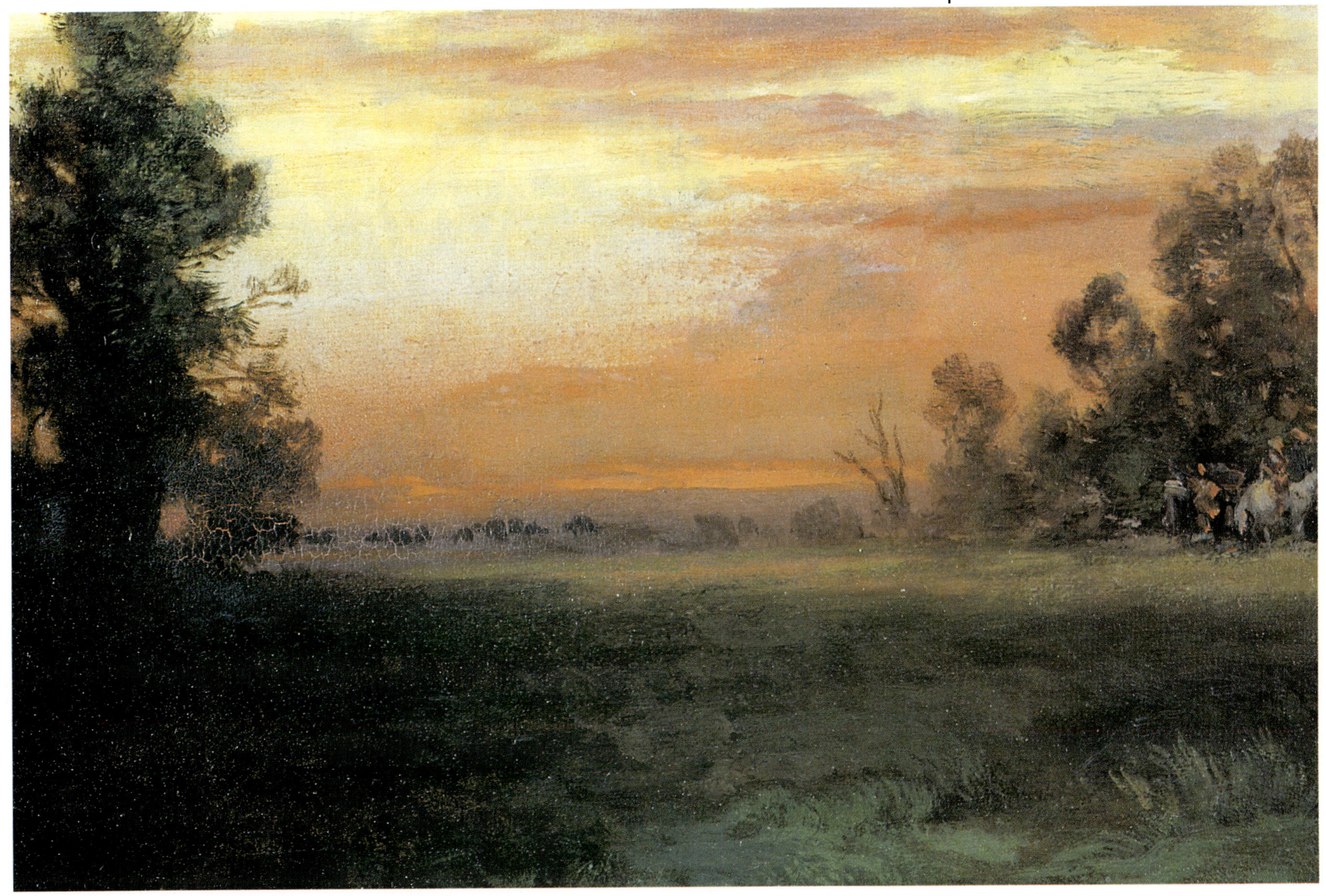

9. DETAIL OF MIDDLE DISTANCE WITH ARTIST'S CHANGES

Moran had worked out the composition for *Indian Village* in detail before applying any paint and he deviated little from his original sketch. Nevertheless, the central landscape initially included mountains in the distance. Also, the grouping of trees and tepees in the middle distance was originally larger and farther forward in the composition. These changes lower the horizon and provide more open space, thus creating a more idealized conceptual landscape.

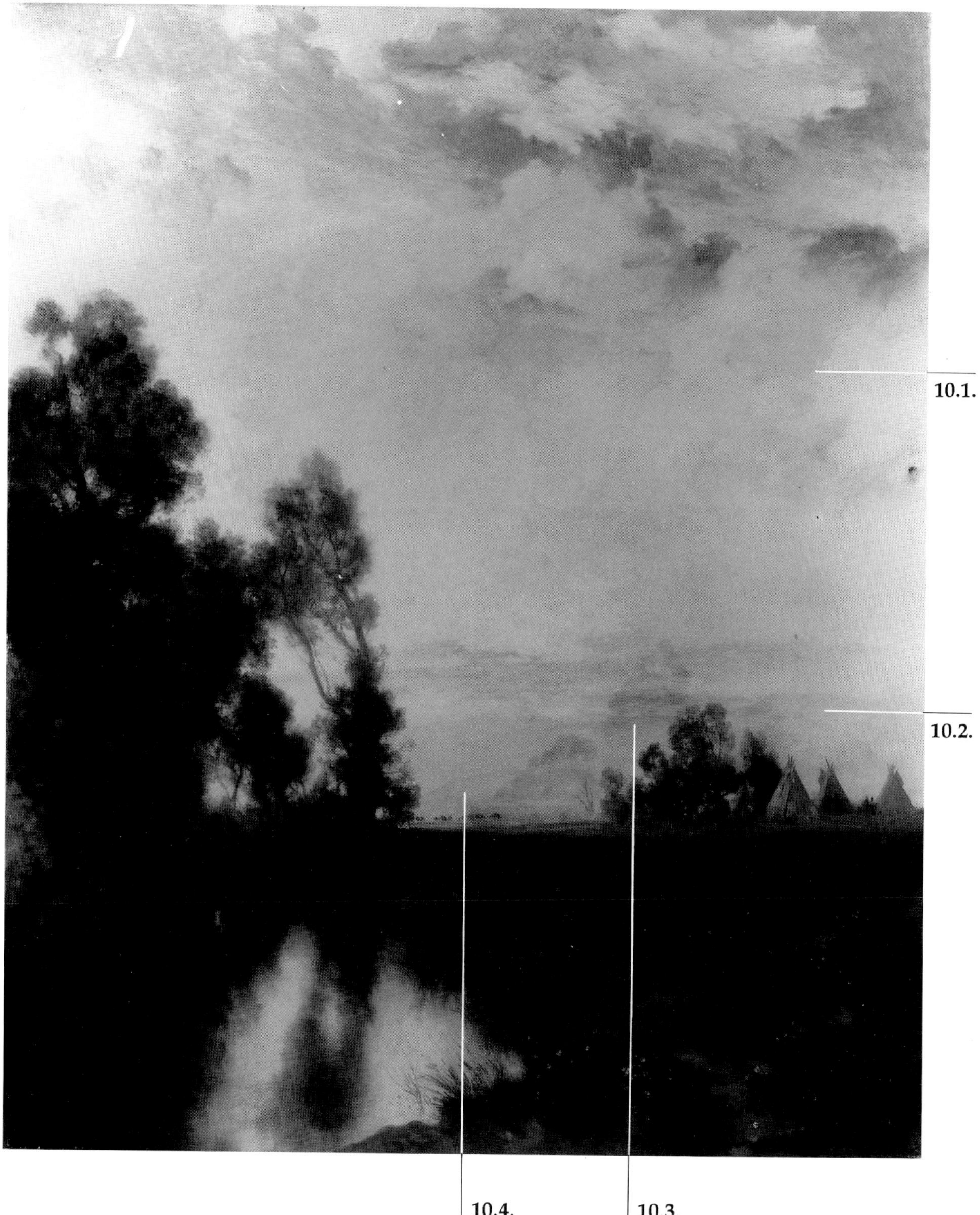

10.1. *The underdrawing.*

10.2. *Here distant mountains have been painted out.*

10.3. *Originally the trees were larger.*

10.4. *A distant mountain has been painted out.*

10. INFRARED PHOTOGRAPH OF PENTIMENTO

The infrared photograph reveals the underdrawing and the artist's changes.

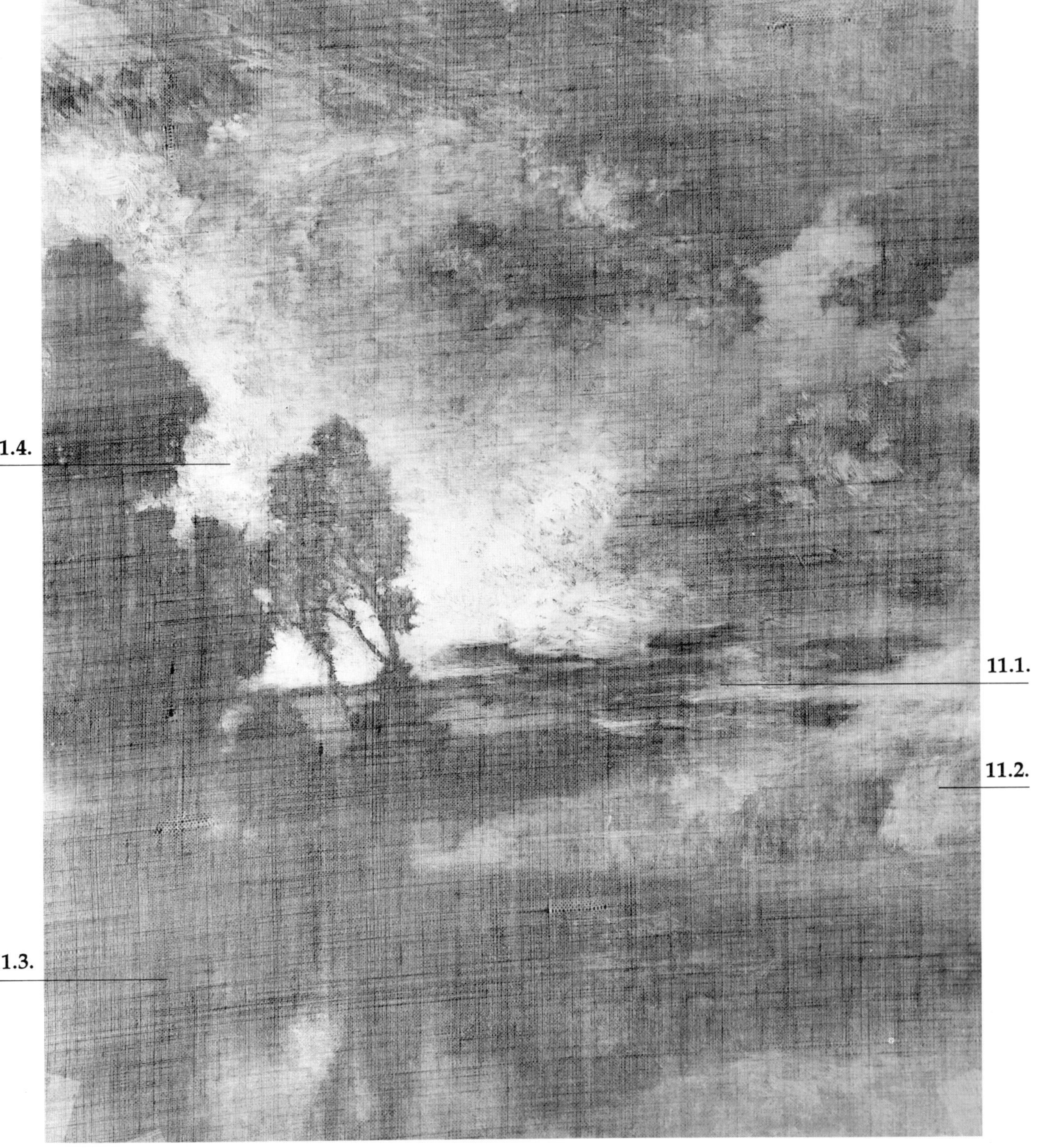

11.1. Lead white paint has covered the larger tree.

11.2. This tepee was originally larger and farther forward in the composition.

11.3. The lead white ground is thicker in the interstices of the canvas weave. This enhances the pattern of the fabric, allowing one to see that the weave is fine with regularly occurring slubs. The canvas has been mounted crookedly on the stretcher. This is odd given Moran's tidiness.

11.4. The paint of the sky was applied around the trees.

11. X-Radiograph of Center of Painting

By revealing areas of lead white, the x-radiograph indicates artist's changes and provides information about the artist's working process.

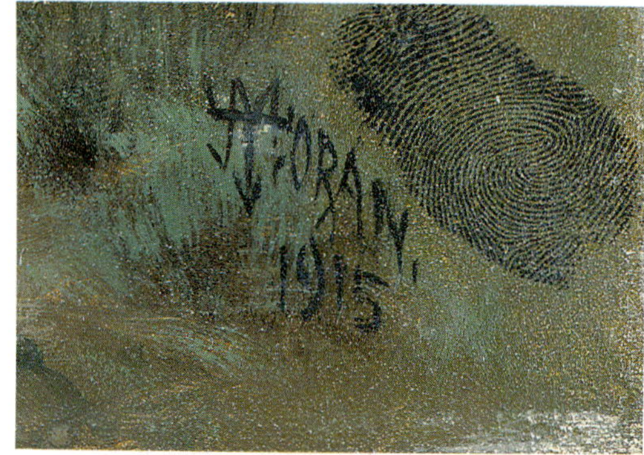

12. DETAIL OF SIGNATURE WITH MONOGRAM AND THUMBPRINT

This is Moran's distinctive monogram, dating from his first trip to Yellowstone in 1871. The T was laid over the M and at the juncture of the two initials a Y was formed. His fellow explorers joked that the presumably accidental Y stood for the Yellowstone.

The artist added the unique thumbprint in 1911 to eliminate the forgeries that accompanied his huge success.

13.a. This cross-section has been taken from the sky. The bottom two layers are ground. Next is blue sky and the top layer is a pinkish cloud.

13.b. This cross-section has been taken from the right edge at the horizon. Again the bottom two layers are ground. Next comes foliage and the top layer is blue sky.

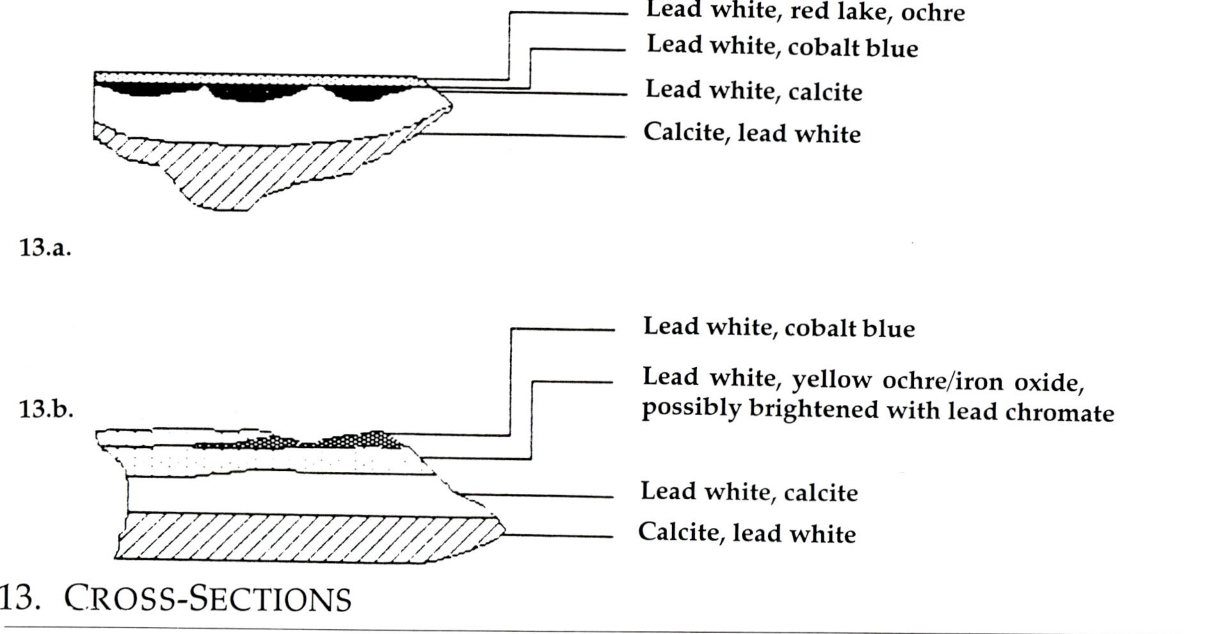

13. CROSS-SECTIONS

SUMMARY OF THE PAINTING TECHNIQUE

a. The canvas was primed by the artist and mounted onto its present stretcher.
b. A sketch was carried out on the white ground.
c. Dark underlayers were applied: brown for trees and landscape, gray for clouds.
d. The modeling was built up with lighter colored, opaque paint layers. The delicate colors of the sky were influenced by glazes, while final touches of paint were applied here and there to adjust forms and to add details.

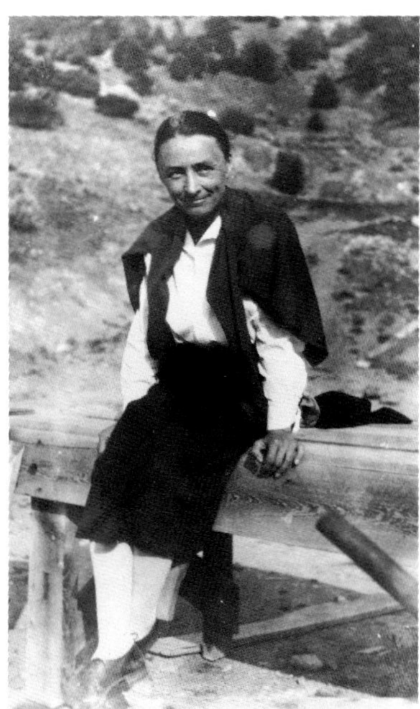

GEORGIA O'KEEFFE

Georgia O'Keeffe was the most individual of the master painters of the American West. The first drawings she offered for criticism were applauded in 1916 by her future husband Alfred Stieglitz: "Finally a woman on paper!"

When the drawings were exhibited, the reviews in the press emphasized that the forms sprang from intriguing mystical and sexual derivations. The sensual aspect of her work was said to provide a feminine tie to the newly popular psychoanalyst Sigmund Freud. Another approving reviewer less involved with her gender commented, "It is only in music that one finds any analogy to the emotional content of her drawings." The impression given was of the then unknown O'Keeffe rising out of these early abstracted drawings as a woman "with a singularly violent intensity." She was soon a celebrity as well as a recognized artist.

She was born November 15, 1887. Her ancestry was a rare mix of Irish and Hungarian. Raised on a prosperous family farm in Wisconsin, she was named for her grandfather. "I grew up," she recalled, "pretty much as everybody else grows up." At 10 she insisted she was going to be an artist.

When she was 20 she studied with the Impressionist painter William Merritt Chase at the Art Students League in New York City. Although she won an important student prize, she felt her technique was merely imitative of her teacher. Rather than spend her career as another Chase, she destroyed her student work and vowed never to paint again. Instead, she became first a commercial illustrator in Chicago and then an art instructor in Virginia.

In 1912 she took a design class for teachers with Alon Bement who was an associate of the painter and theorist Arthur Dow at the Teachers College of Columbia University in New York City. Dow had painted with the Impressionists in Paris while they were ex-ploring the "shadowless space and unreal colors" of the Japanese print makers. After leaving Europe, Dow abandoned both Impressionism and realism to develop his own abstract theory. "The first step," Dow declared, "is the drawing of lines as the boundaries of shapes," as opposed to Impressionist techniques.

O'Keeffe was so impressed with Dow's theories that she went to Columbia to study with him. Later she brought his system to the Texas schools where she taught. Employing Dow principles, she began to paint again. He had opened her eyes to the potentials of a personal approach to the portrayal of beauty.

"One day" in 1916, she explained in the simplistic literary style that is compatible with her painting technique, "I found myself saying to myself–I can't live where I want to–I can't go where I want to–I can't do what I want to–I can't even say what I want to. School and things that painters have taught me even keep me from painting as I want to. I decided I was a very stupid fool not to at least paint as I wanted to and say what I wanted to when I painted, as that seemed to be the only thing that was nobody's business but my own.

"Some of the first drawings done to please myself I sent to a girl friend requesting her not to show them to anyone. She took them to [Gallery] 291 and showed them to Stieglitz and he insisted on showing them to others."

A generation older than O'Keeffe, Stieglitz was an innovative photographer who had adopted a realist idiom. His gallery at 291 Fifth Avenue had been established for 10 years, exhibiting modernist American and European paintings and sculpture.

O'Keeffe quit teaching in 1918 when Stieglitz sent a proxy to bring her to live with him. She became one of the young American artists Stieglitz represented. She also posed for Stieglitz's famous photographic figure studies that were a reflection of their romantic relationship.

Ascetic looking with white skin and black hair drawn back severely from her high forehead, she wore nunnery-black clothes with white accents. Her features were large, her nose was prominent, her chin was firm, and her gray-green eyes were steady. Her smile was enigmatic, her hands were long and sensitive, and her low voice could be intimate. She gave people the feeling that a tiger lurked beneath her impassivity.

Her paintings continued the voluptuously arcane elements that had been perceived in her work from the first drawings. The compositions appeared to be intuitive rather than planned, although the reverse was true. Stieglitz called them color music. He insisted that her images were not translatable into language. She agreed. She said, "I found I could say things with color and shapes I had no words for." She developed a personal vocabulary of forms derived from nature and an equally personal sense of color. They were constantly evolving.

She was among the first American artists to paint American subjects in the modern style. Unlike most of her contemporaries, she had never gone to Europe to learn from foreign masters. Her independence made her a feminist symbol of the newly liberated and unconventional woman. Other women believed they read meanings into her work that men could not understand.

By 1923 she was professionally and financially successful. Critics agreed that she was one of the most original American talents. Her paintings became bigger. She used enlarged flowers as subjects. They filled the entire canvas with surging curves. These giant flowers resembled photographic blow-ups although she denied having been influenced by Stieglitz or his medium. The big flowers made her famous and were regarded as the height of her creativity. Her strange grayed tones of dark green and soft violet suited the simplified natural forms.

She married Stieglitz in 1924. In 1929 she began spending summers in New Mexico, seeking refuge in the high desert. Her work became increasingly majestic and visionary as the sexual charge diminished. To some, however, her "cool clarities" were antiseptic, as if painted at too low a temperature. Her landscapes, "clean-swept as if by a strong wind, lost their sense of specific place."

She observed that "all the earth colors of the painter's palette are there in the many miles of bad lands outside my door: the light Naples yellow through the ochres–orange and red and purple earth–even the soft earth greens." She paid little attention to delicate atmospheric effects.

She stretched her own canvases. After she primed them, generally with a white ground, they became "the hopefuls," waiting their turn. Before she started painting, the picture was complete in her mind, including the colors. She kept sample swatches of her colors brushed onto pieces of cardboard. For each picture she chose the swatches she wanted to use and premixed the hues according to the recorded formulas.

Her careful advance planning resulted in a single unified approach to the handling of the different details of the picture. While painting she adhered to her plan with consistency. In that way she made her job easier, but sometimes she also made the actual painting of the details seem facile and repetitive rather than inventive.

She painted while seated at her easel, dressed in the usual black with an apron protecting her lap. On a table at her side was a very large and very clean white china palette. The colors she had selected and prepared in advance were on the palette, each one carefully separated from the adjacent color. There was a different brush for each hue to avoid contamination. As soon as one color was used, the residue was scraped off the palette which was kept immaculate.

She painted swiftly but surely, pausing only to eat. Small canvases were completed in one day. Larger pictures took longer. They were turned to the wall if anyone entered her studio while the work was unfinished.

After she moved to New Mexico in 1943, she began painting compositions that included the bleached pelvic bones of large animals. She noted that "I was the sort of child that ate around the raisin in the cookie and ate around the hole in the doughnut, saving the raisin or the hole for the last and best. So probably–not having changed much–when I started painting pelvis bones I was most interested in the holes in the bones–what I saw through them."

Some foibles she retained until the end of her career. When she was asked why she never painted the human face or figure, she smiled and replied, "I've always believed that I can get all that into a picture by suggestion. I mean the life that has been lived in a place." She exchanged the presence of people for their artifacts while stripping compositions to their essence.

In addition, she did not see the need for signatures on her paintings. When a stranger asked why, she snapped, "Why don't you sign your face?" As her contemporary Marsden Hartley recalled, "There was no name on the first charcoal drawings. There has seldom been a name on the paintings that followed, for this artist believes that if there is any personal quality, that quality in itself will be signature enough. Over the years we have seen a sequence of her unsigned paintings permeated with an almost violent purity of spirit."

Stieglitz died in 1946 at 82. O'Keeffe died 40 years later at 98. She was a romantic despite the severity of her uncompromising forms and flat colors placed so dramatically on canvases.

The white flower that was the subject of this painting had a special meaning for her as an unspoken tie to New Mexico. The flower was not from a common trumpet vine but rather from the sacred datura used in Indian ceremonials as a narcotic to induce visions. This was "the angel's trumpet" that bloomed in the moonlight and closed in the morning sun along arroyo banks.

Her 30x40 inch *Black Hollyhock with Blue Larkspur* sold for $1,800,000 at public auction in 1987.

1. THE PAINTING

A single flower: Larger than life, by itself, isolated from the usual surroundings such as a

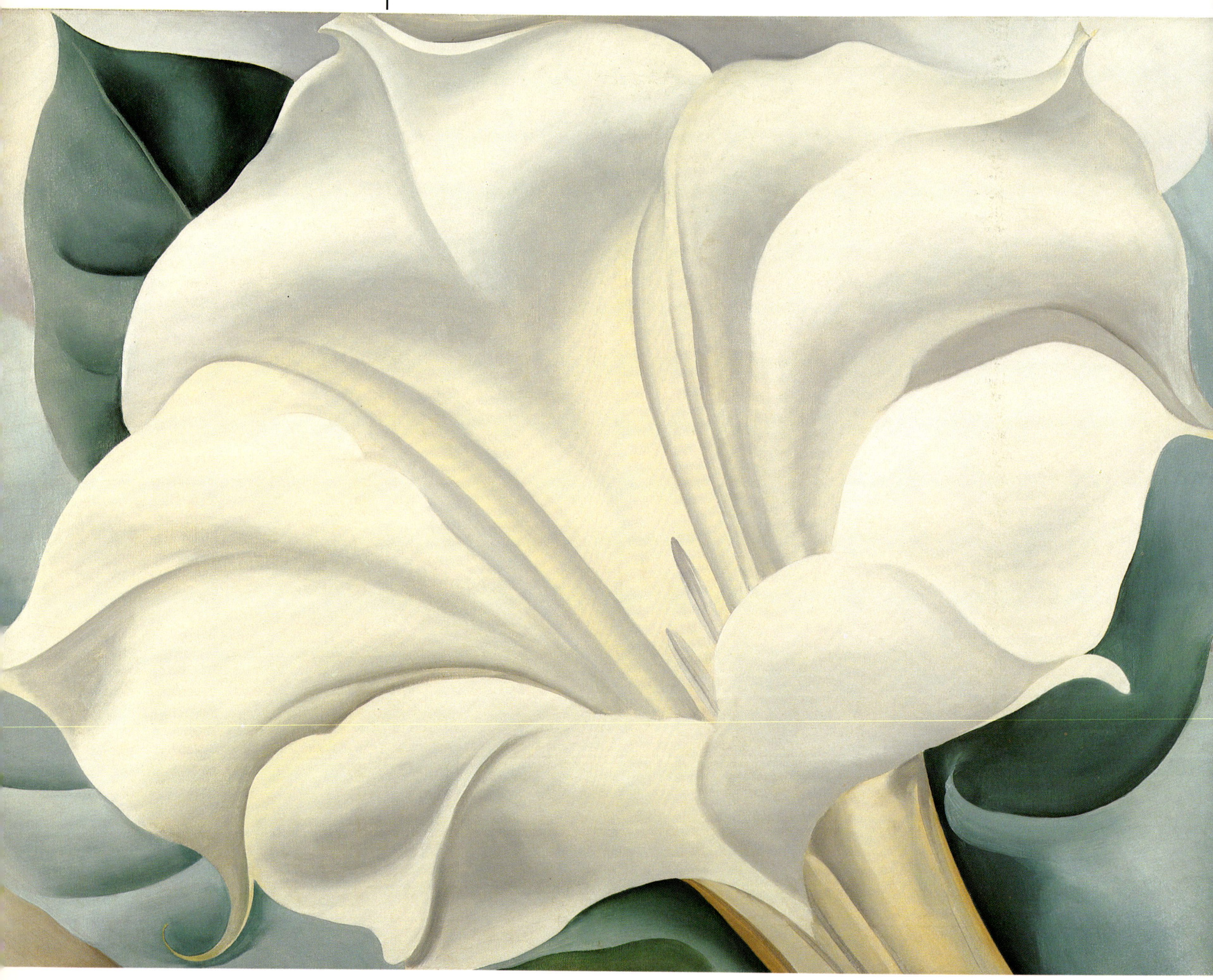

Georgia O'Keeffe. The White Flower *(titled on reverse), also known as* White Trumpet Flower, *is in the collection of the San Diego Museum of Art, California. Oil on canvas, wax lined. 30 1/8 inches (76.5 cm) height x 40 1/16 inches (101.7 cm) width. Not signed. Dated 1932 on the reverse.*

vase or even a stem. The background is adorned with only the flower's shadow. Nothing could be simpler or more real, yet such directness startled the first viewers.

O'Keeffe wrote in 1939, "A flower is relatively small. Everyone has many associations with a flower–the idea of flowers. You put out your hand to touch the flower–lean forward to smell it–maybe touch it with your lips almost without thinking–or give it to someone to please them. Still–in a way–nobody sees a flower–really–it is so small–we haven't time–and to see takes time like to have a friend takes time. If I could paint the flower exactly as I see it no one would see what I see because I would paint it small like the flower is small.

"So I said to myself–I'll paint what I see–what the flower is to me but I'll paint it big and they will be surprised into taking time to look at it–I will make even busy New

Yorkers take time to see what I see of flowers."

In her terse and somewhat impudent manner O'Keeffe explained her motive for painting a flower as an uncomplicated desire to portray the object so people would recognize what she saw in it. Nevertheless, her paintings evoke in some an emotional response not necessarily related to the actual object depicted. Obviously, people with inner life, the sort who are moved by her work, perceive more than just an enlarged flower. Stripped of any association, viewers are free to endow the flower with their own meaning and some part of themselves.

A comparison with the photographs of Stieglitz is easy to make. Stieglitz clearly stated that his photographs, termed by him "equivalents," represented his own feelings, but should induce different responses in others.

O'Keeffe, however, valued her privacy more obsessively and was disinterested in her audience's interpretation: "When you took time to really notice my flower you hung all your own associations with flowers on my flower and you write about my flower as if I think and see what you think and see of the flower–and I don't."

O'Keeffe denied having been influenced by the photographs of Stieglitz. There is, however, an obvious photographic quality to *The White Flower*. The sharp focus, resonant middle tones, incandescent whites, and slightly blurred reflected light are all pictorial devices of black and white photographs. But more important, the simplicity of composition and heightened realism which paradoxically verge on abstraction call to mind the "straight" purely artistic photography of the day as practiced by Stieglitz, Paul Strand, and Edward Steichen.

O'Keeffe modeled her subjects with subtle gradations of light and shadow to produce sensual curvatures. For her inspiration she looked to a personal philosophy based on nature, not to her early training or the avant-garde. She sought natural forms that, by simplification, would represent her dreams and inspirations.

Compositionally, *The White Flower* is uncomplicated and direct. The flower is presented frontally, framed by the leaves which parallel the form of the petals in the upper right and left corners. The inward curve of the lower right leaf directs the viewer's attention up and into the flower.

One enters *The White Flower* with the perspective of an insect about to land on a petal. The flower is tilted up toward the light, responding to the source of energy as any growing thing would. It conveys the positive force intrinsic in nature. The flower is not contained within the picture plane, but reaches slightly beyond the edges of the canvas, again expressing growth and freedom.

The approach taken here, analyzing her work in a series of details, is consistent with her own method of developing a theme. She often painted in series, taking one subject and enlarging the core elements in further paintings, much as the successive detailing does here.

The technique is simple. A sketch was drawn onto plain weave canvas primed with a cream colored ground. A colored paint layer was then applied, usually either green for the leaves or gray for the background and flower. White was blended into this still wet underlayer to produce the graduations of tones that create the contours. Often the ground was left exposed at the tops of the canvas weave where a particularly bright highlight was desired or to depict scattered light.

The brushwork throughout is extremely tidy and controlled. The brush is never free to wander or dab, and the paint rarely trespasses over the neat lines of the underdrawing. The brush remains always sensitive to the most subtle form and delicate curvatures.

The most striking qualities of *The White Flower* are simplicity and clarity. All unnecessary details, anything that could give the flower a context outside of itself, have been omitted. O'Keeffe's refinement of form and color is in keeping with her refinement of technique; her commitment was to craftsmanship. Her brushwork is minimal, con-

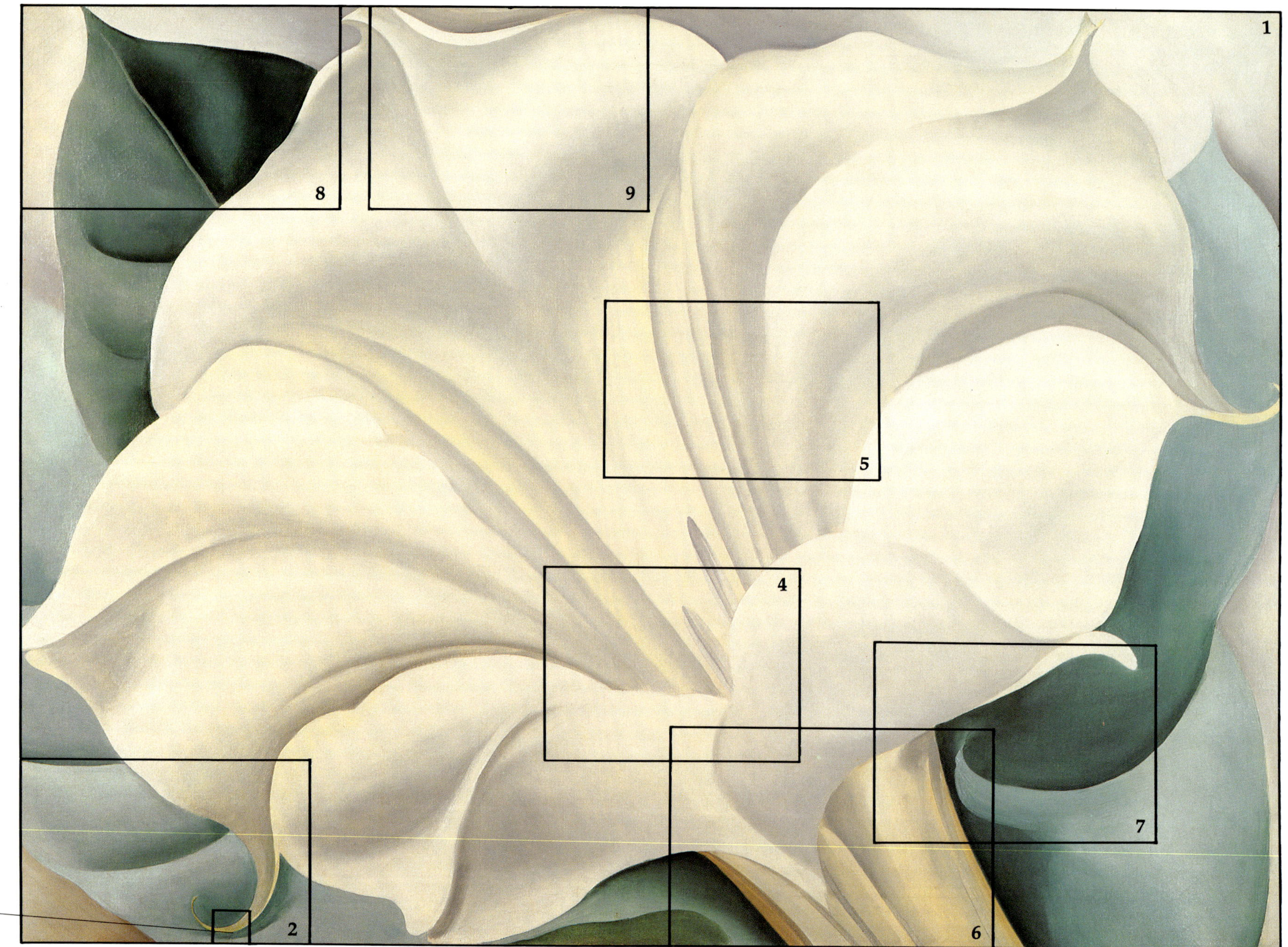

trolled, tidy, yet always delicate and unhesitatingly sure. Hers is a hand that prefers to depict but not intrude.

With most artists, to speak of technique is to open doors of comprehension and vision into the artists' work. With O'Keeffe the opposite is true. Her technique was so controlled that her touch is almost imperceptible. Yet somehow, even more so than with other artists, her presence is felt. Why is this so? The answer has to do with what makes one painting great and another not. Technique, composition, and subject can be described in words, but perhaps words cannot explain what is most important to a painting. The essence of art is its ability to transcend words, to bring one into a deeper understanding of the world. In her utter simplicity, O'Keeffe has done what most are afraid to try. The unembellished forms offer mere suggestions of paths to follow and the viewer is left free to wander unhindered.

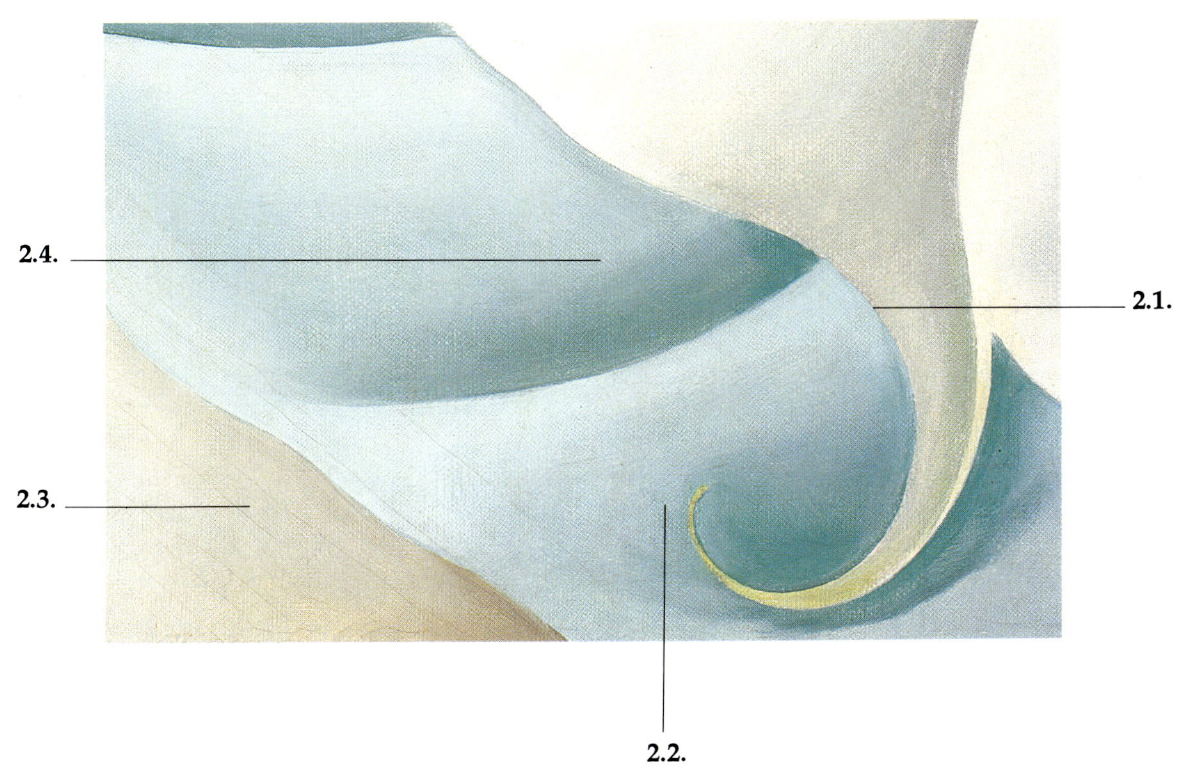

2.4. ———

2.3. ———

2.1.

2.2.

2. DETAIL OF TIP OF FLOWER PETAL IN LOWER LEFT CORNER

2.1. The underdrawing can be seen along the edge of the flower petal. The carefully applied paint stays neatly within the bounds of these drawn lines.

2.2. The transparent green was applied first. The opaque white of the highlights was blended into the still somewhat wet green paint to form the contours of the leaf.

2.3. The white paint strokes give the appearance of having been brushed freely, continuing from one side of the petal to the other. In fact, however, the white has been brushed carefully around the petal.

2.4. These are aging cracks.

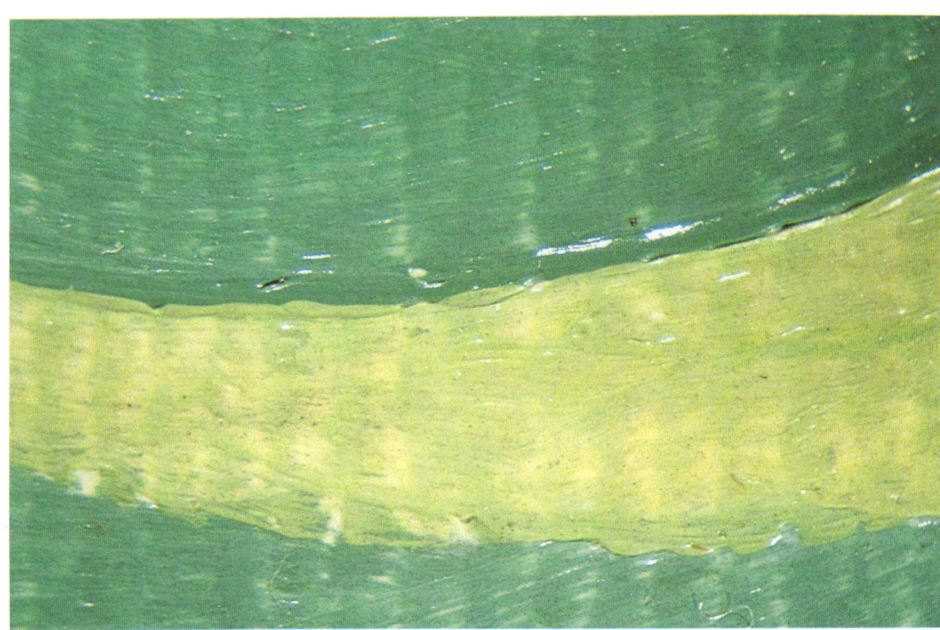

3. PHOTOMICROGRAPH OF PETAL SHOWN IN PREVIOUS ILLUSTRATION

Taken through a microscope, this greatly enlarged detail shows the minimal and tidy brushwork. The green of the leaf was applied first, leaving the ground bare for the petal. Then the yellow-green paint of the petal tip was applied with a deliberate hand that corrected any slight irregularity in the edges of the green. As throughout the painting, the white ground, enhanced by the fabric weave, shows through to create a luminous effect where the paint has been thinly applied.

4.1. The clearly defined edge of the petal il-lustrates the sharp focus.

4.2. Here the edge of the petal is made indistinct by the brightly reflected light, de-picted by bare ground at the tops of the canvas weave.

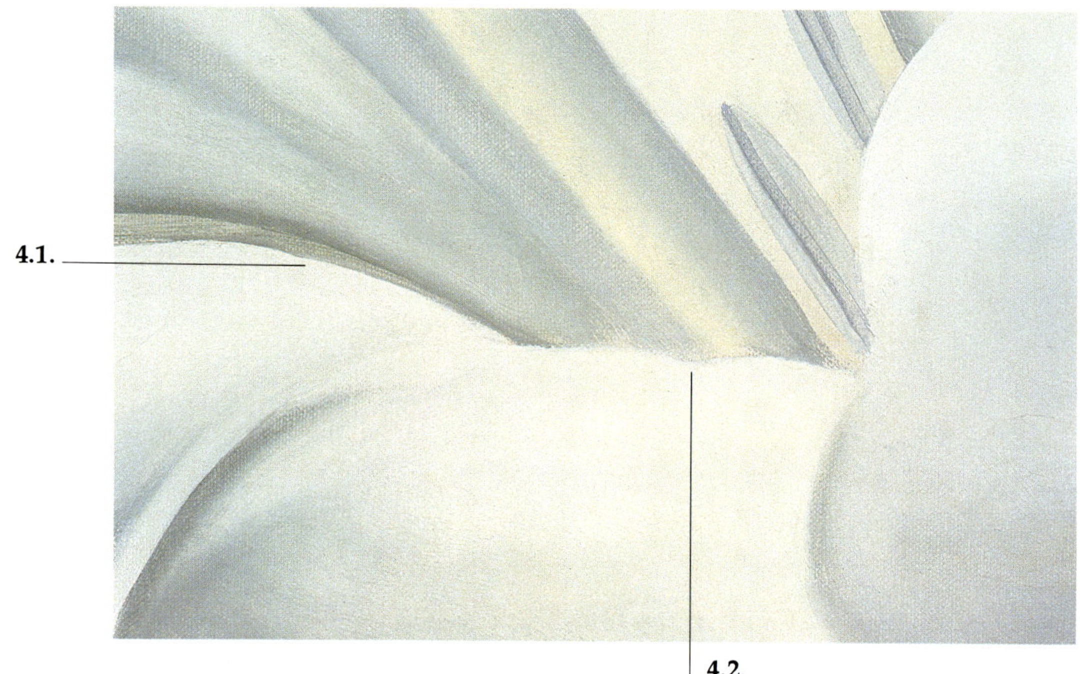

4. DETAIL OF CENTER OF FLOWER

The sharp focus, incandescent whites, shimmering middle tones, and even the graininess of the canvas texture have a photographic quality.

5. SECOND DETAIL OF CENTER OF FLOWER

Blending the white into the gray paint produces a seemingly infinite range of tonal values shaping the contours of the petal. Here again, the points of exposed ground create the effect of scattered light.

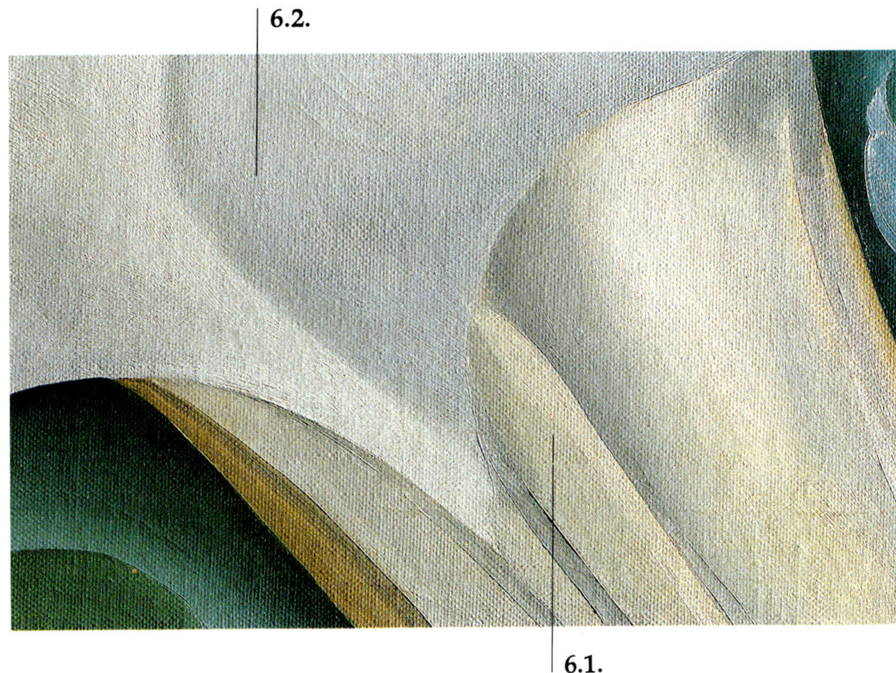

6.2.

6.1.

6. BASE OF FLOWER IN RAKING LIGHT

The smoothness and precision of O'Keeffe's technique makes it difficult to appreciate the hand behind the brush. Only when the brushwork and canvas texture are magnified, as here in raking light, is one startled into taking notice of how such an illusion of reality was created.

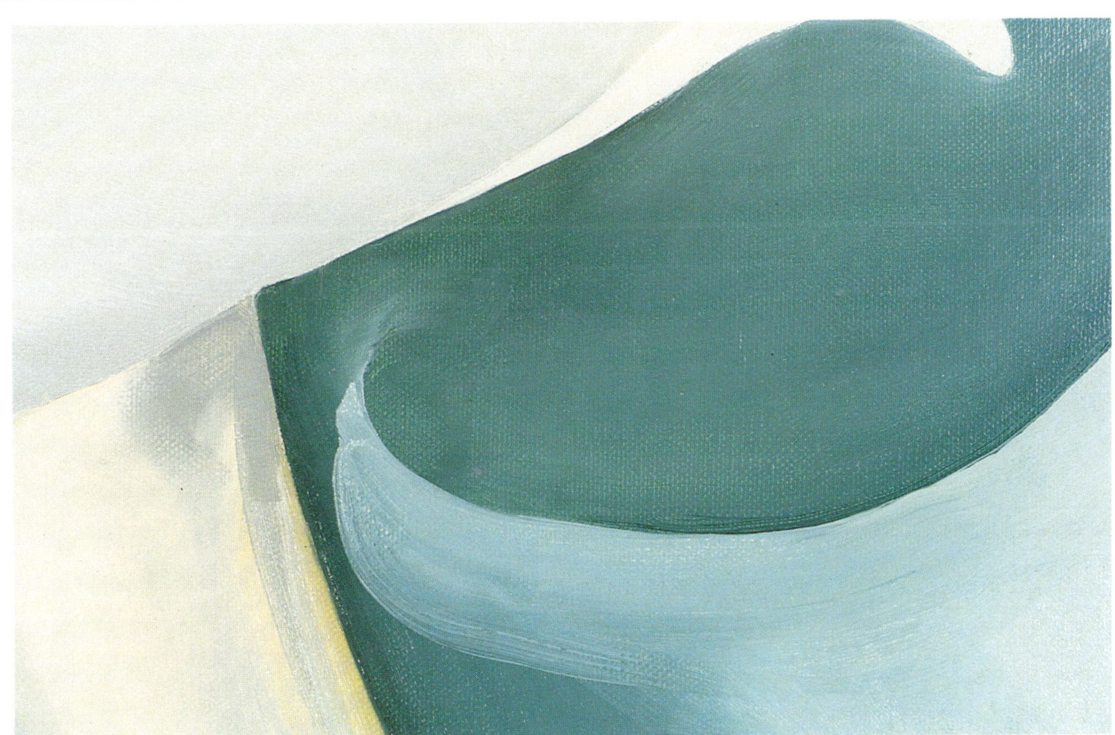

7. DETAIL OF LEAF CURLED INWARD AT LOWER RIGHT

This is the most painterly part of the flower. The white has been freely blended into the green, avoiding sharp lines except along the top of the leaf. The tip of the leaf is a flourish of bright paint creating the illusion of a highlight and its reflection.

6.1. A stiff, color-loaded brush measuring one-quarter inch applied the paint in one stroke. The brush was handled in a slow and determined manner. The pressure produced ridges of paint along the edges of the strokes.

6.2. Here again, the colors were blended on the surface of the canvas to create the delicate transitions in the modeling.

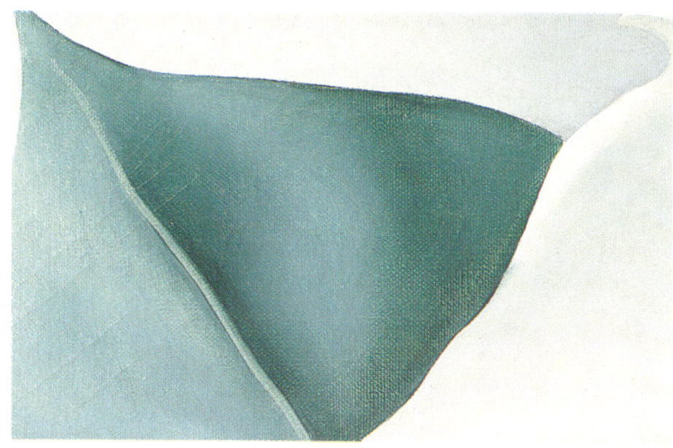

8. Detail of Green Leaf in Upper Left Corner

Form has been achieved with minimal handling of the paint. Again, the transparent green was applied first and the opaque white was blended in while the green was still a bit wet. The fabric texture and points of exposed ground make the paint shimmer. The form is drawn precisely and the focus is sharp as always. The colors are iridescent.

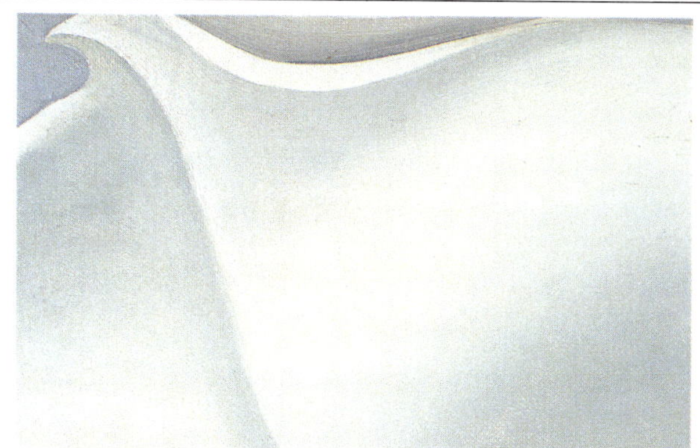

9. Detail of Topmost Petal in Upper Left Corner

The precise undulatory lines along the top of the petal contrast with the softer modeling of the lower curves. The form is at once austerely plain and sensually delicate. One could read into this detail a wave of water or the form of a soaring bird. O'Keeffe herself might have said, If you see it, it's there.

SUMMARY OF PAINTING TECHNIQUE

a. The plain weave fabric was primed with a cream colored ground.
b. A sketch was drawn with pencil or charcoal.
c. The build-up of the paint layers is straightforward and consists of one or two layers. Initially, a thin colored layer closely followed the sketch. For this painting, the colored layer is usually either gray for the flower and background or a transparent green for the leaves.

An opaque white layer was added while the thin layer beneath was somewhat wet. This blending produces the infinite range of tonal values to create the three-dimensional-appearing contours.

The term "blending" is not used here in the academic sense. A smooth paint surface was not desired in this picture and the brush marks were retained. The ground is left exposed to depict scattered light or where a particularly bright highlight was desired.

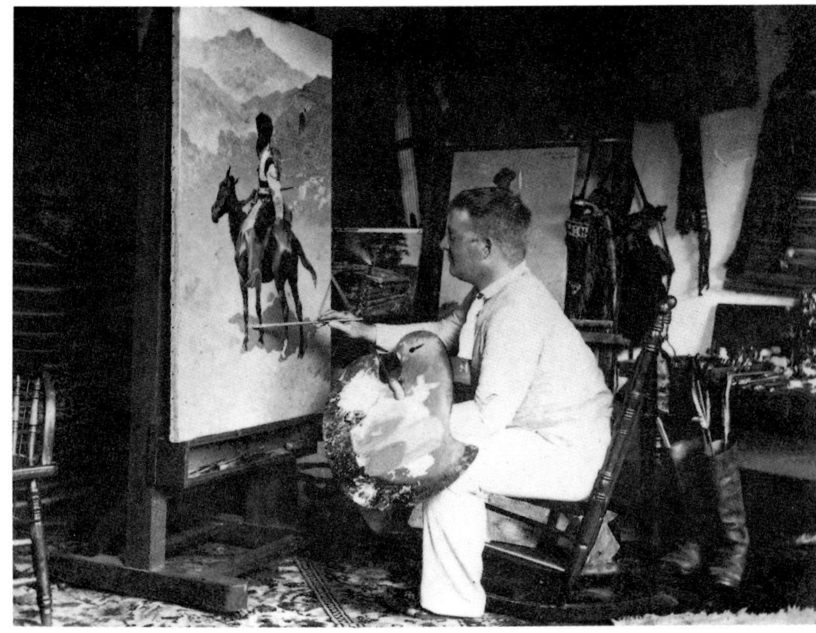

FREDERIC REMINGTON

The first master painters of the Western landscape–Bierstadt, Whittredge, Moran, and Hill–were still working when Frederic Remington was beginning as an illustrator in 1886, but he had no contact with them. They lived in a different, more old-fashioned world of fine art. After Remington quit illustrating to join the American Impressionists, he announced the artistic epitaphs of the antique landscape painters on the basis that, as he put it, they "did not paint 'air'–they saw things darkly."

The mature Remington crammed 300 pounds into his 5 foot 9 inch frame. He carried his heft with a confident, graceful waddle. Blond turning gray and balding, he presented a smooth fair face that was puffed with fat. In the city, he dressed and held himself out to be as worldly as any well-to-do merchant banker but his many friends in all walks of life continued to see him only as a big, good-natured, overgrown boy.

In his day, Remington was the focal point for the practitioners of his type of action-dominated Western figure painting. The big man also set the standard for the Cavalry, Indian, and cowboy genre painters who came after him. They were all on occasion lumped together as followers in "the school of Remington." He was Russell's constant irritant, Schreyvogel's implacable enemy, Dixon's mentor, Berninghaus' inspiration, Johnson's moonlight, Leigh's measurement, and Wyeth's first model. He was the one painter of larger than life Western realism who was the hub for all the rest.

Yet, given his inartistic antecedents and his demonstrated lack of early talent, the young Fred Remington would have been an unlikely choice to become a major American painter and sculptor. The key to understanding the mature Remington with his unique talent is an awareness of the pride that drove him constantly toward self-improvement as an artist. The best things he ever did were in his last few years. If he had lived longer, his paintings would have been even better as he mastered new techniques. He would have tried his hand at murals and original prints. His bronze sculptures would have been more monumental.

Remington was born October 4, 1861 in the village of Canton in the North Country of

New York State. As a child, he learned his aspirations and his limits from his parents: derring-do versus salt pork with milk gravy. He preferred the pork.

An intensive look at his adolescence is almost irrelevant to his art. He was hyperactive as a boy. His father was certifiably a hero as a dashing Cavalry Colonel who was fearless in Civil War battles. The Colonel set high marks for daring that the prosaic Remington could never hope to match. As a military man the Colonel thought artists were sissies and he hung no painting in his house. Remington's mother was a stubborn, sturdy homebody who believed in the efficacy of ingesting a large quantity of food to cure all ills.

As a youth Remington played football for Yale rather than giving his attention to the classical studies in the Yale Art School where he was enrolled briefly. He grew into his father's opposite, a prudent man. He was to become not an actor but a recorder in paint and bronze of the deeds of the valiant figures who were the embodiment of his father. He was to be obese from the overindulgences initiated by his mother.

At 20 he was in Albany, New York working as a disaffected clerk in the state government. For his summer vacation he traveled alone in the West. From Wyoming he mailed a crude little sketch of cowboys to the prestigious *Harper's Weekly* magazine. The sketch was published after it was redrawn by a staff artist. Although Remington was not able to sell the *Weekly* another sketch for three years, his enthusiasts dated his career as an illustrator to 1881, the year of his first appearance in print.

An uncle sponsored Remington's move to New York City in 1885 to find work as an artist. Posing as a cowboy he sold *Harper's* two additional sketches that were rough but had "the ring of truth." In March 1886 Remington entered classes at the Art Students League. His painting technique improved rapidly when he gave 100 percent of himself for the first time in any pursuit.

The brief formal instruction as an artist was his last. In three months he was heading West again. This time he was retained by *Harper's* as the correspondent to search for Geronimo, a wily Apache chief on the warpath. As an example of Remington's prudence, he switched his assignment from tracking the dangerous wild Indians into an article on soldiering in the Southwest. His Cavalry drawings were printed without being redrawn by the staff. The pictures were awkward but they had a special extra fillip of tension in the body language of the figures. By the end of 1886 Remington was an established illustrator of Western subjects.

In another two years Remington was also exhibiting easel paintings at the National Academy of Design. The critics noticed his work and predicted that he would "one day be listed among the great American painters." Remington called this "a grand puff." From the start of his dedication to commercial work that would last for a dozen years, he illustrated the works of Theodore Roosevelt and many other popular authors. In addition, he wrote his own exciting outdoor articles to sell even more illustrations. He could concentrate under any circumstance. When he painted on vacation, the people near him said they "thought we would go mad" while "he'd sit cross-legged painting, diddling his free foot up and down, up and down, and whistling, whistling, whistling."

In 1889, Remington exhibited a painting at the Paris Exposition and won a medal for his native American realism. Older Academic painters like the famous panoramist Albert Bierstadt were deprecated by the judges. To take advantage of Remington's honors in fine art his publisher, the House of Harper, launched a promotional campaign to equate Remington the man with his violent illustrations. The saying was, "He draws what he knows." For publicity, the sophisticated artist was willing to pose as an uncouth Westerner.

The following year Remington had his first one-man show. The subjects were still Western but privately Remington was already certain that "the building up of the West formed an era that is past." He said the time for fascination with the cowboy and the Indian had ended. He intended to proceed to other outdoor and military subjects.

To the Eastern public, however, the land across the Mississippi was still wild and Remington had become the designated pictorial arbiter of what was truly Western. The Harpers wanted only Western images from him and so he remained locked into a mythical West that persisted mainly as a fiction. In addition, he continued to exhibit at the National Academy. He was elected an Associate member in 1891. That was the penultimate step to becoming an Academician.

The following year Remington entered a small pastel in the National Academy exhibition instead of a major oil painting. He meant the pastel to demonstrate his ability as a colorist and was mortified when the hanging committee relegated the piece to a remote location. Tit for tat as he saw it, he refused to enter the 1893 exhibition. As a challenge to the Academy, he put on his own one-man show and sale.

That was the end of Remington's chance to be elected an Academician. For years afterward he rejected peace offerings from members of the Academy. He had insisted on deference from his publishers, his peers, and the public before he was entitled to high rank as an artist. He was no less demanding now that he was becoming the busiest artist in America. His work was recognized internationally. Even Kaiser Wilhelm II of Germany knew about Remington.

In art he was still hyperactive. He described his painting process as wholly an emotional expression. As soon as he would "get my idea on what I am going to do, then the rest of it is nothing. I've made the best things I ever did in two hours. It is all in feeling it. If I don't feel it I work something else till I do feel it."

In late 1894 Remington began sculpting with no training other than brief observation of an established sculptor. The first subject he chose was a rearing *Bronco Buster*, a composition that had never been modeled before because of its problems with balance. He completed the bronze in a year. Remington said the statuette stood for "the wild life of our West in something the burglar won't have, moths eat, or time blacken." The exhibition of the bronze was an art event of the year. The *Bronco Buster* was the first of 21 table-top sculptures and one monument, *The Cowboy*.

Remington's real goal was to be a war correspondent rather than to continue to "pot boil" the Old West. In 1897 the publisher Hearst hired him to accompany the celebrated correspondent Richard Harding Davis to Cuba to report on the insurrection on the island. There was a well-known exchange of cables between Hearst and Remington. The artist wanted to come home. He denied that war existed in Cuba. The publisher told him to stay. He promised to create the war.

After the battleship *Maine* blew up in Havana harbor the next year, Remington sailed to Cuba with the American invasion fleet. Too overweight to handle the rigors of the campaign in the field, he missed the fights and became the chronicler of the battle's rear. He reported on the ordinary soldiers who did their simple best, not on the heroes. While in Cuba he was one of the few correspondents to fail to glorify the exploits of Colonel Theodore Roosevelt, the hero of the charge at San Juan Hill.

When Remington returned to his home in New Rochelle, a suburb of New York City, his friends noticed "he was not happy in his heart." He was drinking heavily. Finally, he gave up his dream of equaling his father's courageous exploits. He confessed, "That old drying up of the West–that is the war I am going to put the rest of my time at." The Cuban experience had matured and mellowed Remington.

Harper's fired him as illustrator because he was too expensive. *Collier's* magazine picked him up, paid more, and gave him the widest exposure. His paintings were reproduced in the magazine in double-page spreads in full color.

In Taos, New Mexico he told European-trained Bert Phillips how to add dash to a picture. He hummed fast popular music and painted in timed strokes. Tum tiddy tum tum was stroke dab dab stroke stroke. He said his own colors were so hot, "passing fire engines will stop." He marveled at his skill in composition. "Some well bred boys called," he remarked. "They take my pictures for veritable happenings & speculate on what will happen next to the puppets, so arduous are boys' imaginations."

His unspoken aim, however, was to paint fine art like the American Impressionists. Paintings that used to take a couple of hours might now take a week as he sought perfection. When paintings were finished he would have a "hanging day" in his studio. According to his friends, he would "tiptoe around and watch your expression. If the picture doesn't strike the observer at once it's all wrong, to Remington's way of thinking, and he forthwith studies it out and works [again] until he puts it there."

"I am learning," Remington wrote in his diary, "to use Prussian [blue] & Ultramarine in proper way," for nocturnes. Soon after, he added, "I have *now* discovered for the first time how to do the *silver sheen* of moonlight." President Roosevelt maintained that "he is one of the most typical American artists we have ever had. The soldier, the cowboy and rancher, the Indian, the horses and the cattle of the plains, will live in his pictures and bronzes for all time."

In less than 20 years of commercial work Remington had drawn or painted at least 2,700 illustrations for most of the leading magazine and book publishers. He quit commercial art, however, to devote himself to fine art full time. His close companions included six of The Ten, the greatest of the American Impressionists.

His best friend was Childe Hassam, a leading Impressionist. Remington thought he caught Western colors better than Hassam. To achieve the new style, his hues were muted. Backgrounds were conceived as simplified patterns. In the figures only the faces in the focus were fully drawn. By 1905 critics began to remark on his growing strength as an artist, but the Academicians continued to charge him with being more of an illustrator than a painter. The subject was more to him, they said, than symbolism or beauty.

His next year's gallery exhibition brought "a softened and harmonized Remington in those tones of mystery he had lacked." Early in 1907 he burned the first of four batches of his old paintings "so they will never confront me in the future." At the same time, he was painting pictures like *Downing the Nigh Leader* to meet *Collier's* demand for violent Western action taking place in the glare of noon. *Downing the Nigh Leader* survived the burnings because it was one of only two pictures sold at the gallery. Today it is regarded as among the most moving of his works.

He considered himself to be a recognized Impressionist by 1908. "Small canvases are best," he stated, "all plein air color and outlines lost." He described his paintings as "quite vibrating." A canvas should, he observed, "glow and quiver until it seems to exude the palpitating quality which light holds." Monet was said to be his primary influence. His December 4, 1909 show was an unqualified success. Remington rejoiced that, "I have landed among the painters and high up too." His brags had all come true.

When Remington died from a burst appendix three weeks later he was in his prime, at the height of his power as an artist. He was admittedly the best in the world at his specialty and he was getting better.

His early demise "nipped his talent at the height of his power, while he was deep in the contemporary art movement, absorbing Monet and approaching Whistler. He was full of enthusiasm for the future, on the verge of something entirely new, something simplified, symbolic, the motif not death but vitality, an application of Western values to his individual view of the American past."

His own more modest claim to fame was that he had been "the first man to do horse action as it is." He wanted to be remembered as the discoverer that all hooves are off the ground at one point in an equine gallop, but his wife refused to permit "He Knew the Horse" to be engraved on his gravestone as his epitaph.

In May 1985 his painting *Assault on His Dignity* sold for $570,000 at public auction.

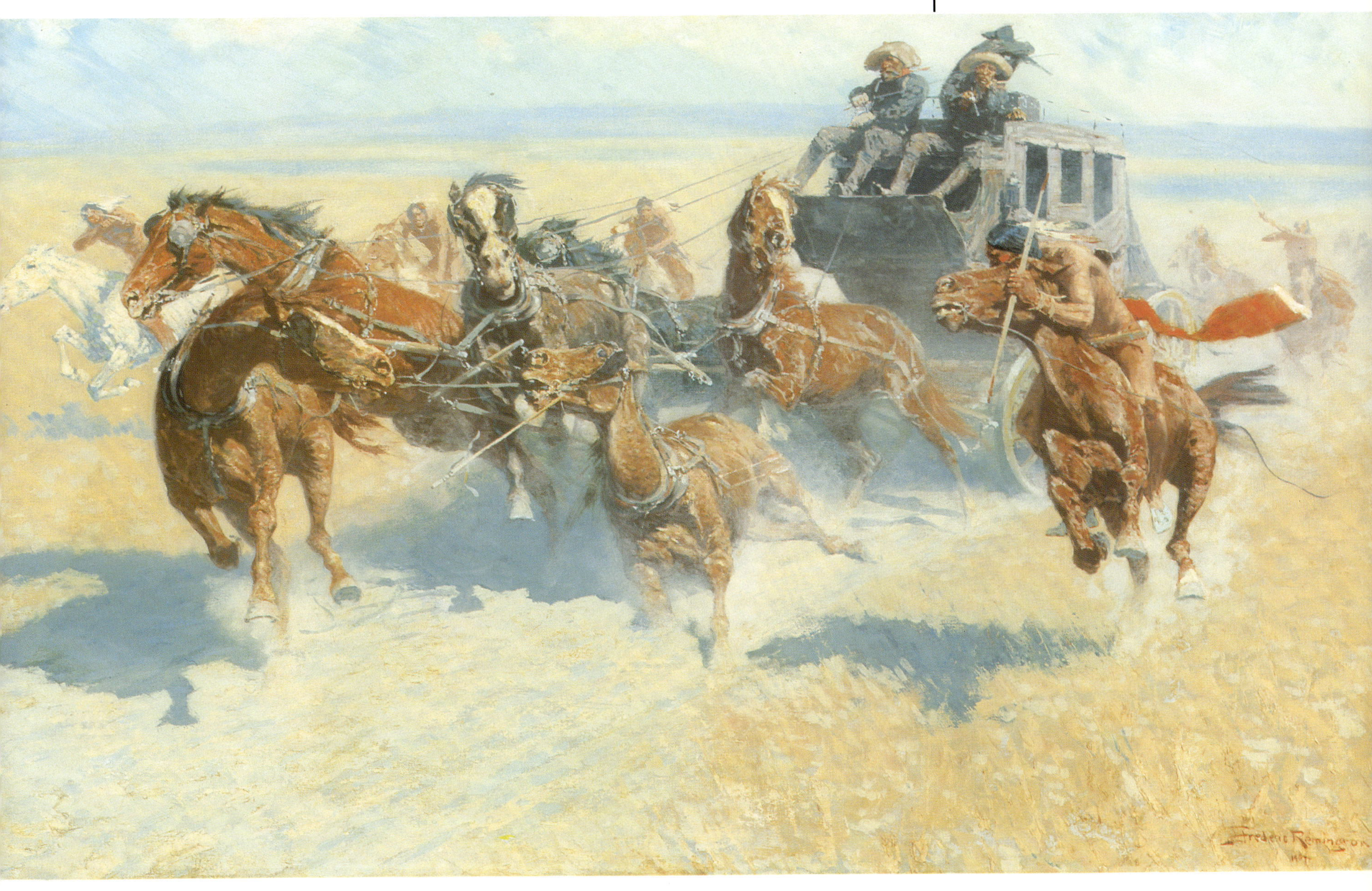

1. THE PAINTING

In *Downing the Nigh Leader* the action is upon us. The horses leap out from a blur of raised dust. A sure hand was at work in a composition that was well thought out in advance. Remington's painting process was practiced and organized in portraying the action at the moment before its climax.

Downing the Nigh Leader was one of many paintings commissioned for reproduction in *Collier's* magazine. The sequence of the action is from left to right. The Indian has driven his lance into the falling left horse, or "nigh leader." The other horses will be down in a moment, the stagecoach will crash to a halt, and all will be at the mercy of the attacking Indians. They haven't a chance.

The essence of the painting is the movement. Remington employed various methods to enhance the excitement and thereby rivet the viewer's attention. Most notable of the devices is the foreshortening of the horses, causing them to explode from the canvas, defying the picture plane in which the rest of the composition is confined. This effect is a trademark of Remington's style.

Among other enhancements Remington used to hold the audience's attention, the skull-like head of the galloping horse in the upper center has dark connotations which

Frederic Remington. Downing the Nigh Leader is in the collection of the Museum of Western Art, Denver, Colorado. Oil on canvas, lined. 30 inches (76.2 cm) height x 51 1/8 inches (129.8 cm) width. Signed lower right and dated 1907.

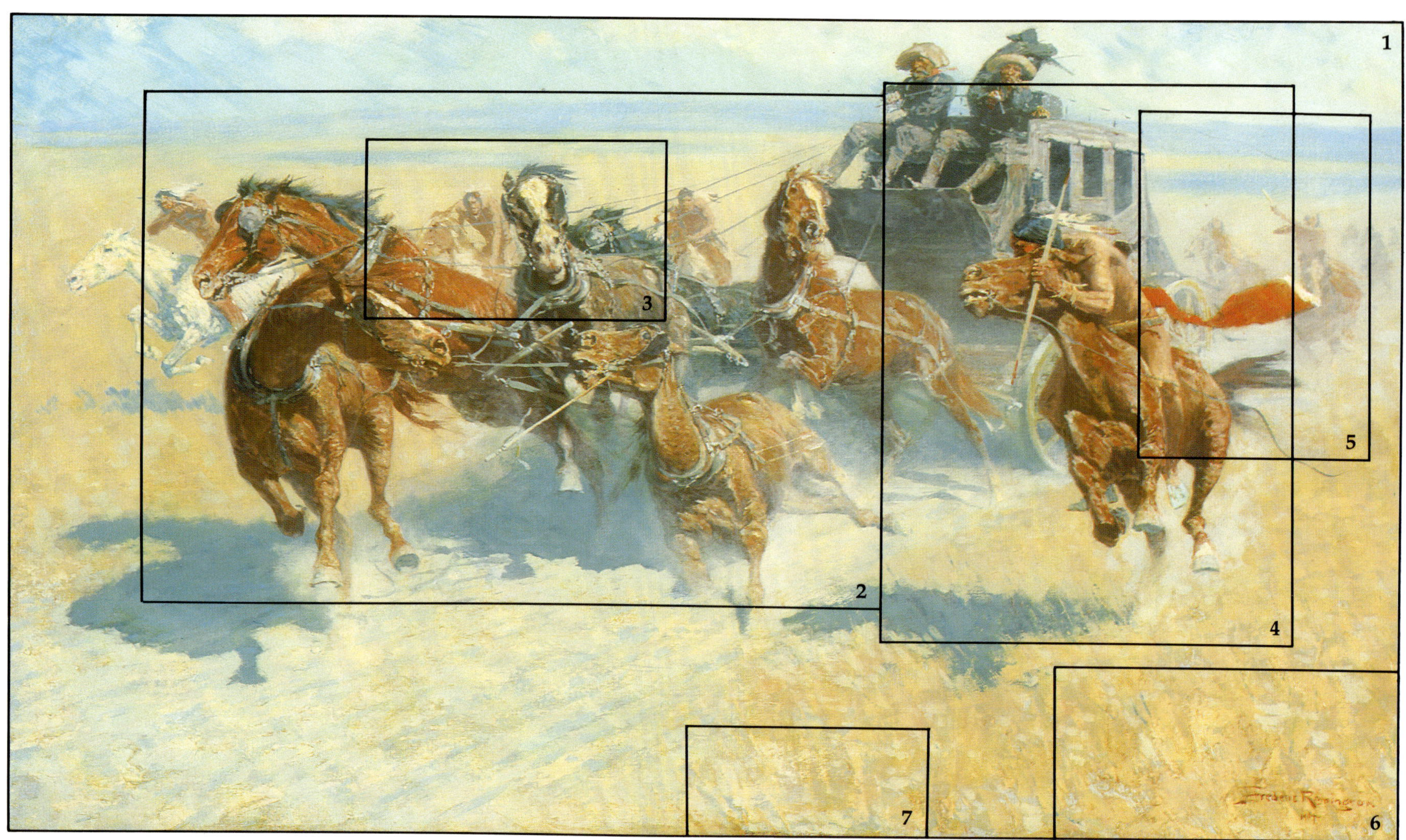

have a subliminal effect. More directly, the use of extra lines drawn parallel to the horses heightens the effect of the motion. Similar simplified lines are commonly drawn in comic book illustrations today to depict swift movement. Remington also used a tool such as a palette knife to draw lines in the wet paint of the foreground grass to direct the viewer's eyes.

Twenty years earlier when Remington was beginning as an illustrator, he had been severely criticized for his reliance on photographic images in his painting. The telltale mark of the camera on his work was said to be the same type of foreshortening as used for the horses. In *Downing the Nigh Leader*, however, there was no way Remington could have photographed a scene that was taken wholly from his imagination. The foreshortening was obviously a considered painterly device. On the other hand, sharp focus of the moving horses set amid a blur of dust is an effect likely to have been derived from stop-action photography, which was one of the technological breakthroughs of the day.

Live models were naturally preferred when a pose was achievable, but Remington did use photographs as *aide-memoires* when confronted with unfamiliar subjects. By the time *Downing the Nigh Leader* was painted, however, horses rolled from the brush of "the man who knew the horse." Remington was past the point of needing equine photos as references. As he put it, "I *have always wanted* to be able to paint running horses so you would feel the details and not *see* them. I am getting so I can stagger at it."

To create atmospheric perspective, Remington used contrasts in color values and in sharpness. The horses and the Indian in the foreground were painted with strong colors and clearly defined outlines. The background was depicted with more subdued tones and less contrast between highlight and shadow. The firm outlines of the foreground also contrasted with parts of the painting made less distinct by sketchily applied paint and scumbles of dust obscuring details.

Remington used a medium weight, plain weave canvas. A warm, light gray ground was applied thinly. The main composition was sketched in with what appears to have been a thin dark oil paint, probably applied with a fine brush. The forms were then blocked in with dark blue paint which provided the color for the shadows. For the most part, subsequent paint was applied from dark to light, that is, from shadows to highlights. The surface is impasted and retains the imprint of vigorous brushstrokes. Finally, Remington added nuances and adjusted contours by superimposing more shadows, highlights, outlines, and scumbles.

Although Remington ate and drank to excess, his painting technique was tight and controlled. The results achieved by formula were dramatic. Rapid execution and a sure hand were the artist's meal ticket.

This is not to imply that Remington was a potboiler. He was driven. His advice to others was paint, paint, paint because he knew from personal experience that his method worked. His serious studies at the Art Students League lasted three months. Beyond that he was self-taught, assimilating every trend and technique he had use for. He was not a fiddler or a fusser, but he approached painting with an energy and inspiration that made self-improvement a compulsion–something to be dealt with so he could get on with the serious business of producing art.

He was a natural. When death took him without warning, he was still racing ahead on the art track, well past his peers and in sight of what was to come.

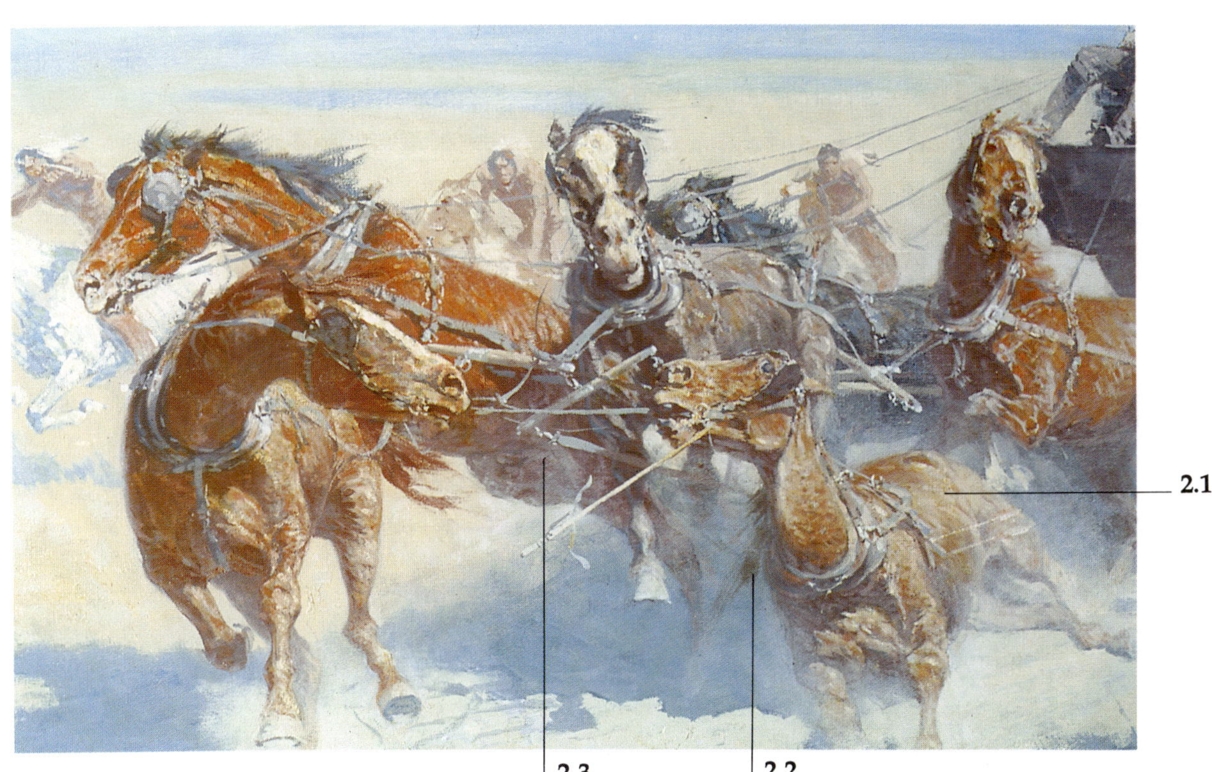

2.1. The "nigh leader" or near leading horse is the forward horse on the driver's left. He is falling, agonized by the lance in his jaw.

2.2. The blue underlayer used for shadows continues under the horses and the coach. Obscured outlines can be seen in places like the hoof of the hind leg of the horse on the far left.

2.3. The horses were painted with a reddish-brown underlayer. Shadows and highlights were added. A fine scumble was laid over the horses to depict the dust thrown into the air by the pounding of the hooves.

2. DETAIL OF HORSES

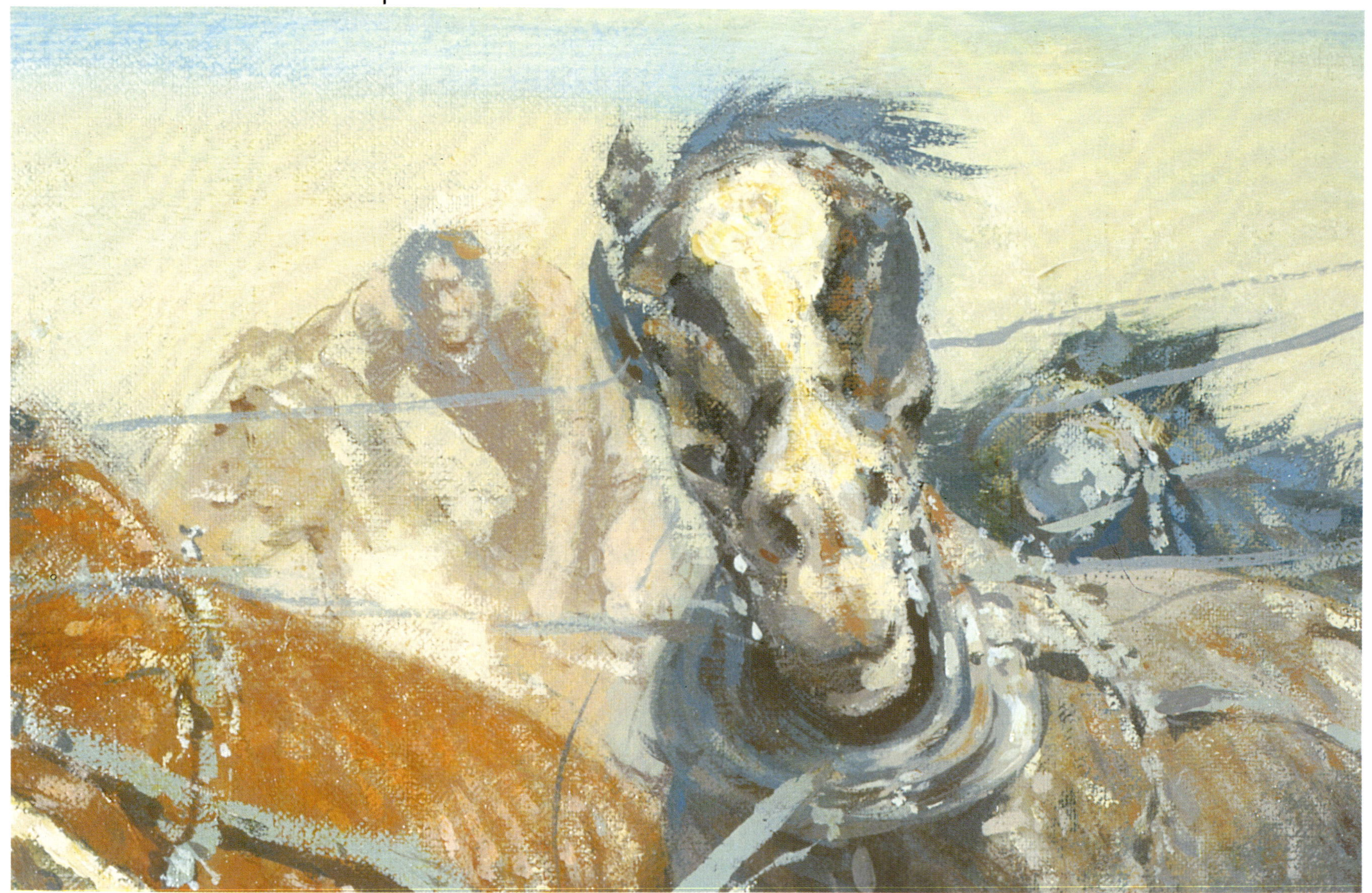

3. DETAIL OF HORSE'S HEAD

The horse's head was constructed systematically. First a violet-brown layer was put in. This was left partially exposed to serve as a middle tone. Thick impasted highlights created the features of the sketchily painted head. The lack of transition between the sparse details makes the head appear skull-like.

Remington directed attention to the focus by giving different color intensities to the elements portrayed. The viewer is drawn into the main action represented in strong dark colors. Less important details were painted in pastel colors. In the horse's head the strong colors were broken by sparkling highlights: dabs of white were used to indicate the burning sunlight reflected from the shiny hardware on the reins. Lastly, blue and gray lines were added. Some of these depict the reins. Others parallel the horses to enhance the movement.

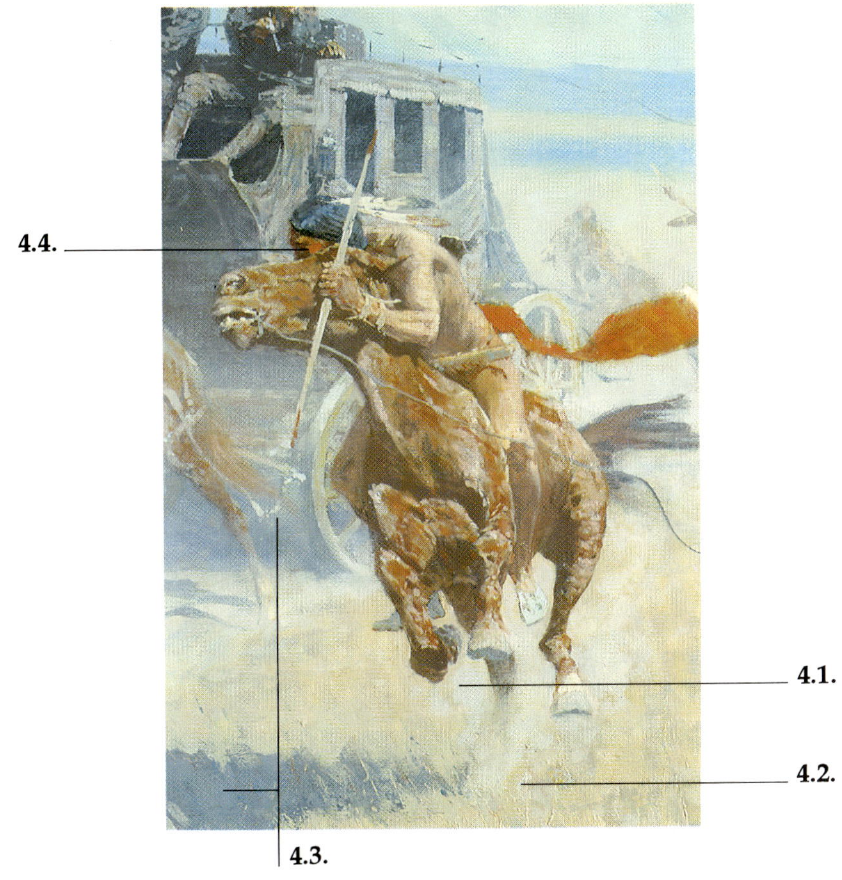

4. DETAIL OF MOUNTED INDIAN

4.1. A fine white scumble was applied around the body of the horse and over the hooves to depict dust.

4.2. The blades of the pale yellow grass were created by cutting into the wet paint with a tool such as a spatula or a palette knife. These cuts follow the direction of the action and energize the painting.

4.3. Here too, the blue underlayer was used as the shadow of the horse and served as a general blue middle tone.

4.4. As noted, the leading Indian and his horse were laid in with strong colors to focus attention.

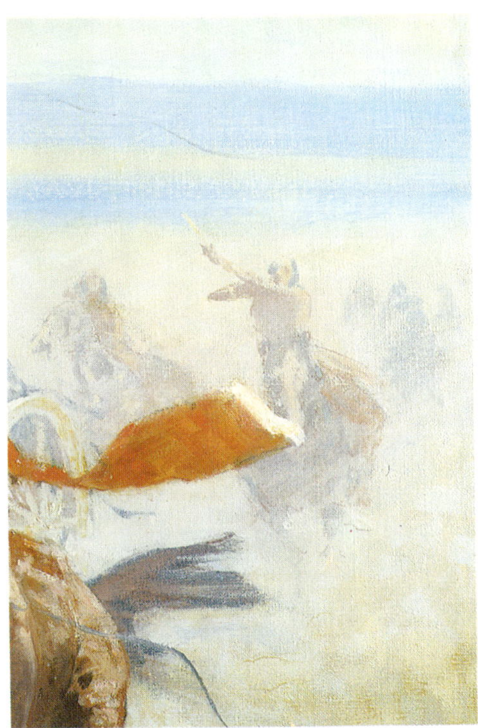

5. DETAIL OF INDIANS IN BACKGROUND

Atmospheric perspective was created by receding color intensities and diminishing focus. As the space recedes, the colors become paler and more subdued and the figures are sketchier.

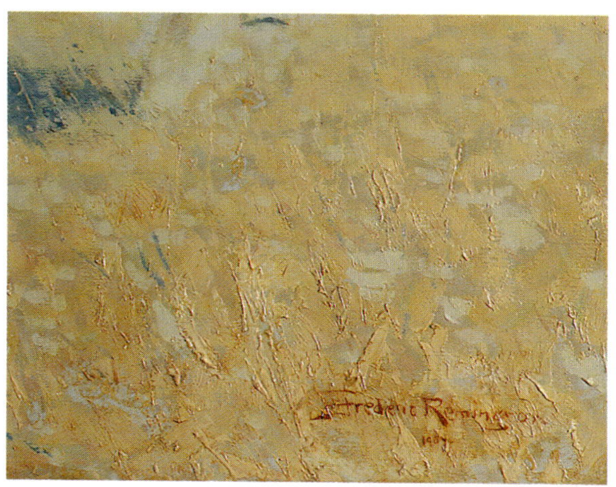

6. DETAIL OF SIGNATURE

Frederic Remington 1907.

    This is a good example of the artist's mature signature. He was one of the most forged American painters, but the spurious signatures were generally more tentative. In gross forgeries Remington's given name was sometimes put down as Frederick.

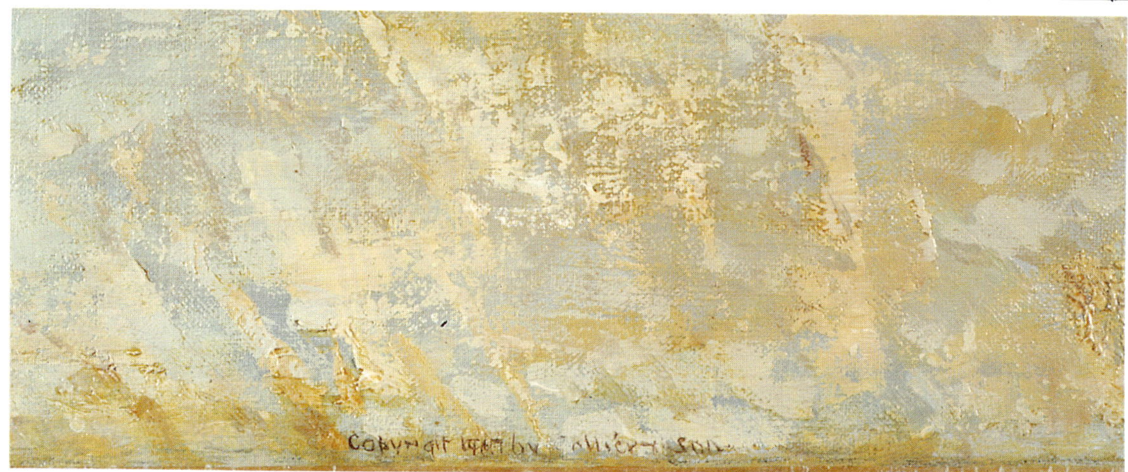

7. DETAIL OF COPYRIGHT NOTICE

Copyright 1907 by Collier & Son.

SUMMARY OF PAINTING TECHNIQUE

a. The fabric was attached to the stretcher.
b. A warm gray ground was applied thinly. As the tacking edges were removed when the painting was lined, it is not possible to determine whether Remington applied the ground himself. It is more likely that he used a commercially prepared canvas, as he did with other paintings.
c. The composition was sketched in with a thin brush and oil paint.
d. The areas representing shadow were blocked in with a dark blue underlayer.
e. The main composition was built up in a very organized way. Generally, Remington worked from dark to light on top of the blue middle tone.
f. Highlights were added in dabs of color. Shadows were used to adjust the contours. Finally, outlines were added to enhance the action and sharpen the focus.

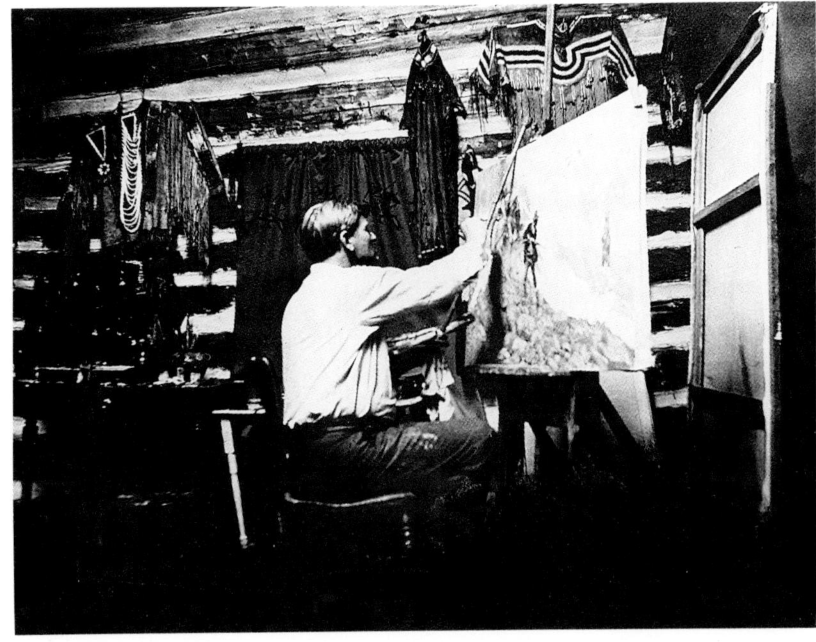

CHARLES MARION RUSSELL

When he was a young man, Charley Russell was one of "the wild 'uns" in Montana's Judith Basin. Off the range he drank to excess, gambled, and consorted with prostitutes. By the time he was married and middle-aged, though, he had been gentled as a man and as an artist.

Compared to the other master painters of the West, he was the most devoted to his adopted land and the most representative of what people expected from a Westerner. He was the most well-known painter among the other cowboys, but he was also the most controversial artistically.

Questions still endure about his art. Were his easel paintings fine art or were they just story-telling illustrations? Were his pictures created to symbolize the general character of the West and its people or were they specific incidents narrated by the artist in paint? Russell's many partisans had no doubt. To them, he stood alone as the greatest painter of the American West. His art was said to be accurate in every historic and cultural detail. Will Rogers maintained that Russell was "the only painter of Western pictures the cow-punchers can't criticize."

Russell's whole body of work was described as a monument to a West that was fading just as he got there. His pictures were praised for their documentary role in the daily life of the Indian and the white man on the frontier of the 1870s and 1880s. To his enthusiasts he was much more than an illustrator. He was a cowboy ethnologist.

Russell was born March 19, 1864 in a suburb of St. Louis, Missouri. His antecedents had been storied notables in settling the West. His father was a Yale graduate who became a rich industrialist. Russell was the black sheep of this prominent family. Neither entreaty nor punishment kept him in school. He liked to draw but he would not accept discipline even in art classes. His only goal was to go West. At 16 he went to Montana to take a temporary job as a sheepherder for a rancher his father knew. In his bag he had a flannel cloth wrapped around a box that held a black crayon, watercolors, small paint brushes, and a ball of beeswax for modeling.

He soon quit tending the flock he learned to hate and said he never thereafter painted or sculpted tame sheep. Instead he took up with a hunter who supplied game for the ranchers' tables. In April 1882 he was hired to night-wrangle horses on a cattle drive. For the next 11 years he "sang to the horses and the cattle" at night. He became a more stereotypical Westerner than men born in the West. He seemed determined to divest himself of every vestige of cultivated speech, manners, and dress.

Although he was totally untrained as an artist, Russell continued to paint in his spare time. At first he gave away or destroyed his primitive pictures. Then he sold them for $5 or $10 to finance his drinking. He was popular with the other cowboys. As he said later, he had friends when he had nothing else. He was "a good mixer," known in every cowboy saloon in the region.

He began to find himself as an artist in 1886. One of his paintings was exhibited in St. Louis. The following year another of his paintings was redrawn for reproduction in a national publication. Soon he was a Montana celebrity as "the cowboy artist." The local newspapers printed his pictures. In 1893 he received a private commission for a group of paintings. This financial cushion allowed him to give up employment as a cowboy and paint full-time.

In 1896 when he was 32 he married a young woman who was working as a maid in the home of a friend. She took care of the business end of his trade and regulated his drinking. She saw him as a kind and considerate man. His deportment with her was always quiet. He asked no question of her and offered no hint of his own lineage or past.

For a cowboy artist he was singularly well-adjusted. By avoiding arguments he had no enemy. He wore a soft shirt with a Stetson shoved to the back of his head. A lock of sandy hair hung down his forehead. His snug riding pants of heavy blue cloth were held up by a red French half-breed sash that was wound around twice, just above the hips. The ends of the sash were twisted into a flat knot, leaving the long fringe dangling.

His voice was deep. His high cheek bones, square jaw, and large mouth made him look Indian. Nothing pleased him more than to be mistaken for an Indian. When he talked, he gesticulated. The slight bow in his legs and his high-heeled riding boots caused him to walk with short delicate steps. He loved jewelry. He wore three or four rings on his long, slender fingers.

As a painter, his forte was the depiction of men and animals in violent action. His paintings were alive and turbulent. They were nostalgic of the heroic Old West. He never worked from live models or photographs but rather from his memory. When a question of human anatomy bothered him, he stripped before the studio mirror to put his own body through the requisite contortions. If he needed representations of larger interactions of people or animals, he sculpted the figures roughly in clay and arranged them on a little stage he kept in the studio.

Around 1900 the way he painted changed markedly. Trained Eastern illustrators John Marchand and Will Crawford met Russell in Montana and discussed his technique. In 1903 Russell visited their studio in New York City and painted with them. There was a new sophistication to his palette as the earth tones gave way to more vivid colors. His compositions were simplified. Critics contend that Russell became a superior artist only after this point in his career.

Russell and Frederic Remington had traveled to the same part of the West at roughly the same time. They painted some of the same subjects so comparisons are inevitable. Russell had the reputation of never expressing a negative opinion about another artist but he made an exception for Remington. The New Yorker never knew, however, that Russell existed. Only after Remington died in 1909 was Russell widely recognized as a Western master.

Russell quit drinking the year before Remington died. His habits became more regular. He arose at sunrise in his Great Falls, Montana home and snuffled cold water up his nose to clear his sinuses. Then he dressed and went outside to feed his horse and chickens. Next he made breakfast for the family, including the sleeping cook. The fare was always hot cakes and bacon with strong boiled coffee. When he finished eating, he walked the few paces to his log-cabin studio built of telephone poles. There he lit a fire.

The composition for the day had been evolved in pencil on a scratch pad the previous evening. He began work in the studio early, concentrating while outlining the drawing on the canvas in charcoal or pencil. Then he relaxed for a moment before proceeding to paint rapidly, without waiting for further inspiration.

He welcomed visitors to his studio and chatted while he painted. Once an hour or so he sat back on his kitchen chair and rolled a cigarette while he evaluated what he had done. If he had doubts, he turned his back to the easel and studied the picture in a hand mirror. He believed that the reversal in the mirror would uncover bad composition but guests unfamiliar with his routine thought he was conceited and looking at himself.

When he hit a snag, that was the end of conversation in the studio. He described trouble with a picture as "fighting it." If he could not find an immediate correction, he moved to another work in progress. He generally had two or three pictures going at a time. A serious problem would lead him to put his palette down, go outside, and twirl his lariat until inspiration came. He sometimes painted and re-painted a portion of a picture for days.

Russell worked by the clock like a clerk. At noon he went into the bathroom and meticulously washed his brushes with Ivory soap. He bought good brushes and they lasted. When he finished the ritual with the brushes, he was ready for lunch. If the food was not on the table he reached for a plate of cookies and ate all but one. Then he was apologetic because he was no longer hungry.

After lunch he rolled another cigarette, went back to the studio, lay down on the couch, and napped for half an hour. When he awoke he ate four or five pieces of candy to resolve the craving for alcohol. Then he hitched up his sash, put his Stetson on the back of his head, and went downtown to the cigar store and to the Great Falls saloons. He bought drinks in his turn but took only Vichy water. The tipplers he talked to were his connection with the old days in the saddle.

He returned home promptly at five. He watered and fed his horse and shut the door to the chicken house. Then he sat at the long table and read the local news in the paper until supper.

He spoke like a provincial but everything was color and light to his eyes. His customers forced him to paint violent action but he said he preferred more contemplative subjects. He worked in what he called impressionist colors. Yet he insisted that "I had a chance to see what those Easterners like. They are all daft on the impressionistic school. I saw a landscape they were raving about. Color! Why, say, if I ever saw colors like that in a landscape I would never take another drink. Them artist fellows study in Europe and they paint what they call technique. You know why painters are impressionistic? 'Cause they can't draw."

He was even-handed in his dislike of the French Academicians. He refused to go to Paris, saying, "who in hell wants to look at miles and miles of entombments and descents from the Cross. I'd just as soon visit the morgue."

Russell died of a heart attack in 1926. He had held successful exhibitions in New York City and in London. His pictures had appeared in at least 50 magazines, 100 calendars, 69 books, and 125 prints. By 1920 he was receiving $10,000 for a painting. A mural brought $30,000.

Many Westerners claimed that there had been only one painter of the American West–Charley Russell. Their appreciation was as much for the artist as for his art.

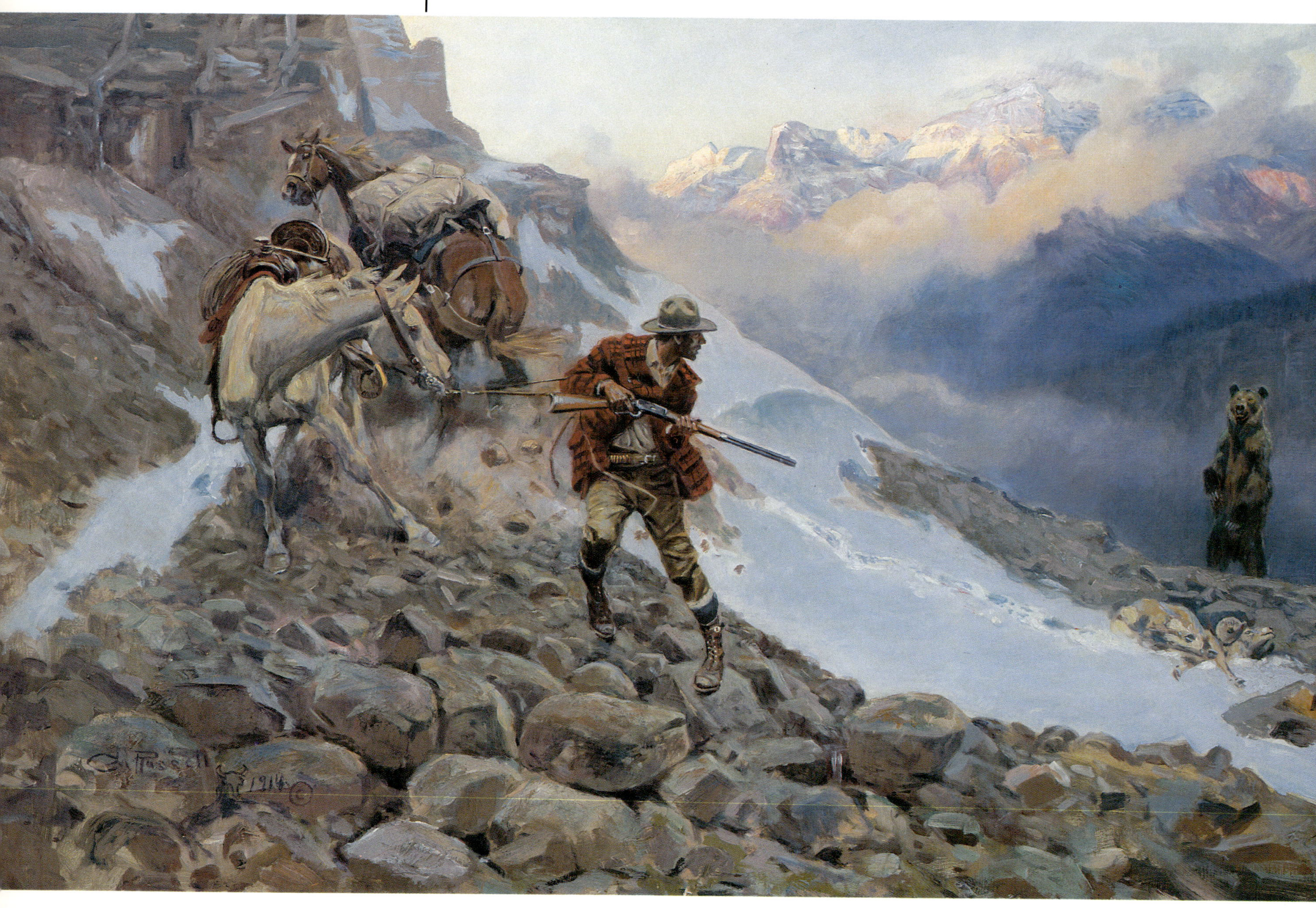

Charles Marion Russell. Whose Meat? is in the collection of the Museum of Western Art, Denver, Colorado. Oil on canvas, wax lined. 30 inches (76.3 cm) height x 48 inches (122 cm) width. Signed lower left and dated 1914.

His 22x36 inch *The War Party* sold for $250,000 at public auction in April 1980.

1. THE PAINTING

Away from his easel, Charley Russell was a master at spinning Western yarns for a male audience. *Whose Meat?* is an image from such a story:

There once was a hunter for skins and meat like the trapper who had befriended the young Russell. The hunter was leading his mount and a packhorse down a rocky trail on the side of a mountain when he spied a fine specimen of mountain sheep around the bend. Grabbing his rifle, he was pleased to dispatch the ram with a single shot. Then he looked up.

That is the moment of suspended action. The picture's title epitomizes the confrontation. Beyond the dead ram the hunter realizes he faces not an apparition but a grizzly rising out of the mist, equidistant from the ram and massively challenging the hunter. The bear is motionless but he represents a serious threat.

The hunter is taken sharply aback. His profile is angular. He holds the rifle, but not at the ready. He is leaning away from the bear, not forward as he was while aggressively shooting the sheep. The horse is obviously frightened, leaning as far back as it can. Its eyes are red and its breath is frozen.

In a saloon with the boys, this would be the time for Russell to sock the punch line to the story. In his painting, however, he holds back.

To Russell, this is a comical situation. The hunter is surprised and in a stance of retreat. So is the horse. Will the hunter abandon his game and depart in a hurry, leaving the bear in command of the field? Or, will he fire his rifle in the air to scare the bear away so he can obtain the ram's skin and meat? Or, since this is an experienced hunter, will he simply recover from his surprise, shoot the bear, and gain twice from the encounter?

In the picture, Russell is not telling the outcome. He leaves the answer to his viewers who will respond according to the bent they bring to the picture. The painting is dated 1914 which was probably the height of Russell's talent. The strong composition was constructed of simple diagonal lines. The effectiveness lies in Russell's intuitive understanding of action and his capacity to capture the essence of conflict.

His depiction of the perspective, however, is inaccurate. Instead of shaping his composition around a main vanishing point, he naively employs several points as they suit him, without conforming to the logical space of the painting. For his enthusiasts, the childlike departures add to the charm.

The fabric support is a plain weave canvas with a light gray ground. The principal composition was sketched in with what appears to be soft pencil. For the outline of the bear, Russell probably used a thin brush.

The paint application is straightforward and was done in one or two layers. The sky and snow have been painted in two layers, using the combined effect of the layers to change the optical properties of the final color. For the sky, the yellow and blue underlayer is covered by a scumble to create a misty, atmospheric effect. For the snow, a white underlayer was applied over the gray ground to achieve a brighter, more reflective appearance.

Russell was spontaneous and direct, working all parts of the painting at the same time, going back and forth, dabbing here and changing there. He added highlights and shadows without any systematic progression and made changes as he saw fit. He would rethink and rework an area until he was satisfied.

For example, the warm rays of a setting sun reflect on the far mountains, but the sun itself is missing from the picture. This suggests that the initial location of the sun was once where the rocks in the upper left are now. The rocks were painted over the sun to remove compositional competition from the main action.

When visitors go to a museum of Western American art, they come out chuckling about Charlie Russell's work. His narratives engage them. People who otherwise would have no use for so-called fine art cannot help but be drawn into his paintings. This raises the age old debate over what is most important in art: subject matter or how it is expressed.

In the end, though, what difference does it make whether Russell's paintings were episodes in narration or fine art? He never pretended to be a fine artist like Remington. He never hinted like Leigh to a National Academician that he wanted to be considered for membership. Instead, he painted subjects that pleased him, for people who appreciated both him and his paintings. The people who relished his paintings also enjoyed his stories.

Conforming to the reports of his early life, his paintings are entertaining. They unfold like a captivating Wild West anecdote told in a barroom, with changes and improvements worked in as required. His seat-of-the-pants approach to his art relied on his sharp eye, memory for detail, and ability to pick up simple techniques from other artists. This instinctive approach is far from the usual procedure of the trained artist.

To Russell, the end was all that mattered in a painting. He may have employed the

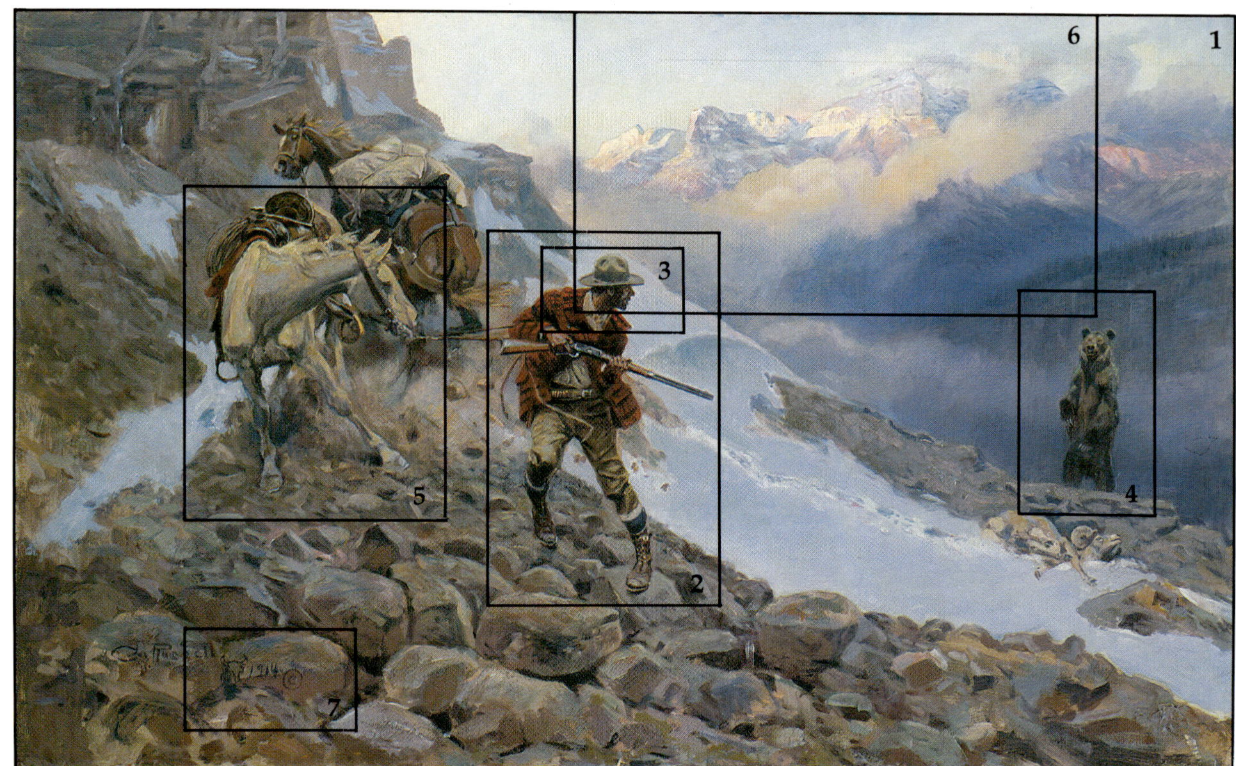

multiple perspectives and the contradictory changes that are the mark of an untutored brush, but if he knew he lacked something in technique, he never let on that he cared. He painted for the feeling of warmth he gave the viewer and for the warmth that came back to him.

2.1. The jacket was changed to be more open than originally depicted. A pentimento of the red of the jacket can be seen showing through the added part of the trousers.

2.2. The snow was painted in two layers. The areas of snow were first blocked in with white paint. Then came a bluish layer. The white underlayer provides a more reflective base for the subsequent paint layer than the gray ground would have. The fairly sophisticated and subtle technique of applying paint in layers to achieve brighter colors is handled skillfully by the untrained Russell. The same effect of brilliant reflective snow could not have been accomplished by mixing the colors on the palette and applying the paint directly onto the gray ground in one layer.

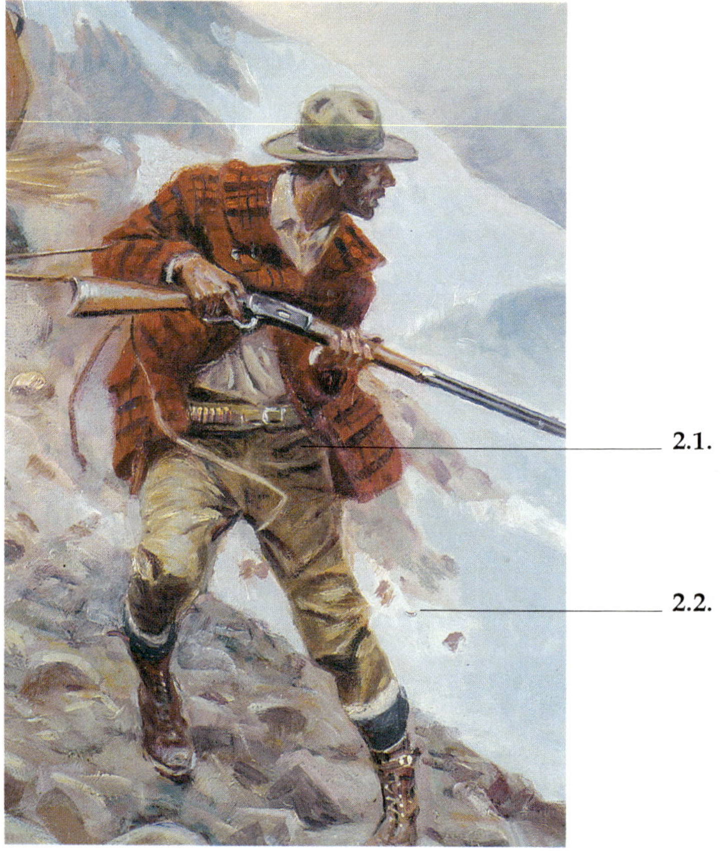

2. DETAIL OF FIGURE

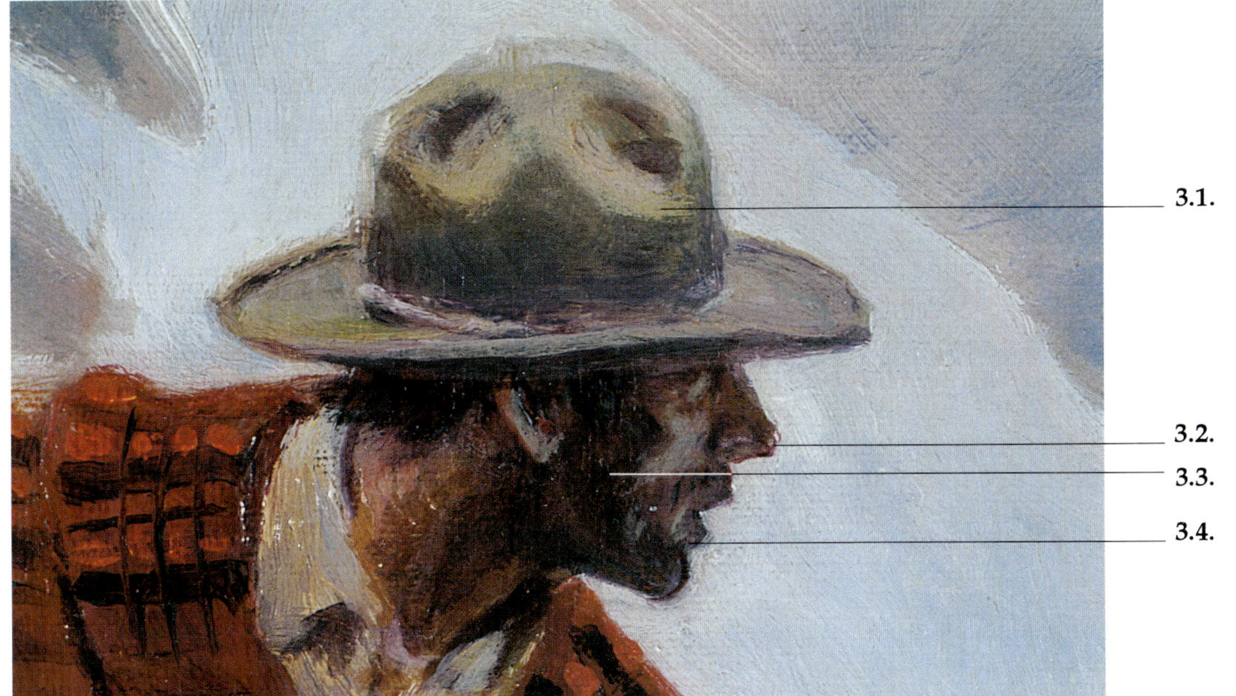

3. DETAIL OF HEAD

3.1. Russell depicted the hat as seen from slightly above whereas the face was painted from the side. The hat seems to float rather than to fit properly because the tilt of the hat does not match the head. Lack of formal training caused the failure to use correct perspective but added to the cartoonish flavor.

3.2. The face has been outlined with a transparent paint such as red lake.

3.3. The colors were not applied in any organized way. Greenish-white highlights were added in a few touches to reflect the bright snow. Warm brown paint was laid over the flesh color to indicate the beard and the shadow on the face. Highlights and shadows were supplied as Russell perceived the need.

3.4. The outline of the hunter's lower lip and chin have been adjusted to render a sharper profile.

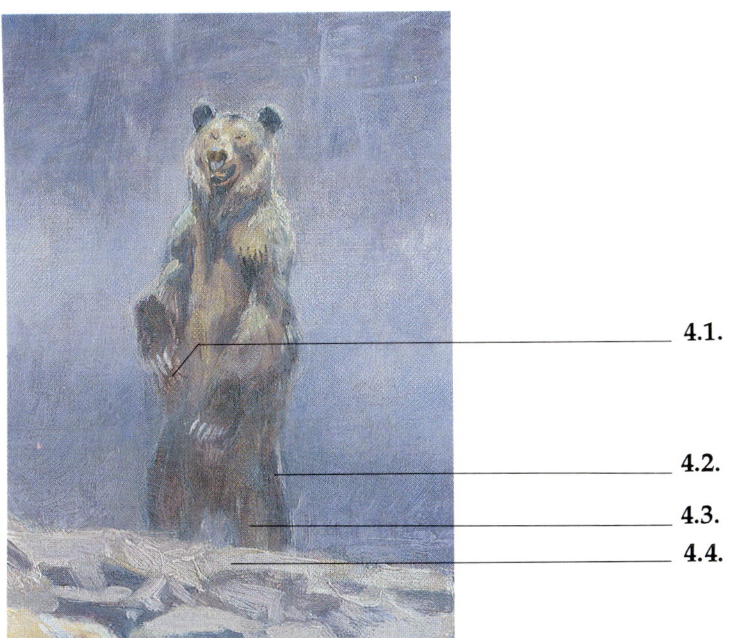

4. DETAIL OF BEAR

4.1. A transparent brown underlayer was applied over the gray ground and left partially exposed as shadows.

4.2. The bear was outlined with a bluish paint.

4.3. The scumble which was added to create the rising mist can be seen clearly in the thin brushstrokes which have been pulled over the bear's legs.

4.4. The rocks in front of the bear have been painted with multicolored brushstrokes. A slight impasto was retained as the texture of the paint was used to create form. The gray ground was left partially exposed. The highlights and shadows were added when the layer beneath was still somewhat wet.

5.1. A dab of pure red color shapes the animal's eye, increasing the tension and dramatic effect.

5.2. There is evidence of underdrawing on the horse's right leg.

5.3. The snow to the left was added after the foreground was painted.

5.4. The gray ground color was left exposed here to create the middle tone of the body. Shadows and highlights were added as Russell's free-form working procedure directed.

5.5. The saddle and reins were painted accurately and with great refinement. A real saddle in the studio may have served as the model or Russell could have relied on his own intimate experience with riding gear.

5.6. The rear horse's warm breath in the cold air was created by a thin scumble of bluish appearing paint.

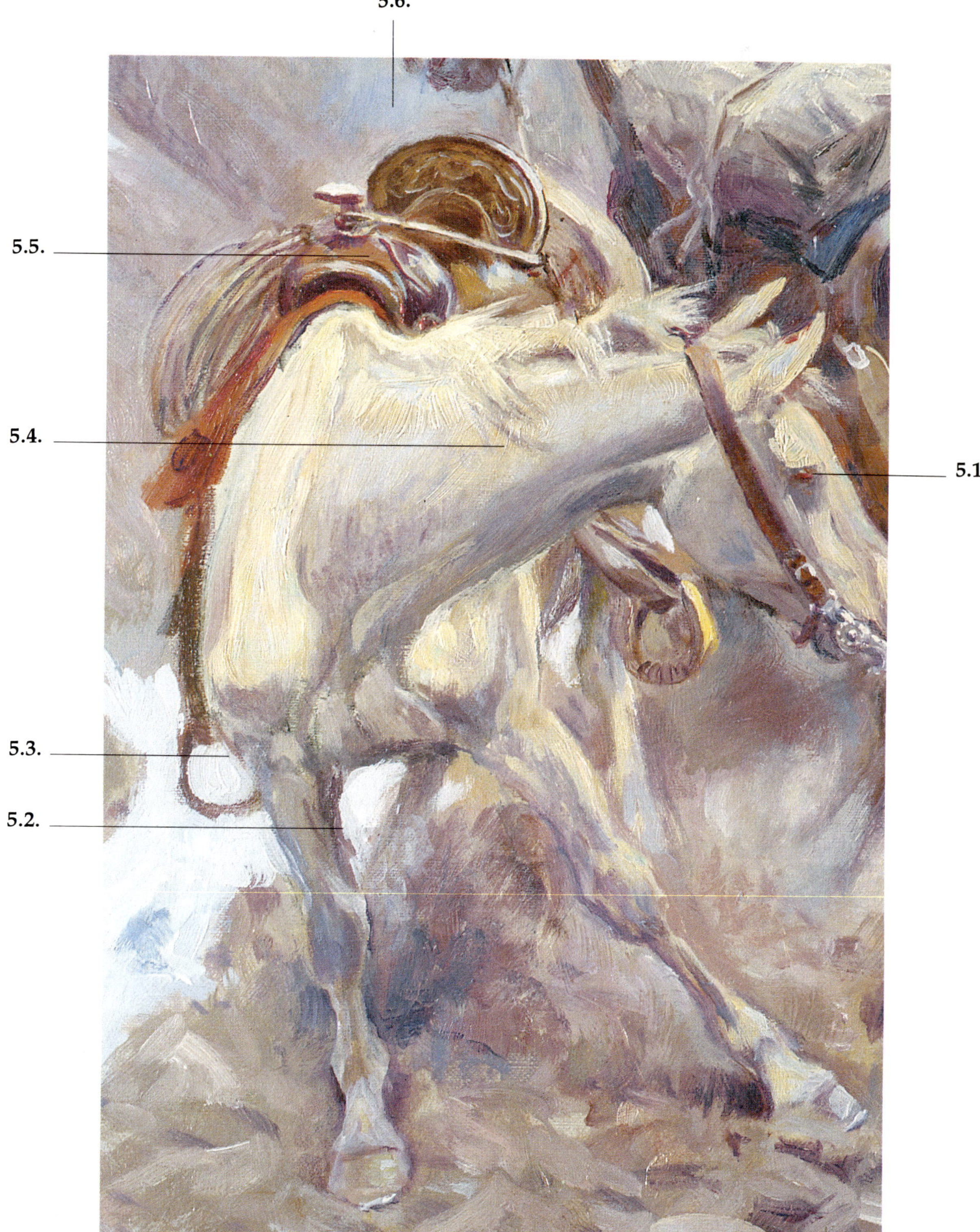

5. DETAIL OF HORSE

Russell captured the image of a frightened horse even though the depiction makes little sense anatomically. The ears and the head of the animal are not in the same plane of perspective. The hind legs are merely suggested. This shows again the lack of formal training, a deficiency Russell compensated for by having a good eye. He knew this type of situation from his own experience.

6.2.   6.1.

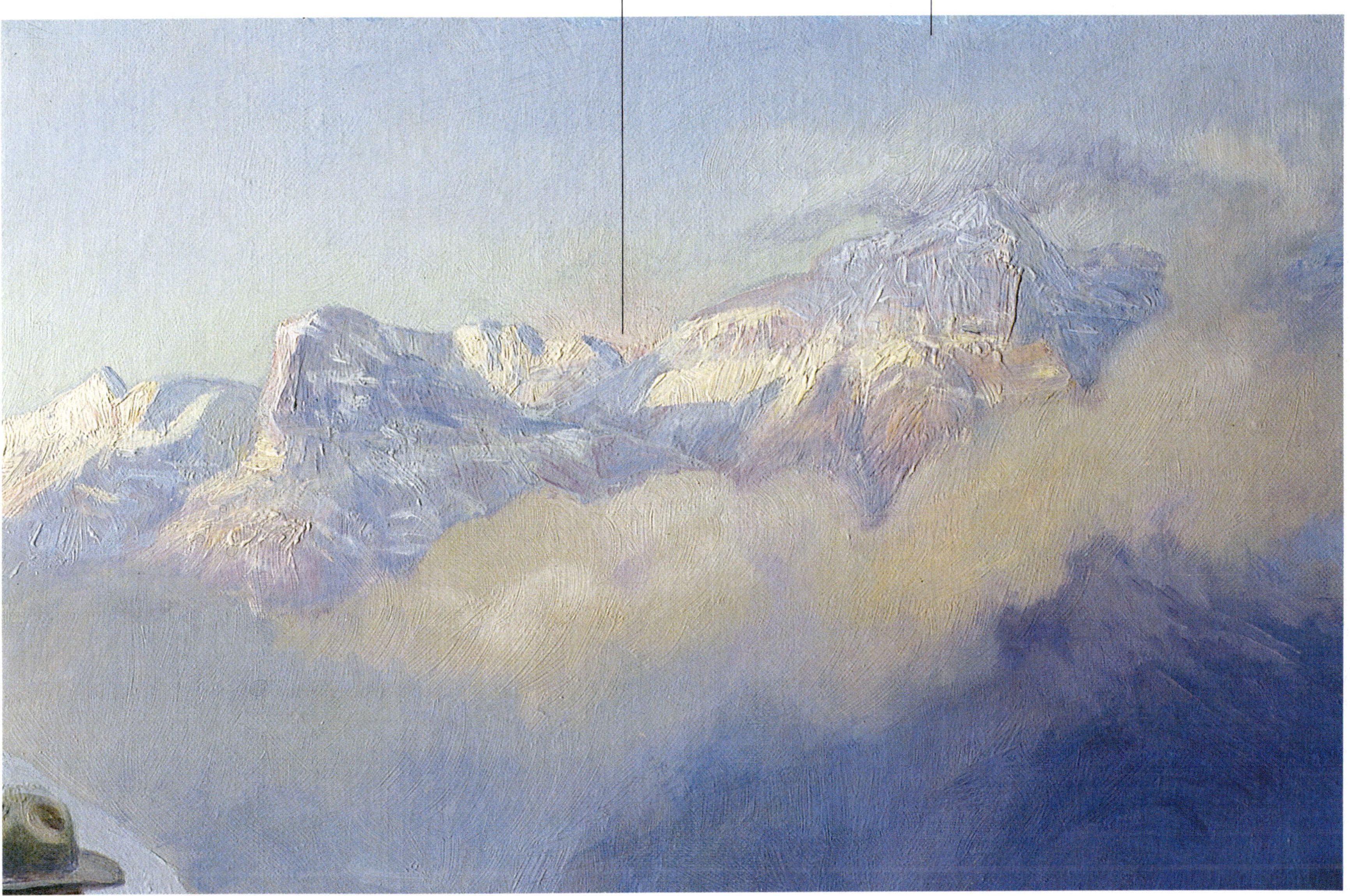

6. Detail of Mountains

The structure of the paint varies from smooth for the sky to impasted in the mountains which almost appear to have been sculpted with the brush.

6.1. The sky here was painted in two layers. The underlayer ranges from yellow near the horizon to a light blue at the top of the picture. A scumble was added to create the clouds and mist.

6.2. Russell made a compositional change where a mountain peak was painted out and then scumbled over with clouds.

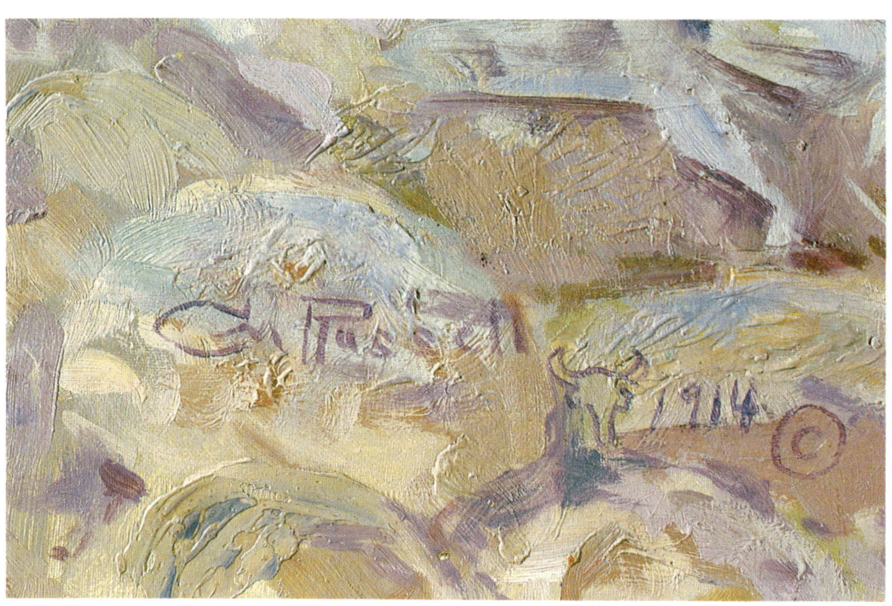

7. DETAIL OF SIGNATURE

C.M. Russell 1914

In the 10 or 11 different versions of Russell's monogram and signature that he employed during his career, this one was the last and the longest in use. The variations over the years were primarily in the placement of the M which wandered around between the C and the R as if it was loose. This particular M inside the C was adopted in 1897 and was employed for 30 years.

SUMMARY OF PAINTING TECHNIQUE

a. Russell used both commercially prepared canvases and ones he primed himself. It is not possible to determine which was used in *Whose Meat?*. The ground is light gray.

b. The composition was sketched on the ground with what appears to be pencil. The bear was done with a fine brush and blue paint. The man's face was brushed in with a line of red lake.

c. Russell blocked in areas of snow with white paint. The white produced a more reflective surface for subsequent paint layers than the gray ground would have. The sky was blocked in with a blue and yellow underlayer which was scumbled over to create the misty atmosphere. A dark brown transparent underlayer was put in for the bear.

d. The thicker paint layers were added for principal parts of the picture. The ground was often left partially exposed. For example, the gray color acts as a middle tone for the body of the horse.

e. Changes in the mountains and the jacket were made during the course of the work. The hunter's face was also adjusted and some of the snow patches were expanded.

f. Refinements were added in the form of highlights and more shadows. Russell did not work methodically but supplemented and altered as he went along. Scumbles were added to depict the rising mist and the horse's hot breath in the cold mountain air.

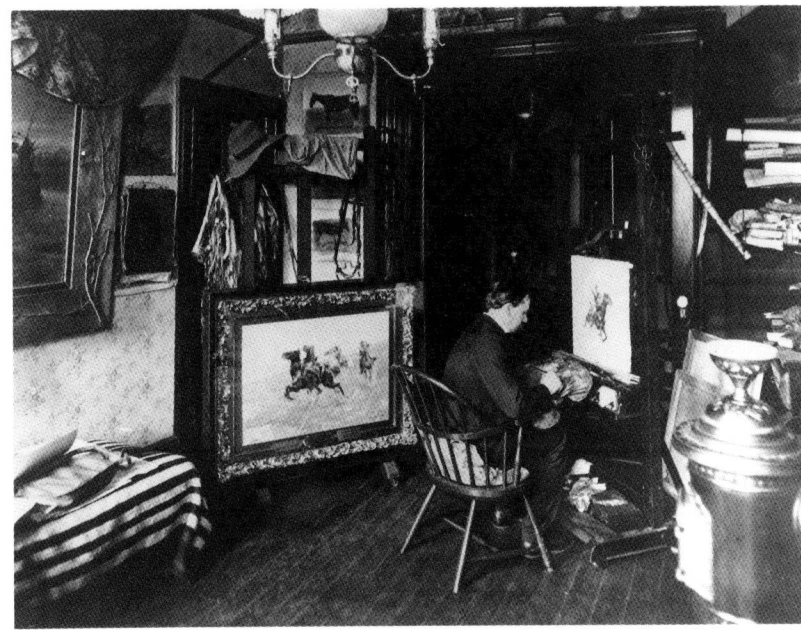

CHARLES SCHREYVOGEL

Most of the master painters of the West had specialties. The genre painters among them dealt with the doings of the people of the frontier. Charley Russell was the cowboy artist. Henry Farny was the Indian painter. Grace Hudson did Pomo babies.

For his part, Charles Schreyvogel was the pictorial recorder of the Indian-fighting United States Cavalry. His short historical period was the quarter century after the Civil War. Because his specialty required him to depict the slaughter of red men by the score, he had the narrowest popular appeal among these master painters. Fortunately, he was a modest man content with the confines of the bloody subject he had undertaken.

There were two high points in Schreyvogel's low-keyed existence as an artist. The first was an unexpected recognition from his fellow artists when he was impoverished and unknown in 1900. The second was the support given him by Cavalry veterans when he was verbally flayed by Frederic Remington in 1903. The one made him financially secure for the rest of his life. The other made the accuracy of his work unimpeachable.

Schreyvogel was born January 4, 1861, a few months before the start of the Civil War. He was the second of three sons of prosperous middle-class immigrants who owned a bakery in Manhattan's German section.

In public school the subject that interested him most was sketching. As he recalled, though, "my parents were adverse to my becoming an artist. They thought all artists were bound to starve." Instead, they apprenticed him to a tool and die maker to assure him of a steady blue-collar job. He quit after a year in favor of more compatible work in lithography. When the family moved to Castle Hills, the German-American section of Hoboken, New Jersey, he took a Hudson River ferry and horse cars to continue working at the print shop in New York City.

One of the other employees was August Schwabe, an older man who was a painter trained in Germany. Schreyvogel enrolled in Schwabe's evening class at the Newark Art League and went on Sunday sketching trips with him.

In 1886 his father died, making dedication to art easier. His brothers sacrificed to finance his voyage to Munich for study at the Art Academy. When his money was gone, his father's family in Stuttgart helped him. He returned to Hoboken in 1890 in frail physical condition. His chronic asthma had worsened. Doctors prescribed weeks in bed.

After he recovered, he rented a small Hoboken apartment he also used as a studio. From these modest surroundings, he offered his Munich-trained services as portrait painter and commercial artist. Though he found few takers, the frugal Schreyvogel saved enough to go West for the first time in the late spring of 1893 when he was 32. Part of the reason for the trip was to improve his health, so he solicited an invitation to stay with the Army post surgeon at the Ute Reservation in Ignacio, southwestern Colorado.

The Indian uprisings that had grown in intensity after 1865 ended in 1890 with the defeat of the Sioux at Wounded Knee. No one knew then, however, that the bitterest part of the warfare was over. In 1893 there were still rumors of large-scale Indian attacks in the vast arena from the Mississippi River to the Rockies and from Arizona to Montana. The 14,000-man Army on Indian duty was responsible for 100 square miles per soldier, all for a dollar a day. The men faced 25,000 off-reservation Indian warriors who were determined to retain their heritage by halting the westward expansion of the whites.

In Ignacio where Schreyvogel spent the summer there were plenty of Cavalrymen to tell him their version of the heroic experiences of the soldiers during fierce battles with the villainous Indians. In the field, the servicemen taught him to ride and shoot. He also learned sign language from the peaceful Indians on the reservation. He sketched the men and their horses, and accumulated boxes of Cavalry and Indian artifacts to be used as studio props. Then he moved on to the Army post at San Carlos in Arizona.

In November Schreyvogel went back to Hoboken loaded with photographs as well as the sketches and artifacts. He began to paint pictures of the Cavalry engaged in the thrilling episodes that had been described to him. The New Jersey sunrise reminded him of the Western plains so he painted in the open air on the flat tar roof of the building where he lived. For realism in his compositions, he first sculpted the horses in clay. Friends were his models and the backgrounds were the flat-topped Palisades which resembled Western buttes.

Schreyvogel completed only a small number of pictures because he did not begin to paint until he had done elaborate research on the historical accuracy of every composition. The pictures were placed on consignment with New York City art dealers but there were no sales. The Indian-fighting Cavalry was ignored as a subject. Despite a few purchases made privately by Schreyvogel's loyal German-American neighbors, canvases began to accumulate in his studio, even at his low rate of production.

To earn a bare living he turned to painting miniature portraits on ivory, but the use of a magnifying glass strained his eyes. He also imitated European pastoral scenes on canvas, but the potboilers that sold for some mediocre landscape painters did not sell from his brush.

In a momentary flush of income from the sale of a portrait in 1894 he married Lulu, the daughter of one of the affluent German-Americans in Hoboken. His pet name for her was Schnuck. So was hers for him. Her father did not attend the ceremony.

Within weeks they were squeezed into poverty. At one point their cash on hand was 13 cents. His wife made soup for them from bones they shared with his hunting dog Spot. The stoic artist recalled that, "I guess you can say it was a time when I was hard up." He contemplated dropping the Cavalry as his subject but unexpectedly another portrait sold and he was spared the decision.

Schreyvogel had been exhibiting paintings at the National Academy of Design since 1892, without recognition. In 1897 he entered a Western subject, *Over a Dangerous Pass.* The painting was chosen for reproduction as part of the review in *Harper's Weekly.* However, the picture was poorly hung in the exhibition hall, was not mentioned in other important reviews, and remained unsold. Schreyvogel was hurt by the relative inattention to a painting he had expected to sell. He declared that he would never show his work at the Academy again.

As he reconstructed the next episode, it was early in 1899 when Schreyvogel remembered an Ignacio tale about a Cavalryman who was rescued by his bunkmate after his horse was shot by Indians during a battle. Schreyvogel labored for months over a 25x34 inch portrayal of the scene, only to discover that no dealer he approached would buy the painting or take it on consignment. Dismayed, he sold the picture cheaply to a lithographer for use on a commercial calendar but in a few days the lithographer asked him to take the picture back. The shape of the composition did not lend itself to the layout.

Schreyvogel had to be persistent. He was still as he said "hard up." He had previously sold a few paintings by showing them at Luchow's German-American restaurant in Manhattan so he took this one there, too. The proprietor did not care for the picture. He failed to hang it for easy viewing and Schreyvogel was obliged to take his picture back once again. "I was put out by that," he declared in an understatement. Finally a collector of Western art saw the painting in Schreyvogel's studio and agreed to come back in November to complete the purchase. The agreed date arrived but not the collector.

The difficulty was that the leading Western artist, Frederic Remington, had sculpted a well-publicized bronze statuette *The Wounded Bunkie* in 1896. Schreyvogel's painting followed exactly the same theme and he gave his picture the derivative title of *My Bunkie*. Even if Schreyvogel's choice of subject was as original as he later claimed, the similarities made dealers and collectors uncomfortable.

With none of the usual marketing outlets available, Schreyvogel was unable to dispose of the picture. His wife advised him to offer *My Bunkie* for the National Academy's annual exhibition but he replied, "I entered one Western painting and see what they did to me."

At the last moment for submission to the show he gave in. "You win," he sighed. "I'll bring it over today." He took *My Bunkie* to the Academy building in New York and put it on the floor against the wall with the other 297 offerings. His name and the title were on the picture's nameplate but he did not stop to fill in the entrance slip with his address. There was not much hope of recognition at the highest level for a painting nobody really wanted.

This was the 1899 Christmas season, ending Schreyvogel's worst year. He was broke. When his older brother died he could barely raise the money for the December 29 funeral. On the 31st, however, he was visiting a potential patron when the phone rang. His wife informed Schreyvogel that *My Bunkie* had won the important Clark prize of a medal and $300 they desperately needed. The award was given for "the best American Figure Composition painted in the United States by an American citizen."

Schreyvogel hurried to meet his wife. He didn't want to see the reporters until she could share the honor with him. They went to the Academy together to collect the prize money but all they could get was the medal. The $300 was delayed until the ceremony a month later.

The painter was chagrined to find that he had not been notified directly by the Academy. No official there had known who he was. The secretary, Henry Watrous, told an inquiring critic, "You are about the hundredth person who has asked me but I can't answer your question. I have never heard of the artist. I have asked every artist whom I met here today but they know as little as I do. We will just have to wait until he comes in."

Actually, the standard reference book for artists, the *American Art Annual* for 1898, listed Schreyvogel both as a painter and as an exhibitor. Watrous had a copy of the *Art Annual*. The difficulty was that Schreyvogel's address in the *Annual* was in care of the National Academy rather than his home, probably because he was embarrassed at having no studio.

On New Year's Day 1900 the New York *Herald* printed a four-column cut of *My Bunkie*, adding, "In subject the picture is akin to those of Frederic Remington. But it is wholly different in treatment. The instantaneous photographic effects which Remington is so fond of are wholly absent." Schreyvogel told the writer that the two bunkies "are now serving in the Philippines." They were too far away to be questioned, but Schreyvogel's hard times were over. Ahead were financial security and an associate membership in the Academy, along with Remington's undying enmity.

As a German joke "schreyvogel" was taken to mean a shrieking bird, but his daughter described him as a happy man who loved to laugh and sing German songs. Though his paintings were bloody he himself was gentle and kind-hearted. He loved carbines and revolvers. A crack shot, he wanted his young daughter to snap the triggers of unloaded guns to enjoy them as he did. Instead, she was frightened.

Others saw him as a slender, dark-haired, dark-eyed man of medium height, modest and shy, with old-world manners. When he painted on the roof of his red-brick row house he dressed as formally as Oscar Berninghaus did in Taos. He wore a dark suit and derby. A thick gold chain was strung across his vest. His friends were the rich German-American businessmen from Hoboken. He looked like them and away from his easel he acted like them. They bowled together at the German Club on Saturdays. Schreyvogel was intrigued by the legends about General George Armstrong Custer, particularly by the lesser known incident of Custer's confrontation with the war chief Santana in 1869. The General had faced down 7,000 sullen warriors and had forced them back onto their reservations without a fight.

Schreyvogel began to paint the scene in December 1902. Most of the troopers who were present at the dramatic meeting had died with Custer at the Little Big Horn in 1876, but the Colonel's widow, Elizabeth, was still active. So was Custer's aide-de-camp in 1869, Lieutenant Colonel Schuyler Crosby.

Schreyvogel researched the event thoroughly. He obtained gear and advice from Mrs. Custer. He also induced the retired Crosby to search through his old trunks for bits of costume he had worn 23 years earlier. The painting was titled *Custer's Demand*. It was exhibited in April 1903. The reviews stressed the artist's historical accuracy.

Nine days later Remington sent a vitriolic letter to the *Herald*. He claimed that Schreyvogel's painting was half-baked and unhistorical and he listed specific points on which he said Schreyvogel had erred.

Schreyvogel refused to respond to Remington's attack but he released a letter to him from Mrs. Custer confirming his accuracy. Schreyvogel named his daughter after Mrs. Custer. Then Colonel Crosby wrote to the *Herald*, siding with Schreyvogel. President Roosevelt told Schreyvogel that Remington had made "a perfect jack of himself." If the Schreyvogels' child had been a son, he would doubtless have been named either Schuyler or George Armstrong.

Schreyvogel died January 27, 1912. A sliver of chicken bone pierced his gum at dinner, causing blood poisoning. In his short life he had considered only 62 of his paintings to be important enough to be registered in the copyright office. Museum founder Bill Foxley said that a convention of all of the owners of Schreyvogel paintings could be held inside one tepee.

1. THE PAINTING

The Messenger shows a young Cavalry soldier racing toward the viewer while he turns to try to fend off the enemy. The horse is tersely rendered with the most detail given to its panicked expression.

Unlike most other Western painters, Schreyvogel saw himself solely as a narrative painter whose pride was historical truth. One can be sure that the particulars of military

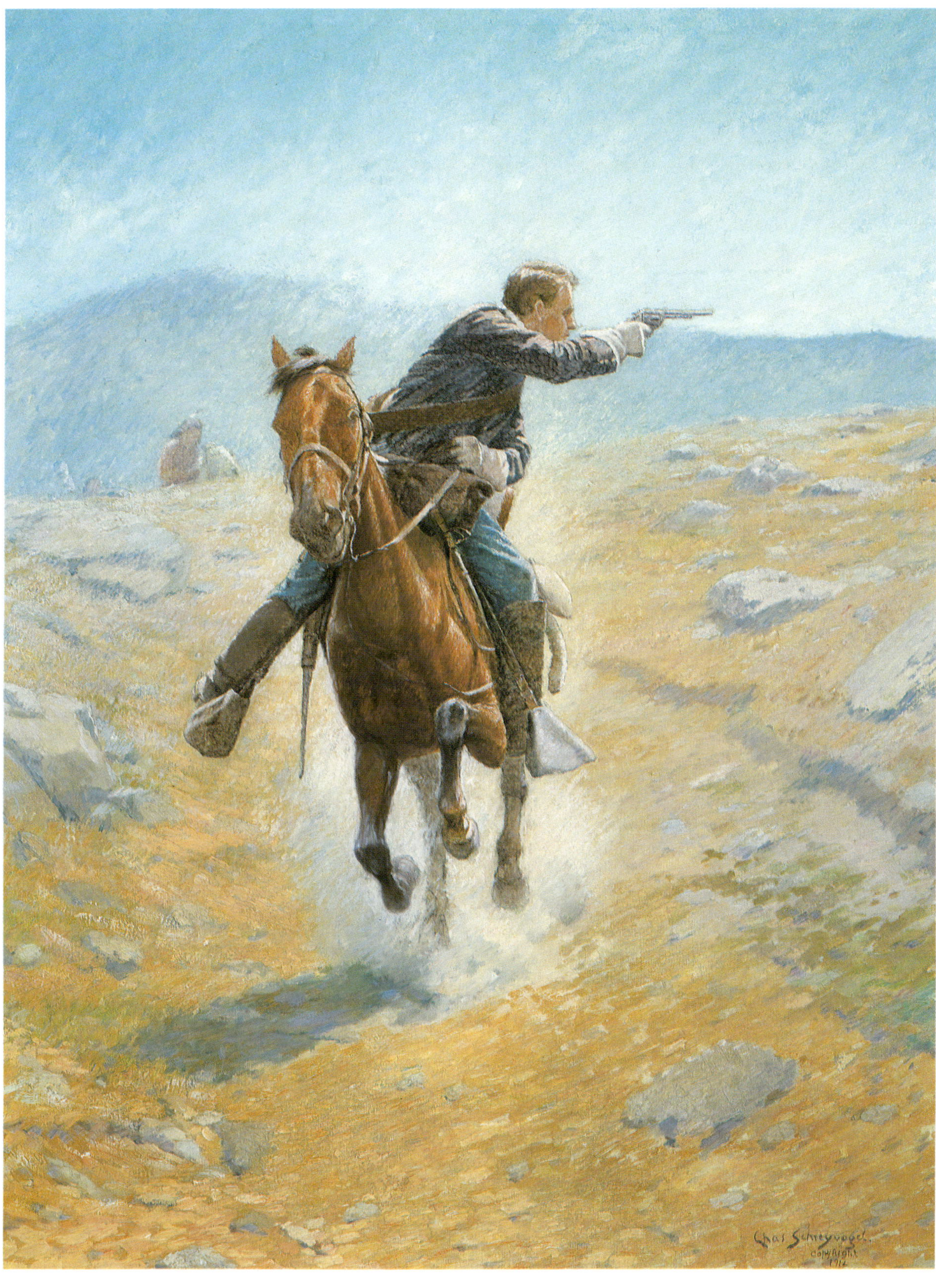

Charles Schreyvogel. The Messenger is in the collection of the Museum of Western Art, Denver, Colorado. Oil on canvas, wax lined. 34 inches (86.5 cm) height x 25 inches (63.8 cm) width. Signed lower left and dated 1912.

dress, weapons, and accoutrements are depicted as accurately as Schreyvogel's thorough research permitted. In preparation for each painting he read military records, interviewed veterans, sought old uniforms, and collected memorabilia. For this reason his total output was very small, numbering less than 100 paintings. In comparison his contemporary, Frederic Remington, who lived an equally brief life span, produced more than 20 times as many works of art.

Furthermore, after Schreyvogel was established he hesitated to paint for reproduction.

He claimed that the printing process could not do justice to an original oil, though some of his pictures were reproduced as a result of their popularity. He painted entirely for himself and for his dedication to the recording of this brutal period of American history.

The Messenger was painted on a lightweight plain weave fabric. The ground is gray. The tacking edges which usually contain information about how the ground was applied have been removed in the course of a lining process. Therefore, it is not possible to determine if the ground was artist applied.

The soldier and horse were underdrawn with thin hard lines, probably from a sharp pencil. This hairline sketch is very exact. Some softer lines were used for the horse's rear legs, perhaps to produce a less distinct focus. The Indians in the background were underdrawn more sketchily with brief broken lines.

The paint for the figure and the horse was applied directly onto the ground with a single dilute layer. Lighter paint was added wet-into-wet for highlights and darker areas were created simply by applying the paint more thickly. The paint stays neatly within the bounds of the drawn lines, often leaving them clearly visible. Schreyvogel had a controlled hand and a clear conception of what he wanted to paint. Once the exact sketch was made, the paint was applied with meticulous, painstaking precision.

Schreyvogel used the ground in various ways. It was left uncovered for light areas such as the whites of the horse's eyes. For the ghostlike Indians in the background, the paint was thinly applied, allowing the ground to show through at the tops of the fabric weave to create a shimmering light effect. The most distinctive use is the gap of exposed ground that the artist often left around brightly lit edges. For example, the glinting shape of the moving gun was enhanced by a jagged space of ground left showing.

Schreyvogel also added paint to create a similar effect of blurred edges to indicate swift motion. At the underside of the soldier's arm the artist chose to add small touches of paint from the distant mountain range over the edge of the jacket rather than leave a gap of exposed ground. Both the exposed ground and the blurred edges are equally effective.

The foreground, middle distance, and sky were painted with drier, slightly impasted paint which was more freely applied with short diagonal brushstrokes. This paint was generally mixed with white, giving it opaque, pastel-like qualities that contrast with the thinner, more translucent paint of the horse and figure.

The composition of *The Messenger* is straightforward, yet effective. The pose is dramatic. The horse veers to the left while the rider shoots to the right. The pursuing Indians rise out of the dust from his blind side. The action is enclosed in the V of the arroyo. The tilt of the horizon line energizes the painting. The blue mountain in the distance balances the composition and creates a transition between what would otherwise be a jarring contrast of sky and foreground.

Depth is achieved by a combination of linear perspective and the more natural atmospheric perspective. The diagonal line of the edge of the arroyo leads the eye back to a vanishing point located behind the main figure. In addition to making the distant Indians smaller than the figure in the foreground, atmospheric perspective is utilized by muting the colors as the space recedes. These methods mimic the way one's eye perceives distance. The farther away something is, the smaller it appears, and the closer the color values are.

The striking pose of the horse and rider coming directly out of the picture plane brings to mind a scene described by the artist's daughter. Dressed as a cowgirl, her mother galloped on horseback toward Schreyvogel over and over again while he worked. He preferred live models, though he was familiar with Eadweard Muybridge's stop-action studies and was known to photograph people and horses in motion. In addition, he would sculpt clay models from his many field sketches.

Schreyvogel was a quiet man who enjoyed brief excursions to the West but was happiest painting on his rooftop in Hoboken, near family and friends. His passion was the

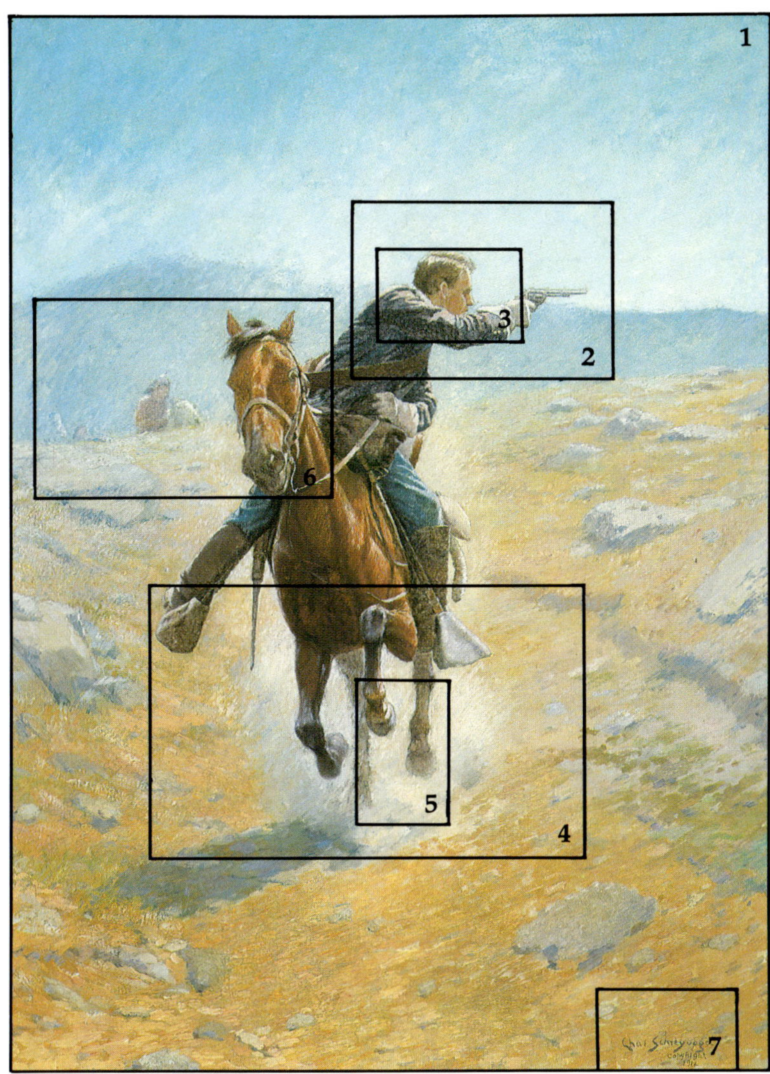

military campaigns waged against American Indians and his fetish was historical accuracy. As a white man, his bias was understandably in favor of the Army and he was naturally closest to officers as sources of information. The Indian point of view had not yet been given much consideration. The Indian could be romanticized as noble but justifiably defeated. Soldiers were brave and loyal heroes.

Schreyvogel's closest contemporary was his ideal, Frederic Remington. Their careers paralleled in subject matter and productive years. Schreyvogel was a Remington fan and said, "He's the greatest of us all."

It was an odd twist that Schreyvogel unwittingly made Remington look ridiculous in the newspaper war over the historical accuracy of the details in *Custer's Demand* completed by Schreyvogel in 1903. Remington attacked the painting in the press: "I saw in the Sunday *Herald* a print of ....*Custer's Demand*–a so-called historical picture. I have studied and have ridden in the waste and made many notes for 23 years and I would set down the following on that painting. While I do not want to interfere with Mr. Schreyvogel's hallucinations, I do object to his half baked stuff being considered seriously as history." Remington was quickly rebutted by many public figures including Custer's widow.

If Remington had been a less confident man, he might have kicked himself for stirring up so much trouble over minutiae such as what shade of blue a trouser leg was. He should have realized that this sort of trivia was secondary to the aesthetic qualities of the work of art.

Remington was no doubt driven by continuing jealousy over the success of the derivative *My Bunkie* and by his dislike of Germans, but he unintentionally became the single greatest boon to the popularity of the previously little known Schreyvogel.

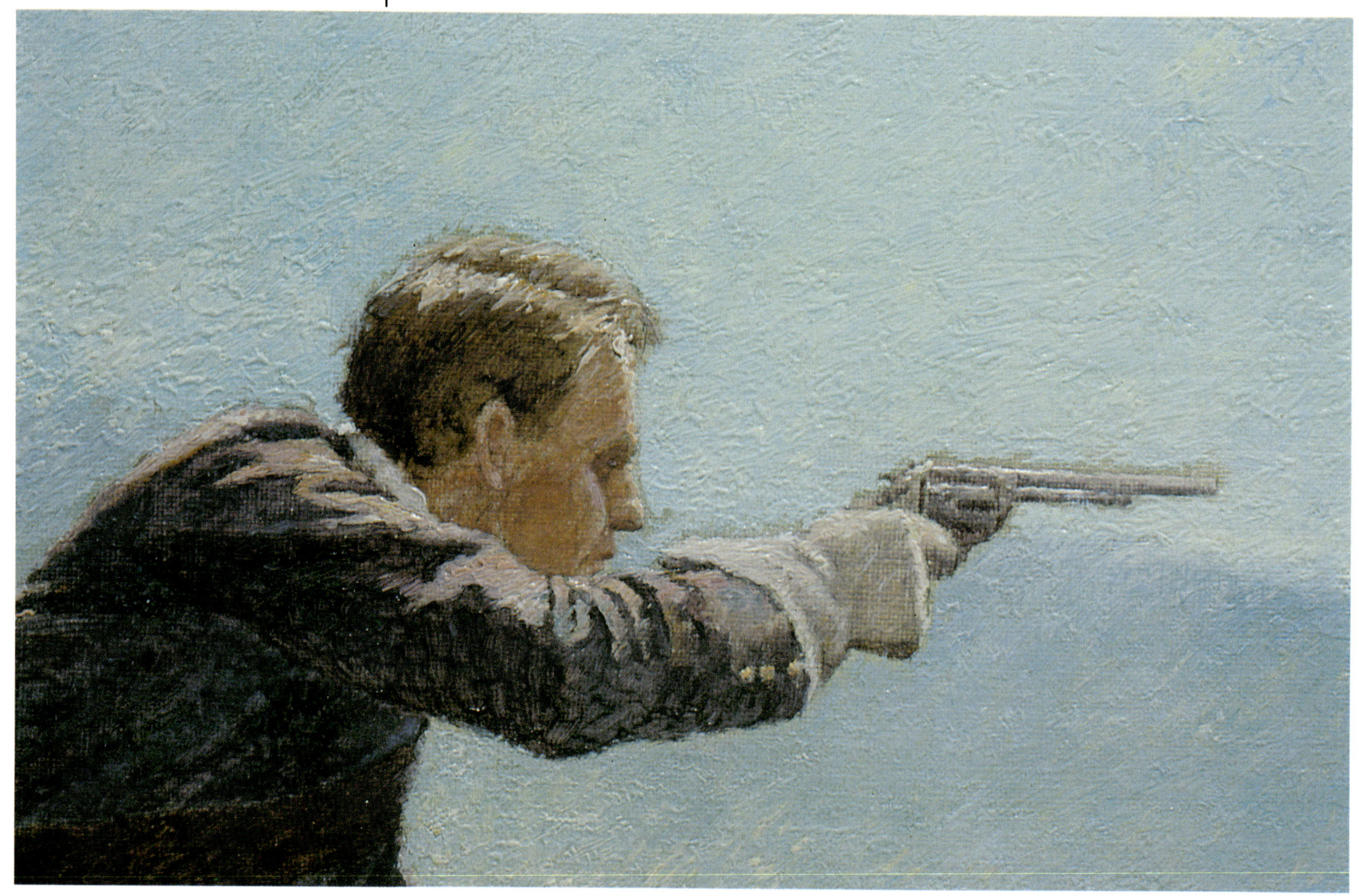

2. DETAIL OF MESSENGER'S HEAD

Schreyvogel let the ground work for him extensively throughout the painting. The glove, for example, is composed almost entirely of the ground color with only some bluish shading and white highlights added. The accurately painted gun was done with blue for the detail. White was added for highlights and black for shadow. Yet, the gray ground shows through for the body color.

As mentioned, the ground was left exposed around the edges of the glove and gun, creating the indistinct outline of shimmering metal reflecting the burning overhead sun. This uneven line also enhances the slightly blurred effect of a moving object caught in motion.

The sky was added around the soldier and in places this blue paint overlaps the figure, breaking up the edges. This can be seen under the raised arm where the slightly blurred line of the added paint creates an effect of motion similar to the fringed edges of the bare ground around the gun.

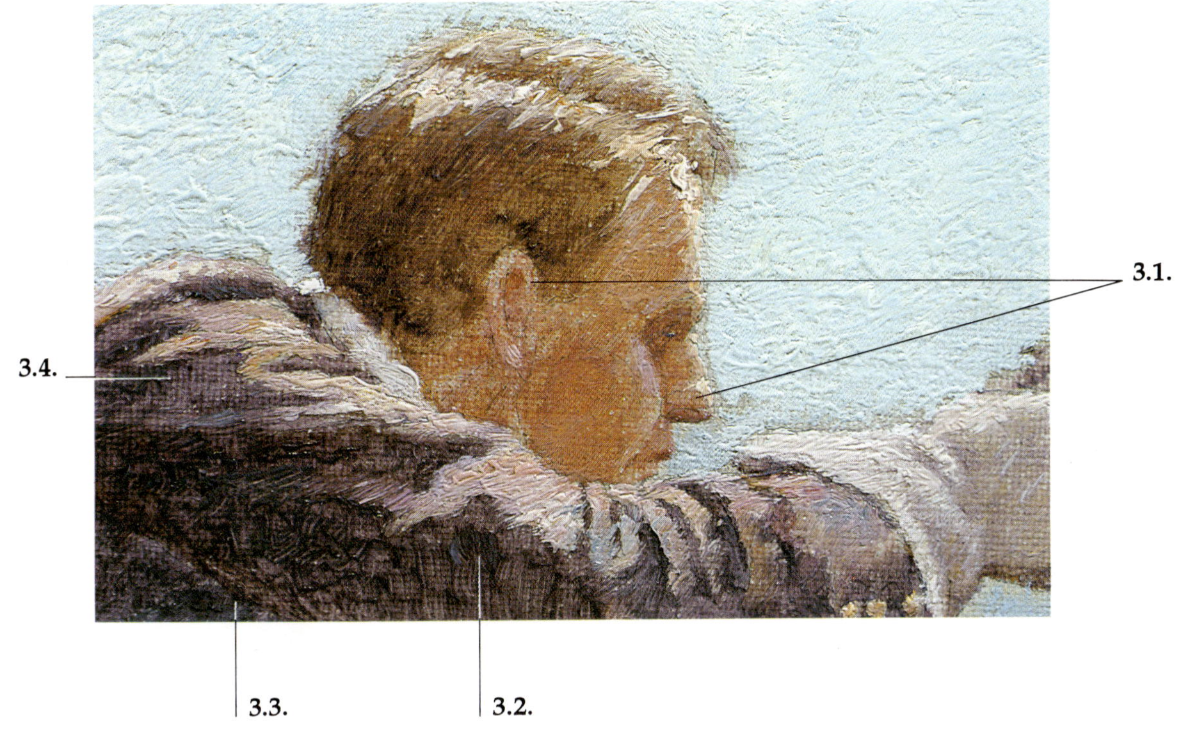

3.1. The fine lines of the underdrawing can be seen clearly through the thin paint of the face, especially in the ear and nose where the details are defined by the sketch.

3.2. The distinct strokes retain the imprint of a very narrow stubby brush.

3.3. Vivid purple-blue pigments retain their saturated and transparent qualities.

3.4. The rich medium gives the paint a very viscous consistency and further enhances the deeply saturated nature of the color.

3. FURTHER ENLARGEMENT OF SOLDIER'S FACE

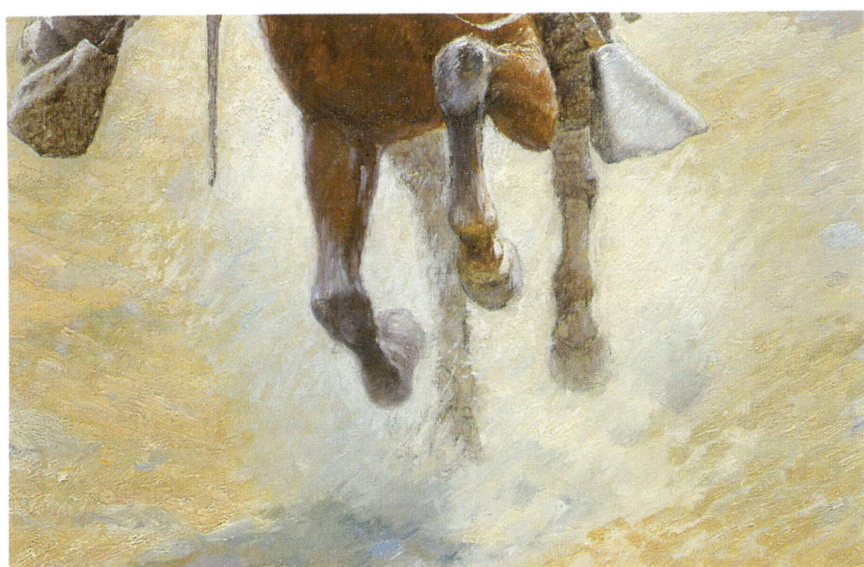

4. DETAIL OF LOWER PART OF HORSE

Speed and the exaggeratedly shortened perspective of the horse galloping directly out of the picture plane have been achieved by the use of selective focus.

The foremost leg and hoof have been depicted in sharp focus. The underdrawing has been done with a sharp pencil and highlights and shadows are strongly contrasted. On the other hand, it can be seen that the rear leg which has been positioned next to the front leg has been underdrawn with softer, broader lines and further blurred with a combination of exposed ground and added paint to create the clouds of dust.

5.1. As for the horse's face, a sharp pencil was used for the underdrawing which was left visible through the subsequent paint to form the details of the front hoof and leg.

5.2. The opacity of the freely applied paint of the foreground contrasts with the thinner and more translucent paint of the horse.

5.3. Cream colored paint was dragged across the leg for dust clouds.

5.4. A slightly softer drawing implement was used to create the less distinct lines of this rapidly moving leg.

5.5. The gray ground was exposed to create the raised dust which partially obscures this leg.

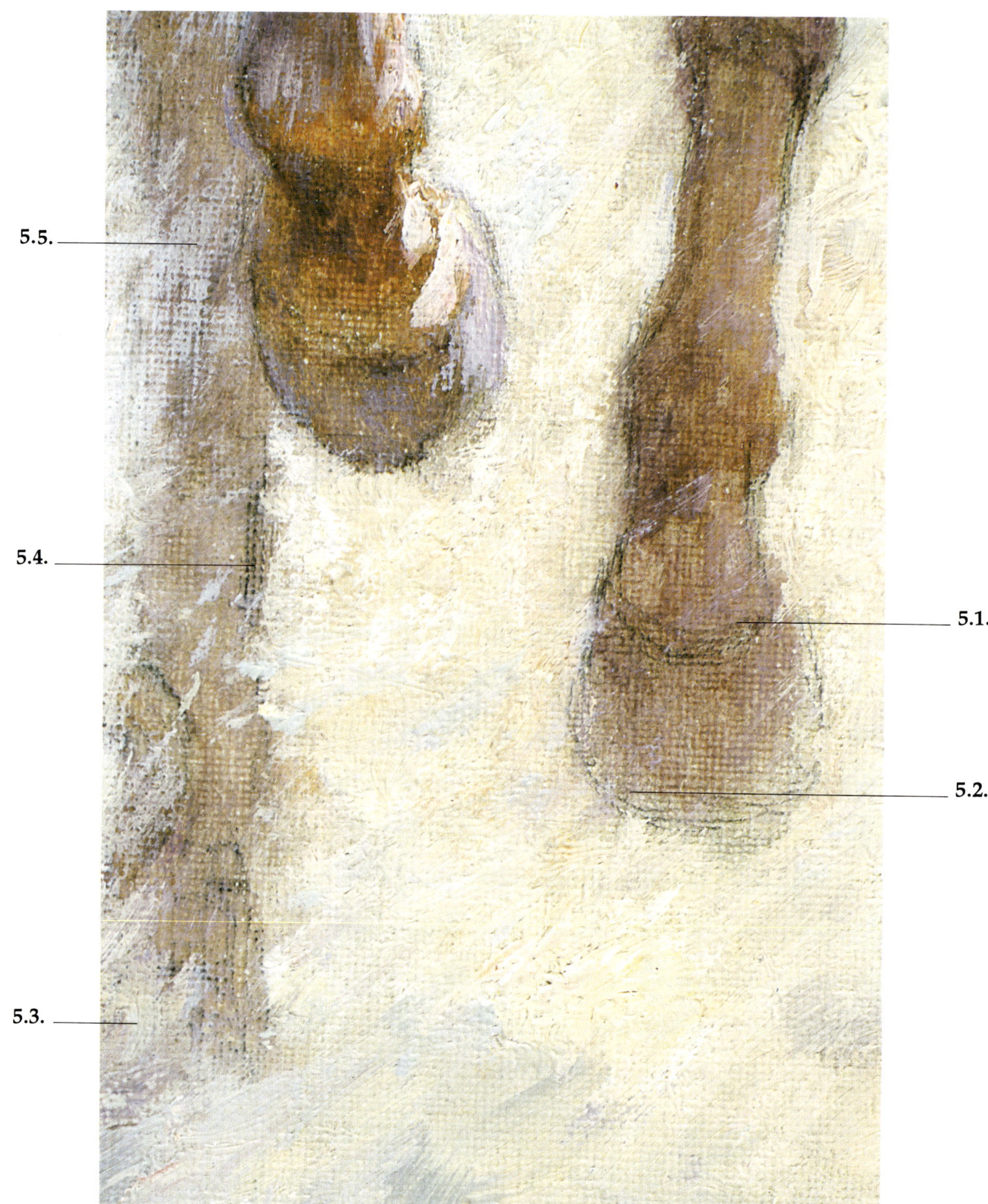

5. DETAIL OF HORSE'S LEGS

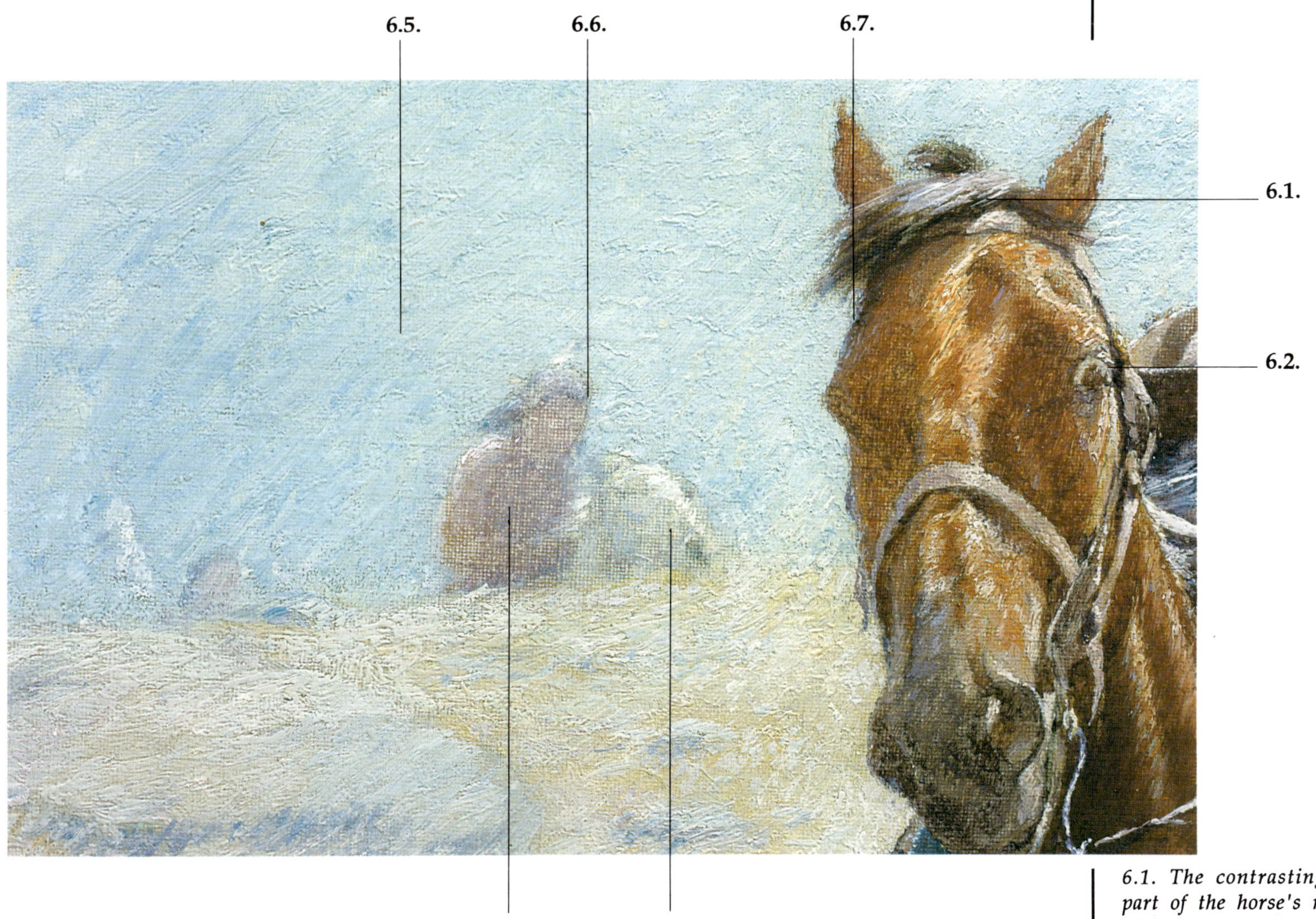

6. DETAIL OF HORSE'S HEAD AND PURSUING INDIANS

Exaggerated foreshortening causes the pursuing Indians to loom over the horizon, seemingly on top of the panicked Cavalry horse. The close proximity of the pursuers and the pursued within the picture plane belies the actual distance between them, heightening the overall tension. Yet Schreyvogel's use of atmospheric perspective holds the image together.

6.1. The contrasting direction of the front part of the horse's mane blowing to the left while his eyes and nose point to the right add to the frenzied appearance of the tightly reined animal.

6.2. This shows the gray ground left exposed as a pictorial effect to define the white of the eye. Leaving bare ground next to opaque paint creates three-dimensionality.

6.3. The Indian pony is largely composed of the gray ground with minimal detailing added. The edges have been left indistinct, again with the ground left uncovered, to make a hazy outline.

6.4. The broken appearance of the thin paint caught in the texture of the plain weave canvas enhances the out of focus quality of the distant Indian.

6.5. The cool blue of the sky has been warmed with touches of red madder lake.

6.6. The Indian was underdrawn with terse, non-continuous lines.

6.7. The blue of the sky has been mixed with white giving it an opaque, pastel like quality which contrasts with the thinner paint of the horse to enhance depth and form.

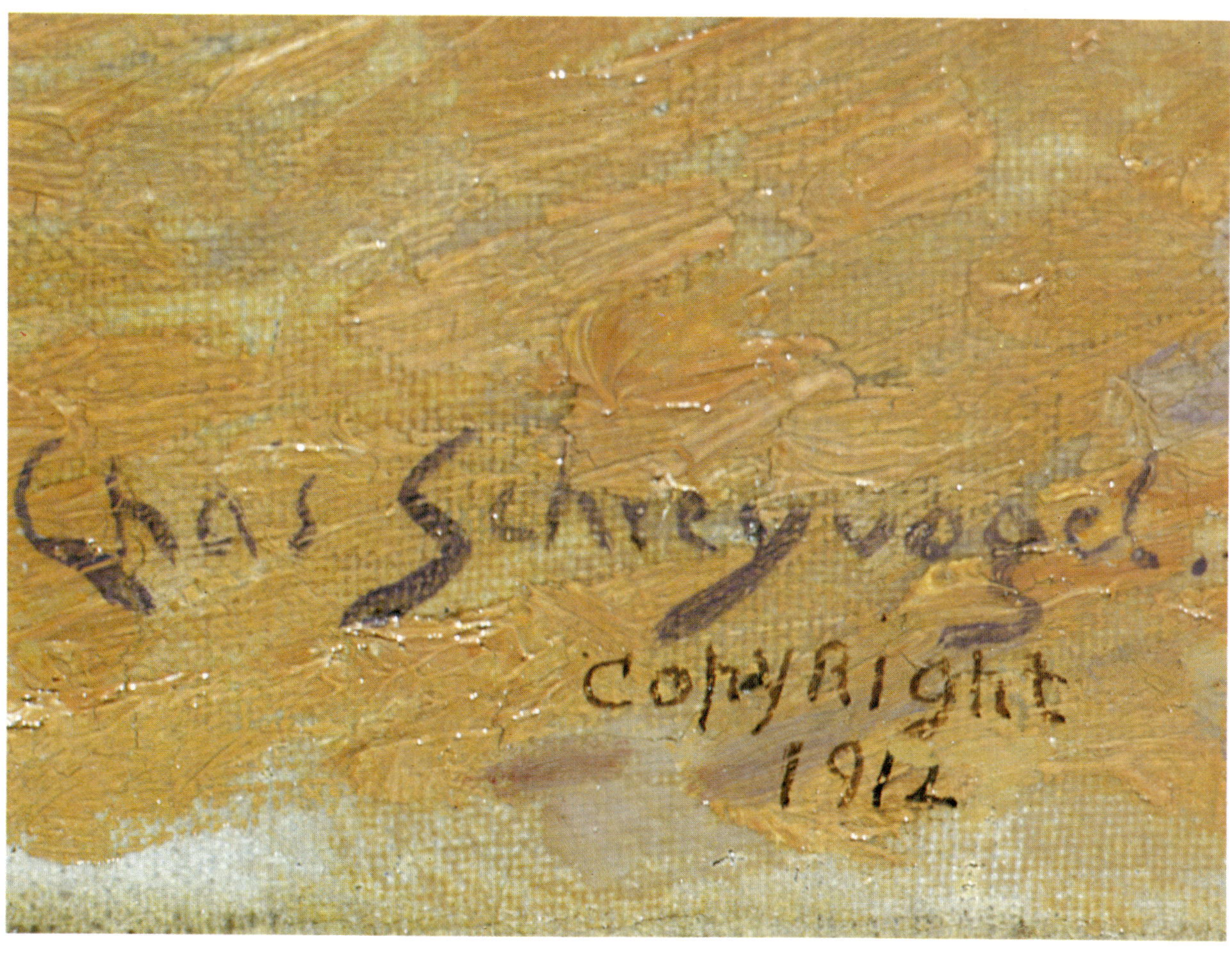

7. DETAIL OF SIGNATURE

Chas. Schreyvogel. Copyright 1912.

SUMMARY OF PAINTING TECHNIQUE

a. A detailed sketch was drawn onto the gray ground.
b. The soldier and horse were painted first with meticulous brushstrokes.
c. The sky and foreground were added around them, in places overlapping the edges slightly and in other places leaving a distinct gap of exposed ground, creating faintly hazy outlines.

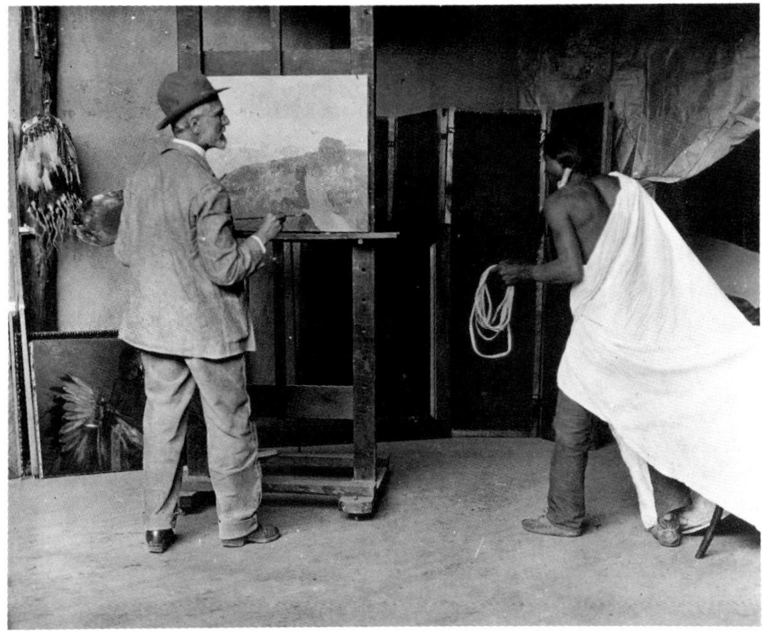

JOSEPH HENRY SHARP

Henry Sharp was not the most technically adventurous of the six artists who were based in Taos, New Mexico in the early 1900s. His work was never honored by the National Academy of Design, as paintings by other Taos artists were. He was just a romantic realist, painting in the style he thought suited to America.

He had, however, three special things going for him. He was the founder of the Taos colony for these artists portraying the sentimental aspects of an unspoiled corner of the tranquil West. As he said succinctly, "I discovered it and told the other boys." Second, he painted more Indian subjects than anyone in Taos. Third, his paintings brought him a larger income than other Taosenos earned. The clever ones were depending on prize money or illustrating for their living while he was selling easel paintings by the dozen.

Sharp's great-grandparents on the paternal side had emigrated from Ireland to New York State, but the artist was born September 27, 1859 in Bridgeport, Ohio, a town on the Ohio River. After squandering investments, his father died when Sharp was 13. The impoverished family moved westward across the state to Cincinnati, the city Sharp thought of as his home.

His friends called him Henry. He was totally deaf as the result of nearly drowning in an accident when he was a boy. He was not self-conscious about his disability. He talked freely, without inflection. People communicated with him by writing in pencil on a 5 inch pad he carried.

Sharp credited two childhood events for his lifelong involvement with Indians. He claimed that when he was six, he saw a band of Indians across the river from Bridgeport in Wheeling, West Virginia. At other times he maintained that reading the novels of "Fenimore Cooper first attracted me to the Indian. It was the romance of boyhood." Whichever the reason, his interest in the red man was deep and permanent.

Sharp's father had been an amateur painter. Sharp was determined to become an artist although his mother was without money to pay for lessons. He found a job in a nail factory and in one year saved enough to enter the McMicken School of Design in Cincinnati. He was 14, 5 feet 6 inches tall with dark hair, a thin face, bright eyes, and a smiling mouth.

One of Sharp's teachers was Henry Farny, putting him in the fourth tier behind Whittredge who had encouraged Bierstadt who had encouraged Farny. Although Farny's popular genre and portrait paintings of Indians were not published until 1881, he already claimed to be the paramount Indian painter.

According to Sharp, Farny expressed a proprietary interest in the subject that was dearest to them both: "When I went to the Academy, I wanted to paint Indians. Farny dissuaded me by telling of hardships and dangers, and made me feel I didn't exactly have the right to paint Indians. After a couple of years when he saw I was determined to go West he gave me books on Pueblo Indians of New Mexico and wanted me to take that up." Farny's concession was easy to make. His lucrative specialty was the Plains Indians.

Despite Sharp's small-town origins and proletarian beginnings in the nail factory, he developed into a perpetual art student, influenced by great teachers in four European art centers. His first trip abroad was to Antwerp, Belgium in 1881. He grew a mustache he waxed at the ends in the Continental manner and affected a "Vandyke beard" in honor of the 17th century Flemish-born artist. He even copied Van Dyke paintings.

Back in the United States in 1882, Sharp indulged his dreams about Pueblo Indians by visiting Santa Fe, New Mexico the next spring. He said he was thrilled by the Indian villages all around him. After returning to Cincinnati, however, he painted commissioned portraits of local notables.

In 1886 he went to Munich where he was exposed to the facile academic style of the German masters who had influenced other Cincinnati painters. With his hometown teacher and friend Frank Duveneck, Sharp also traveled to Spain to study Velasquez paintings in the Madrid museums. He copied works by Velasquez, Goya, and El Greco to retain as guides.

By this time he was 30 and had been studying art for 14 years. His forte was the human figure. He began teaching life and portrait classes at the Cincinnati Art Academy in 1892. The following summer he returned to New Mexico where he discovered Taos and its two cultures, Spanish and Indian. The first artist to live in the village, he divided his work between Indians and all other subjects. He charged five times more for the Indians. Two Indian paintings from sketches Sharp made during the eight weeks he spent in Taos were reproduced in *Harper's Weekly* in 1894.

Schooling abroad had become a way of life for Sharp. In 1895 he went to Paris to study quick depiction of the figure because Indians would not hold lengthy poses despite inducements of candy, cloth, cigarettes, or even a little money. Three of his Indian paintings were exhibited at the Paris Salon. He earned his sobriquet as the father of the Taos art colony by praising the picturesqueness of the village to Ernest Blumenschein and Bert Phillips. They were younger painters who shared a New York City studio and also studied in Paris with the French Academicians.

Sharp came back to Cincinnati in 1897 to resume his own teaching. Portraiture was his bread and butter. Easel paintings were offered for about $30 and he averaged two a week. At the same time, Blumenschein and Phillips were actively seeking uniquely American subjects. They found their way to Taos by accident in the summer of 1898. Phillips remained there while Blumenschein, like Sharp, became a summer resident.

Sharp was torn between depicting the Pueblo and the Plains Indians. Finally, he said, "I went north because I realized that Taos would last longer." He started painting and photographing at the Crow Agency in Montana in 1899. To him, the Crow were more interesting to look at. They were "the old plains fighters." His goal was to put on canvas the portraits of the surviving Plains Indians who had annihilated Custer in the battle of the Little Big Horn 25 years earlier. He pictured some Indians with their weapons but none in violent action.

He did not forget Paris, though. He exhibited Indian portraits at the Exposition in 1900 as well as in Washington, D.C. where the Smithsonian Institution bought 11 paintings for $800. These first major sales were because of his ethnological fidelity. The Smithsonian's curator volunteered that "I regard you as among the first, if not the very first, painter of Indian portraits." He meant first in quality. The Smithsonian already had Catlin paintings.

Through the courtesy of President Theodore Roosevelt he was able to build a log-cabin studio at the Crow Agency in 1901. By the end of the year he had completed 79 Indian paintings. They were all purchased by Mrs. Phoebe Hearst, the mother of the publisher William Randolph Hearst. She donated the pictures to the University of California at Berkeley, bought eight more the next year, and commissioned another 15.

The proceeds from this huge sale let Sharp resign his teaching position in Cincinnati to paint full time beginning in 1902. He reversed the seasons, wintering at the frigid Crow Agency and summering in warmer Taos. He said Montana was "too green" in summer. The fall was his favorite because of the changing colors and the Indian gatherings. In winter, the Crow had time to pose and the snowy landscape was more suited to his style.

Sharp painted portraits of more than 200 Plains Indians of the thousands who had fought in the Custer battle. This was a greater number of portraits than he later accomplished in 40 years in Taos, although he liked to do "heads" in New Mexico as well as Montana. He achieved this large body of work despite the handicap of a serious accident at the Agency. While he was chopping blocks of coal to heat the studio, a splinter flew into his left eye. The injury bothered his vision the rest of his life.

Obtaining models was his primary problem but he saw humor in the obstacles. Red Cloud, he recalled, objected to posing. The chief complained that "I do all the work. You have all the fun." The Crow named Bill Jones said he couldn't sleep because Sharp had painted him with his eyes open.

In the field, Sharp wore a Tyrolean felt hat and a safari jacket. For local scenes he walked with a box of paints and canvas under one arm, a folding easel and stool under the other. For travel he used a sheepherder's wagon made into a studio.

After the pictures he had set out to paint in Montana were finished in 1912, Sharp moved to Taos permanently. For $700 he bought an old dance hall he remodeled as a residence. The front of his home faced the street though access was only through a long side porch. For another $240 the church sold him an abandoned Penitente chapel on adjacent land that he made into his first Taos studio. Droplets of dried blood from the Penitentes' lashings of themselves stained the ceiling of the studio where Sharp's copies of the Spanish masters were hung for inspiration.

He was the senior artist in Taos. A small man, he looked European with his dark eyes, dark Vandyke beard, and now trim mustache. Cheerful, gentle, and kind, he was said to be the most lovable of the Taoseno painters. Women thought he was handsome. His eyes sparkled behind steel-rimmed spectacles that were shaded by the brim of his Tyrolean felt.

Sharp collected Navaho rugs. When Indians from other pueblos came to Taos for a ceremonial gathering, Sharp would wander among their wagons. Surreptitiously, he fingered their handmade quilts. That way he could tell whether there was a rug inside the quilt for extra warmth. He would then offer to buy quilts he knew to contain the rugs he really wanted.

His profound deafness did not hinder him. He could not read lips, except with his wife, so he always carried the small pad and pencil for use in communicating. He also employed the pad for his sketching. He took hundreds of photographs, too. They were what he called his "notes," along with the sketches. However, he seldom worked directly from either.

His routine was Spartan. He rose early, sponge bathed in a bowl, went to the studio, did light exercises, and painted until one. After lunch he took a short nap. If he had errands to run in town, he put on a jacket and vest and a broad-brimmed Stetson with a low crown. Afterward he returned to the studio. In the evening he sat on the side porch with his second wife who was his first wife's younger sister. He described himself physically as having "no scars or repairs. Eyes like a terrier–can't tell if growling or smiling." He followed fad diets, avoiding a combination of starches and meat.

In his portraits he generally used lights and darks as strong diagonals to try to ease static poses. Instead of the $2 he had paid Crows to pose, Taos Indians received 25 cents an hour until they found out what paintings of them sold for. Despite his pride in ethnological accuracy, he dressed Taos models in Crow garb when he thought the subject required it. In Montana, he had painted a birchbark canoe in a Crow camp when a movie crew left the canoe behind.

He conceived of each picture as a romantic idea and made the titles fit the concept. Sometimes he decided on the titles in advance of doing the work. When he finished a painting, his usual practice was to write the title, date, and place on the reverse or on the stretcher. He claimed to be least involved with technique and most concerned with color and light. The choice of subjects fell somewhere in between.

From 1916 to 1925 sales were so slow, he once lied about Duveneck's health to stop a client from buying from Duveneck instead of him. He told other customers, "If my price is too high you can have it for less." After 1925, however, painting sales were strong. He had no more financial worries, even during the Depression.

Later in his career when his eyesight worsened, he avoided details by painting still-lifes of flowers from his garden. He would not do "very fine work, like placing a highlight in an eye." Outdoors, he sat on a folding three-legged stool under an umbrella to shade him from the strong Southwestern sun. His large palette was on his left arm. The box of paints was at his feet. He said "I want to be known as a Taos painter."

Sharp was an accomplished academic artist in the straightforward style he had learned in Munich. His success came from conforming to the artistic values of his day as well as from his early meticulousness in recording ethnographic details.

In 1946 Sharp complained that "Taos isn't Taos any more." Stooped, frail, and white haired, he resented the inroads of civilization, even though the crowds he hated were partially the result of his own founding of the famous art colony. Although he was no longer painting, he said he was "still on deck" even if he "felt the age a bit in eyes and bones." He died in his sleep August 29, 1953 in Pasadena, California. More than 500 of his paintings were in museums.

His 25x30 inch painting *Elk Foot Taos* sold for $100,000 at public auction in 1981.

1. THE PAINTING

After 16 years of training in Europe, Sharp was a well prepared, very experienced, and highly individual painter. His accuracy in recording Indian life brought him early recognition. The Anthropology Department of the University of California acquired 87 of his paintings through Mrs. Hearst. His *oeuvre* consists of more than 10,500 oil paintings. Over 7,800 of them are Indian related.

Sharp brought numerous Indian artifacts back from his trips through the West. This extensive collection served as an *aide-memoire* for objects to incorporate into his paintings. One artifact was a prime elk skin that was a present from the aging warrior Flat Iron. "The best you could find in two days' ride in any direction," it had a green scorpion painted on the inside. The edges of the holes made by the bullets that killed the elk were beaded. This skin was used in many of Sharp's pictures of the interior of a tepee, including *Pipe Song* where it appears as the backdrop. The scorpion design is upper left and one beaded bullet hole is located in the center of the skin.

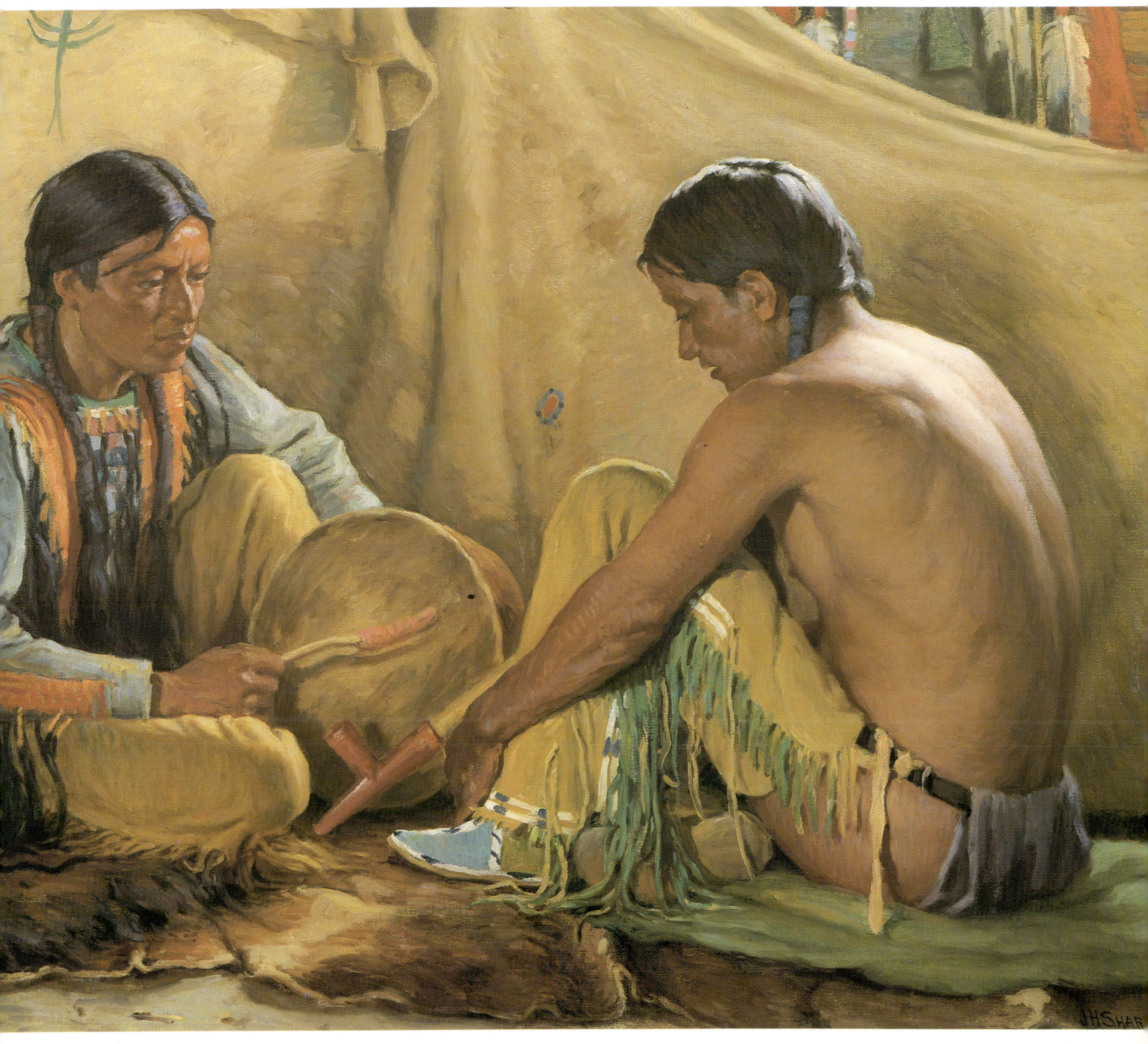

Sharp enthusiastically took many photographs of Indians in their daily life. He also had a large collection of photographic portraits of Indians which he had snapped during his many visits. Back in the studio, he referred to the various photographs to compose his portraits and other representations of Indian life. He once commented in *Pen and Brush* on the difficulty of painting the Indians: "As a model the Indian is not a great suc-

J.H. Sharp. Pipe Song is in the collection of the Museum of Western Art, Denver, Colorado. Oil on canvas, wax lined. 25 inches (63.5 cm) height x 30 1/8 inches (76.5 cm) width. Signed lower right. Not dated.

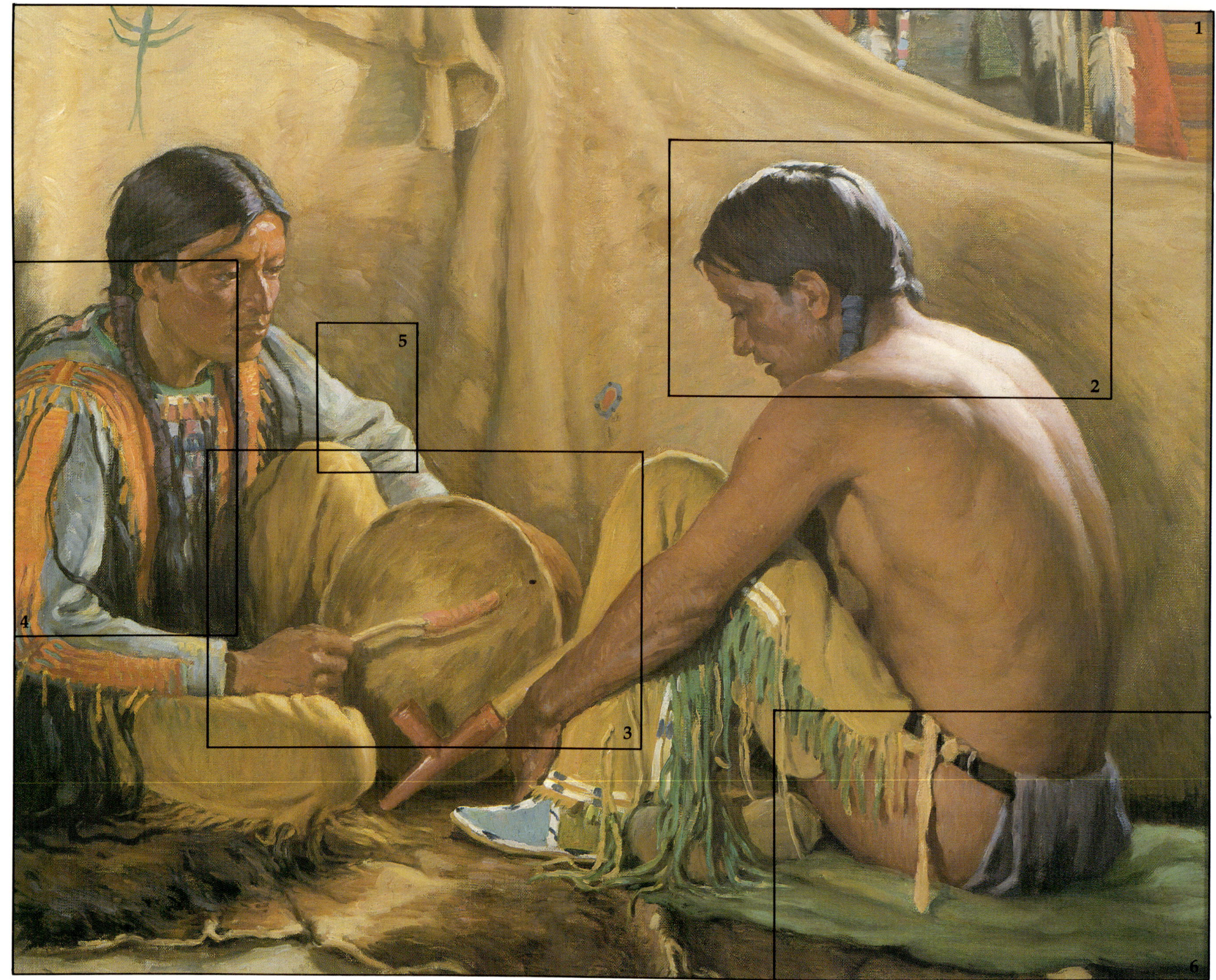

cess. After various tribulations to get him to pose, it is impossible to make him unbend. If it is his first attempt he will invariably take a pose of majestic and often ludicrous stiffness. Having used much persuasion, time and patience in breaking one in, he soon becomes indifferent, often gets too familiar, goes on a strike for more pay, or stays away altogether...."

Despite his complaints about the models, Sharp was liked and respected by the Indians. Many of his sitters can be recognized again and again in his paintings. They preferred posing for him to serving as models for any other Taos artist. When not posing, they gathered in his studio, greatly amused by Sharp's working methods as he dabbed paint on the canvas and then danced backward to view the painting from a distance. Behind the artist's back, the Indians would mock and mimic his unrestrained gestures.

For *Pipe Song*, Sharp used a plain weave, medium weight canvas with a thin white commercially-applied ground. There is no visual evidence of an underdrawing.

Like many other Sharp paintings, *Pipe Song* was probably done from Indian models in the artist's studio. No artist's changes are apparent in the composition. Rather, the painting procedure was very methodical. Sharp seems to have started with the background, that is, with the elk skin at the top of the picture, and worked consistently toward the foreground, or bottom.

The technique used for *Pipe Song* is straightforward and efficient, yet productive of a powerful impact. The painting was executed rapidly with a practiced hand. Dilute colored underlayers were laid in carefully to block in the main composition. The overall texture is influenced by the pronounced canvas weave which is not concealed by the thinly applied paint. The white ground shows through at the tops of the weave, further accentuating the fabric texture and providing a glistening effect.

While Sharp painted the underlayers, he was already thinking in terms of the composition, palette, and modeling of the finished picture. In most cases, the colors of the underlayers are related to the colors of the subsequent paint. The underlayers were usually left exposed to provide the middle tone of the main body color, though they are often darker where there are shadows. There are dark brown underlayers for the shadows, beige for the background, red for the flesh, violet-blue for the hair, green for the drum and the yellow trousers, red for the feathers in the background, and so on.

For the most part, the underlayers are followed by a single layer of paint that is thicker and richer in medium than the dilute underlayers. The thicker paint was applied in short and sure strokes that retain brushwork, indicating that Sharp used fairly stiff brushes for his application. In this stage, forms were painted systematically, working from dark to light.

The highlights for the skin were done with fairly opaque paint that was smoothly blended, creating subtle transitions in the modeling. This paint appears satiny and smooth against the translucent underlayers. The contrast fills out the forms, giving them a strong sense of roundness and solidity.

The colors are clean and fresh throughout the painting. Sometimes the colors were mixed on the canvas rather than on the palette, but traces of one color rarely appear in a brushstroke of another color. This implies either that the artist used different brushes to apply the various tones or that he cleaned his brushes carefully before proceeding to the next color. The former explanation is more likely. Some photographs of Sharp in his studio show him holding a great many brushes.

The viewer is led into the scene by the diagonal arm of the bare chested Indian. The strong composition consists of simple diagonal lines with the drum at the confluence. The vivid palette and fiery highlights are contrasted with warm shadows to create full modeling and provide depth. Yet, the tableau is kept intimate by the warm color of the elk-skin backdrop.

The Taos artists were brought together by their joint isolation. They enjoyed the selective seclusion of the artists' colony, the rugged northern New Mexican landscape, the primitive lifestyle, and the inspiration drawn from the Indians and the terrain.

How they responded to their surroundings and how they expressed themselves artistically varied. Technically, the paintings of Sharp and Blumenschein in this book have similarities. Both used dilute colored underlayers that were built up with subsequent strokes of impasted paint. The renderings are straightforward and bold. The difference here is that Sharp painted a realistic record of Indian customs and artifacts while Blumenschein used a cartoon style to evoke a response to a particular incident.

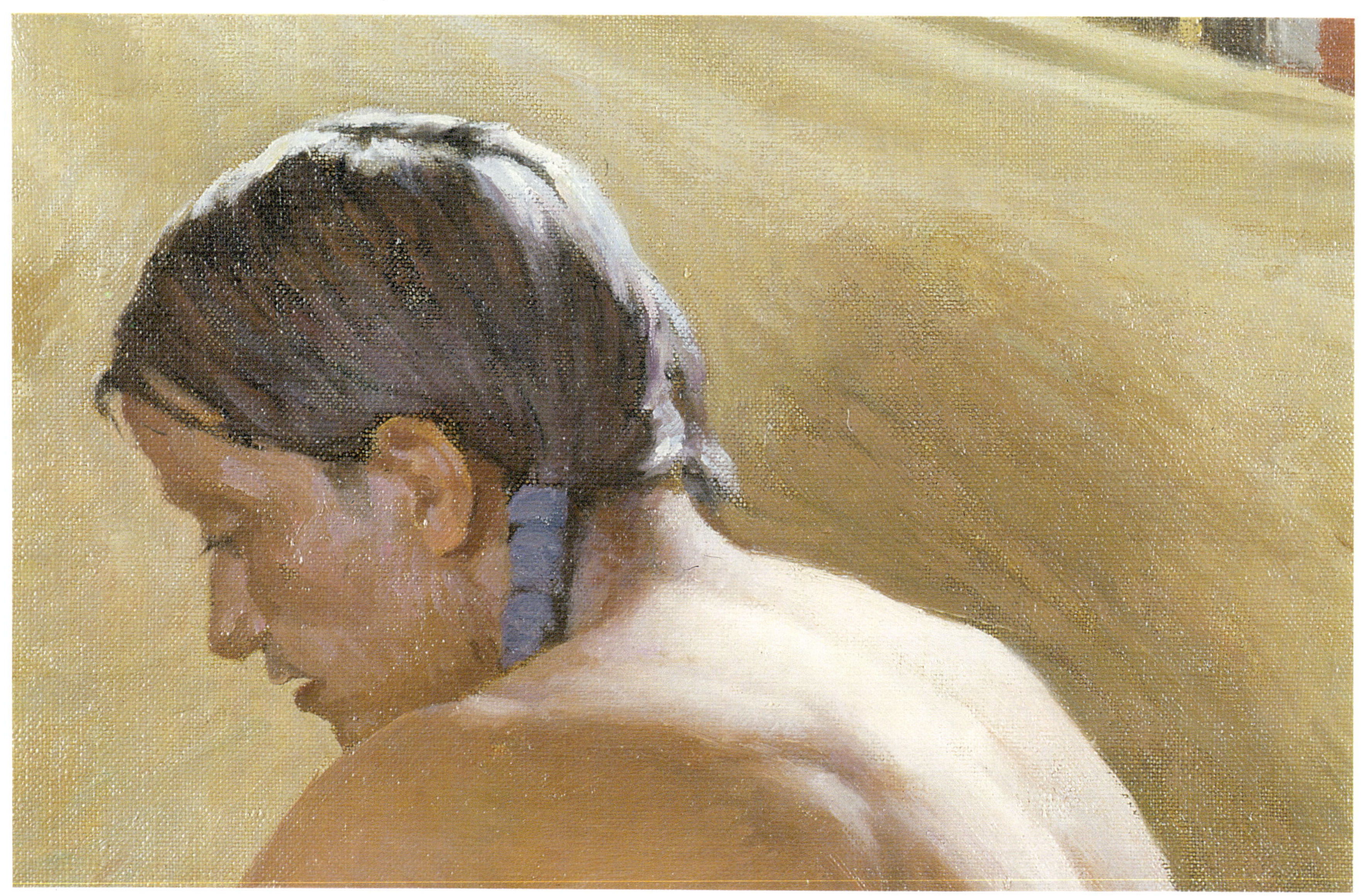

2. Detail of Head on Right

The Indian on the right was painted after the elk-skin background. The flesh color was laid in much more opaquely with rather thick paint for the highlights on his back. The contrast between the intense highlights on the figure's bare back and the warm shadows emphasizes the fullness of the form. The individual brushstrokes are distinct and were applied with short stubby movements. In places the paint was partially blended on the canvas itself to create smooth transitions for the modeling of the figure. Highlights in the face were added and refinements such as the eyelashes were put in last.

As noted, a dark blue-violet underlayer was used beneath the Indian's hair. The underlayer was applied very thinly. The ground showing at the tops of the canvas weave creates a bright, shimmering effect. Dark reddish-brown individual brushstrokes on top of the underlayer represent the hair. A blue such as ultramarine was mixed with white and applied in short vertical brushstrokes for the braid holder.

The color variation for the underlayer in the background is from dark brown to beige. The dark brown corresponds to the location of the shadows, which were then strengthened in the top paint layer by using an appropriately darker paint than for the rest of the background. This implies that Sharp knew exactly where to put the shadows at a very early stage. The background was then probably painted with an earth color such as yellow ochre mixed with white.

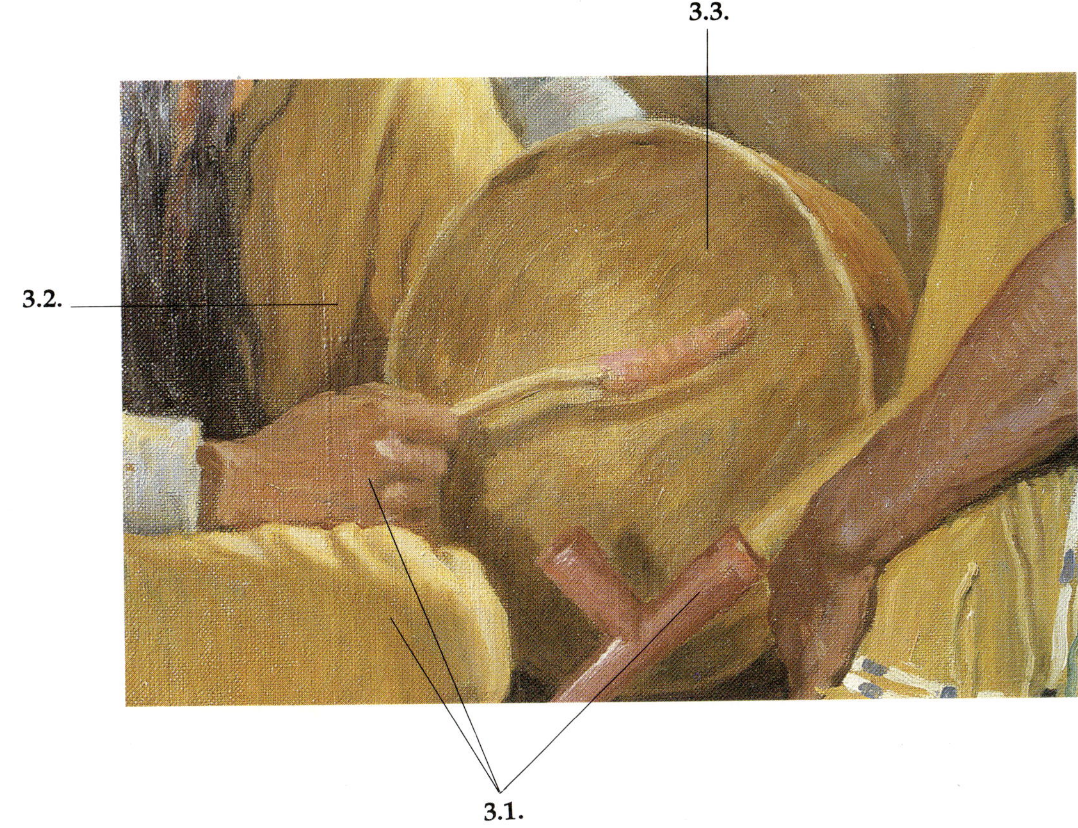

3.1. The work sequence for the trousers was from dark to light. The pale yellow highlights were added last. The same procedure can be observed for the pipe and the flesh tone.

3.2. Sharp used the canvas texture throughout the picture to break up the surface and reflect light. The thinly applied paint layers do not cover the texture of the fabric. The white ground shows through, again creating a luminous effect.

3.3. A greenish underlayer was put beneath the yellow of the drum. Fairly dry paint was partially mixed on the painting surface. The distinct brushwork adds shadow and shape to the instrument.

3. DETAIL OF DRUM

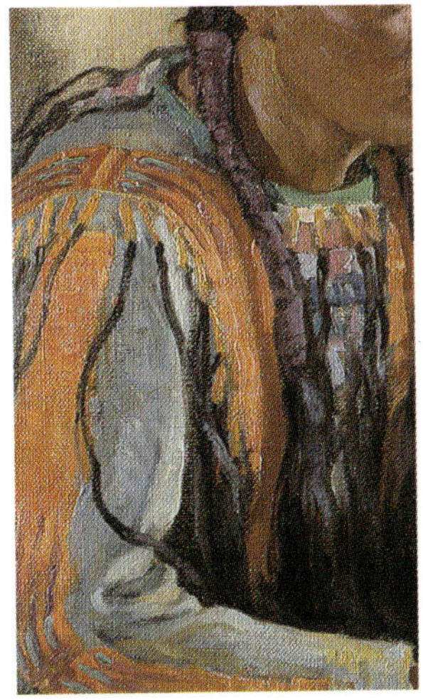

4. DETAIL OF DRUMMER'S VARIEGATED OUTFIT

Here too, the white ground was often left exposed to produce glistening colors. Also, the application of the differently colored underlayers is visible. The dark violet for the drummer's hair, dark brown for his shadow in the background, blue for the sleeve, orange for the decorations, and brown-black for the shadow on his chest can all be seen.

In this detail, the underlayer serves as the shadows while the top layer provides the highlights. The rich paint was applied with a somewhat stiff brush that retained its typical imprint. Although a varied palette was employed, the individual colors in this example have a pure appearance.

The light blue was mixed with white wet-into-wet. Fringes were added last as refinements. The orange fringe was applied with short brushstrokes wet-into-wet.

5.1. The background paint was mixed on the canvas in a wet-into-wet technique, picking up some of the darker color of the underlayer. The paint is rich and buttery, retaining some traces of the brushwork.

5.2. What appears to be an underdrawing or sketch on the ground is in fact the dark brown underlayer for the drummer's shadow. The underlayer is visible in the space between the elbow and the background. Sharp intentionally left the gap to form the exposed underlayer into a dark outline to further define the arm of the figure.

5.3. The white ground of the arm was left exposed to provide the color of the sleeve. Highlights and shadows for the folds were added in single concise brushstrokes. In this detail, the usual work order was reversed. That is, shadows were painted on top of the highlights.

5.4. Particulars such as the dark brown line were added last with somewhat drier paint that was dragged across the surface in a fast movement, catching only on the raised texture of the weave.

6.1. A dark green underlayer creates a shadow for the green blanket.

6.2. A dark brown underlayer was used for the foreground.

6.3. The slightly impasted fringe was done on top of the underlayer with distinct, narrow brushstrokes, leaving little ridges at the edges.

6.4. Violet was used as an underlayer for the loincloth.

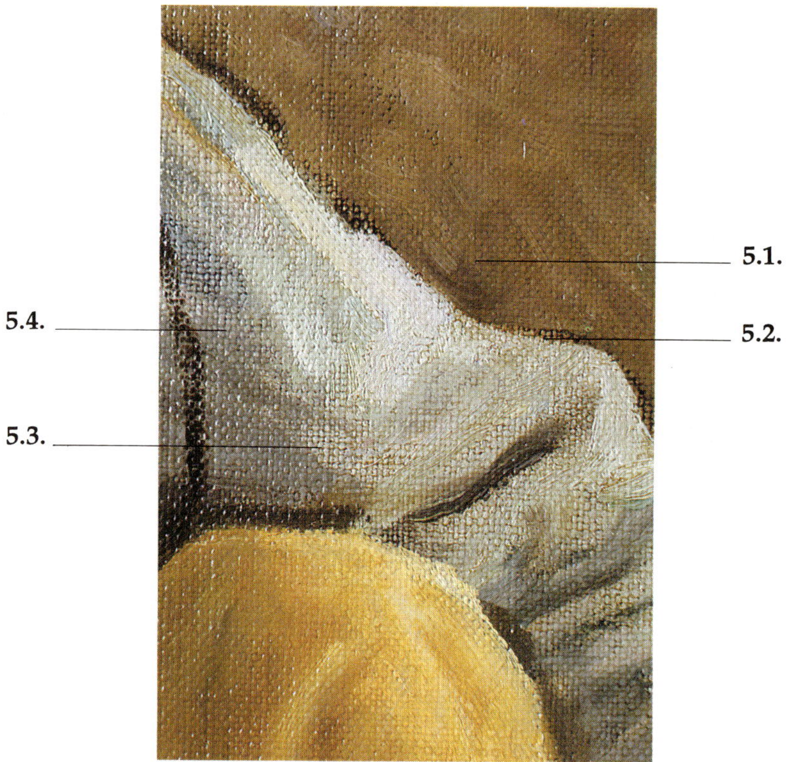

5. DETAIL OF DRUMMER'S ELBOW AND KNEE

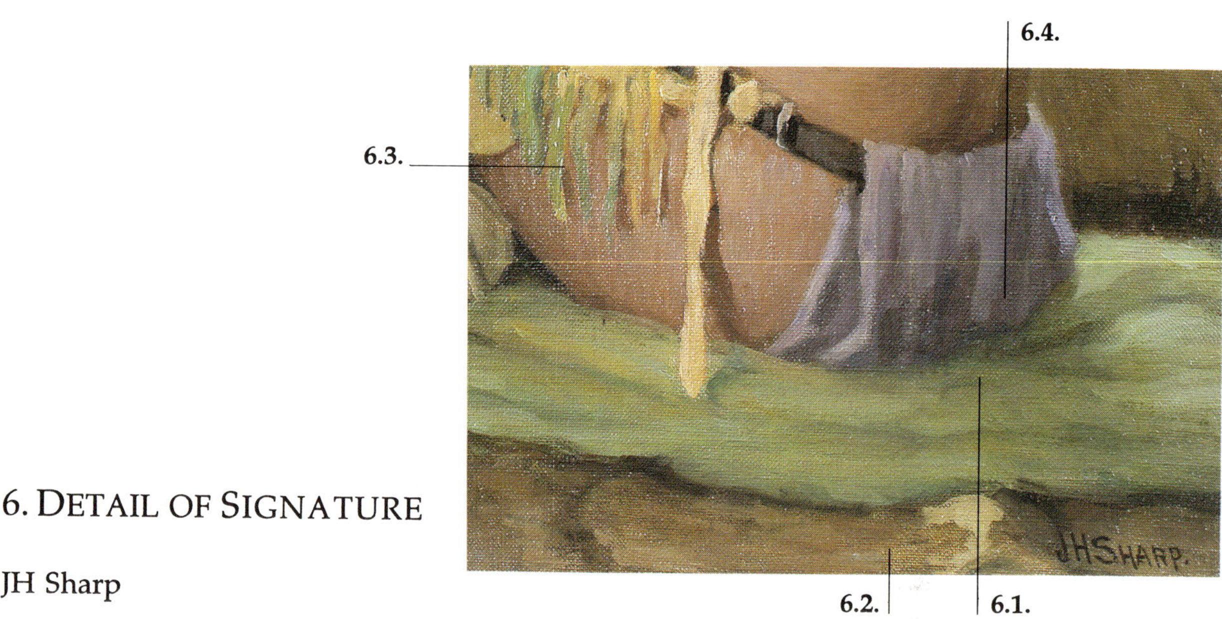

6. DETAIL OF SIGNATURE

JH Sharp

As they do throughout the picture, the thin colored underlayers remain visible in the final composition as glistening middle tones or luminous shadows.

SUMMARY OF PAINTING TECHNIQUE

a. A thin white ground was commercially prepared.
b. There is no underdrawing visible.
c. There was an extensive application of thin and transparent colored underlayers leaving the ground partially visible.
d. Thicker paint was applied to develop the modeling of the forms. Some particulars were added. There are no apparent changes in the composition.

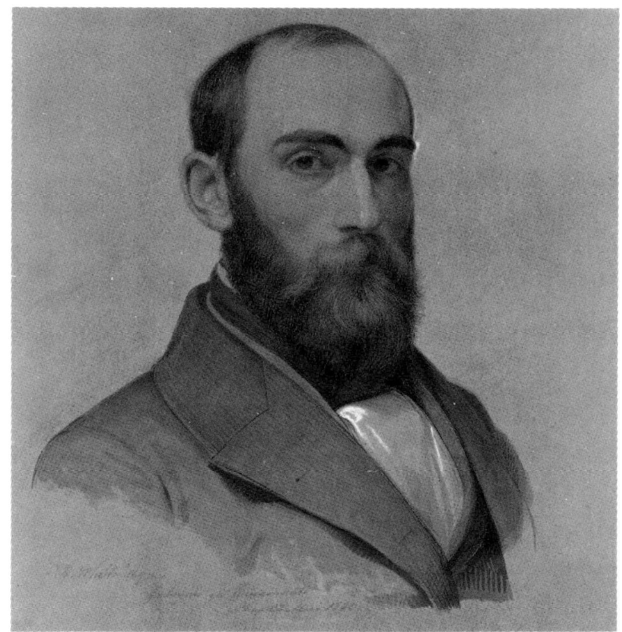

WORTHINGTON WHITTREDGE

Among the master painters of the landscape of the American West, Worthington Whittredge was unique. When he entered the Rockies in 1866 he was not interested in depicting the grandeur and the immensity of the towering mountains as were Bierstadt and Moran. He said he was not impressed by perpendicularity. Instead, he climbed the elevations mainly to look back at the endless, horizonless plains.

It was the vastness of the silent grassland and the forests stretching eastward from the foothills that intrigued him. His paintings were generally smaller and simpler than the panoramas. Over the years, however, his more intimate works came to mean almost as much to American art as the larger pictures did.

"I was born in Ohio in 1820," Whittredge wrote, "the youngest of the family. My boyhood was spent on my father's dairy farm near Springfield. He had been a sea captain. Where we lived there were great expanses of prairie and woodland. The Shawnee Indians were still in the vicinity.

"Game was abundant. I was a born trapper. My father had in his keeping $400 which I had made from the sale of my pelts before I was 16. My formal education was extremely limited. Farmers' boys could not be spared to go to school. I applied to my father for my money to go to High School but my father refused. He considered it his own. When my unmarried brother returned home, I seized the opportunity to go away.

"I had promised to learn a trade. Already I had a longing to be an artist. But I could not speak of this to my father. The word 'artist' was anathema. When the time came, my mother put $2.50 in my pocket. With this patrimony I made my way to a sister in Cincinnati. Her husband was a house-and-sign painter. He set me at it immediately.

"I spent all my evenings over drawing books. I was getting to be an artist. In a little while I was painting pictures on firemen's hose-wagons as well as on temperance banners.

"A friend proposed that we go into the daguerreotype business. I soon came to grief in Indianapolis for lack of money. Besides being destitute, I fell ill and returned home in a miserable condition. I painted a portrait of my father. This was the end of his objections that I should become a painter. Portraits occupied my attention then for a few years, but my love of outdoor life was too strong and it was not long before I took up landscape.

"Returning to Cincinnati, I painted a landscape which I sent to the National Academy in New York. This picture was hung in the exhibition. This was a great encouragement. When I decided to go to Europe, friends secured work for me for all the time I expected to be away.

"I went abroad in 1849. I made sketches along the Rhine that summer, returned to Brussels, then went to Paris. I found no landscape painter in Paris that I cared to go with. I went to Barbizon but did not think much of the pictures. Leutze was in his prime when I came to Düsseldorf. In his 'Washington Crossing the Delaware' I was made to do service [as a model] twice, once for the steersman and again for Washington himself. Leutze mixed the colors for the sky and invited Andreas Achenbach and myself to help him cover the canvas the next day.

"I had concealed my baldness from my friends. I had worn a toupee. One day [on an outing] the conversation turned to American Indians. One of the girls asked what scalping was like. Suddenly I had an idea that would let me get rid of my wig. Seizing a knife, I emitted a war-whoop, climbed a tree, hung to a branch by my legs, cut the toupee from my head and threw it to the ground. Three girls fainted. I never wore the toupee after that.

"In July [1854] I started for Rome, sketch book in hand. Switzerland was not a subject for my pictures. I never measured grandeur in a perpendicular line. [In 1859] I had been in Europe ten years. I came back to New York and fit up my studio in the old Tenth Street building. It was the most crucial period of my life. I knew I must produce something inspired by my home surroundings. I hid myself for months in the Catskills. To my surprise I was elected an Academician.

"At the close of the Civil War I was invited by General [John] Pope to accompany him on a tour of inspection through the eastern portions of the Rocky Mountains and New Mexico. I went as a civilian. We left Fort Leavenworth [Kansas] on the first of June 1866 with a detachment of cavalry. I rode that summer over 2,000 miles on horseback, passing up the Platte River to Denver and along the base of the mountains until we crossed them at the Spanish Peaks and went over to Santa Fe and Albuquerque on the Rio Grande, returning over the old Cimarron trail the end of September.

"I had never seen the plains or anything like them. I cared more for them than for the mountains. My own pictures have been produced from sketches made on the plains with the mountains in the distance. Whoever crossed the plains, notwithstanding its herds of buffalo and flocks of antelope, wild horses, deer, and rabbits, could hardly fail to be impressed with its vastness and silence. On reaching an elevation we had a remarkable view of the great plains. No definite horizon was visible.

"We usually made a march of 33 miles a day, between daybreak and 1 o'clock in the afternoon. On arriving in camp I went at once to make a sketch. Then I had to partake of a cold dinner.

"We encamped one night near the Garden of the Gods. I made a sketch but it grew dark before I finished. I mentioned my disappointment to the General. He said he would leave me an ambulance [wagon] and two orderlies and I might follow in the afternoon. At that time the Indians were none too civil. We had met plenty of ghastly evidence. With the usual reminder from the General about Indians, I set out alone before sunrise to find some elevation. Finally I wandered four miles and there on a hill I stuck up my umbrella and went to work.

"Before long my eye caught a dark figure of a man who seemed to be approaching. When he was out of sight I set down my sketch box and examined my revolver, then resumed work. The fellow at last approached me from behind, without uttering a word.

Then he said, *'Harper's Weekly*?'

"I met Kit Carson, the famous scout, in Santa Fe. One day he asked if he might go with me to sketch. He described a sunrise he had seen and wanted to know if I could paint it for him.

"At Santa Fe I met another character. I was making a sketch of Santa Fe itself. The picture was nearly finished when a rough-looking fellow stepped up behind me and demanded to know what I asked for the picture. I told him it was not for sale. He broke out with a volley of cuss words and drew his pistol: 'You think that I haven't any money to buy your picture. I have got money enough to buy all the pictures you could paint and I want that picture and I'm going to have it.' He kept brandishing his pistol.

"I finally got on my feet and said: 'My friend, you look pretty rough but I don't believe you are a fool. You can't have the picture. It is a sketch to make a large picture from. I live in New York and my business is to paint big pictures and sell them at a thundering price, and if you have money enough I can accommodate you after I get back to New York.' 'Money,' he ejaculated, 'What will the big picture cost?' I told him $10,000 without the frame. The frame would cost him $2,000 more. This silenced him and I handed him my studio address. He took it and I have never seen him since.

"At Santa Fe we saw a cloud of dust and presently a herdsman riding for his life. Behind him was 25 Utes in pursuit. The herdsman had been appointed to take care of a small drove of cattle. He had the pluck to tell the Indians that if they killed one of his steers he would kill one of them, which had been carried out.

"As I wanted to make sketches of the Indians the Major took me with him to sittings for six days. The Major represented that I was the Chief Justice of the United States and had the settlement in my hands, and while I was trying to make sketches I was interrupted by the Major asking me if that was not so. All this palaver was to gain time, until one evening the Indians stole three of our best horses and departed. The Utes murdered every white man, woman and child on the entire route.

"We set out from Albuquerque early in September. Our way lay over the old Santa Fe trail. On leaving our troops, I gave my orderly a dollar to buy oats for the old cavalry horse I had ridden over 2,000 miles. I thought some recognition of his services was due.

"I went twice to the Rocky Mountains after my first visit, these last times by railroad [in 1870 and probably in 1871]. The first of these later visits was undertaken because on my first visit I had made a sketch from which I had begun a large picture. Looking out from under trees were the plains. The trees did not suit me. I remembered a group I had seen 50 miles from Denver which I thought would suit my picture better. I undertook the journey to make sketches of them. They were introduced into the picture, much to its improvement.

"The early landscape painters of America thought the only way to get along was to paint *scenery*. This led to much wandering of our artists. Simplicity of subject was not in demand. It must be on a big canvas. Bierstadt and Church answered the need. For more homely scenery there was the Hudson River School, one of whom I was. Their pictures were 'got together' either out of doors or from sketches. Study was directly from nature.

"The subjects of my pictures have been extremely varied. I have tried everything until I am hardly known as the painter of any particular class of landscape. Coast scenes, brook scenes, scenes of the plains, interiors of old New England houses, I have tried to depict."

In 1859 when Whittredge returned from Rome after 10 years abroad, his compelling need had been to free himself from the artificial mannerisms of the stiff and colorless Düsseldorf school. His capacity for hard work had helped. To overcome the European training, he had sketched along the Hudson River and in the Catskills for months.

By 1866 when he went to the Rockies, the Düsseldorf finish had been replaced by looser and fresher brushwork. He was able to visualize the West not merely as invasive mountains but also as consonant with the gentler prairies and woodlands of his childhood in frontier Ohio. He made the West into the familiar, not the fantastic.

Whittredge's contemporaries described him as attractive, sensible, outgoing, and self-reliant. They said his 90 years of life were a constant joy.

His 22x33 inch *Indian Encampment* dated 1868 sold for $280,000 at public auction in September 1981.

1. THE PAINTING

On the Cache la Poudre provides a rare opportunity to study a mid-19th century landscape done in an *alla prima* manner. It is the artist's preparatory painting for a larger work and was done almost entirely in one sitting in the field. Whittredge's heightened awareness of his surroundings can be read in every brushstroke. The fluid paint was applied quickly and surely, touching wet paint into wet paint with an eye to palette and composition.

Back in the studio with controlled lighting, unlimited time, an accumulation of sketches, and no mosquitoes, a final painting can be done with forethought and careful preparation. Rendered out-of-doors in one sitting, however, a field sketch conveys the artist's immediate impression by means of direct paint application. It is an unconscious effort intended to record, not impress. Yet, this small picture is a virtuoso achievement.

There are no distinct paint layers, indicating that the paint was applied throughout in a wet-into-wet technique. Final refinements such as individual tree branches, touches of foliage, and perhaps even the deer were added while the paint was still wet. Despite its relatively small size and rapid execution, the painting is a highly finished work with a carefully chosen composition rendered with full regard to color value and the essential nuances.

The original fabric support has a twill weave and is covered with a white ground which incorporates distinct coarse particles. It cannot be determined if the ground was applied by the artist because he painted to the edge of the canvas. The sketch was executed on a lapboard, a common plein air practice. The fabric was tacked to the lapboard at the extreme edges. Evidence of these tack holes can still be seen, evenly spaced around the edges.

Once back from his sketching expedition, Whittredge had the sketch lined to a new fabric so that it could be mounted on a stretcher without losing any of the image. This was probably done so that the artist could have a frameable and thus salable work rather than an unmounted sketch. The paint that has been added to the new edges to extend the image to the slightly increased size closely matches the palette and handling of the original paint, making it clear that Whittredge himself painted the edges.

The sketch has been attributed to Whittredge's third Western trip made to Denver and adjacent areas, probably in 1871. The visit was reported in the local paper: "Whittredge, a New York artist of no little celebrity ... has been stopping several weeks in our town, making sketches of mountain and river scenery.... Some of his views of the Cache la Poudre are charming, for there can be no more picturesque stream in the world; these, however, have been painted this summer, and are not wholly completed.

"This is a field almost wholly new to artists, for those who visit Colorado seem to think [there are] no studies worth their attention below the mountains. With rare and good judgment,... Whittredge has lingered lovingly along the Cache la Poudre ... and he has reproduced some of their loveliest aspects."

This small scene conveys the intimate atmosphere of moist soft air which the artist himself experienced and retains the freshness and uninhibited brushwork of the plein air piece it is. No doubt it served as the model for the larger and later painting in the collection of the Amon Carter Museum, a picture done in Whittredge's studio in 1876 and considered to be one of the artist's Western masterpieces.

The Hudson River School and Asher B. Durand in particular were Whittredge's self-

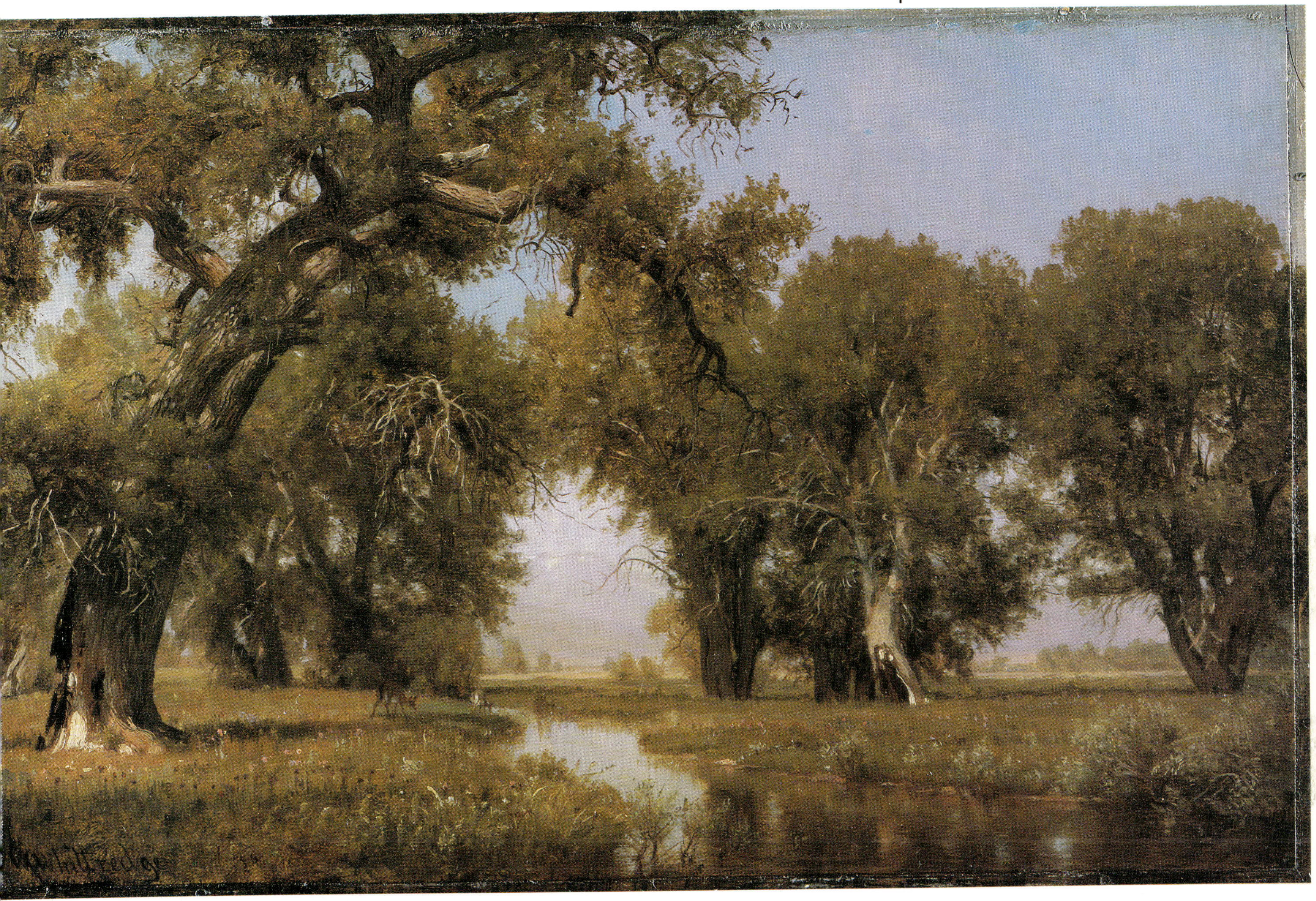

proclaimed influences. This is evident in the treatment of nature as a simple and pure subject: arched foliage over a tranquil pastoral scene creates a meditative, reverential mood. The romantic poet William Cullen Bryant, whom Whittredge knew and admired, expressed this sentiment in *A Forest Hymn*: "... forlorn bowers [leaning] toward each other like the vaulted nave of a cathedral.... The groves were God's first temples."

The influence of the Barbizon School which Whittredge had renounced is also unmistakable in the subdued palette and hazy outlines. Yet, Whittredge seems to have shaken off the rigors of his German training and French and Italian experiences to become part of the movement to establish something new, "something peculiar to our people, to distinguish it from the art of the other nations and to enable us to pronounce without shame the oft repeated phrase, 'American Art.' "

In 1871, Whittredge wrote in a letter to the *Greeley Tribune*: "Those who have claimed so much for the atmosphere of Italy, never saw the atmosphere of our plains near the mountains, and it is pretty evident that they never dreamed of it, for they spent

Worthington Whittredge. On the Cache la Poudre River is in the collection of Fine Arts Museums of San Francisco, California. Museum Purchase, Roscoe and Margeret Oakes Income Fund. Oil on canvas, glue lined. 15 1/4 inches (38.7 cm) height x 22 7/8 inches (58.2 cm) width. Signed lower left. Not dated.

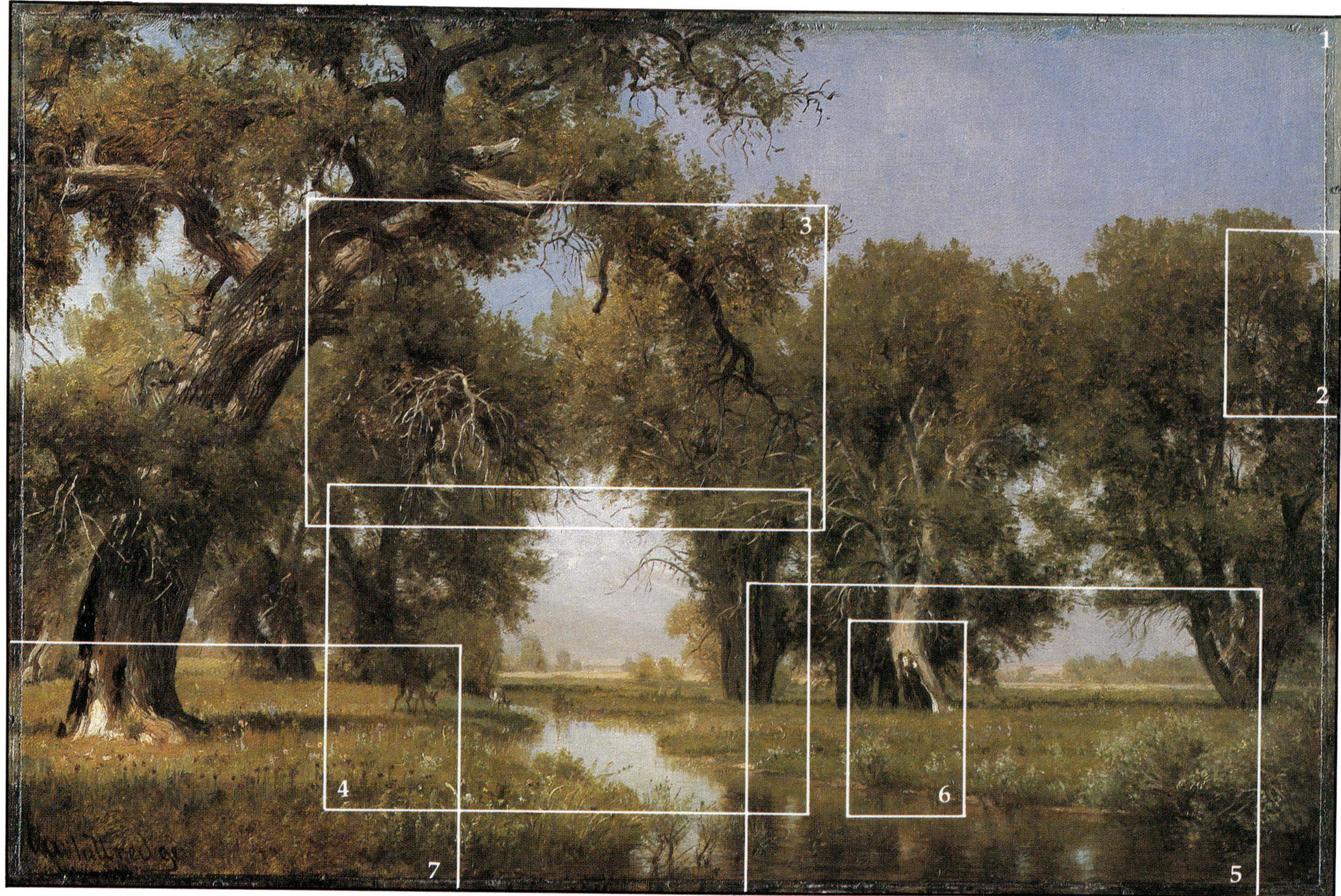

all their energies in glorifying what was around them, and declaring that there was nothing else in this world like it.... We need age, historical associations, and great poets and painters to make our land as renowned as the ash heaps of the Old World; but we need nothing of this kind to enjoy its beautiful scenery when it is before our eyes, if we will but strip ourselves of old prejudices, and use our common senses."

Whittredge is frequently grouped with Thomas Moran and Albert Bierstadt as painters of realistic Western vistas. The painting styles of Bierstadt and Whittredge overlapped somewhat and their paths certainly crossed. They became acquainted in Europe and shared a studio in Düsseldorf. Bierstadt went West first and the success of his panoramas may have influenced Whittredge to seek his fortune there. Their intent and outlook, however, were dissimilar.

If all three produced a painting at the same location, the results would be vastly different. Moran sought the fantastic: unusual cloud, land, or rock formations often depicted at sunset so that the strong light and vivid colors would accentuate the strange shapes into semi-abstract forms.

Bierstadt preferred the grand view with a pastoral foreground, hazy middle distance, and a vast, distant, mountainous panorama. Strong light was used to sharply delineate closer objects, while veiled light produced a slightly out of focus distance. When Easterners viewed the paintings of Moran and Bierstadt, they felt that they had travelled to strange and far away places.

Whittredge brought the West home. He chose tranquil scenes where trees form an intimate shelter. The middle distance is a stone's throw away and the background mountains melt into the sky. Outlines appear fuzzy through the soft diaphanous light. Except for the suggestion of the far away mountains, the scene could be any place.

For Whittredge, nature was nature the world over. It had become a metaphor for peace and repose in a world that 19th century man realized was quickly changing.

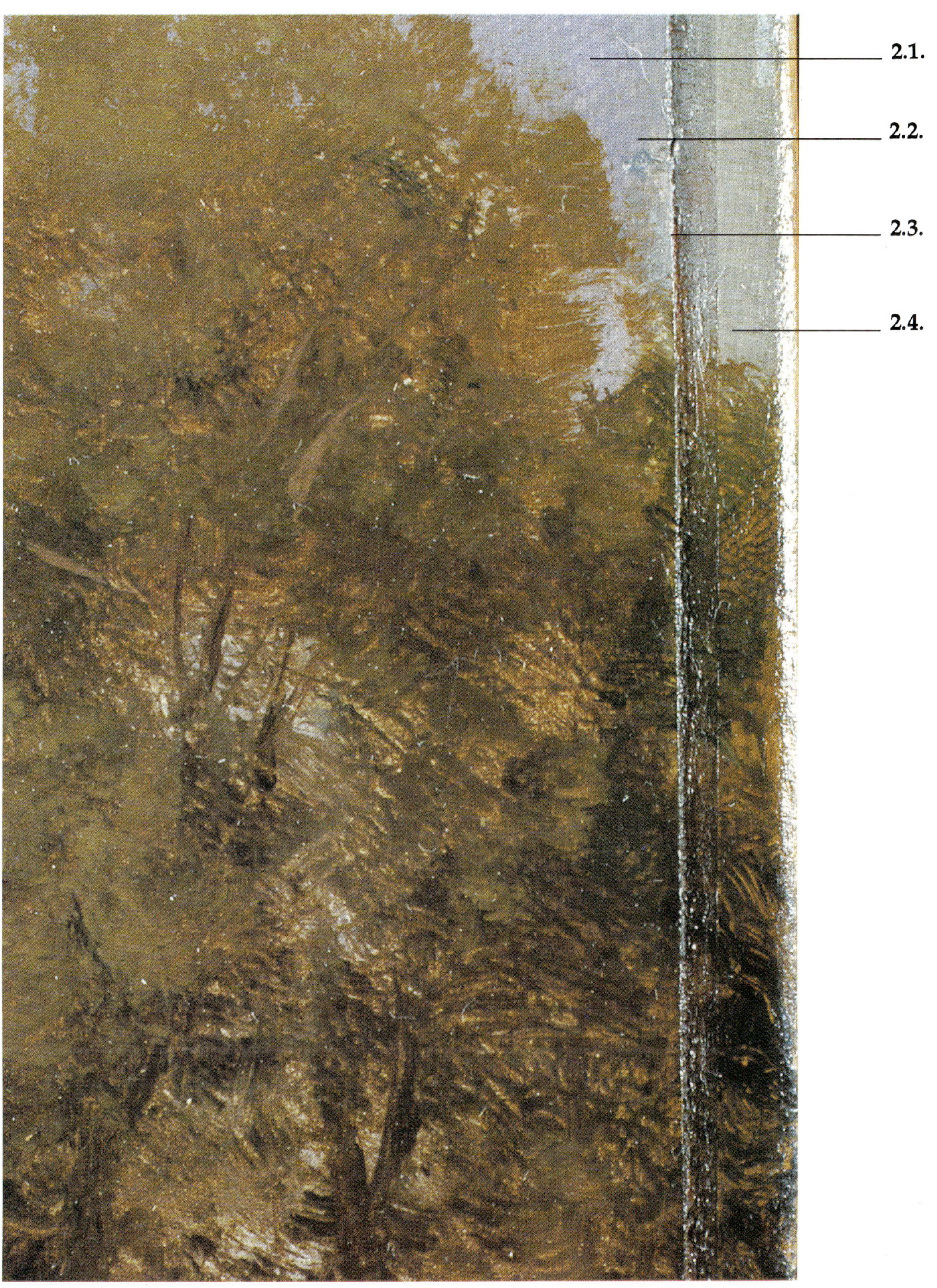

2. Detail Along Right Edge

2.1. *The diagonal pattern is from the twill weave of the canvas.*

2.2. *This is a painted-over tack hole which resulted from the canvas' temporary attachment to a lapboard when the picture was executed in the field.*

2.3. *This is the edge of the original fabric.*

2.4. *This paint was applied to the new edges after the painting was lined. The size of the image was increased slightly, beyond the original perimeter. As noted, the palette and handling match the original closely, indicating that the peripheral paint was also applied by Whittredge. The tonality of the blue is somewhat warmer because it was applied directly onto the brown paper tape rather than onto a white ground. Paper tape was commonly attached to the borders of lined paintings to protect the edges.*

3.1. A dilute warm brown was applied first. With a scrubbing motion of the brush, the paint was thinned in some places to expose the white ground, creating a luminous effect. This effect is heightened by the coarse particles in the ground which reflect light, thus producing a shimmering surface.

3.2. The foliage was added with more opaque greens.

3.3. The tip of the brush handle was used here to draw a line in the wet paint.

3.4. The highlighted opaque white of a dead branch stands out against the transparent brown shadow.

3.5. Short broken strokes were quickly hatched to create the rough textured bark.

3.6. The green paint has mixed with the wet blue paint of the sky.

3.7. Final refinements such as small branches have been applied wet into the wet paint of the sky.

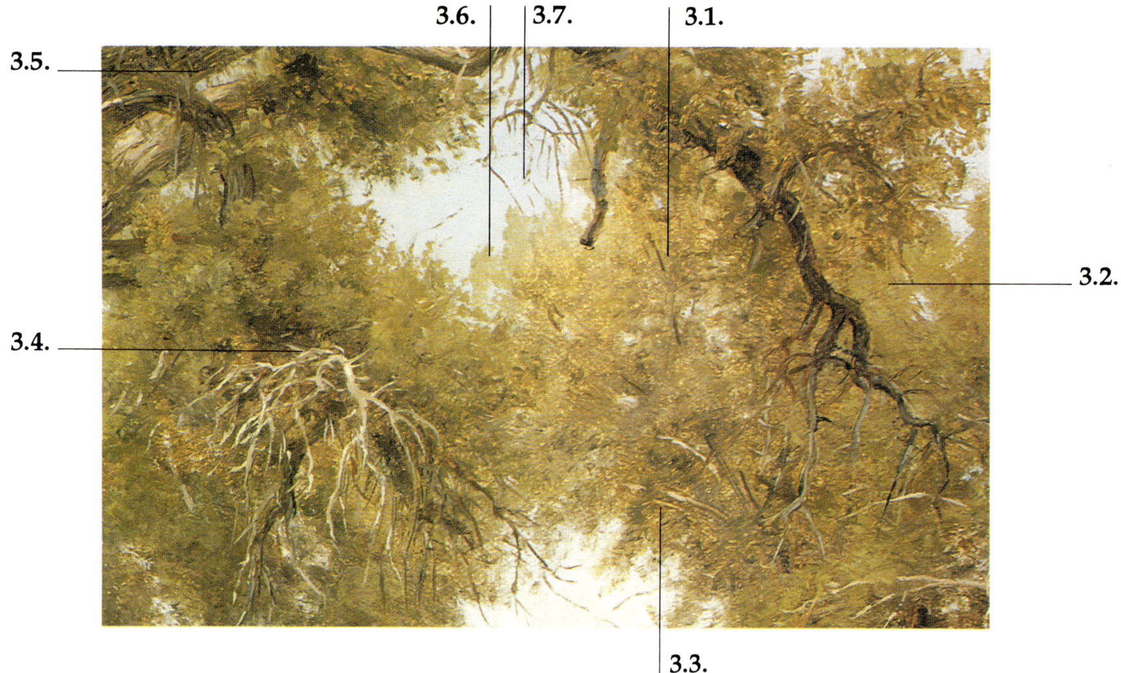

3. DETAIL OF BRANCHES AND FOLIAGE

The arched branches create the cathedral-like dome over the intimate landscape. The sense of depth is heightened by the sunlight which makes its way through the dense foliage, highlighting certain branches and leaving others in shadow. The rough texture of the bark has been achieved with short, alternating light and dark brushstrokes.

4.1. The blue has been very thinly applied, perhaps even rubbed down, allowing the white ground and diagonal texture of the twill weave fabric to remain visible in places and to create a softly incandescent sky
.

4.2. A snowcapped mountain has been faintly suggested in the hazy distance. The thin tree branches were applied into the still wet paint of the sky.

4.3. A narrow band of pinkish-white paint sets off the sunlit middle distance.

4.4. The twill weave of the canvas has been used to create softly blurred edges.

4.5. The fringed grass and bright dabs of flowers bring to mind Barbizon painters like Corot.

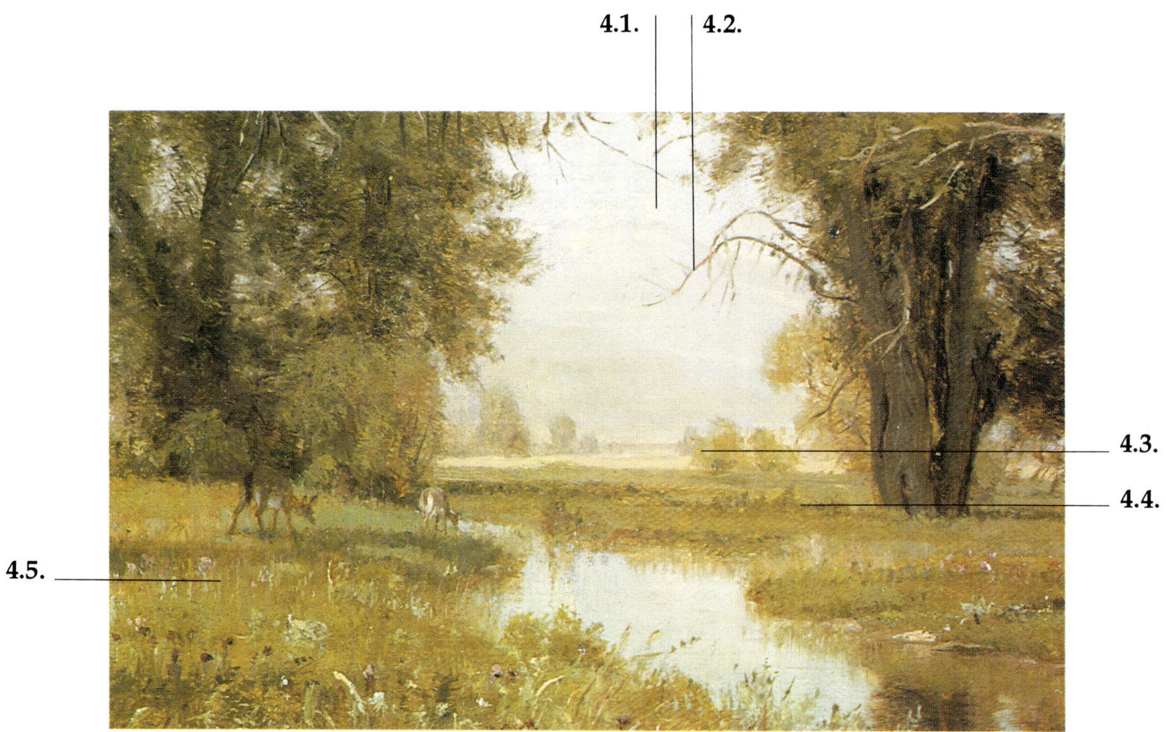

4. DETAIL OF CENTER

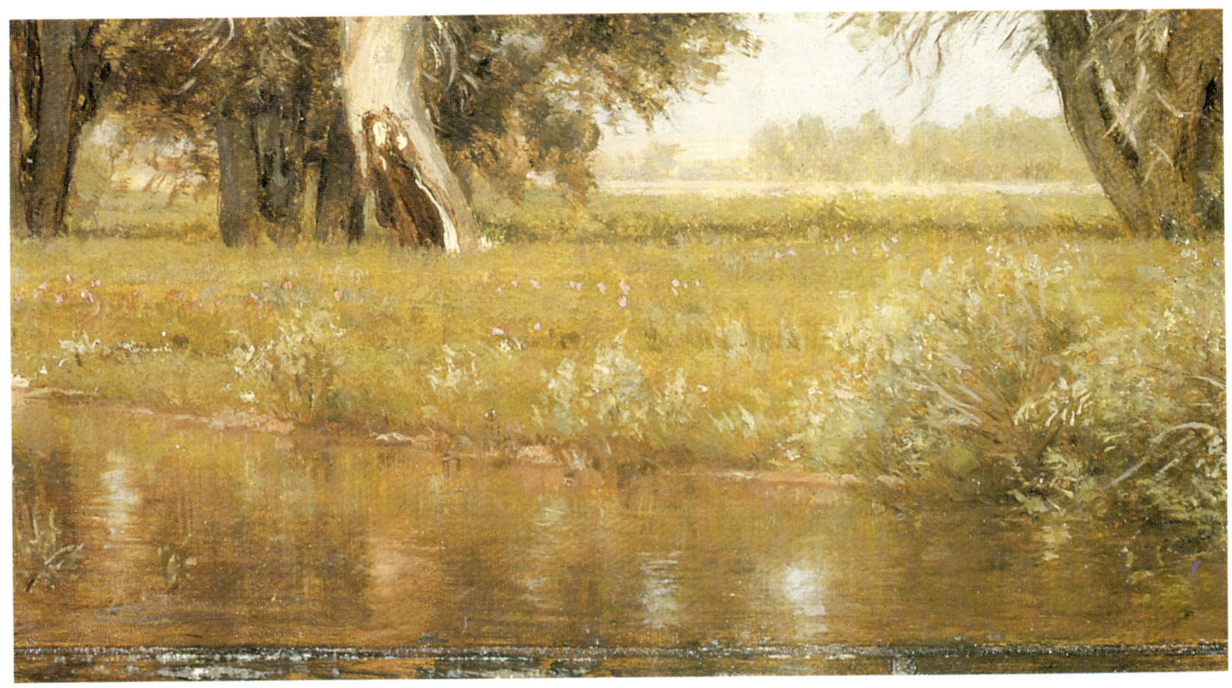

5. DETAIL OF RIGHT FOREGROUND

Horizontal brushstrokes that have been delicately blended at the edges create the wavering reflections of the foliage in the stream. Using a very subdued palette restricted primarily to values of brown and green, Whittredge has given the picture life with subtle and precise touches of bright highlights and colorful flowers.

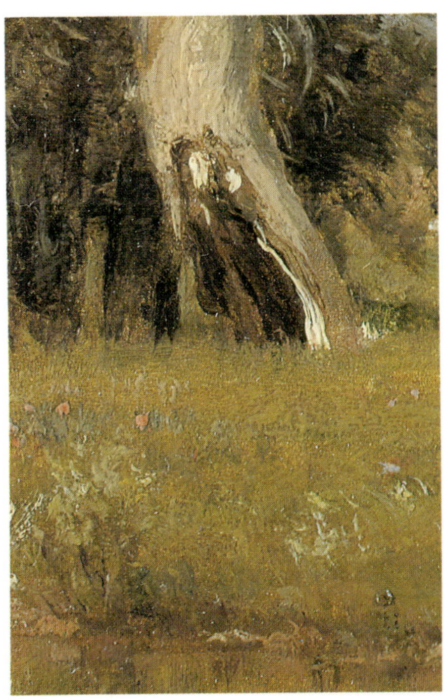

6. DETAIL OF HOLLOW TREE TRUNK

Rich dark brown paint that was thinly applied produced a deep yet transparent shadow. This dark cavity was offset by the impasted white highlight and opaque gray of the bark to create the hollow tree trunk.

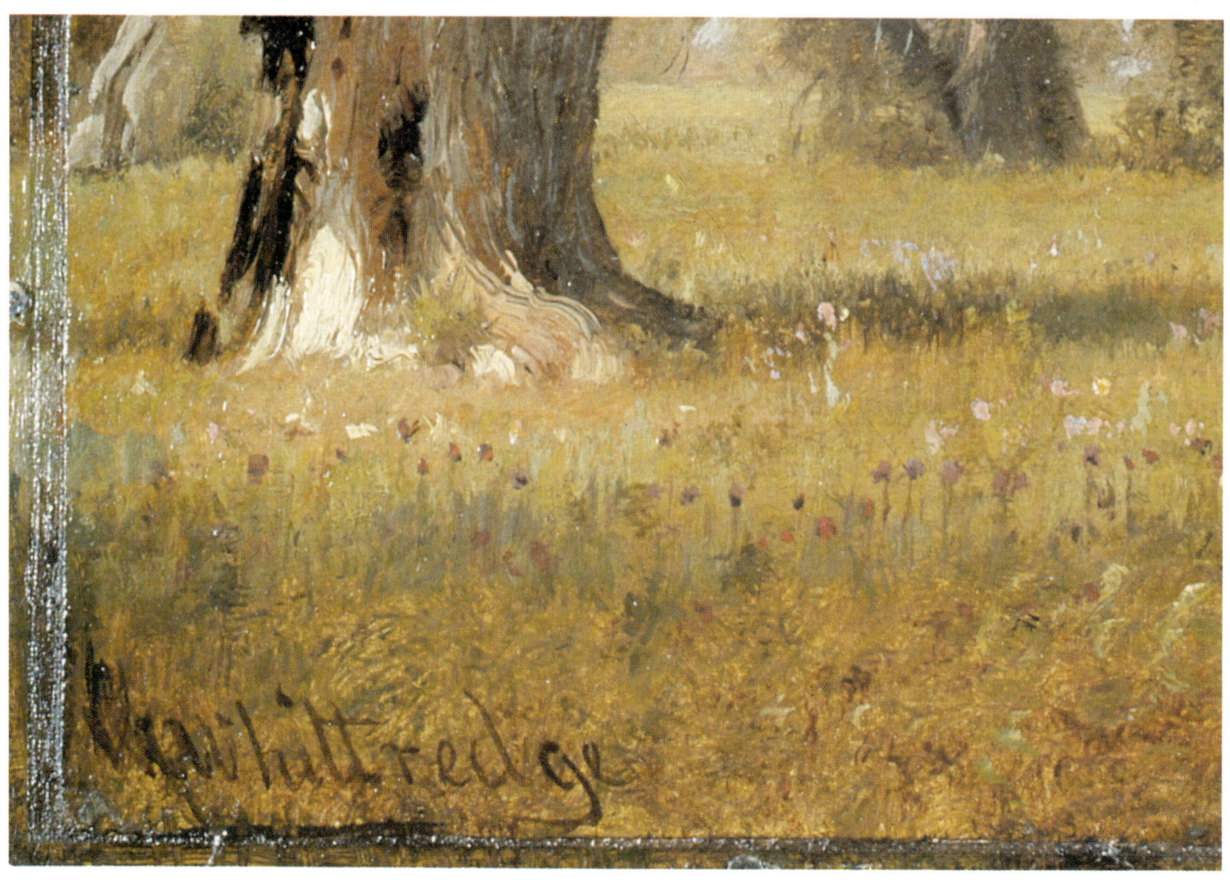

7. DETAIL OF SIGNATURE

W. Whittredge

It is likely that the signature was added by Whittredge after the original painting was lined when he considered the work to be finished.

SUMMARY OF PAINTING TECHNIQUE

a. The primed fabric was tacked to a lapboard on all four edges.
b. The painting was almost entirely executed in one sitting in the field. The paint was applied wet-into-wet, from the first paint strokes to the smallest detail.
c. Back in New York, Whittredge had the oil sketch glue-lined to a plain weave fabric, which is larger than the original fabric, thus retaining the entire image and providing tacking edges. After the lined sketch was stretched, the artist painted over the exposed edges of the lining fabric and over the brown paper tape that was affixed around the tacking edges.

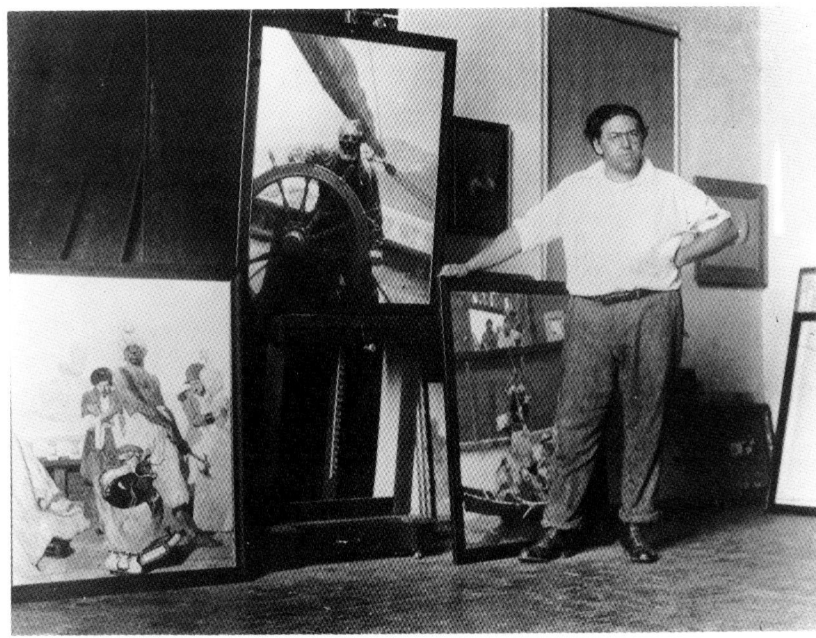

NEWELL CONVERS WYETH

Newell Convers Wyeth earned his place as a master illustrator early in the 20th century by specializing in action pictures of the American West. Once he was solidly established in the business of producing cowboy and Indian art, however, he complained that the Western assignments he received had begun to "plague" him. Frontier subjects appealed only to the frivolous child in him, he grumbled, and not the man, the one who counted.

After just five years of illustrating the West, he insisted he had matured beyond the point where he was willing to confine himself to what he saw as merely adolescent material. Because he was a New Englander by choice as well as family tradition, he was now convinced that the West was alien to him. He was exuberantly self-directed, not one to suffer without taking corrective action, so he replaced the cowboys and Indians in his repertory with three other subjects that were more acceptable to him: Colonial America, medieval England, and the Bible.

"New England was where I was born, raised and educated," Wyeth explained. "My ancestor, Nicholas Wyeth, came from Wales to Massachusetts in 1647. I was born in Needham, not far from the town of Plymouth to which I made many pilgrimages during my boyhood. The spirit of the early days on the Massachusetts coast was an oft-discussed subject in my home. All creative expression, be it in painting, writing, or music, must spring from the artist's own factual and emotional experience."

He was born October 22, 1882 on a farm on the banks of the Charles River near Boston. The land had been owned by the Wyeths since 1730. "From the time I could walk," he recalled, "I was conscripted into doing every conceivable chore there was to do about the place."

His father expected him to remain a farmhand, but he wanted to be an artist. Because he was unhappy with a public school education that could only lead back to the farm, his mother interceded with a compromise. He was permitted to enter the Mechanics Art School in Boston to learn drafting, related to art but more practical in his father's eyes.

Instead of getting a job as a draftsman when he graduated in 1899, however, he persuaded his father to pay for further studies in art education at Massachusetts Normal Arts School. The instructors there told him his proficiency was in illustration rather than in teaching art. Wyeth was encouraged. He transferred to the new Boston art school founded by Eric Pape who had studied with academic painters in Paris before working as an illustrator. One of Wyeth's fellow students under Pape was Clifford Ashley who persuaded him to apply for admission to the more prestigious Howard Pyle School of Art.

Pyle had been a major American illustrator for 25 years. He started teaching in Philadelphia in 1894 because he saw a scarcity of trained illustrators. When the classes became overcrowded he quit in 1900 and started his own smaller facility in Wilmington, Delaware. He was looking for total commitment from a carefully selected group of young men and women who already knew how to paint. The number of students was limited to 20. The entrance examination tested them for enthusiasm and imagination as well as artistic technique.

Winters were spent in Wilmington and summers in an old grist mill near Pyle's home in Chadds Ford, Pennsylvania. The cost of materials and the rental of a studio were nominal. Pyle charged no tuition or fee. His goal was to show his students how to visualize themselves as active participants in the stories they would be illustrating. He called this mental projection, an arts forerunner of the Stanislavsky method for the theater. The artist, he insisted, "must live in the picture" like an actor subordinating his own personality in a play. He told them, "you must do your best in a simple life and work hard."

From the start, Wyeth was intrigued by the illustrative opportunities in the Wild West of Frederic Remington who was a friend of Howard Pyle. A generation older than Wyeth, the well-to-do Remington had already retired from illustration in favor of producing monthly easel paintings for *Collier's* magazine.

Wyeth had never been in the West, but he was an accomplished horseman after his years on the farm. He studied Remington's work, added a few of his own touches, and turned out a painting of a Remington-style rough rider with the derivative title *The Bronco Buster*. Through Pyle's contacts, he sold the picture to *The Saturday Evening Post* for the front wrapper of the February 21, 1903 issue. Wyeth wrote, "The *Post* went wild over my cover and gave me $60 for it." This was a remarkable achievement for a young artist who had been with Pyle less than four months, though he actually received only $50 from the penny-pinching *Post*.

Additional illustrations were sold to other magazines for appearances in March, August, November, and December 1903. Wyeth had arrived. By 1904 he was a successful illustrator with enough assignments to make him financially independent. In August he graduated from the Pyle School although he remained in Wilmington with other former Pyle students who were now professional commercial artists. They continued to solicit Pyle's advice.

Most of Wyeth's illustrations at that time were Western. When he left the Pyle School he was fortunate to have in hand a commission from the *Post* to illustrate another frontier story, but Pyle was perturbed. Wyeth had never been West and yet he was willing to paint what he had not seen. Pyle insisted there was no way a young artist could mentally project himself into a context so foreign to him. To avoid this challenge to the school's methodology, Pyle persuaded *Scribner's* to give Wyeth an advance to be deducted from compensation for unspecified future work which Pyle promised would be authentic beyond question.

With both the *Post* and *Scribner's* as his sponsors, Wyeth left for the West in late September 1904. For three months he immersed himself in the land and the people in the territory. According to him, he explored Colorado mountains and New Mexican deserts, stayed in remote trading posts, and bedded down with Indian tribes. Wherever available he bought typical cowboy and Indian gear to use as studio props for future paintings. When the money from the advances ran out, he found part-time jobs as range rider, mail carrier, and stage driver. Every place he stopped he sketched until at last his portfolios were full.

As soon as he arrived back in Wilmington in late December he was inundated with requests for Western illustrations. *Scribner's* treated him as a celebrity to get a quick return on its advance. The magazine announced the forthcoming publication of Wyeth's own story of his experiences "in the cattle country, engaged in the work of a cowboy in order to become thoroughly familiar with his subject." Wyeth wrote and illustrated two articles for *Scribner's*, just as his predecessor Remington had done for *Harper's*. He gave precedence to new work so the articles did not appear until 1906 and 1909. By then Wyeth had made his second and last foray into the West. He went off to Colorado for *Outing Magazine*.

The high point of Wyeth's involvement beyond the Mississippi was with Cream of Wheat. At a small mid-Western flour mill one of the millers had been taking home the rough residue of the wheat berry that was discarded after the production of fine flour. His wife cooked these middlings into a hot cereal they enjoyed. When the company was in financial distress after the panic of 1893, the managers tested this by-product by shipping ten cases of handmade cereal to their New York City brokers, along with a carload of the regular flour. The brokers replied by telegraph, "Forget the flour. Send us a car of Cream of Wheat," and a new American industry was born.

By 1906 the wheat cereal was an international staple. The company began an advertising campaign using the principal Eastern illustrators. Wyeth had returned from his second Western trip when "Mr. Mapes of the Cream of Wheat Company telegraphed for me to run up and see him at the Waldorf-Astoria. I have just completed two pictures for him, $250 each, which he is immensely pleased with." Wyeth also received the commission for a third illustration.

Mapes should have been pleased. These illustrations were Wyeth at his best, which meant anyone's best. The first was the still famous *Where the Mail Goes Cream of Wheat Goes* with the Cream of Wheat crate as the cowboy's mailbox on the plains. Second was *The Bronco Buster* at the rodeo with a Cream of Wheat billboard in the background. Shortly after Christmas Wyeth started the third, *The Yukon Freighter*, "with an Esquimaux Half-Breed protecting himself from a pack of wolves. There is a case of Cream of Wheat amongst the canned goods." Although all three were variations on Remington paintings, prints were issued for framing in 1907 and the series was repeated beginning in 1917.

Just as the demands on him for Western illustrations were reaching a crescendo, Wyeth rebelled. He said he did not want to become captive to his subject, as Remington had been. "With five years of mostly Westerns," he confessed, "my ardor for the West has slowly been dwindling, until my desires to go there to paint are lukewarm. The West appealed to me as it would to a boy. An artist may start out in search of the great Western Plains but he has got to come back to the soil he was born on."

Even when he painted Indians from then on, he chose the noble woodland Indians of the Northeast, not the warlike Sioux or the Apaches. His lasting fame came from the series of Scribner's Classics books beginning with *Treasure Island* in 1911. By 1919 he was able to turn down $1,500 for a single drawing to be used in advertising. His interest shifted to murals done on a massive scale that suited him.

Wyeth was as big as his murals, with a large head featuring brilliant eyes. He stood 6 feet 2 inches and weighed 210 pounds. His chest was broad but his legs and arms were slender. Hands were small and delicate. His voice was surprisingly high-pitched, but his size and vitality made his presence commanding. He was a good conversationalist and a graceful dancer. For exercise he rode and hiked.

He painted large canvases, up to 50 inches, even for small illustrations. He worked with broad brushes. Where he wanted a pronounced impasto he switched to his palette knife. Assertive brushstrokes transferred juicy pigments to the canvas while his entire body was continually in motion like a fencer. Periodically he would back away from his easel to squint at the canvas before returning to the attack. Some illustrations he finished in one day.

From the beginning he had wanted to be a landscape painter. His inspiration was New England transcendentalism starring Nature with a capital N. Like Whittredge, he loathed the landscapists who explored the country "like hunters with guns over their shoulders, to 'shoot the landscape' and nothing more."

He was convinced that seeking exotic scenery was a mistake for an artist. "I don't believe any man who ever painted a great big picture did so by wandering from one place to another searching for interesting material. I have come to the conclusion that a man can only paint that which he knows even more than intimately; he has got to know it spiritually." He was implicitly deprecating the successful Western panoramists Albert Bierstadt and Thomas Moran.

Unhappily, illustration was Wyeth's cross to bear. He hated being labelled an illustrator because he thought his commercial work was deprecated by the fine artists. Becoming a success as an easel painter obsessed him. The need distressed him for months at a time. He produced his fine art paintings very slowly but he was never wholly satisfied with them. Even after the National Academicians elected him a member in 1941 the grapes were sour. He knew the recognition was for his illustrations, not his landscapes.

October 19, 1945 was exactly 45 years after the day the young Wyeth had boarded the Century Express train from Boston en route to Wilmington to see Pyle for the first time. He was now 63 years old, driving his car with his grandson Newell Convers II at his side. Just two miles from home, bushes blocked his view of an unguarded railroad crossing. He did not see or hear the approaching train. Both Wyeth and his grandson were killed in the crash.

One lasting monument to Wyeth has been the fine figurative artists among his descendants. He taught three of his own children, Andrew, Caroline, and Henriette, and two sons-in-law, John McCoy and Peter Hurd, demanding the same total commitment Pyle had asked from him. The third generation includes Jamie Wyeth and George Weymouth who married a granddaughter. In addition to his own body of work he created the Wyeth dynasty.

He qualifies as a master painter of the American West, despite the relatively few years he devoted to cowboys and Indians, because he produced pictures like the Cream of Wheat series that are enduring classics in reproduction.

Indians Watch with Astonishment is equally a masterpiece.

1. THE PAINTING

Wyeth gave the following account of his technical procedure. While this does not describe the identical method used for *Indians Watch in Astonishment*, it does express Wyeth's deep knowledge and appreciation of the proper technique of painting as well as the artist's role in creating a work of art. For him, craftsmanship and artistic inspiration went hand in hand.

He wrote about a particular painting that it "was made entirely from memory, which is my customary practice in creative painting. It is painted in egg tempera on a gesso ground, and the method used in painting it strictly conforms, I believe, to directions handed down to us from the time of the Renaissance.

"After weeks–or months, as the case may be–have gone into the intensive preliminary phases of compositional effort and the motive has been completely realized in black and white cartoon (charcoal perhaps) then, by means of a lantern slide, a careful map-like tracing is made directly upon the prepared panel. This pattern is carefully drawn in with

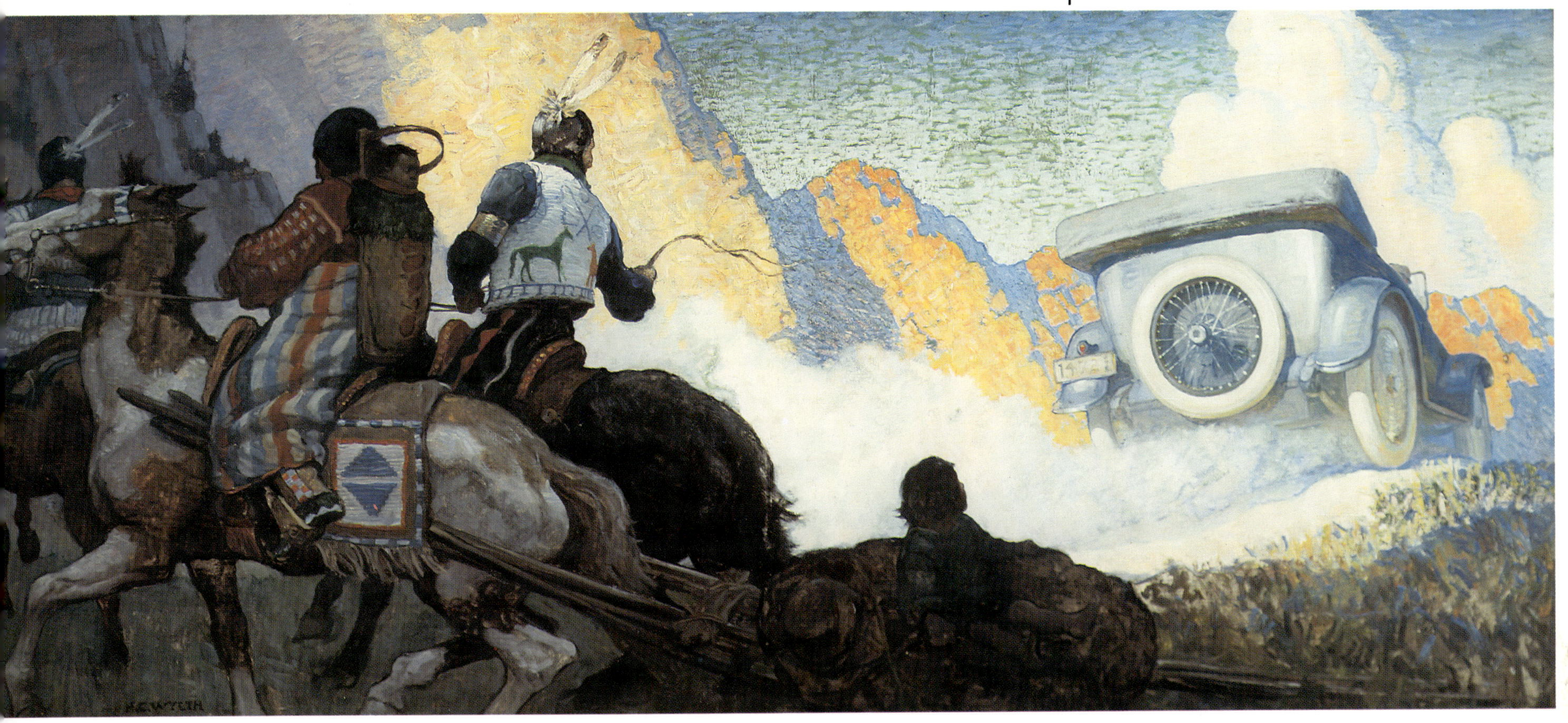

brush and india ink to such a degree of completeness that an excellent and complete tonal drybrush drawing results. This is all imperatively necessary in order to give the over-painting in color full body and power–it can make the shadows deeply rich and luminous and will give the over-all pattern in its finality a unified and richly fabricated surface.

"Following the completion of the ink rendering, the entire surface is evenly coated with a thin solution of egg yolk and distilled water. This makes an adhesive ground for the color.

"Painting in egg tempera is strictly a process of building one color over another, seeing to it that, in the end, every inch of surface carries a faintly equalized weight of pigmentation. Opaque painting must be observed throughout, depending upon transparent glazing over the opaque to achieve glowing depth or luminous brilliance.

"The method of applying color, or the sequence of color overlays or glazes, is something for the individual to find out for himself through patient and incessant practice.

"True tempera painting is not a fortuitous procedure, but on the contrary is very painstaking and methodical. Accidental flourishes of the brush do not count, and one achieves only so far as he feels and sees things definitely.

"... the safe methods of preparing dry color, and its application is a precise affair, but once grasped, it is all very simple.

"Every illustration or painting I have made in the last thirty years has been done from the imagination or the memory. However, I have constantly studied from the figure, from animals and from landscape, and have especially stressed the training of my memory. This I've done from the time I was seventeen. An early and greatly valued teacher of mine, one Carles W. Reed of Boston, insisted that the faculty of memory had become a lost function among American artists and he blamed much of the lack of mood and imagination in their work to this fact."

N.C. Wyeth. Indians Watch with Astonishment as Car Speeds By *is in the collection of the Museum of Western Art, Denver, Colorado. Mixed media on canvas glued to masonite. 32 inches (81.2 cm) height x 71 1/2 inches (181.6 cm) width. Signed lower left. Not dated.*

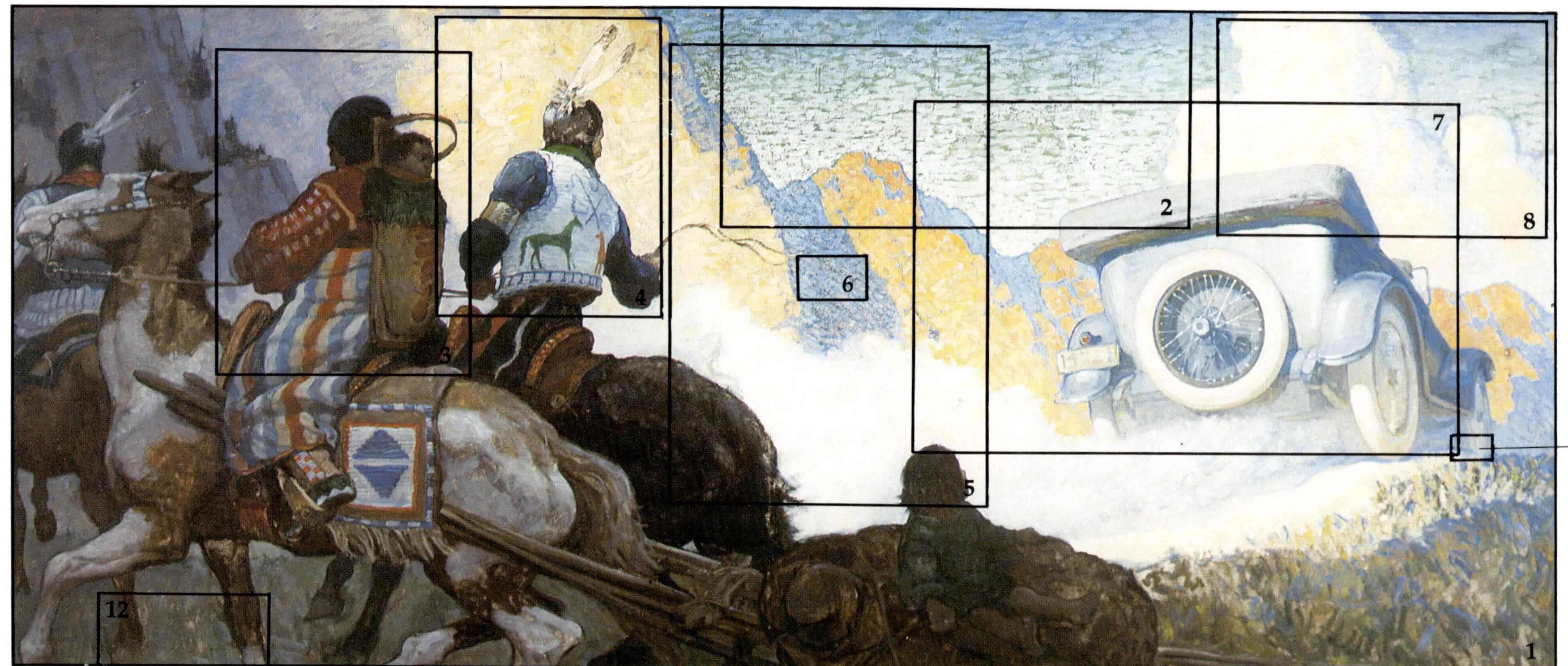

Indians Watch with Astonishment was painted on a fine, plain weave canvas that has been glued to a masonite panel. There is evidence that the canvas was originally mounted on a five member stretcher since the paint film retains a crack pattern corresponding to the center bar and right member. The ground is a light gray color.

For this painting, both tempera and oil paint were used. Analysis shows that the orange background paint is egg tempera and the more fluid paint used for the figures, horses, and the rest of the background is an oil medium. The dense orange paint has been applied with short, hatched brushstrokes typical of egg tempera. Unlike the long working time retained by oil paint, the rapid drying of tempera precludes manipulation of the paint.

The light gray ground was left partially exposed to influence the allover tonality of the painting and brighten the palette. The paint was applied in multiple distinct layers. The underlayers, for the most part, are of dilute color, applied to block in major compositional areas and forms. Then details and highlights were added with thicker, often quite impasted paint. The underlayers are left visible to provide color throughout. There is no overall varnish, though varnish was locally applied to the white portions of the tires, probably to enhance them for the advertisement.

Throughout, the brushwork is bold and sure. In the background especially, the paint seems to have exploded from the brush. One can easily picture Wyeth wielding a loaded brush with a strong, deliberate hand. Despite this sureness of execution, changes in details of the automobile can be seen clearly in raking light, a technique that exaggerates the profile of paint strokes. These changes could be Wyeth satisfying the wishes of his client or his own artistic instincts.

The painting was originally commissioned as an advertisement for Fisk Tires. It appeared in *Country Life Magazine* as well as *Collier's Weekly*. Then, probably when its usefulness as an illustration was through, the inscription "FISK" was painted out. As with the compositional changes, raking light shows the shapes of the letters in profile.

Even though *Indians Watch in Astonishment* was originally conceived as an illustration for an advertisement, the painting holds its own as a work of fine art. The composition is dramatically organized with the Indian group located in shadow, separated by a strong diagonal from the brightly lit landscape containing the automobile. Not only is this arrangement a way of highlighting the client's product, but it could also stand as a social statement: the old world and the new are separated by a stark line of incompatibility. The Indians, in the prophetic shadow, travel out of the picture plane. They look at the intruder that is pushing them from their native land.

With only a few strokes to paint out the client's logo, *Indians Watch with Astonishment* was changed from an advertising illustration to a finished work of fine art. The painting is not only appreciated for its masterful technique and dramatic composition, but the meaning of the painting was subtly changed as well by obscuring the logo. The automobile with its sturdy new tires that bring it over the unpaved western roads is no longer a hero but becomes the faceless intruder into the Indian world. It would appear that Wyeth had more to say beyond the promotion of Fisk Tires.

Wyeth remained an illustrator, yet he was frustrated that he was not referred to as a "fine artist," and in the end he thought less of himself for being an illustrator. Nevertheless, his illustrations are not just pictures to go along with a story, they were shaped by Wyeth's own experiences and emotions. He felt his subject strongly and painted it masterfully. His prowess as an artist comes from a lifelong study of painting techniques and traditions as well as an eye for subjects to be stored in his prodigious memory for future reference.

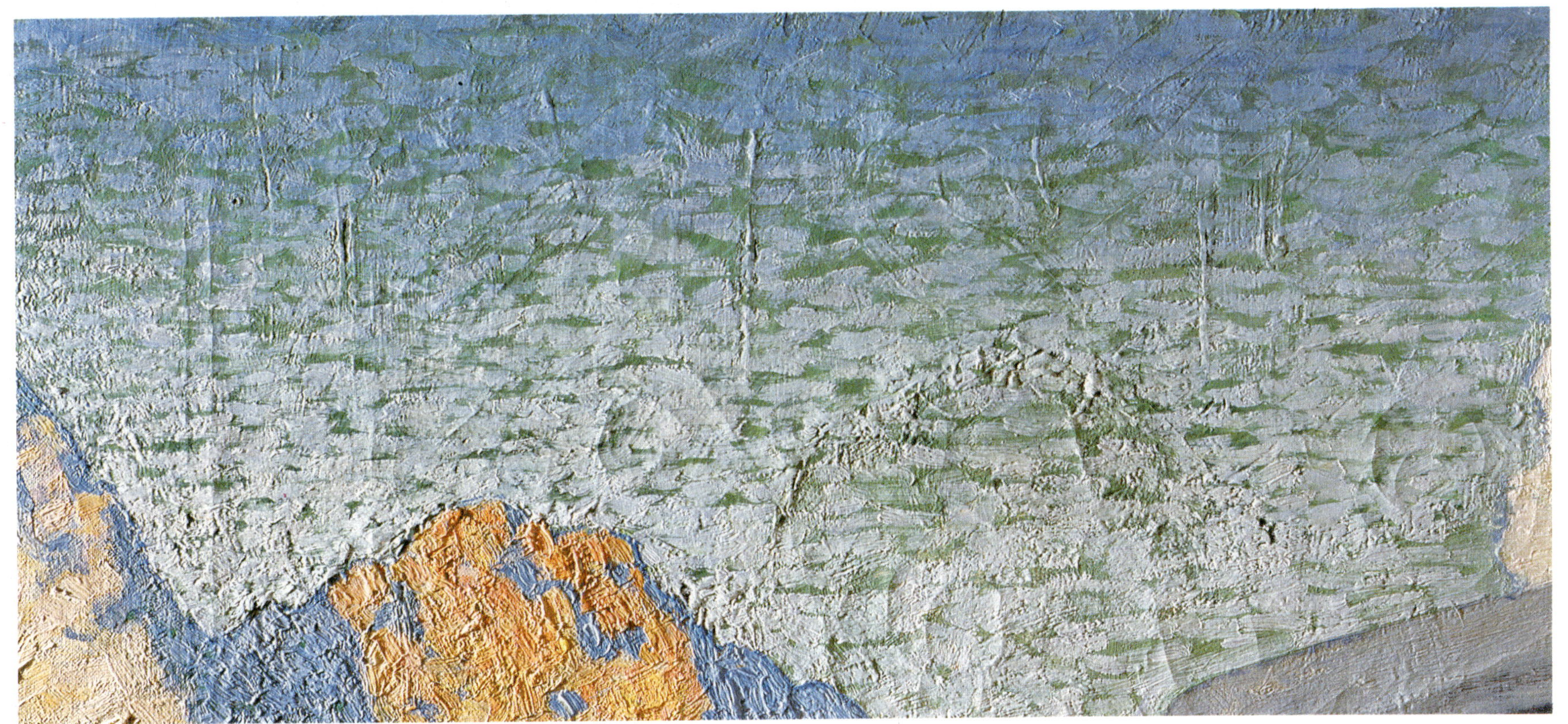

2. DETAIL OF INSCRIPTION IN RAKING LIGHT

The shape of the letters F (partially) S K (partially) for Fisk Tires can be seen when the picture is lit from one side. The background was reworked and the inscription painted out.

3.1. The papoose was painted with a thin earth color, leaving some of the ground exposed. Lighter scumbles were added to create the highlights of the face. A few brushstrokes form the baby's skeptical expression.

3.2. For the blue stripes of the blanket, an underlayer of dilute blue paint was followed by a more opaque mixture of blue and white. Lines representing folds were added.

3.3. A thin brown underlayer was painted for the saddle. Contours were added with a thicker layer. Lines were incised into the still wet paint of the front part of the saddle, using a tool such as the tip of the brush handle.

3.4. For the woman's dress, a thin dilute red paint was laid in first, followed by a more opaque red paint layer. Details were added in white paint.

3.5. The shadow of the mountain was first blocked in with purple, followed by a layer of darker blue paint, and finally scumbled over with lighter paint.

3.6. The dark outline on the sleeve extends to outline the woman's facial features.

3.7. The short distinct brushstrokes and opaque silky appearance of the yellow-orange paint of the background indicate that egg tempera was the medium used. The bright yellow paint of the sunlit mountain was made of a mixture of cadmium yellow, cadmium red, and zinc white. This bright color has also been painted on top of the rim of the papoose-holder. Then details of the baby's hair were added.

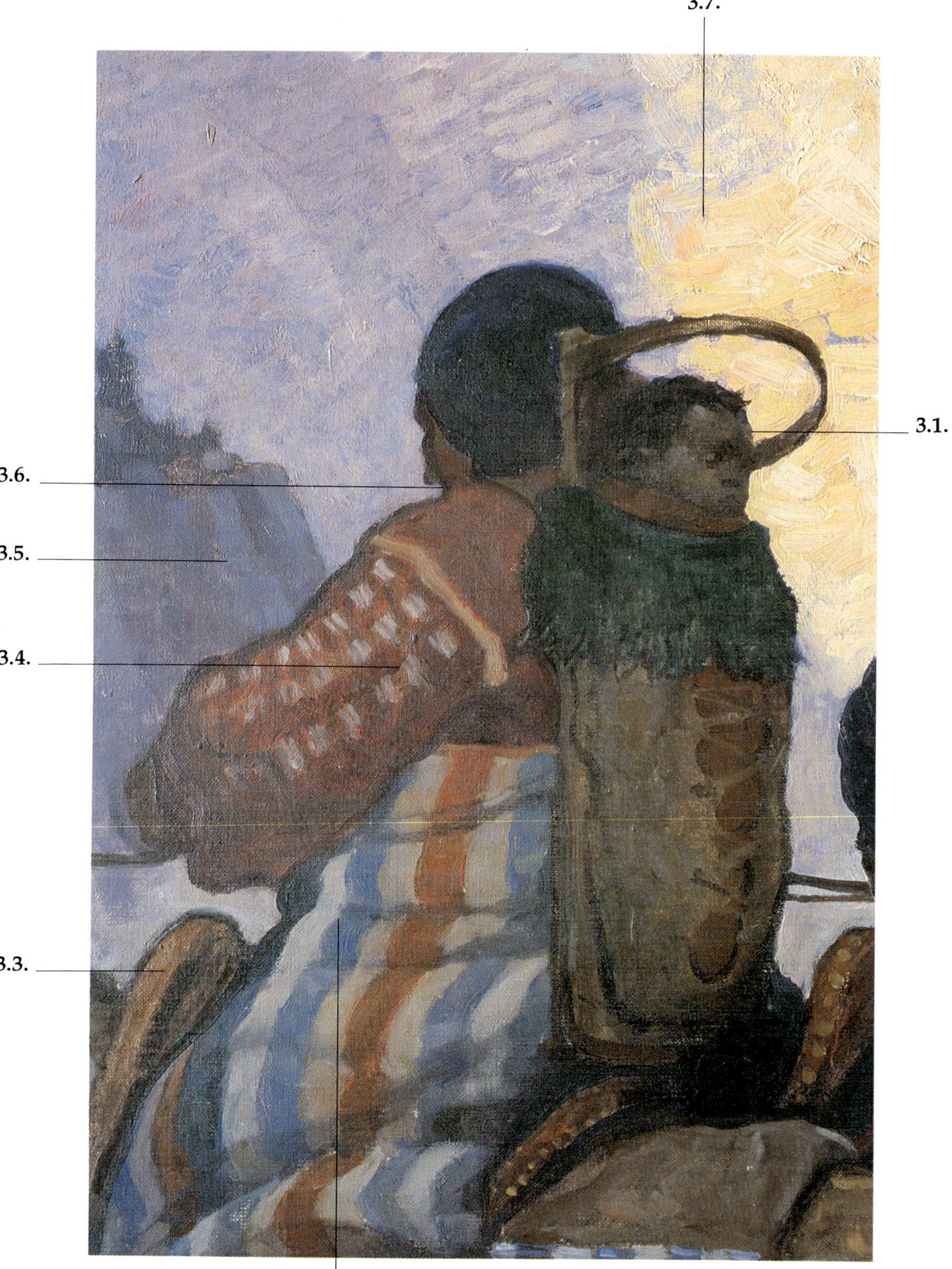

3. DETAIL OF PAPOOSE

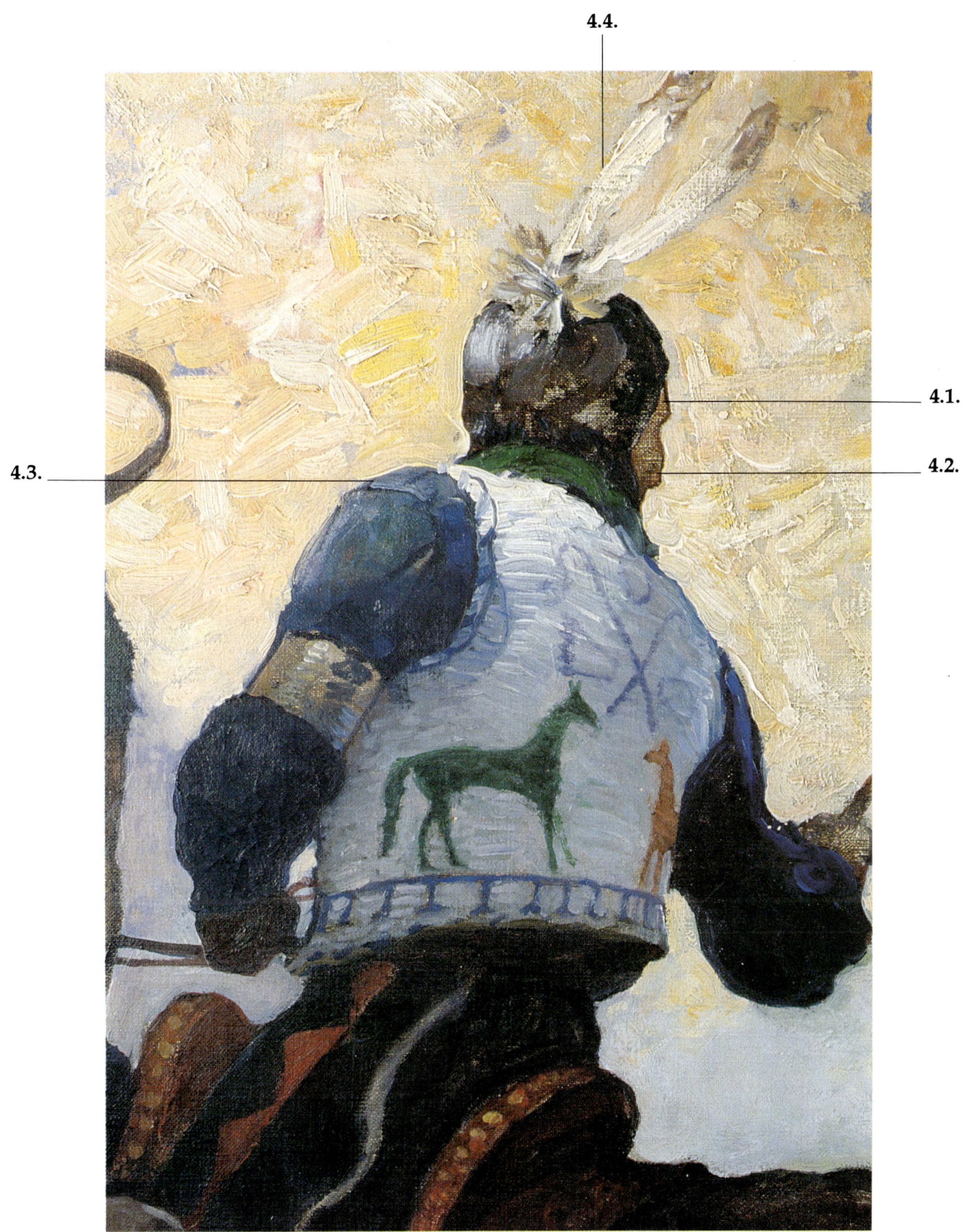

4. DETAIL OF INDIAN MAN

4.1. The paint of the underlayer seems to have been rubbed away by Wyeth, leaving the ground partially exposed as a highlight. Thicker black and gray paint were added for the details of the hair and head. This gray paint is mixed with white at the crown of the head to create another highlight.

4.2. The fierce yellow of the sunlit mountain was applied over and around the head, defining its shape. The dynamic brushwork of the background seems to burst around the face.

4.3. The tip of the paintbrush handle was used to incise the line defining the shoulder seam of the shirt.

4.4. Rich white paint was dragged for the fringed shape of the feathers.

The gesture of this proud man in the direction of the automobile points to the end of an era and borders on social commentary. The two horses embroidered on the back of his vest symbolize the old way of life for the Indians and form a contrast with the passing car. Wyeth's vivid yellow brushstrokes indicate a world blown asunder by the intruder into the Indian land.

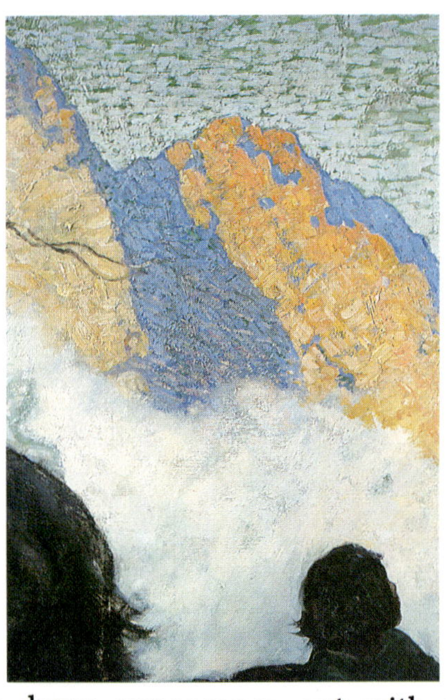

5. Detail of Mountains

The paint for the mountains has a dense appearance, yet with a sheen from a medium such as egg tempera. Multiple colored layers are intermingled as Wyeth worked back and forth between blue and orange with the lighter blue on top and a darker blue as an underlayer. The darker blue was left exposed to form an outline.

The dust cloud frames the Indian child's head. The hair was added over the white. Wyeth applied the paint by a variety of techniques including dragging, scumbling, and blending.

Analysis indicates that the orange is composed of cadmium yellow, cadmium red, and zinc white and that the blue is synthetic ultramarine mixed with zinc white.

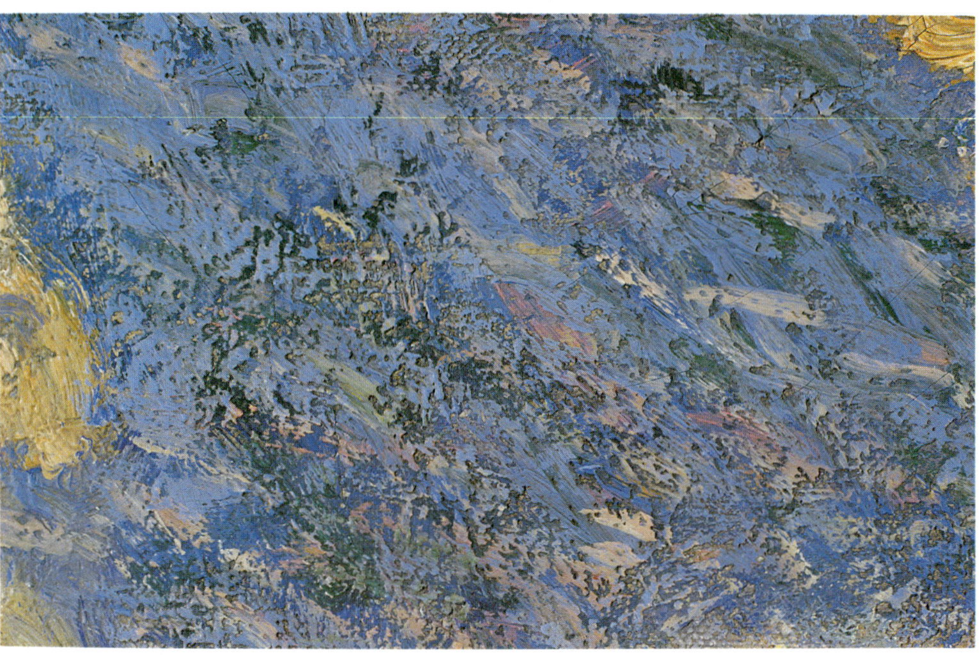

6. Detail of Shadow of Mountain

The blue shadow was created by using multiple colors ranging from pink to yellow, white, green, and blue. The texture of the canvas can be seen in the lower paint layers which were not completely concealed when the subsequent paint was dragged across the surface, catching on the tops of the weave. Some wet-into-wet technique was used to blend the colors directly on the surface.

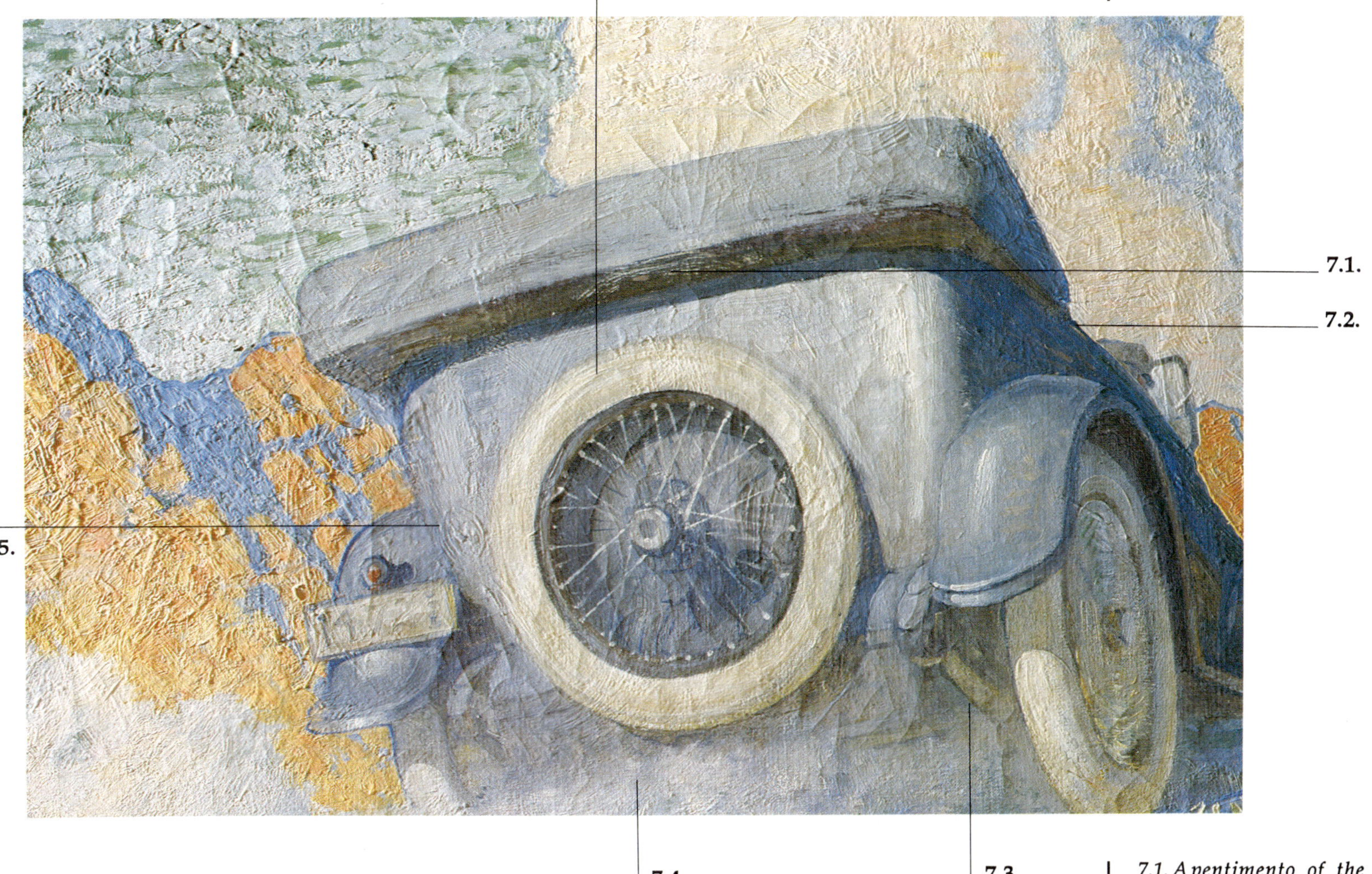

7. Detail of Rear of Car in Raking Light

Painters have long struggled with human anatomy. Here Wyeth has drawn the humans easily while he worked and reworked the anatomy of the automobile.

7.1. A pentimento of the previous higher position of the spare tire can be distinguished when viewed in raking light. The impasted paint in the shape of a tire does not relate to the image seen at the surface, indicating artist's changes. Wyeth might have found this necessary to please either the client or himself.

7.2. The orange of the mountains was painted around the car, defining its outline.

7.3. The paint application for the underside of the vehicle is thin and does not conceal the ground completely. Thicker and darker paint was added for detail and shadow.

7.4. Scumbles of lighter paint were added for the semi-opaque effect of the dust cloud raised by the passing car.

7.5. The pentimento of a previous location of the red taillight can be seen.

7.6. The only varnished and glossy parts of the painting are the whites of both rear tires as well as the spare. This was probably done to emphasize the advertiser's product. A faint spatter of varnish around these areas indicates that the varnish was applied with some sort of spray device such as a mouth blower.

8.1. The majestic cumulus clouds were painted with short horizontal strokes. The blue shadow was added while the lighter color was still wet.

8.2. The blue sky was painted over a green paint layer consisting of viridian and zinc white. This might have been the original background color where the FISK inscription was located for the advertisement. Blue mixed with pink was applied over the green in horizontal strokes. One can surmise that Wyeth liked the effect of the green underlayer showing through the blue because dabs of green paint were added on top of the blue sky on the other side of the cloud.

8.3. A purple underlayer was left partially exposed in the car roof. Highlights for the car were added over the shadows, indicating a work sequence from dark to light.

8.4. As mentioned, darker green was added on top to match the broken effect on the other side of the cloud.

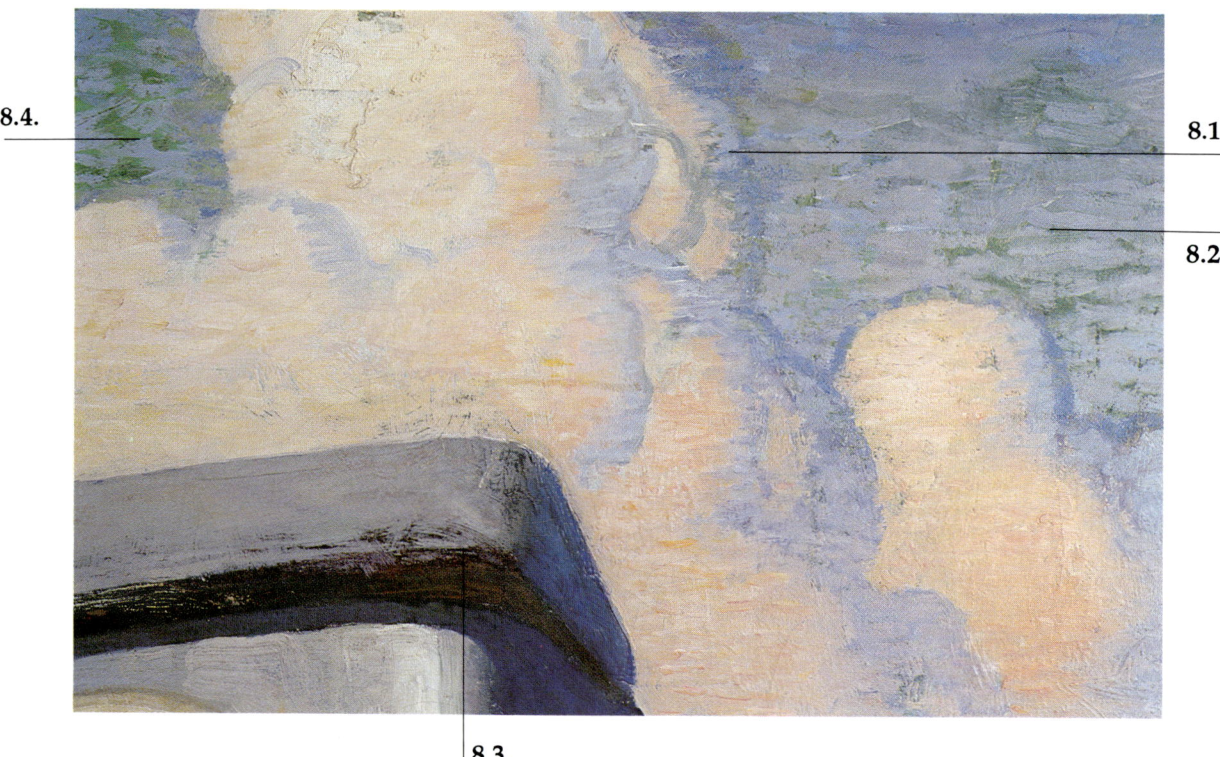

8. Detail of Clouds

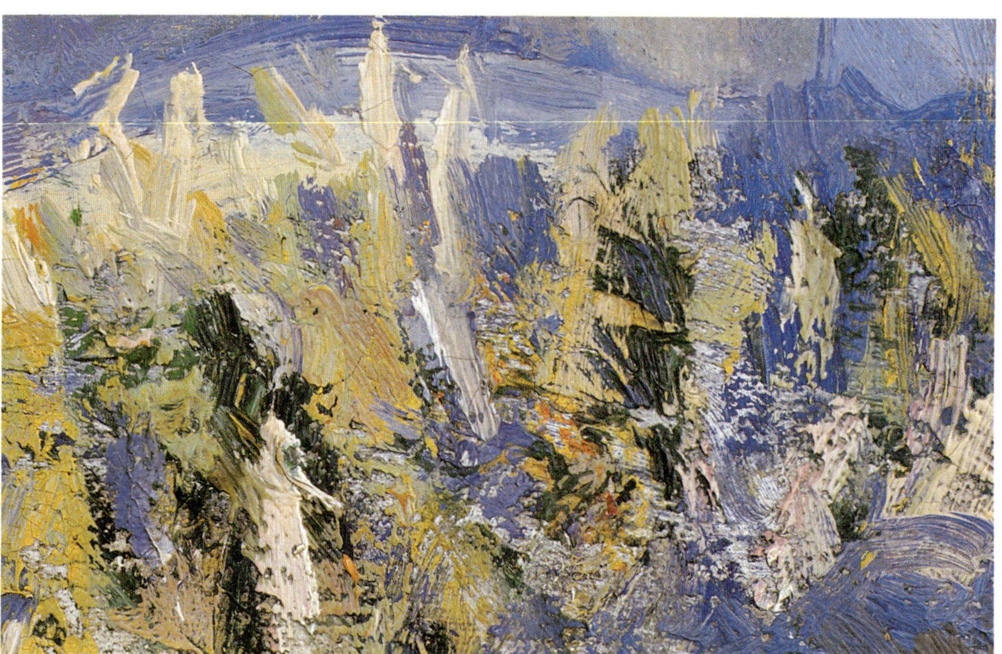

9. Detail of Grass in Foreground

A wide range of colors was applied in broad and generous brushstrokes. Yellow, white, orange, blue, and green were used, partially in a wet-into-wet technique. The multicolored brushstrokes were applied in a fast motion. Still, the sense of pure and fresh color remains. The gray ground was left partially exposed.

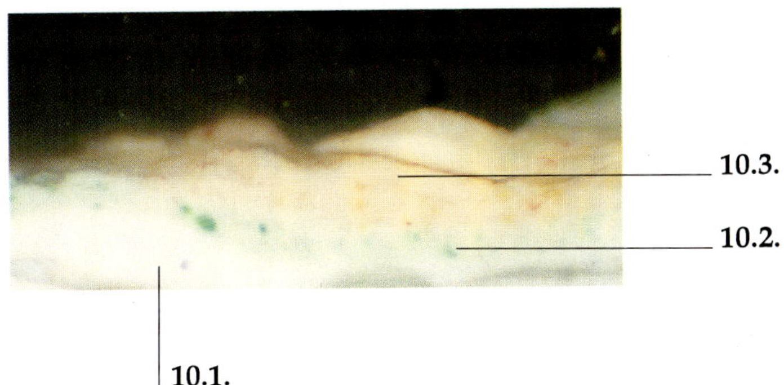

10.3.

10.2.

10.1.

10. CROSS-SECTION OF SKY

Media analysis shows that Wyeth used a mixed media technique. The orange paint contains a protein binder, such as egg tempera, and the green paint beneath contains an oil medium.

10.1. The pale blue is made up of zinc white with a few particles of artificial ultramarine.

10.2. The green is made up of zinc white and viridian.

10.3. The orange is made up of zinc white, cadmium yellow and cadmium red.

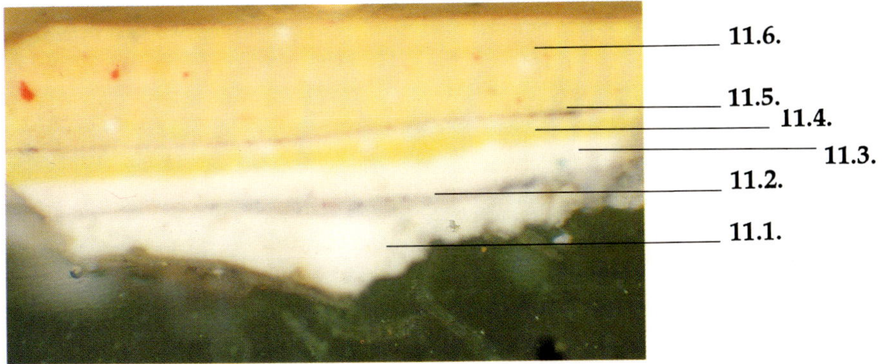

11.6.

11.5.
11.4.
11.3.

11.2.

11.1.

11. CROSS-SECTION OF MOUNTAINS ALONG RIGHT EDGE

This complicated build-up shows Wyeth's multilayered technique.

11.1. The ground containing lead white.

11.2. The thin multicolored layer could be underdrawing.

11.3. A white layer with a trace of viridian.

11.4. A bright yellow layer (probably cadmium yellow).

11.5. This thin dark layer could be a grime layer between work phases.

11.6. This layer contains zinc white, lead white, cadmium yellow, and cadmium red.

12. DETAIL OF SIGNATURE

N.C. Wyeth

SUMMARY OF PAINTING TECHNIQUE

a. The fabric was primed with a light gray ground.

b. Sections of the composition were blocked in with dilute colors, then rubbed down to create tonal variations and highlights. These thin underlayers were often left exposed as body color, shadows, or highlights.

c. Form and detail were built up with thicker paint, often quite impasted. The thicker paint was frequently used in the background to form the outline of the figures. Finer details were added on top.

d. Scumbles were added for highlights and further detail.

e. The painting originally showed the name of the product being advertised, FISK, but this was later painted out.

f. Varnish was applied only locally to the white portions of the tires, probably to enhance the product.

g. At some later time the painting was glued to a masonite panel.

NOTES

(Berninghaus) "From my Studio window..." from Gordon Sanders, *Oscar E. Berninghaus*. New Mexico: Taos Heritage Publication, 1985.
(Bierstadt) "That name had appeared pedantic..." from Fitz Hugh Ludlow, *The Heart of the Continent*. New York: Hurd and Houghton, 1870, page 421.
    "...most of them got up..." Ludlow, page 436.
    "Bierstadt, who is one of the most..." New York *Evening Post*, June 9, 1864.
(Blakelock) "...had a strongly sensuous feeling..." from Lloyd Goodrich, *Ralph A. Blakelock, Centenary Exhibition*, Whitney Museum of American Art, April 22 to May 29, 1947.
    "...many canvases were painted...," Goodrich.
    "...his process was slow and laborious..." Frederick W. Morton, "Work of Ralph A. Blakelock." *Brush and Pencil*, Chicago, February 1902, page 264.
    "He could paint a really good picture..." a letter Mrs. R.A. Blakelock to Robert C. Vose, February 26, 1908.
    "...until it seems to flow..." Mrs. Blakelock letter.
    "Blakelock was a very uneven painter." Morton.
(Dixon) "To see much and observe the things..." Letter dated September 3, 1891, quoted from *Maynard Dixon* by W.M. Burnside.
(Farny) "It breaks my heart..." from Denny Carter, *Henry Farny*. New York: Watson-Guptill, 1978, page 28.
    "Breaking Camp," an 1891 gouache and watercolor on paper 10x17 inches, is in the University of Texas, Austin, C.R. Smith Collection. The original photograph is in Farny's papers in the Archives of American Art.
    "Personally (*Nomads*) pleases me–as one of the most..." William C. Foxley, *Frontier Spirit*. Denver: Museum of Western Art, 1983, page 25.
(Fechin) "a high degree of expertise in technique..." from Nicolai Fechin: *Notes on Art*, translated by Eya Fechin Banham, Albuquerque, New Mexico, 1953-54.
    "The pigments mix together and cannot..." Fechin *Notes on Art*.
    "If one wishes to produce this living..." Fechin *Notes on Art*.
(Hill) "...is awfully careless." from Margarie Dakin Arkelian, *Thomas Hill: The Grand View*. Oakland, California: The Oakland Museum, 1980, page 26.
    "Don't paint paws" Arkelian, page 36.
(Hudson) "This is Alice..." from Grace Carpenter Hudson, Unpublished Notes, 1898, in *The Pomo: Gifts and Visions*. Palm Springs, California: Palm Springs Desert Museum, 1983, page 19.
    "Mrs. Hudson's pictures of Indians..." Clara Erskine Clements, *Woman in the Fine Arts from the Seventh Century B. C. to the Twentieth Century A. D.* Cambridge: Houghton, Mifflin and Co., The Riverside Press, 1905, pages 166, 167.
(Laurence) "...pupil of Edward Moran." from Robert Shalkop, *Sydney Laurence His Life and Work*. Anchorage Historical and Fine Arts Museum, 1982, page 23.
(Leigh) "When our country was first invaded..." from *Frontier Spirit*, Denver: Museum of Western Art, 1983. (Quoted from D. Duane Cummins, *William Robinson Leigh: Western Artist*. Norman: University of Oklahoma Press and Thomas Gilcrease Institute of American History and Art, 1980.)
(Moran) "I place no value upon literal..." from Robert Taft, *Artists and Illustrators of the Old West*. New York: Charles Scribner's Sons, 1953.
(O'Keeffe) "A flower is relatively small..." from Lloyd Goodrich and Doris Bry, *Georgia O'Keeffe*. New York: Whitney Museum of American Art, 1970.
    "When you took time to really notice my flower..." Georgia O'Keeffe, *Georgia O'Keeffe*. New York: Viking Press, 1976.
(Remington) "I have always wanted to be able to paint..." from Peggy and Harold Samuels, *Frederic Remington A Biography*. Garden City: Doubleday & Co., 1982, page 418.
(Schreyvogel) "He's the greatest of us all." from James D. Horan, *Life and Art of Charles Schreyvogel*. New York: Crown Publishers, 1969.
    "I saw in the Sunday *Herald*..." Horan page 36.
(Sharp) "The best you could find in two days' ride..." from *Pen and Brush*, April 1899.
    "As a model the Indian..." *Pen and Brush*.
(Whittredge) "Whittredge, a New York artist of no little celebrity..." from Greeley (Colorado) *Tribune*, June 19, 1871, quoted in *The Rocky Mountains–A Vision for Artists in the 19th Century* by Patricia Trenton and Peter Hassrick, University of Oklahoma Press: Norman.

"...forlorn bowers..." from Anthony F. Janson, "Worthington Whittredge: The Development of a Hudson River Painter, 1860-1868." *The American Art Journal*, April 1979.
"something peculiar to our people,..." John I.H. Baur, ed. *The Brooklyn Museum Journal*, 1942.
"Those who have claimed so much..." Trenton and Hassrick.
(Wyeth) "...was made entirely from memory..." from Ernest W. Watson, *Forty Illustrators and How They Work*. New York: Watson-Guptill, 1946.

BIBLIOGRAPHY: BIOGRAPHIES

(Berninghaus) Sanders, Gordon E. *Oscar E. Berninghaus*. New Mexico: Taos Heritage Publication, 1985.
(Bierstadt) Anderson, Nancy K. *Albert Bierstadt: Cho-looke, The Yosemite Fall*. San Diego: Timkin Art Gallery, 1986.
Britsch, Ralph A. and Charles E. Merrill. *Bierstadt and Ludlow*. Monograph No. 5. Brigham Young University, 1980.
Hendricks, Gordon. *A. Bierstadt*. Fort Worth: Amon Carter Museum, 1972.
Hendricks, Gordon. *Albert Bierstadt: Painter of the American West*. Harry Abrams Inc. in association with Amon Carter Museum of Western Art, 1974.
Hoopes, Donelson F. *The Düsseldorf Academy and the Americans*. Atlanta: The High Museum of Art, 1972.
Ludlow, Fitz Hugh. *The Heart of the Continent*. New York: Hurd and Houghton, 1870. *New York Evening Post*, June 9, 1864.
Trump, Richard. *Life and Works of Albert Bierstadt*. A Dissertation. Ann Arbor: University Microfilms, 1964.
(Blakelock) Coates, Robert M. "Blakelock." *The New Yorker*, May 3, 1947.
Blakelock, Susielies M. *Ralph Albert Blakelock N. A. 1847-1919/ Drawings*. Boston: Vose Galleries, 1981.
Daingerfield, Elliot. *Ralph Albert Blakelock*. New York: Privately printed, 1914.
Geske, Norman A. *Ralph Albert Blakelock*. Nebraska Art Association, 1975.
Goodrich, Lloyd. *Ralph Albert Blakelock Centenary Exhibition*. New York: Whitney Museum of American Art, 1947.
Monroe, Harriet and James William Pattison. *Loan Exhibition of Important Works by George Inness, Alexander Wyant, Ralph Blakelock*. Chicago: Moulton and Ricketts Galleries, 1913.
Morton, Frederick W. "Work of Ralph A. Blakelock." *Brush and Pencil*, Chicago, February 1902.
National Endowment for the Humanities, "Of Moonlight and Forgery: The Blakelock Problem." March 1972, Vol II, No. 2.
Stuurman, Phyllis and David Gebhard. *The Enigma of Ralph A. Blakelock*. Santa Barbara: The Art Galleries, University of California, 1969.
Tanzer, Jack. *Ralph Albert Blakelock*. New York: M. Knoedler & Co., 1973.
Young, J. W. *Paintings by R. A. Blakelock and His Daughter Marian Blakelock*. Chicago: Young's Art Gallery, 1916.
(Blumenschein) Henning, William, Jr. *Ernest L. Blumenschein Retrospective*. Colorado Springs Fine Arts Center, 1978.
(Catlin) Catlin, George. *Letters and Notes on the Manners, Customs, and Conditions of North American Indians*. New York: Dover Publications, 1973.
Haberly, Loyd. *Pursuit of the Horizon*. New York: The Macmillan Co., 1948.
Hassrick, Royal. *The George Catlin Book of American Indians*. New York: Watson-Guptill, 1977.
Millichap, Joseph R. *George Catlin*. Boise, Idaho: Boise State University.
Truettner, William H. *The Natural Man Observed: A Study of Catlin's Indian Gallery*. Washington: Smithsonian Institution Press, 1979.
(Dixon) Burnside, W. M. *Maynard Dixon, Artist of the West*. Utah: Brigham Young University Press, 1973.
(Farny) Carter, Denny. *Henry Farny*. New York: Watson-Guptill, 1978.
Henry F. Farny. Catalog. Cincinnati, Ohio: Indian Hill Historical Museum Association, 1975.

(Fechin) Balcomb, Mary N. *Nicolai Fechin*. Flagstaff, Arizona: Northland Press, 1975.
Branham, Eya Fechin. *Nicolai Fechin-A Catalogue*. Santa Fe: Fenn Galleries, 1975.
(Hill) Arkelian, Marjorie Dakin. *Thomas Hill: The Grand View*. Oakland, California: The Oakland Museum, 1980.
(Hudson) Boynton, Searles R. *The Painter Lady Grace Carpenter Hudson*. Eureka, California: Interface California Corp., 1978.
Clements, Clara Erskine. *Women in the Fine Arts from the Seventh Century B. C. to the Twentieth Century A. D.* Cambridge: Houghton, Mifflin and Co., The Riverside Press, 1905.
The Pomo: Gifts and Visions. Palm Springs, California: Palm Springs Desert Museum, 1983.
(Johnson) McCracken, Harold. *The Frank Tenney Johnson Book*. Garden City: Doubleday & Company, 1974.
(Laurence) Jones, H. Wendy. *Life of Sydney Laurence Alaska Painter/Man of the Mountain*. Anchorage, Alaska: Alaskan Publishing Co. and Graphics Arts Press, 1962.
Laurence, Jeanne. *My Life with Sydney Laurence*. Seattle, Washington: Salisbury Press/Superior Publishing Co., 1974.
Shalkop, Robert L. *Sydney Laurence His Life and Work*. Anchorage, Alaska: Anchorage Historical and Fine Arts Museum, 1982.
(Leigh) Cummins, D. Duane. *William Robinson Leigh Western Artist*. Norman: University of Oklahoma Press, and Thomas Gilcrease Institute of American History and Art, 1980.
(Moran) *The Moran Family*. Huntington, New York: Heckscher Museum, 1965.
Bassford, Amy O. and Fritiof Fryxell. *Home-Thoughts from Afar*. East Hampton, New York: East Hampton Free Library, 1967.
Clark, Carol. *Thomas Moran Watercolors of the American West*. Austin: University of Texas Press, 1980.
The Drawings and Watercolors of Thomas Moran (1837-1926). University of Notre Dame, 1976.
Fryxell, Fritiof, editor. *Thomas Moran/Explorer in Search of Beauty*. New York: East Hampton Free Library, 1958.
Wilkins, Thurman. *Thomas Moran Artist of the Mountains*. Norman: University of Oklahoma Press, 1966.
(O'Keeffe) *Georgia O'Keeffe, An Exhibition of the Work of the Artist from 1915 to 1966.* Amon Carter Museum of Western Art, 1966.
Goodrich, Lloyd and Doris Bry. *Georgia O'Keeffe*. New York: Whitney Museum of American Art, 1970.
Lisle, Laurie. *Portrait of An Artist*. New York: Seaview Books, 1980.
The M. Carey Thomas Awards. Bryn Mawr College, 1971.
O'Keeffe, Georgia. *Georgia O'Keeffe*. New York: Viking Press, 1976.
Rich, Daniel Catton. *Georgia O'Keeffe*. Chicago: Art Institute of Chicago, 1943.
Rose, Barbara. *American Art Since 1900*. New York: Frederick A. Praeger, 1967.
Rose, Barbara. *American Painting/The Twentieth Century*. Distributed by The World Publishing Co., n.d.
Tompkins, Calvin. "The Rose in the Eye Looked Pretty Fine." *The New Yorker*, date unknown.
Wilder, Michell A., editor. *Georgia O'Keeffe/An Exhibition of the Work of the Artist from 1915 to 1966*. Amon Carter Museum of Western Art, 1966.
(Remington) Hassrick, Peter. *Frederic Remington*. New York: Harry N. Abrams, Inc., 1973.
McCracken, Harold. *Frederic Remington, Artist of the Old West*. Philadelphia: J. B. Lippincott Co., 1947.
Samuels, Peggy and Harold. *Frederic Remington A Biography*. Garden City: Doubleday & Co., 1982.
(Russell) Adams, Ramon F. and Homer E. Britzman. *Charles M. Russell/The Cowboy Artist*. Pasadena, Califonia: Trail's End Publishing, 1948.
Dippie, B. W. *"Paper Talk" Charlie Russell's American West*. New York: Alfred A. Knopf, in association with the Amon Carter Museum of Western Art, 1979.
Linderman, F. B. *Recollections of Charley Russell*. Norman: University of Oklahoma Press, 1963.
McCracken, Harold. *The Charles M. Russell Book*. Garden City: Doubleday & Co., 1957.
Renner, Frederic G. *Charles M. Russell*. Austin, Texas: University of Texas Press, 1966.
Russell, Austin. *Charles M. Russell Cowboy Artist*. New York: Twayne Publishers, 1957.

(Schreyvogel) Horan, James D. *The Life and Art of Charles Schreyvogel.* New York: Crown Publishers Inc., 1969.

(Sharp) Fenn, Forrest. *The Beat of the Drum and the Whoop of the Dance.* Fenn Publishing, 1983.

J. H. Sharp Among the Crow Indians 1902-1910. El Segundo: Upton and Sons, 1985.

(Whittredge) Baur, John I. H., editor. "The Autobiography of Worthington Whittredge." *Brooklyn Museum Journal,* 1942.

Draper, Benjamin. "Worthington Whittredge in the West." *Antiques,* January 1949.

Dwight, Edward H. *Worthington Whittredge (1820-1910).* Utica, New York: Munson-Williams-Proctor Institute, 1969.

Dwight, Edward H. "Worthington Whittredge, Artist of the Hudson River School." *Antiques,* October, 1969.

Greeley (Colorado) *Tribune,* July 19, 1871.

Janson, Anthony F. "Worthington Whittredge: The Development of a Hudson River Painter,1860-1868." *The American Art Journal,* April 1979.

(Wyeth) Allen, Douglas and Douglas Allen Jr. *N. C. Wyeth.* New York: Crown Publishers, 1972.

Duff, James H. "The American West of N. C. Wyeth." *The American West,* July/August 1980.

Johnston, Patricia. "N. C. Wyeth and Cream of Wheat." *The American West,* July/August 1980.

Meyer, Susan E. "N. C. Wyeth." *American Artist,* February 1975.

Watson, Ernest W. *Forty Illustrators and How They Work.* New York: Watson-Guptill, 1946.

BIBLIOGRAPHY: GENERAL

Ainsworth, Ed. *The Cowboy in Art.* New York: The World Publishing Co., 1968.

Curry, Larry. *The American West.* New York: Viking Press in association with the Los Angeles County Museum of Art, 1972.

Foxley, William C. *Frontier Spirit.* Catalog of the Collection of the Museum of Western Art. Denver: The Museum of Western Art, 1983.

Hassrick, Peter. *The Way West.* New York: Harry N. Adams, 1977.

Kovinick, Phil. *The Women Artist in the American West 1860-1960.* Fullerton, California: Muckenthaler Cultural Center, 1976.

La Farge, Oliver. *American Indian.* New York: Crown Publishers, 1956.

Larkin, Oliver W. *Art and Life in America.* New York: Rinehart & Co., 1949.

Luhan, Mabel Dodge. *Taos and Its Artists.* New York: Duell, Sloan and Pearce, 1947.

Nelson, Mary Carroll. *The Legendary Artists of Taos.* New York: Watson-Guptill Publications, 1980.

Prown, Jules David. *American Painting From Its Beginnings to the Armory Show.* Cleveland: The World Publishing Co., n/d.

Rewald, John. *The History of Impressionism.* New York: The Museum of Modern Art, 1961.

Rosenberg, Pierre and H. Barbara Weinberg. *A New World: Masterpieces of American Painting 1760-1910.* Boston: Museum of Fine Arts, 1983.

Taft, Robert. *Artists and Illustrators of the Old West.* New York: Charles Scribner's Sons, 1953.

Von Kalnein, Wend and Donelson F. Hoopes. *The Düsseldorf Academy and the Americans.* Atlanta, Georgia: The High Museum of Art, 1972.

White, Robert R., editor. *The Taos Society of Artists.* Albuquerque: University of New Mexico Press, 1983.

Witt, David L. *The Taos Artists.* Colorado: Ewell Fine Art Publication, 1984.

BIBLIOGRAPHY: TECHNICAL

Bottler, M. and A. H. Sabin. *German and American Varnish Making*. Wiley & Sons, 1912.

Carpenter, J. M. *Color in Art*. Cambridge: Fogg Art Museum, Harvard University, 1974.

Church, A. H. *The Chemistry of Paints and Painting*. Seeley and Co. Ltd., 1892.

Coke, Van Deren. *The Painter and the Photograph*. Albuquerque: University of New Mexico Press, 1964.

Cotter, M. J. *A Study of the Materials and Techniques Used by Some 19th Century American Oil Painters by Means of Neutron Activation Autoradiography*. Privately Printed, 1973.

Davis, P. *Photography*. William C. Brown Co. Publishers, 1977.

Gettens, R. J. and G. L. Stout. *Painting Materials, A Short Encyclopedia*. New York: Dover Publishing Co. Inc., 1966.

Harley, R. D. *Artist's Pigments c. 1600 - 1835*. American Elsevier Publishing Co., Inc., 1970.

Hours, M. *Conservation and Scientific Analysis of Paintings*. New York: Van Nostrand, 1976.

Levinson, H. W. *Artist's Pigments*. Colorlab, 1976.

Mayer, R. *The Artist's Handbook of Materials and Techniques*. New York: The Viking Press, 1982.

A Dictionary of Art Terms & Techniques. Thomas Y. Crowell Co., Apollo Edition, 1975.

The Painter's Craft. Penguin Books, 1986.

National Gallery Technical Bulletin. London: Publication Department, National Gallery.

Newhall, B. *The History of Photography*. New York: The Museum of Modern Art, 1964.

Stout, G. L. *The Care of Pictures*. New York: Dover Publications, 1975.

Taubes, F. *The Painter's Dictionary of Materials and Methods*. New York: Watson-Guptill Publications, 1976.

Toch, M. *Materials for Permanent Painting*. New York: D. Van Nostrand Co., 1911.

van Asperen de Boer, J. R. J. *An Introduction to the Scientific Examination of Paintings*. Nederlands Kunsthistorisch Jaarboek, 1975, Deel 26.

Watson, Dori. *The Technique of Painting*. New York: Van Nostrand Reinhold Co., 1970.

GLOSSARY

academic: In painting, a discipline based on and conformed to the standards set by the academies of the main European art centers. The philosophies though varied, tended to be conservative, promoting traditional methods and styles, derived from classical principles.

aging cracks: See CRACKING

alla prima: Technique in which the artist works directly, in one sitting, characterized by a simple paint build-up without underlayers. From Italian meaning "at first."

asphaltum: A brown PIGMENT that was commonly used in underlayers, especially in the 19th century. It is no longer used because of its poor drying abilities. Also called bitumen.

binder: See MEDIUM.

blending: Separate colors are blended together until the gradations of tone and the marks of the brush are imperceptible. Blending is commonly carried out with a special brush that is lightly tapped or dragged on the surface of the still wet PAINT.

calligraphic: A term descriptive of a fluid or rhythmic line. Derived from calligraphy, meaning the fine art of handwriting.

canvas: Refers to the fabric SUPPORT which is most commonly used for painting. The canvas is attached to a STRETCHER or STRAINER. Better quality canvas is made of linen; cotton is generally considered to be a less satisfactory, albeit less expensive alternative. See PLAIN and TWILL WEAVE CANVAS.

complementary colors: A pair of colors that are considered to be the opposite of each other. When colors are circularly arranged in the order of the spectrum, complementary colors naturally fall opposite each other. The complement of a primary color is made by mixing the other two primaries. For example red and green (blue and yellow) are complements. These combined colors are called secondary colors. By following this system an infinite range of complements can be formed. The color circle illustrates this principle.

conservation: The field that encompasses the RESTORATION and preservation of works of art. Duties of a conservator include investigation into proper conditions under which works of art may be stored, exhibited, and transported, as well as examinations and treatments.

cracking: Cracks may appear in the GROUND, PAINT, and/or VARNISH layers. AGING or mechanical cracks may be a result of movement in the SUPPORT due to climatic changes, improper KEYING out, or a blow to the reverse. When the stress is too great, the cracks form to release tension. A fine network of cracks is known as craquelure. DRYING CRACKS occur when the top paint layer is less flexible than the under layer. Upon drying of the latter, the top layer is pulled apart. Also known as alligatoring.

cross-section: A tiny sample (approximately 0.5 mm in diameter) of the GROUND, PAINT, and sometimes VARNISH layers is taken from the edge or an area of existing damage of a painting. This sample is embedded in resin, and polished to reveal the stratification of the layers. The sample is examined under a microscope to determine the nature of PIGMENTS, the order in which the layers were applied, and the sample can be stained for media analysis.

cusping: See SCALLOPING.

diluent: A thinner for oil PAINTS, such as turpentine or mineral spirits, that evaporates quickly and can be used to accelerate drying.

dragging: Denotes the movement of a stiff brush loaded with PAINT. In dragging, the wet paint only catches on the raised parts of the dry texture, allowing the colors beneath to show through and hence create the effect of broken color.

drying cracks: See CRACKING.

drying oil: The MEDIUM or binding material of oil PAINT that has the property of forming a solid, elastic substance when exposed to air. Linseed oil is most commonly used; poppyseed and walnut oils are less frequently used.

gesso: A GROUND made of usually chalk or whiting, and sometimes a white pigment, in a water-based BINDER.

glaze: A transparent coating made up of a PIGMENT within a quantity of MEDIUM large enough to allow light to penetrate and be reflected from the surface beneath. The main characteristic is transparency.

ground: Compound of a MEDIUM, a filler and sometimes an opaque PIGMENT. It is usually white though its color can be affected by added pigment or by subsequent layers such as an imprimatura or a TONED GROUND. Applied onto the SIZED SUPPORT to provide a satisfactory painting surface. See PRIMING.

hue: The variety of a color such as red, green, blue, etc., excluding achromatic colors such as black, white and gray.

impasto: Thick and heavily applied paint that stands out in relief produced by pronounced brush work or PALETTE KNIFE application.

infrared: A technique useful in detecting carbon containing UNDERDRAWING, such as charcoal. When used in the examination of paintings, these rays can penetrate superficial layers of VARNISH and overpaint. They are part of the invisible spectrum that is contiguous to the red end of the visible spectrum and are comprised of electromagnetic radiations of wavelengths of 760 to 2000 nanometers.

key: Wooden wedges inserted in corners of a STRETCHER. Keying out a stretcher means to expand its size.

lining: New fabric attached to the reverse of the original CANVAS, in picture RESTORATION.

matte: A dull, nonreflective surface.

medium: The BINDER or vehicle that holds together PIGMENT particles in paint.

middle distance: The portion of a pictorial representation that lies between the foreground and background. Also called middleground.

modeling: In painting and drawing, the depiction of three-dimensional form by means of light and shadow.

paint: The compound of a MEDIUM and PIGMENTS.

paint layers: PAINT applied in one or more stages. Also called paint film. GROUND and VARNISH are not considered to be paint layers.

palette: An artist's choice of colors for a painting. Also, the surface on which the artist arranges and mixes the colors while painting.

palette knife: A spatula, usually with a flexible metal blade, used for mixing and applying paint. Its use is commonly characterized by thick, broad IMPASTO that retains the imprint of the knife's edge.

pentimento: An artist's change or improvement carried out by overpainting the dissatisfactory portion. Pentimento often become visible later as a result of PAINT LAYERS becoming more transparent with age. Artist's changes can be detected by observing, with the aid of RAKING LIGHT, where brushwork does not match what is depicted, and can often be confirmed by means of X-RADIOGRAPHY.

perspective: A method of representing three-dimensionality on a two-dimensional plane. The most commonly used method is linear perspective in which objects become smaller as they recede in space and lines converge at vanishing points. This is often used together with the more naturalistic atmospheric perspective in which colors become paler and there is less contrast between light and shade as the space recedes.

picture plane: The imagined plane between the artist/viewer and the subject, represented by the surface of the picture.

pigment: A finely ground coloring matter.

pigment analysis: The method of identifying PIGMENTS, usually by examining small samples taken from the edge or area of existing damage of a painting. Some of the means of examination used in this book are optical microscopy, chemical microscopy, x-ray diffraction, laser microspectral analysis, and scanning electron microscope. See CROSS-SECTION.

photomacrograph: A photograph taken under some magnification.

photomicrograph: A photograph taken through a microscope.

plain weave canvas: A CANVAS weave in which each warp thread passes under one and over one weft thread.

plein air painting: A painting executed outdoors as opposed to in the artist's studio.

priming: The process of preparing a CANVAS with SIZE and GROUND layers before the paint is applied. A canvas is normally single or double primed, that is with one or two layers of ground. A single priming is more flexible and usually retains more canvas texture; a double priming is stiffer and smoother. A canvas may be primed by the artist, or commercially, referred to as pre-primed. A pre-primed canvas can often be detected because the ground is applied uniformly and extends over the TACKING EDGE.

raking light: A technique used when examining paintings in which the source of illumination is from one side only and at a flat angle. This technique is also used in photography to emphasize the structure of the CANVAS texture or brush strokes.

restoration: An aspect of the field of CONSERVATION that deals with the examination and repair, or restoration of works of art that have deteriorated due to the artist's improper use of materials, exposure to a detrimental climate, and/or damage. Common practices are cleaning, LINING, and retouching losses in the original image. When looking into artist's technique it is important to take into consideration the effects restoration may have had on a work of art.

saturation: The attribute of a color that allows one to judge the amount of pure chromatic color present, the vividness or intensity of a color. The term is also used with VARNISH application to refer to the degree to which colors are made more intense.

scalloping: A series of curves along the edge of CANVAS, the tips of which correspond to the points of attachment to the STRETCHER. Also called CUSPING.

scumble: Similar to a GLAZE, but instead of a transparent PIGMENT, an opaque and pale pigment is present.

sizing: The application of, usually, an animal glue to the SUPPORT to render it less absorbent for the subsequent layers of GROUND and PAINT.

sketch: A preliminary drawing or model which captures the essential elements of the subject without going into much detail. It is rapidly executed, usually on a separate surface and then copied onto the final SUPPORT of the work of art. It is often carried out in charcoal, ink, crayon, pencil, dilute paint, or in the case of a model, clay or wood. See UNDERDRAWING.

slub: A lump in thread or fabric that, in the case of CANVAS, can be desirable to provide TOOTH or an irregular surface.

strainer: A non-expandable rigid wooden frame over which a CANVAS is held taut for the painting process.

stretcher: A wooden frame with mortised and mitered corners over which a CANVAS is pulled and held taut, usually with tacks. Expandable with KEYS.

support: Any surface upon which a painting is executed. The most common supports used in paintings are CANVAS, panel, artist's board, etc.

tacking edge: The margin of fabric, pulled around the edge of the STRETCHER, into which tacks are inserted in a row for attachment to the stretcher. Also called turn-over edge or margin.

tempera: An emulsion-type PAINT with a water-miscible BINDER, usually egg. The term is also used broadly for a variety of aqueous paints, such as casein.

toned ground: A transparent or thin layer of color applied over the usually white GROUND, thus adding a color effect without sacrificing the bright, reflective qualities of the ground.

tooth: A slight roughness in a GROUND, caused by the addition of coarse particles or by the canvas texture, that provides a good surface for the paint to adhere to.

turbid media effect: An optical phenomenon in which a thin layer, applied over a dark layer, appears bluish, without necessarily containing blue PIGMENT. This is also the reason cigarette smoke appears blue against a dark background.

twill weave canvas: A CANVAS weave in which each warp thread passes under one and over two or more weft threads, producing diagonal ribs.

ultraviolet light: A method used to examine paintings to determine the nature of VARNISH and PIGMENTS and to identify later additions of paint to the surface. It consists of electromagnetic waves beyond the violet in the spectrum, having wavelengths between 400 and 140 nanometers.

underdrawing: A SKETCH made directly on the SUPPORT before the painting is executed.

value: The degree of lightness or darkness of a color. Darker colors are said to be lower in value.

varnish: A protective, transparent coating, usually with a resin content, laid over a PAINT film. Common natural resin varnishes are dammar and mastic. Since the 1940s, synthetic resins have been used with increasing frequency. Traditionally, most paintings were intended to be varnished. More recently, particularly beginning with the Impressionists when artists became interested in the optical properties of the paint itself, paintings have been intentionally left unvarnished by the artist. The permanence and pervasive effects of varnish are important considerations for both collectors and conservators.

wet-into-wet: A painting technique in which PAINT is applied into a still wet paint surface.

x-radiography: A method used to reveal artist's changes, damages, and to gain insight into the nature of the CANVAS, STRETCHER and/or panel. Elements of high atomic weight, lead white in particular, are recorded on a photographic negative, which in turn is used to produce an image of their distribution. Also called Roentgen rays.

PHOTO CREDITS: ARTIST'S PORTRAITS

Oscar E. Berninghaus, Taos, New Mexico, about 1927. Courtesy Museum of New Mexico, Santa Fe, New Mexico, negative number 40393.

Albert Bierstadt. Courtesy Photographs of Artists, Collection I, Archives of American Art, Smithsonian Institution.

Ralph Albert Blakelock. Courtesy Photographs of Artists, Collection I, Archives of American Art, Smithsonian Institution.

Ernest L. Blumenschein in his studio, Taos, New Mexico. Courtesy Museum of New Mexico, Santa Fe, New Mexico, negative number 20566.

Wagon breakdown near Taos, New Mexico. Photo by Bert Phillips, September 4, 1898. Courtesy Museum of New Mexico, Santa Fe, New Mexico, negative number 40378.

A painting of George Catlin by William Fisk. Courtesy National Portrait Gallery Smithsonian Institution, transfer from the National Museum of American Art: Gift of Miss May C. Kinney, Ernest C. Kinney and Bradford Wickes, 1945.

Maynard Dixon painting on location. Courtesy Edith Hamlin.

Henry Farny. Courtesy Cincinnati Art Museum, Library Archives, Cincinnati, Ohio.

Nicolai Fechin at his easel. Courtesy Forrest Fenn, Santa Fe, New Mexico.

Thomas Hill. Courtesy of the United States Department of the Interior, National Park Service, Yosemite National Park.

Grace Hudson working in her studio. Courtesy Grace Hudson Museum, Sun House, City of Ukiah, California.

Frank Tenney Johnson in his studio. Courtesy Buffalo Bill Historical Society, Cody, Wyoming.

Sydney Laurence painting in his studio. Courtesy The Anchorage Museum of History and Art, Lathrop Collection, Anchorage, Alaska.

William R. Leigh sitting for his N.A. portrait. Courtesy Traphagen School of Fashion, New York, New York.

Thomas Moran with his wife Mary Nimmo Moran. Courtesy Thomas Moran Biographical Art Collection, East Hampton Library, East Hampton, New York.

(Moran) Infrared photograph. Courtesy Janos Novak, Preparer, Balboa Art Conservation Center, San Diego, California.

Georgia O'Keeffe near "The Pink House," Taos, New Mexico, 1929. Courtesy Museum of New Mexico, Santa Fe, New Mexico, negative number 9763.

Frederic Remington in his studio. Courtesy The Kansas State Historical Society, Topeka, Kansas.

Charles M. Russell painting *Whose Meat?* Courtesy Museum of Western Art, Denver, Colorado.

Charles Schreyvogel in his studio. Courtesy National Cowboy Hall of Fame and Western Heritage Center, Oklahoma City, Oklahoma.

Joseph Sharp with an Indian model, Taos, New Mexico. Ca 1915-16. Courtesy Museum of New Mexico, Santa Fe, New Mexico, negative number 1176767.

A portrait of Worthington Whittredge by Carl Friedrich Lessing. Courtesy of Cincinnati Art Museum, Cincinnati, Ohio, gift of Joseph Longworth.

N.C. Wyeth in his studio. Courtesy Delaware Art Museum Archives, Wilmington, Delaware.

PHOTO CREDITS:
COLOR TRANSPARENCIES

Museum of Western Art, Denver, Colorado:
  Oscar Berninghaus, *The Ceremony of the Rabbit Hunt.*
  Ernest Blumenschein, *Jury for the Trial of a Sheepherder for Murder.*
  Henry Farny: *Nomads.*
  Sydney Laurence, *Mount McKinley.*
  William R. Leigh, *Hopi Indian Runners.*
  Frederic Remington, *Downing the Nigh Leader.*
  Charles Russell, *Whose Meat?*
  Charles Schreyvogel, *The Messenger.*
  Joseph Sharp, *Pipe Song.*
  N.C. Wyeth, *Indians Watch with Astonishment as Car Speeds By.*
Fine Arts Museums of San Francisco, California:
  Ralph Albert Blakelock, *Indian Encampment, North Dakota.*
  George Catlin, *Fire in a Missouri Meadow, and a Party of Sioux Indians Escaping From It: Upper Missouri 1871.*
  Worthington Whittredge: *On the Cache la Poudre.*
Palm Springs Desert Museum, Palm Springs, California:
  Thomas Hill, *Hunter and Setters in the Foothills with the Great Basin Beyond.*
  Grace Hudson, *Love's Labor.*

All other color and black and white photographs not credited were taken by Daniel Fabian and Joan Samuels with the assistance of Janos Novak, Balboa Art Conservation Center, San Diego, California.

TECHNICAL ANALYSIS

R.A. Blakelock, *Indian Encampment*. Analysis was done by D. Fabian using the facilities of the Swiss Institute for Art Research, Zurich, Switzerland.

E. Blumenschein, *Jury for the Trial of a Sheepherder for Murder*. Infrared photograph was taken by D. Fabian and J. Samuels.

M. Dixon, *Apache Land*. Analysis was done by Eugene Farrell, Center for Conservation and Technical Studies, Fogg Art Museum, Harvard University, Cambridge, Massachusetts.

N. Fechin, *Indian Maid*. Analysis and cross-section photography were done by Richard Wolbers, Winterthur, University of Delaware Program in the Conservation of Artistic and Historic Works, Winterthur, Delaware.

F.T. Johnson, *In Old Isleta*. Analysis was done by Eugene Farrell, Center for Conservation and Technical Studies.

T. Moran, *Indian Village*. Analysis was done by E. Farrell, Center for Conservation and Technical Studies. Infrared photograph and x-radiograph were taken by D. Fabian and Janos Novak, Balboa Art Conservation Center, San Diego, California.

N.C. Wyeth, *Indians Watch in Astonishment as Car Speeds By*. Analysis was done by D. Fabian using the facilities of the Swiss Institute for Art Research.

ACKNOWLEDGMENTS

We thank the institutions that generously allowed us to examine their paintings and reproduce them in this book. Martin Peterson, Curator of American Art, San Diego Museum of Art was the first to encourage and advise us. We especially want to thank William Foxley, Chairman of the Board, The Museum of Western Art, Denver, Colorado for his assistance. We also thank Kristin Hoermann and James Wright, Paintings Conservators, and Mark Simpson, Curator of American Art, Fine Arts Museums of San Francisco; Kathy Clewell, Registrar, Palm Springs Desert Museum; and Nancy Peterson, Director, Timkin Museum of Art.

For technical assistance and advice we thank Betsy Court, Chief Paintings Conservator, Janet Ruggles, Director, Janos Novak, Preparator, and Gary Alden, Balboa Art Conservation Center; Richard Wolbers, Associate Paintings Conservator, Winterthur Museum, University of Delaware; Eugene Farrell, Chief Scientist, Center for Conservation and Technical Studies, Harvard University; and Dr. Bruno Muhlethaler, Head of Research, Swiss Institute for Art Research.

Also Charles Patterson, Director, Rocky Mountain Regional Conservation Center; Carl Grimm, Western Center for Conservation of Fine Arts; Kathryn Hird, Assistant Paintings Conservator, The Panhandle-Plains Historical Museum; and Steven Prins, Conservator, Prins-Wait Studio.

Finally, we are appreciative of the help we received from Paul Bingham, Westview Gallery, San Jose; Forrest Fenn, Santa Fe, New Mexico, and from all the members of the Research and Information Center at the Main Library, Albuquerque, New Mexico.

INDEX

Page numbers in italics indicate illustrations.